REBUILD BY DESIGN

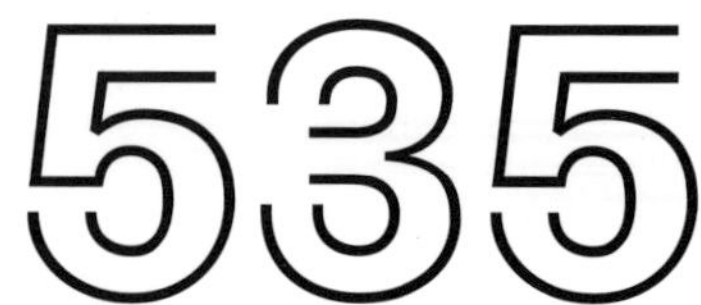

Community
Organizations

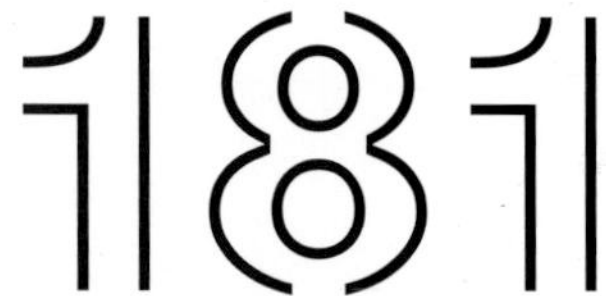

Government
Agencies

10

Teams

4

Partner
Organizations

1

Region

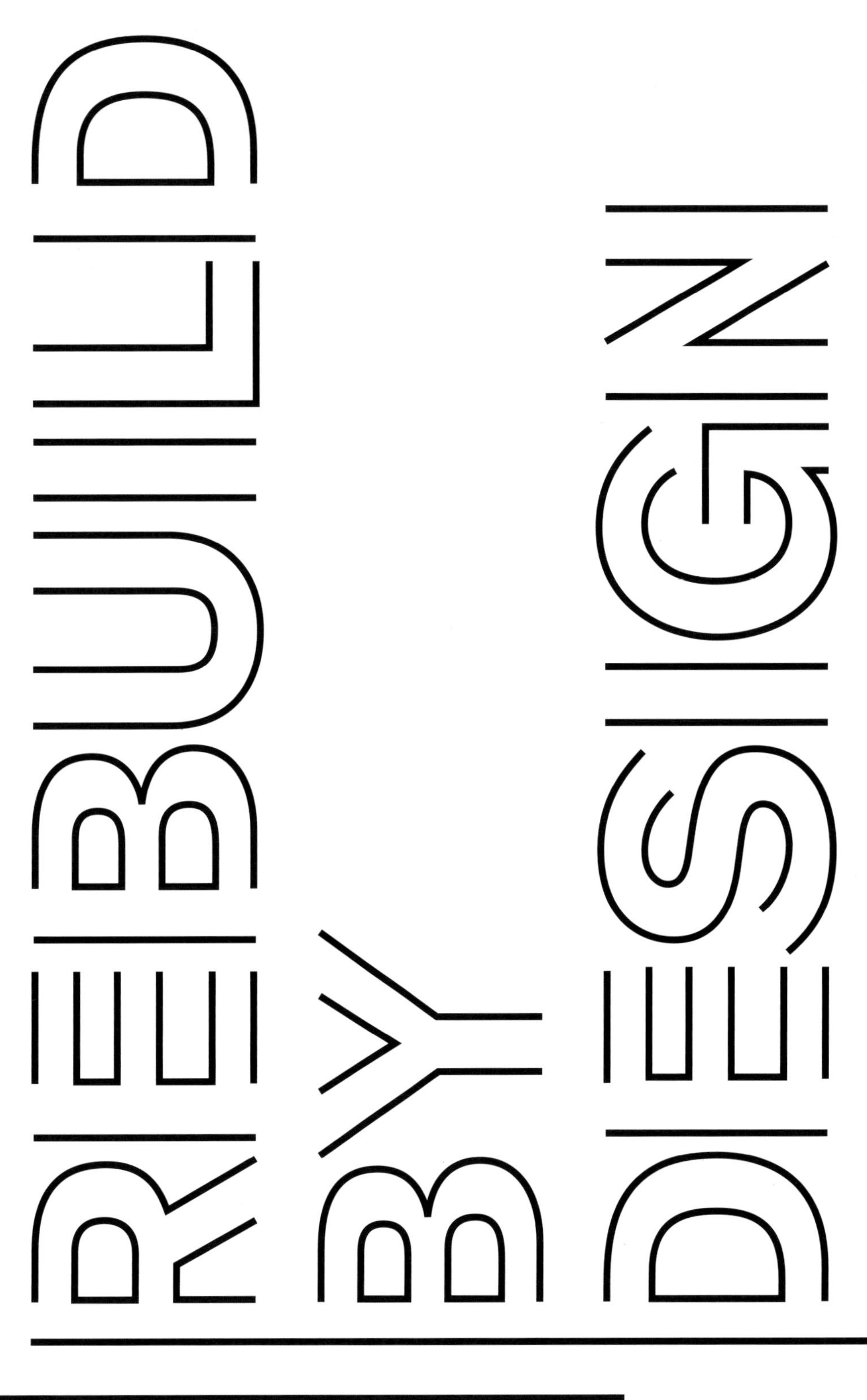
REBUILD
BY
DESIGN

This publication has been made possible thanks to the generous support of The Rockefeller Foundation.

Consulting Editor:
John Gendall

Additional Writing:
Josh Bisker

Editors:
Josh Bisker, Amy Chester, Tara Eisenberg

Additional Editorial Support:
Scott Davis, Henk Ovink

Book and infographic design:
Pentagram: Natasha Jen, Jeffrey Waldman

Printing:
American Printing Co.

Contents

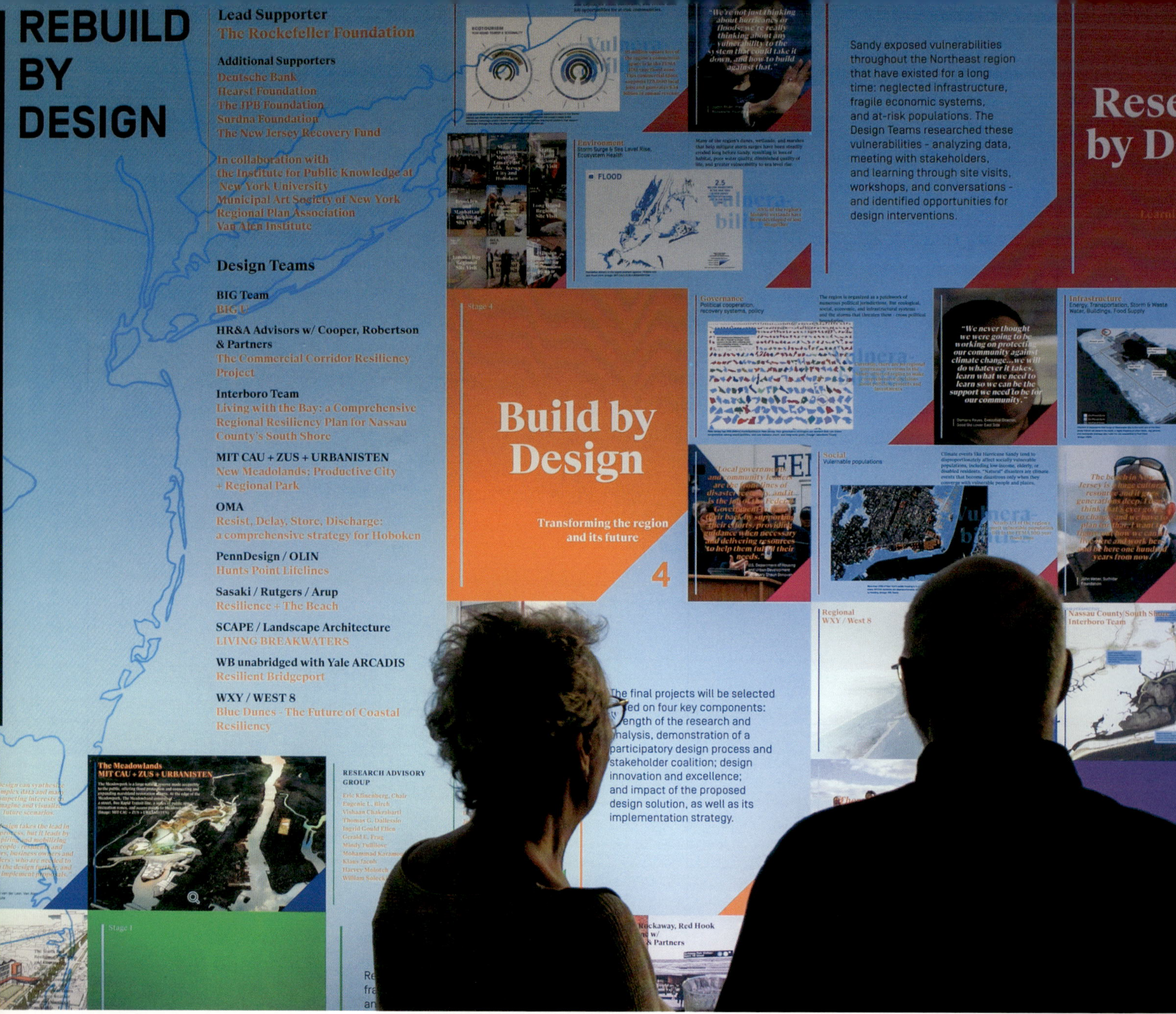

In April, 2014, at the competition's final exhibition, members of the public explore an overview of the Rebuild by Design process, from concept to collaborative design.

Preface

Named first among CNN's Top 10 Ideas of 2013, Rebuild by Design began as a new kind of design competition in the devastating aftermath of Hurricane Sandy. It represents a new process for collaboratively researching, developing, and implementing ideas for a more resilient future and constitutes a new model for how government can partner with philanthropy, academia, the nonprofit and private sectors, and the design world to bring impacted communities into the heart of the design process.

The leadership and support from federal and local governments, in particular the Department of Housing and Urban Development, have been vital to every element of Rebuild by Design's success. Critical financial support came from The Rockefeller Foundation – which continues to rally the globe toward a more resilient future – along with the JPB Foundation, Deutsche Bank Americas Foundation, Surdna Foundation, Hearst Foundation, and New Jersey Recovery Fund. The NYU Institute for Public Knowledge, Municipal Art Society, Regional Plan Association, and Van Alen Institute provided invaluable regional knowledge and programmatic coordination. The talent of the region was joined by the talent of the world through ten interdisciplinary design teams who accepted an unprecedented challenge. Thousands of local community stakeholders – residents, business owners, academics, government officials, and others – made the process part of their lives and futures.

The ten final designs, much like the process itself, represent the expertise, vision, enthusiasm, and perseverance of countless individuals and organizations. The sum of their contributions has transformed an ambitious goal into a reality — and will continue to define how to confront the uncertain horizon of a changing world for years to come.

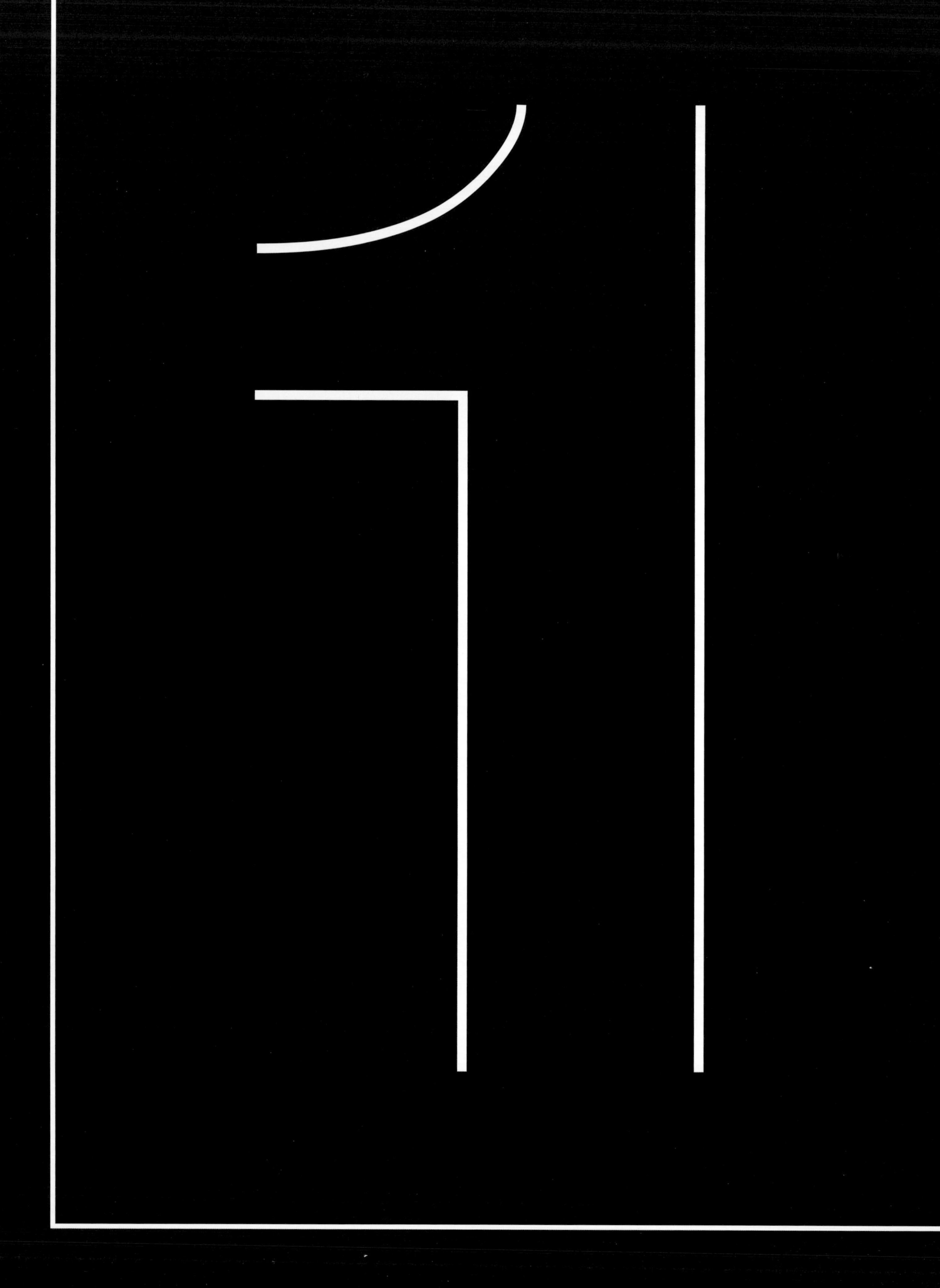

THE STORM & THE RESPONSE

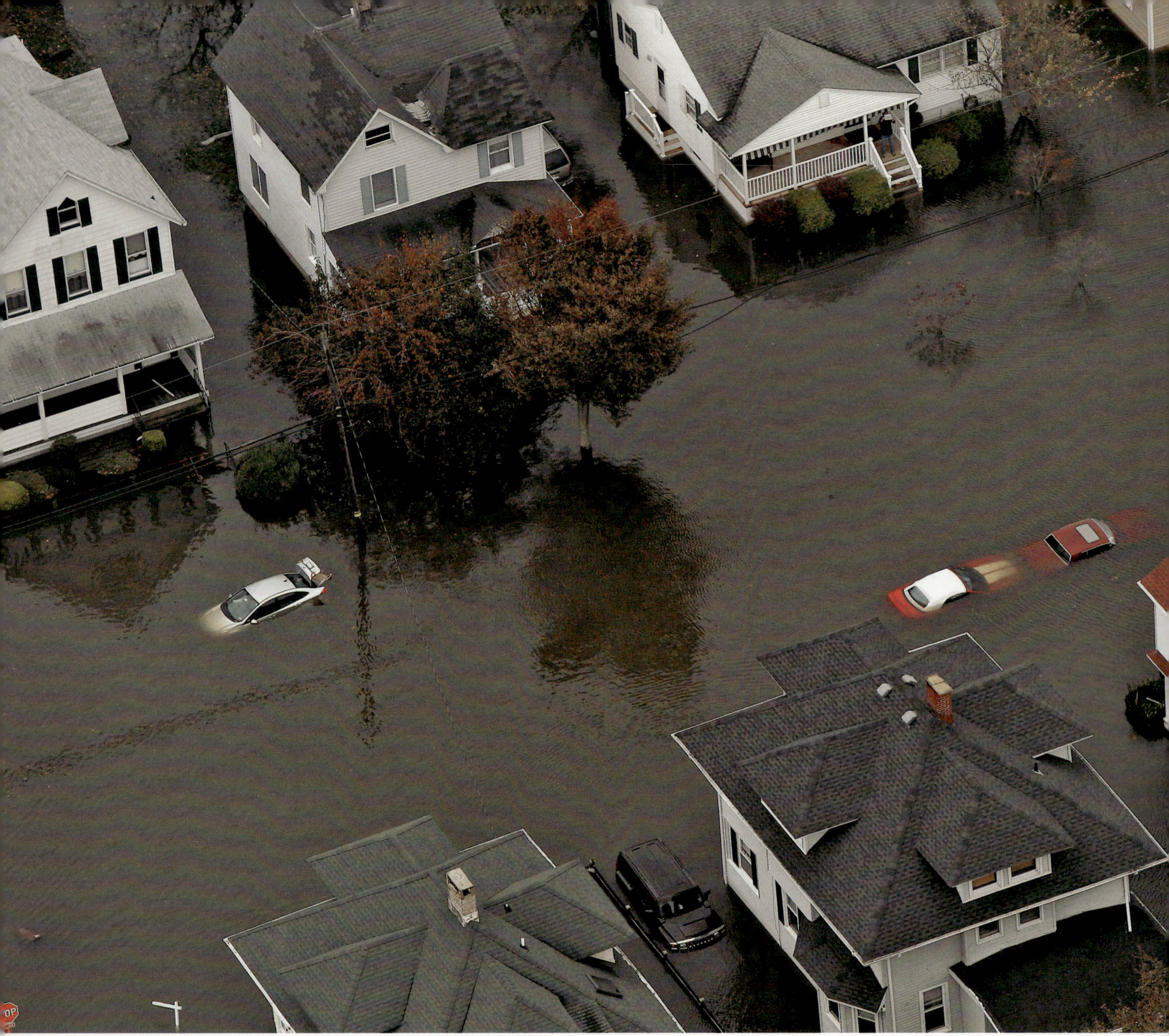

"Understanding what really is at stake and what happened during Hurricane Sandy informs a path forward that can reconnect the social, the economy, and the ecology. Design can bridge these gaps and marry science and politics, the real world with imagination. Rebuild by Design is not about making a plan, but about changing a culture."

—

Henk Ovink, Principal, Rebuild by Design and Special Advisor to Secretary Shaun Donovan, Chair of Hurricane Sandy Rebuilding Task Force

Above: Pictured are homes in Belmar, New Jersey, where the storm surge rose to more than six feet during Hurricane Sandy.

Following Spread: Darkness engulfed much of Lower Manhattan after Hurricane Sandy's storm surge crippled a power station in the East Village.

Impact

1

On October 29, 2012, Hurricane Sandy made landfall in the northeast United States. At least 186 people were killed, more than 600,000 homes were damaged or destroyed, and critical infrastructure was crushed across the region.

Several elements converged to give the storm its devastating impact. In what was so far the hottest year in recorded US history, rising temperatures at the ocean's surface intensified the hurricane's strength and magnitude. One thousand miles in diameter when it descended upon the shore, Sandy pummeled coastal and inland communities with 80-mile-per-hour winds, while the slow-moving eye of the storm dragged out the duration of the assault. Meanwhile, a full moon meant that the tide of the sea was higher than average, adding volume to the water at the land's edge and increasing the storm's surge levels to catastrophic proportions. All told, Sandy left behind more than $65 billion in damages and economic loss.

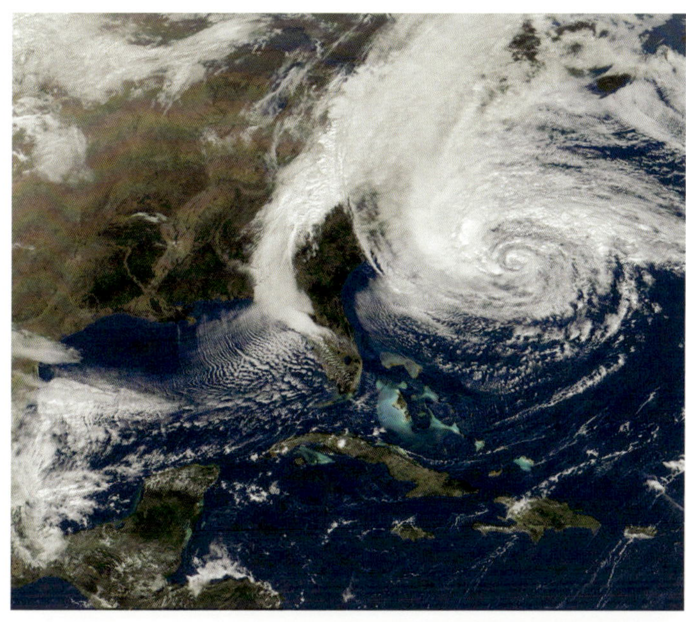

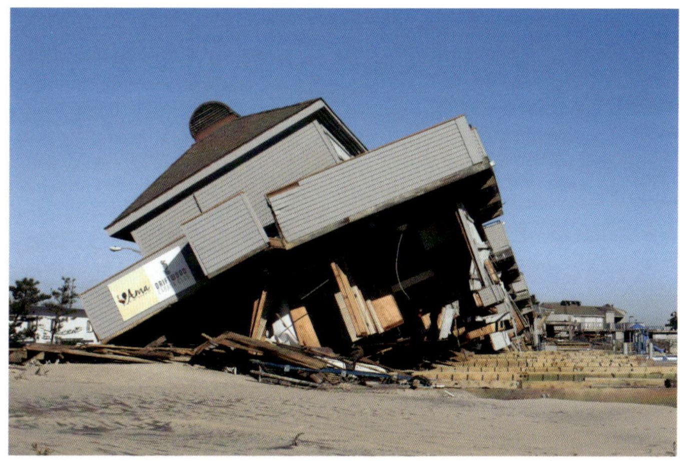

Above: The demolished remains of the Driftwood Cabana Club in Sea Bright, New Jersey.

Left: Satellite image of Huricane Sandy

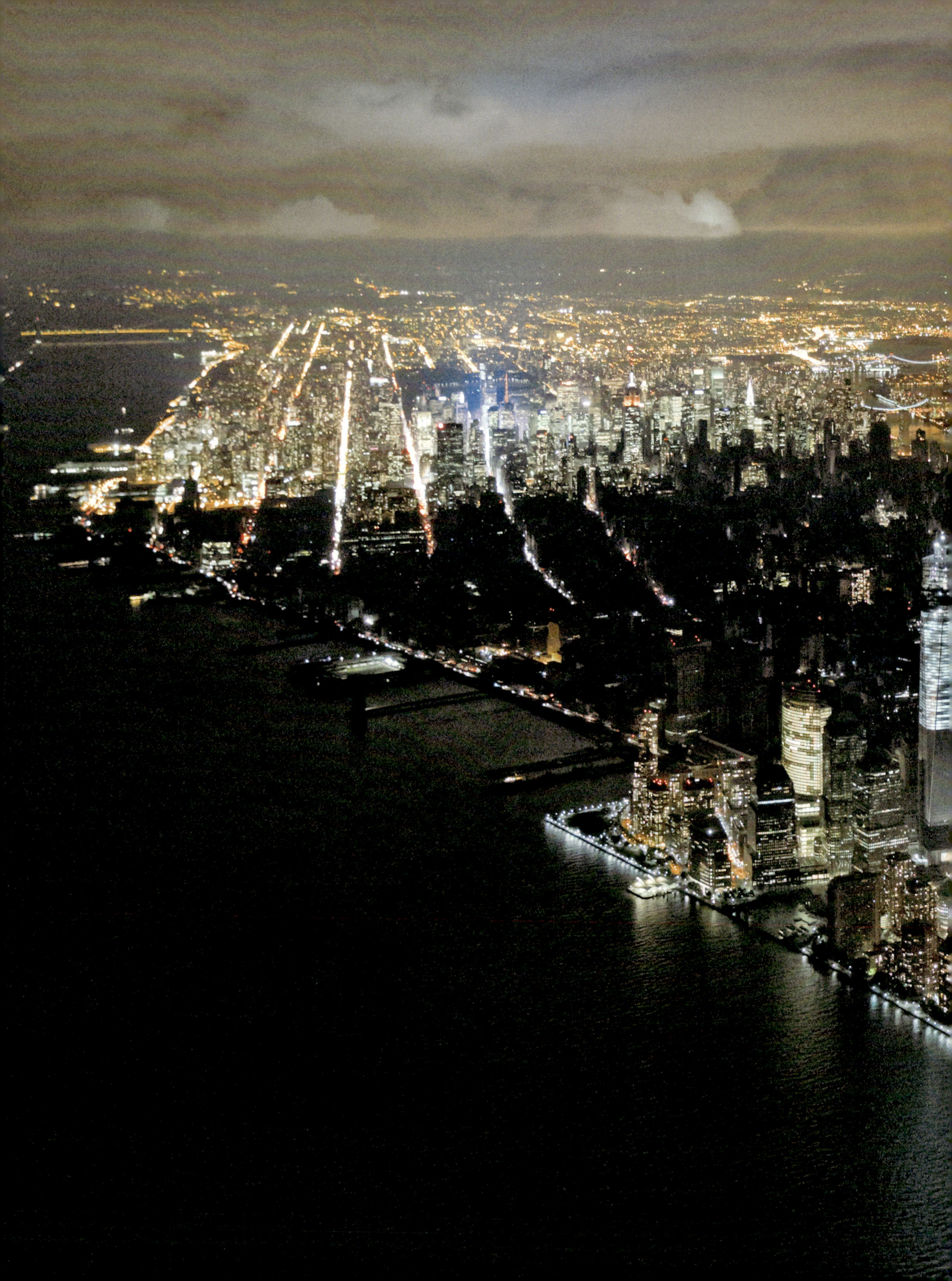

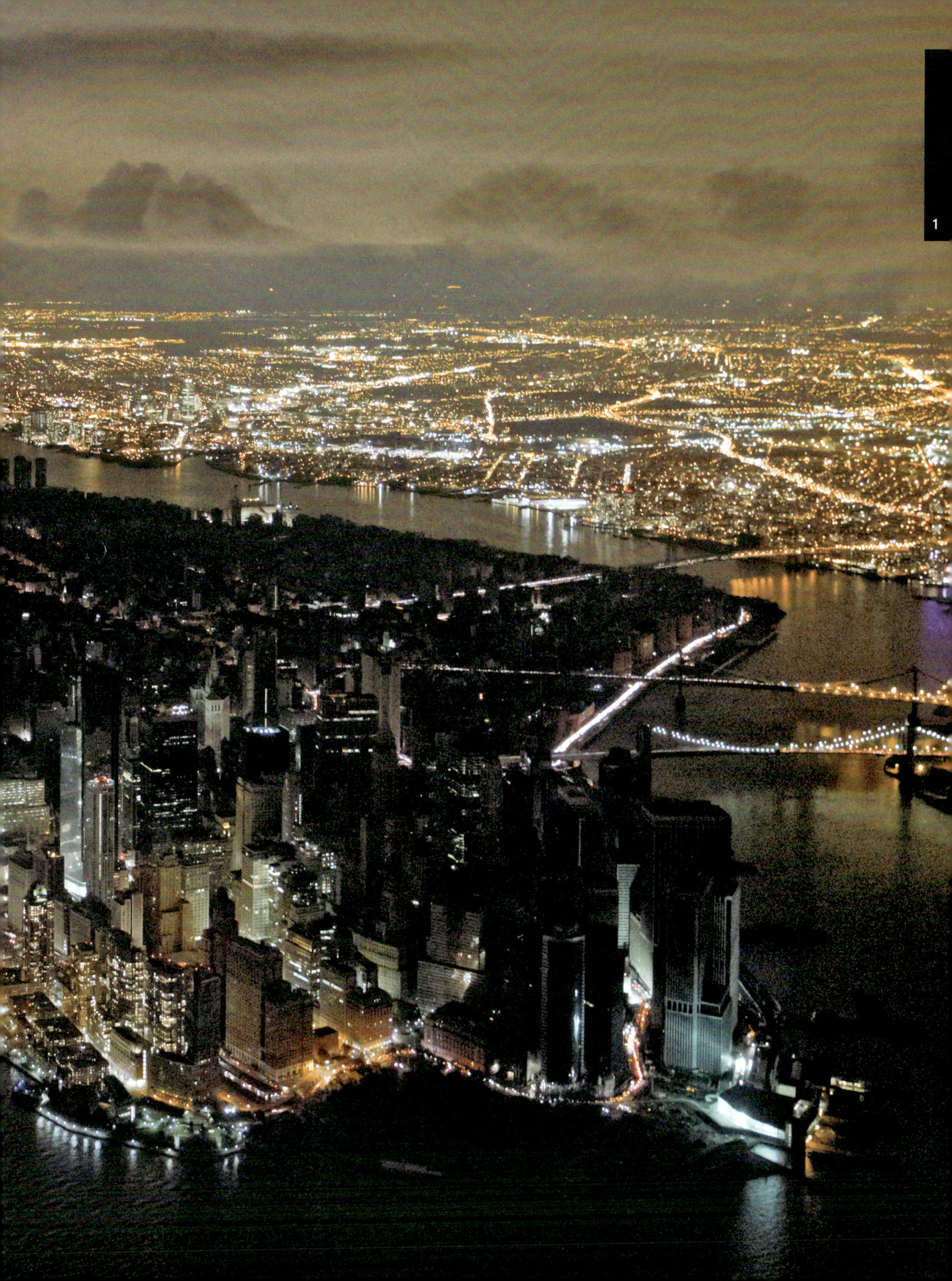

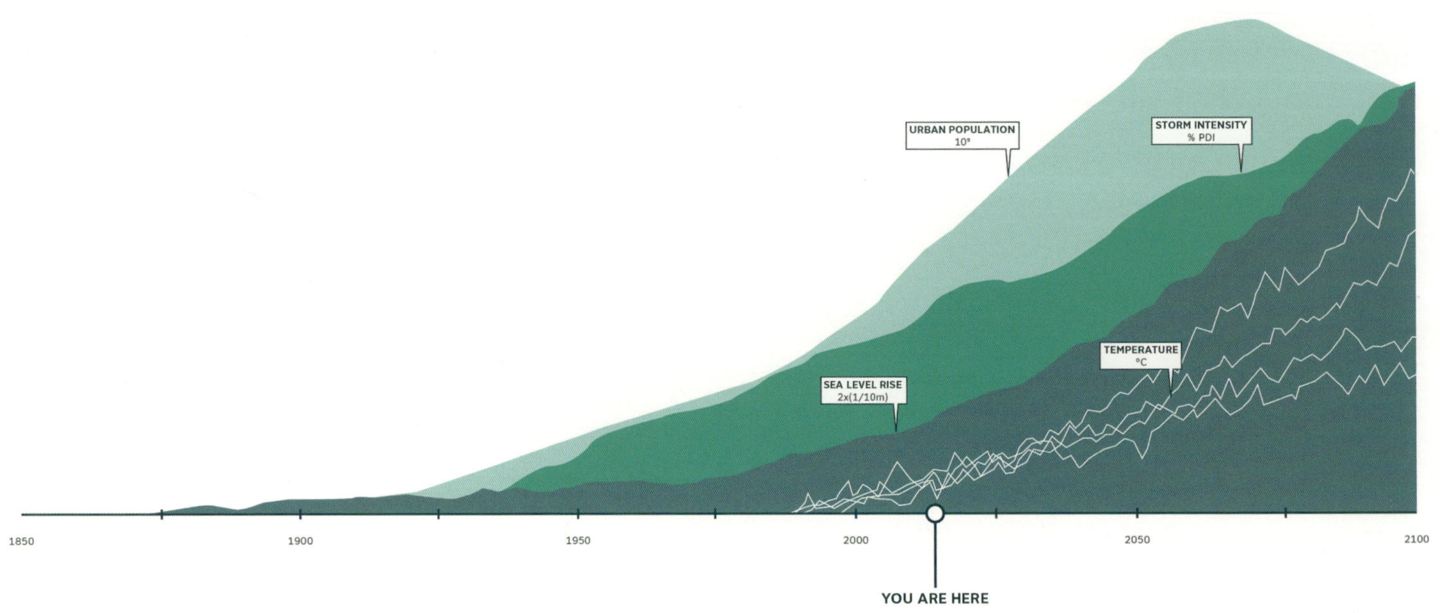

"Sandy was the most sizable storm to hit in 100 years, bringing billions of dollars in unprecedented destruction to New Jersey's communities, businesses, infrastructure, and natural and cultural resources. Through the work of these talented Rebuild by Design teams, we have the opportunity to strengthen our communities in New Jersey and throughout the region to make them more resilient in the face of future storms."

—

New Jersey Governor Chris Christie

"Superstorm Sandy was the latest example of a worsening trend in recent years toward highly destructive extreme weather. ... Rebuild by Design is leading the way in the development of resilience projects that are not just about brick and mortar; they create jobs, promote business and education, and ensure safety in waterfront communities."

—

New York State Governor Andrew M. Cuomo

Above: The SCAPE team pondered the question of how to design for an uncertain future while addressing long-term resilience. Reducing fragility and increasing the perception of risk will help to move beyond current design paradigms and address larger issues of ecosystem collapse, cycles of regional decline, and calmer, non-disastrous inundation events.

Right: HUD Secretary Shaun Donovan tours Hurricane Sandy damage in Jersey City.

Following Spread: Streets and homes in Ortley Beach, New Jersey.

Storm Surge Meets Groundswell

1

Government agencies, businesses, nonprofits, grassroots organizers, and countless individual volunteers sprang up to tackle Sandy's challenges. They wasted no time in transforming public and private spaces into emergency response centers, innovating and coordinating complex relief operations, and organizing support for those affected by the storm.

These efforts to respond to the region's most urgent needs underscored some of the broader dimensions of the risks ahead. Hurricane Sandy had sent the message that coastal communities would continue to face weather-related crises. Building back to pre-storm conditions would not prepare them for the inevitable future of increasing storms. For many it was clear that the storm's most devastating effects were not simply the results of a natural disaster. Instead, they were the products of a long history of planning decisions that had created or exacerbated vulnerabilities throughout the region. Damaged ecosystems, altered topography, high-density and high-value development in flood-prone areas, and other factors had contributed to – if not defined – the fragility of life on the coasts.

Rebuilding would have to holistically examine and address these interconnected physical, social, and ecological vulnerabilities to respond to the region's complex needs. The process would require unprecedented collaboration, creative interdisciplinary research, broad and meaningful citizen engagement, visionary engineering, and close cooperation between government, philanthropy, community, business, academia, and design. The challenge would be formidable. The answer would be to "Rebuild by Design."

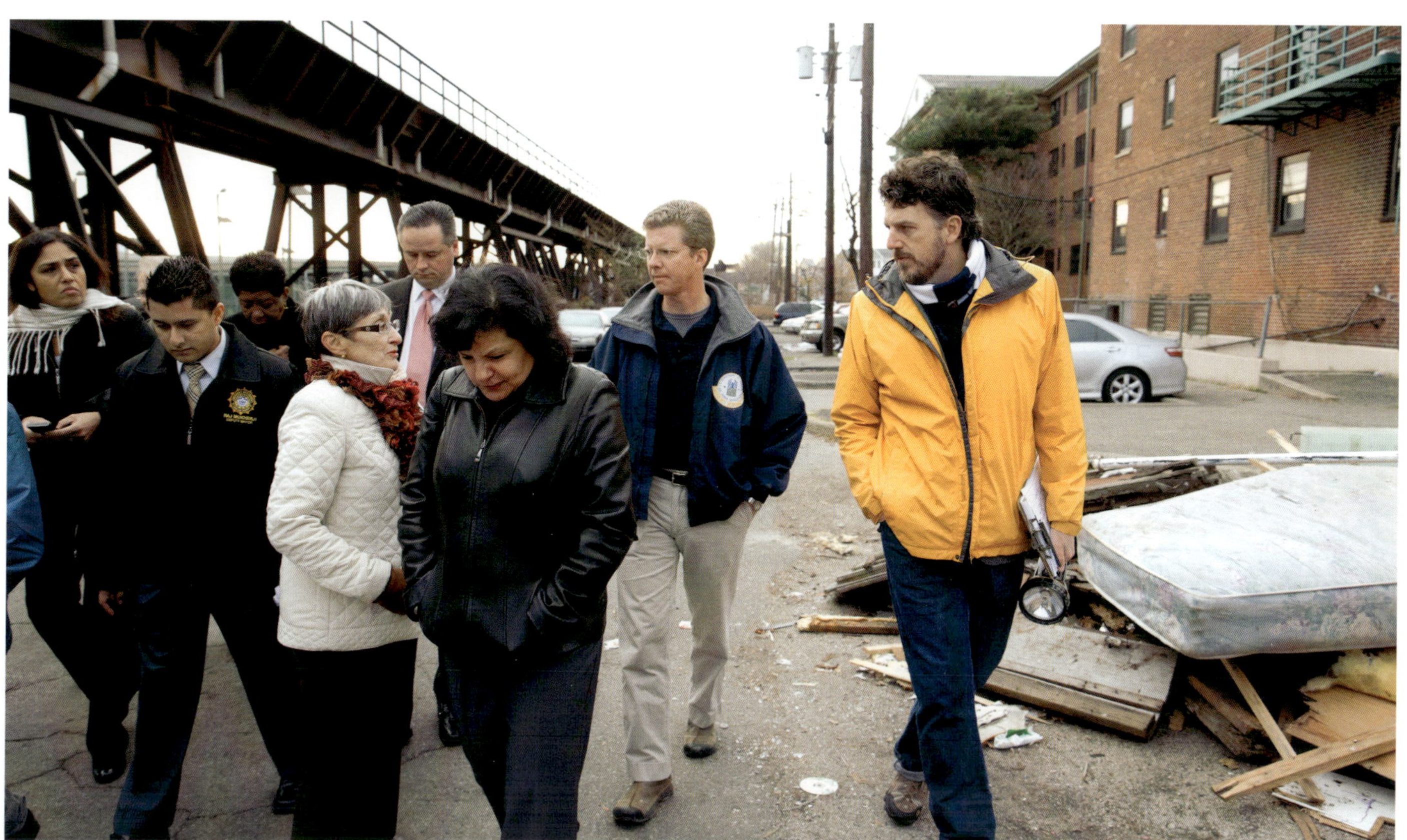

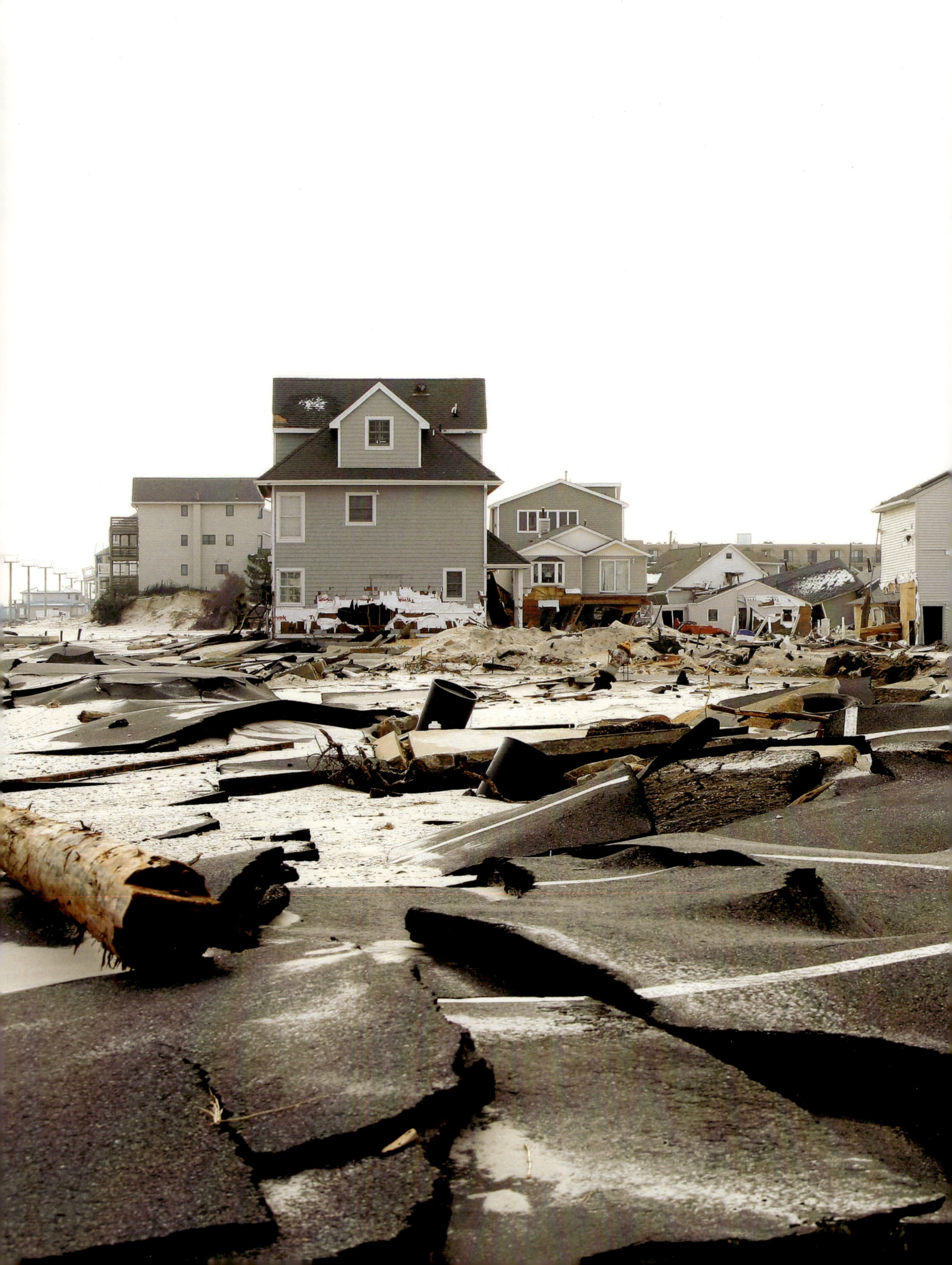

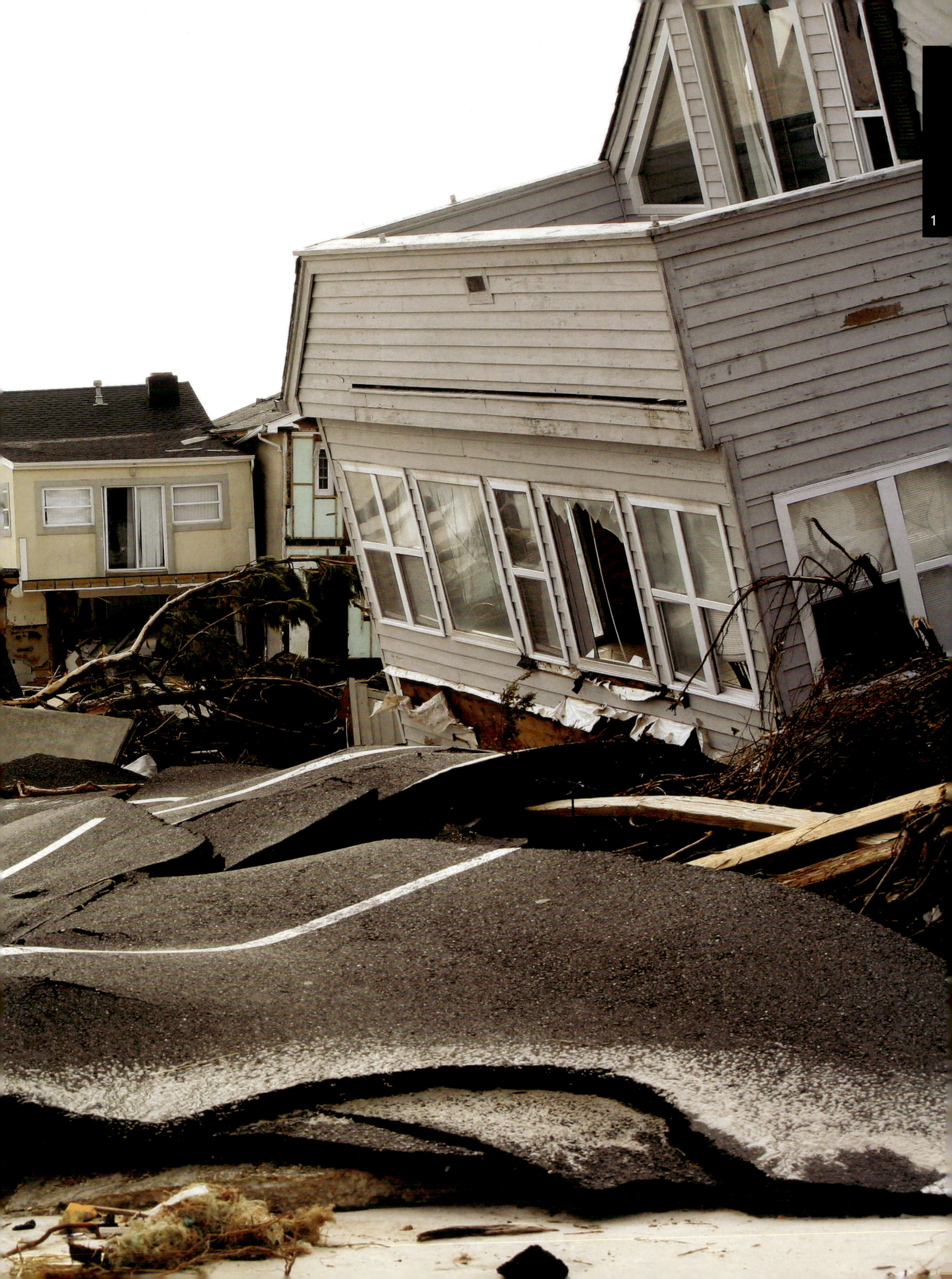

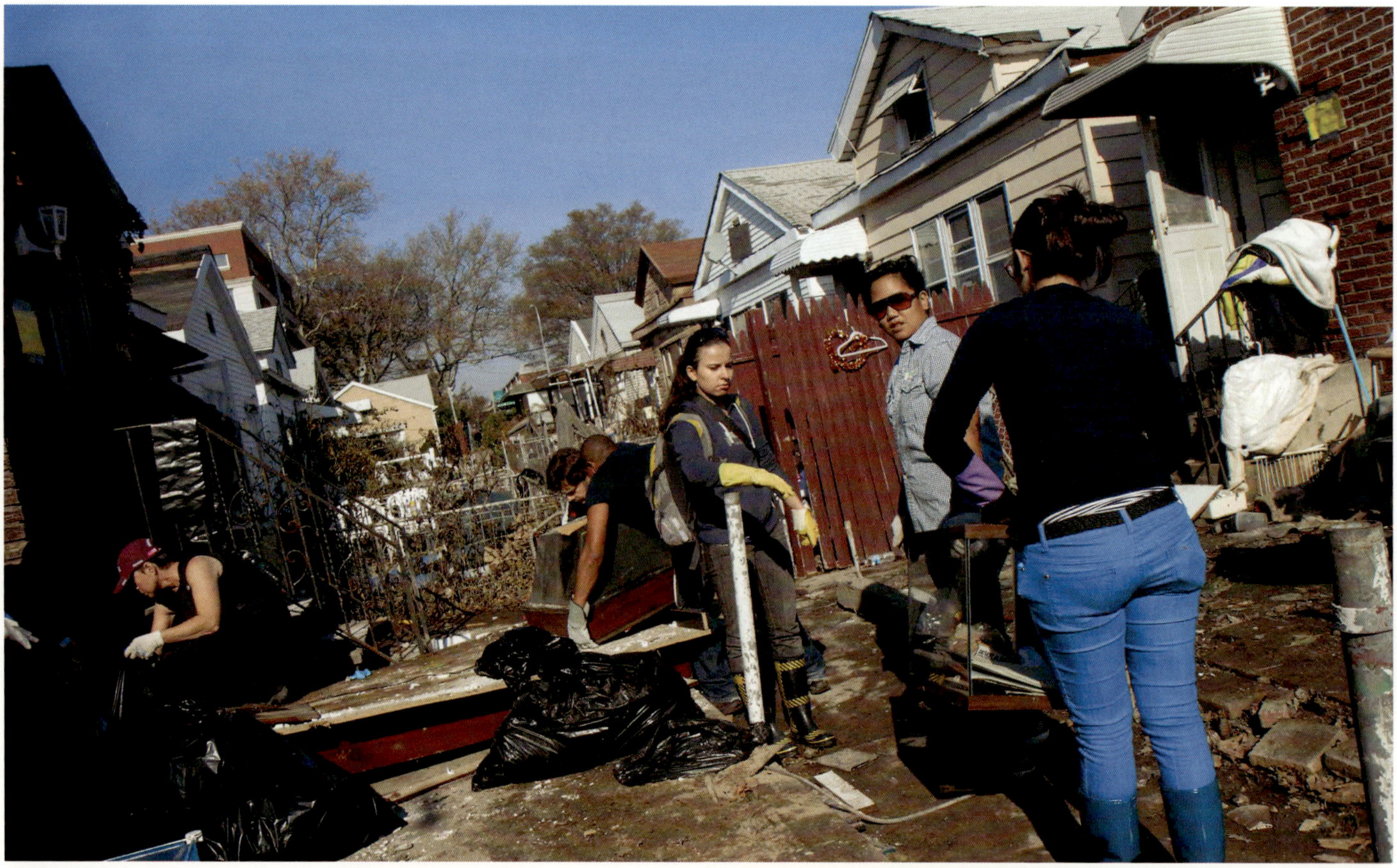

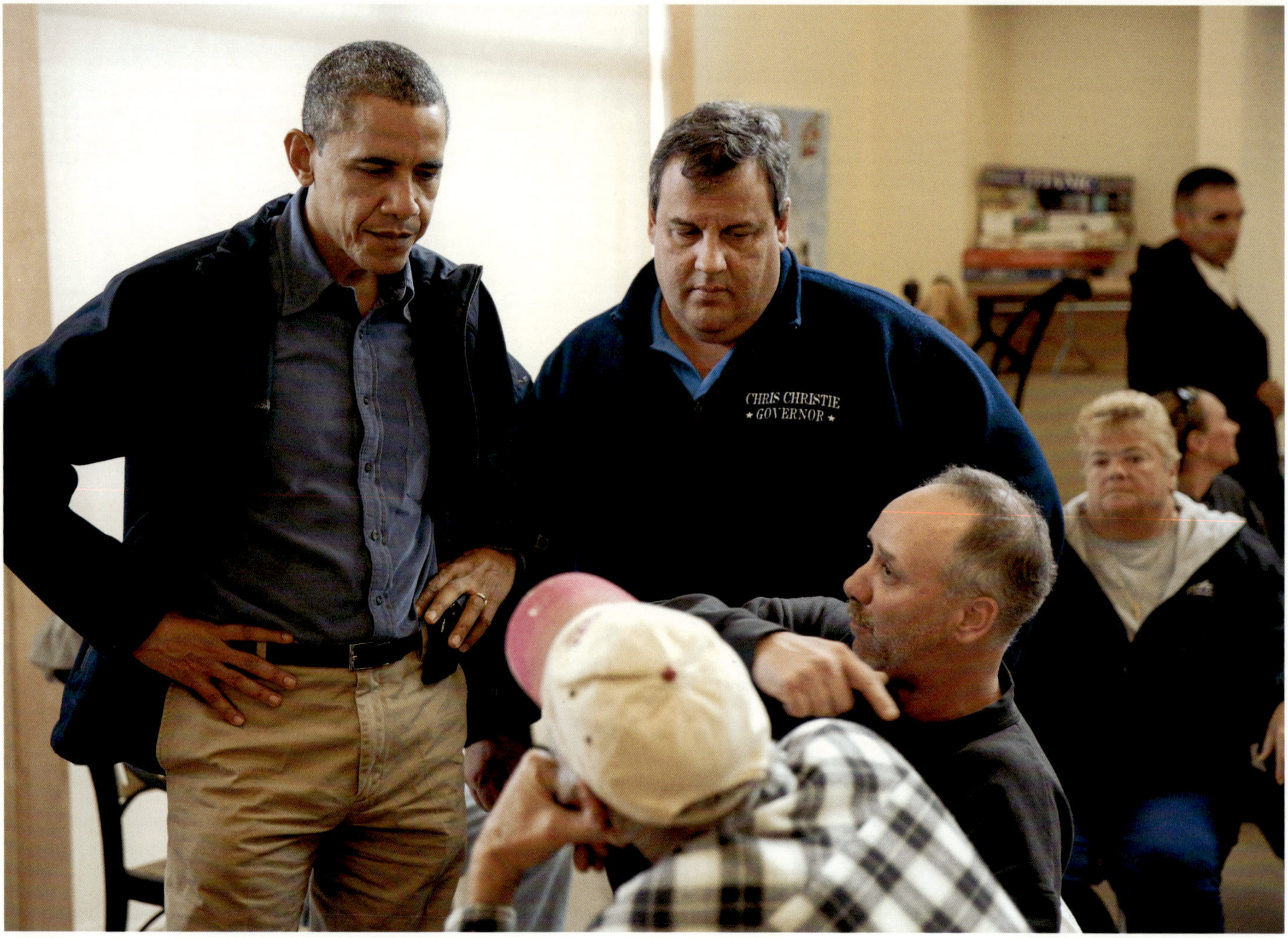
CHRIS CHRISTIE
★ GOVERNOR ★

Responding to the Needs of the Region

State and local governments launched a variety of recovery efforts, but fully addressing Sandy's devastation was beyond the resources or expertise of any individual community. Furthermore, the storm doled out damage that crossed numerous political borders – from ruptured railway lines to disrupted reef systems that stretched across municipal boundaries – requiring an unprecedented level of coordination across jurisdictions.

President Obama launched the Hurricane Sandy Rebuilding Task Force to align federal policies and resources with local needs and priorities. Chaired by Shaun Donovan, then Secretary of the Department of Housing and Urban Development, the Task Force was also charged with furnishing recommendations for rebuilding towards long-term resilience. As the Task Force began developing its understanding of the situation on the ground, Donovan made contact with the water management administration in the Kingdom of the Netherlands, home to some of the world's leading water experts. This collaboration between the Dutch and US governments was of great value to the Task Force's approach. By appointing Henk Ovink to the Task Force as special advisor and Principal of Rebuild by Design, the Dutch government's insights into the intersection of politics, design, and planning became embedded into the Task Force's work.

The international perspective suggested that rebuilding would require a process fundamentally different from the regular federal model. Designing successful interventions would rely upon intensive collaboration between community members, government agencies, and talented experts from a variety of fields. Additionally, the process would have to start with regional research and analysis, wherein a "design thinking" approach would help collaborators develop a highly nuanced understanding of the region's vulnerabilities before they began identifying critical problems or envisioning solutions. Last but not least, making an up-front commitment to funding the first phases of implementation for the best designs would incentivize participation.

With these conditions and guidelines in place, the Task Force formally recommended "creat[ing] a design competition to develop innovative resilient design solutions that address the Sandy-affected region's most pressing vulnerabilities." That competition became Rebuild by Design.

"Local governments and community leaders are at the front lines of disaster recovery, and it is the job of the Federal Government to have their back by supporting their efforts, providing guidance when necessary, and delivering resources to help them fulfill their needs."

—

Secretary Shaun Donovan, Hurricane Sandy Rebuilding Task Force Report

Above: Two weeks after the storm, community members from the Sheepshead Bay, Brooklyn bungalow community returned to clean their homes.

Below: President Barack Obama and New Jersey Governor Chris Christie talk with residents at the Brigantine Beach Community Center, where a temporary shelter was developed for displaced families.

Following Spread: Donations flooded in from across the country to help local residents after the storm. Many aid centers were ad hoc sites set up by grassroots responders.

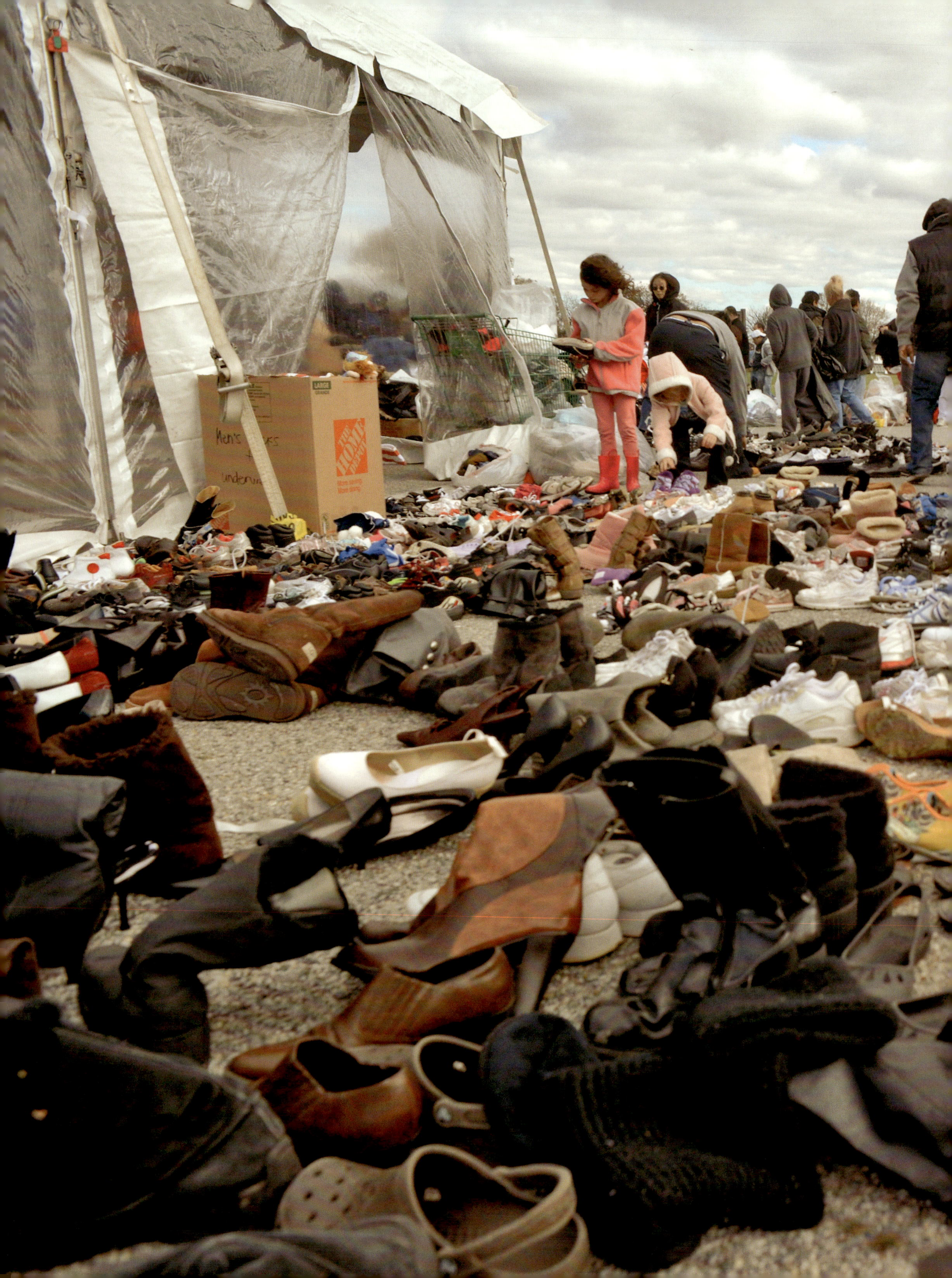

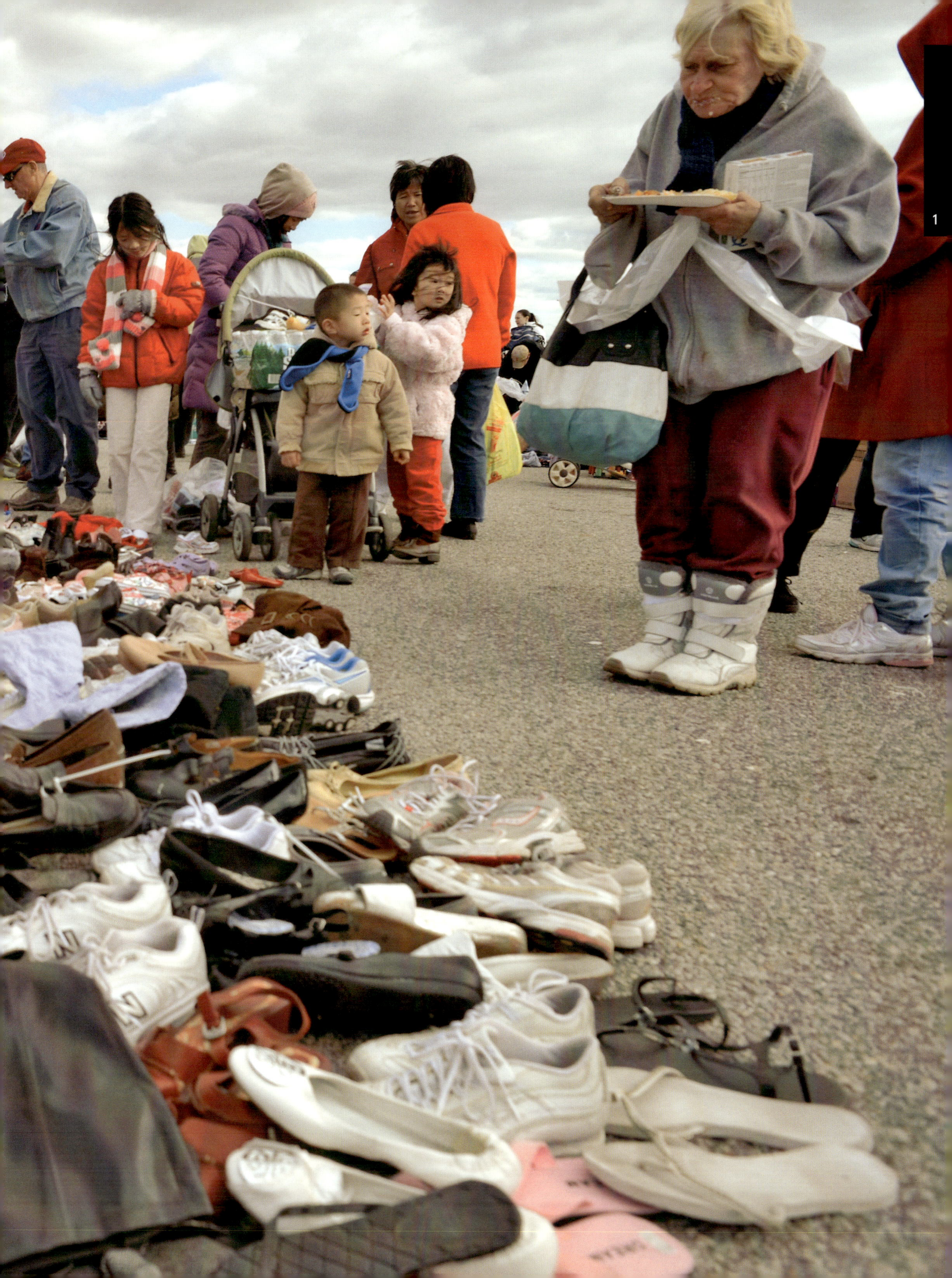

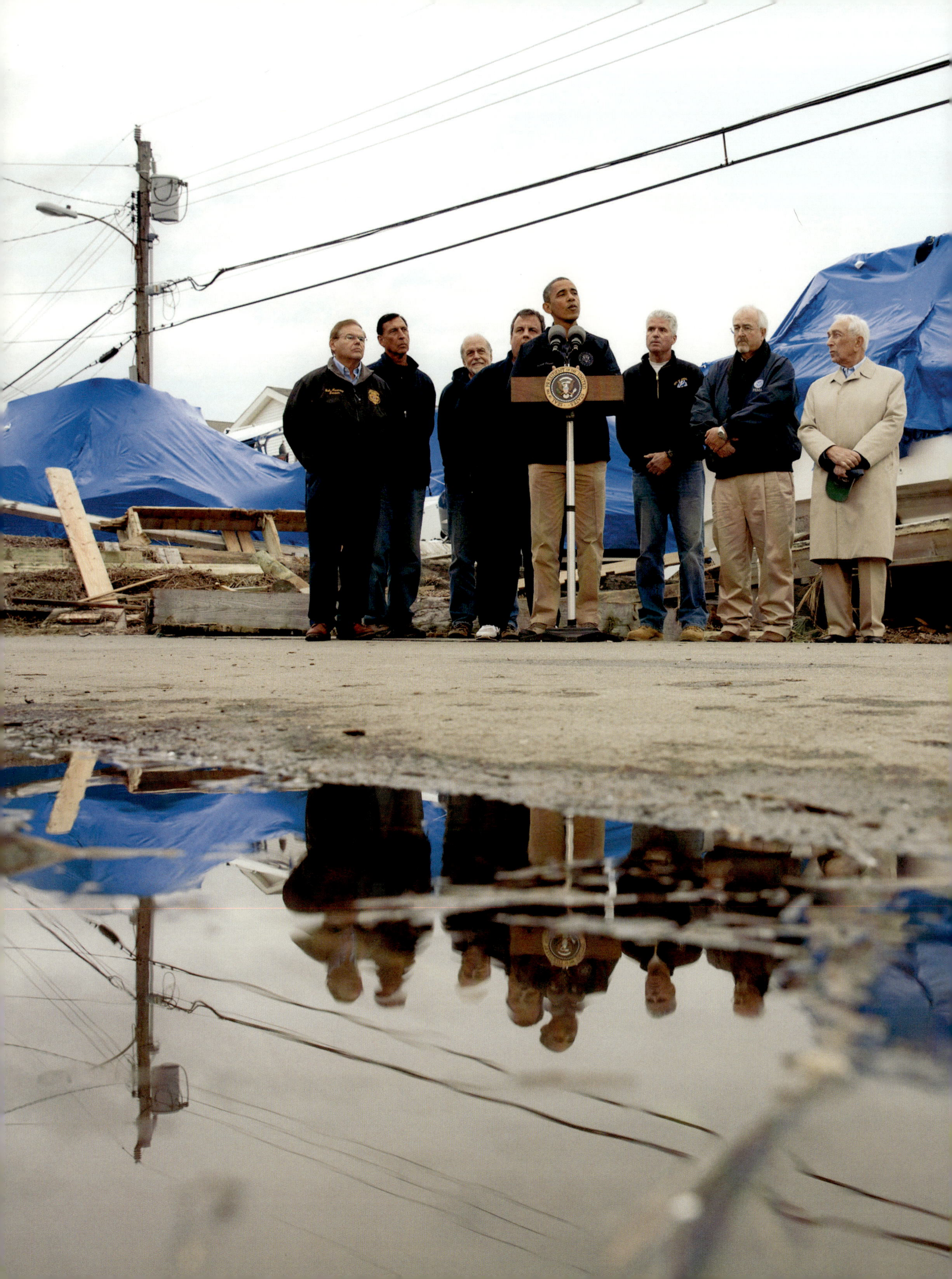

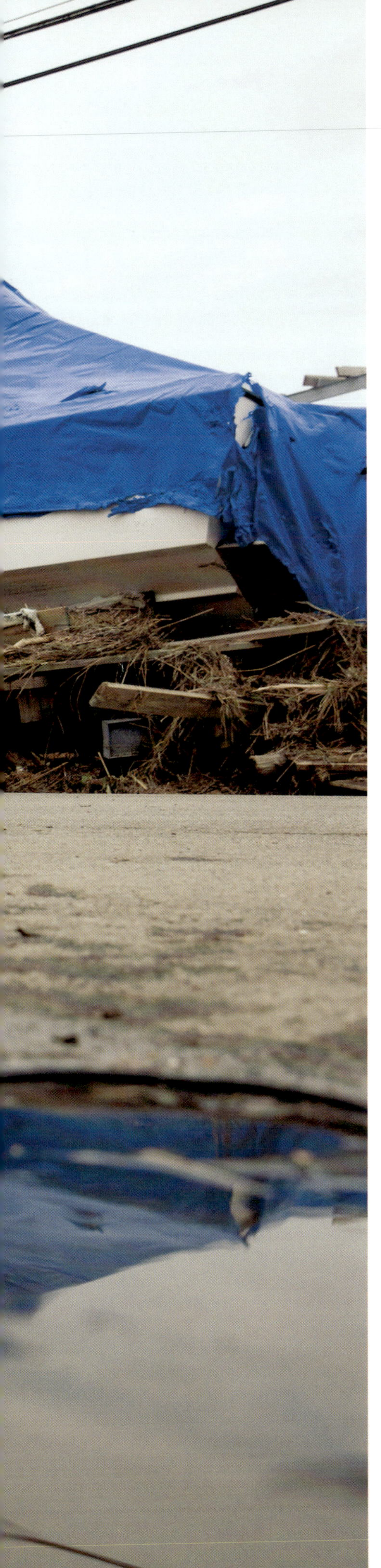

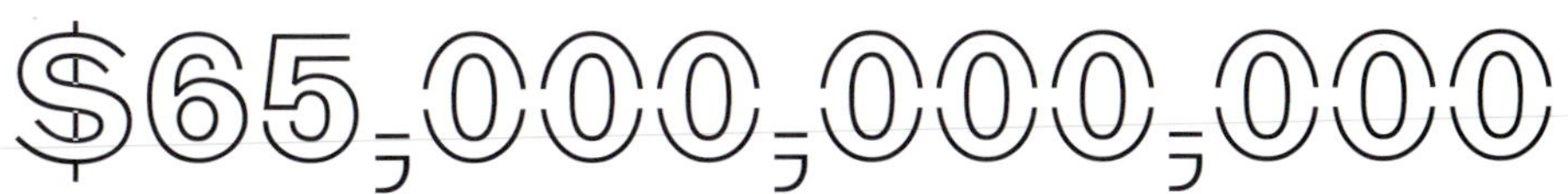

$65,000,000,000

IN DAMAGES AND ECONOMIC LOSS OVER 24 STATES

200,000

SMALL BUSINESS CLOSURES

100,000,000

GALLONS OF RAW SEWAGE RELEASED IN HEWLETT BAY

2,000,000

WORKING DAYS LOST

8,500,000

CUSTOMERS WITHOUT POWER

650,000

HOMES DAMAGED OR DESTROYED

All data from Hurricane Sandy Rebuilding Task Force, "Hurricane Sandy Rebuilding Strategy," August 2013.

President Barack Obama, center, along with New Jersey Governor Chris Christie, FEMA Administrator Craig Fugate, and other officials, makes a statement after touring Hurricane Sandy storm damage in Brigantine, New Jersey, October 31, 2012.

Designing the Process

The Task Force, with a core group of advisors and staff, created a unique structure for the competition. A successive and connected set of stages was established to orient the design process around in-depth research, cross-sector, cross-professional collaboration, and iterative design development. The design process incorporated a variety of inputs to ensure that each stage's deliverables were based on the best knowledge and talent, and that the final proposals would be replicable, regional, and implementable.

Making room for a collaborative and innovative approach was a side step away from the institutional world. A detour around negotiations, the process aimed to build understanding and trust.

2 RESEARCH

Objective Establish the broadest possible understanding of the region's vulnerabilities to future risks and uncertainties, to enhance resilience.

Process Rebuild by Design's local partner organizations create an intensive, three-month program of field research to introduce teams to a variety of local stakeholders, providing a comprehensive view of the storm's effects — the damage it created as well as the long-standing problems it uncovered or exacerbated.

A Research Advisory Board leads the teams through the region to learn from a variety of perspectives, and teams conduct additional research to supplement this on-the-ground work. Research is collaborative across teams and focuses on typologies as well as locations.

Result A public presentation from each team that includes three to five "design opportunities" describing conceptual approaches for interventions and an overall compilation of research submitted by all teams.

1 TALENT

Objective Gather the talent of the world to work with the talent of the Sandy-affected region.

Process Task Force issues a Request for Qualifications and Approaches calling for teams to assemble themselves in interdisciplinary partnerships to tackle the region's physical and social vulnerabilities.

To incentivize participation, the Federal Government pledges funding to implement the winning designs while private philanthropy pledges prize money for competitors.

Result Ten finalist design teams are selected comprising a diverse set of complementary skills and approaches.

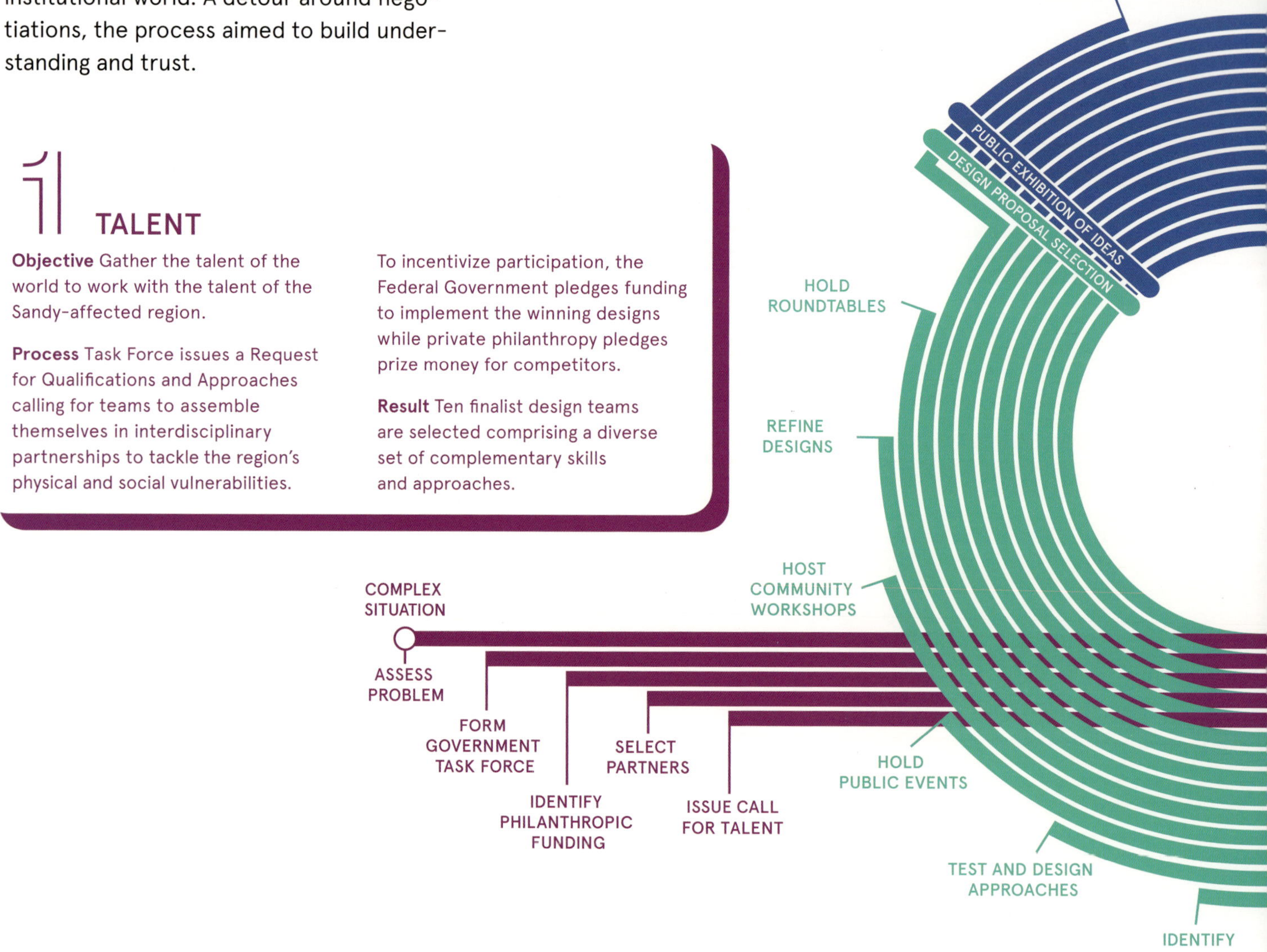

3 DESIGN

Objective Develop implementable solutions that have support from local communities and governments.

Process HUD Secretary Shaun Donovan selects, on average, one design opportunity for each team to develop. Teams then gather diverse local stakeholders into community coalitions, with whom they begin a four-month process of co-designing the final interventions. Using meetings, colloquia, charrettes, and non-traditional events to gain the broadest perspectives, they create solutions that not only address disaster scenarios, but also enrich the daily life of community members.

Result Ten fully developed, implementable resilience proposals champion communities' visions for future development and have support from the local governments.

1

4 IMPLEMENTATION

Objective Governments and community stakeholders work together to build the projects.

Process A jury evaluates the projects. HUD Secretary Shaun Donovan designates which are eligible to receive federal funds. HUD allocates disaster recovery funds to city and state governments for the implementation of the projects' first stages. HUD sets strong guidelines for community involvement to ensure that the coalitions formed during the competition continue to be involved through implementation. Teams are poised to work with government and communities to refine the interventions.

Result A more resilient region achieved through collaboration and design.

CRITIQUE DESIGNS

PARTICIPATE IN LECTURES, SITE VISITS, WORKSHOPS

CONDUCT INDIVIDUAL RESEARCH & INVESTIGATIONS

FORM WORKING GROUPS & SHARE KNOWLEDGE

WORK WITH GOVERNMENT PARTNERS

SELECT TALENT

BUILD RESEARCH ADVISORY GROUP

FINAL PUBLIC PRESENTATION

JURY JUDGEMENT AND WINNERS SELECTED

FUNDING ANNOUNCED

ALLOCATE FUNDING

CONTINUE REFINING DESIGNS

BEGIN CONSTRUCTION

CONTINUE ENGAGING STAKEHOLDERS

LD TIONS

Collaboration Is Key

A powerful core of talented individuals and organizations provided the leadership, logistics, and support necessary to realize the competition's ambitious aims. Four organizations with on-the-ground experience in the Sandy-affected region brought different areas of expertise to the table. Financial support came from a combination of public capital for implementation and private capital for the process. Research advisors helped lead the teams through the process of design. Across the region, residents and government officials grounded the process in local needs, ensuring the approaches would be implementable.

Federal Support

In 2013, Congress appropriated approximately $60 billion for disaster relief and recovery, including $15.2 billion in Community Development Block Grant Disaster Recovery funds, which HUD could award to state and local governments' rebuilding projects. The Task Force reached out to philanthropy for their regional network, local insights and knowledge, as well as their capacity to fund the administration of the competition's creative process and award prizes to offset the design teams' participation costs.*

Philanthropic Support

Philanthropic organizations played a key role in transforming the idea for the competition into a reality. The Rockefeller Foundation, in particular, embraced Rebuild by Design's potential to transform how societies respond to disaster. Along with the Deutsche Bank Americas Foundation, Hearst Foundation, JPB Foundation, New Jersey Recovery Fund, and Surdna Foundation, they provided financial incentives for the research and design stages, underwrote prizes for the design teams, and provided communities with organizing funds and a central project manager to help coordinate the complex enterprise.

Partner Organizations

To bring local experience and specialized expertise into the heart of the competition, HUD brought together a dynamic coalition of four partner organizations: New York University's Institute for Public Knowledge, the Municipal Art Society, Regional Plan Association, and Van Alen Institute. Each partner organization dedicated full-time staff to execute the competition's day-to-day operations; along with staff from HUD, more than a dozen individuals became the backbone of the effort. They led the teams through the region, facilitated relationships with community stakeholders and government officials at the local, state, and federal levels, and tackled a complex and protean set of logistics. The partner organizations also brought a diverse cohort of scientists, academics, and local experts into the process, ensuring that the design teams had the best access to a rich field of information as they undertook their research.

"The Rockefeller Foundation funded the Rebuild by Design competition to create a space for talents of every stripe to break the models and construct innovative and creative ways to build for our future. The winning proposals will be beneficial to all of us in both directly improving Sandy-impacted communities, and also by providing models around which successes can be replicated."

—

Judith Rodin, President,
The Rockefeller Foundation

* HUD's ability to award funding to state and local governments was granted by the Disaster Relief Appropriations Act of 2013. The America COMPETES Act governed HUD's jurisdiction during the competition itself.

1

Partners

The NYU Institute for Public Knowledge (IPK) is dedicated to bringing robust academic scholarship to bear on issues of public concern. Understanding social vulnerability is one of IPK's primary areas of concern, and the Institute brought this focus to its participation in post-Sandy projects including the Superstorm Research Lab and Rebuild by Design. IPK orchestrated the competition's initial three-month research stage and brought together a Research Advisory Group of experts in a variety of fields to enhance the design teams' insight, research, and analysis.

The Municipal Art Society (MAS) promotes the New York metropolitan area's economic vitality, cultural vibrancy, environmental sustainability, and social diversity. Even before the research stage, MAS helped inform the Task Force's understanding of the region. Once the competition began, the organization was instrumental in co-creating and leading the critical community engagement process.

The Regional Plan Association (RPA) is a leader in understanding and advocating for issues such as transportation, the environment, and economic development across New York, New Jersey, and Connecticut. RPA brought crucial technical expertise, region-specific knowledge, and an informed understanding of how to work with local communities.

The Van Alen Institute (VAI) jumpstarts innovation to transform cities and landscapes in ways that improve people's lives. For the competition, VAI orchestrated and executed an innovative outreach strategy that was vital to bringing stakeholders into the process through communications and public programs.

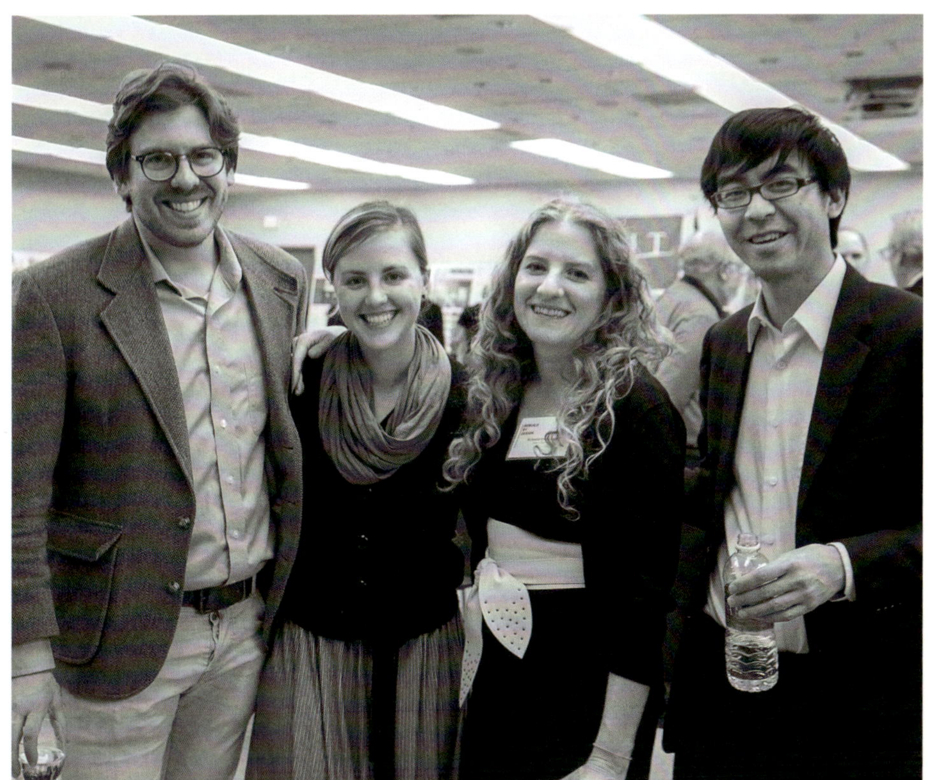

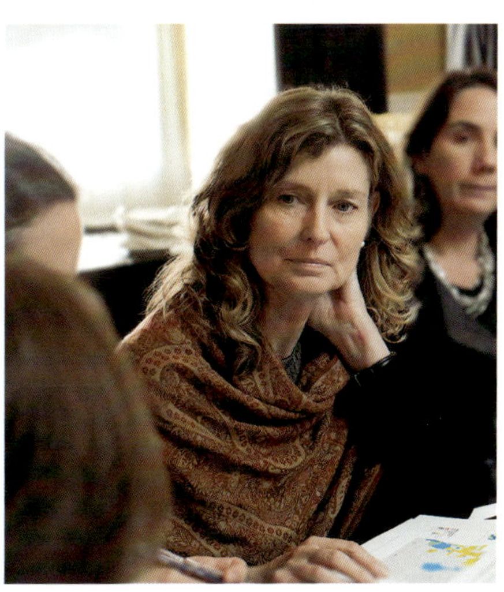

Left: Staff from partner organizations gathered for the October 2013 unveiling of teams' "design opportunities." Pictured are Sam Carter, Institute for Public Knowledge; Courtney Smith, Municipal Art Society; Amy Chester, Rebuild by Design; and Jerome Chou, Van Alen Institute.

Above: Nancy Kete, The Rockefeller Foundation, was a critical supporter of the competition.

Design Teams

Planning for climate change necessitates insights from a broad spectrum of highly specialized fields. Ecology, engineering, planning, sociology, landscaping, architecture, water management, climate forecasting, and a number of other disciplines are crucial to successfully addressing the region's vulnerabilities.

HUD issued a design brief calling for teams from around the world with interdisciplinary qualifications to articulate their approach to resilience. 148 teams from 15 countries applied for the chance to compete in Rebuild by Design. The applicants represented firms and individuals from a broad range of fields. The Task Force selected ten teams who would bring the greatest level of talent and the most diverse and complementary set of approaches to the competition.

With the funding, partners, and design teams in place, the next step was diving into the region's communities to learn about the challenges at hand. After that, the competition set off in earnest.

"The key here is to recognize that government is not known for its innovation. The onus is on us to go out and find people who are innovative. But the burden is also on us to make sure that the end result has credibility. That means buildability."

—

Holly Leicht, HUD Regional Administrator for New York and New Jersey

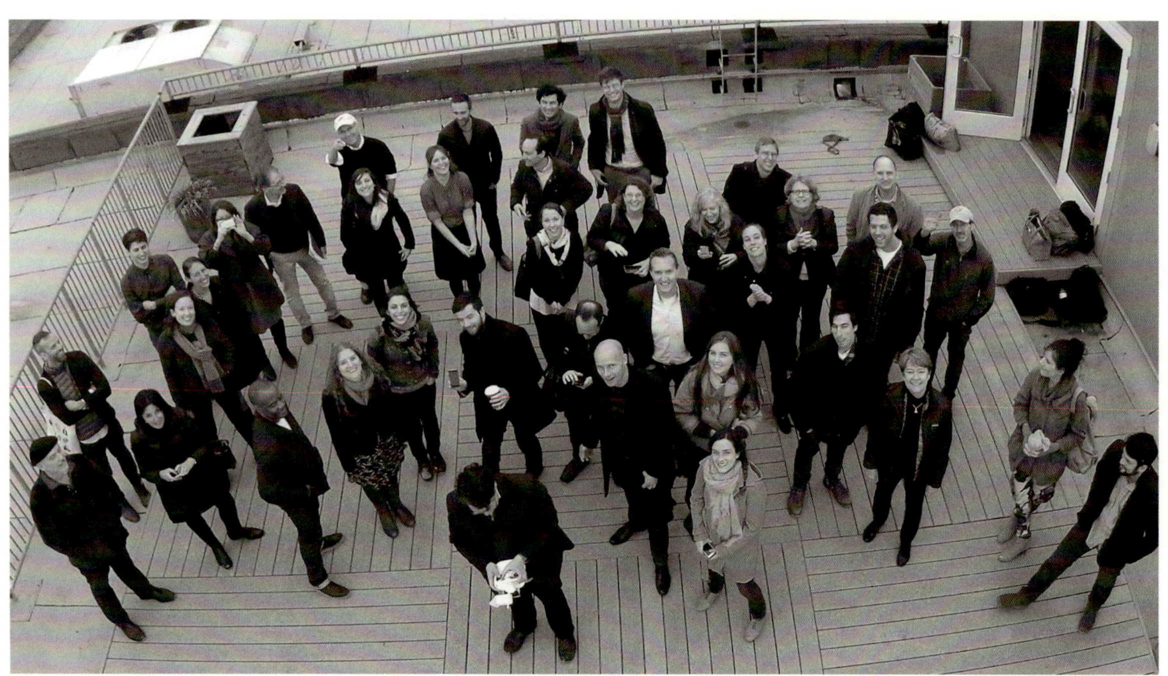

Above: Design team members tour New Orleans to learn about the development of flood protections after Hurricane Katrina.

Following Spread: Design team members from the SCAPE, Interboro, Penn/OLIN, and BIG Teams gather at the Jacob Riis Houses on New York City's Lower East Side for the announcement of winning designs in June 2014.

Team Members

BIG Team
Bjarke Ingels Group: Lead, Urban Design and Architecture
AEA Consulting: Cultural Resources
ARCADIS: Coastal Resilience Engineering
Buro Happold: Energy and Structural Engineering
Green Shield Ecology: Ecological Services
James Lima Planning + Development: Planning and Development
Level Agency for Infrastructure: Infrastructure Engineering
One Architecture: Urban Planning
Starr Whitehouse: Landscape Architecture

HR&A Advisors with Cooper, Robertson & Partners
HR&A Advisors, Inc: Lead, Economic Strategist/Project Management
Cooper, Robertson & Partners: Lead, Planning and Architecture
Dewberry: Hazard Mitigation/Disaster Planning
Southwest Brooklyn Industrial Development Corporation: Economic Development
W Architecture and Landscape Architecture: Public Realm Design

Interboro Team
Interboro Partners: Lead, Urban Design and Community Engagement
Apex: Infrastructure Engineering
Bosch Slabbers: Urban and Landscape Design
Center for Urban Pedagogy: Education
IMG Rebel: Economics and Finance
David Rusk: Governance
Deltares: Infrastructure Engineering
H+N+S: Urban and Landscape Design
NJIT Infrastructure Planning Program: Academic Research Partner
Palmbout Urban Landscapes: Urban and Landscape Design
Project Projects: Communication Design
RFA Investments: Community Building, Economics, Finance
TU Delft: Academic Research Partner

MIT CAU + ZUS + URBANISTEN
MIT Center for Advanced Urbanism: Lead, Landscape Architecture, Urban Design, Systemic Design, and Environmental Planning
ZUS - Zones Urbaines Sensibiles: Lead, Architecture and Urban Design
De Urbanisten: Lead, Urban Design
75B: Graphic and Communication Design
Deltares: Eco-Engineering
Volker Infradesign: Infrastructure Engineering

OMA
OMA: Lead, Architecture and Urban Design
Balmori Associates: Ecology and Landscape Design
HR&A Advisors, Inc: Economics and Policy
Royal HaskoningDHV: Water Management and Engineering

PennDesign/OLIN
PennDesign: Lead, Geospatial Analytics, Landscape Architecture, Urban Design, and Civic Engagement
OLIN: Lead, Landscape Architecture, Urban Design, and Green Infrastructure
Barretto Bay Strategies: Community Engagement
Buro Happold: Structural Engineering
eDesign Dynamics: Environmental Engineering
HR&A Advisors, Inc: Economic Strategy
Level Agency for Infrastructure: Infrastructure Planning
McLaren Engineering Group: Marine Engineering
Philip Habib & Associates: Civil and Transportation Engineering

Sasaki/Rutgers/Arup
Sasaki: Lead, Urban Planning
Rutgers University: Lead, Ecology, Biology and Sociology
Arup: Lead, Coastal Engineering

SCAPE/LANDSCAPE ARCHITECTURE
SCAPE/LANDSCAPE ARCHITECTURE: Lead, Landscape Architecture
LOT-EK: Architecture
MTWTF: Graphic Design
Ocean and Coastal Consultants: Coastal Engineering
Parsons Brinckerhoff: Engineering/Planning
Paul Greenberg: Author/Advisor
SeArc Ecological Marine Consulting: Marine Biology
Stevens Institute of Technology: Hydrodynamic Modeling
The New York Harbor School: Education/Oyster Restoration

WB unabridged w/Yale ARCADIS
Waggonner and Ball Architects: Lead, Urban Design and Water Management
unabridged Architecture: Lead, Resilience, and Architecture
Yale University: Lead, Ecology and Urban, and Landscape Design
ARCADIS: Lead, Engineering
BumpZoid: Architecture
Dorgan Architecture & Planning: Community Outreach and Implementation
Gulf Coast Community Design Studio: Landscape, Planning, and Community Engagement

WXY/WEST 8
WXY Architecture & Urban Design: Lead, Architecture, and Planning
West 8 Urban Design & Landscape Architecture: Lead
AIR Worldwide: Risk Modeling
ARCADIS: Engineering and Technical Feasibility
Columbia University Center for Urban Real Estate: Development
NowHere Office: Graphic Design
Parsons the New School for Design: Community and Planning
Rutgers University: Landscape Ecology
Stevens Institute of Technology: Climate Science
BJH Advisors: Financial Modeling
Griffith Planning & Design: Planning and Design

1

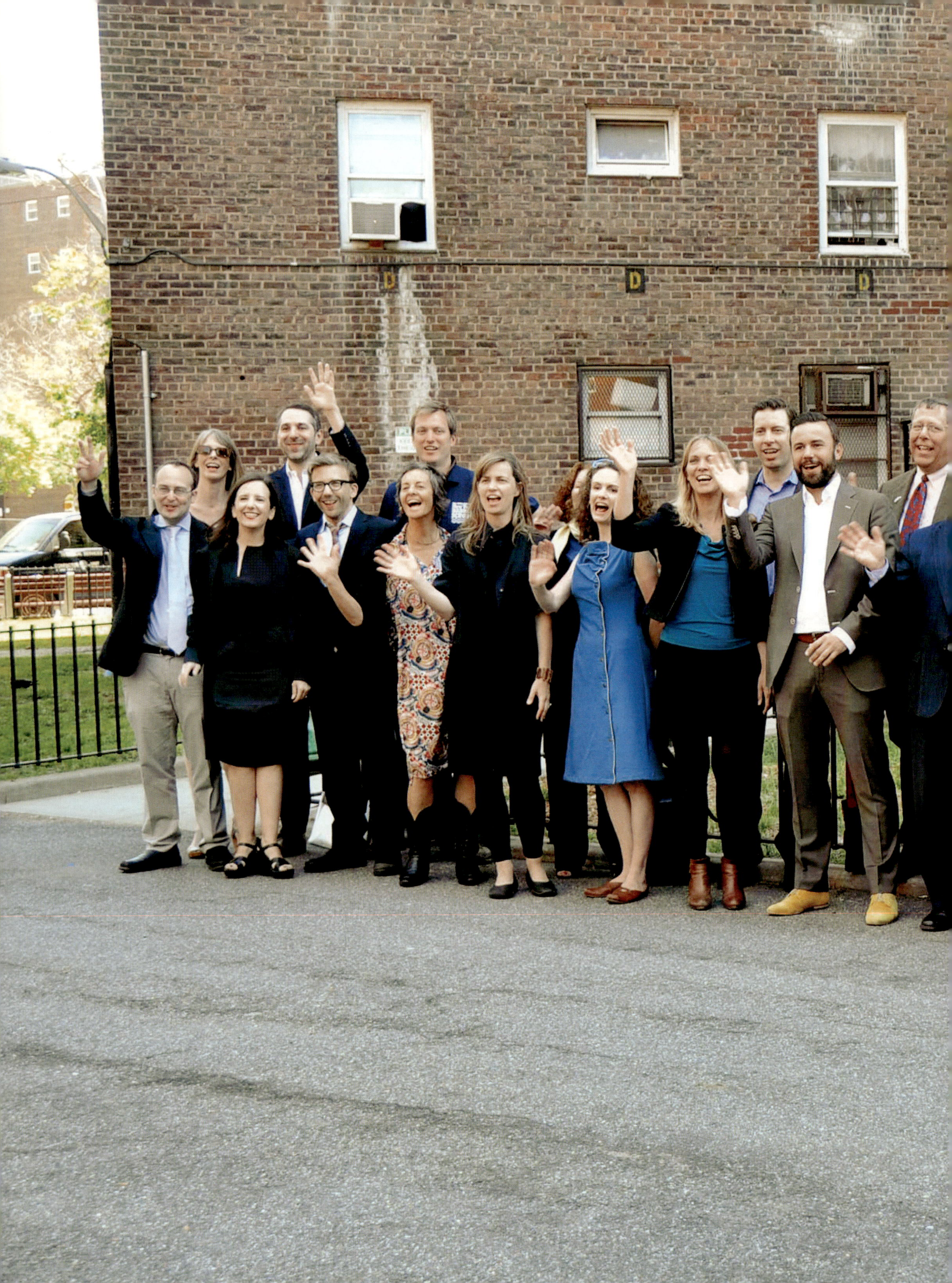

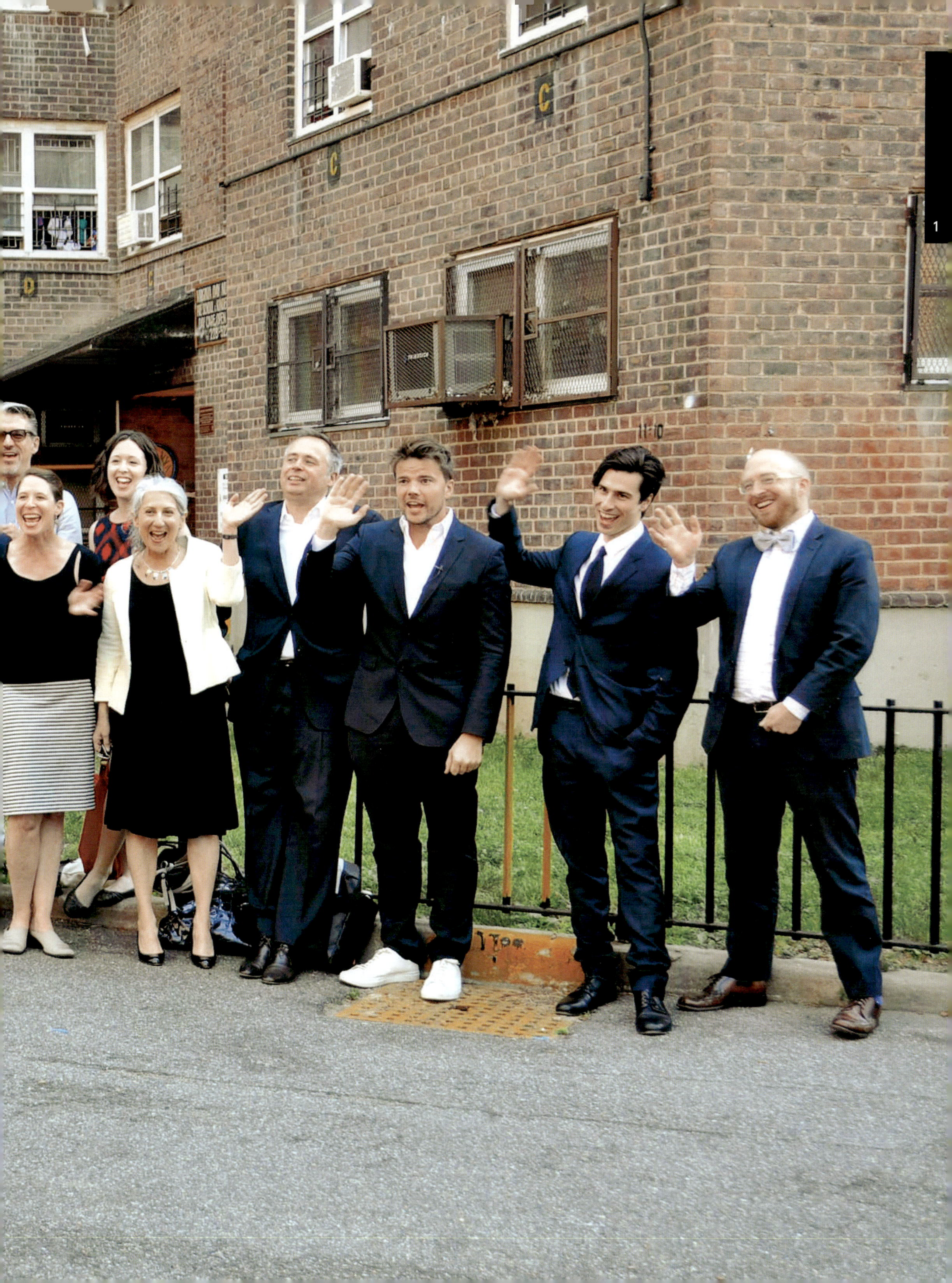

1

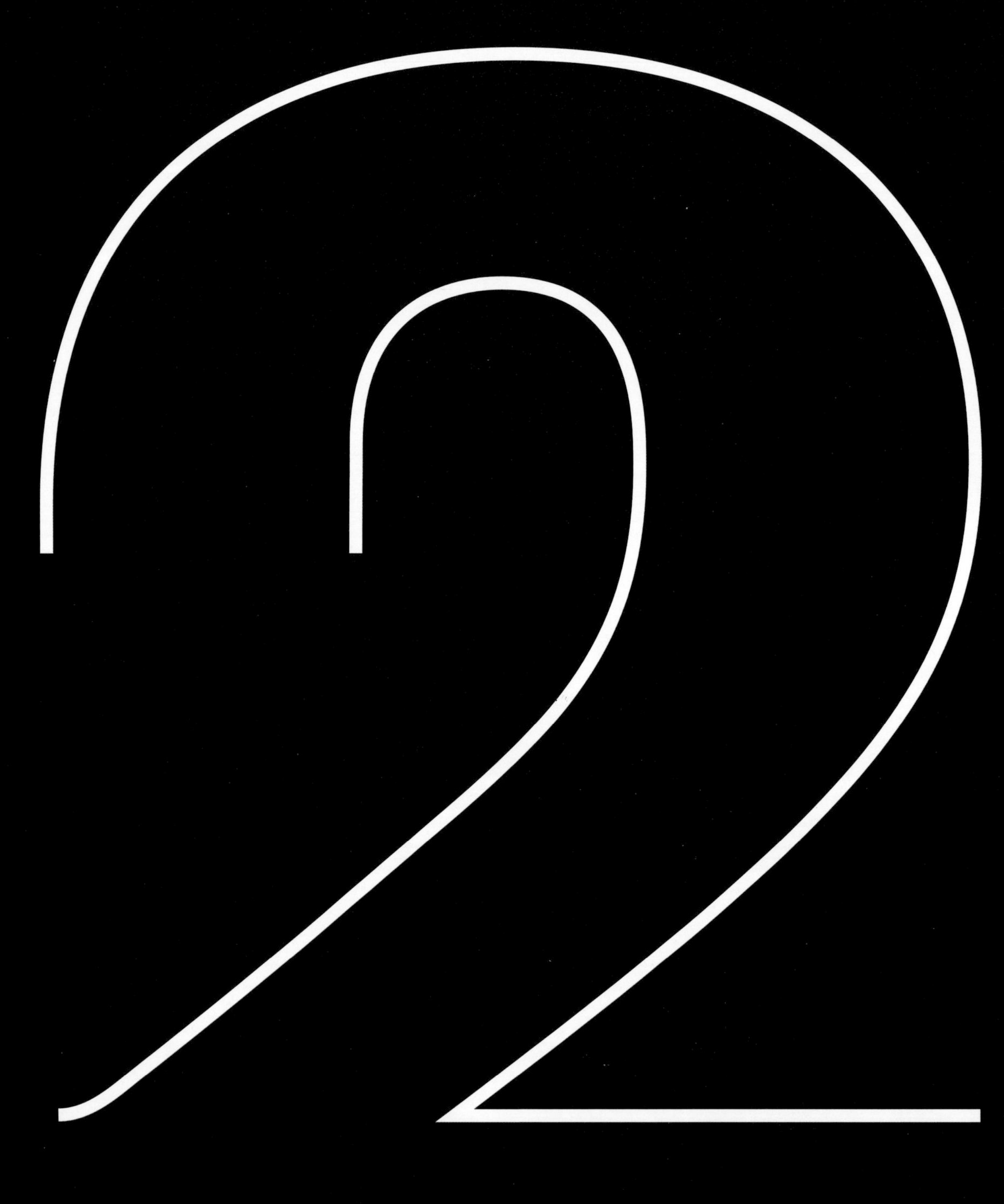

RESEARCHIN
THE REGION

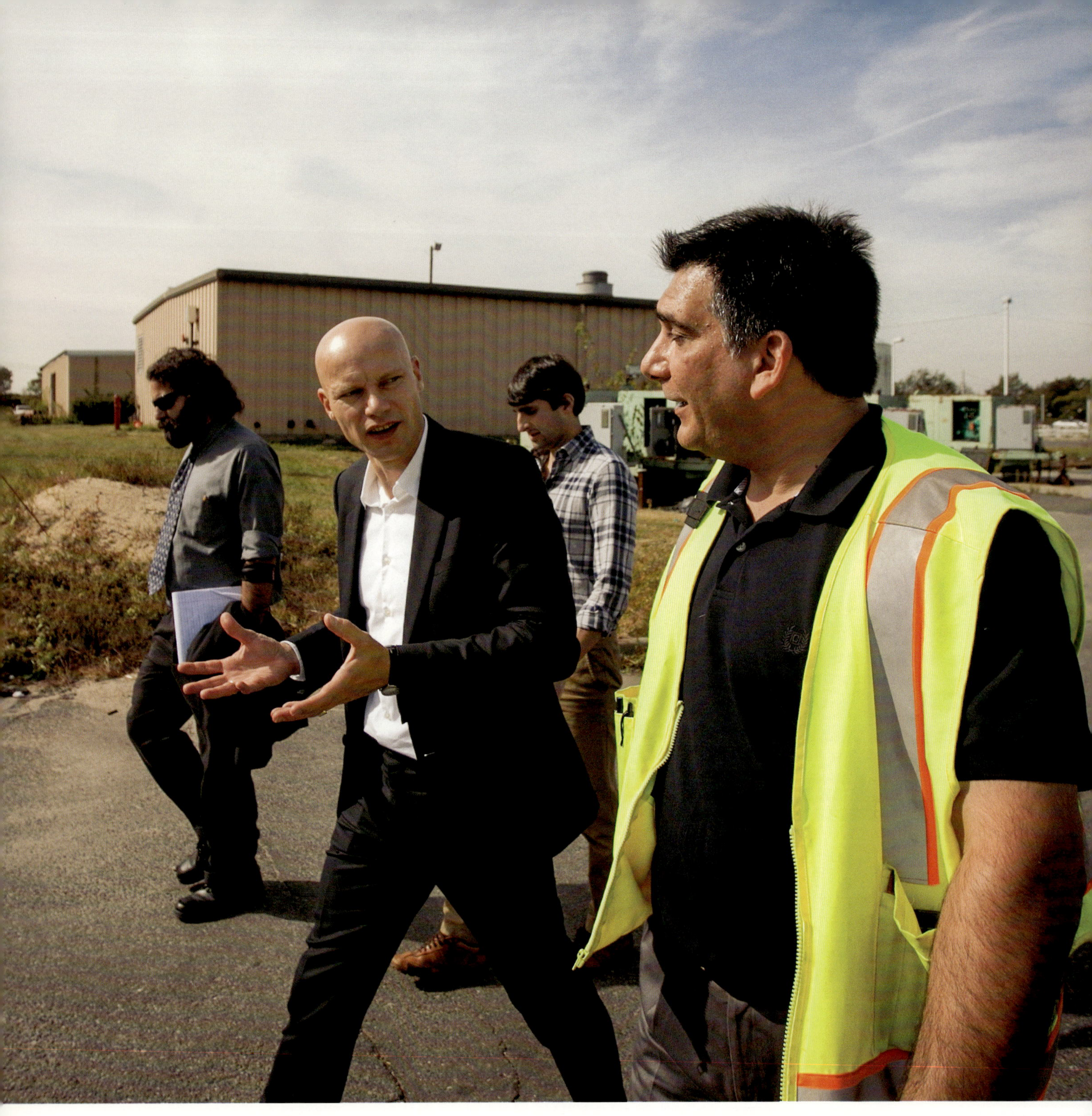

Henk Ovink, Principal Rebuild by Design and Special Advisor to Secretary Shaun Donovan, Chair of Hurricane Sandy Rebuilding Task Force, joins the design teams to tour the Bay Park Sewage Treatment Plant on Long Island, learning from managers and workers about infrastructure issues and flooding that pollutes the local area and the bay. The Plant dumped over 68 million gallons of raw sewage into the Great South Bay during Hurricane Sandy.

Understanding the Region

Designing infrastructure to promote a resilient future required thoroughly understanding the region's current challenges. Just as Sandy had ripped the walls from houses, exposing the structures beneath, its devastation revealed a range of vulnerabilities that had existed in communities since long before the storm. The design teams had to assemble a picture of the region's sociological, political, economic, infrastructural, and ecological vulnerabilities – and the ways in which they intersected – in order to design effective solutions.

With the ten teams in place, Rebuild by Design began a three-month enterprise in collaborative, in-depth research. Co-led by the four partners – NYU's Institute for Public Knowledge, Municipal Art Society, Regional Plan Association, and Van Alen Institute – the design teams toured disaster-strewn locations over five two-day trips in New Jersey, New York, and Connecticut. The Institute for Public Knowledge took the lead as the four partners facilitated walking tours, lectures, workshops, meetings with volunteer responders, and other events to give the teams a greater understanding of the issues at stake — including housing, infrastructure, economy, public health, insurance, access to public services, and ecology.

To expand the depth and reach of the teams' research, the Institute for Public Knowledge assembled an eleven-member Research Advisory Group composed of luminaries from a variety of academic disciplines who could consult on issues such as hydrology, risk management, social displacement, insurance, and climate change forecasting. The Research Advisory Group accompanied the teams on site visits, helping to ensure that each team had the best available material to work with, and reinforced the competition's foundational emphasis on a collaborative research and design process.

As they assembled information, the teams quickly came to work together and rely on one another for support and development. They shared data and observations, presented ideas to each other for assessment and feedback, pooled expertise, and formed working groups on social infrastructure, data analysis, ecology, policy, and planning. The competition's organizers emphasized from the start that until the moment their final proposals went before the judges, Rebuild by Design was intended to function as a collaborative enterprise. The teams took this message to heart as they assessed the region's vulnerabilities and began designing their interventions.

Research Advisory Group

Eric Klinenberg, Chair, Director, New York University's Institute for Public Knowledge
Eugenie L. Birch, Co-Director, Penn Institute for Urban Research, University of Pennsylvania
Vishaan Chakrabarti, Director, Center for Urban Real Estate, Columbia University Graduate School of Architecture, Planning and Preservation
Thomas G. Dallessio, Director, Center for Resilient Design, College of Architecture and Design, New Jersey Institute of Technology
Ingrid Gould Ellen, Director, Urban Planning, New York University Robert F. Wagner School of Public Service
Gerald E. Frug, Professor of Law, Harvard Law School
Mindy Fullilove, Co-Director, Community Research Group, New York State Psychiatric Institute, and Mailman School of Public Health, Columbia University
Mohammad Karamouz, Director of Environmental Engineering, New York University Polytechnic School of Engineering
Klaus Jacob, Special Research Scientist, Lamont-Doherty Earth Observatory, Columbia University Earth Institute
Harvey Molotch, Professor of Sociology and Metropolitan Studies, New York University
William Solecki, Director, CUNY Institute for Sustainable Cities

Regional Site Visits

The ten teams toured 41 neighborhoods during the course of five multi-day site visits, traversing storm-tossed wetlands, desolated beachfront towns, and city streets marked by boarded-up shops and damaged infrastructure. They met with residents, community organizations, activists, business leaders, experts, and many local government officials who shared their experiences of the storm's effects, provided perspectives on the ongoing response, and offered insights on their communities' priorities for long-term recovery. In addition to gathering insights on these excursions, each team was charged with producing new research that would enhance and deepen their design approaches.

Jamaica Bay

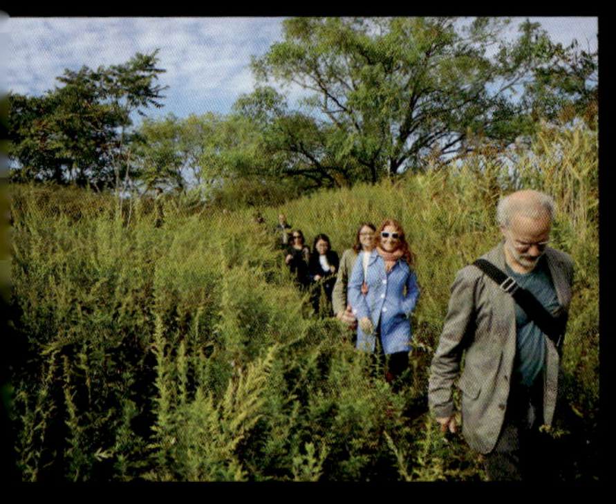

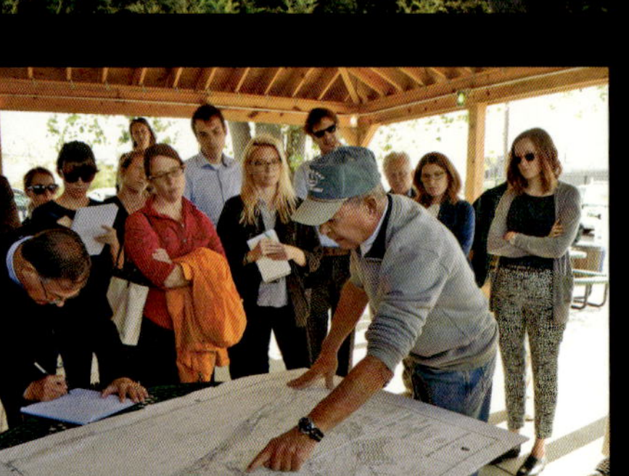

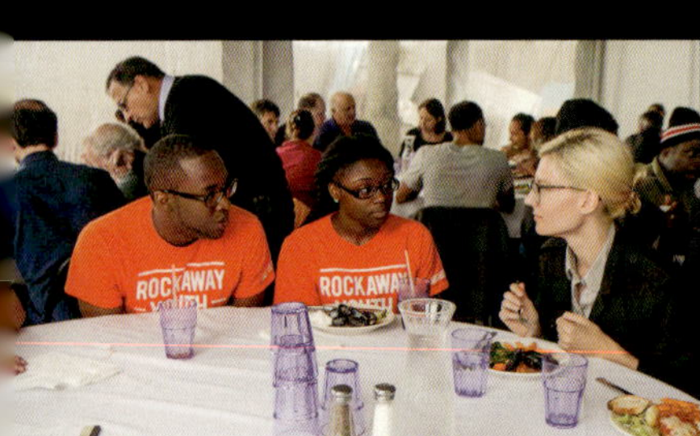

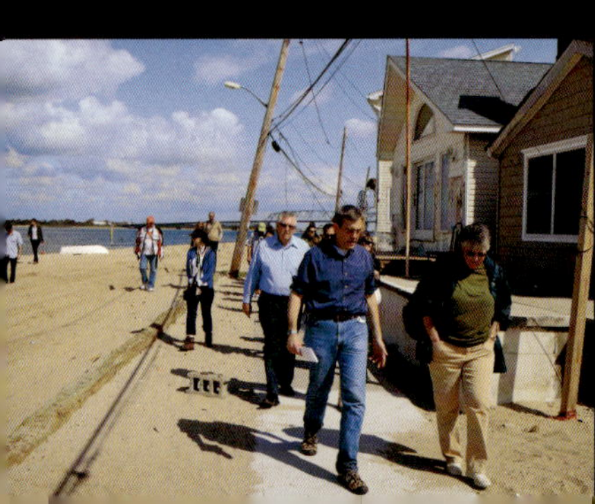

Jersey Shore

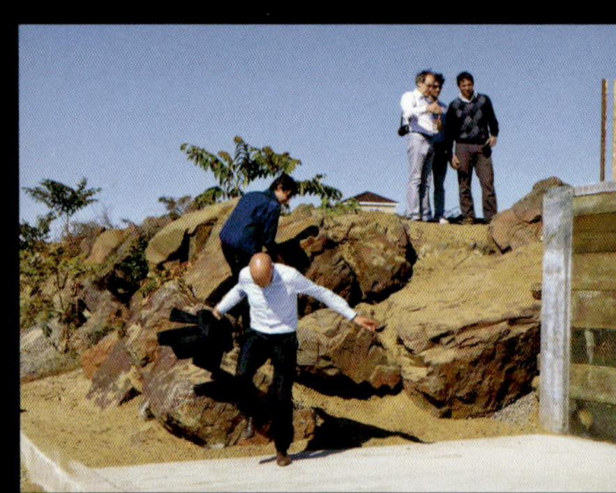

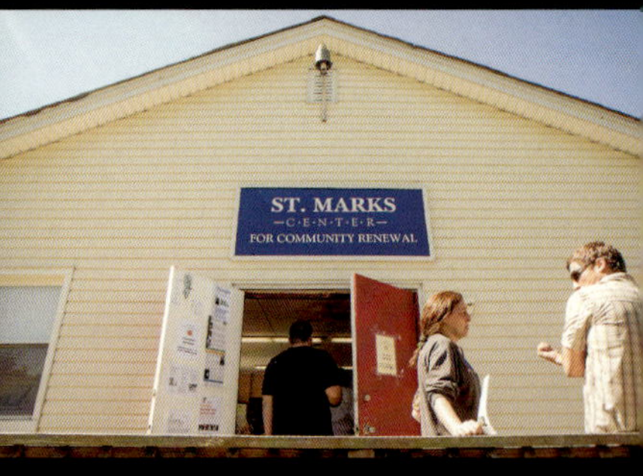

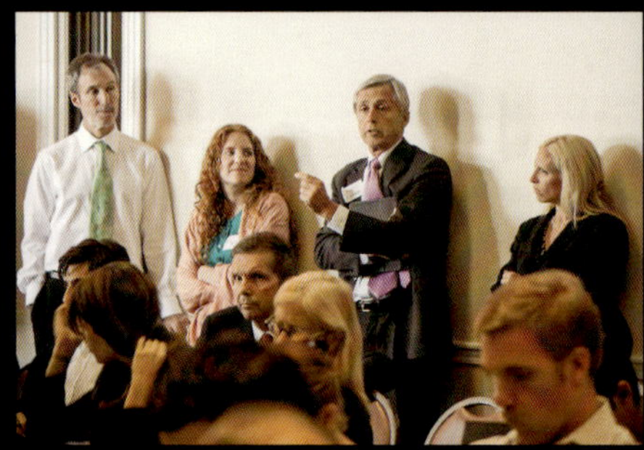

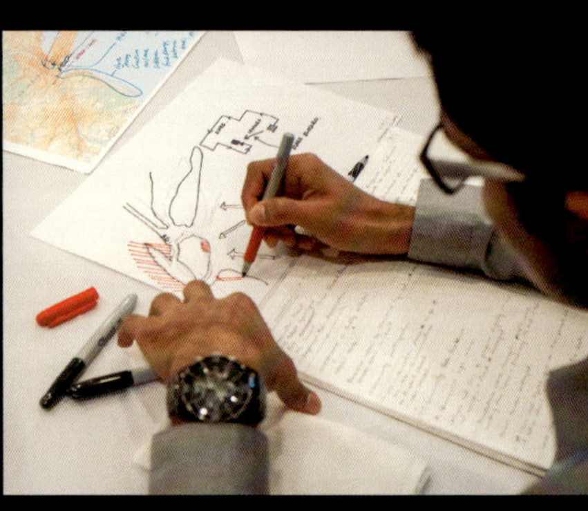

Lower East Side, Hoboken, and Jersey City

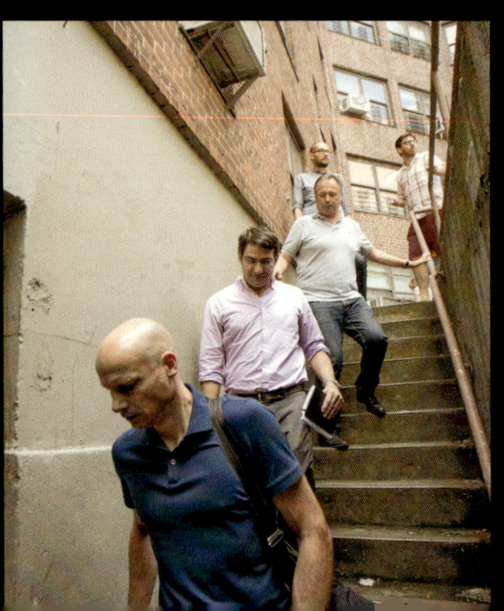

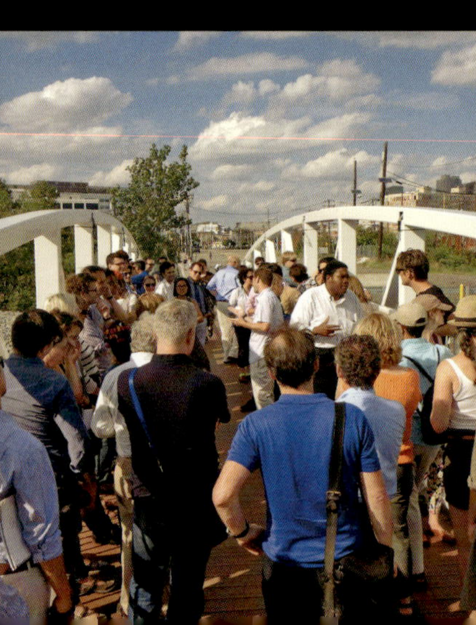

Bridgeport, Milford, and Fairfield

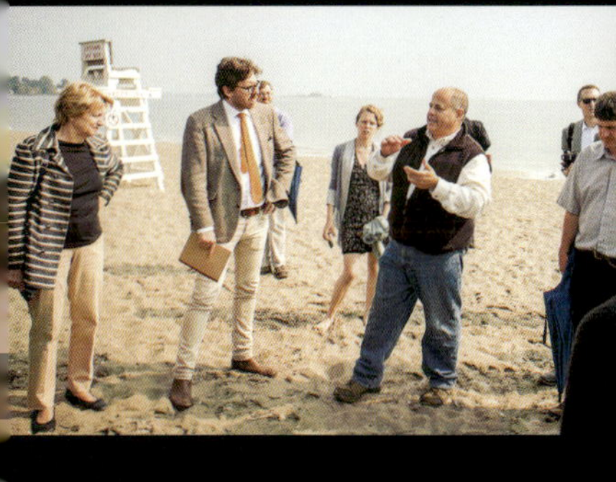

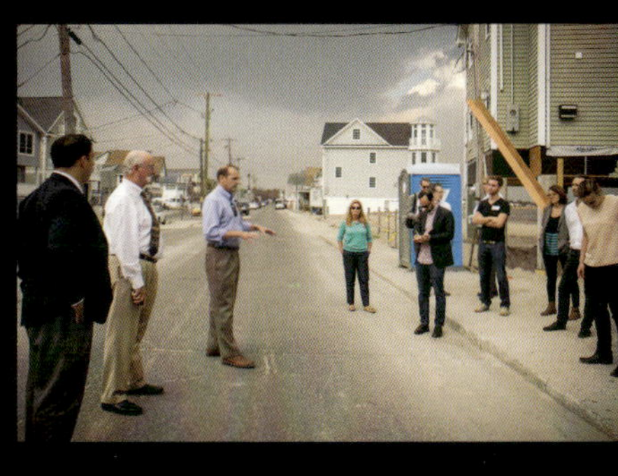

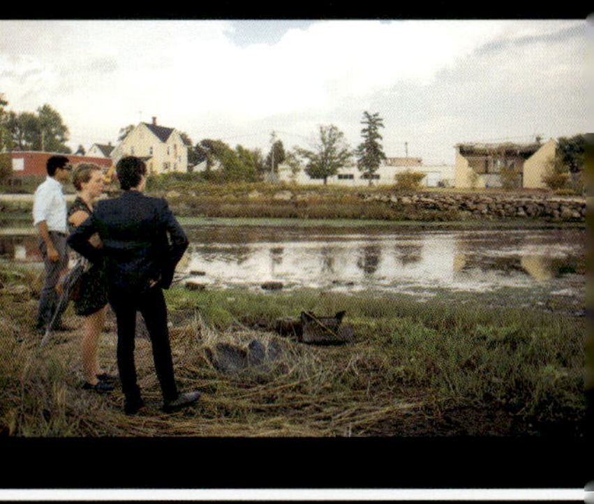

Long Island

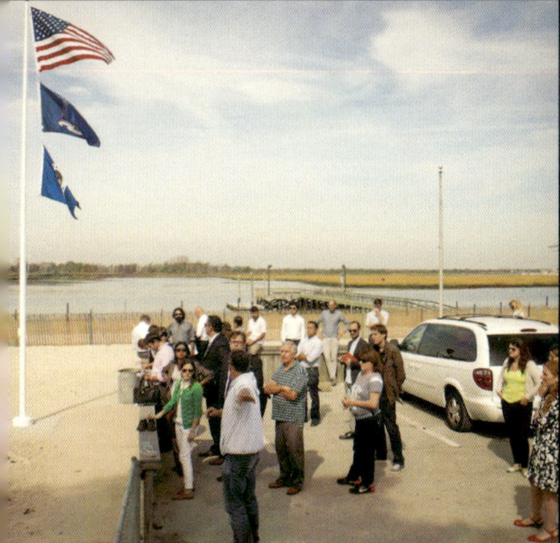

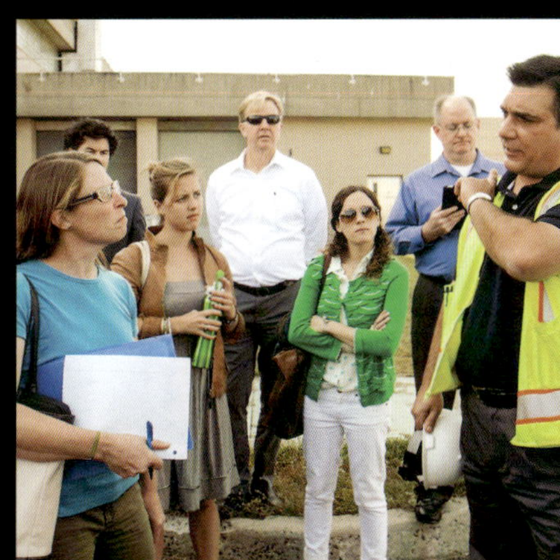

Red Hook and Lower Manhattan

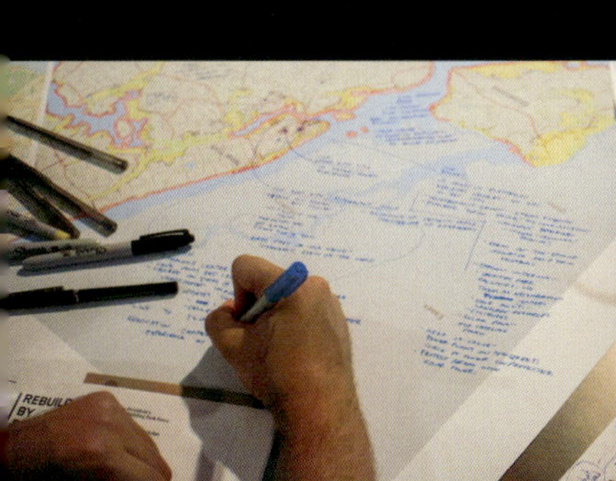

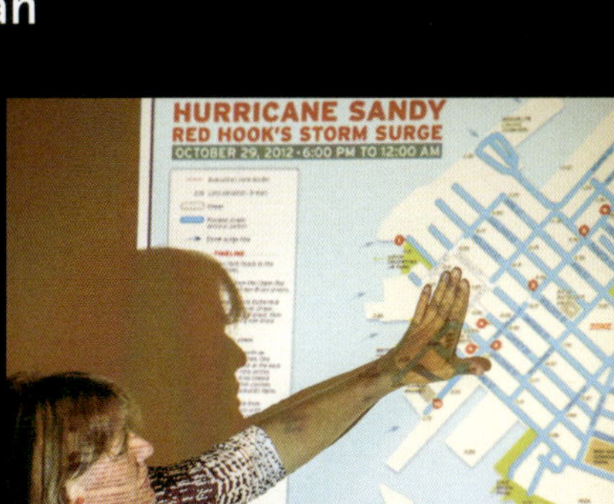

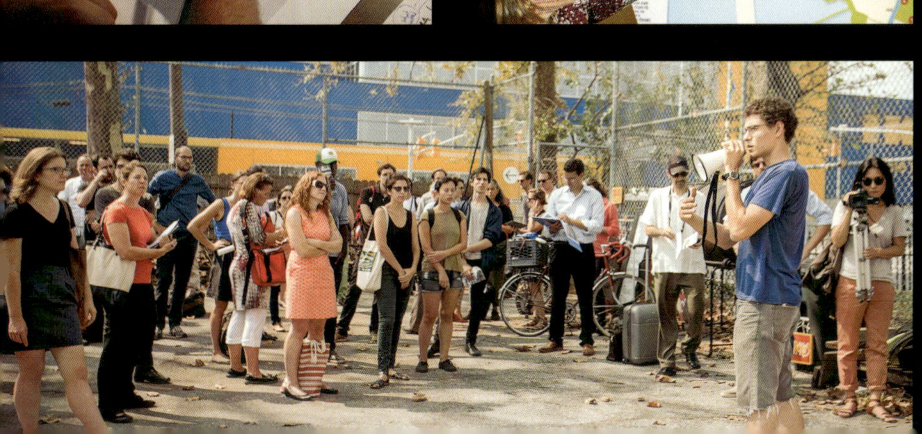

Staten Island

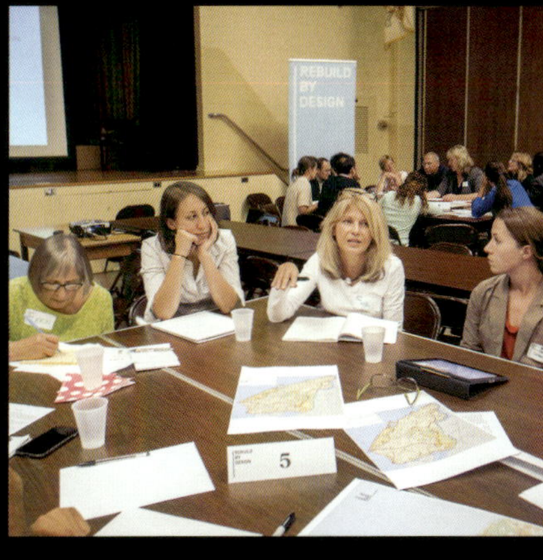

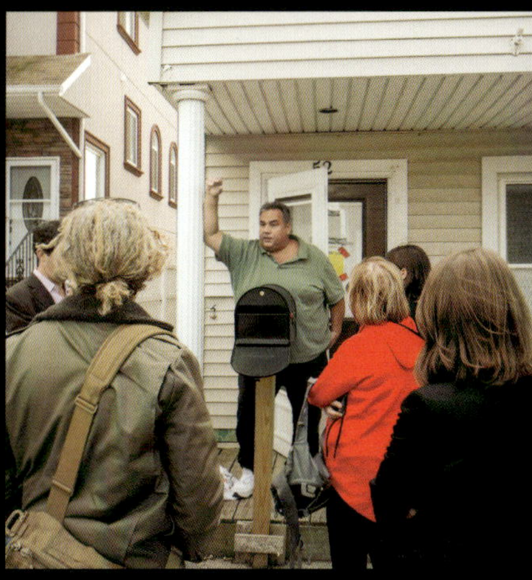

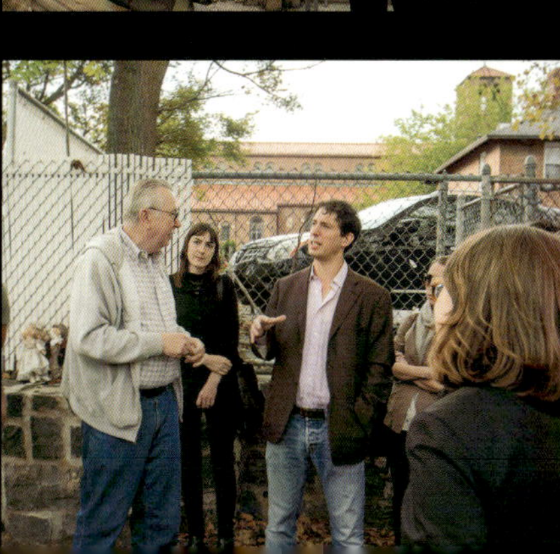

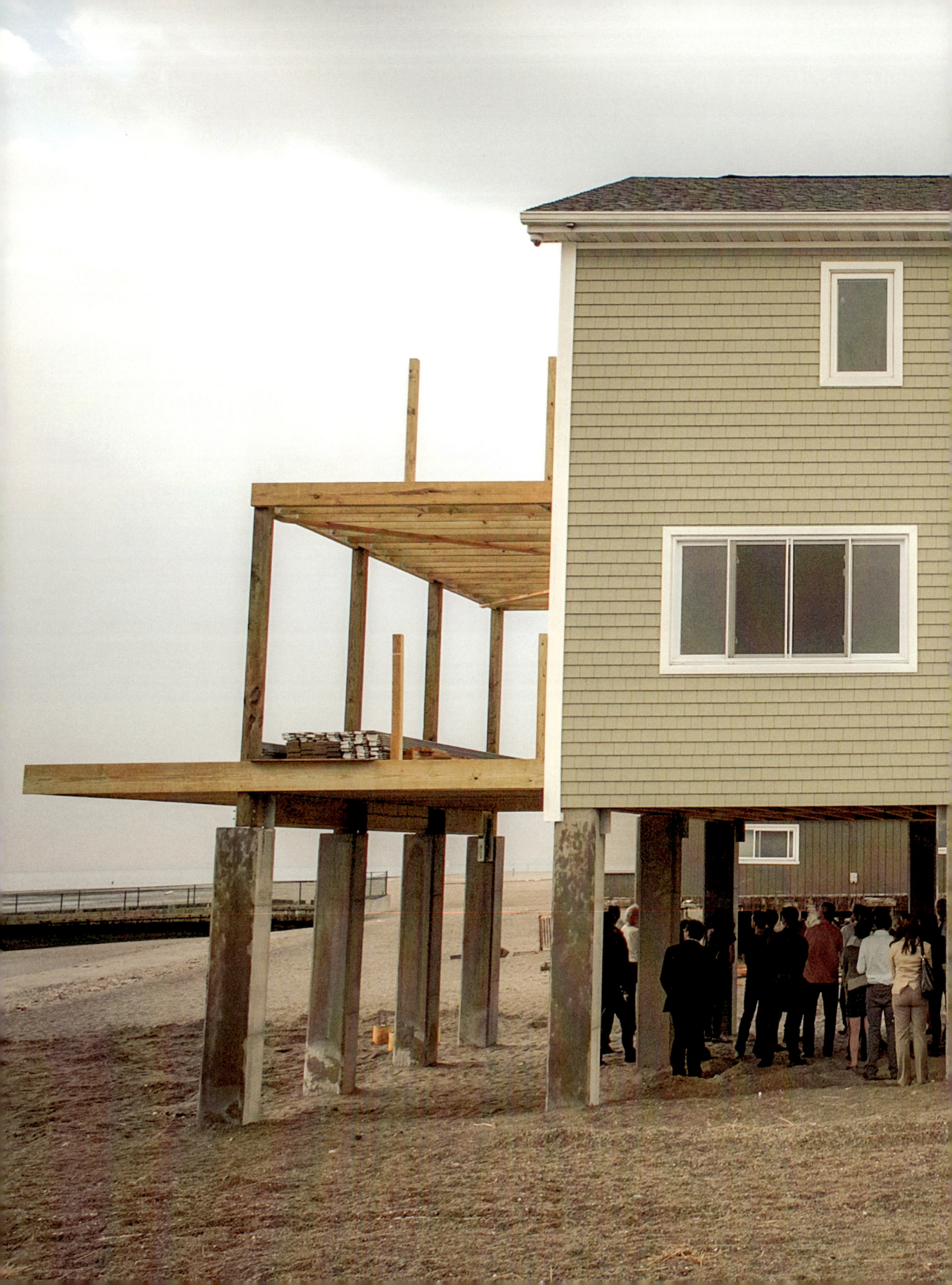

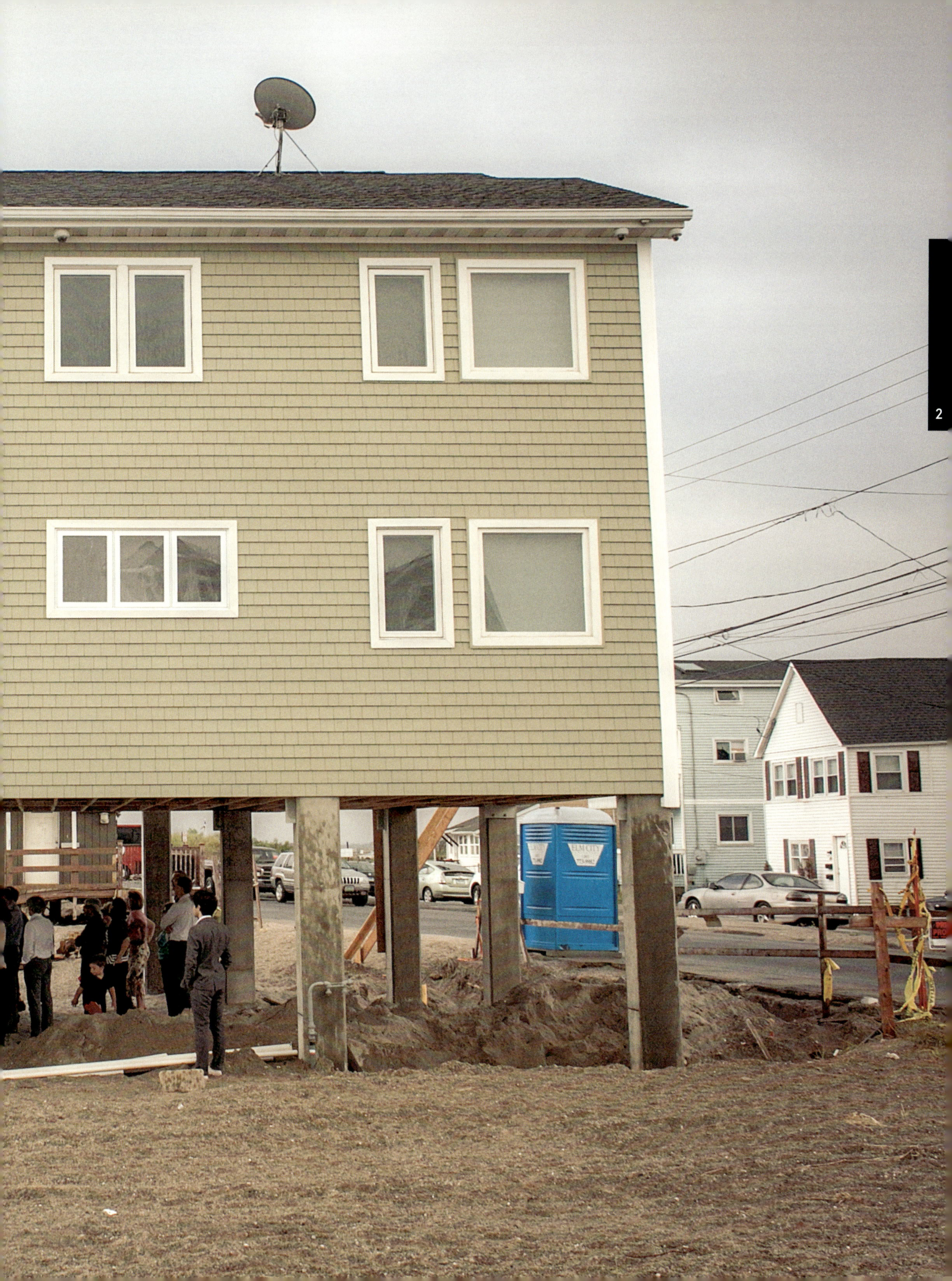
ELM CITY

Listening to Communities

Throughout the research stage, roundtable community meetings addressed questions such as "What makes a community resilient?" and "What does resilience mean to you?" Community residents and leaders from affected areas worked directly with team members, exploring these questions through discussions and drawing exercises to better inform design teams about issues and solutions on the ground.

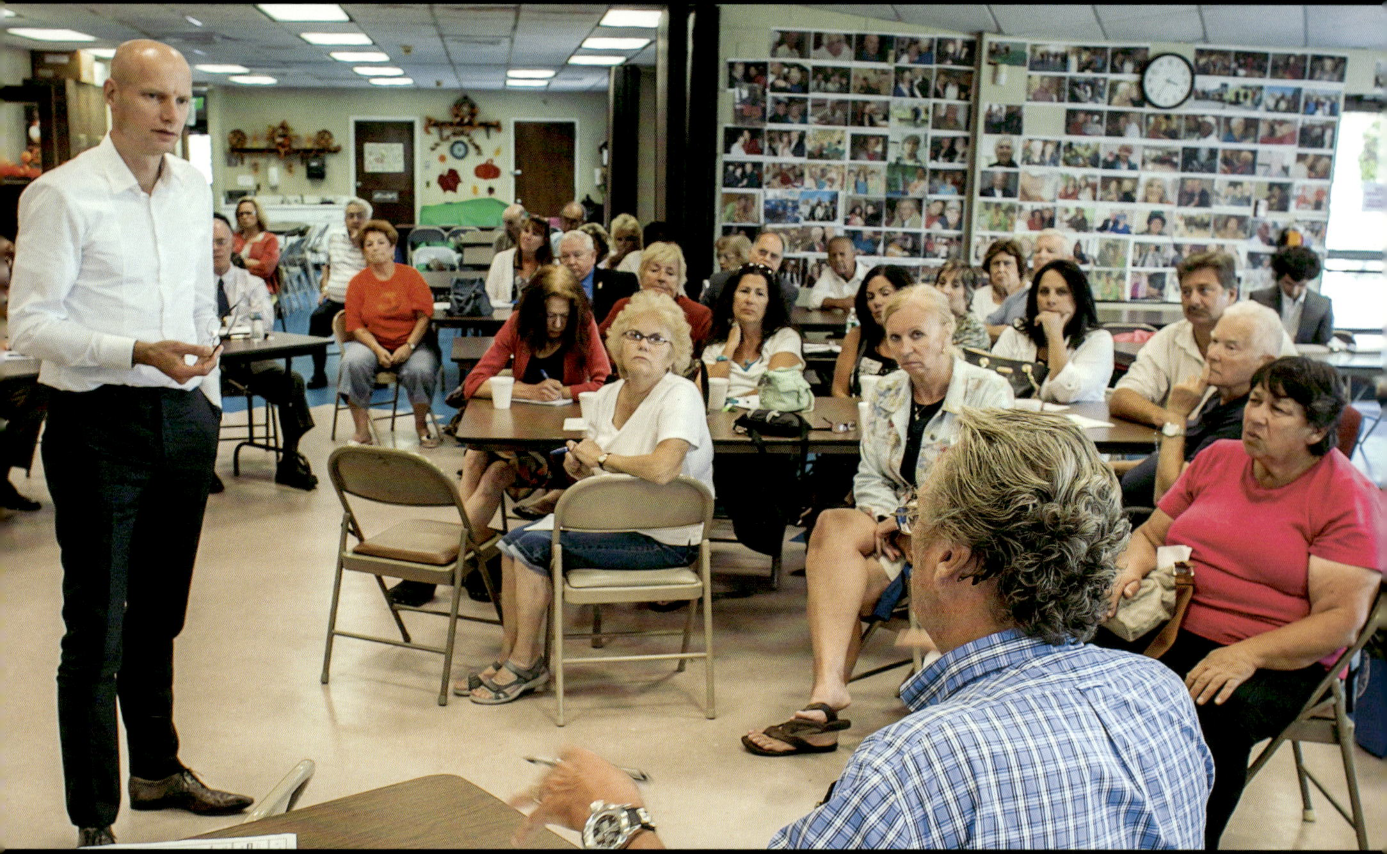

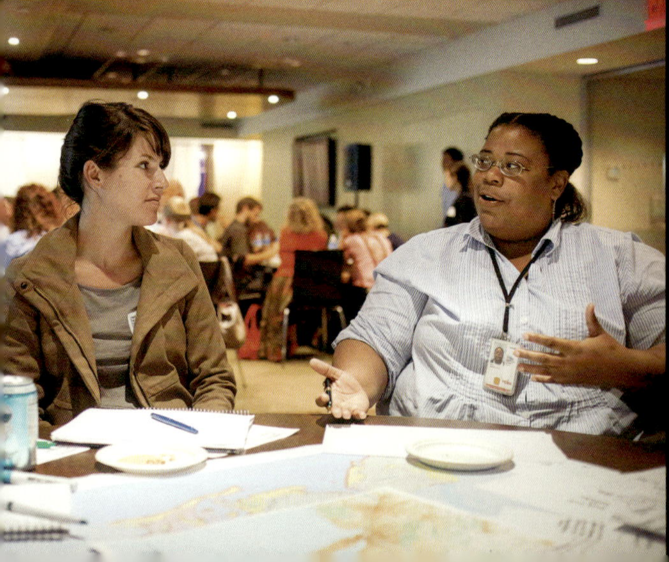

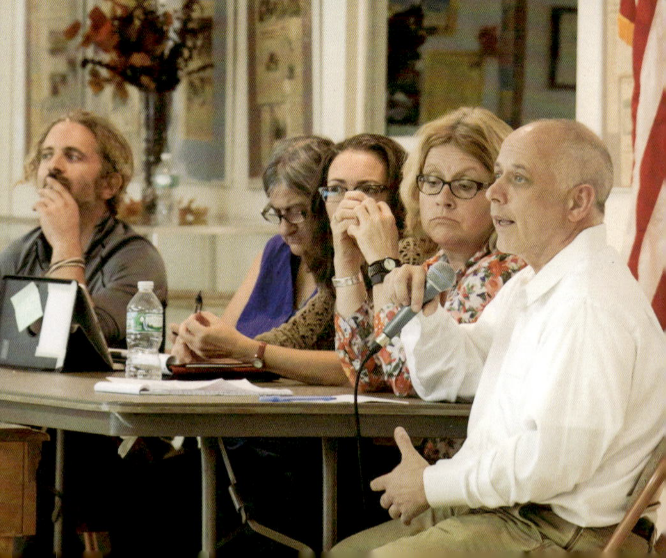

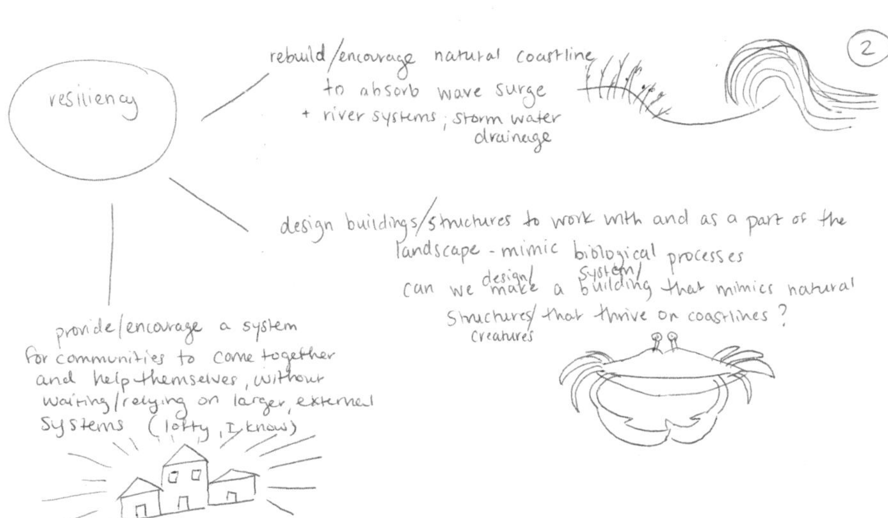

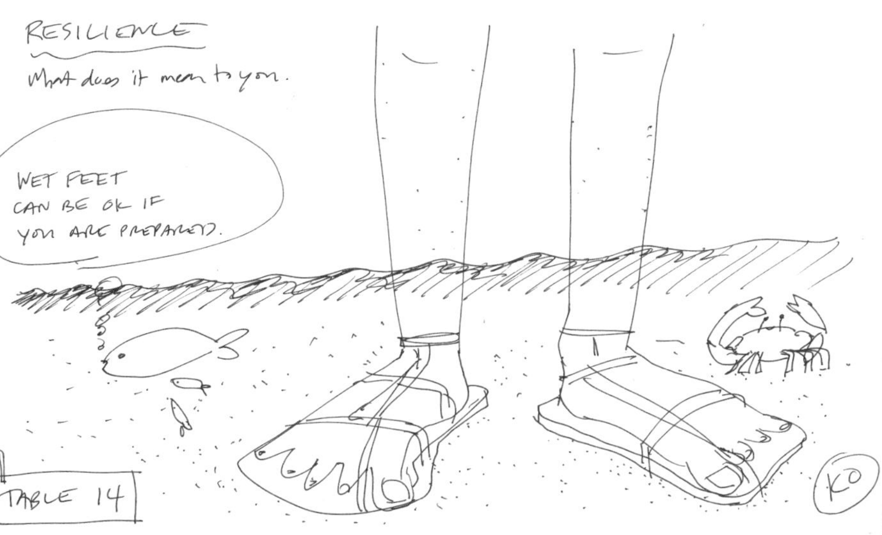

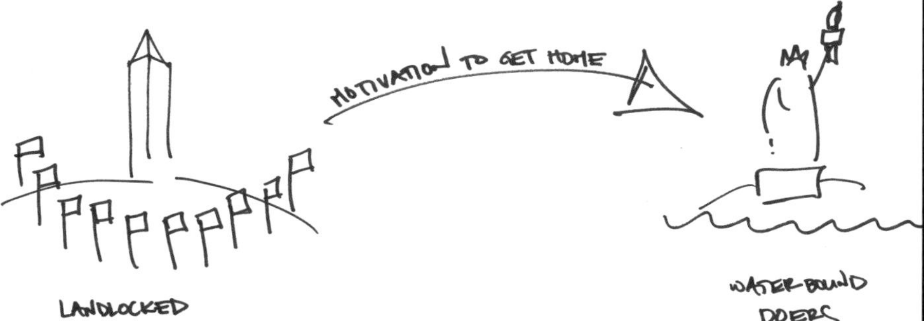

Opposite Page, Top: Task Force Special Advisor Henk Ovink at a community conversation on Long Island, New York.

Opposite Page, Below Left and Right: Grassroots organizers, researchers, and community leaders discuss the storm's challenges and opportunities for rebuilding.

This Page: At community meetings, residents were encouraged to provide sketches that illustrated their own experiences and of how they imagine

Mapping the Region's Vulnerabilities

The competition was structured to generate a nuanced and comprehensive understanding of the region's varied vulnerabilities and their interdependencies. It asked the teams to conduct independent research into the region's environmental, infrastructural, governmental, economic, and social systems and to synthesize their findings with the results of their combined field work. Using a wide array of metrics alongside their experiential data, the teams created a picture of where the region's vulnerabilities existed, intersected, and affected each other. Conceptually, this translated into a map of opportunities to develop opportunities for regional resilience.

"The Meadowlands has an incredible confluence of infrastructure, nature, and transportation, but it's all incredibly vulnerable. Every network of roads, every rail line, every power plant in this region is built below what we would consider to be a safe location."
—
Alex Klatskin, General Partner, Forsgate

Graphics from the MIT CAU + ZUS + URBANISTEN team show infrastructural, environmental, and social vulnerabilities, helping the team determine where to investigate design interventions.

Environment

Teams assessed present and future environmental risks, including storm surge and sea level rise. With consultation from Stevens Institute of Technology and Rutgers University, the teams synthesized data from the Intergovernmental Panel on Climate Change (IPCC) and the National Oceanographic and Atmospheric Administration (NOAA) to establish 100-year projections for sea level rise and other changes in coastal ecology. Additionally, because neither IPCC nor NOAA includes storm surge projections, the teams coupled their data with storm-related inundation projections from the from different sources to assemble a comprehensive picture of the risk levels they would need to address.

2.5 million inhabitants in the New York and New Jersey metropolitan area live in the flood zone.

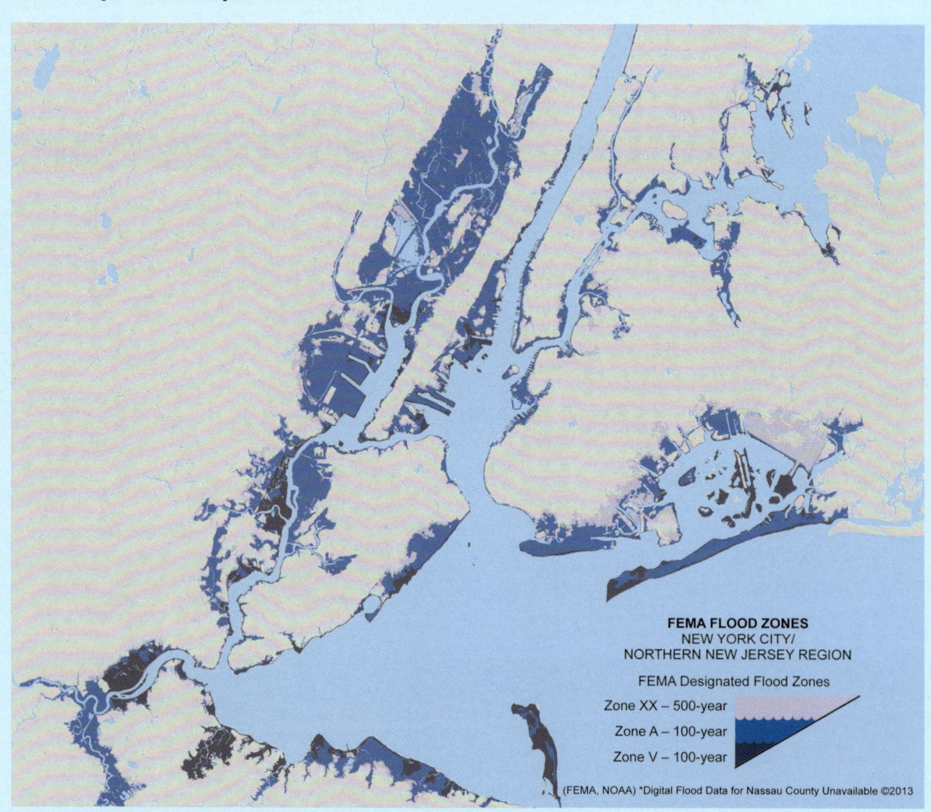

Infrastructure

Sandy destroyed or disrupted critical infrastructure across the region, with disastrous results: hundreds of millions of gallons of sewage were unleashed into waterways, millions of travelers were immobilized, and millions of homes lost power and heat. Teams used fieldwork and research to identify a complex pattern of the region's vulnerable infrastructure.

75% of the net annual power generation is in the 100-year flood zone.

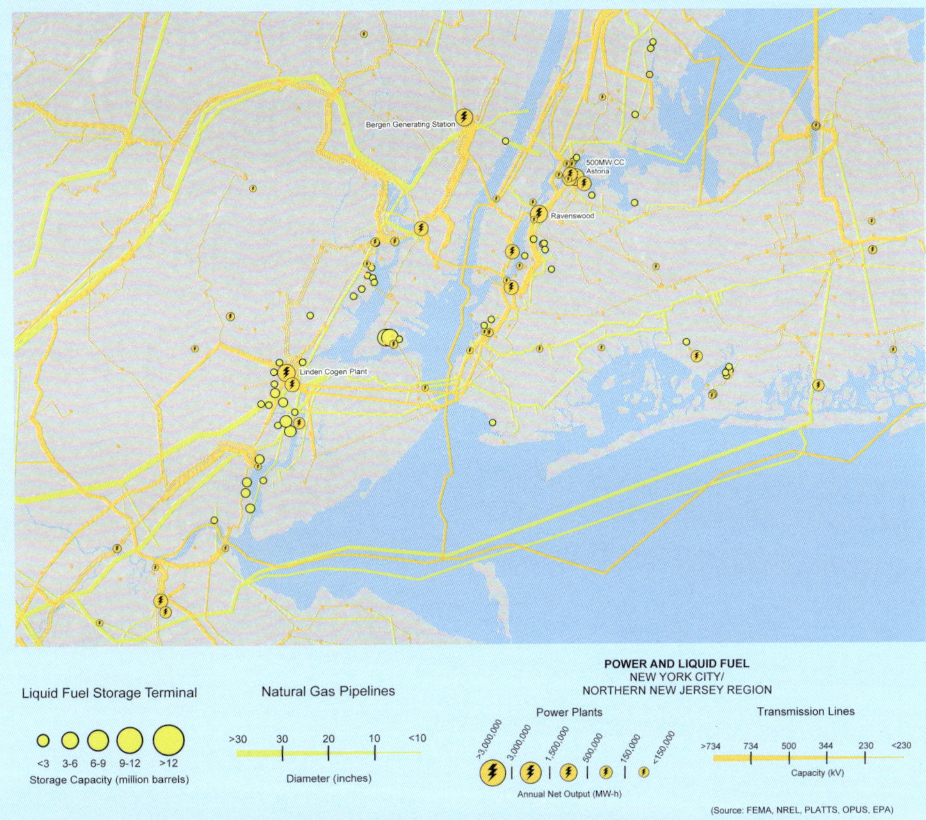

Social

To diagnose social vulnerability, teams relied on tools such as the University of South Carolina's Social Vulnerability index,* which standardizes indicators of vulnerability based on data such as income levels, poverty rates, ethnicity, language, and access to transportation. Additionally, on-the-ground fieldwork helped the teams gather knowledge beyond what they could glean from the data alone. A wide range of community members shared critical first-hand insights and experiences, providing a nuanced picture of different communities' capacities to respond to crisis.

66% of the most vulnerable communities live within a 1/2 mile of the flood zone.

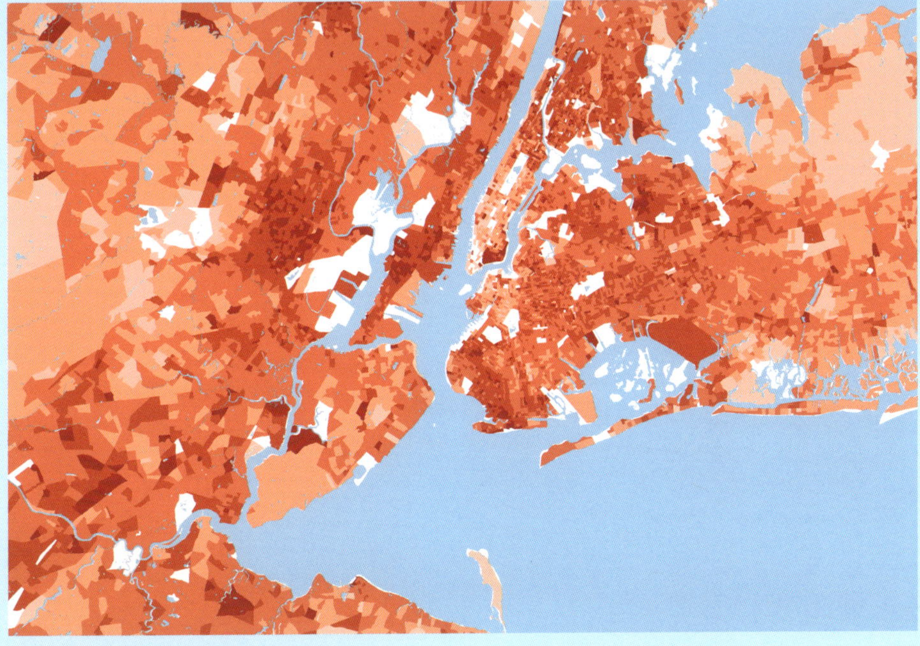

SOCIAL VULNERABILITY INDEX
NEW YORK CITY/
NORTHERN NEW JERSEY REGION

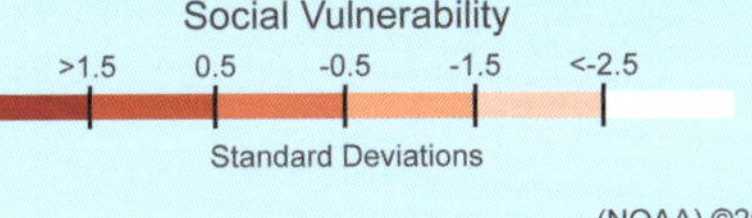

(NOAA) ©2013

* Developed by Susan Cutter of the University of South Carolina for NOAA

Economy

The storm left an estimated $65 billion dollars in damages and economic loss. For the first time in well over a century, the New York Stock Exchange closed because of weather, causing an estimated $7 billion in lost productivity. Over 200,000 small businesses reported closures, and people in the region lost a collective 2 million working days. New Jersey reported a whopping $8.3 billion in business losses; 75% of the state's small businesses were adversely affected.

Governance

As highlighted in the image to the right from the BIG Team, natural disasters cut across political jurisdictions, confronting different governments with the challenges of addressing vulnerable infrastructure and ecology. Teams had to determine where a cross-jurisdictional response was called for and examine the barriers and incentives for government cooperation.

At-Risk Commercial *

12,000

BUSINESSES

175,000

JOBS — 20% OF COASTAL EMPLOYMENT

100,000,000 FT^2

10% OF THE REGION

$34,000,000,000

ANNUAL SALES

* For the purposes of this analysis by the HR&A and Cooper Robertson and Partners Team, the region is defined as coastal communities on the Jersey Shore and the New York City coastline. Floodplains based on best available data from FEMA.

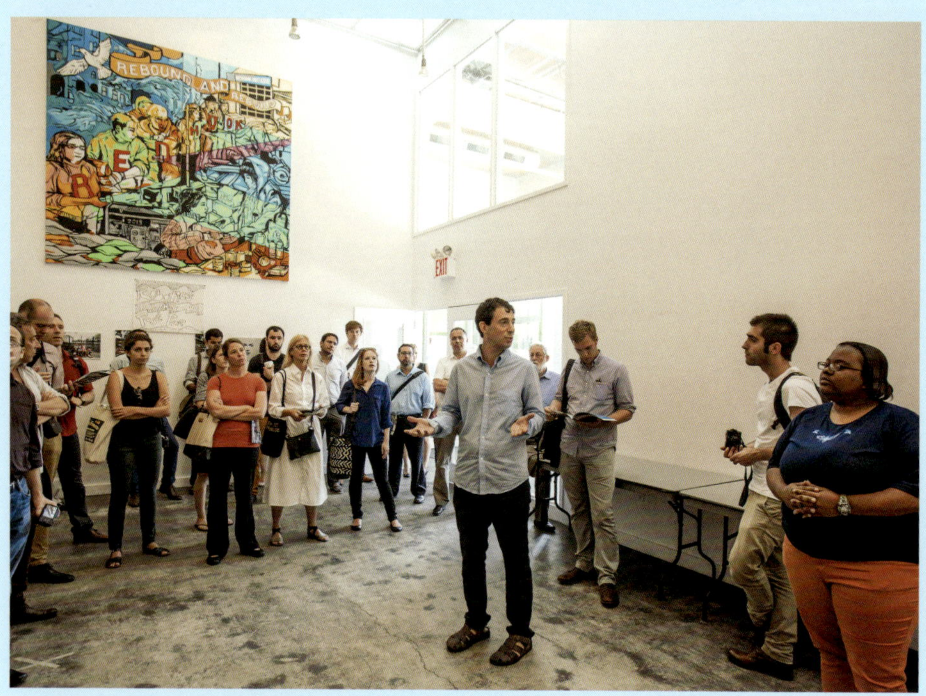

Eric Klinenbeg, Director of the NYU Institute for Public Knowledge, chair of the Rebuild by Design Research Advisory Group, and Director of Research led teams on a field excursion to the Red Hook Initiative, which became a hub for local businesses to coordinate their response in Brooklyn, New York.

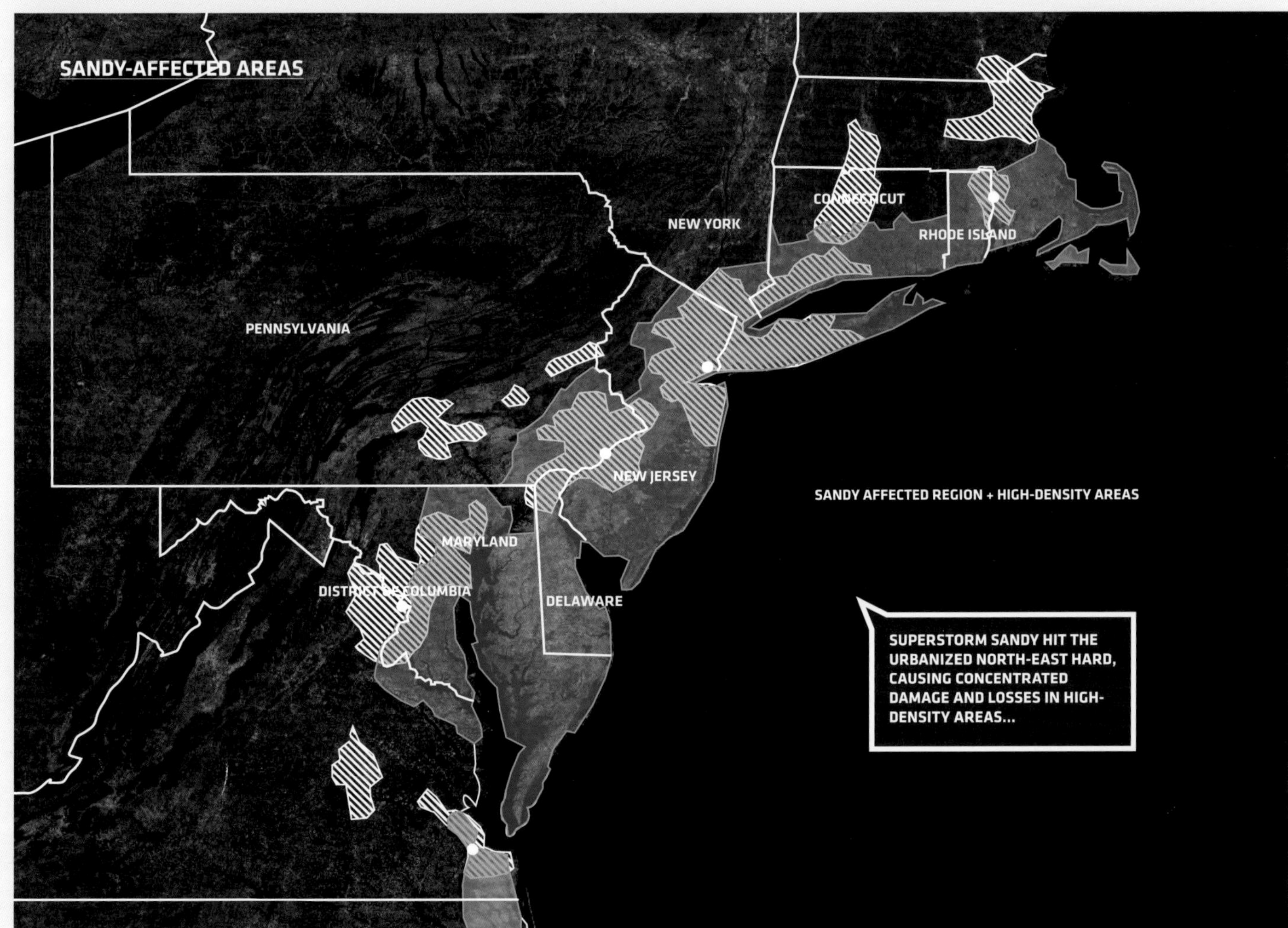

2

Interconnected Vulnerabilities

Synthesizing their findings, the teams uncovered complex intersections between the region's varied vulnerabilities: connections that explained how the physical damage of a critical weather event could precipitate crises in public health, housing, mobility, social services, and more. These intersections also revealed promising opportunities to address interdependent vulnerabilities with interventions that aspired to improve comprehensive resilience.

Physical, social, economic, political, and ecological vulnerabilities intersected, for example, in small-scale coastal communities. In many such locations, the built environment occupied historic floodplains and development eroded natural protections, raising the risk for locally-owned small businesses near the shore. These businesses, meanwhile, were anchor institutions whose destruction not only disrupted the community's ability to create and retain capital but also eroded the local culture and character that are vital to long-term recovery. By mapping the region's various vulnerabilities, the design teams came to understand how they might propose design strategies to address those challenges.

The teams indexed their findings into comprehensive maps of the region's social infrastructure — a cartography of community resilience. Broadly, it revealed that socially vulnerable communities are triply challenged: they are less able to undertake costly risk mitigation measures, have fewer resources to react to unexpected emergencies with contingency solutions, and are often situated in areas of highest risk (including flood-prone locations, areas near potentially hazardous infrastructure, or places with few transportation options). Along with this detailed picture of the stakes facing the future, local government officials helped the teams understand their communities' existing visions for long-term development. This intricate perspective on what the region wanted and needed let the teams identify the most promising locations and approaches for designing new structures to promote resilience.

"Rather than beginning the competition with pre-conceived ideas, the Rebuild by Design finalists entered with questions, inclinations, and a catalog of opportunities. Every member of every team built a new set of relationships and developed a new set of design ideas for dealing with the threat of climate change."

—

Eric Klinenberg, Director, NYU Institute for Public Knowledge and Director of Research, Rebuild by Design

"The proposals delivered by the Rebuild by Design teams demonstrate the importance of enabling professionals and community leaders to work together to solve problems. The plans and partnerships created as a result will help the New York-New Jersey-Connecticut region prepare for a changing climate."

—

Robert Yaro, President Emeritus, Regional Plan Association

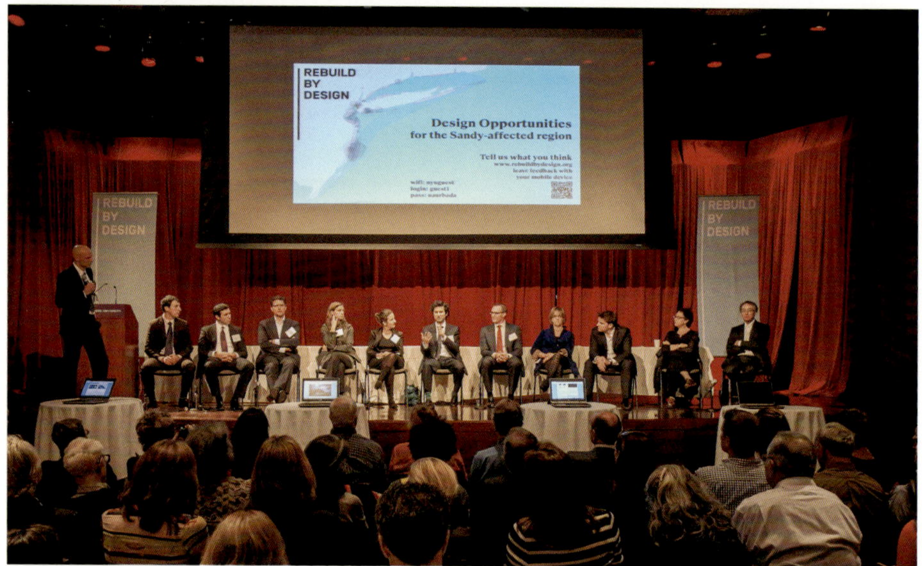

Left: At the end of the research phase, the teams unveiled their design opportunities to the public at New York University and New Jersey Institute of Technology.

Below: a member of the public examines design opportunities in Jamaica Bay.

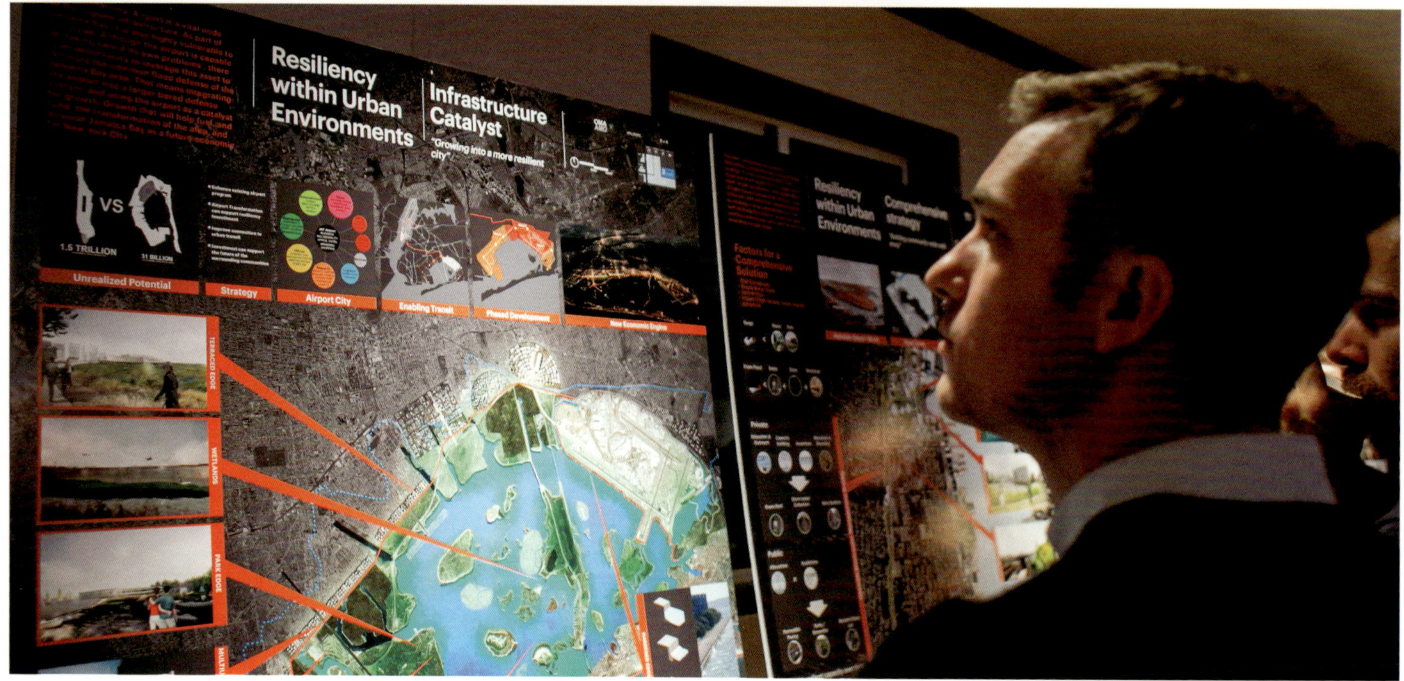

Designing Opportunities

By the end of the research phase, the teams had collectively created 41 concepts for possible interventions: early-stage proposals that described a multifaceted vision for a more resilient region. During a pair of events at New York University and New Jersey Institute of Technology, the teams unveiled their "design opportunities" to local officials, federal representatives, the press, and more than 1,000 members of the public.

Each team presented their design opportunities, and HUD selected an average of one per team for further development. Rebuild by Design compiled and published the research phase's overall findings in an online research database, as the teams began a period of intense community collaboration and iterative design.

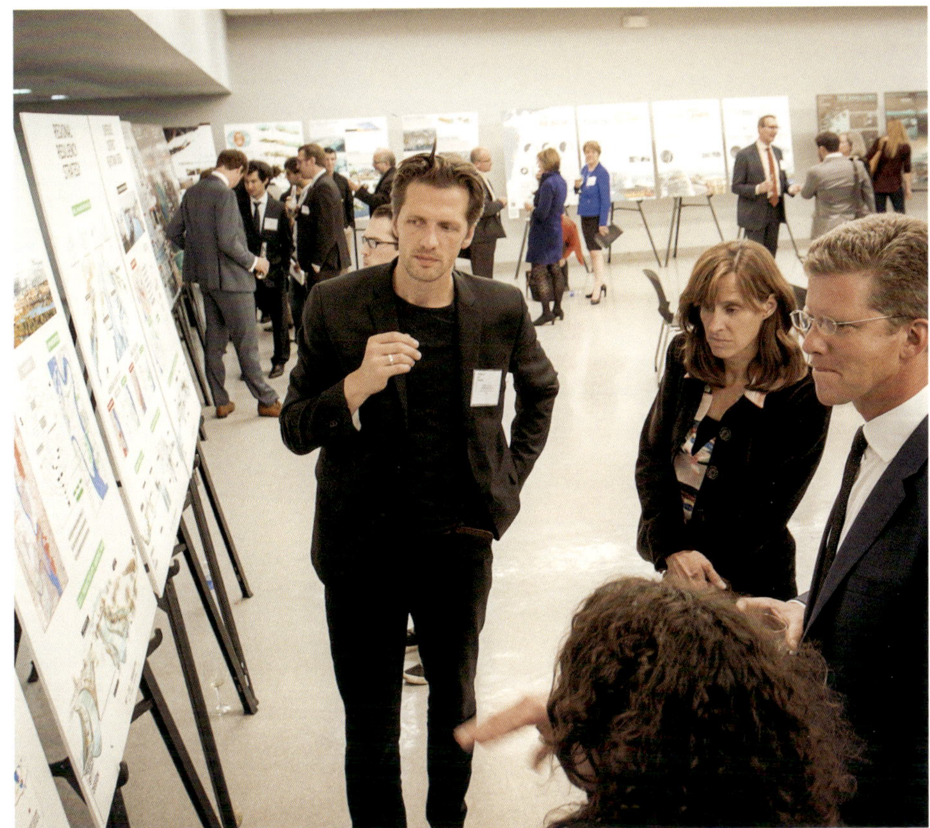

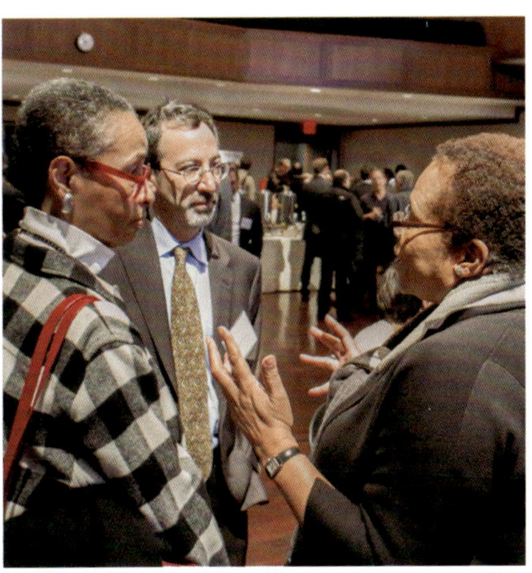

Above: Rob Pirani of the Regional Plan Association discusses resilient design solutions with team members.

Left: Secretary Shaun Donovan and Hoboken Mayor Dawn Zimmer observe opportunities for the region with design team members from the MIT CAU + ZUS + URBANISTEN team.

Competition Stages

The competition proceeded in stages, each of which informed the next set of goals, participants, and outcomes.

IMPACT

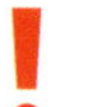

October 2012
HURRICANE SANDY strikes the Northeast United States. It is the second costliest/most destructive storm in the nation's history.

Executive Order establishes Hurricane Sandy Rebuilding Task Force.

Task Force announces Rebuild by Design competition.

TALENT

The Task Force issues a Request for Qualifications and Approaches, calling for teams to assemble themselves in interdisciplinary partnerships to tackle the region's physical and social vulnerabilities.

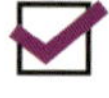

148 interdisciplinary, international teams apply.

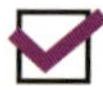

10 design teams are selected.

RESEARCH

Teams are lead through an intensive program of field research to introduce them to a variety of local stakeholders, providing a comprehensive view of the storm's effects – the damage it created as well as the long-standing problems it uncovered or exacerbated. The teams undertake five multi-day excursions and a variety of research projects, culminating in a body of regional research and 41 design opportunities that can be developed into full proposals.

SITES VISITED

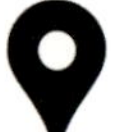

New York

Brooklyn: Red Hook

Queens: Breezy Point, Broad Channel, Howard Beach, Rockaways

Staten Island: Midland Beach, New Dorp, Oakwood Beach, South Beach, St. George

Manhattan: Downtown, Lower East Side

Suffolk County: Copaigue, Port Jefferson

Nassau County: Freeport, Bay Park, Oceanside, Island Park, Long Beach, East Rockaway

New Jersey

Essex County: Newark

Hudson County: Kearny, Hoboken, Jersey City

Mercer County: Trenton

Monmouth County: Asbury Park, Highlands, Keansburg, Sea Bright, Union Beach

Ocean County: Toms River

Connecticut

Fairfield County: Bridgeport, Milford, Fairfield

THEMES EXPLORED

Social Infrastructure
Multi-Family Housing
Major Infrastructure
Public Transit
High-Density Urban Development
Vulnerable Populations
Small Businesses
Environmental Justice
Single-Family Housing
Economic Development
Beach Access
Tourism
Insurance
Health Care Infrastructure
Capacity Needs of Small Communities
Emergency Response
Disaster Management
Governance and Federally Funded Rebuilding
Displacement
Climate Change and Risk
Ecosystem Services
Conservation
Ecological Barriers

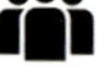
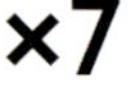

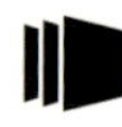
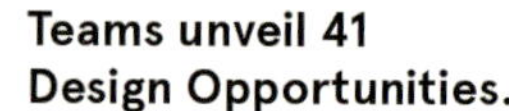

10 proposals are selected.

DESIGN

Ten proposals are selected to move to the design phase.
HUD and the partner organizations work with teams throughout the design stage to gather diverse local stakeholders into community coalitions with whom they begin to co-design the final interventions.

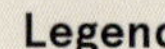

Legend

 Site Visit

 Community Meeting

 Stakeholder Meeting

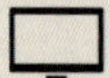 Webinar

 Teacher Training

REBUILD BY DESIGN GUIDES ALL TEAMS

Throughout the design stage, Rebuild by Design continues to gather teams for distinct moments of design critique and widespread public involvement. A series of interactive, community-driven activities brings Rebuild by Design to new audiences around the region.

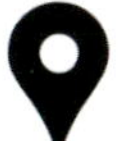
New Orleans
Site Visit

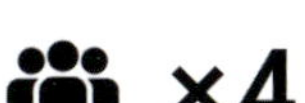

Thank you LES Dance Party
Manhattan, NY

I <3 My Shoreline Resiliency Fair
Staten Island, NY

Rebuild One City Parade
Asbury Park, NJ

Citymaking Bike Ride
Bridgeport, CT

Earth Day, Rockaway
Queens, NY

BIG TEAM

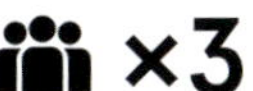

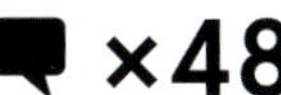

OMA

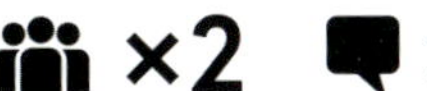

SCAPE/LANDSCAPE ARCHITECTURE

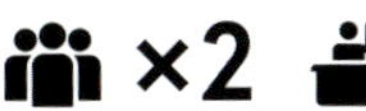

×60

HR+A WITH COOPER ROBERTSON AND PARTNERS

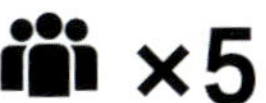

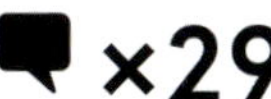

PENNDESIGN/OLIN

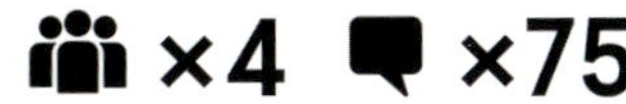

WB UNABRIDGED WITH YALE ARCADIS

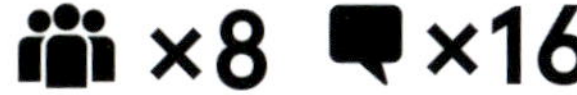

INTERBORO TEAM

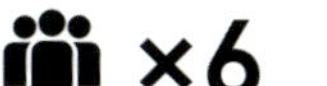

SASAKI/RUTGERS/ARUP

×2
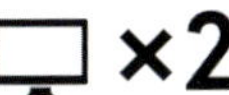

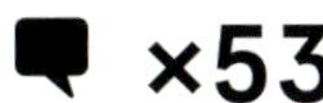

WXY/WEST8

×2 ×16

MIT CAU + ZUS + URBANISTEN

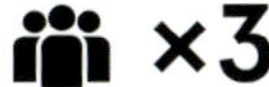

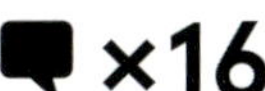

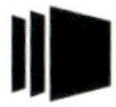

Teams showcase their final proposals.
The Rebuild by Design jury assesses their proposals, including the designs, coalition involvement, and implementation plans.

HUD Secretary Shaun Donovan, as Jury Chair, selects winning proposals.

IMPLEMENTATION

June 2014
Winning proposals are announced.
HUD allocates $930 million to city and state governments to carry out the first stages of implementation for six winning and one finalist design.

City and state governments have until September 30, 2022 to spend federally allocated money.

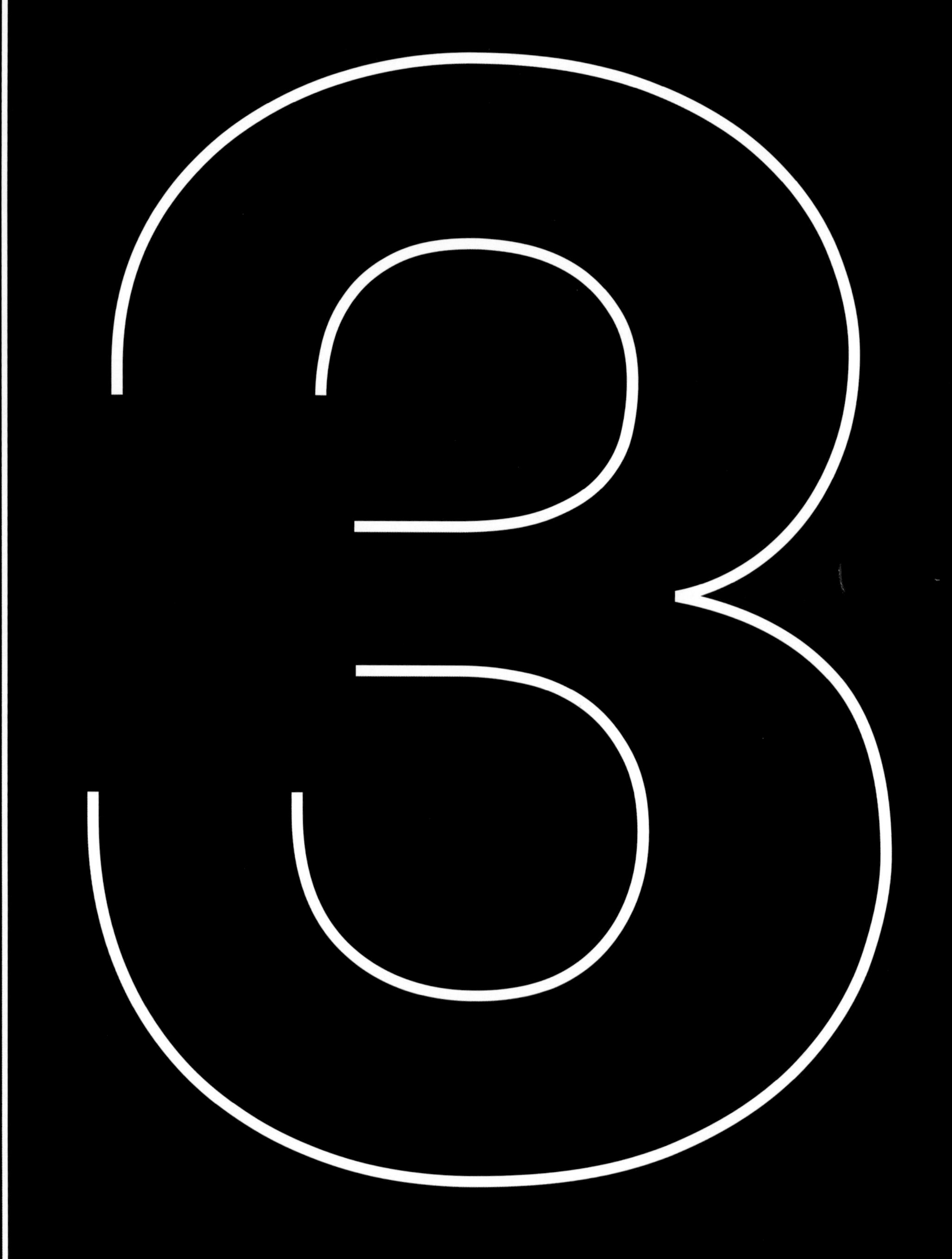

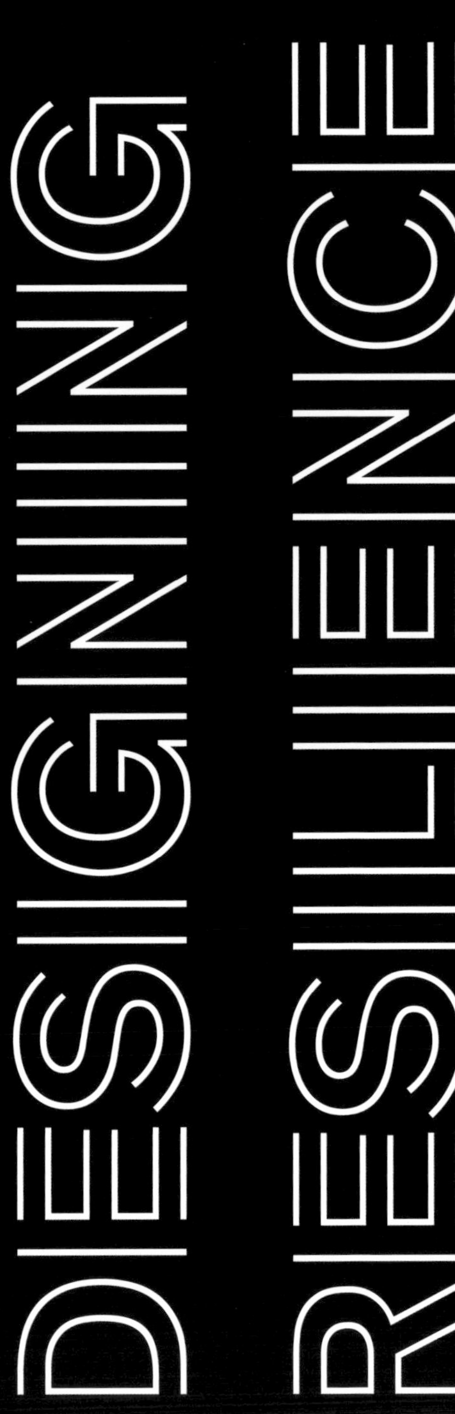
DESIGNING
RESILIENCE

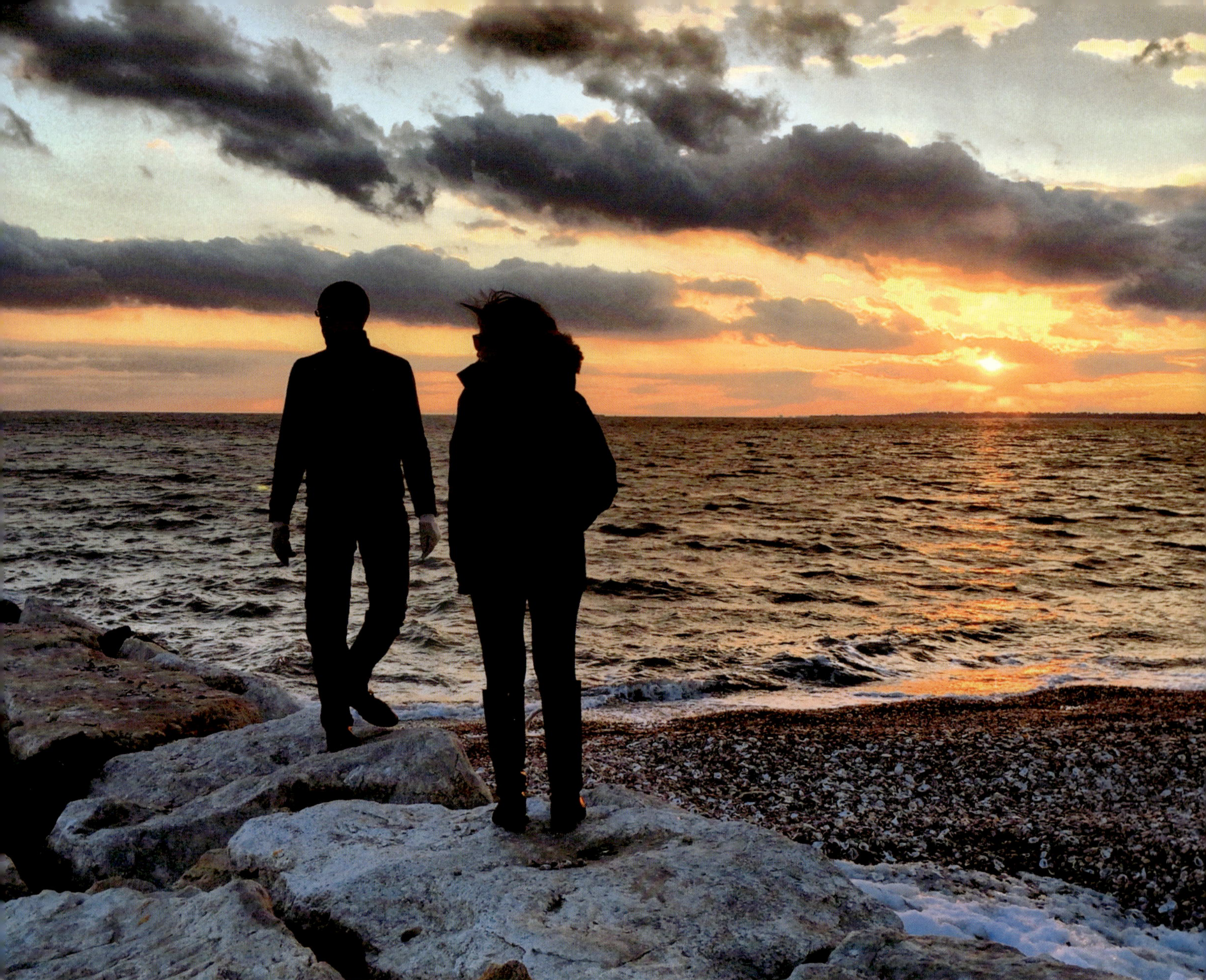

"Local people living and operating businesses in neighborhoods know best the real challenges and opportunities around which they've been improvising for years. The Rebuild by Design process gave them tangible channels to share both their concerns and solutions. The design teams recognized how important it is to listen to the locals and that the design process itself helps these communities build their own resilience."

—

Mary Rowe, Director of Urban Livability and Resilience Initiatives, Municipal Art Society of New York

Members of the WB Unabridged with Yale ARCADIS team explore the shoreline of Bridgeport, Connecticut.

Collaborate, Iterate, Create

With the Design Opportunities selected, the teams moved forward into the design phase. Their challenge was to work closely with community stakeholders and local governments to design interventions that were inclusive, representative, and responsive to the needs and lived experiences of the local residents. To achieve this, collaboration remained central to every part of the process.

The Municipal Art Society, Regional Plan Association, and Van Alen Institute took the lead to help the teams establish links with local government officials, residents, businesses, landowners, community-based organizations, academics, and scientists. The teams worked intimately with these community coalitions to co-design the final proposals. The process incorporated the teams' expertise and knowledge from the research phase with the needs and concerns of local participants representing diverse constituencies.

With the coalitions leading the charge, flood protection measures soon became multifaceted interventions to protect or enhance critical infrastructure, local economic structures, public health, transportation networks, and access to public spaces. Stakeholders brought their concerns and histories to the table – including, in many cases, previous master plans for development or preservation – helping the teams shape their proposals around the vision of the communities they were meant to serve.

The teams spent considerable time with these communities building relationships and testing their proposals. Collectively, the ten teams staged 64 large public meetings, immersed themselves in hundreds of smaller events, and enthusiastically engaged in countless interactions with stakeholders. They continually honed their proposals based on the guidance they received. Residents shared insights, challenged ideas, and enhanced the projects at every stage of design development. Local government agencies and officials guided the evolution of the proposals to ensure that the designs would be implementable using existing governmental framework.

The competition's emphasis on inclusivity and the teams' creative and tireless dedication to engaging the community gave stakeholders a true sense of ownership over the design process and the designs. Community members' willingness to invest their time, spirit, and insight into the process reinforced their commitment to seeing the designs become a reality. As the teams, government, and communities worked together to forge the final proposals, their final designs reflected more than merely infrastructural fixes: they embodied a uniquely local, comprehensive vision for long-term resilience.

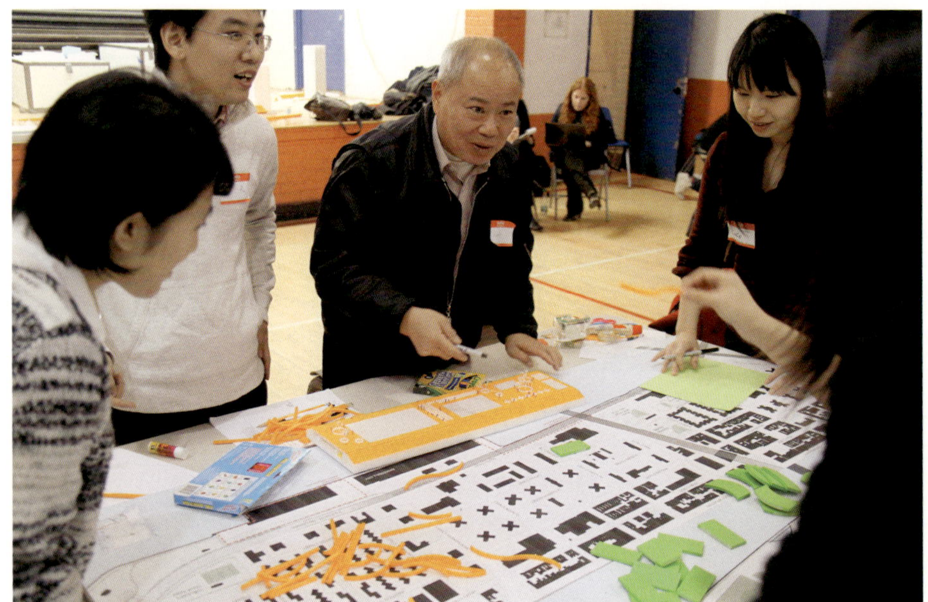

Left: In the Lower East Side, the BIG Team used a technique they traditionally use with colleagues in their office when developing a project. Creating a series of interchangeable models for workshop participants to interact with allowed LES residents to visually understand the look and implications of BIG's proposed resilience infrastructure approaches. The BIG Team worked with the LES Ready! Coalition to help develop and deliver community meetings.

Below, Left: In a planning meeting for the New Meadowlands project, the MIT CAU + ZUS + URBANISTEN team engaged stakeholders to help them devise their proposal.

Below, Right: Jeremy Alain Siegel and Laura Starr of the BIG Team tweak their designs on the go.

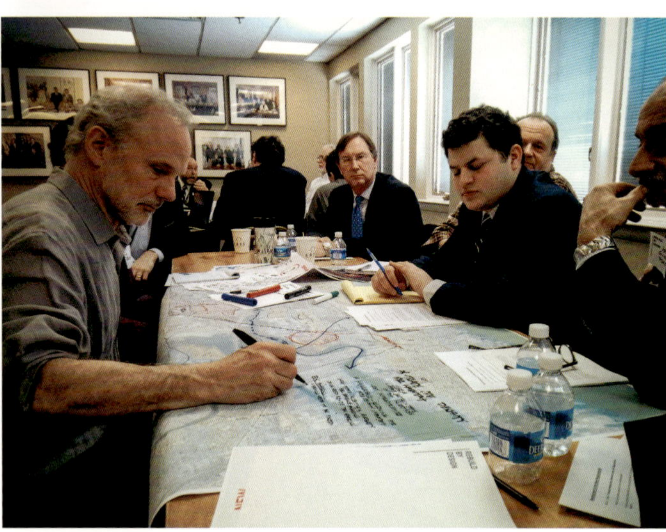

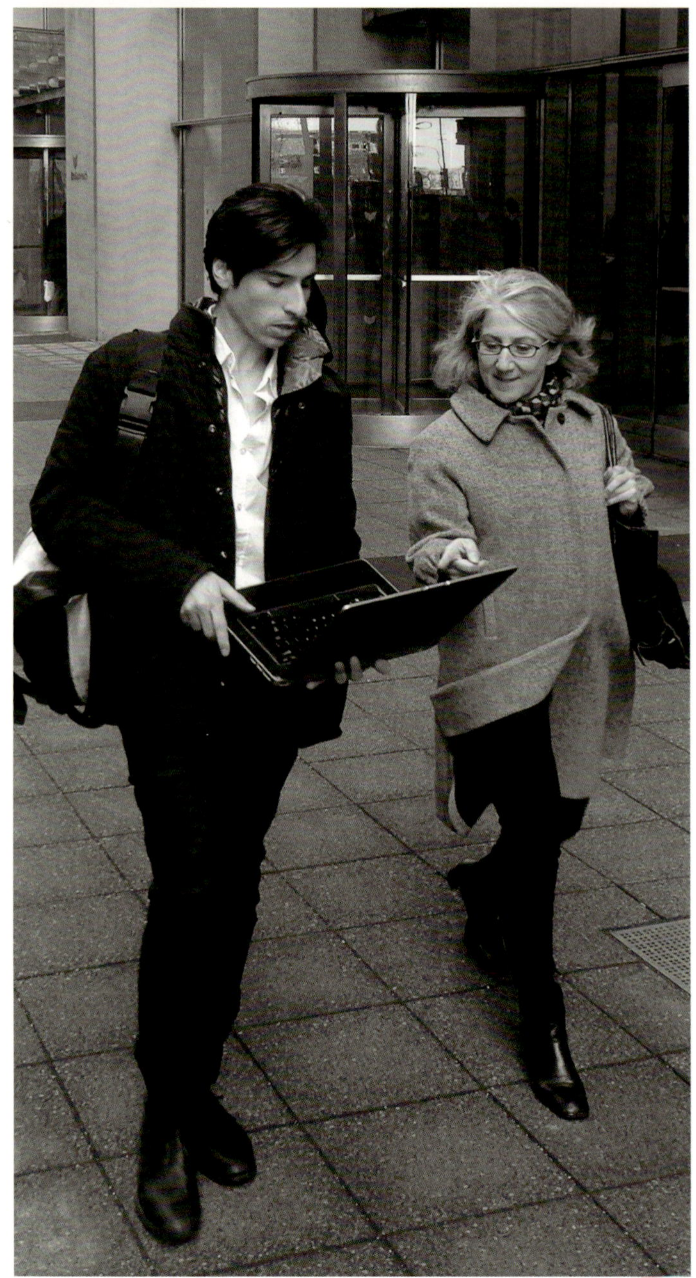

"We never thought we were going to be working on protecting our community against climate change. We will do whatever it takes, learn what we need to learn so we can be the support we need to be for our community."

—

Damaris Reyes, Executive Director, GOLES (Good Old Lower East Side)

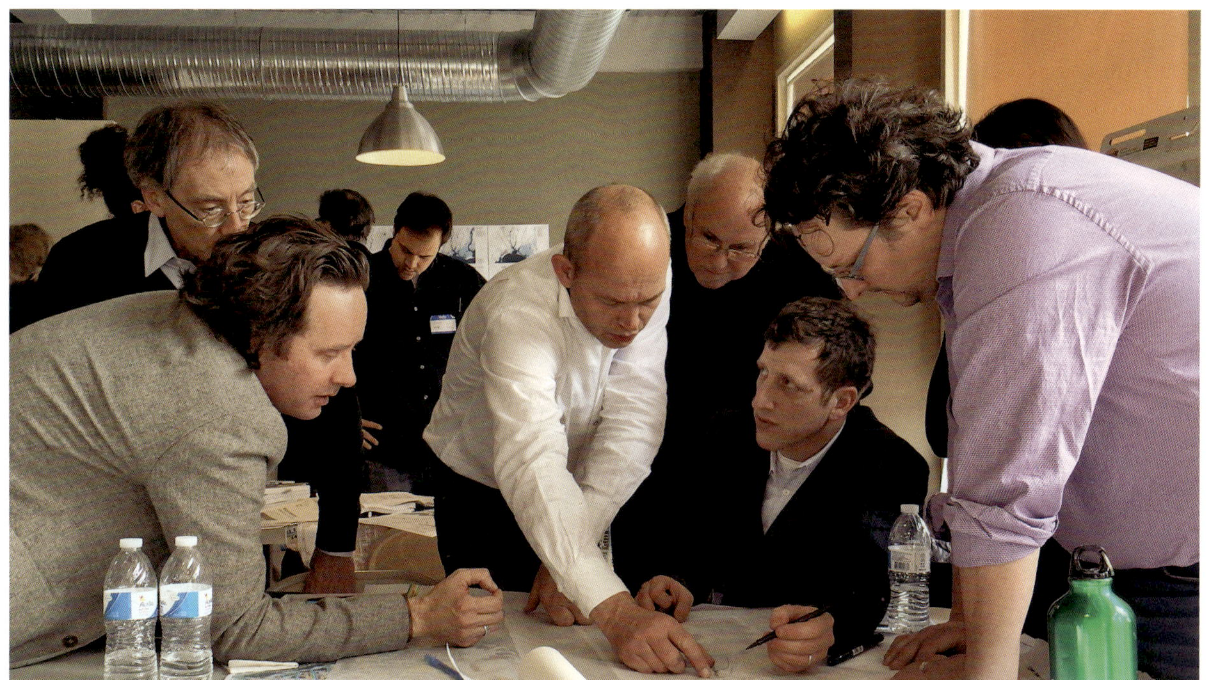

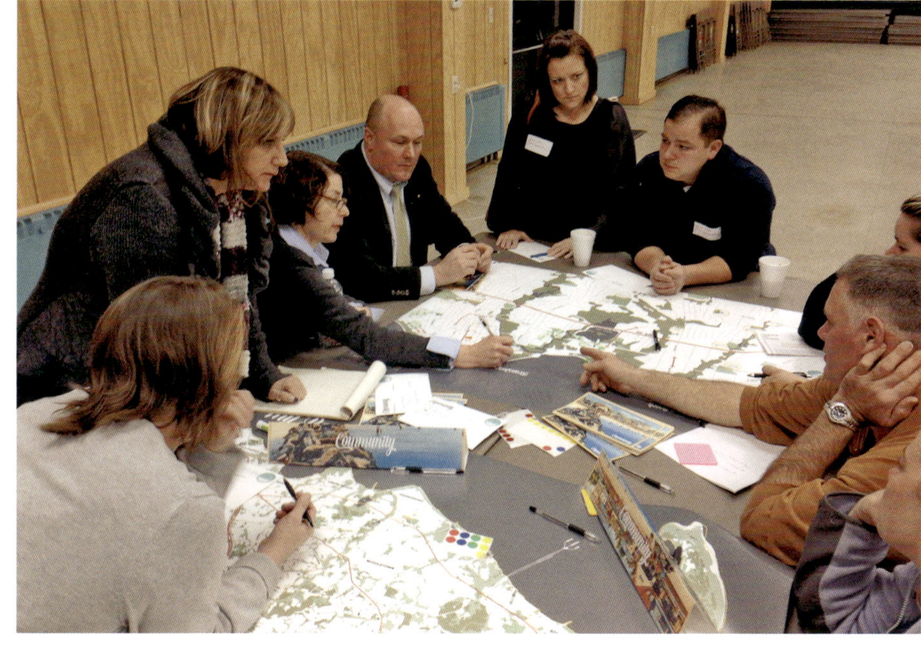

Above: WB unabridged with Yale ARCADIS held multiple workshops with residents across the greater Bridgeport area to present their approach, gather feedback, and refine their plan.

Middle: The Sasaki Team held workshops along the Jersey Shore to engage residents iin making their neighborhoods more resilient.

Below: WXY/West 8 focused on a regional research opportunity. Considering the scope and scale of their work, their workshops took the form of a research colloquium, bringing together industry experts to analyze the feasibility, effectiveness, and associated risk of their potential project.

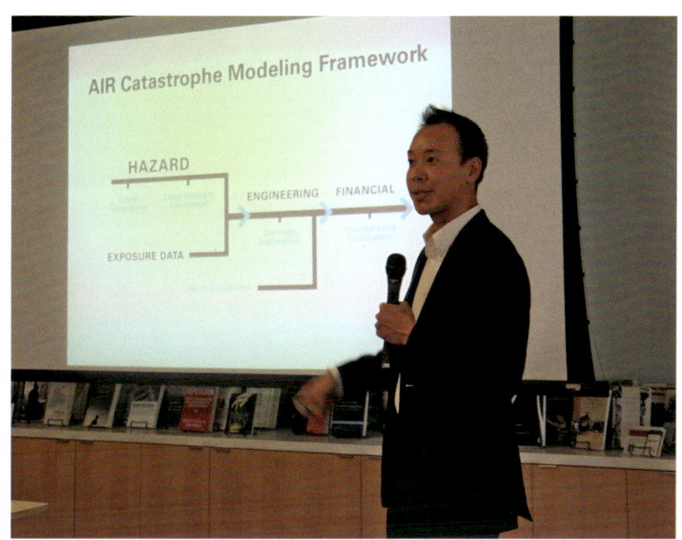

"The beach in New Jersey is a huge cultural resource and it goes generations deep ... I want to figure out how we can all live here and work here and be here one hundred years from now."

—

John Weber, Mid-Atlantic Regional Manager, Surfrider Foundation Asbury Park

A Complex Network

Rebuild by Design is a consortium of stakeholders working together toward a shared vision of a more resilient region.

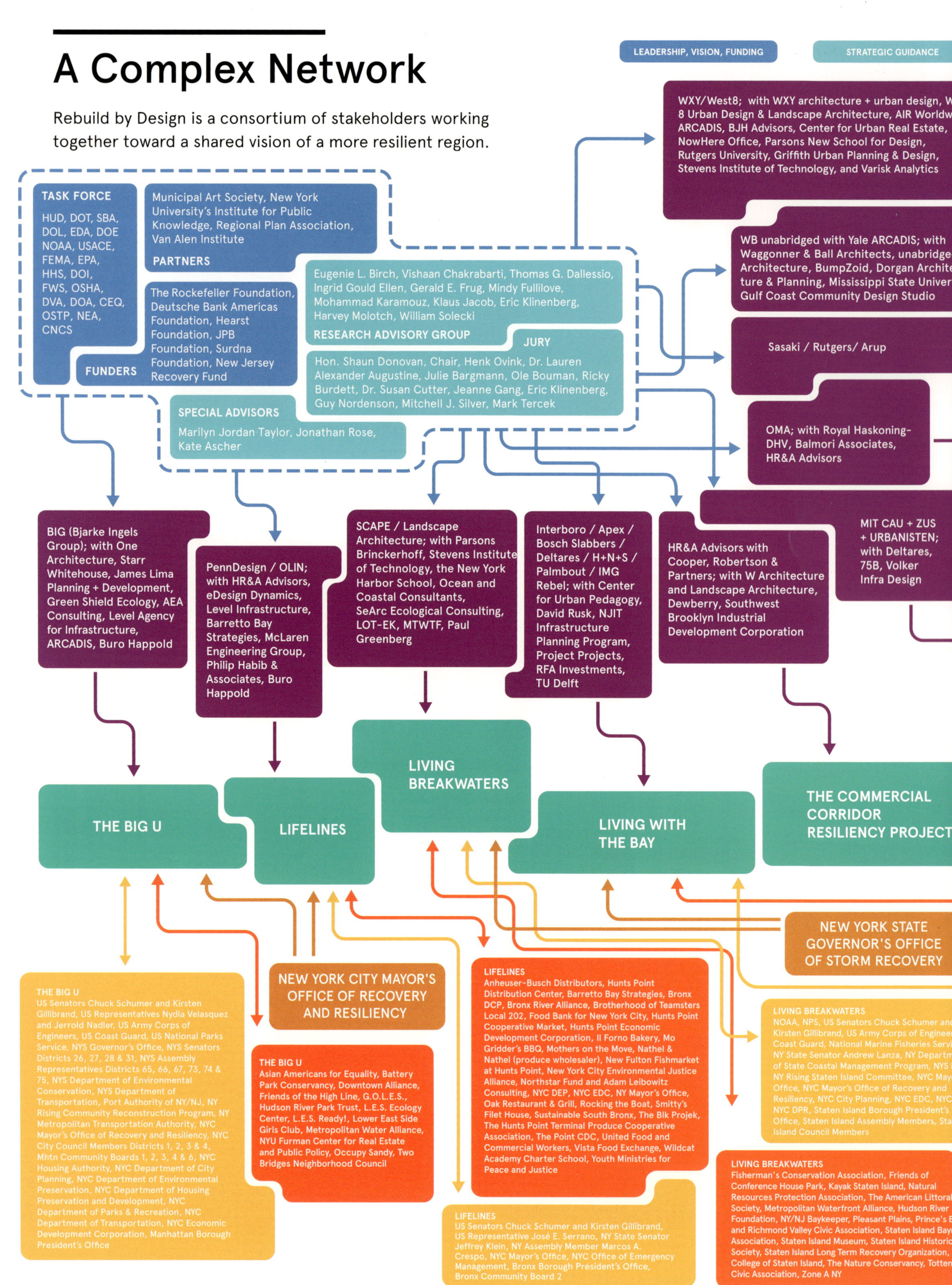

INTERNATIONAL TALENT

TEN PROJECTS

LOCAL & STATE GOVERNMENT

COMMUNITY COALITION PARTNERS

GOVERNMENT COALITION PARTNERS

BLUE DUNES

RESILIENT BRIDGEPORT

RESILIENCE + THE BEACH

RESIST DELAY STORE DISCHARGE, COMPREHENSIVE URBAN WATER STRATEGY

NEW MEADOWLANDS

STATE OF CONNECTICUT, DEPARTMENT OF HOUSING

NEW JERSEY GOVERNOR'S OFFICE FOR RECOVERY AND REBUILDING

BLUE DUNES
Columbia University, The New School, New York University, Rutgers University, Stevens Institute of Technology, SUNY Stony Brook, University of Delaware, Ballard Spahr LLP, Center for Architecture, Empire State Future, Great Lakes Dredge & Dock Company, HDR/HydroQual, Jamestown Properties, Karbone, Lisa Miller & Associates, Louis Berger Group, Maracoos, Meridian Institute, Metropolitan Waterfront Alliance, National Institute for Coastal Harbor & Infrastructure, The Nature of Cities Blog, NYC Environmental Justice Alliance, Real Estate Board of New York, Rockaway Waterfront Alliance, Sandy Hook Pilots Association, Sive, Paget & Riesel, PC, Structures of Coastal Resilience, Surfrider Foundation, SwissRe, Verisk Analytics, Vickerman & Associates LLP, WaterWorks LLC, The Water Institute of the Gulf

BLUE DUNES
US Senators Chuck Schumer and Kirsten Gillibrand, HUD, NASA, NOAA, US Army Corps of Engineers, NJ Governor's Office of Recovery and Rebuilding, NJ Department of Environmental Protection, NJ Department of Transportation Office of Maritime Resources, NYS Department of Environmental Conservation, NYS Department of Transportation, Port Authority of NY/NJ, NYC Mayor's Office of Recovery and Resiliency, NYC Department of City Planning, Royal Embassy of the Netherlands, Netherlands Consulate General in New York

RESILIENT BRIDGEPORT
EDA, NOAA, CT Department of Economic & Community Development, CT Department of Labor, CT Department of Transportation, CT Department of Energy & Environmental Protection, CT Division of Emergency Management & Homeland Security, City of Bridgeport, Bridgeport Housing Authority, Bridgeport School Board, City of Stamford, City of Norwalk, City of New Haven, Royal Netherlands Embassy, City of Amsterdam

RESILIENT BRIDGEPORT
Emergency Operations Center, Regional Business Council, D+G Industries Inc, Greater Bridgeport Community Enterprises, Hill Neighborhood House (NHN), Long Island Sound Futures, Metro North, PT Partnership, South End Neighborhood Revitalization Zone, The Nature Conservancy, University of Bridgeport, Yale Urban Design Workshop, Freeman Center, Yale Urban Ecology and Design Laboratory, Save the Sound, UConn Landscape Design, Mercy Learning, B:Hive, BGreen 2020 Committees, Greater Bridgeport Regional Council CTAC, Jonathan Rose Companies, JHM Consulting, Poko Partners, O&G, PSEG, Wheelabrator, Santa Energy, Marina Village Tenants Association, Seaside Village Board of Directors, Sierra Club, Trust for Public Land, American Planning Association, Bridgeport Neighborhood Trust, Groundwork Bridgeport, Bridgeport Regional Aquaculture Science & Technology Education Center, Charles Island Oyster Farm, Bridgeport Lobster and Shellfish, Bridgeport SDAT, Shiloh Baptist Church, Connecticut Coalition for Environmental Justice

RESILIENCE + THE BEACH
US Department of Commerce, NJ Governor's Office, NJ Secretary of State, NJ Department of State, NJ Division of Travel & Tourism, NJ Department of Environmental Protection, NJ Economic Development Authority, NJ Transit, NJ Department of Planning Advocacy, NJ State Parks, NJ Department of Transportation, City of Asbury Park, Asbury Park Planning Department, City of Keansburg, Monmouth County, Monmouth County Planning Office, Ocean County, Borough of Union Beach, Berkeley Township

RESILIENCE + THE BEACH
Asbury Park Press, Asbury Park's Environmental and Shade Tree Commission, Barnegat Bay Partnership, Community Affairs & Resource Center, Creative NJ, Deal Lake Commission, Department of Planning Advocacy, Division of Travel & Tourism, Faith Based Initiative Group, Greater Media Newspapers, Interfaith Neighbors, Inc., International Flavors and Fragrances, Jersey Shore Partnership, Langosta Lounge, League of Municipalities, Littoral Society, Monmouth University, New Jersey Future, NJ EDC, NJ Future, NJTPA, Occupy Sandy, Our Lady of Mt. Carmel 21st Century Learning Center, Rare Find Nursery, Rutgers, State of New Jersey Travel & Tourism, Surfrider, T&M Associates, Table Talk, Art Helps, Together North Jersey, Toms River/Berkley Township, Union Beach Strong, Urban Coast Institute at Monmouth University

RESIST DELAY STORE DISCHARGE
FEMA, US Senators Bob Menendez and Cory Booker, NJ Governor's Office of Recovery and Rebuilding, NJ Department of Environmental Protection, NJ Economic Development Authority, City of Hoboken, Hoboken Mayor Dawn Zimmer, Hoboken City Council, Hoboken Housing Authority, Township of Weehawken, Weehawken Mayor Richard Turner, Weehawken City Council

RESIST DELAY STORE DISCHARGE COMPREHENSIVE PLAN FOR HOBOKEN
Bike Hoboken, Community Emergency Response Team, County of Hudson Division of Planning, Hoboken Boys and Girls Club, Hoboken Catholic Academy, Hoboken Chamber of Commerce, Hoboken Commuter Community, Hoboken Cove Community Boathouse, Hoboken Day Care, Hoboken Developers, Hoboken Dual Language Charter School, Hoboken Green Infrastructure Strategic Plan, Hoboken Jubilee Center, Hoboken Resident Community Hopes, Jersey City Division of City Planning, Louis Berger (Together North Jersey), Mayor of Jersey City Steven Fulop, Mile Mesh, New Jersey Transit, North Hudson Sewerage Authority, Port Authority of NY/NJ, PSEG, Stevens Institute, Re:Focus

NEW MEADOWLANDS
NJ Governor's Office, NJ Meadowlands Commission, NJ Meadowlands Conservation Trust, Jersey City, City of Kearny, Borough of Little Ferry, Borough of Moonachie, Town of Secaucus, Hudson County, Bergen County, Port Authority of NY/NJ, Public Service Enterprise Group, Meadowlands Environmental Research Institute

NEW MEADOWLANDS
Forsgate Industrial Partners, Hackensack Riverkeeper, Hartz Mountain Industries, Kearny Point Industrial Park, Meadowlands Chamber of Commerce, Center for Urban Environmental Sustainability, Rutgers University, RTL Services Inc., Russo Development LLC., CSX Transportation

LIVING WITH THE BAY
US Senators Chuck Schumer and Kirsten Gillibrand, US Representative Carolyn McCarthy SW Brooklyn District Office, US Department of Health and Human Services, NY Governor's Office of Storm Recovery, NYS Department of Transportation, NY Rising, Long Island Railroad, Long Island Regional Planning Council, Long Island Regional Economic Development Council, Nassau County, Nassau County Department of Public Works, Nassau County Executive Office, Nassau County Legislature, City of Long Beach, Town of Hempstead Department of Conservation and Waterways, Town of Hempstead Department of Engineering, Village of East Rockaway, Village of Freeport, Village of Lynbrook, Village of Rockville Centre

LIVING WITH THE BAY
Peconic Baykeeper, Adelphi University, Association of Marine Industries, Baldwin Civic Association, Bellport High School Students for Environmental Quality, Brookhaven Baymen's Association, Brookhaven League of Women Voters, Captain Don's Nautical Adventures, Center for Estuarine, Environmental and Coastal Oceans Monitoring, Child Care Council of Long Island, Citizen's Campaign for the Environment, Coastal Research and Education Society of Long Island, Community Development Corporation of Long Island, Empire Justice, ERASE Racism, Family Service League, FEGS, Fire Island Association, Garden Club of Long Island, Great South Bay Audubon Society, Health and Welfare Council of Long Island, Hofstra University Suburban Studies Program, Islip Town Leaseholders Association, Kimmel Housing Foundation, Knights of Columbus, Long Island Housing Partnership, LIVOAD Long Term Recovery Group, Local NY Laborers 66, Long Beach COAD, Long Island Association, Long Island Housing Partnership, Long Island Index, Long Island Sierra Club, Long Island Volunteer Center, Lutheran Counseling Center, Lutheran Social Services, Mastic Beach Property Owners Association, National Center for Suburban Studies, New York Committee for Occupational Safety and Health, New York Sea Grant, New York Seafood Council, New York Sportfishing Federation, Operation SPLASH, Pattersquash Creek Civic Association, Presbyterian PBA, Presbytery of Long Island, Project Hope, Rebuilding Together of Long Island, Renaissance Downtowns, Seatuck Environmental Association, Sheet Metal Workers Local 28, Society of Vincent de Paul, South Bay Cruising Club, South Shore Audubon Society, South Shore Bayhouse Owners Association, South Shore Estuary Reserve, South Shore Waterfowlers Association, Stony Brook University Department of Geosciences, Suffolk Alliance of Sportsmen, Sustainable Long Island, The Nature Conservancy on Long Island, Trout Unlimited, United Methodist Church, United Way of Long Island, Vision Long Island, Western Bays Coalition

THE COMMERCIAL CORRIDOR RESILIENCY
NJ Governor's Office of Recovery & Rebuilding, NJ Economic Development Authority, NYC Mayor's Office of Long-Term Planning and Sustainability, NYC Department of City Planning, NYC Economic Development Corporation, NYC Department of Small Business Services, City of Asbury Park

THE COMMERCIAL CORRIDOR RESILIENCY
Beach 116th Street Partnership, Dry Dock, Flickinger Glassworks, Fort Defiance, Home/Made, IKEA, iStar Residential, Kevin's Restaurant, Linda Tool, Madison Marquette, The O'Connell Organization

Scale It Up

To gain momentum for the projects as they were being developed and to broaden the opportunities for individuals to become involved, Van Alen Institute took the lead to organize "Scale It Up," a series of public events in five locations selected for geographic and demographic diversity: Asbury Park, New Jersey; Bridgeport, Connecticut; and, in New York City, Far Rockaway, Queens; Lower East Side, Manhattan; and the North Shore of Staten Island. Organizers invited resident committees, community-based organizations, businesses, and government officials to co-create events that would have a uniquely local flavor in order to make the teams' work accessible through hands-on activities and engaging site installations.

Rebuild One City: Asbury Park, New Jersey

A bombastic parade led by local marching bands wound through Asbury Park to connect the city's disparate communities together in pursuit of a common vision for resilience. Research and design work from the Rebuild by Design teams that related to Asbury Park was on display; the Monmouth County Division of Planning sponsored interactive mapping stations showing disaster preparedness information; Hope Academy middle school students built an installation on the theme of resilience; and Lakehouse Music Academy students, the St. Stephen gospel choir, and the Eloquent Orators provided a musical backdrop for the entire event.

Following Spread: The Asbury Park One City parade brought together disparate parts of the Asbury Park community.

Citymaking: Bridgeport, Connecticut

A festival showcased transportation and other urban issues at the city's main public library. The teams exhibited research and designs that directly concerned Bridgeport; Los Angeles-based planner James Rojas held a design workshop; and local bicycle advocates convened hands-on bike repair workshops and led youth and teens on a group ride. Rebuild by Design supplied funding for bicycles, helmets, and a mobile trailer that functioned as a pop-up bicycle repair station. Once the event finished, these items became part of the foundation for the Bridgeport Community Bike Center, which would continue to hold similar events at libraries around the city.

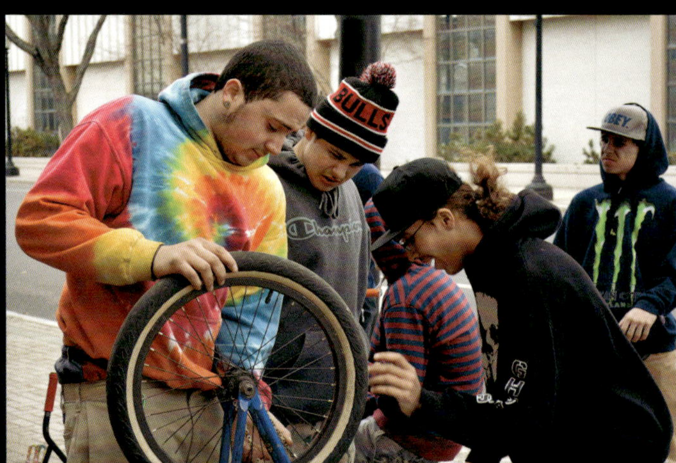

Thank You LES: Lower East Side, New York City

A dance party and a storytelling workshop helped infuse energy and excitement into a series of planning and visioning exercises. Local and visiting artists made interactive stations for people to develop creative ideas about community resilience. Sandy Storylines, an oral history group, led a writing workshop that asked participants to describe or draw their vision for the Lower East Side waterfront, asking "What makes a good community?" "What do you love to do in the park?" and "What future waterfront do you see?" Residents spent the afternoon dancing, creating, and learning about local resilience.

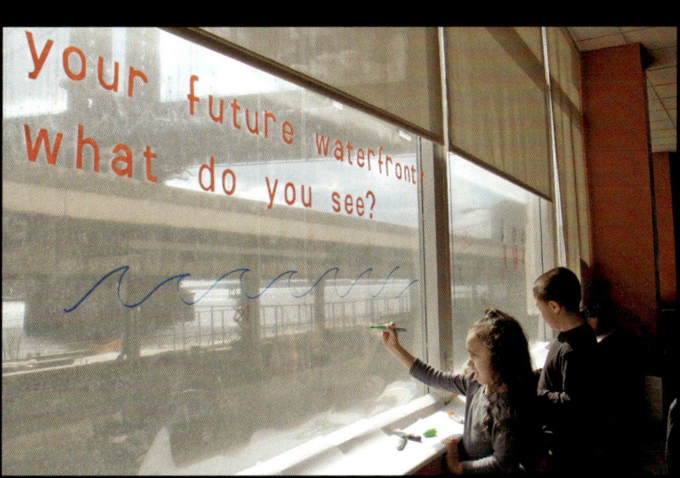

I <3 My Shoreline: Staten Island, New York City

Community members gathered at the Staten Island MakerSpace to construct a model oyster reef that demonstrated the SCAPE team's Living Breakwater project. Exhibited at the Staten Island Museum, the concept brought community members of all ages together through experiential education about resilience.

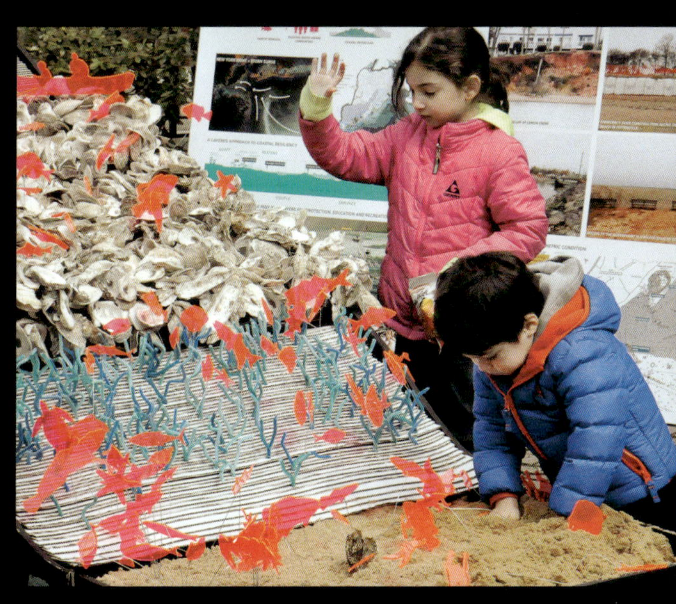

Earth Day: Far Rockaway, New York City

The final Scale It Up celebrated Earth Day in a community that had lost much of its green public space to Hurricane Sandy. Neighborhood members gathered to pot plants and re-establish a space for residents to congregate, enhancing their neighborhood's social resilience, and a visiting architect was commissioned to design and build seating, shade structures, and solar power generators with local youth.

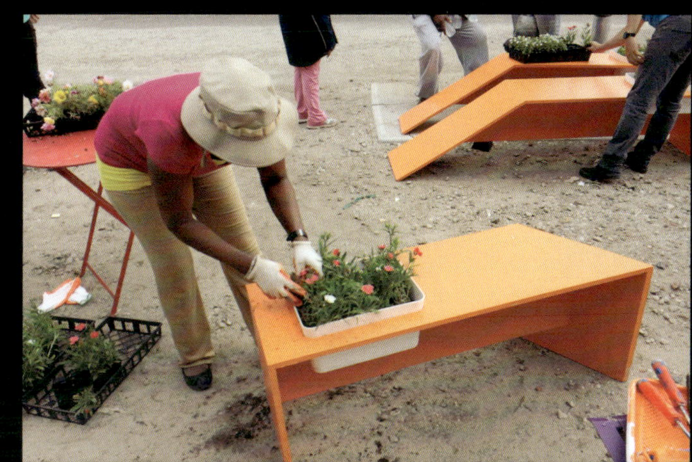

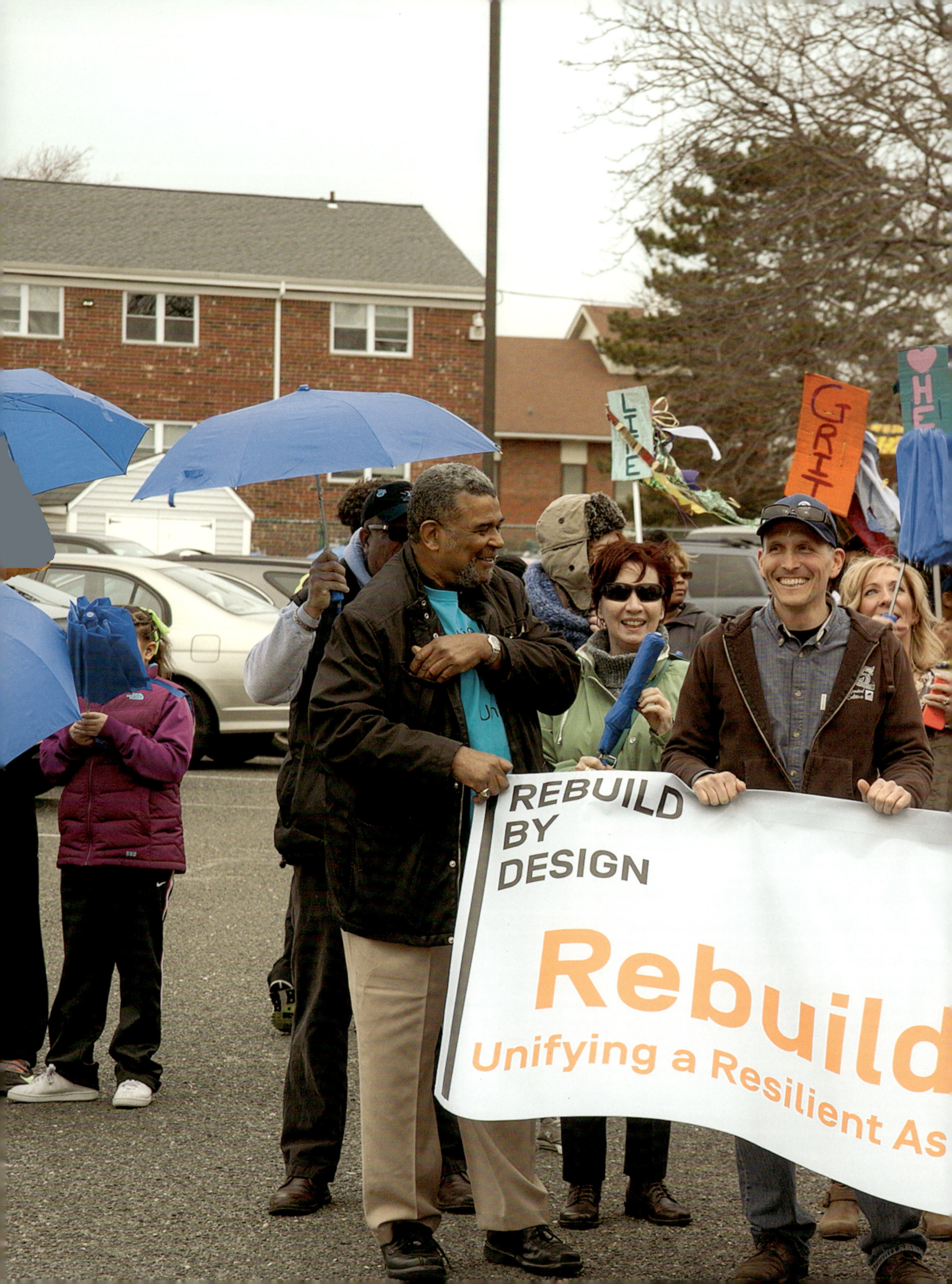
GRIT
REBUILD
BY
DESIGN
Rebuild
Unifying a Resilient As

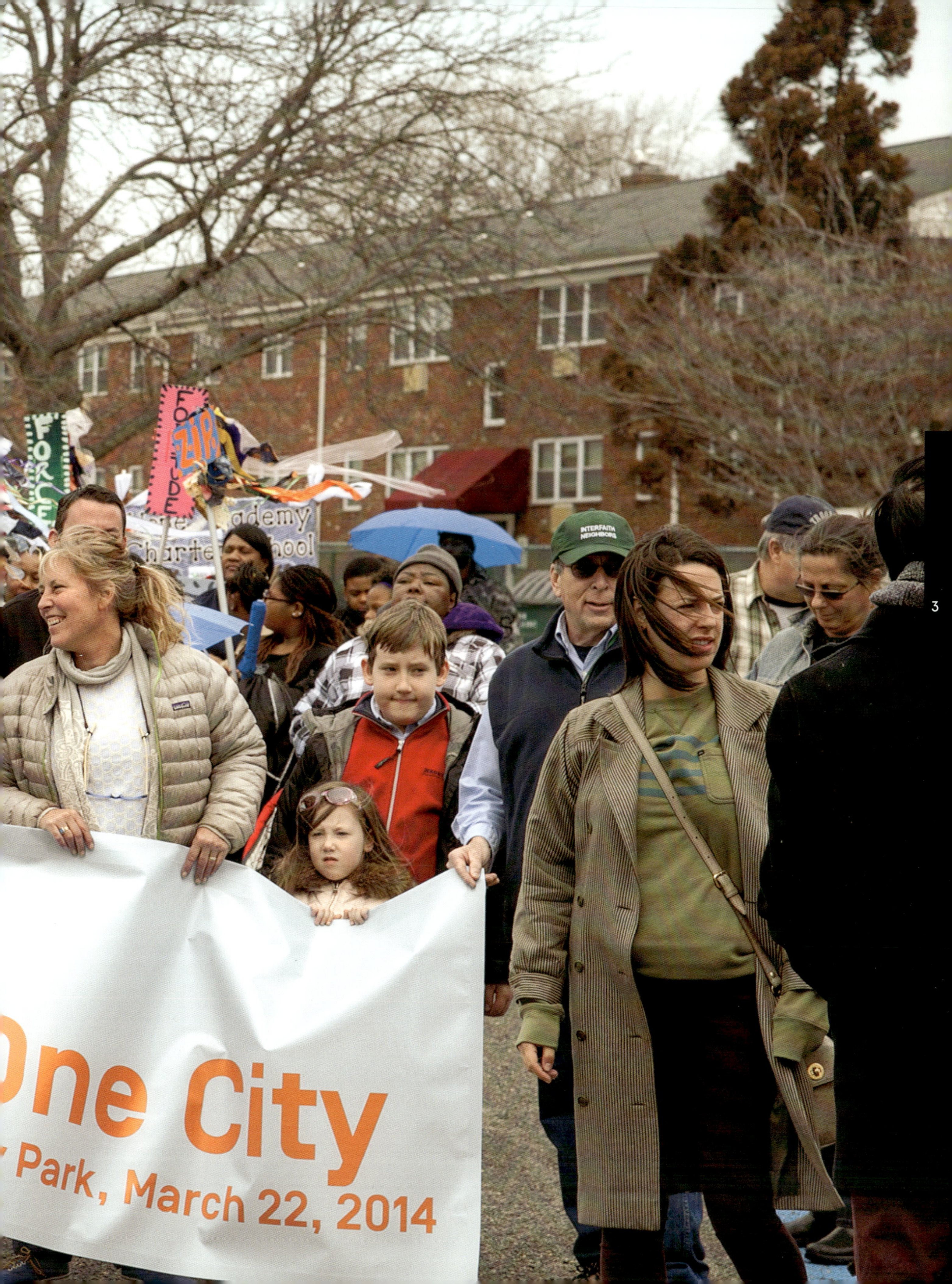
One City
Park, March 22, 2014
INTERFAITH NEIGHBORS
FORCE

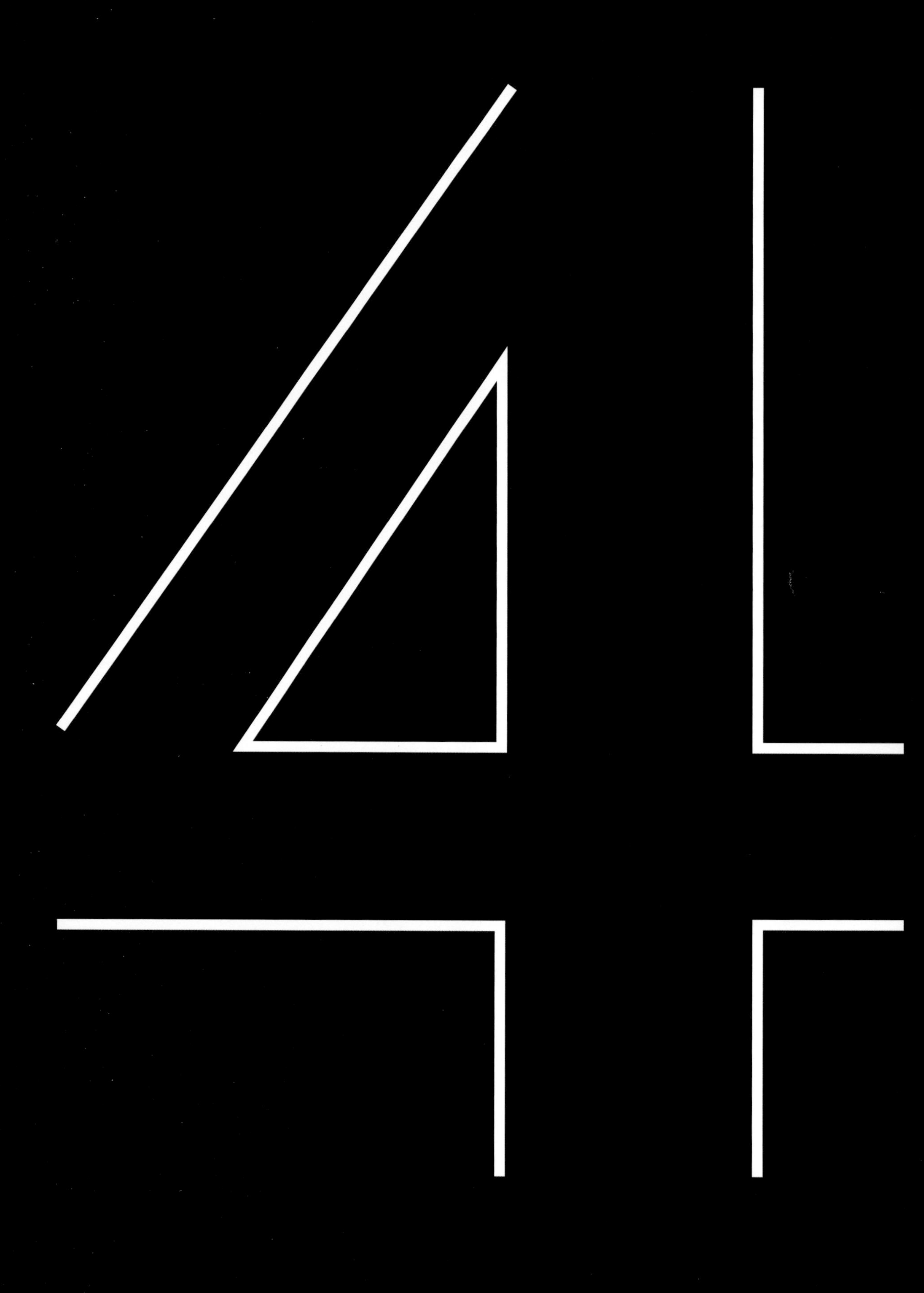

PROJECTS

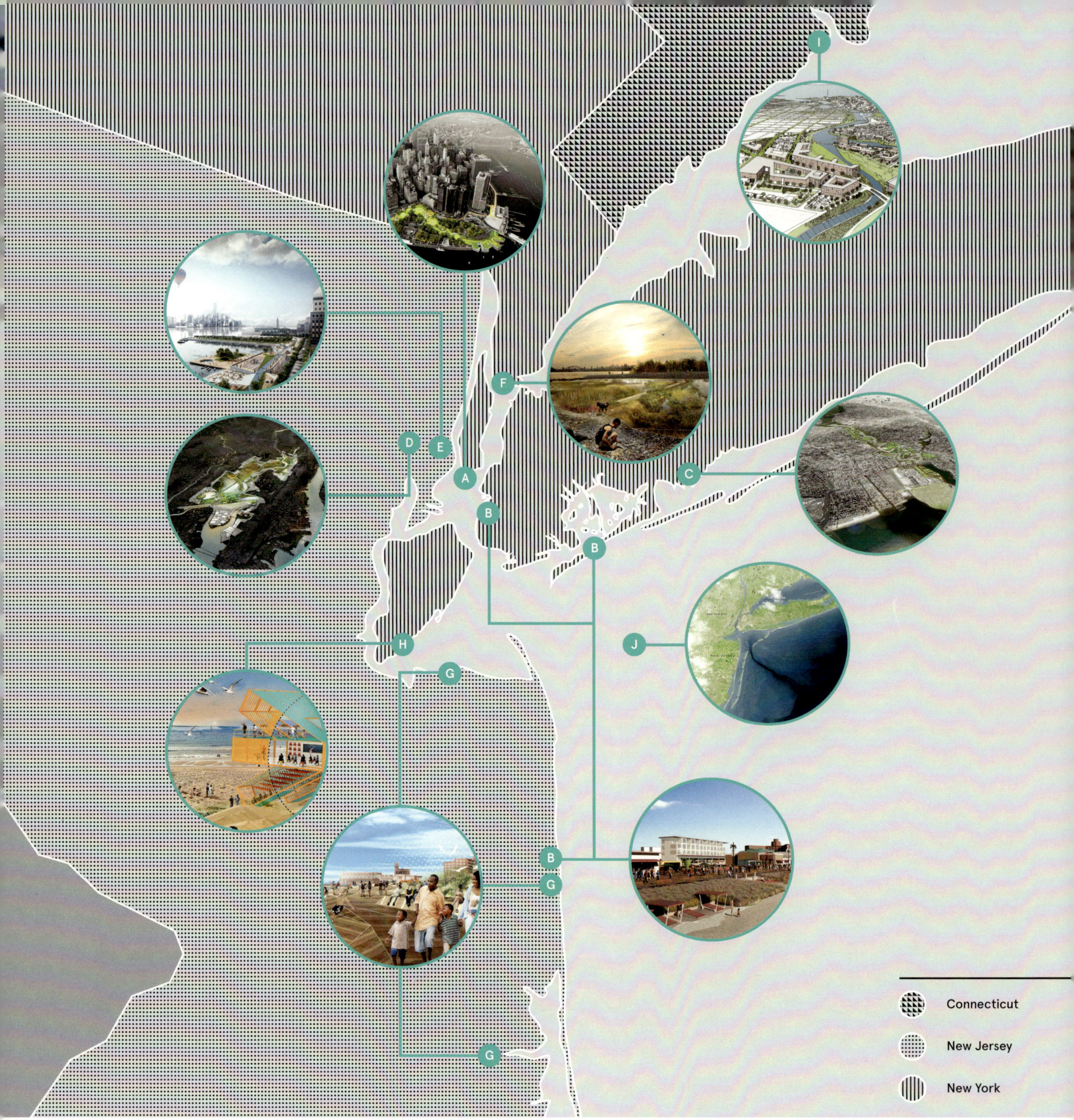

Connecticut

New Jersey

New York

BIG Team
The BIG U
Manhattan, NY

HR&A Advisors, Inc. with Cooper, Robertson & Partners
Commercial Corridor Resilience Project
Asbury Park, NJ; Rockaways, NY; Red Hook, NY

Interboro Team
Living with the Bay: A Comprehensive Regional Resilience Plan for Nassau County's South Shore
Nassau County, NY

MIT CAU + ZUS + URBANISTEN
New Meadowlands: Productive City + Regional Park
Meadowlands, NJ

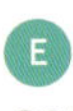

OMA
Resist, Delay, Store, Discharge
A Comprehensive Urban Wate
Strategy
Hoboken, NJ

PennDesign/OLIN
Hunts Point Lifelines
Bronx, NY

Sasaki/Rutgers/Arup
Resilience + The Beach
Union Beach, Asbury Park, Toms River, NJ

SCAPE/Landscape Architecture
Living Breakwaters
Staten Island, NY

WB unabridged with Yale ARCADIS
Resilient Bridgeport
Bridgeport, CT

WXY/West 8
Blue Dunes – The Future of Coastal Protection
Atlantic Coastline

Final Design Projects

After months of collaborative design, learning, and community engagement, the ten teams finalized their proposals: ten visionary designs aimed at making the region more resilient in the face of future risks.

Because of the interdisciplinary nature of the process and the diverse expertise represented amongst the teams, the ten projects range in scale, typology, location, and approach. They incorporate the tools of architecture, landscape architecture, urban planning, environmental science, and engineering to address issues as varied as ecology, urban density, and coastal communities — from dense housing projects to marine environments far offshore. Despite their differences, the projects all grew from the same soil: the comprehensive vulnerability assessments made during the Rebuild by Design research phase. As each unique project sprouted up, the teams' close collaborations with local communities helped the projects mature into the complex, robust strategies they finally became.

The following pages present each of the final ten proposals along with the process each team traversed to arrive at their final solutions.

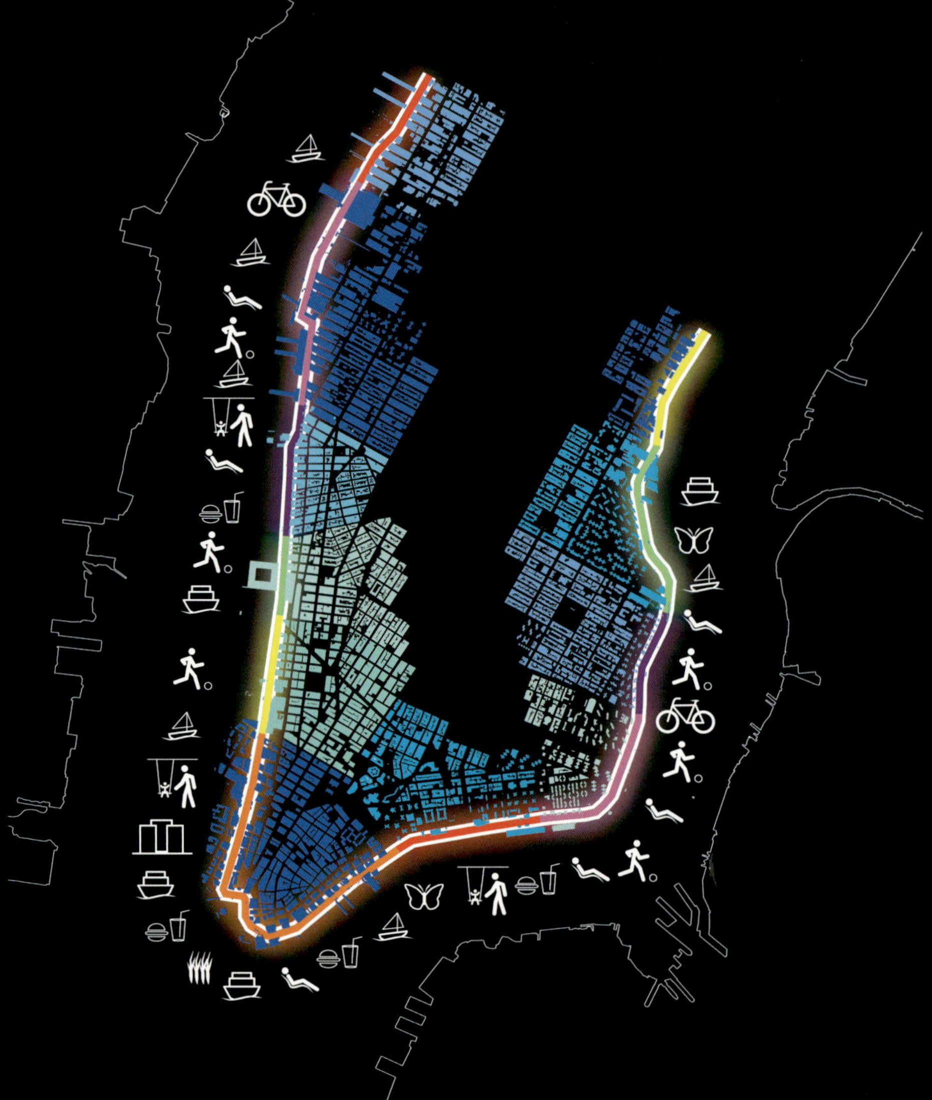

Team Lead
Bjarke Ingels Group (BIG)

Urban Planning
One Architecture

Landscape Architecture
Starr Whitehouse

Planning and Development
James Lima Planning + Development

Infrastructure Engineering
Level Infrastructure

Energy and Structural Engineering
Buro Happold

Coastal Resilience Engineering
ARCADIS

Ecological Services
Green Shield Ecology

Cultural Resources
AEA Consulting

The BIG Team

The BIG Team explored the problem of how flood protection could be designed for the coastline of New York City without creating a seawall that segregates the life of the city from the water around it. For inspiration, the team looked to the newly revitalized High Line, a stretch of decommissioned railway that has become one of the city's most popular promenades. Could lessons learned from the High Line be incorporated into a flood barrier? Instead of waiting for the infrastructure to be shut down to become a public amenity, could these protections be designed to come with intended social and environmental benefits? And what if this large-scale state-of-the-art coastal flood protection were planned in such a way that it could be tailored to the character of each neighborhood it protects and informed by input from resident communities? To achieve this, the multidisciplinary team brought together a diversity of knowledge, from urban ecology to infrastructure engineering. The collaboration combined local expertise in community outreach with global experience protecting the world's most vulnerable coastlines. The resulting proposal is unified in function but diverse in character. It responds to the specific needs of communities today but remains flexible enough to develop over time, as sea level and climate continue to change.

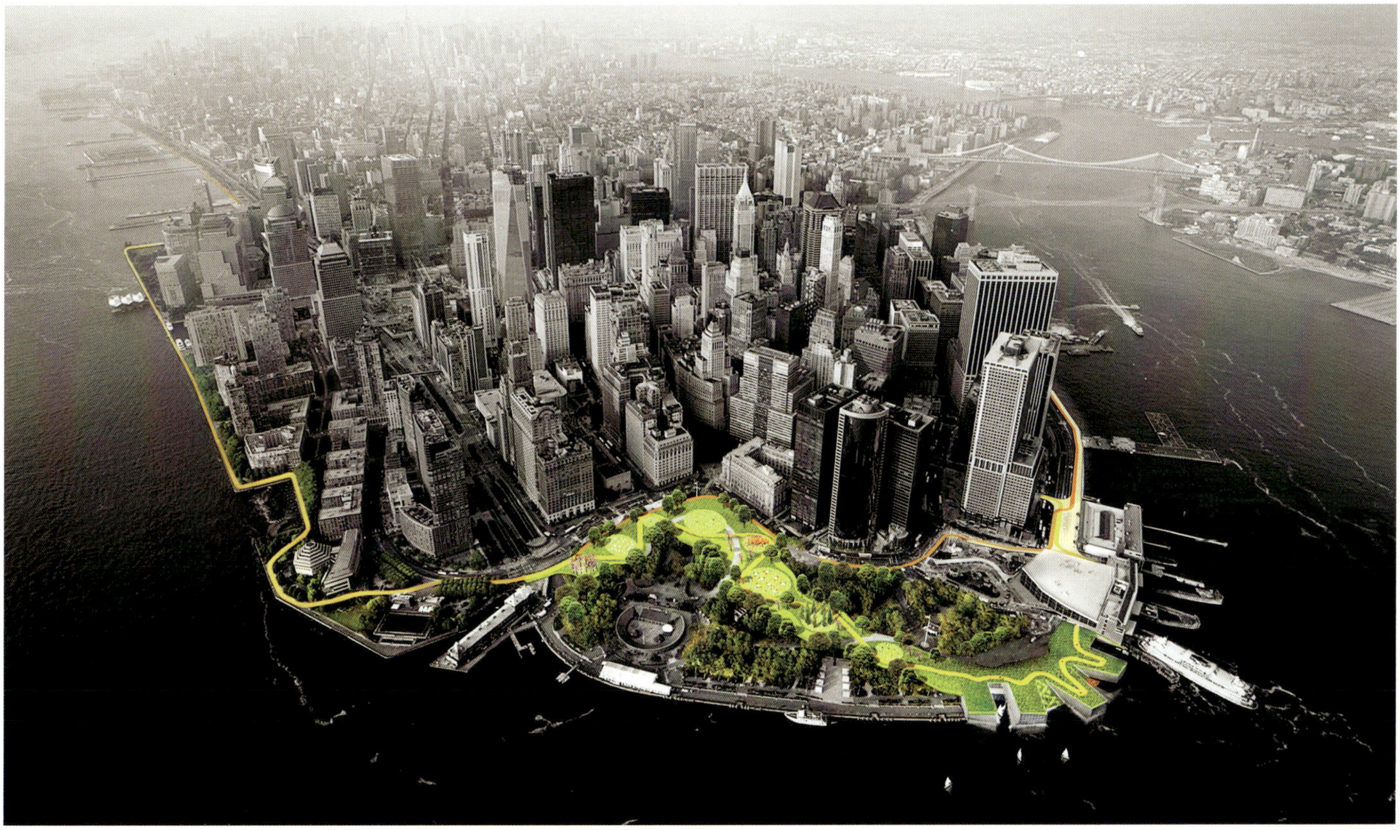

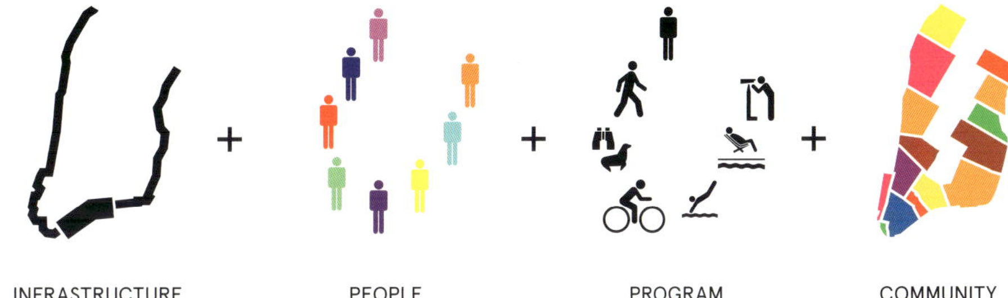

The BIG U combines the infrastructure required to protect the coastline of Manhattan from flooding with the desire to bring people to the waterfront in places where the existing coastline prevents it. The plan builds into that infrastructure an array of programs and amenities envisioned in collaboration with local communities.

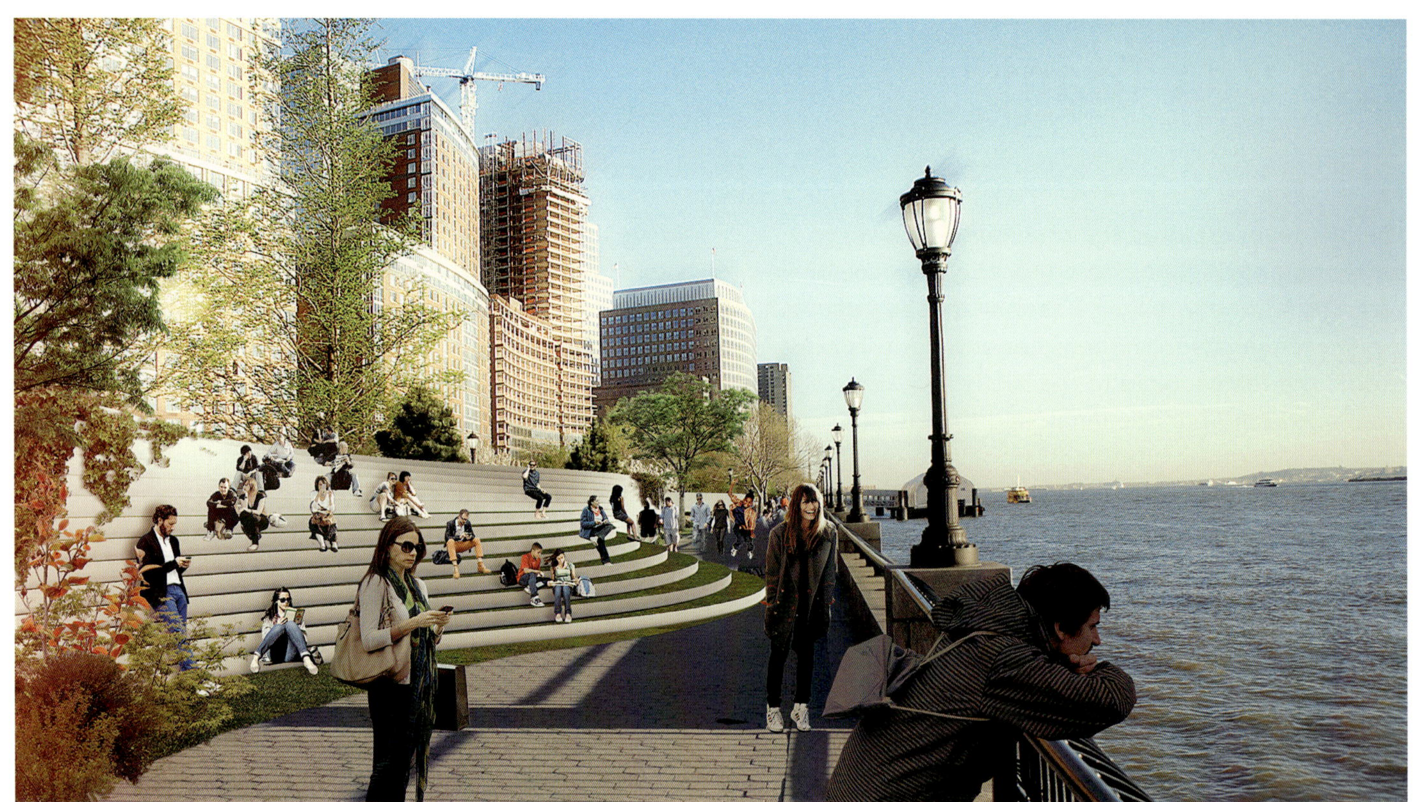

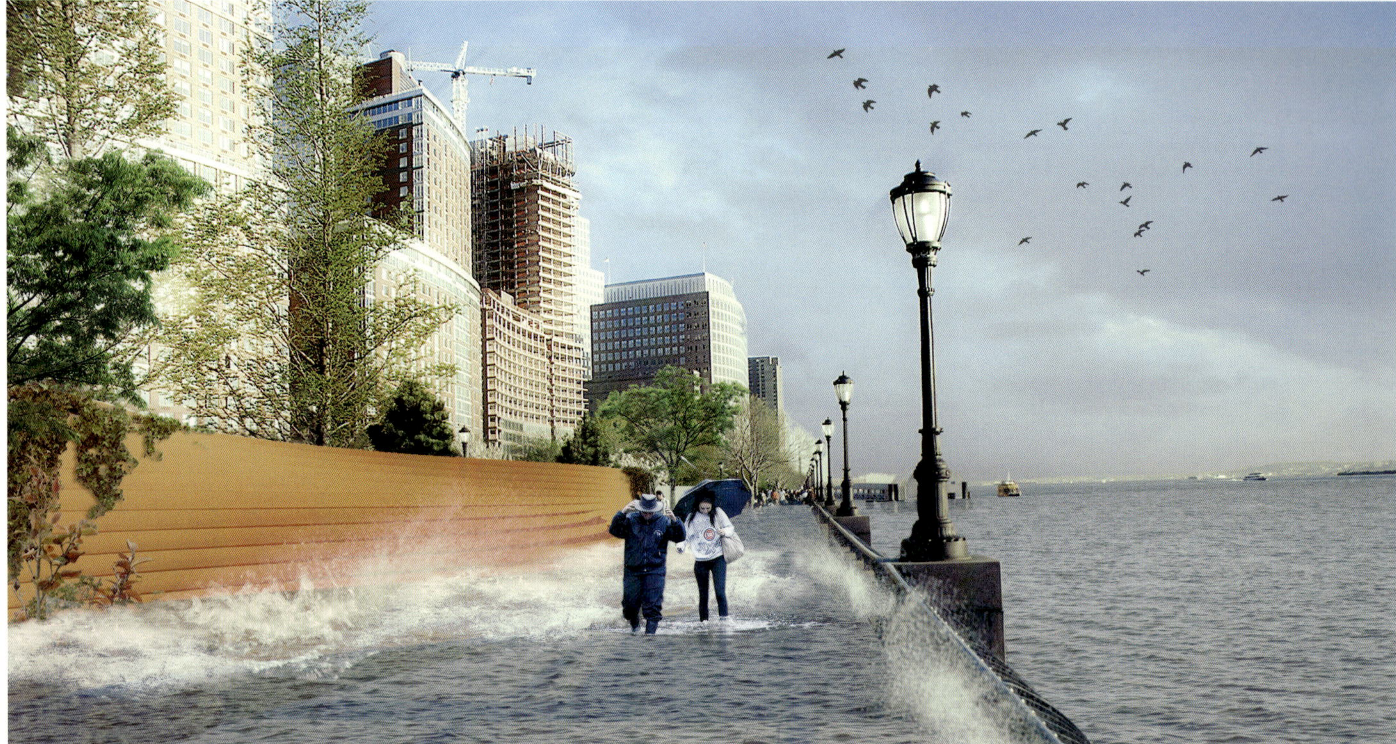

The flood protection that keeps Manhattan dry during extreme weather events will only serve this purpose for a small percentage of its lifetime. The other 99% of the time, it is essential that it be designed as an improvement to the city's coastline, which can be enjoyed by citizens on a daily basis. To make this work, flood protection features must become part of the life of the city. The same grandstand where people sit to watch a performance on a sunny day, for example, doubles as a seawall preventing storm surge waters from flooding the neighboring community.

A Hybrid Approach

New York's modern development has been shaped by a clash of ideologies personified by two individuals. On one side Robert Moses, "the Power Broker," championed a top-down approach to realize a series of colossal projects, including highways, social housing, and public parks. Unfortunately, these interventions came at a terrible cost to existing neighborhoods, as new highways blocked the waterfront and divided communities. When he attempted to cut a highway through Greenwich Village, he met fierce opposition from Jane Jacobs – the other side of New York's historic planning struggle. She rallied local grassroots sentiment and, in a David versus Goliath struggle, managed to defeat the plan.

The BIG Team calls the BIG U the "love-child of Moses and Jacobs." Its ten miles of coordinated flood protection requires a big-picture approach, but its success in New York's urban environment requires close dialogue with local communities. Each flood threat needs to be countered by a particular geometry, which can be achieved with a variety of innovative forms that serve social purposes beyond functioning as a flood barrier. Through dialogueS with community groups, the team developed an array of flood protection features, ranging from informal hangout areas to sculptures nested in highway medians. In each case, the proposed intervention is tailored to the neighborhood to provide enhancements, rather than barriers, to the waterfront.

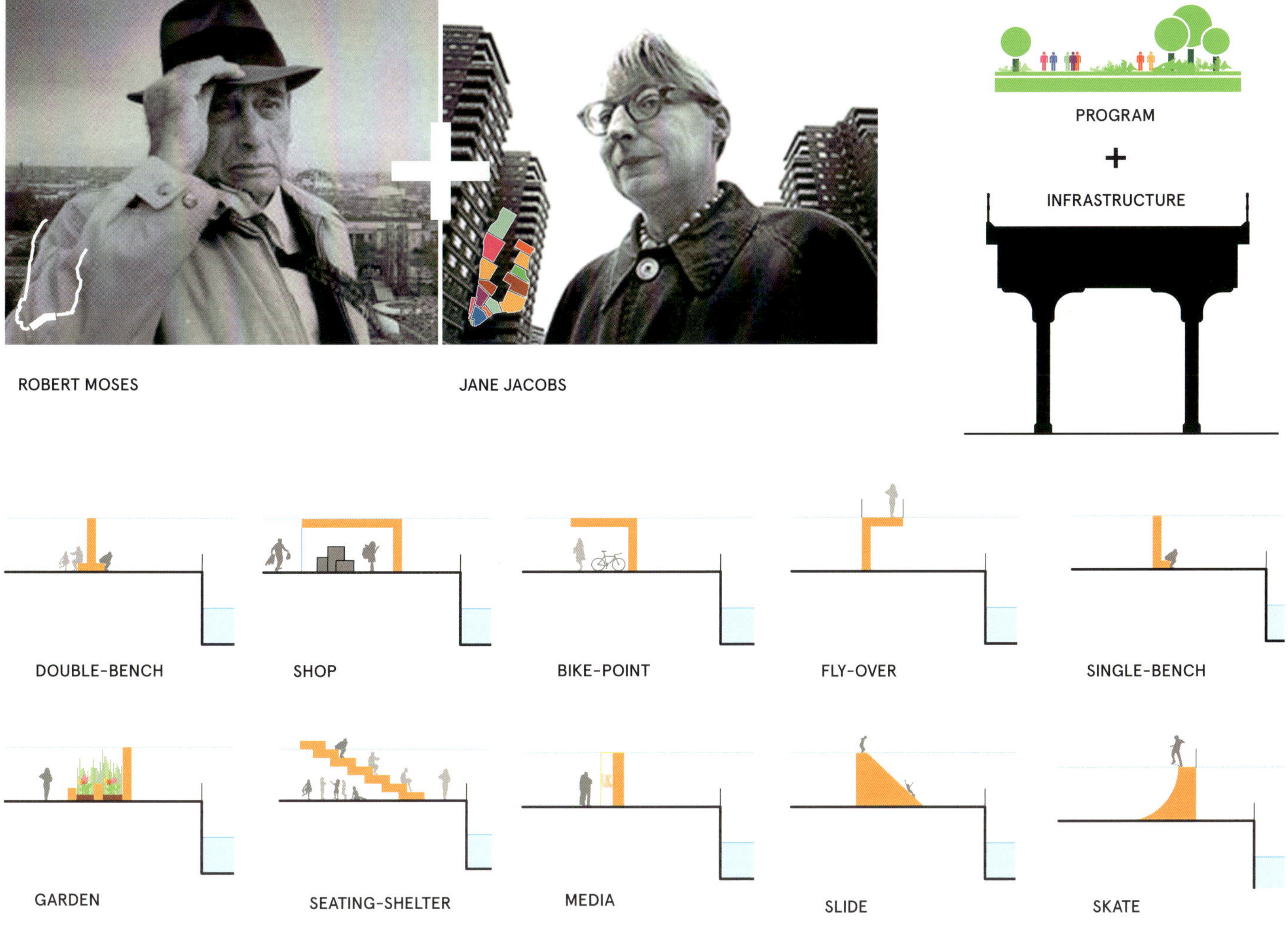

ROBERT MOSES

JANE JACOBS

4

Design Opportunities

The BIG Team began by focusing on New York's urban core — a dense and diverse economic engine for the region and country that was hit hard by Hurricane Sandy. In the process of exploring the potential of pairing growth with resilience, the team identified several potential sites with different waterfront and urban conditions: Manhattan, Red Hook, and the South Bronx.

These investigations led to a number of techniques, typologies, and mechanisms that informed the team's design opportunities and helped them consider urban challenges in an integrated way. Forecasting more than 500,000 new units of housing by 2040 and an increased exposure of assets to extreme weather, the team was determined to think big. It also recognized that it would need to start small. In the proposal for Resilient Community Districts, community planning, social resilience, water management, utilities, and financial instruments were organized on a district scale and an urban scale. This partial decentralization of critical infrastructure would increase the resilience of the whole. Community micro-grids and water-management plans create redundancies that decrease the risk posed by storms and allow incremental adaptation to climate change. District-organized social infrastructure and emergency preparedness provide a cohesive response to unforeseen emergencies. Finally, leveraging local investment in coastal protection, matched with government investment as needed, would engage neighbors in developing protective measures that provide for other district needs, creating tremendous economies of scale that could directly benefit end users.

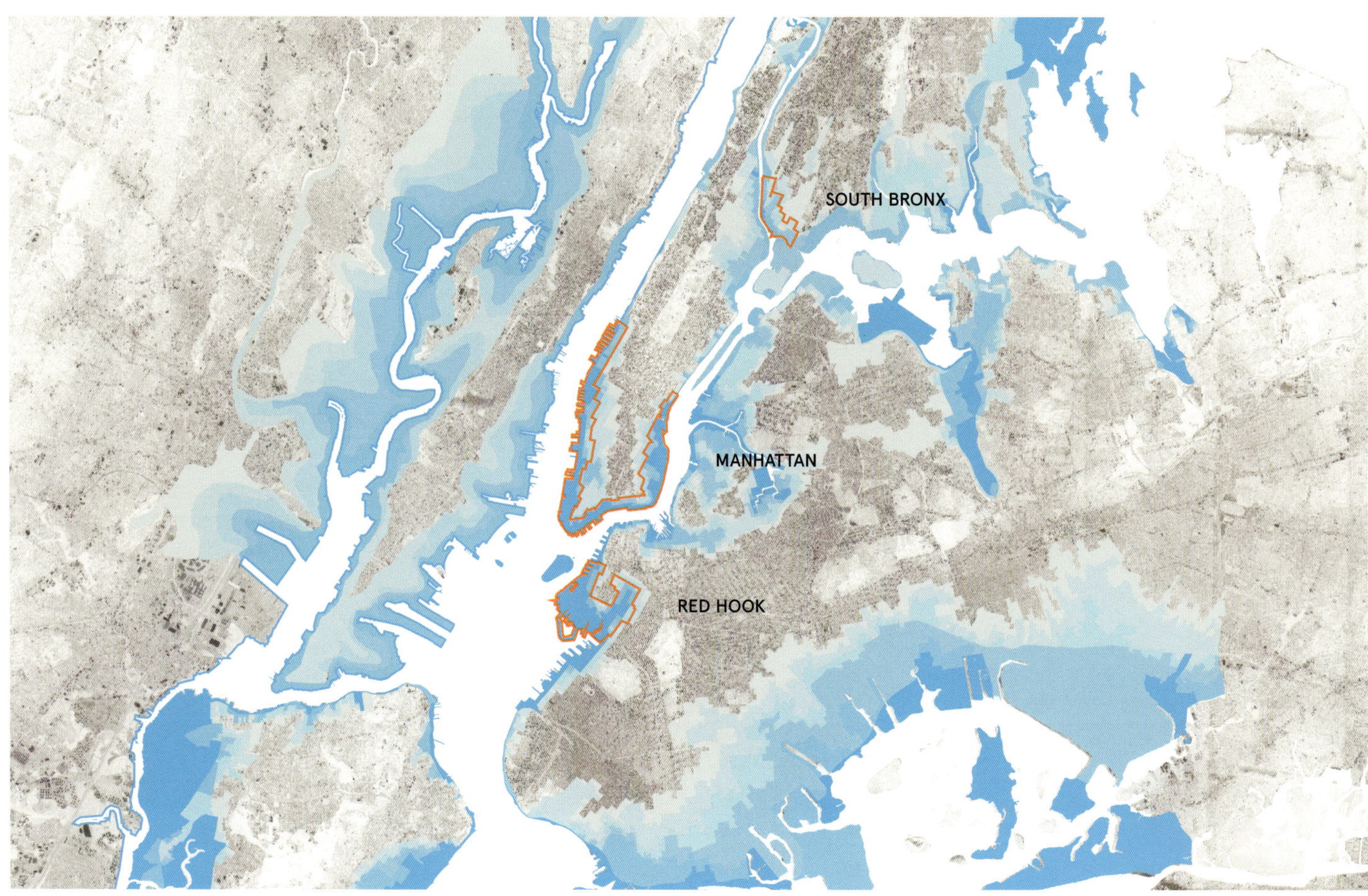

Manhattan

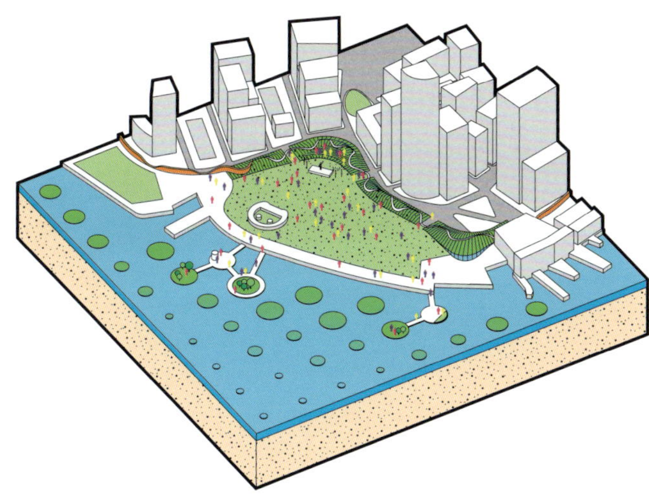

The development of a series of adaptive flood-protection measures around Manhattan – from West 57th Street down to the Battery and up to East 42nd Street – would allow Manhattan to link growth with protection and tailor flood measures to each district. The BIG U can bundle infrastructure into new robust energy districts that increase redundancy and reliability. On a longer timescale, the BIG U proposes to lower FDR Drive and cover it with a seamless park to connect the city to the waterfront. The new tunnel could support a U-Line subway to reach currently under-served areas. The BIG U would be a new infrastructure linking resilience efforts on the waterfront to the city's ongoing social and ecological goals.

Red Hook

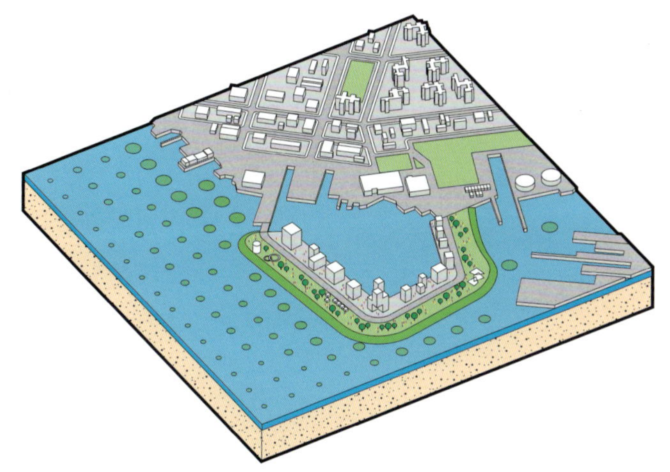

Significant investments are needed in Red Hook to buffer against flooding, retrofit existing buildings, harden critical infrastructure, and revitalize commerce. Planning for growth in Red Hook through a Resilient Community District (RCD) strategy would engage local stakeholders to find the right balance of diverse land uses. The RCD would prioritize creating spectacular public waterfront parks, which would become the organizing element for new affordable housing, enhanced transit connections, and a working waterfront industry. The RCD would also support new food services and other creative industries, as well as encourage tourism and other new uses on Governors Island and other nearby areas in the burgeoning New York Harbor District.

South Bronx

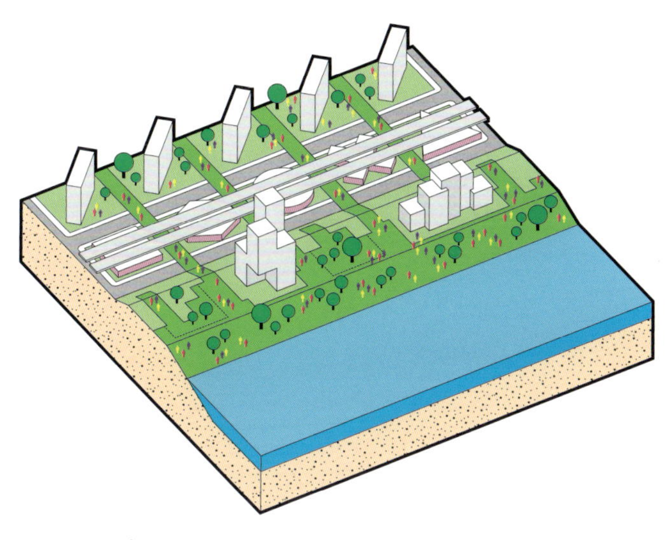

The notion of social infrastructure is particularly relevant to the challenges of vulnerable affordable housing, where necessary resilience measures can be an important first step toward further improvement. This led the BIG Team to seek opportunities for waterfront place-making and increased economic investments in this area. With good transit connections and adjacency to a developing Harlem, the South Bronx Waterfront offers great potential for the development of mixed-income and affordable housing. Such development would serve three major purposes: to give the South Bronx a clear, public front toward Manhattan, to connect the area to Harlem via the Third Avenue Bridge, and to reinvigorate the surrounding neighborhoods.

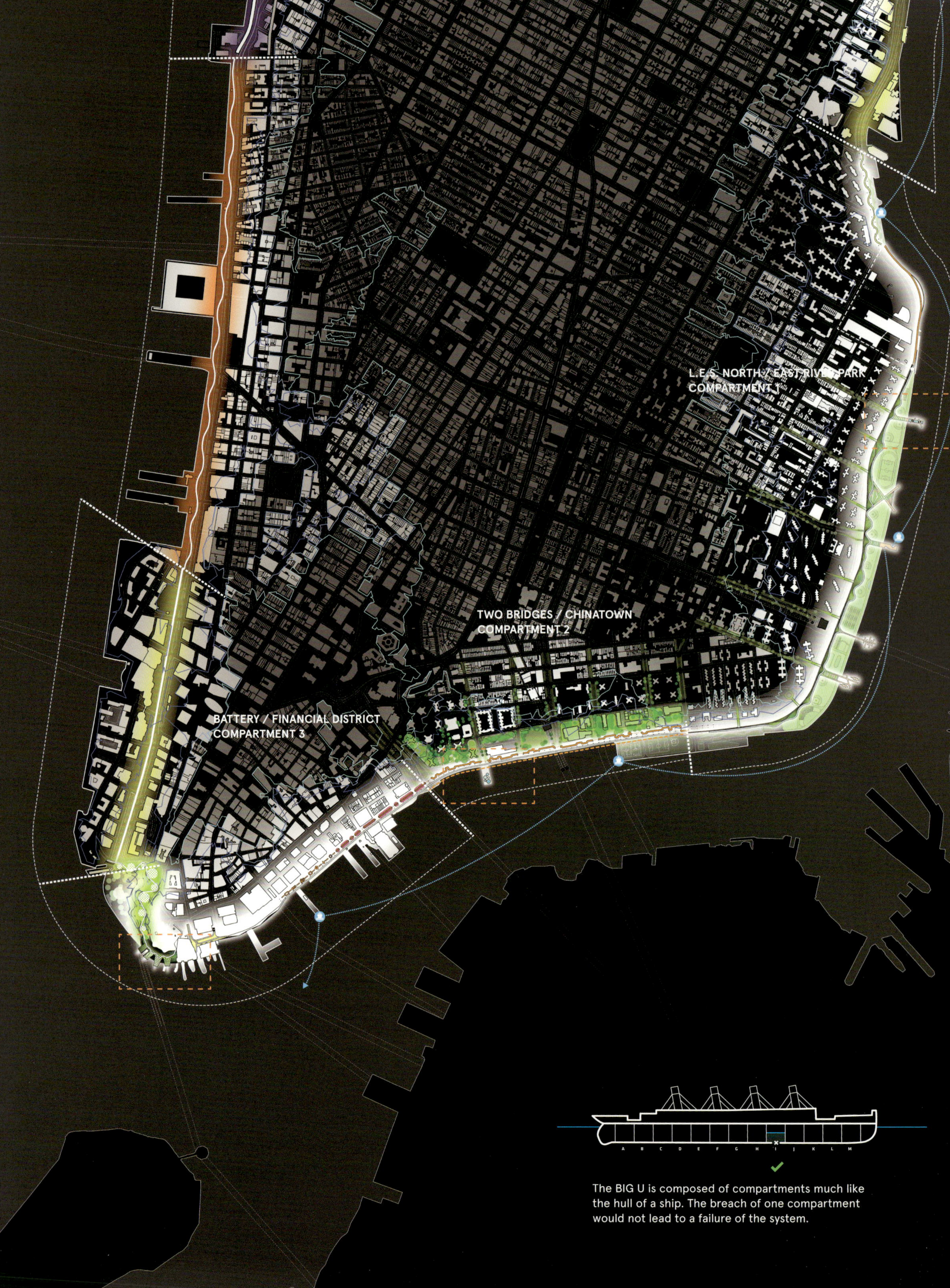

The BIG U is composed of compartments much like the hull of a ship. The breach of one compartment would not lead to a failure of the system.

Final Proposal: The BIG U

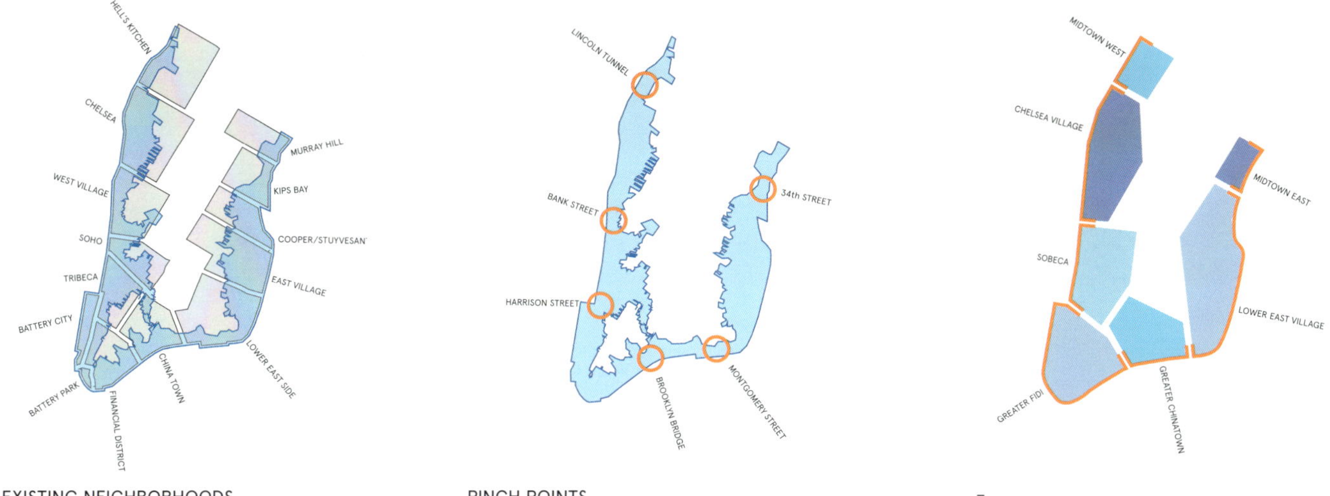

EXISTING NEIGHBORHOODS PINCH POINTS =

For its final proposal, the BIG team created coordinated plans for three contiguous but separate waterfront regions that it dubbed "compartments." Each compartment comprises a physically discrete flood-protection zone that can be isolated from flooding in adjacent zones. Each presents unique opportunities for integrated social and community planning. Proposed solutions for the components were designed in close consultation with the associated communities along with many local, municipal, state, and federal stakeholders to ensure they would be flexible, easily phased, and able to integrate with existing projects.

The designs propose not only to solve existing problems but also to prevent the formation of new ones, proactively enhancing the city and channeling its future growth in desirable directions. This approach creates an opportunity to work with communities to ensure that the resilience measures function as social, economic, and environmental assets. As a dynamic process, linking resilience with growth enables planners to adapt to emergent developments, such as global climate change and shifting policy priorities.

These first compartments in the BIG U combine the mandate to create large-scale protective infrastructure with a commitment to meaningful community engagement. Through this process, the structures that provide flood protection double as attractive centers of social and recreational activity that enhance the city and commit positive groundwork for its future.

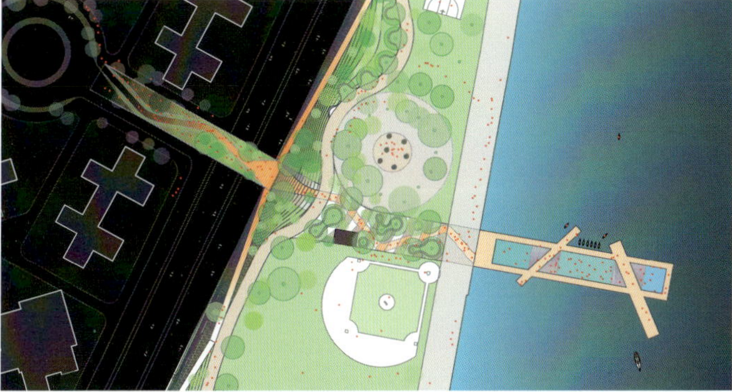

Harbor Bath - L.E.S. North / East River Park

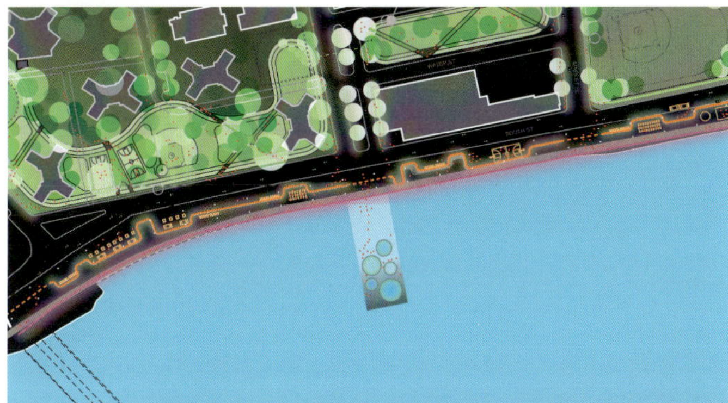

Eco Dock - Two Bridges / Chinatown

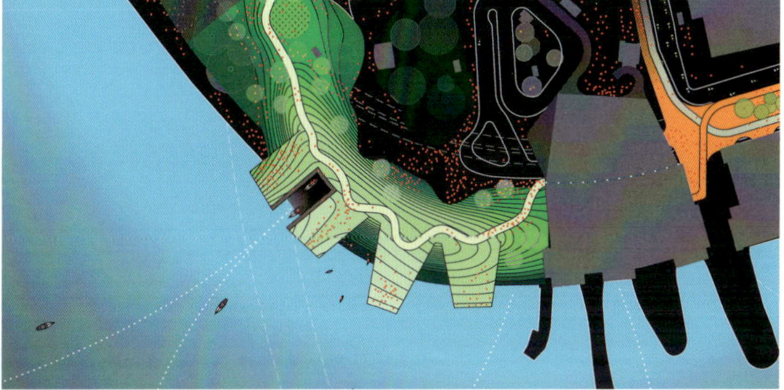

Harbor Museum - Battery / Financial District

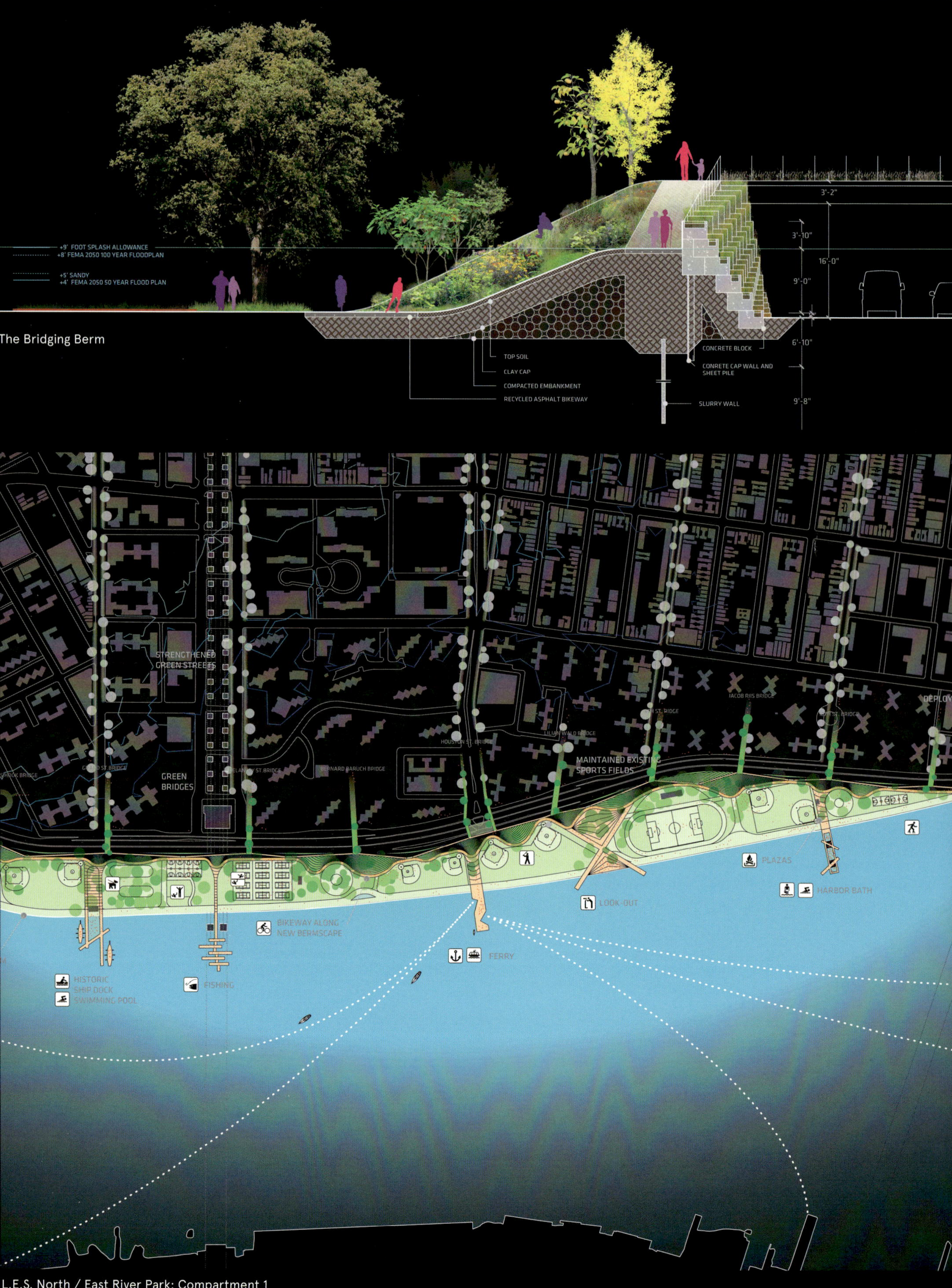

The Bridging Berm

L.E.S. North / East River Park: Compartment 1

East River Park

At East River Park, an undulating berm along the path of an existing service road would provide a new flood protection measure. Contoured to avoid interfering with existing sports fields, the berm provides topographic relief and new vistas for the back of the park. New landscape also increases the resilience of the park with more diverse, salt-tolerant trees and plantings. Generous landscaped bridges connect East River Park to the community, enhancing existing bridges and adding new bridges between major streets.
A series of ramps allow residents and visitors a way to move between the park and the bridges. Plazas connect the park with a new scenic bikeway, and they enhance access to the East River, where a series of new waterfront activities are arrayed along the edge. The flood protection continues to Montgomery Street by fortifying the new Pier 42 Park, where a deployable barrier helps protect the on-ramp to the FDR Drive.

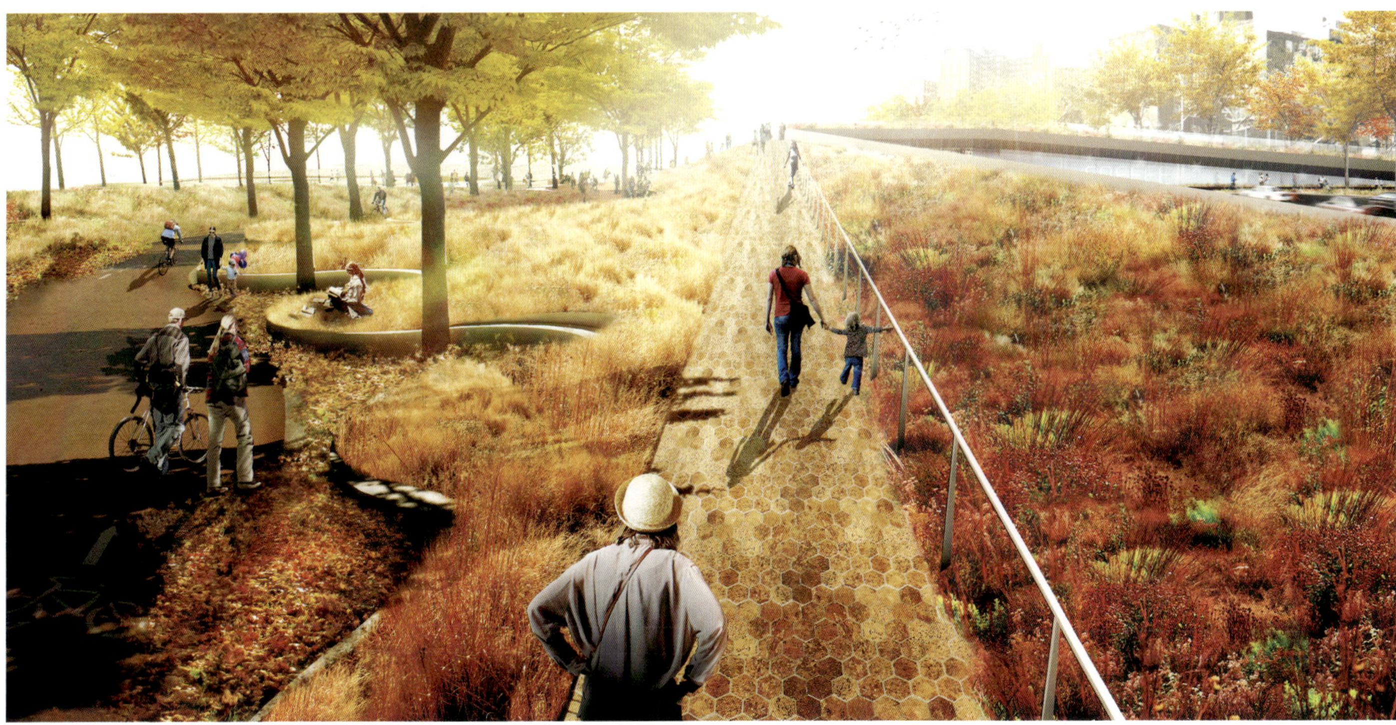

New Resilient Landscape

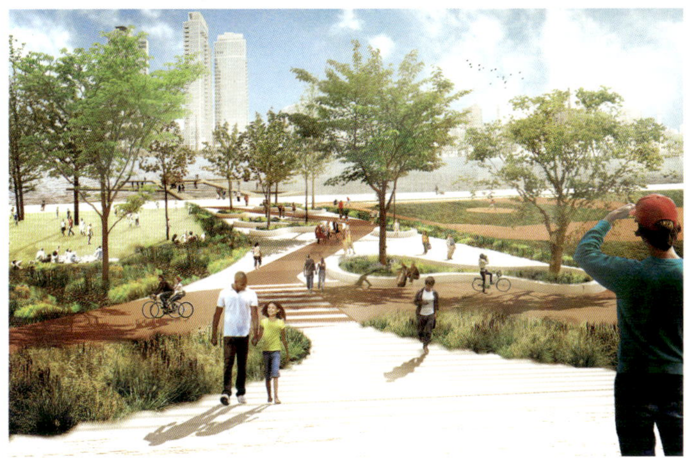

10th Avenue Bridge

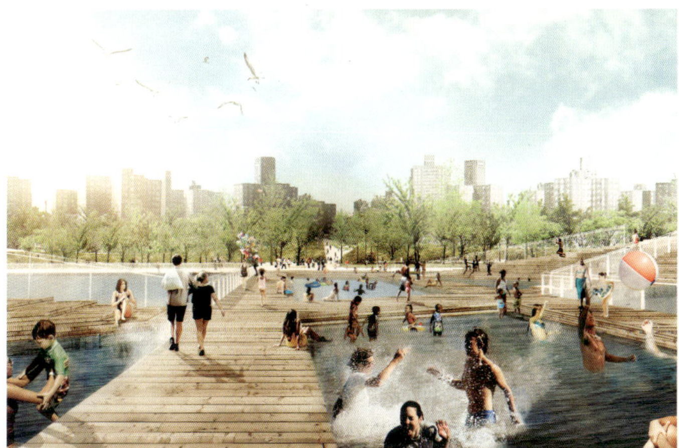

Harbor Bath

4

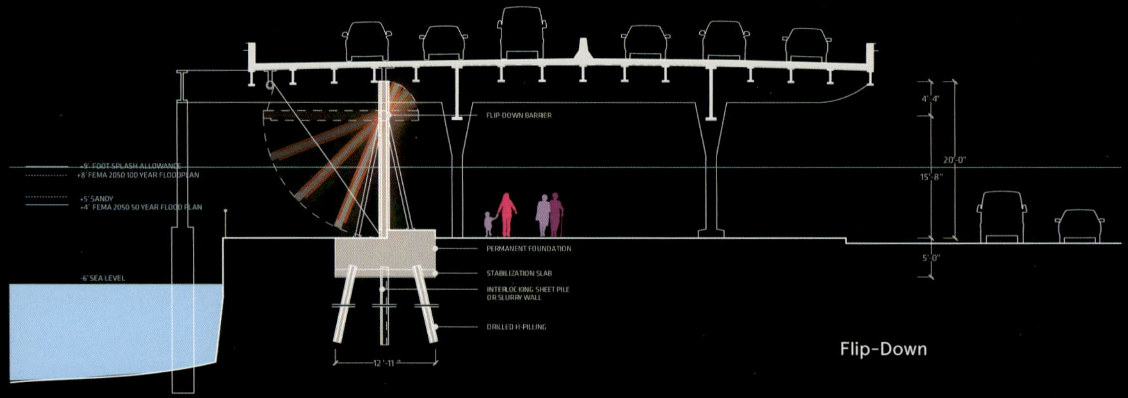

+9' FOOT SPLASH ALLOWANCE
+8' FEMA 2050 100 YEAR FLOODPLAN
+5' SANDY
+4' FEMA 2050 50 YEAR FLOOD PLAN
-6' SEA LEVEL
FLIP-DOWN BARRIER
PERMANENT FOUNDATION
STABILIZATION SLAB
INTERLOC KING SHEET PILE OR SLURRY WALL
DRILLED H-PILLING
12'-11"
4'-4"
20'-0"
15'-8"
5'-0"

Flip-Down

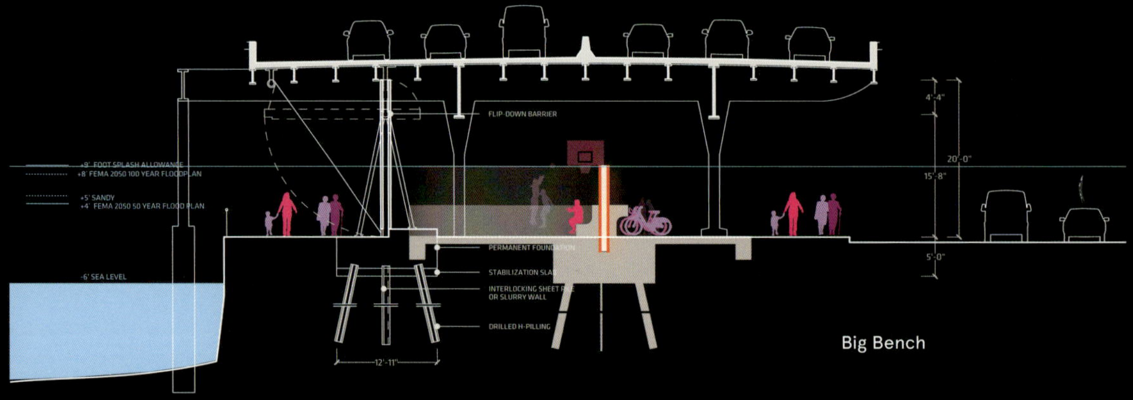

+9' FOOT SPLASH ALLOWANCE
+8' FEMA 2050 100 YEAR FLOODPLAN
+5' SANDY
+4' FEMA 2050 50 YEAR FLOOD PLAN
-6' SEA LEVEL
FLIP-DOWN BARRIER
PERMANENT FOUNDATION
STABILIZATION SLAB
INTERLOCKING SHEET PILE OR SLURRY WALL
DRILLED H-PILLING
12'-11"
4'-4"
20'-0"
15'-8"
5'-0"

Big Bench

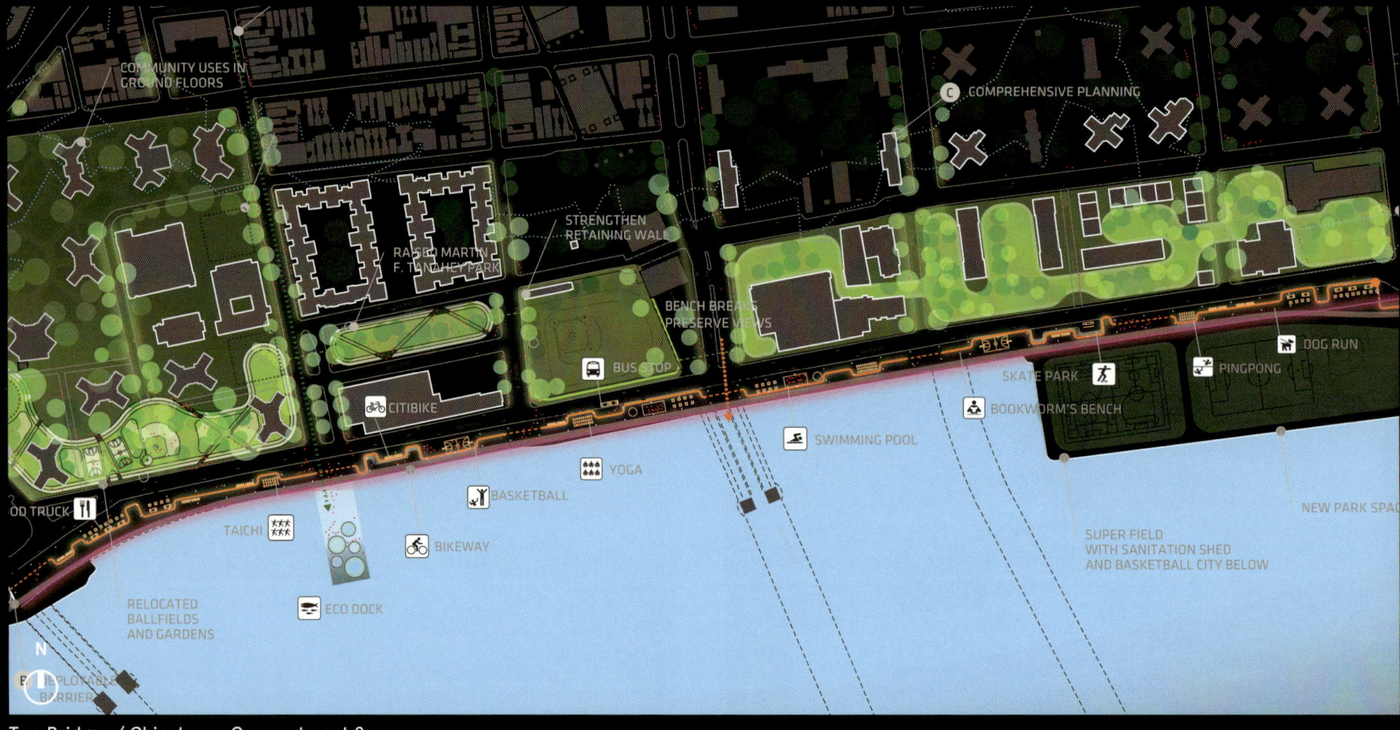

COMMUNITY USES IN GROUND FLOORS
COMPREHENSIVE PLANNING
STRENGTHEN RETAINING WALL
RAISED MARTIN F. TANAHEY PARK
BENCH BREAKS PRESERVE VIEWS
BUS STOP
CITIBIKE
DOG RUN
PINGPONG
SKATE PARK
BOOKWORM'S BENCH
SWIMMING POOL
YOGA
BASKETBALL
OD TRUCK
TAICHI
BIKEWAY
NEW PARK SPAC
SUPER FIELD WITH SANITATION SHED AND BASKETBALL CITY BELOW
ECO DOCK
RELOCATED BALLFIELDS AND GARDENS
DEPLOYABLE BARRIER
N

Two Bridges / Chinatown: Compartment 2

Two Bridges

At Montgomery Street, in front of the Pier 36 Sanitation Department facility, the team proposed the use of deployable barriers on the underside of FDR Drive. These flood protection devices, which would double as a public art project, are designed to provide lighting and security in these now-dark spaces. Opposite the Smith Houses, flood protection would come in the form of benches, skate parks, tai chi platforms and a pool, which would be enclosed in glass from four feet up. These features will enliven the waterfront and provide amenities such as laundromats, shops, and spaces for community functions. One of the ground floors is fortified, housing a cogeneration plant for the entire Smith Houses campus. Limited-height flood barriers shield the area against most recurrent floods while allowing waterfront views.

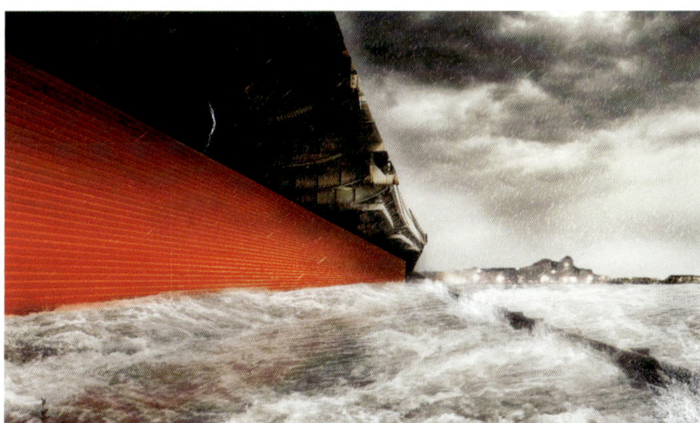

Lowered Flip-Downs

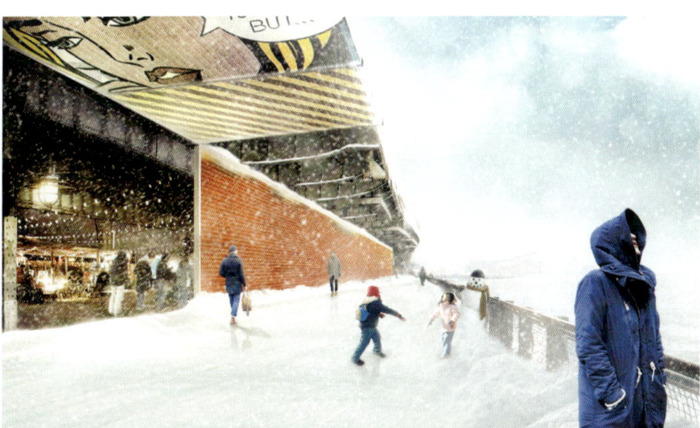

Winter Market

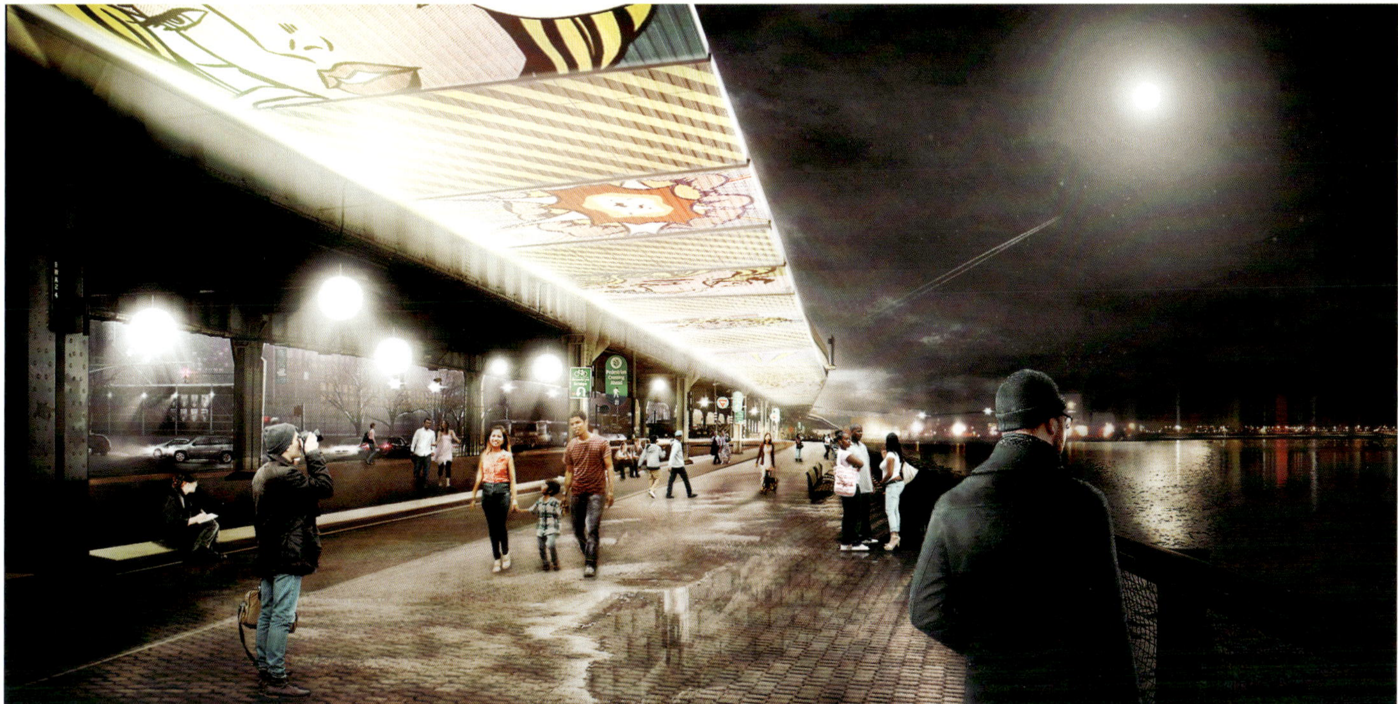

Raised Flip-Downs

4

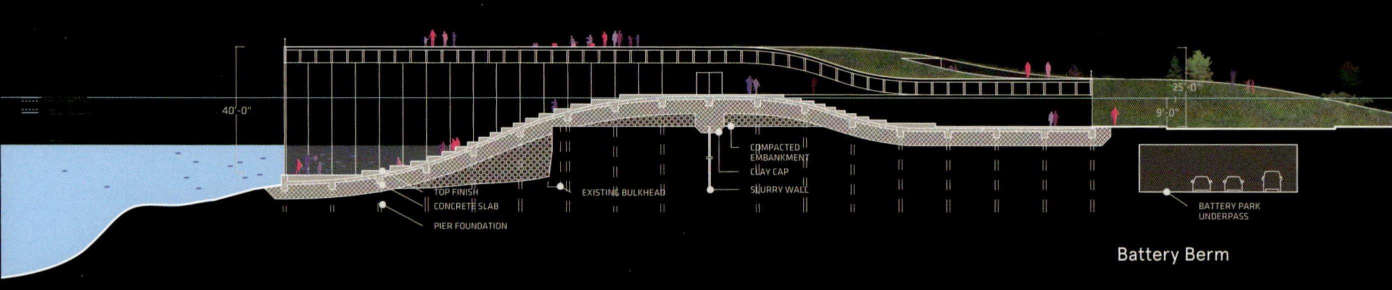

Battery Berm

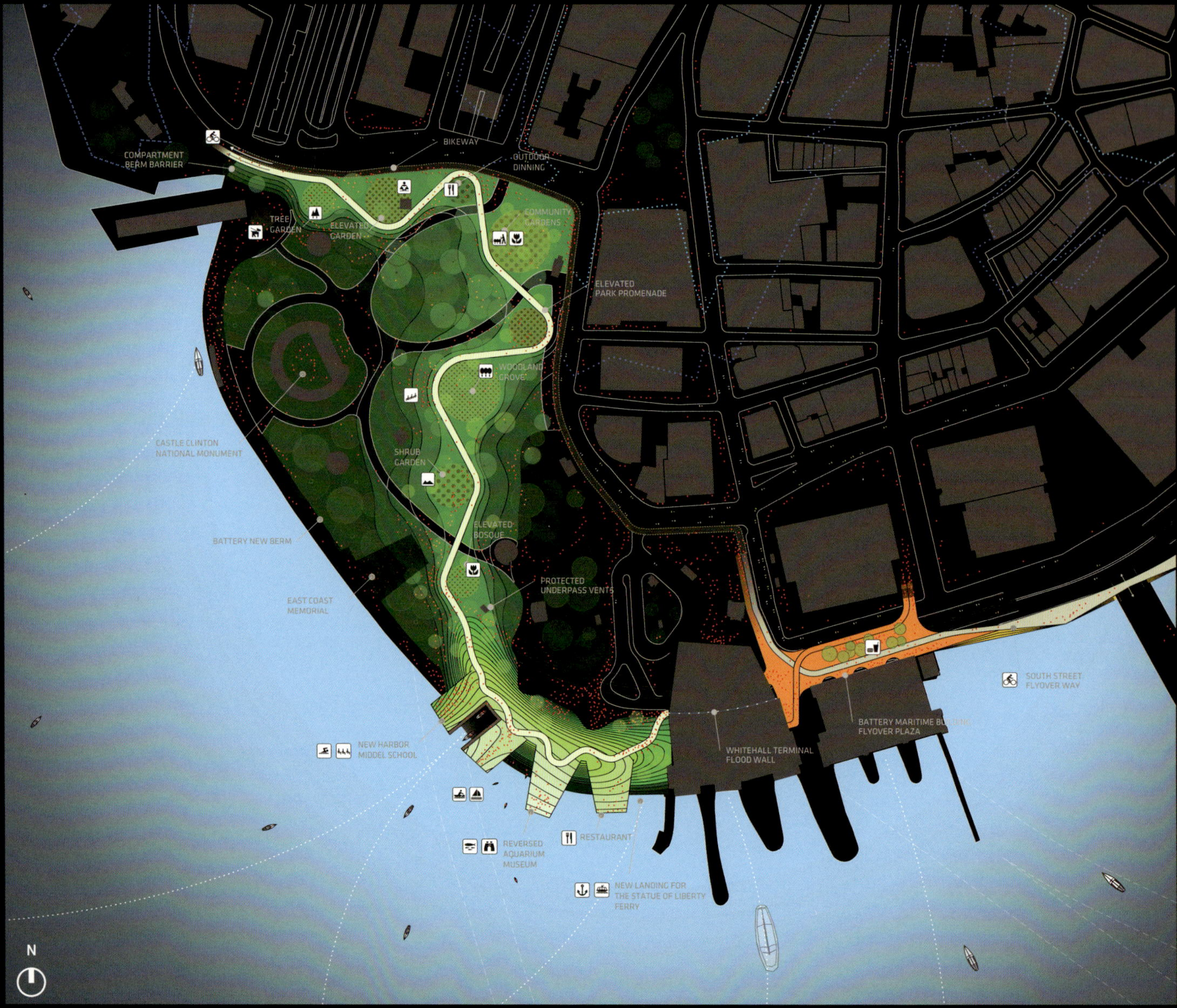

BIKEWAY
COMPARTMENT BERM BARRIER
OUTDOOR DINNING
TREE GARDEN
ELEVATED GARDEN
COMMUNITY GARDENS
ELEVATED PARK PROMENADE
WOODLAND GROVE
CASTLE CLINTON NATIONAL MONUMENT
SHRUB GARDEN
BATTERY NEW BERM
ELEVATED BOSQUE
PROTECTED UNDERPASS VENTS
EAST COAST MEMORIAL
SOUTH STREET FLYOVER WAY
BATTERY MARITIME BUILDING FLYOVER PLAZA
WHITEHALL TERMINAL FLOOD WALL
NEW HARBOR MIDDEL SCHOOL
RESTAURANT
REVERSED AQUARIUM MUSEUM
NEW LANDING FOR THE STATUE OF LIBERTY FERRY
N

Battery / Financial: Compartment 3

Battery Park

Berms in the Battery, strategically located to protect ducts to critical infrastructure, create a continuous protective upland landscape. In place of the Coast Guard building, the plan envisions a new maritime museum and environmental education facility. This signature building features what the team calls a "reverse aquarium," with its form derived from the flood protection at the water-facing ground floor, as well as a new Harbor Middle School. Continuing east, a flood wall connects through the Staten Island Ferry building and aligns with the FDR Drive at the Battery Maritime Building. An elevated plaza brings the latter's monumental mezzanine floor level with its surroundings. The plaza connects to an elevated bikeway, which, in turn, connects to a series of pavilions providing flood protection in conjunction with sliding flood gates. A sequence of attractive urban spaces on the waterfront protect the city while serving and delighting the millions of visitors and thousands of workers in the area.

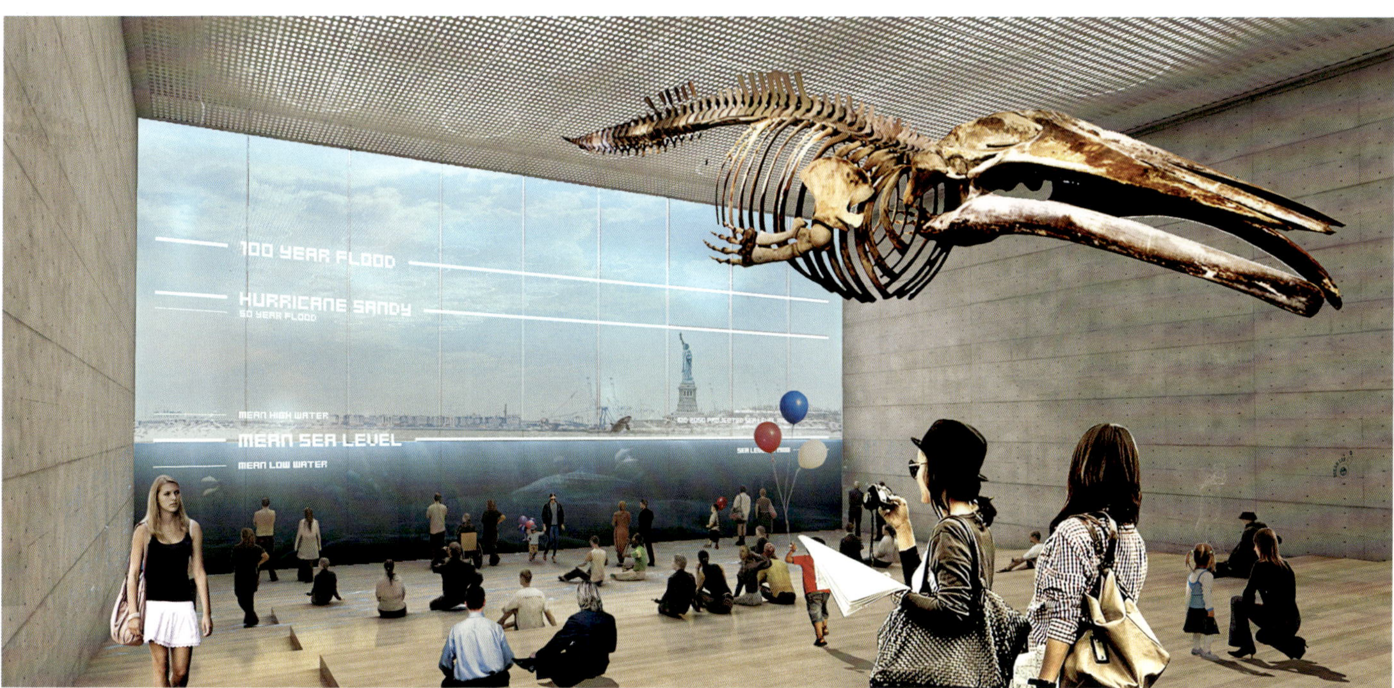

Reverse Aquarium

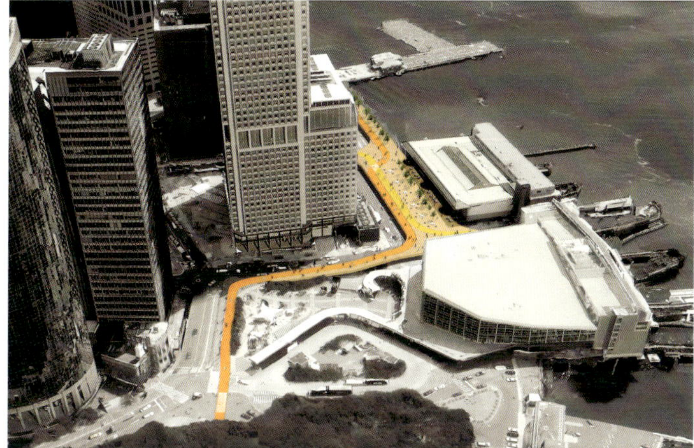

Battery Maritime Plaza

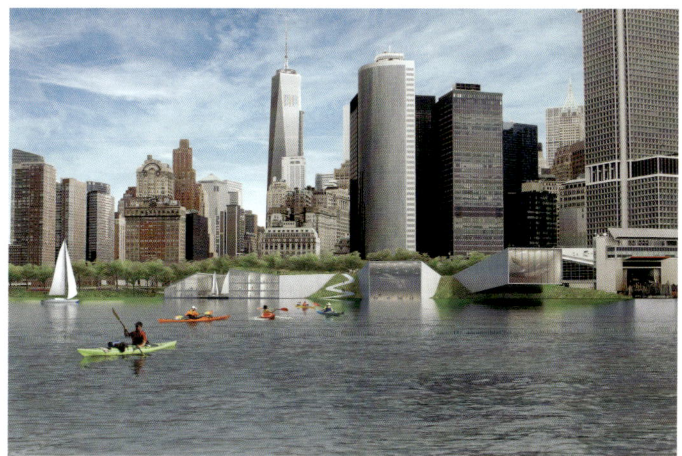

Harbor Museum

4

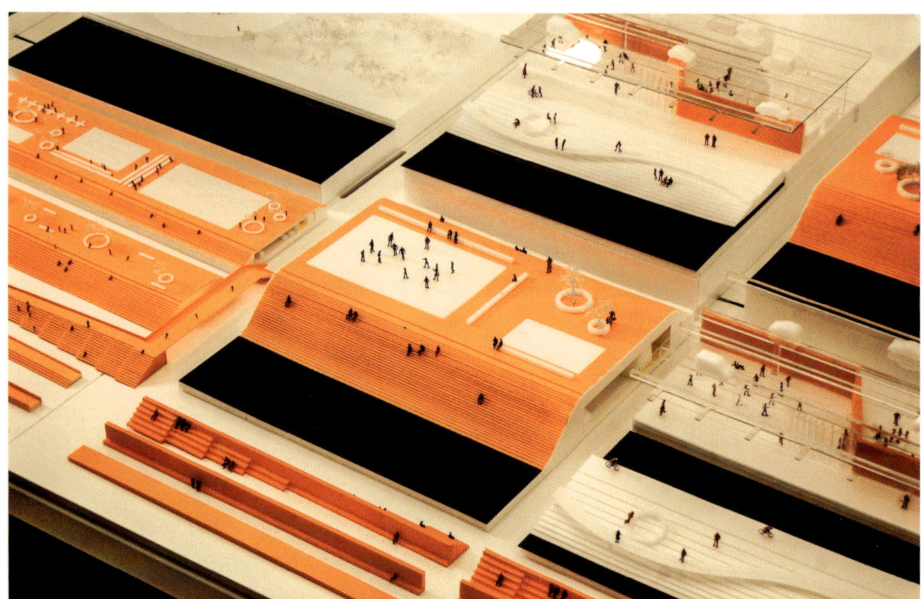

Interactive Models
To make the schemes accessible, the team constructed a collection of models showing different scenarios for flood protection at different points along the Lower East Side waterfront. Using these to guide the conversation, community members engaged in a process of critical discussion similar to what would happen in a design office.

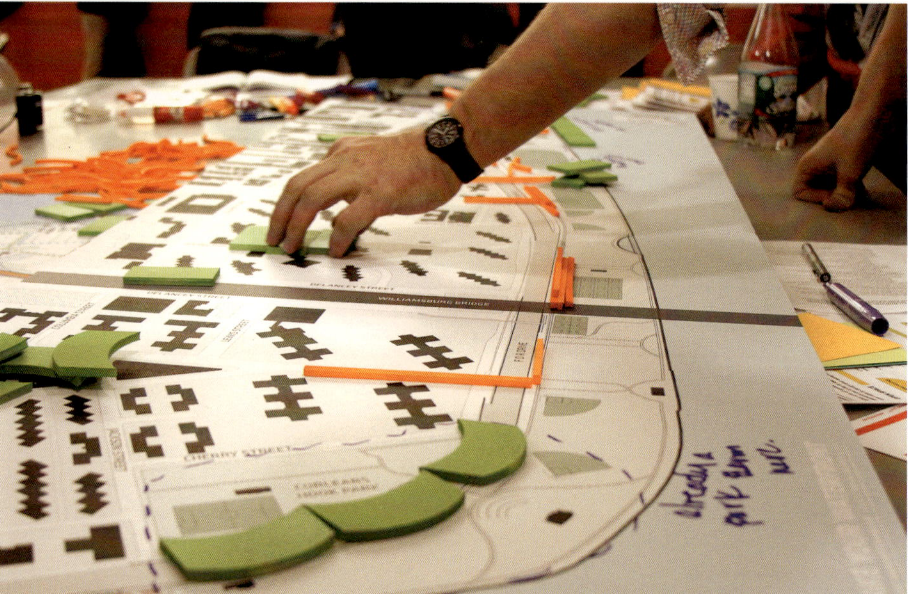

Build Your Own Waterfront
In another design collaboration with the neighborhoods, the community members built their own waterfront using foam models of berms, flood walls, and public amenities. Locals worked together to develop plans that suited their desires for different community improvements and protection from storms like the one that flooded them in 2012. The knowledge and insights gained from this process became critical features of the team's proposal.

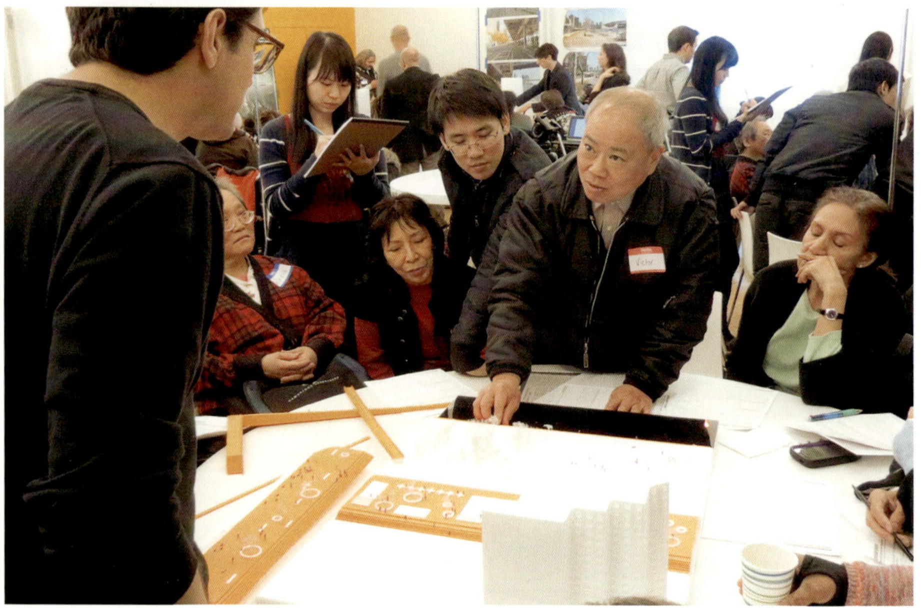

Collaborating With The Community
Members of the community were encouraged to change out parts, compare options, and imagine the effect of each proposal on their neighborhood. The models facilitated conversation and made the project instantly understandable to the group. Some members of the BIG TEAM acted as facilitators, while others recorded input and distributed surveys to document the conversation. The process fostered a collaboration with the community that allowed its ideas to be incorporated into the final design.

Design Process

The communities of the Lower East Side have participated in seven separate waterfront-planning processes over the past decade. Before engaging residents in yet another dialogue, the team reviewed these earlier plans to better understand local needs and desires. On the Lower East Side, the team worked intensively with LES Ready!, an umbrella organization of 26 community groups focused on coordinating emergency response and preparedness. With LES Ready! and Rebuild by Design's support, the team held a series of workshops at various locations in the neighborhood.

During the first workshops, the community debated the merits of various flood protection approaches using the team's models of different prototypical solutions. In the second series of workshops, the results of those discussions were incorporated into two possible design solutions for each compartment. These designs were also discussed by community members, whose feedback was used to refine the final proposal. Over 150 community members attended these workshops, and many returned to join the team for a celebration at the end of the process.

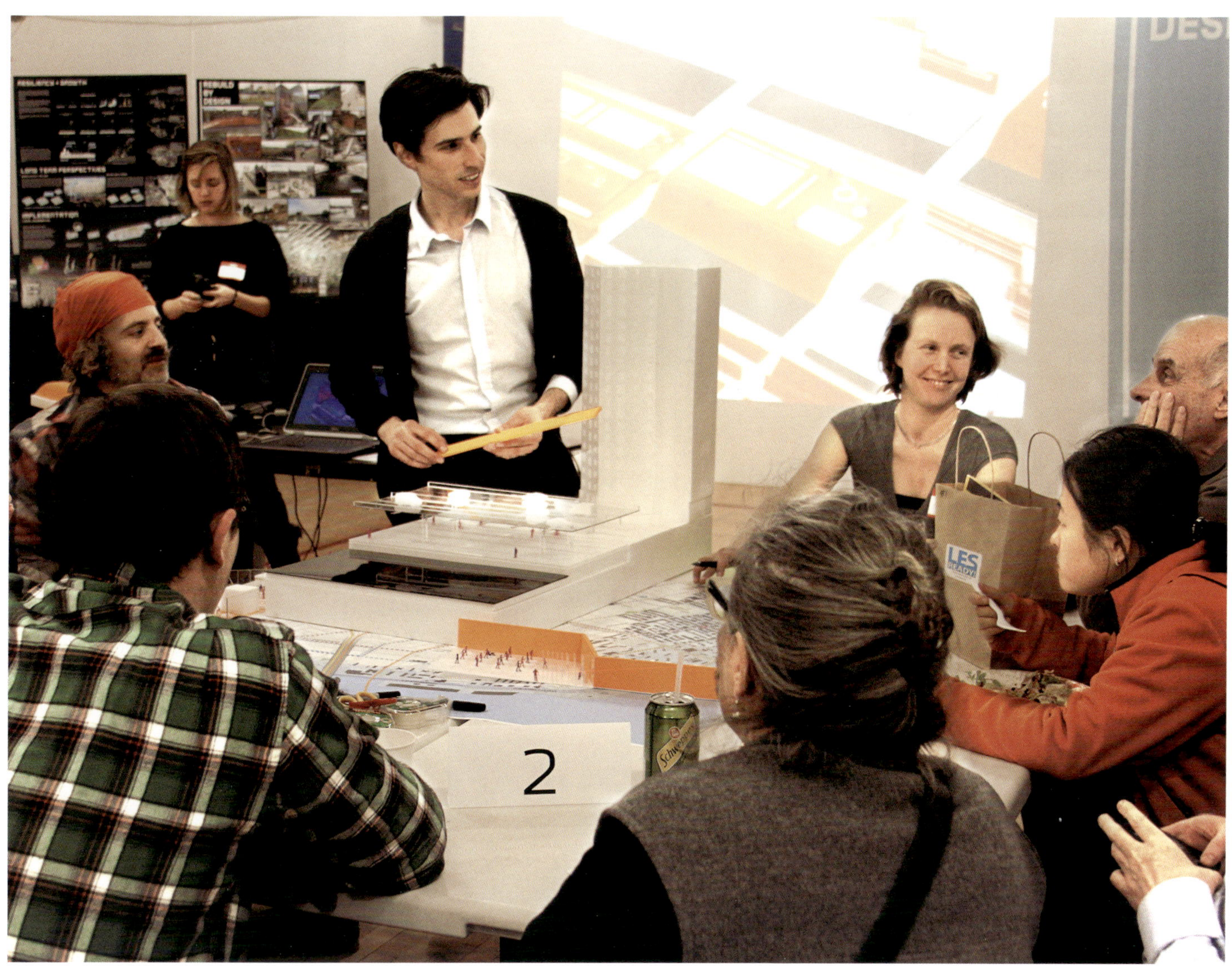

4

COMMERCIAL CORRIDOR RESILIENCE PROJECT

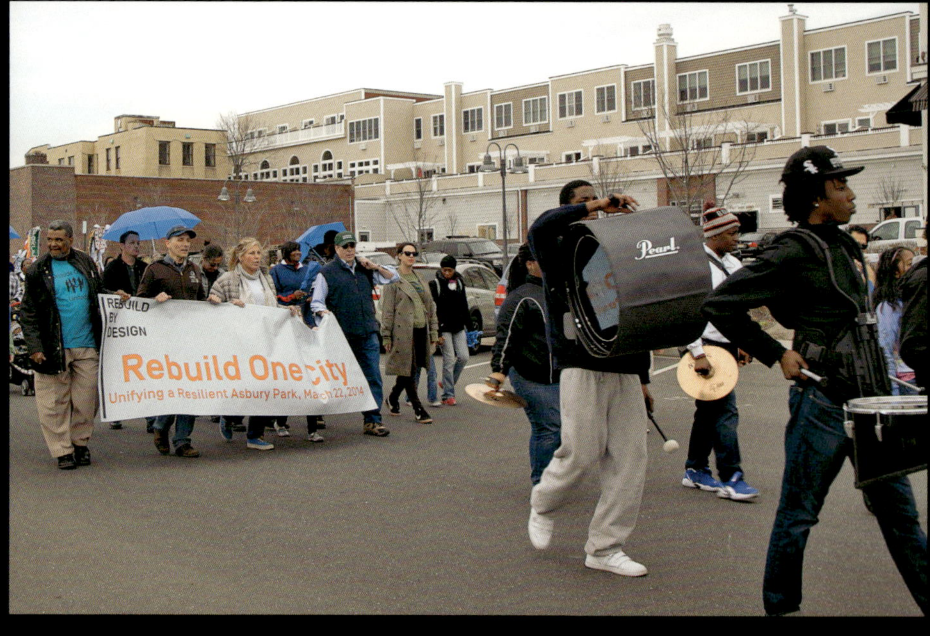

Team Leads
HR&A Advisors
Cooper, Robertson & Partners

Hazard Mitigation/Disaster Planning
Dewberry

Economic Development
Southwest Brooklyn Industrial Development Corporation

Public Realm Design
W Architecture and Landscape Architecture

HR&A Advisors with Cooper, Robertson & Partners

The HR&A with Cooper, Robertson & Partners team focused on creating innovative strategies to enhance the resilience and economic vitality of the Sandy-affected region's coastal commercial corridors and the neighborhoods that surround them. As the lifeblood of coastal cities and towns, commercial corridors and districts generate important economic activity, serve as sites of social and cultural exchange, and can become critical platforms for coordinating emergency services in the event of extreme climate events. However, in many cases, these corridors are highly vulnerable to flooding, and, when inundated, can dramatically impact community recovery. The team's proposal was based on the close relationship between the resilience of commercial corridors and the physical and economic resilience of entire communities. Protecting these areas helps protect whole neighborhoods.

The team, composed of real estate and economic development company HR&A Advisors, Inc. and architecture firm Cooper, Robertson & Partners, created pilot proposals for commercial corridors at three different sites: Beach 116th Street, in the Rockaways; Red Hook, in Southwest Brooklyn; and Asbury Park, on the New Jersey Shore. Proposals included a series of context-specific and replicable strategies, including building-level mitigation that would address tenant space and exterior flood-protections; corridor and neighborhood-wide protection and revitalization strategies; and organizational capacity-building to provide technical assistance and funding to small businesses in at-risk areas.

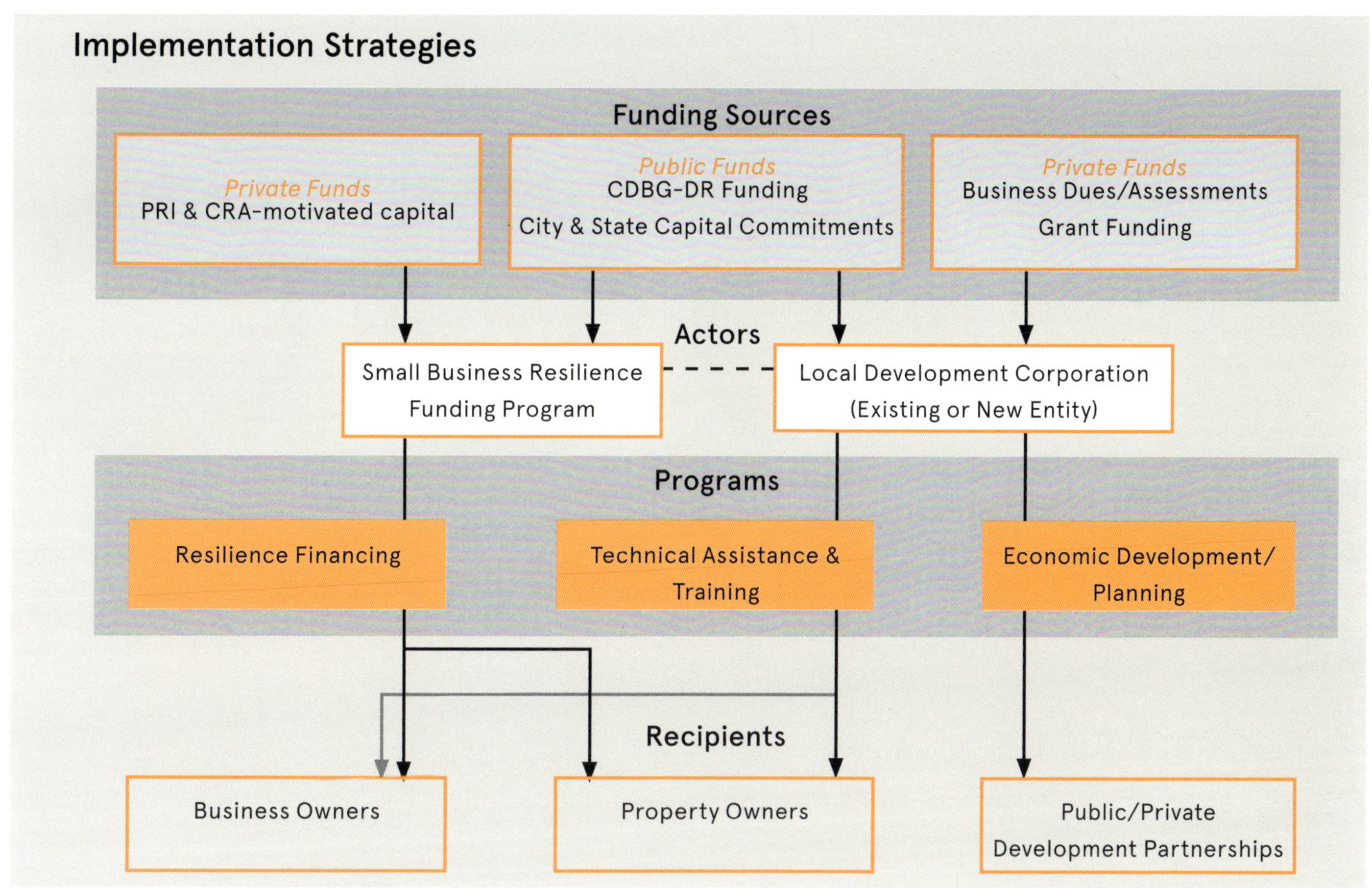

4

Approach to Commercial Resilience

The team conducted two main phases of research: the first, a regional analysis to identify test sites for project development, and the second, a targeted analysis of the site conditions that represent typologies found throughout the region.

Within the 100-year floodplain alone, the team identified 100 million square feet of retail space representing $34 billion in annual sales and over 175,000 jobs — amounting to 20% of the employment in these coastal zones. Most of this activity comes in the form of small businesses dependent on waterfront visitors and tourists. Following Hurricane Sandy, 74% of these businesses closed for an average of seven days.

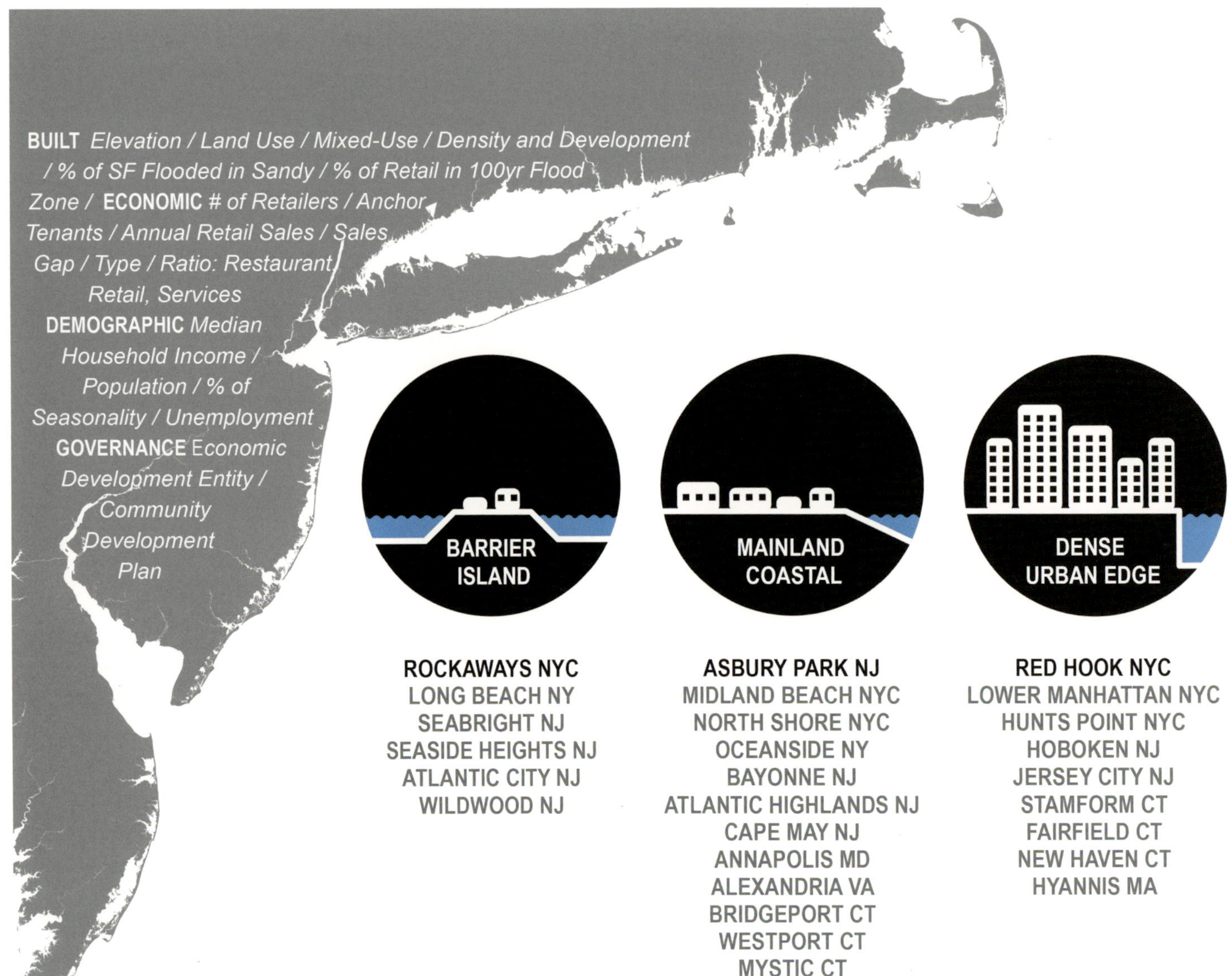

The team also identified three central challenges to implementing commercial resilience, including: difficulty accessing capital for small businesses and incentivizing business owners to make physical improvements, information asymmetry and a lack of organization within small businesses and those charged with providing technical assistance, and, in key study areas, a lack of density and coordination between businesses, weakening their ability to advocate for necessary improvements and aid.

The team categorized sites based on physical and economic vulnerabilities, including elevation, demographic characteristics, and other attributes. Using that information, they identified three environmental typologies prevalent throughout the region: barrier islands, mainland coastal communities (semi-urban edge), and dense urban edges. The team then selected sites representing these environments for more in-depth research and a study of pilot programs.

Design Strategies

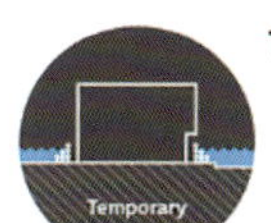

TEMPORARY
- Sand bags/earth sacks
- Sheeting/panel/barrier systems
- Sump pumps and generators

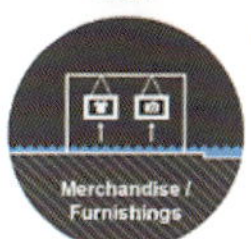

MERCHANDISE/FURNISHINGS
- Elevate merchandise
- Move displays above BFE

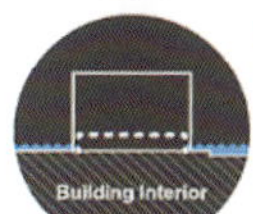

BUILDING INTERIOR
- Water/mold resistant finish materials
- Safeguard hazardous materials

BUILDING FAÇADE
- Watertight and reinforce doors, windows, storefront and hatches
- Sliding/hinged gasketed gates or anchors for shutter systems at openings
- Plug utility and service openings
- Operable fenestration for ventilation
- Anchor elements that could become wind-blown debris
- Secure roofing and façade materials
- Add waterproofing layer underneath cladding, above sheathing
- Water/mold resistant cladding materials

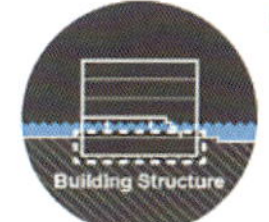

BUILDING STRUCTURE
- Raise building
- Raise ground floor level
- Secure load path from roof to foundation
- Floodproof foundations

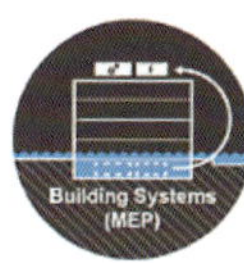

BUILDING SYSTEMS (MEP)
- Raise or isolate critical equipment
- Seal fuel tanks
- Raise fuel oil and plumbing vents
- Add backwater valves
- Add quick connection points for temporary systems
- Raise ventilation intakes and exhausts
- Additional ventilation and extract fans
- Protect emergency power equipment
- Add battery powered emergency lighting
- Add redundant telecomm and fire-safety

LANDSCAPE
- Defensive landscape barriers/berms
- Absorptive landscape/softscape - open space, bioswales and tree-pits
- Plant wind and floor resistant plants

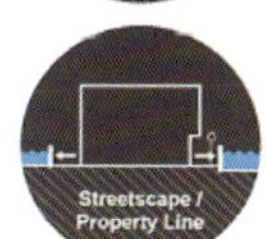

STREETSCAPE/PROPERTY LINE
- Raise sidewalks
- Secure street furnishings
- Sheeting/panel/barrier system pre-set clips and anchors

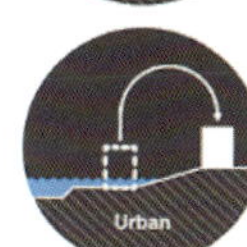

URBAN
- Temporary or deployable pre-fabricated structures
- Relocate buildings
- Add compatible uses to support existing businesses
- Flood shield sharing program
- Evacuation signage/wayfinding
- Evacuation centers
- Shared back-up power sources

Opposite: The team identified three sites for further study based on their unique economic, demographic, and physical qualities, which are representative of typologies throughout the Sandy-affected region.

Above: To categorize the scales and typologies of risk, the team created a matrix of physical interventions that were then simulated in each pilot study site to test for potential project applications.

Design Opportunities

Red Hook

Red Hook, a post-industrial maritime community in southwest Brooklyn, was hard hit by Hurricane Sandy. Its 12,000 residents (6,000 of whom live in public housing) are situated almost entirely in the 100-year floodplain, while its 400,000 square feet of retail space, which supports about 650 local jobs, is fully in this high-risk zone. The neighborhood has a 24% unemployment rate and many small businesses struggle because of relatively low foot traffic.

The team proposed a flood protection system that would be integrated with a community-based planning process meant to promote commercial revitalization. Physical proposals include shoring up waterfront edges along the New York Harbor and the Gowanus Canal and retrofitting historic architecture not originally designed to withstand flooding.

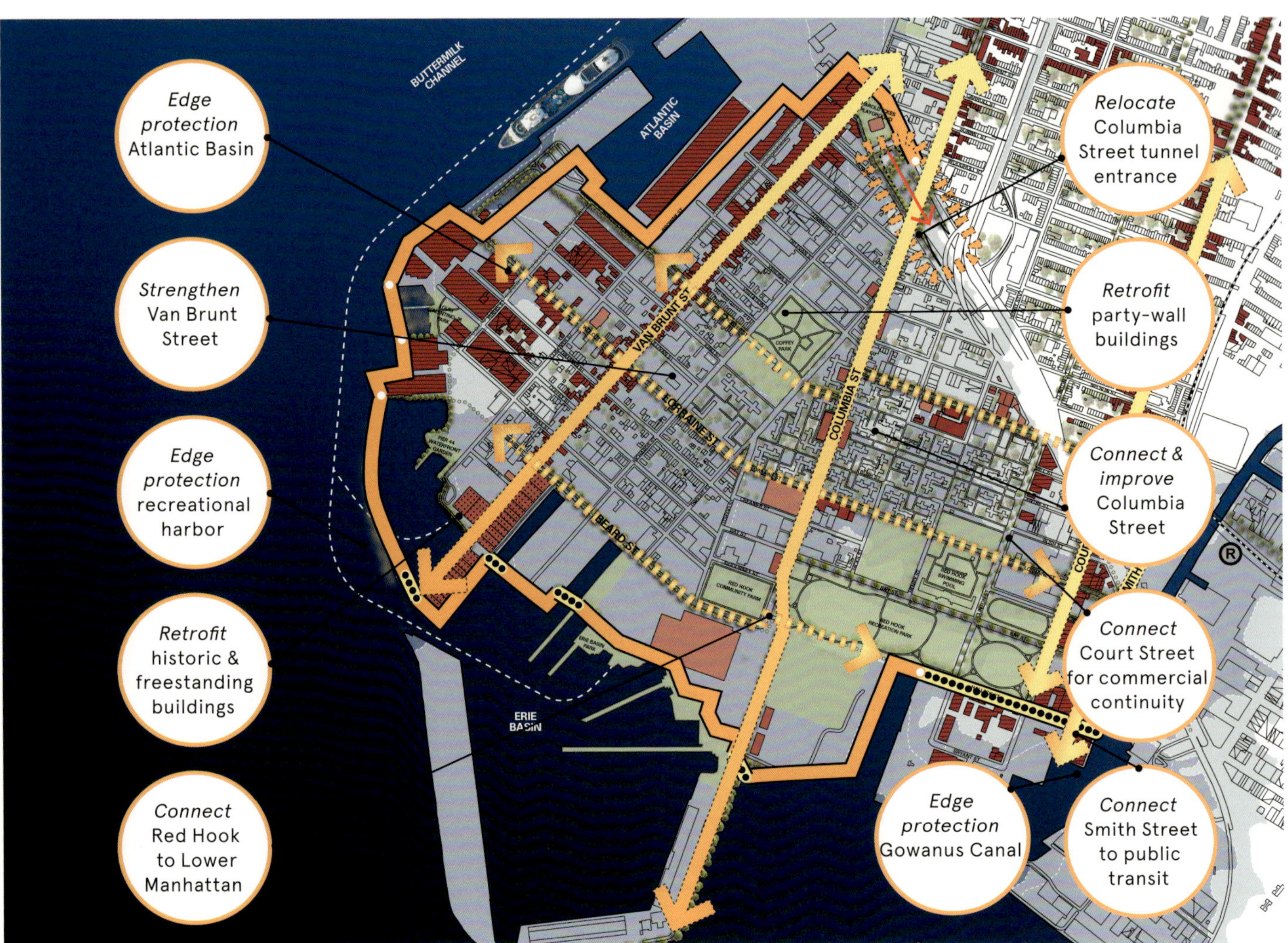

Opportunities for Red Hook

Beach 116th Street

On Beach 116th Street, a central commercial strip on the Rockaway peninsula in Queens, the HR&A with Cooper, Robertson & Partners team identified another site severely impacted by Hurricane Sandy. Essential services, such as grocery stores and gas stations, as well as office space and amenities, were not equipped to withstand flooding — even though they sit fully in the 100-year floodplain. To make this district more resilient, the team proposed strategies at a range of scales, including the creation of a public space on the Jamaica Bay side of the corridor to absorb storm surge and wave action, the relocation of commercial buildings situated on the waterfront, and the use of new construction to create protection around a vital public transportation node in the middle of the district.

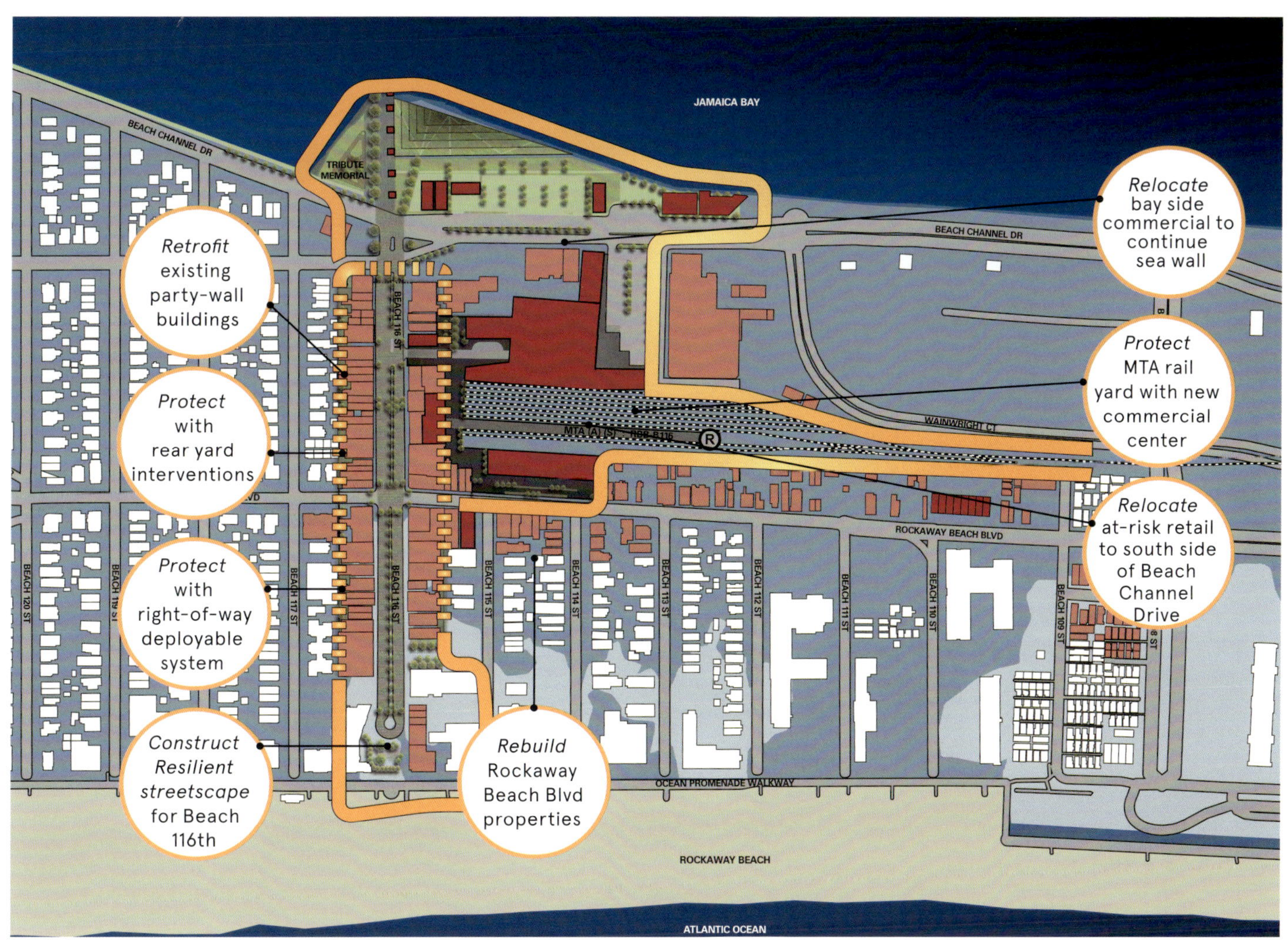

Opportunities for Beach 116th Street

Asbury Park

The team also assessed Asbury Park, a popular destination on the Jersey Shore. There, 14% of retail square footage – approximately 200,000 square feet – sits in the 100-year floodplain. With several commercial nodes, including an oceanfront boardwalk and others along coastal lakes, the area is susceptible to numerous risks: sea-level rise, storm surge, and lake flooding. The team developed several concepts that would improve flood protection and, at the same time, enhance connectivity among neighborhoods and stimulate economic activity. These designs aimed to introduce protective edges, both soft and hard, while preserving recreational access to the beachfront and reintroducing lakefront recreation, a historic use and an important feature of Asbury Park. The team proposed elevating beachfront buildings, structures, and a roadway as a way to maintain the vibrancy of these businesses and to encourage infill development.

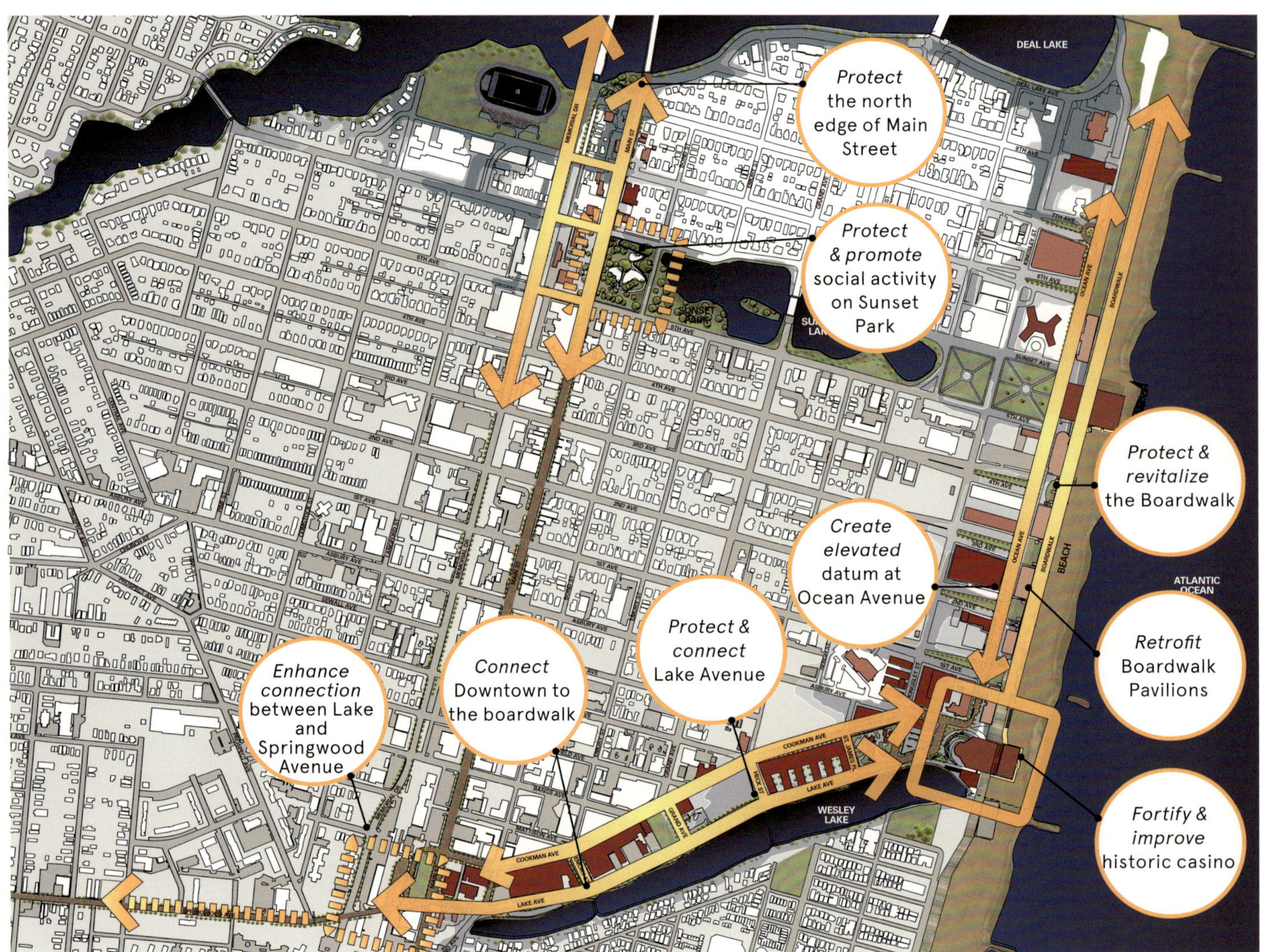

Above: Opportunities for Beach 116th Street

The team developed corridor- and district-level strategies aimed at enhancing commercial vibrancy and providing flood protection. In these areas, building-level protections could be too expensive for tenants to bear, or they might not protect an exposed area as efficiently as a more broadly based strategy. Integrated corridor or district strategies have the potential to act as multiple pieces of a larger protective system, with each portion created to suit its surroundings during normal and acute conditions. These improvements would be coupled with urban design elements, including transit connectivity and streetscape improvements that include resilient features to enhance drainage and stormwater management. They would also encourage collective adoption of resilient behavioral and physical strategies, such as investment in deployable flood protection systems for business clusters.

Corridor Strategies

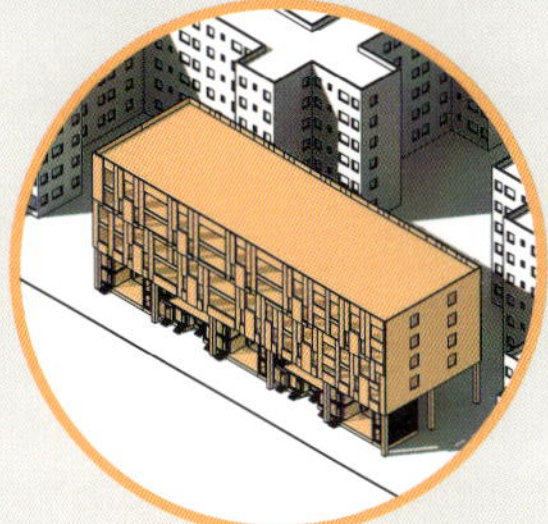

Commercial Infill
Create new resilient commercial buildings and activate corridors
Application: Red Hook, Beach 116th St Asbury Park

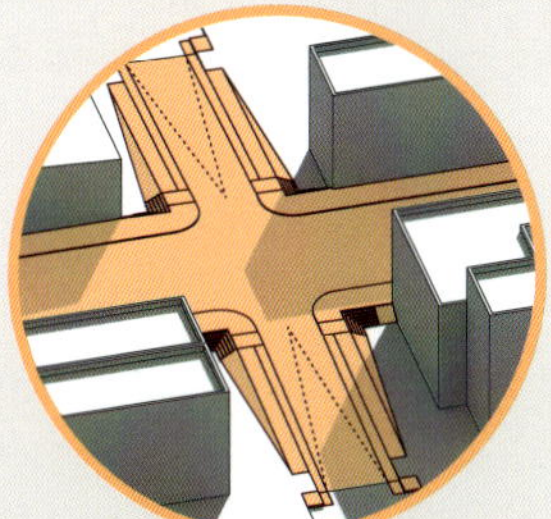

Elevated Road
Raise roads above flood and place deployable barriers to provide robust protection
Application: Red Hook

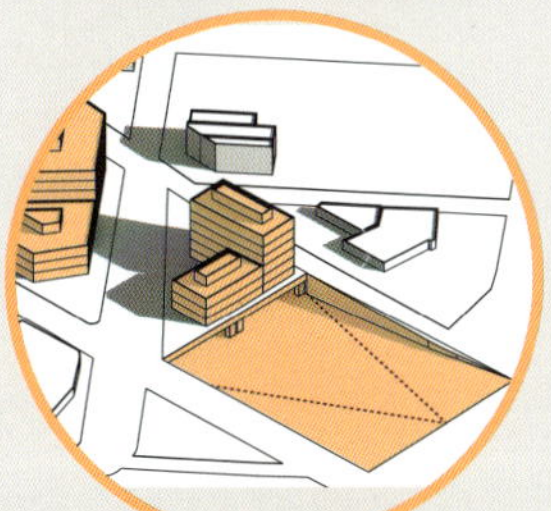

Cut and Cover
Move tunnel infrastructure out of flood zone, providing new development and connectivity opportunities
Application: Red Hook

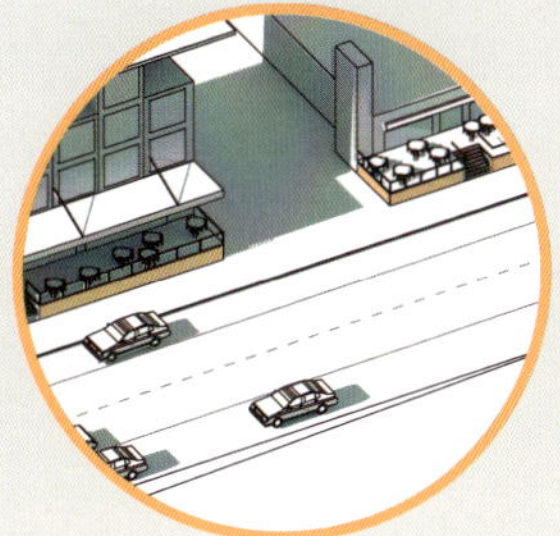

Road Diet
Reduce street width with parking reductions, improving corridor quality and enabling the inclusion of flood-protection components
Application: Asbury Park

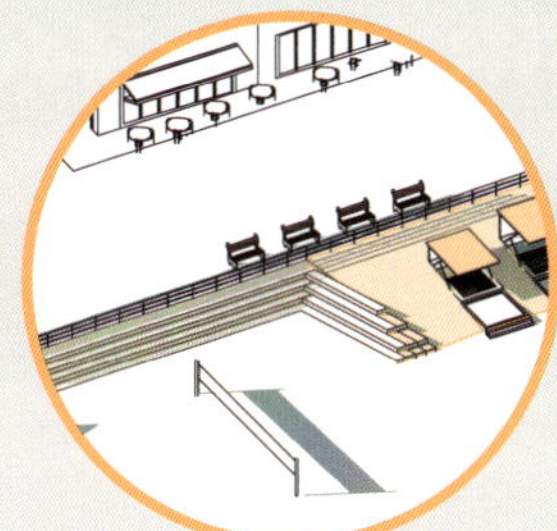

Boardwalk Reinforcement
Fortify the boardwalk and add seating and recreational elements
Application found in:
Asbury Park

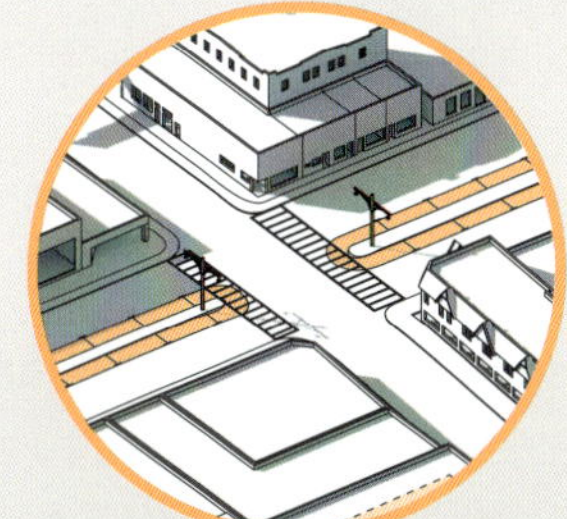

Streetscape Improvements and Green Infrastructure
Improve stormwater management along with the quality of the commercial corridor experience
Application found in:
Red Hook, Beach 116th St
Asbury Park

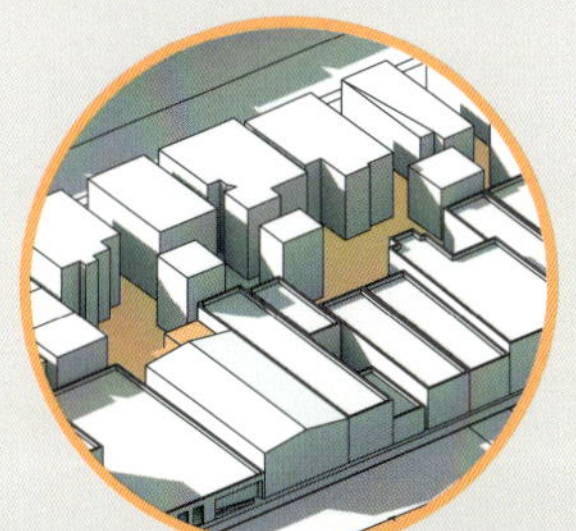

Rear Yard Commercial Perimeter
Expand building areas to protect commercial corridors crucial for relief and recovery
Application: Beach 116th St

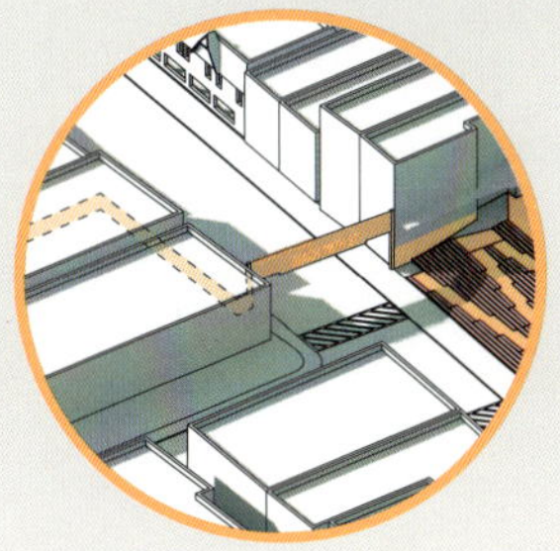

Right-Of-Way Deployable Systems
Use deployable flood protections as gateway entry points to commercial corridors
Application: Beach 116th St

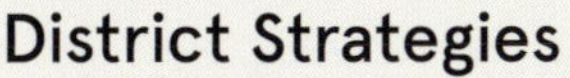

District Strategies

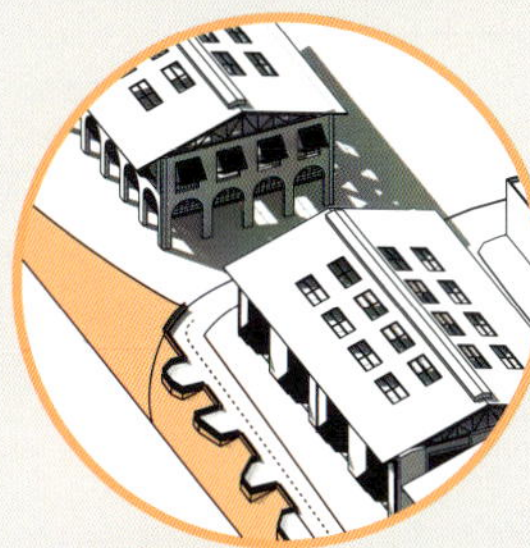

Integrated Flood Protection
Install new landscape and esplanade features, deployable components, and building walls as flood protection
Application: Red Hook, Beach 116th St Asbury Park

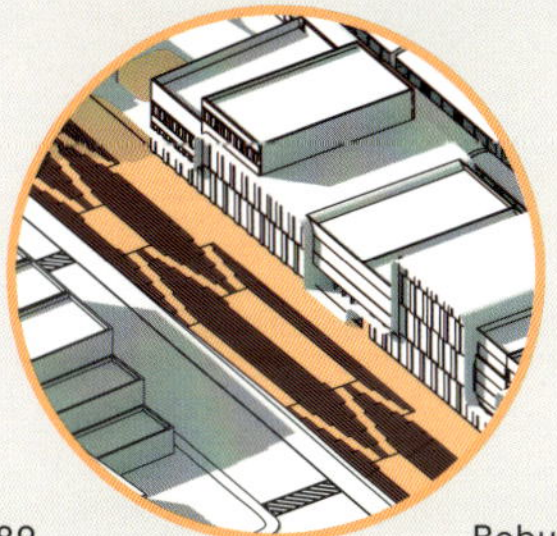

Stepped Plaza
Create new open-space amenity to elevate commercial areas
Application: Beach 116th St

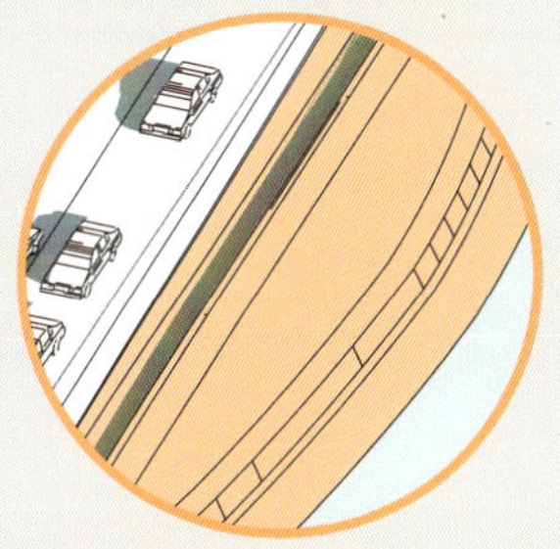

Landscaped Berm
Slope open space or landscaped edge to reduce flood risk and provide a path for human access for recreation
Application: Red Hook, Beach 116th St, Asbury Park

Ferry Access
Connect communities to the regional economy through enhanced transportation options
Application: Red Hook, Beach 116th St

Final Proposal: Commercial Corridor Resilience Project

The team proposed strategies that focused on three highly vulnerable sites, with the potential to be replicated in locations with similar characteristics. Red Hook addressed conditions along dense urban edges, Beach 116th Street spoke to the challenges on barrier islands, and Asbury Park resonated with other coastal communities. For these sites, the team developed a "Design Toolkit," a set of interventions that could be applied to business operations and physical environments at various scales, including the tenant space itself, single buildings, the corridor, and the district. It also included programmatic recommendations to overcome key implementation challenges facing small businesses in vulnerable areas.

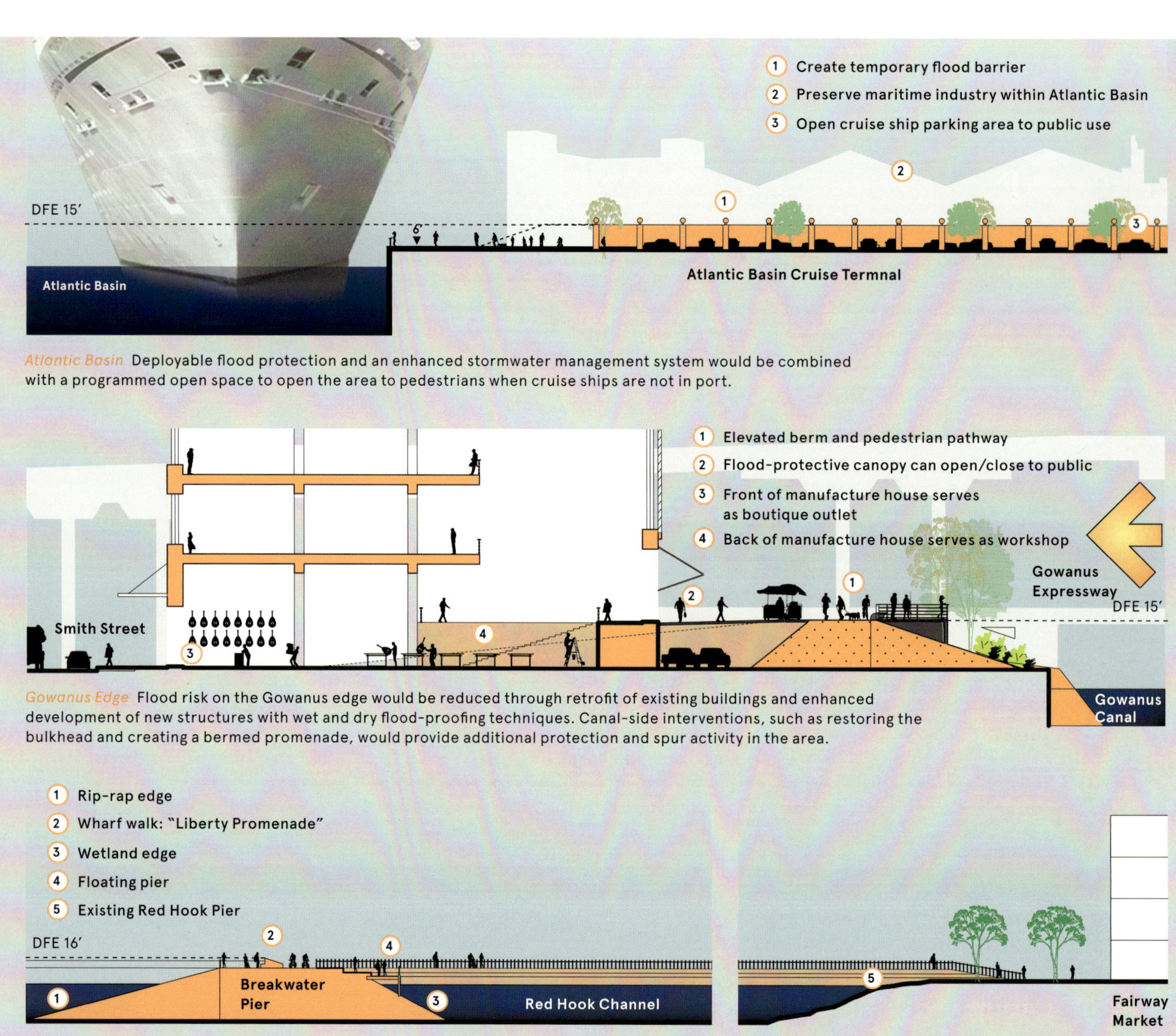

Atlantic Basin Deployable flood protection and an enhanced stormwater management system would be combined with a programmed open space to open the area to pedestrians when cruise ships are not in port.

Gowanus Edge Flood risk on the Gowanus edge would be reduced through retrofit of existing buildings and enhanced development of new structures with wet and dry flood-proofing techniques. Canal-side interventions, such as restoring the bulkhead and creating a bermed promenade, would provide additional protection and spur activity in the area.

Liberty Promenade A recreational harbor, created through development of a jetty that acts as a wave barrier, would be accessible from the land side and provide recreational access to the waterfront in non-storm conditions.

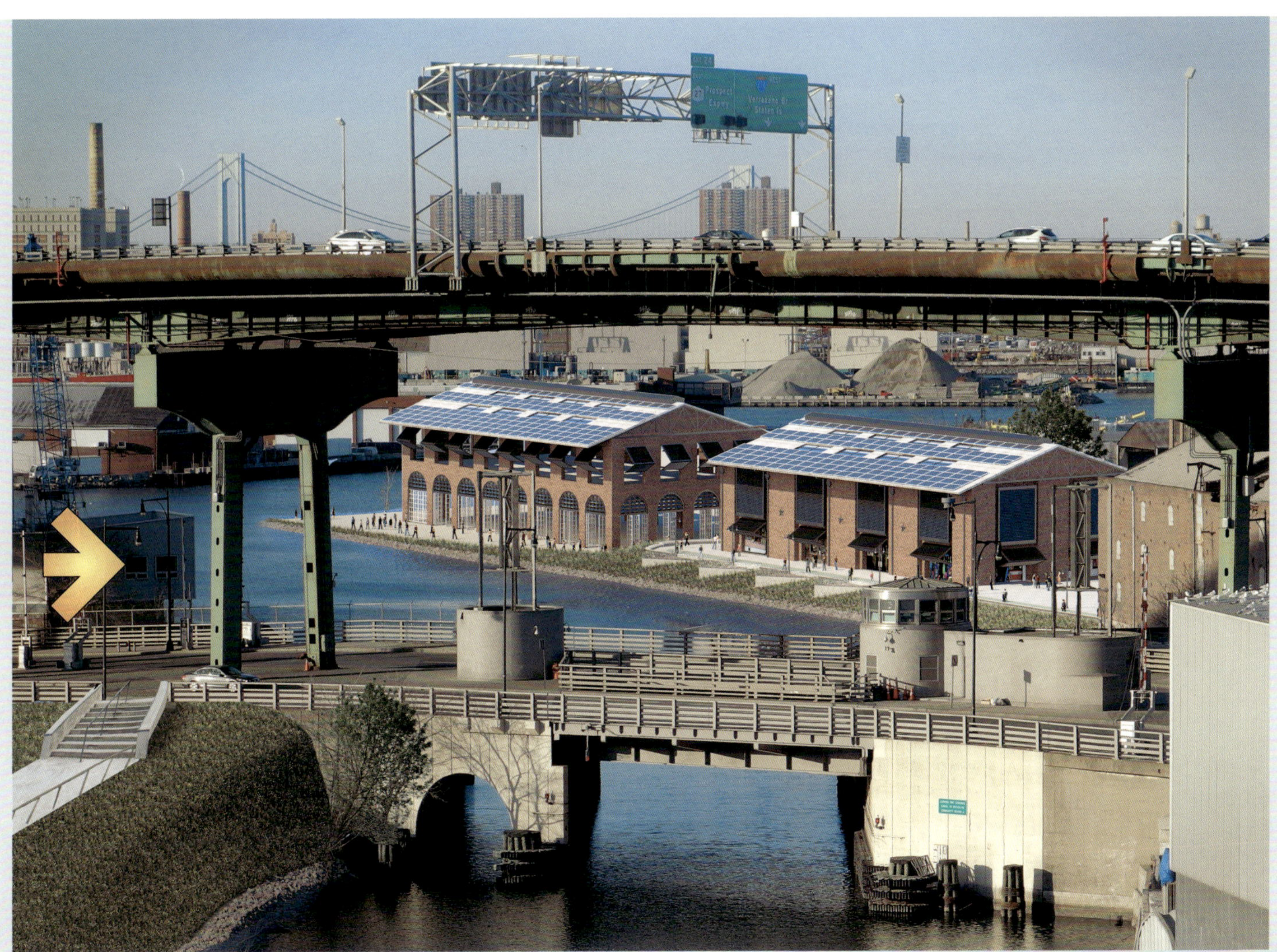

Gowanus Edge On Red Hook's Gowanus edge, a source of flooding would become a revitalized and resilient "Maker's District," where manufacturing and production businesses would thrive in dry and wet flood-proofed buildings. A raised promenade would encourage activation and access.

Shuttering small businesses during and after climate events can trigger many collateral setbacks for the community because it can hamper response efforts and slow the rebuilding process. With this in mind, the team created a set of guidelines that would allow small businesses to open their doors more quickly after a storm and support their preparation for future extreme weather events. These strategies ranged from operational steps, such as backing up business files and storing crucial documents in elevated, off-site locations, to physical improvements such as elevating inventory on existing structures and installing tracks for deployable flood gates. By formalizing these simple steps, the team provided a valuable resource to small businesses that may not have had the capacity to invest in costly flood-protection retrofits.

For individual building-scale tools, the team compiled a set of strategies ranging from simple, low-cost ideas (using suspended ceilings or ring shank nails) to more expensive, complex techniques (relocating utilities and elevating sales floors). Together, these were meant to protect small businesses from flood damage, prevent inventory and equipment loss, avert contamination from mold and sewage, and avoid significant damage to the building.

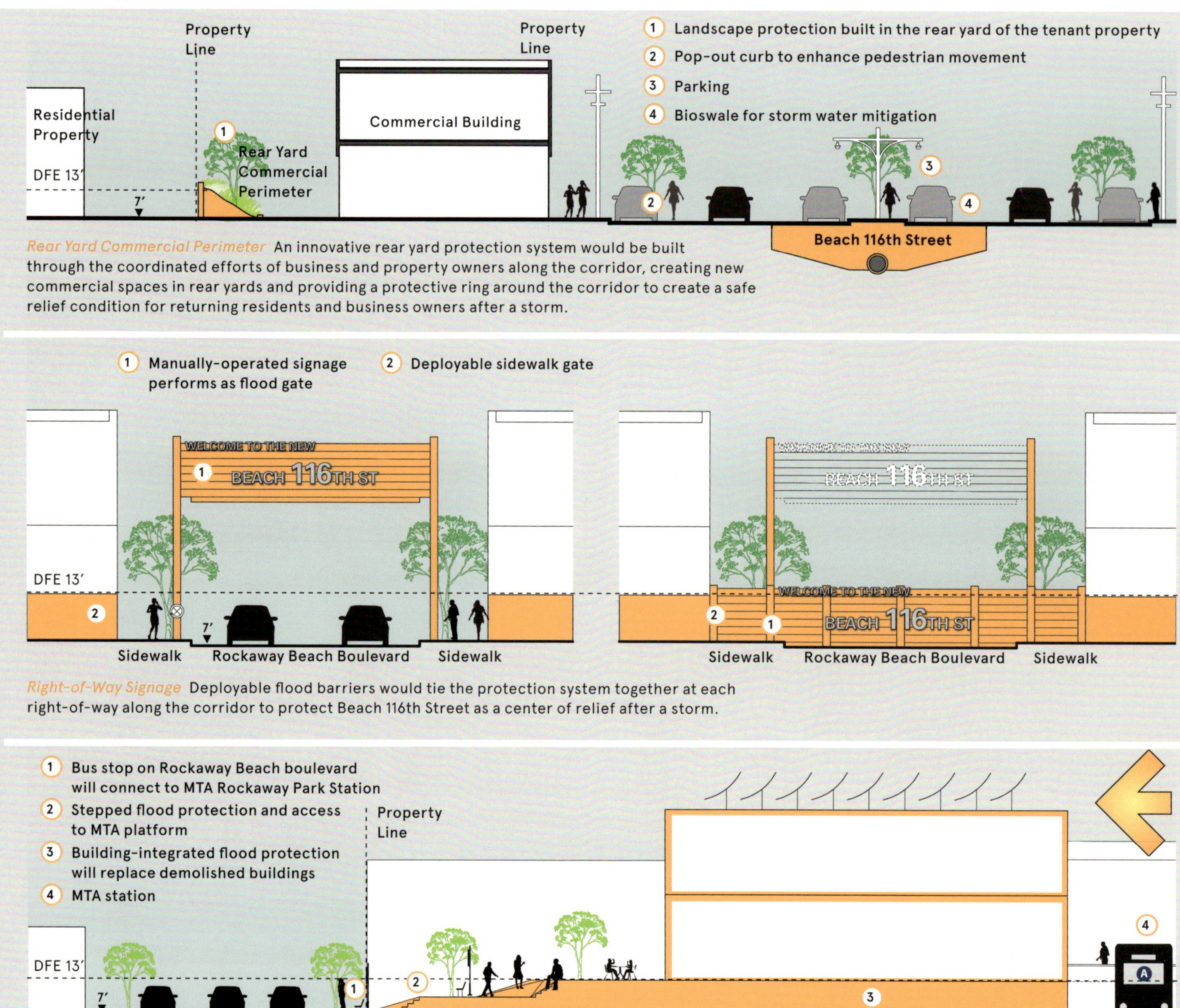

Rear Yard Commercial Perimeter An innovative rear yard protection system would be built through the coordinated efforts of business and property owners along the corridor, creating new commercial spaces in rear yards and providing a protective ring around the corridor to create a safe relief condition for returning residents and business owners after a storm.

Right-of-Way Signage Deployable flood barriers would tie the protection system together at each right-of-way along the corridor to protect Beach 116th Street as a center of relief after a storm.

MTA Railhead Development An elevated platform (at design elevation of 13 feet) would wrap around the east and south sides of the MTA rail yard, open to the municipal lot to the north, now activated, and open Rockaway Beach Boulevard and new development to the south (shown), where buildings were destroyed by a fire during Sandy.

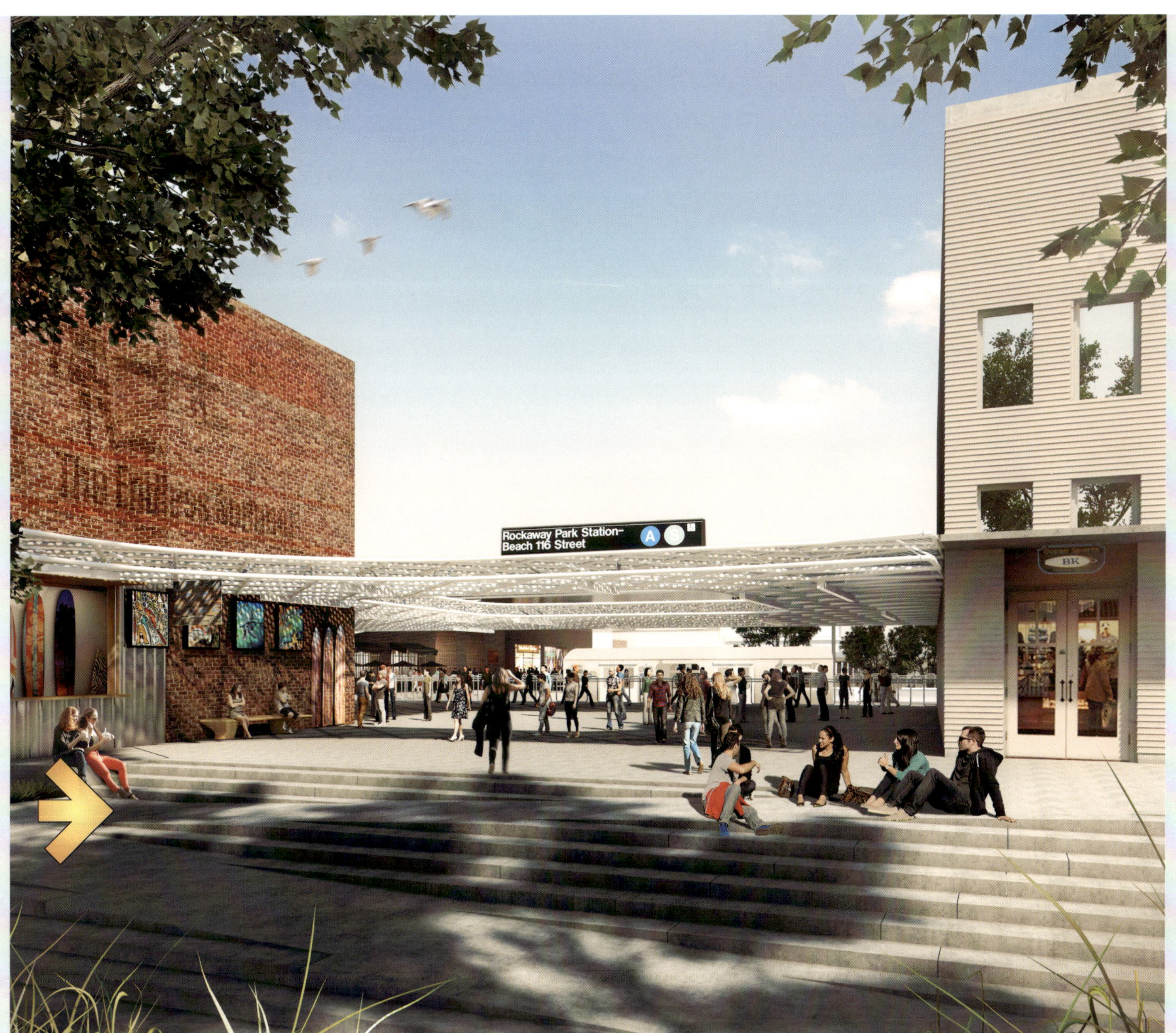

MTA Railhead Development The A train station becomes a vibrant hub of activity as an elevated platform connects to new commercial destinations and public space at a higher elevation to the north and south. This level ties into the street level at the north, south, and west, creating an active, resilient entrance to the corridor.

At the corridor and district scales, proposals included flood-protective elements in public spaces (such as those included in the Red Hook design), elevating critical transportation infrastructure (the MTA subway terminus on Beach 116th Street), and reinforcing the boardwalk (Asbury Park) to improve the commercial experience while protecting the district from ocean storm surge.

As a complement to designing physical improvements, the team also developed strategies that focused on providing sustainable funding sources and technical assistance and expanding the capacity of business advocacy organizations. These proposals included:

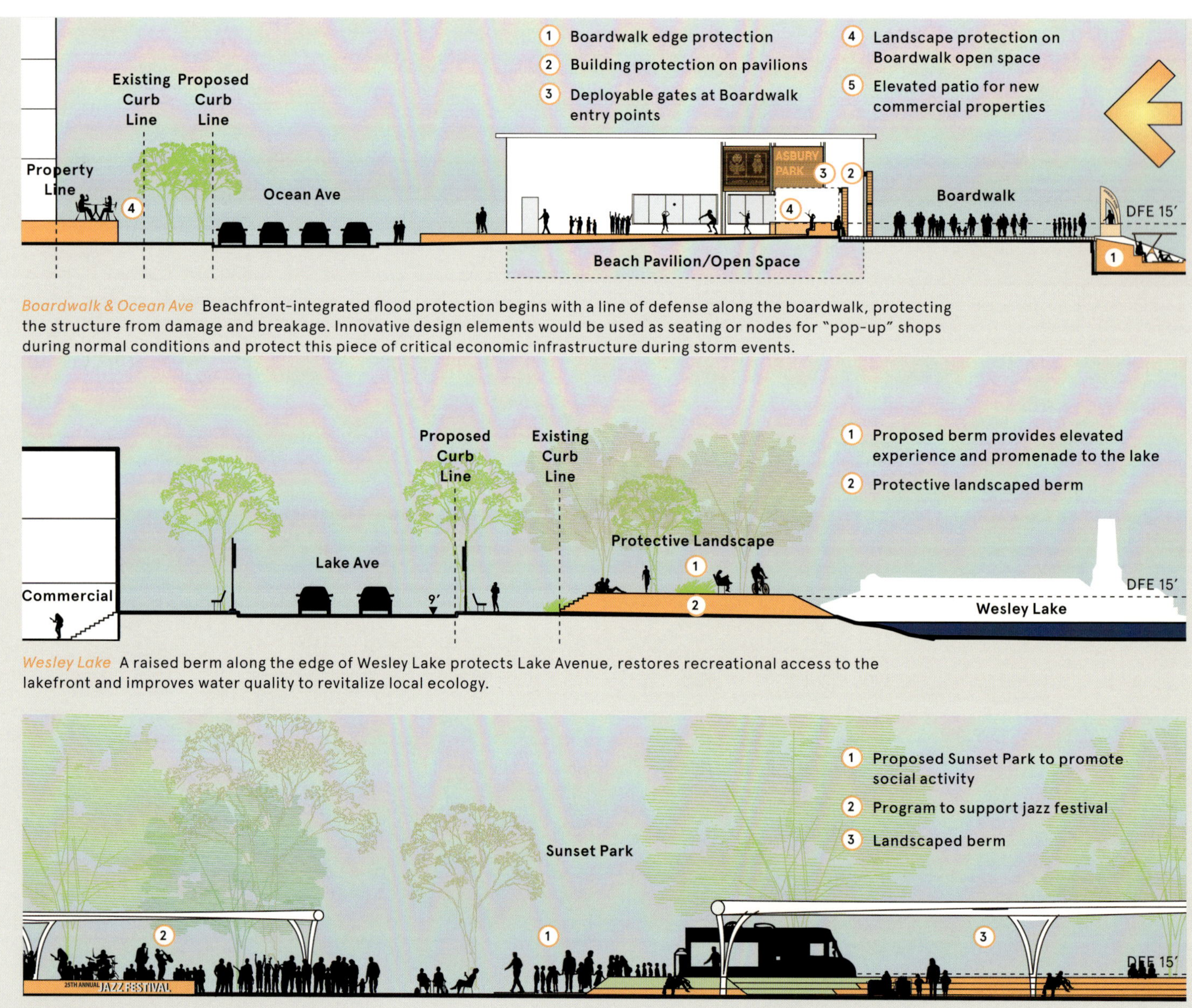

Boardwalk & Ocean Ave Beachfront-integrated flood protection begins with a line of defense along the boardwalk, protecting the structure from damage and breakage. Innovative design elements would be used as seating or nodes for "pop-up" shops during normal conditions and protect this piece of critical economic infrastructure during storm events.

Wesley Lake A raised berm along the edge of Wesley Lake protects Lake Avenue, restores recreational access to the lakefront and improves water quality to revitalize local ecology.

Sunset Park Expanded programming and resilient landscaping at Sunset Park provide an enhanced open space for Asbury Park's communities to meet and enjoy outdoor entertainment. In times of recovery, Sunset Park could provide a central location for residents and business owners to receive information and assistance.

· A small business resilience fund that would leverage diverse resources, including federal Community Development Block Grant Disaster Recovery (CDBG-DR) funds, Community Reinvestment Act-motivated investment capital, and philanthropy to reduce interest rates.

· An intermediary to administer the fund and provide technical assistance to support businesses in accessing capital improvement funds.

· A network of community organizations to provide technical assistance to local development corporations, organizational support for behavioral changes by small businesses, and technical assistance to fund applicants. It could also potentially provide loan guarantees for corridor-wide improvements.

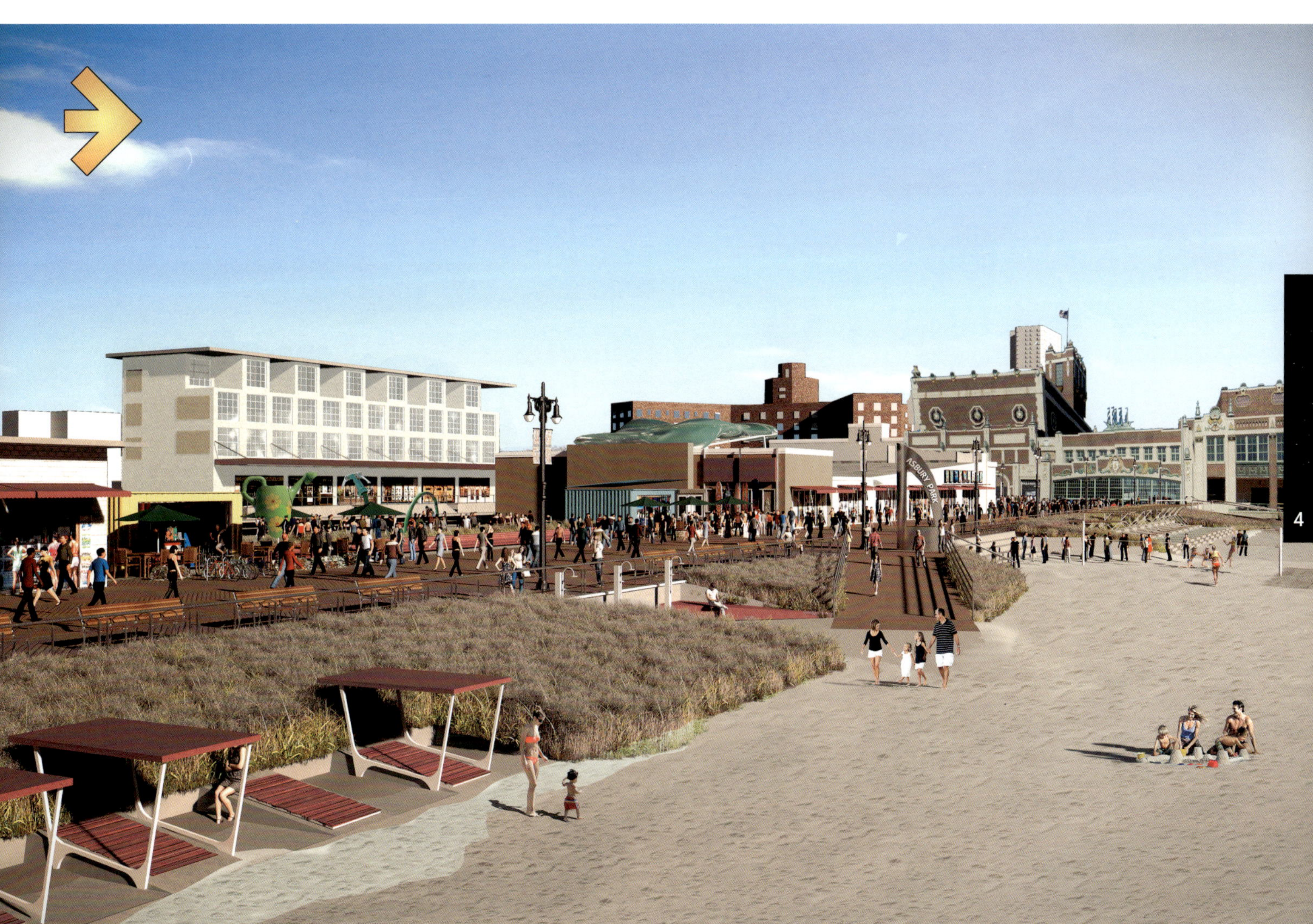

Boardwalk & Ocean Ave On the beachfront, resilient infrastructure would fortify the boardwalk and could be used as seating or for recreation during normal conditions. Resilient interventions for commercial buildings and open space lining the boardwalk would include deployable flood and debris barriers, protecting storefronts from severe damage, but leaving them open to normal activity during the high season.

Opportunities for Asbury Park

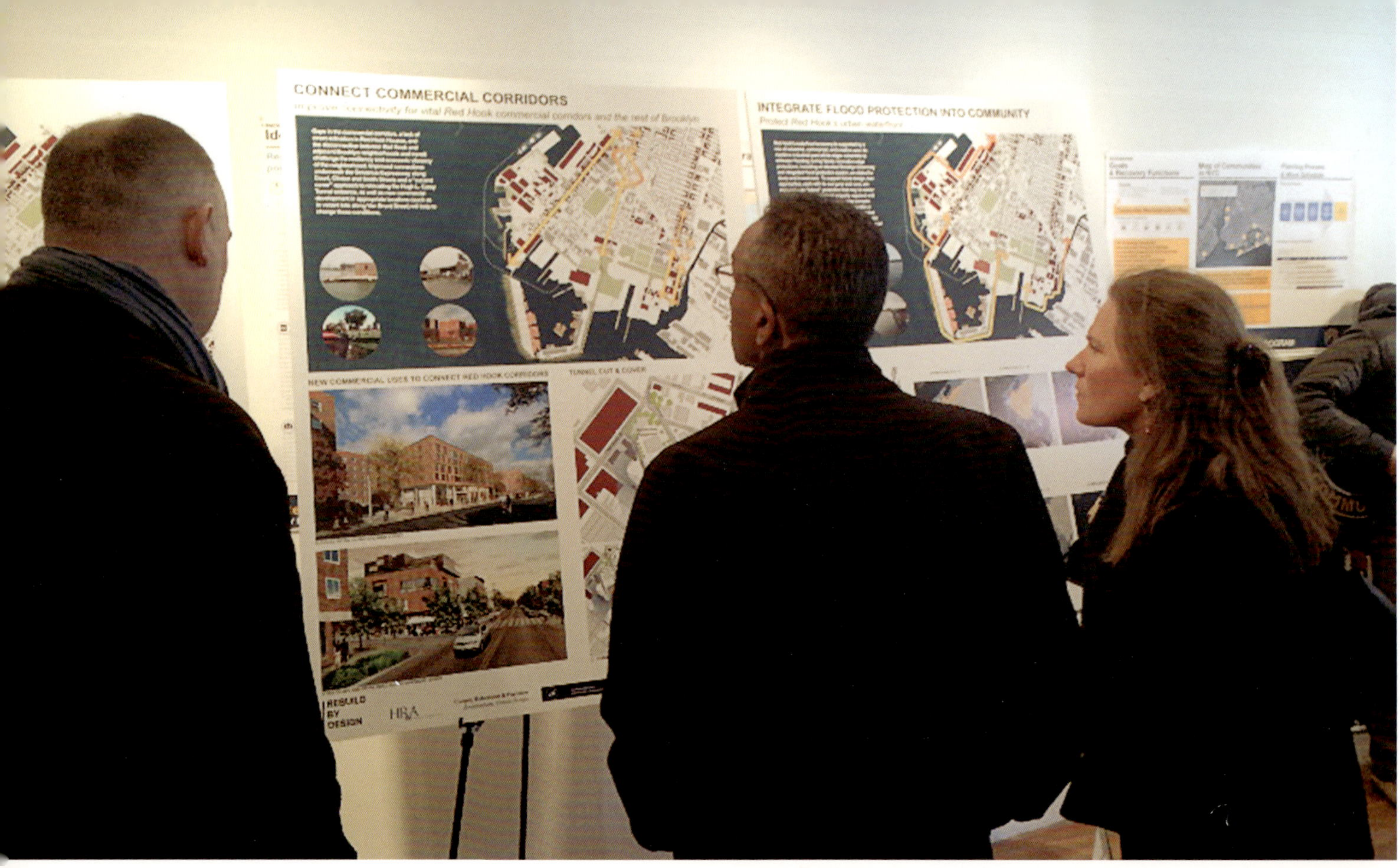

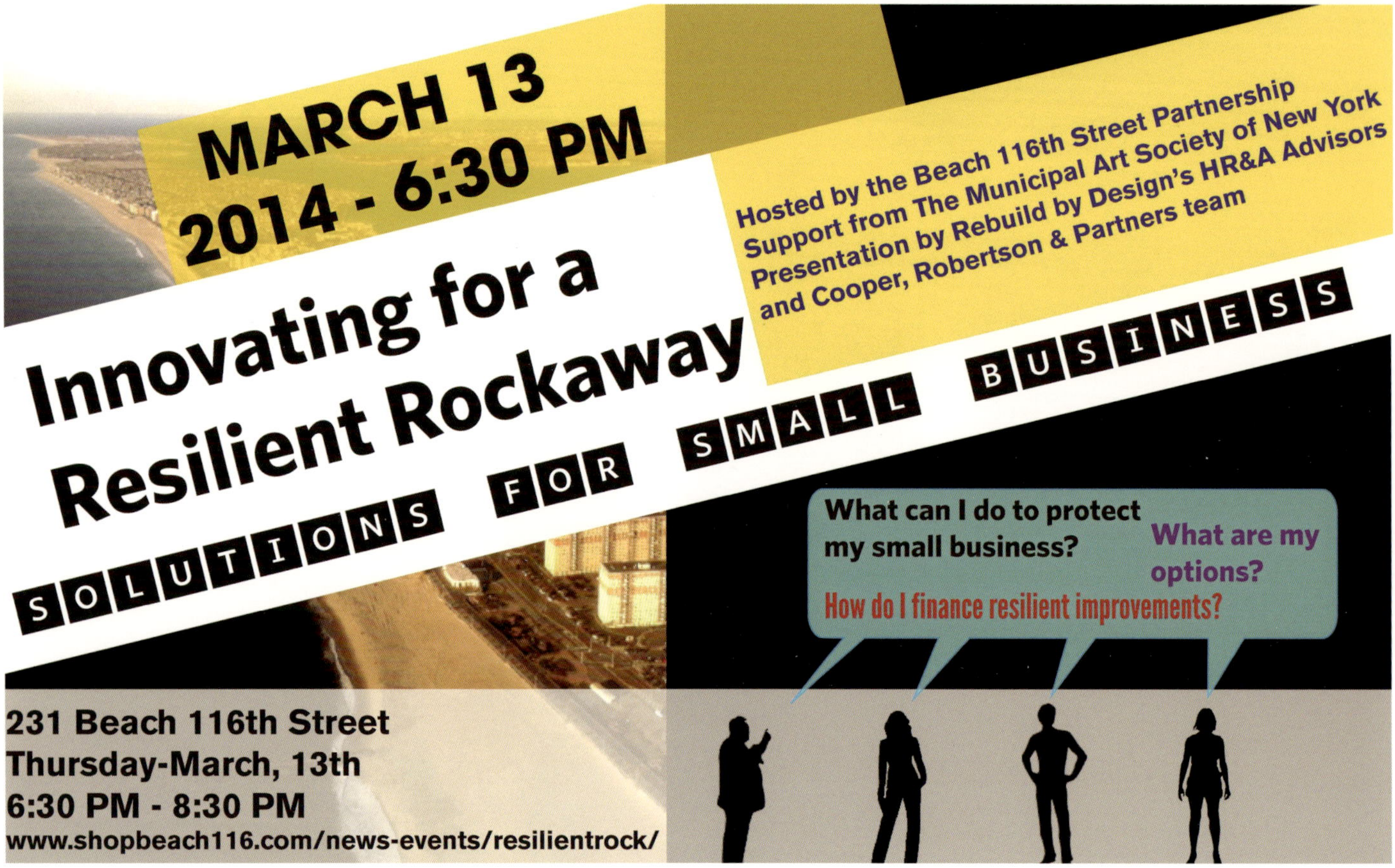

MARCH 13
2014 - 6:30 PM

Hosted by the Beach 116th Street Partnership
Support from The Municipal Art Society of New York
Presentation by Rebuild by Design's HR&A Advisors
and Cooper, Robertson & Partners team

Innovating for a
Resilient Rockaway

SOLUTIONS FOR SMALL BUSINESS

What can I do to protect my small business?
What are my options?
How do I finance resilient improvements?

231 Beach 116th Street
Thursday-March, 13th
6:30 PM - 8:30 PM
www.shopbeach116.com/news-events/resilientrock/

Design Process

HR&A with Cooper, Robertson & Partners engaged each community as it undertook its research and design process, holding meetings with over 30 local stakeholders and organizations. In Red Hook, the team developed a partnership with the Southwest Brooklyn Industrial Development Corporation, worked with local business owners, and participated in the New York State-sponsored Community Reconstruction Planning process. The team also held a public workshop in the Rockaways, which provided a forum to discuss the Beach 116th Street design through a dialogue with community members and local business owners. In Asbury Park, the team participated in the Rebuild One City Parade, which wound through the streets drawing attention to the project and inspiring a lively public exchange between residents and designers. Throughout this engagement process, which also included a series of individual interviews and informational meetings, the team advanced design through an iterative process with local business community stakeholders, getting feedback to refine its ideas.

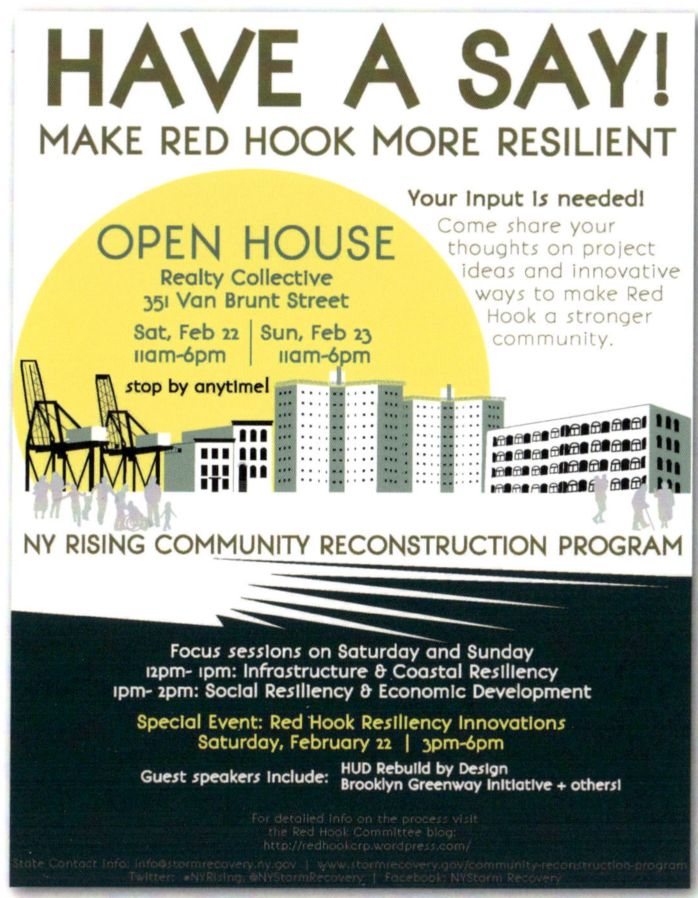

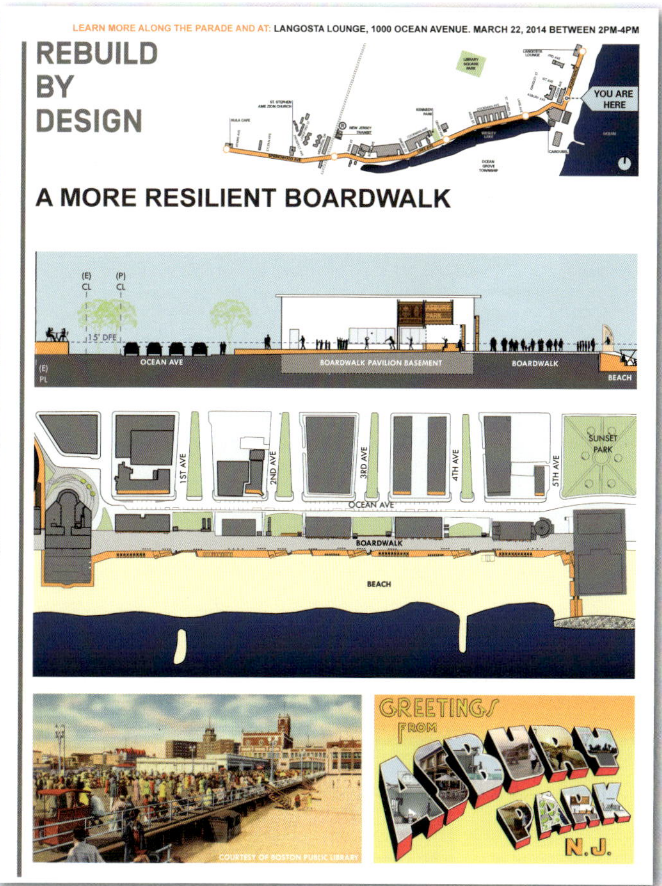

LIVING WITH THE BAY

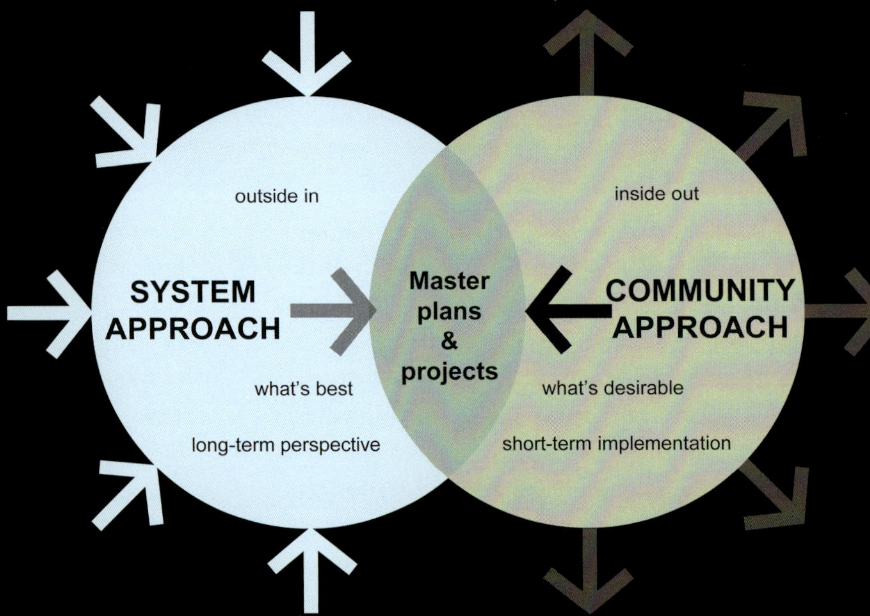

Team Lead
Interboro Partners

Infrastructure Engineering
Apex

Urban and Landscape Design
Bosch Slabbers

Infrastructure Engineering
Deltares

Urban and Landscape Design
H+N+S

Economics and Finance
IMG Rebel

Urban and Landscape Design
Palmbout Urban Landscapes

Education
Center for Urban Pedagogy

Governance
David Rusk

Academic Research Partners
New Jersey Institute of Technology (NJIT)
Infrastructure Planning Program and
TU Delft Faculty of Architecture

Communication Design
Project Projects

Community Building, Economics, Financee
RFA Investments

The Interboro Team

The Interboro Team proposed four projects on sites including Long Island, the Jersey Shore, Staten Island, and New Jersey's Monmouth County. In each, the team looked beyond the confines of a single site to consider strategies that worked at the scale of both an ecosystem and a region. In addition to assessing vulnerability to sea-level rise, the team selected its sites by identifying low and medium density and income communities with critical infrastructure. Led by Interboro Partners, an architecture, urban design, and urban planning firm based in New York, the team combined the best of Dutch land-use planning, environmental and coastal engineering, and urban water management with the best of American participatory planning, community development, financial-economic advising, and engineering. Together, they developed a novel way to link environmental resilience designs with policy questions and social objectives.

For its selected project, Living with the Bay, in Long Island's Nassau County, the team considered bay flooding, but it treated the bay as part of a larger ecosystem, including the river and creek system and areas farther inland. Decisions far upstream, the team reasoned, had direct a impact on the relative vulnerability of communities living on the water. Linked with environmental plans and designs, the team also proposed policy and governance strategies that would be needed to implement a project between different municipalities. They positioned the proposal as a way to instigate greater cooperation between municipalities that may consider themselves otherwise unaligned.

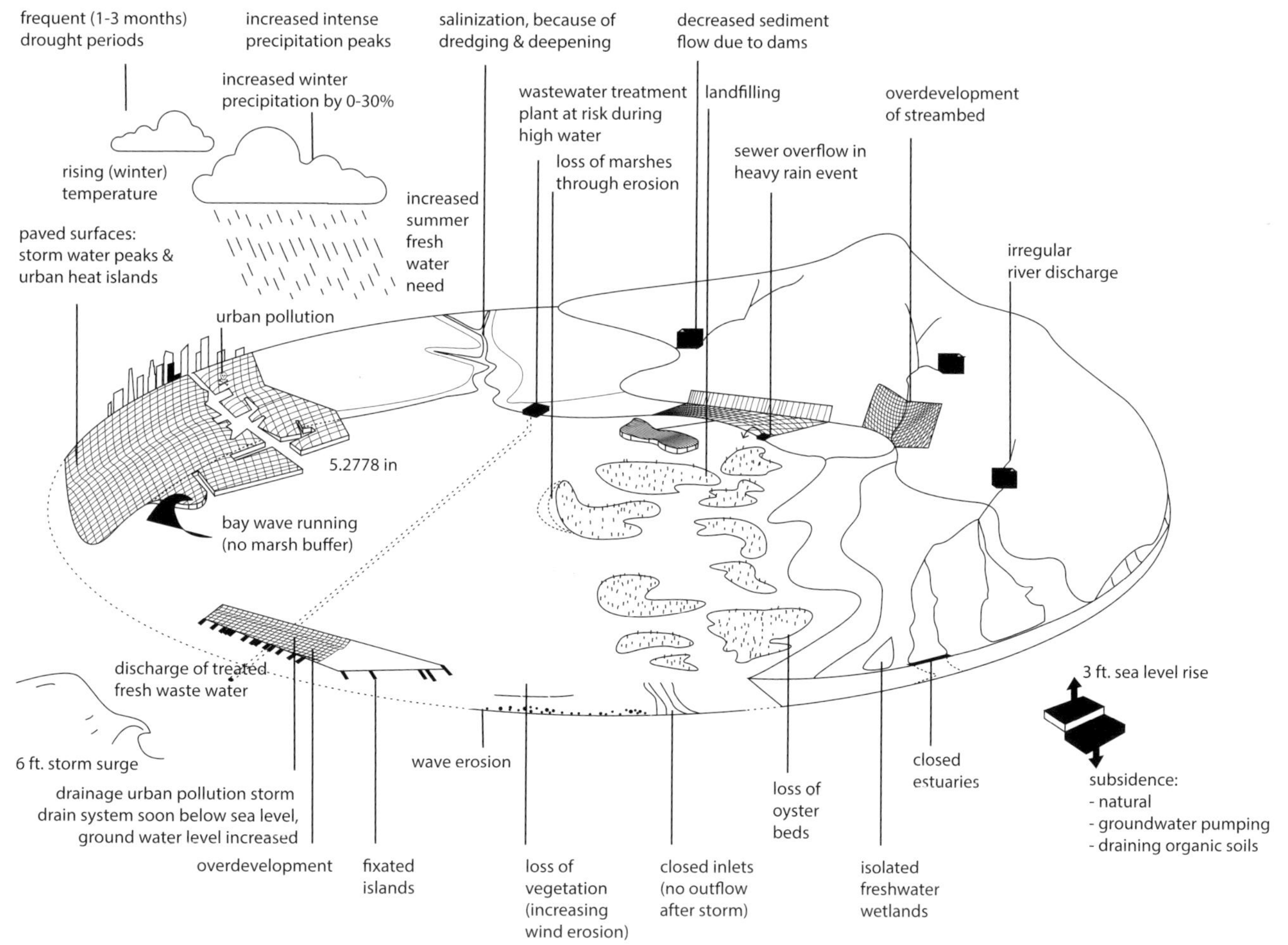

4

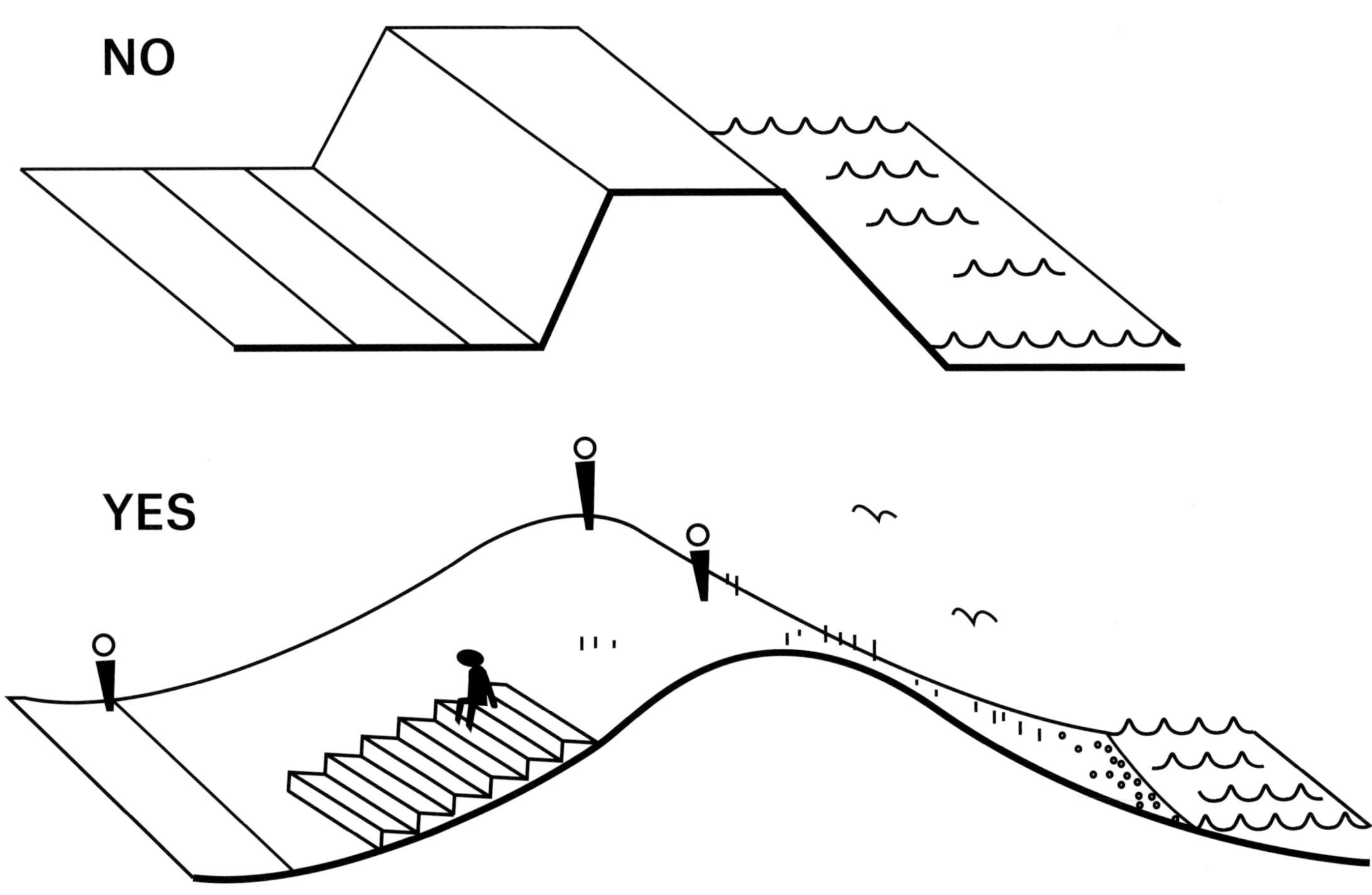

Plan and design for the storm and the norm
Architecture that protects from the occasional disaster (for example, a terrorist attack or a flood) too often requires sacrificing enjoyable aspects of more everyday, non-disaster moments. Each and every investment in flood protection should improve everyday life. In building protective structures, there is simply no reason not to add value to them so that they do more than merely protect.

An Inclusive Approach

The Interboro Team treated environmental vulnerability and issues of policy and governance as a unified challenge, exploring the ways in which each affects the other. Throughout their study, they documented social vulnerabilities, assessed the enforcement of public trust doctrine, and accounted for affordable housing, infrastructure, and access to transportation. In response to their research findings, the team articulated guiding principles for their work.

In the first, "Grassroots Regionalism," the team set out to create a way for different municipalities to cooperate toward shared goals. Because of the home rule system in the U.S., individual municipalities have autonomy over local decision-making. Some decisions, however, can negatively impact other municipalities, as can be the case when it comes to environmental issues. Even with home rule governance, communities are intrinsically linked in a shared ecology, so the Interboro Team was determined to create designs and policies that acknowledged those important commonalities. The second guiding principle, "The Storm and the Norm," underscored the importance of ensuring that protective measures meant for sporadic emergencies enhanced everyday life around the calendar year. For its third principle, "Low Risk, No Regrets," the Interboro Team proposed that planning should include features that would be beneficial in any future scenario. For example, more affordable housing options would benefit communities regardless of sea level rise, with or without the construction of a big surge barrier.

4

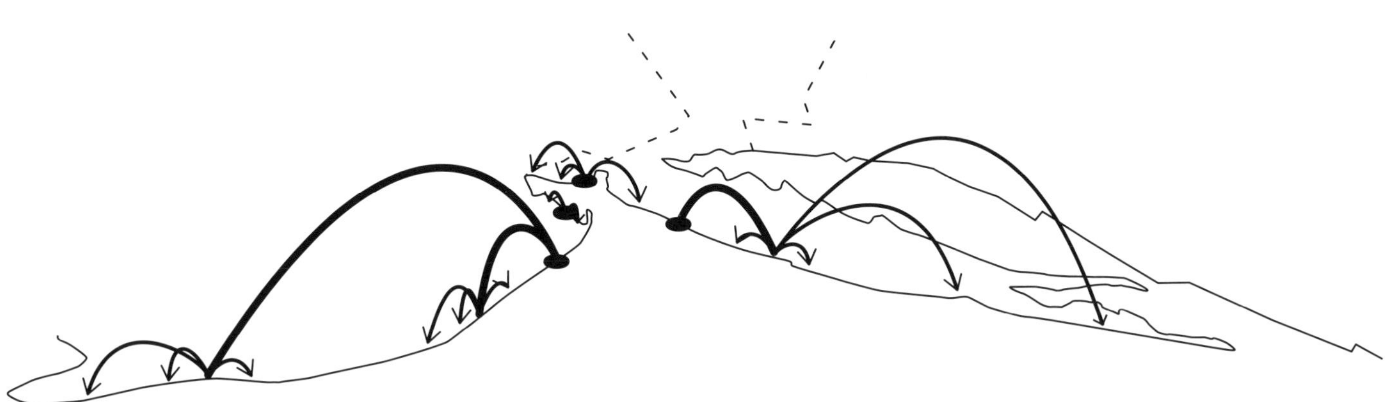

Plan and design interventions that are prototypical and catalytic
Many Sandy-damaged communities are still recovering, and still struggling to determine where and how to find the resources to rebuild, adapt, or move on. How do architects, planners, engineers, and policy makers ensure that their projects help those who need help the most? How can designers ensure that projects are maximally impactful? The Interboro Team strived to identify design opportunities that are prototypical and catalytic. They are prototypical in that they address common problems, and offer solutions that may be applicable elsewhere. They are catalytic in that each one can be conceived of as a concrete starting point capable of catalyzing other desired outcomes.

Design Opportunities

At the culmination of its research investigation, the Interboro Team proposed four design opportunities. Though each was tailored to a specific site – and each represented a different coastal type/landscape: ocean fronts, rivers, marshes, bays – the principles that underlie each one were designed to be adaptable to other similar contexts.

Living with the Marsh

For its study of the east shore of Staten Island, the team took on one of the more intractable issues of climate adaptation: managed retreat. On a site where 170 of 184 residents opted for a New York State-administered buy-out program, the designers saw an opportunity to test strategies for communities that go in this direction. The opportunity would implement a very participatory process, transforming once-privately-owned lots into recreational public spaces that help to attenuate storm surge.

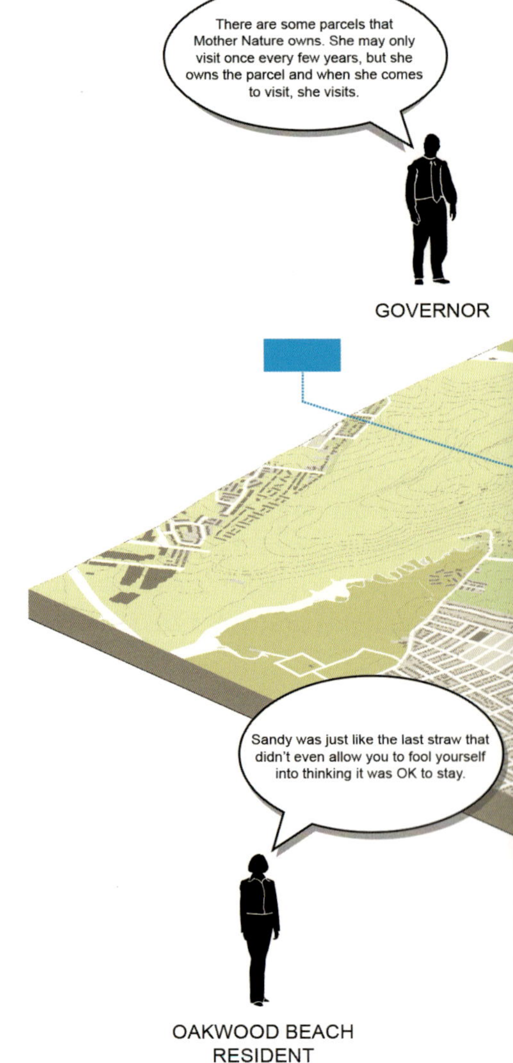

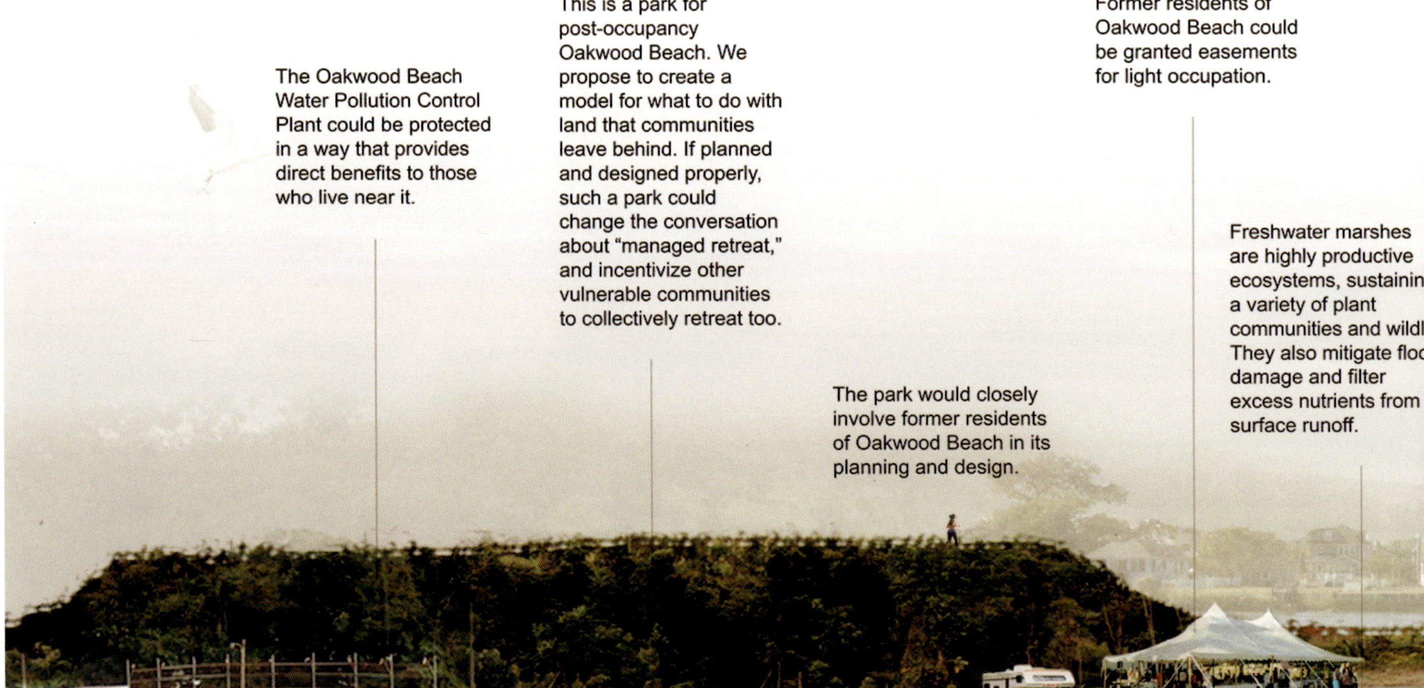

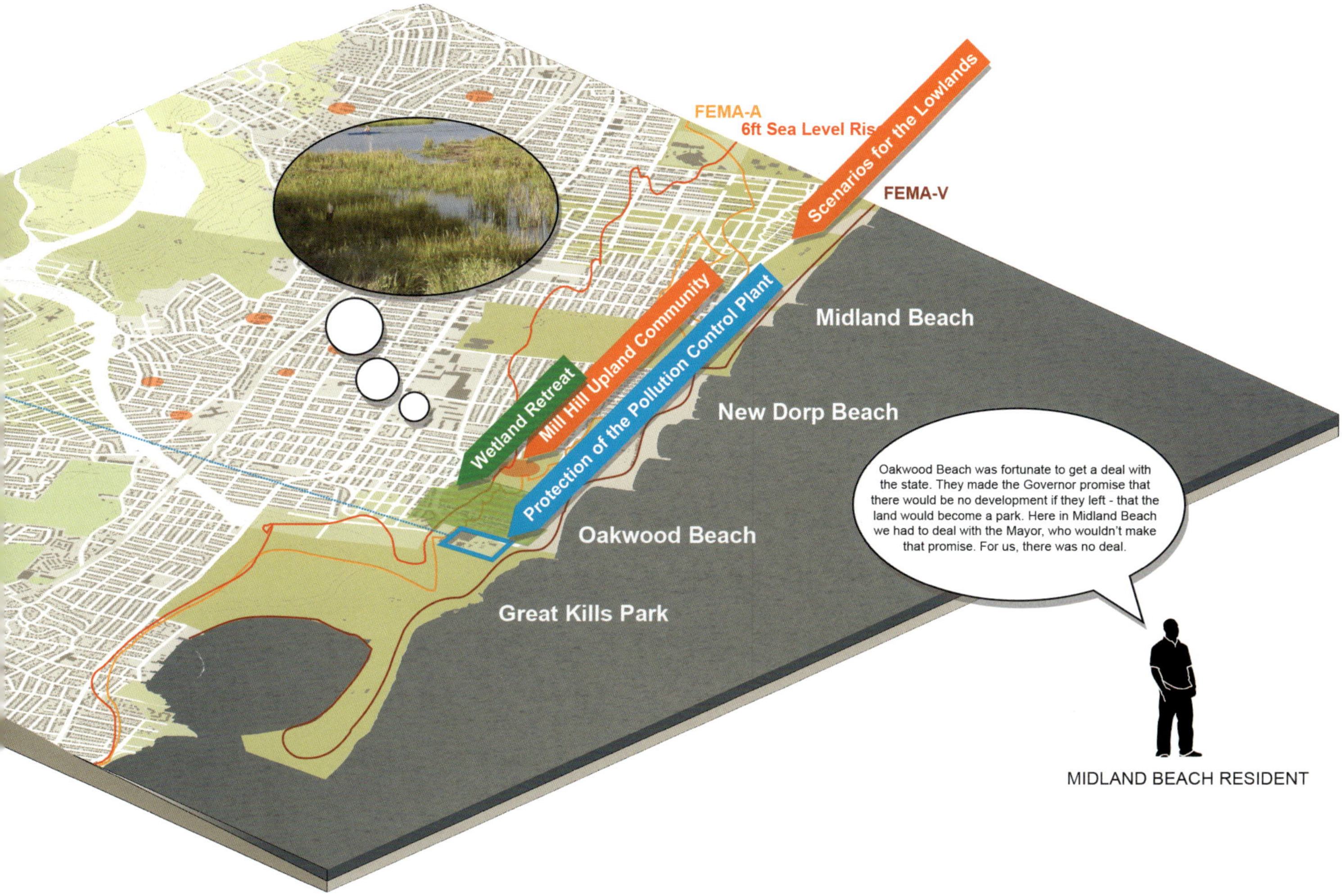

FEMA-A

6ft Sea Level Rise

Scenarios for the Lowlands

FEMA-V

Midland Beach

Mill Hill Upland Community

Protection of the Pollution Control Plant

Wetland Retreat

New Dorp Beach

Oakwood Beach

Great Kills Park

Oakwood Beach was fortunate to get a deal with the state. They made the Governor promise that there would be no development if they left - that the land would become a park. Here in Midland Beach we had to deal with the Mayor, who wouldn't make that promise. For us, there was no deal.

MIDLAND BEACH RESIDENT

4

Sites in high and dry, high opportunity communities should be identified for those who opt to retreat.

Fill from the bay could be used to create new high and dry mounds for residents who opt to remain.

Cut and fill development could contribute to watershed restoration and the health of the Lower Bay.

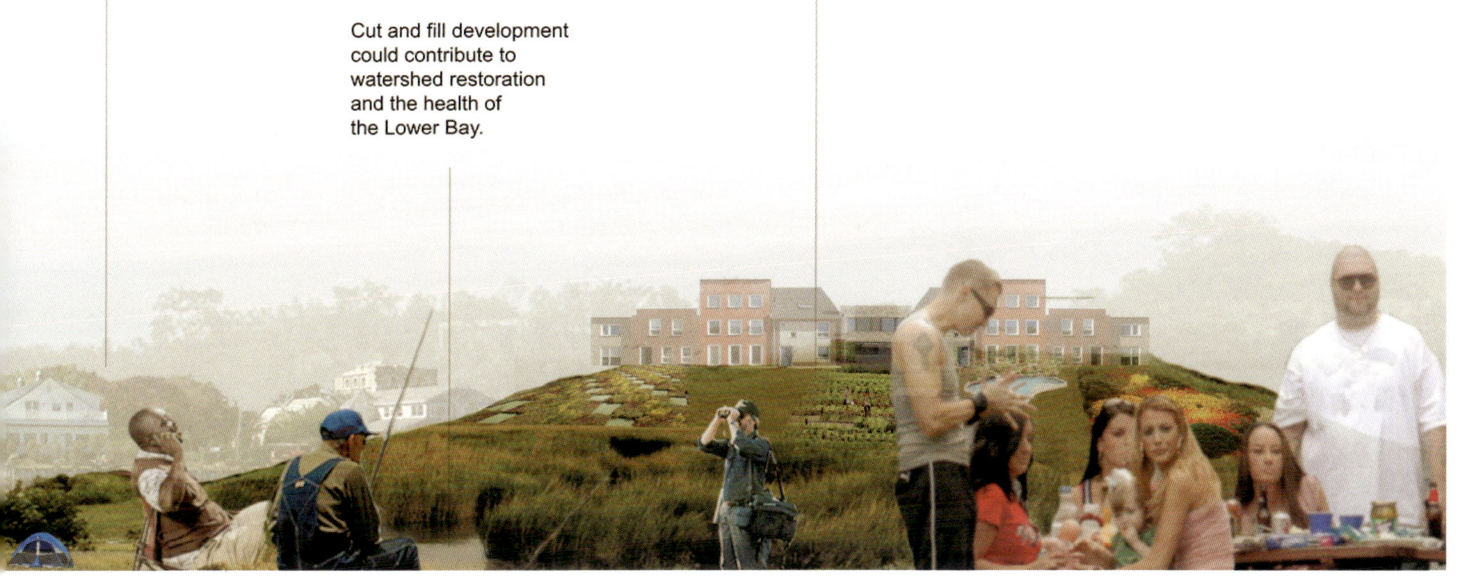

Living with the Creek

During its research in New Jersey's Monmouth County, the team identified a troubling pattern: there was a close relationship between socioeconomic status and vulnerability to climate events. Though each community in the county's watershed system shares in the same ecology, those with higher real estate values and other economic metrics fared much better during Hurricane Sandy. As a way to overcome these disparities, the Interboro Team geared resilient environmental designs – wider creek beds, absorptive open spaces, and levees – to double as connective areas that would make a more socioeconomically equitable watershed system. As such, part of its proposal included building affordable housing in upland, high and dry, high-opportunity areas that have affordable housing obligations under the Mount Laurel doctrine.

Living with the Coast

The team set out to capitalize on the New Jersey Shore's cherished role in the region, making it less susceptible to climate-related damage while making it more publicly accessible. The team's research highlighted two stark realities about the shore: first, it is highly vulnerable to extreme weather events; second, the Public Trust Doctrine, which is meant to ensure open, public access to New Jersey's beaches, tends to be dubiously enforced. As the Interboro Team saw, these two deficits could be addressed simultaneously with a coastal trail that would ensure unimpeded public access to the coastline, built to make the shore more resilient and robust.

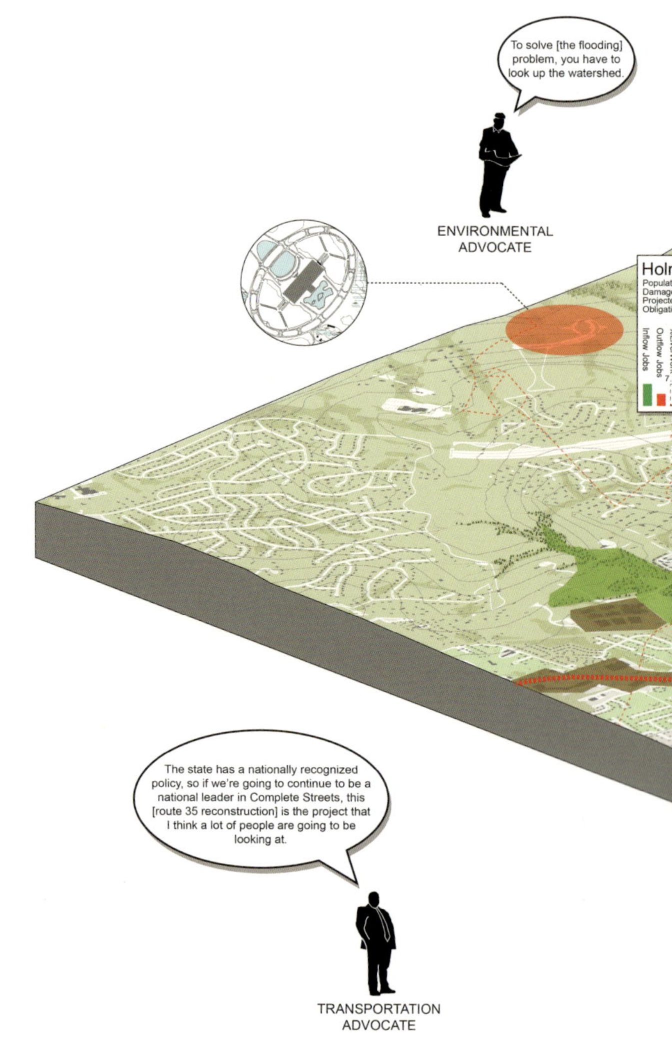

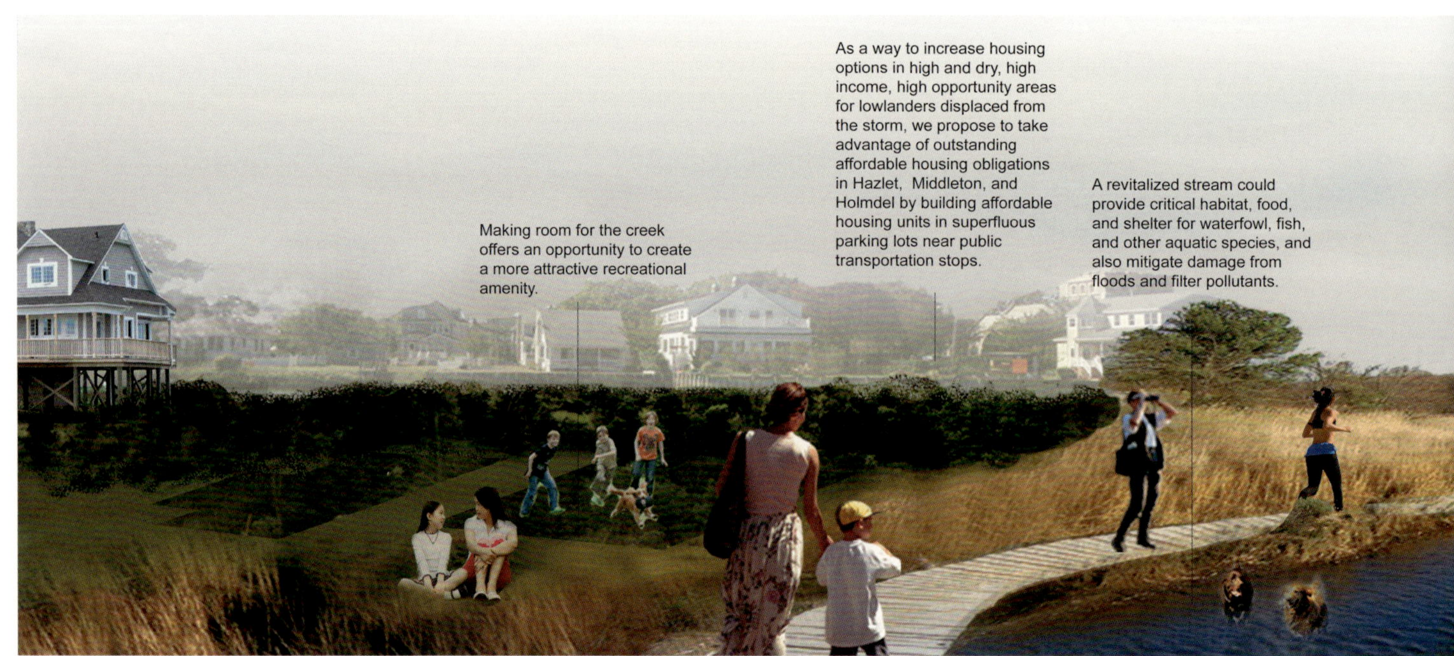

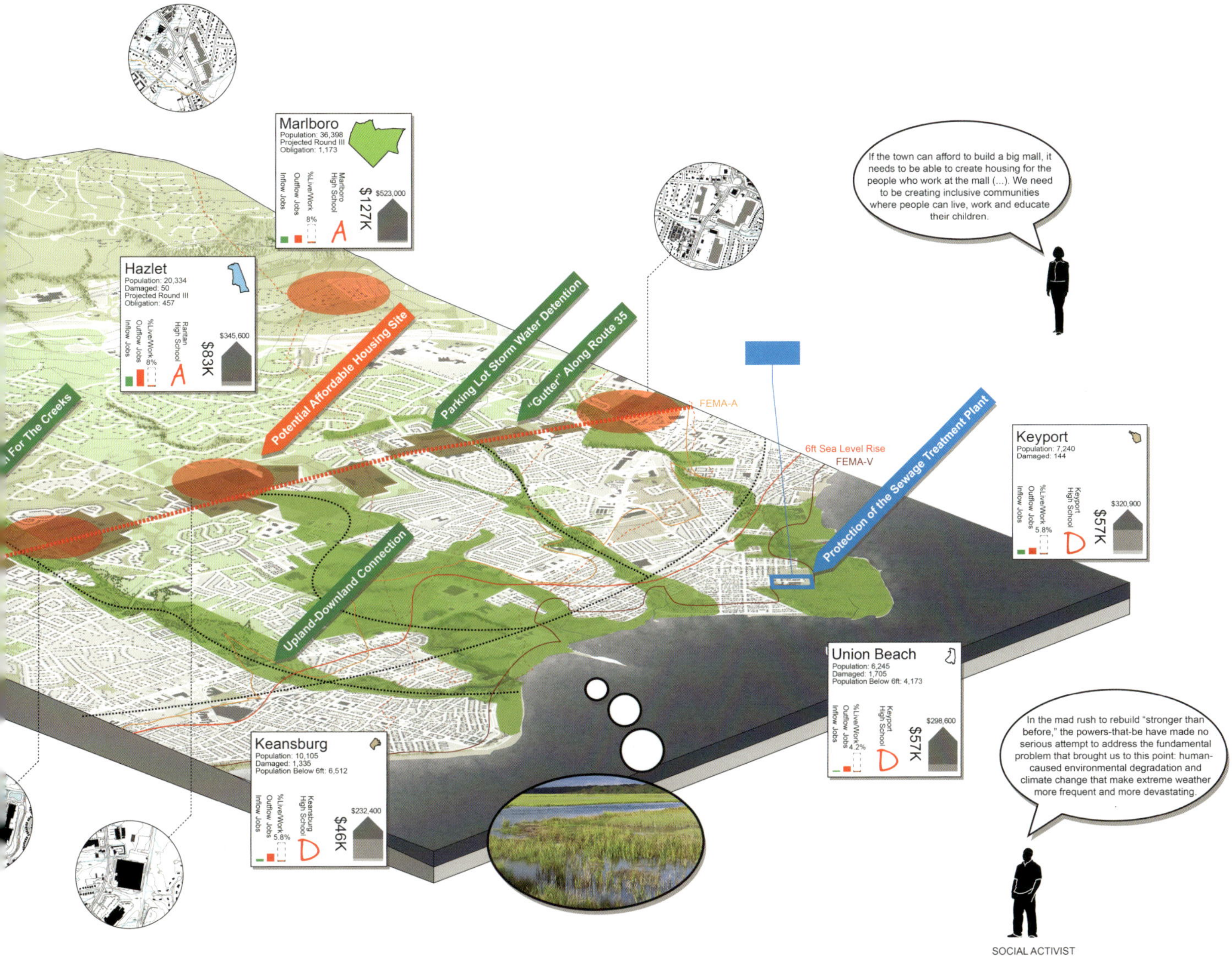

Marlboro
Population: 36,398
Projected Round III
Obligation: 1,173
Marlboro High School
$523,000
$127K
A
%Live/Work 8%
Outflow Jobs
Inflow Jobs

Hazlet
Population: 20,334
Damaged: 50
Projected Round III
Obligation: 457
Raritan High School
$345,600
$83K
A
%Live/Work 8%
Outflow Jobs
Inflow Jobs

If the town can afford to build a big mall, it needs to be able to create housing for the people who work at the mall (...). We need to be creating inclusive communities where people can live, work and educate their children.

For The Creeks
Potential Affordable Housing Site
Parking Lot Storm Water Detention
"Gutter" Along Route 35
Upland-Downland Connection
Protection of the Sewage Treatment Plant
FEMA-A
6ft Sea Level Rise
FEMA-V

Keyport
Population: 7,240
Damaged: 144
Keyport High School
$320,900
$57K
D
%Live/Work 5.8%
Outflow Jobs
Inflow Jobs

Union Beach
Population: 6,245
Damaged: 1,705
Population Below 6ft: 4,173
Keyport High School
$298,600
$57K
D
%Live/Work 4.2%
Outflow Jobs
Inflow Jobs

Keansburg
Population: 10,105
Damaged: 1,335
Population Below 6ft: 6,512
Keansburg High School
$232,400
$46K
D
%Live/Work 5.8%
Outflow Jobs
Inflow Jobs

In the mad rush to rebuild "stronger than before," the powers-that-be have made no serious attempt to address the fundamental problem that brought us to this point: human-caused environmental degradation and climate change that make extreme weather more frequent and more devastating.

SOCIAL ACTIVIST

4

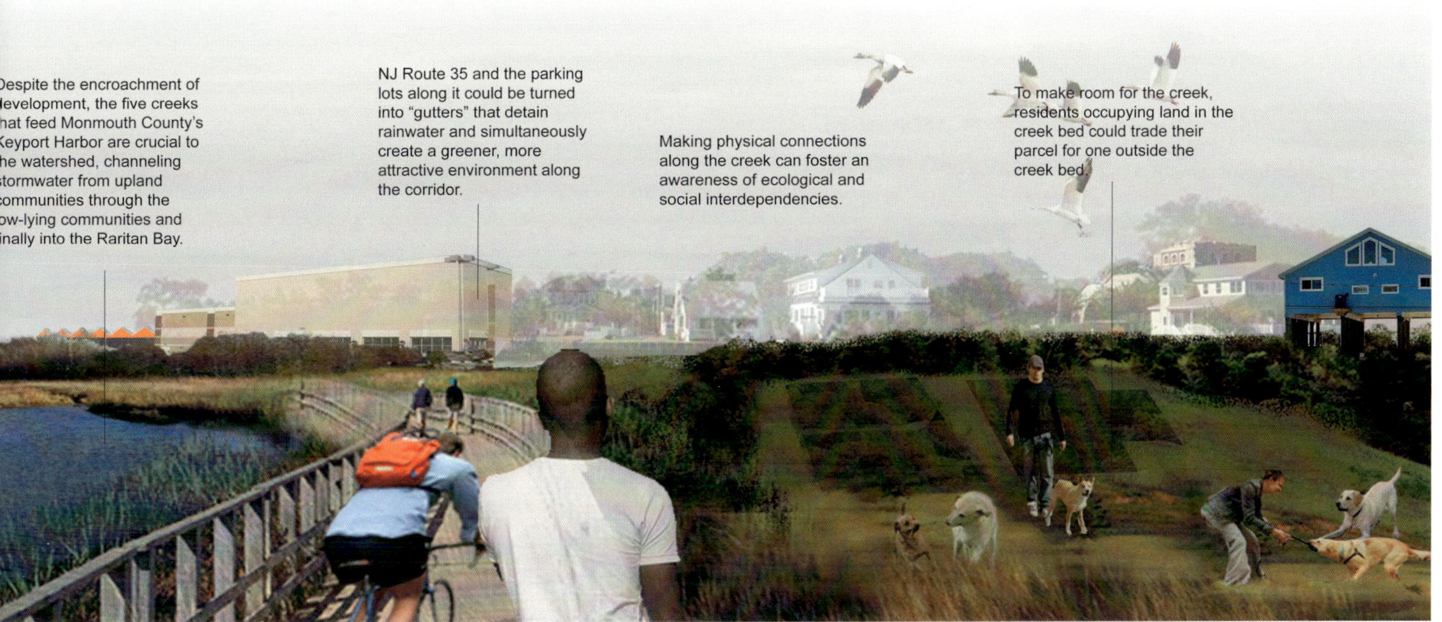

Final Proposal: Living with the Bay

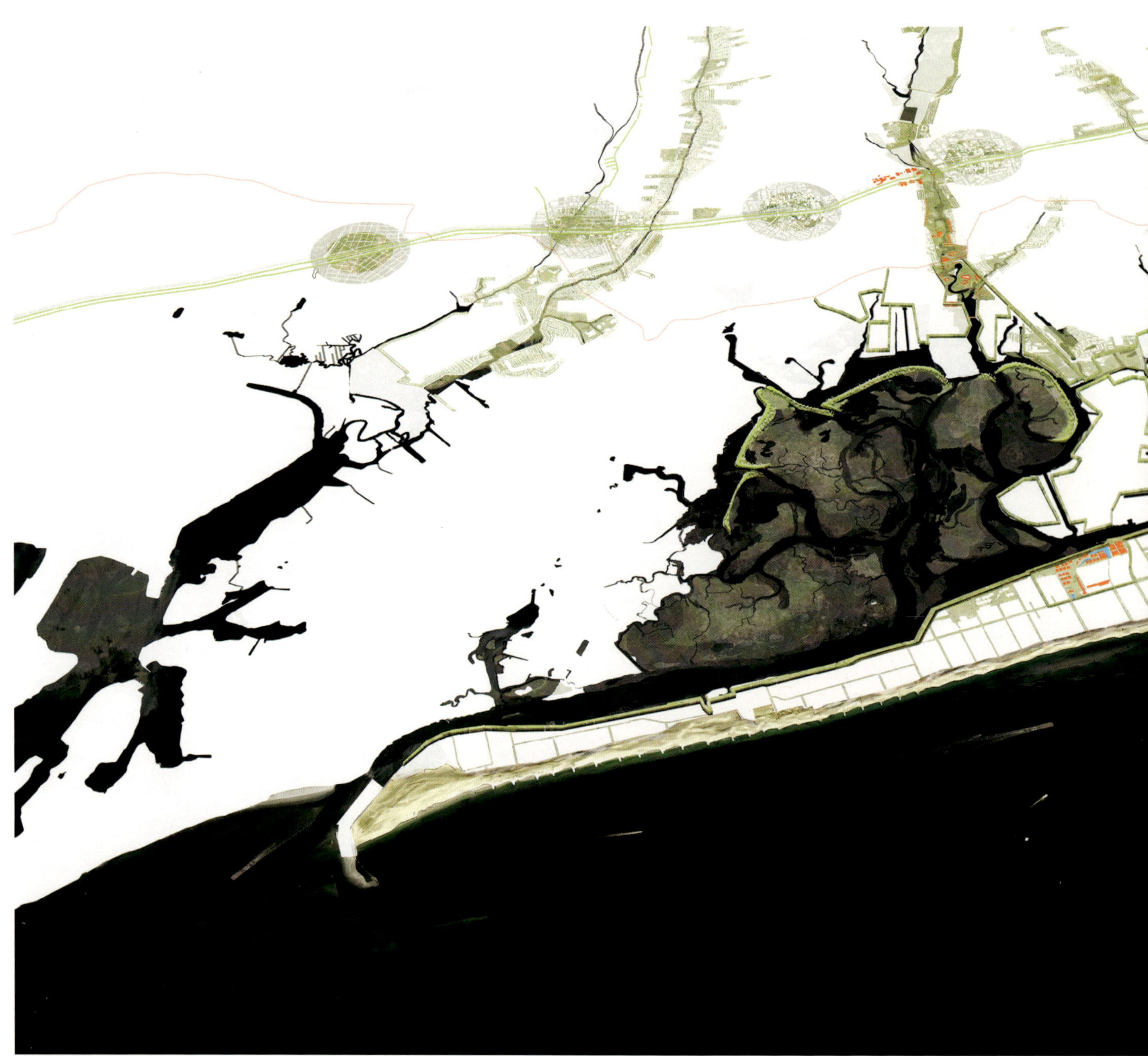

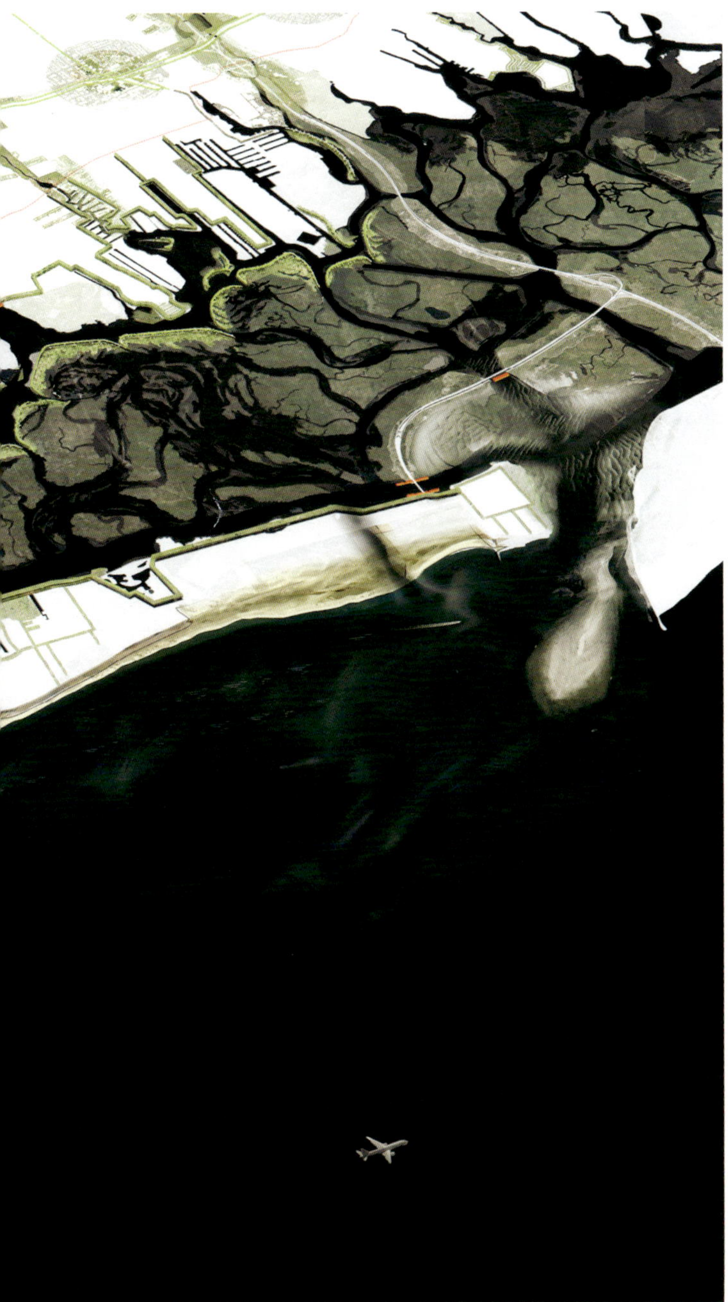

The team's proposal, Living with the Bay, considered the south shore of Nassau County on Long Island in New York. The bay itself is framed by Long Island and Long Beach Island, a pencil-thin barrier island and a popular recreational landscape. The area has to confront different types of water threats, including flooding from storm water runoff, bayside inundation, and coastal wave action; these are underscored by sea level rise, ecological failures from overdevelopment and pollution, and the lack of access to housing and public space. This landscape of vulnerability is built up with infrastructure that, in many cases, lacks the capacity to fully address these threats.

Because the challenges are too complex for any single off-the-shelf solution, the Interboro Team conceived a multi-pronged approach that could be implemented at specific sites to regional effect. The team broke the project into five constituent ecological components: ocean shore, barrier island, saltwater marsh, river estuary, and highlands. This approach acknowledged that each component is integrated with the others —that storm water in the highlands, for example, has a direct impact on the ocean shore.

Sediment Flow

For the ocean shore element, the Interboro Team set out to preserve the vital wave-attenuating marshlands in the bay. Building up oceanfront dunes to capture and manage sediment would create stable conditions for the beach to grow stronger. This would raise a multi-layered buffer between the open ocean and Long Island.

Living with the Bay is a comprehensive regional resilience plan for Nassau County's South Shore.

Smart Barrier

On the barrier island, the team proposed a dike on the bay side to protect critical infrastructure and a densely populated public-housing community. Coupled with absorptive landscapes and water retention features, this would protect residents and establish better connections between different neighborhoods, as well as between the community and the bay. North Park suffers as a result of negative environmental externalities produced in surrounding areas. Part of the Interboro Team's proposal recommended removing some polluters and shrinking the footprint of others to improve health of the residents in North Park.

The Eco-Edge

Historically, wetlands and marshes have provided a critical buffering effect for wave energy and storm surge. Development and contaminants from urban run-off, however, have compromised these landscapes, lessening their effectiveness at mitigating water risks. To counteract this trend, the Interboro Team called for the development of new marsh islands in the bay. These would not only buffer against surge, they could also provide wildlife habitat and recreational opportunities.

Slow Streams

Many rivers and creeks empty into the bay from further inland. Estuaries, areas where rivers meet open water, are critical sites for water management, since flooding can come from two directions: from storm water run-off, and from coastal flooding. To give these critical ecologies room to swell, the team proposed publicly accessible greenways along the banks of tributaries, enhancing their absorptiveness and adding a civic amenity. By filtering water, too, these landscapes would help cut down on the contaminants that threaten nearby wetlands.

Green Corridor

The team also addressed conditions farther inland, along the Long Island Rail Road line. There, on a corridor outside of FEMA-designated flood zones, the team saw an opportunity to insert absorptive green infrastructure and to develop transit-oriented affordable housing, which the team found to be in short supply in Nassau County.

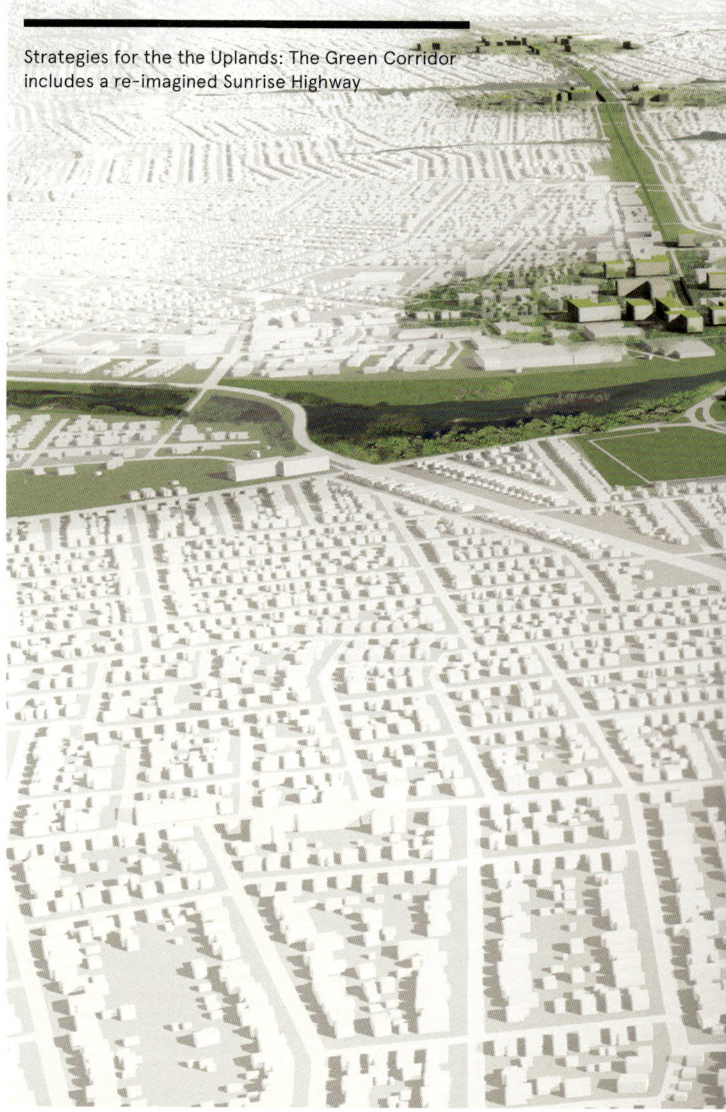

Strategies for the the Uplands: The Green Corridor includes a re-imagined Sunrise Highway

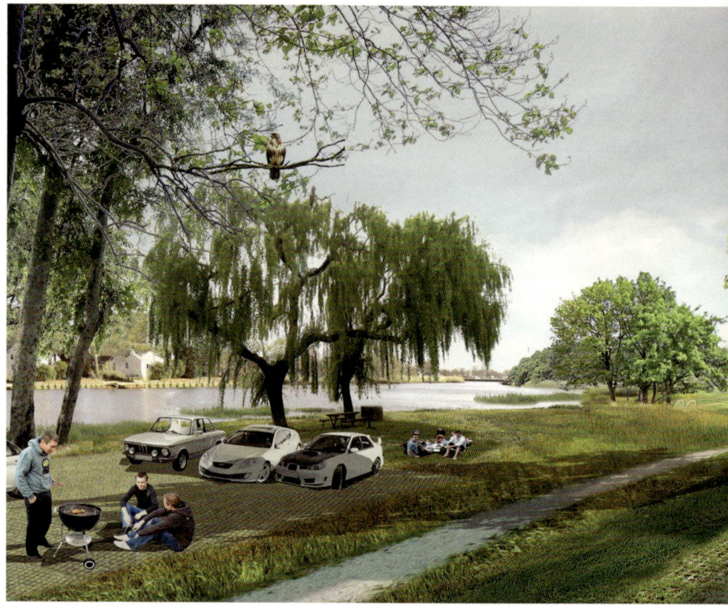

For the lowlands, the team envisioned a future river park

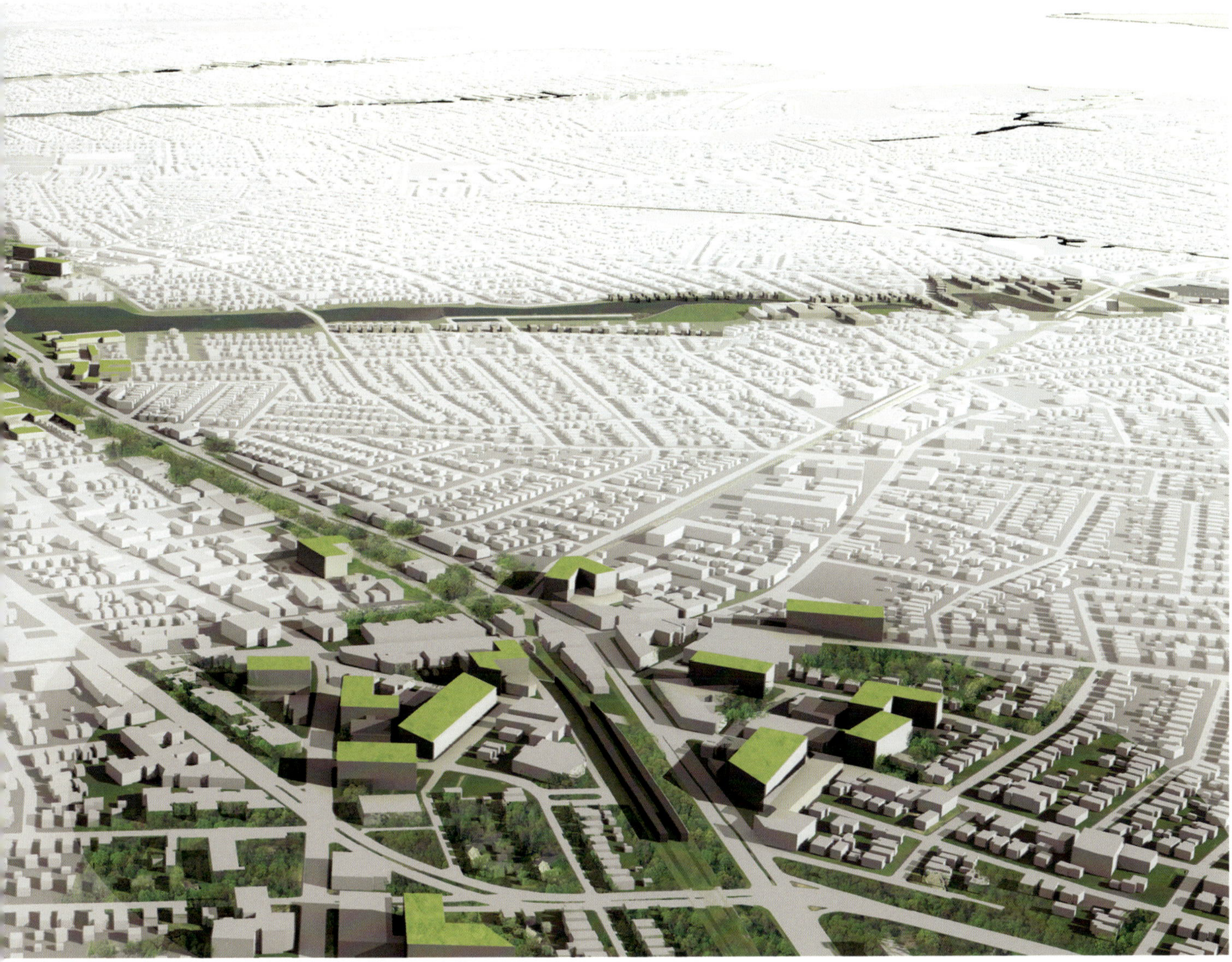

4

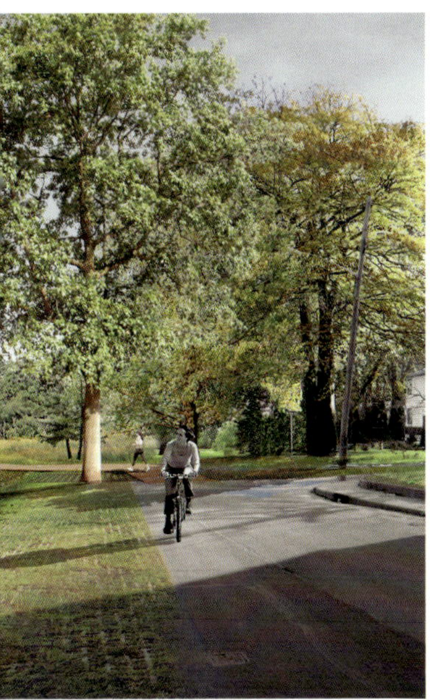

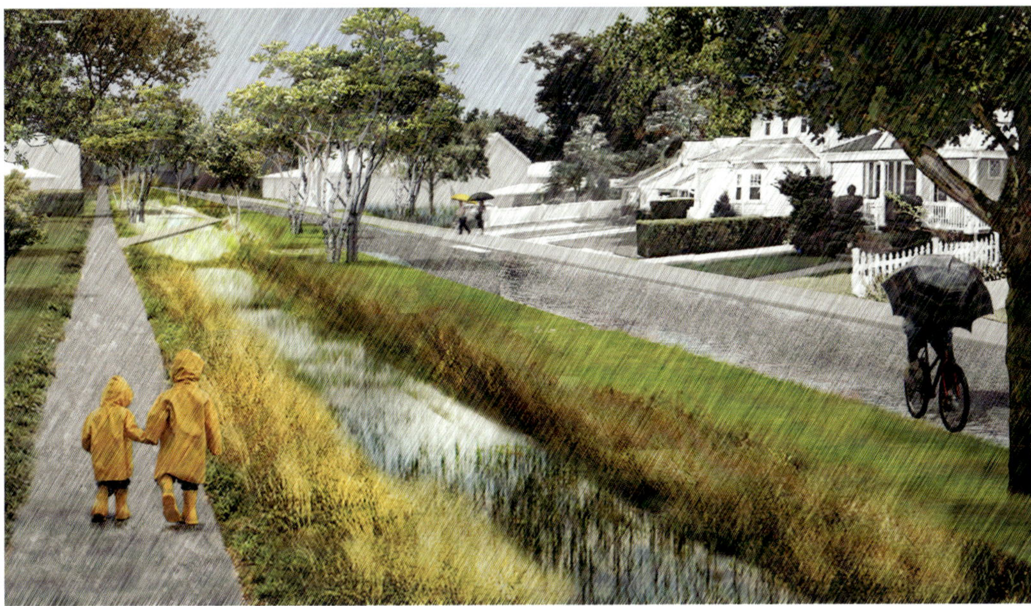

Bio-swales would become a neighborhood amenity in the lowlands

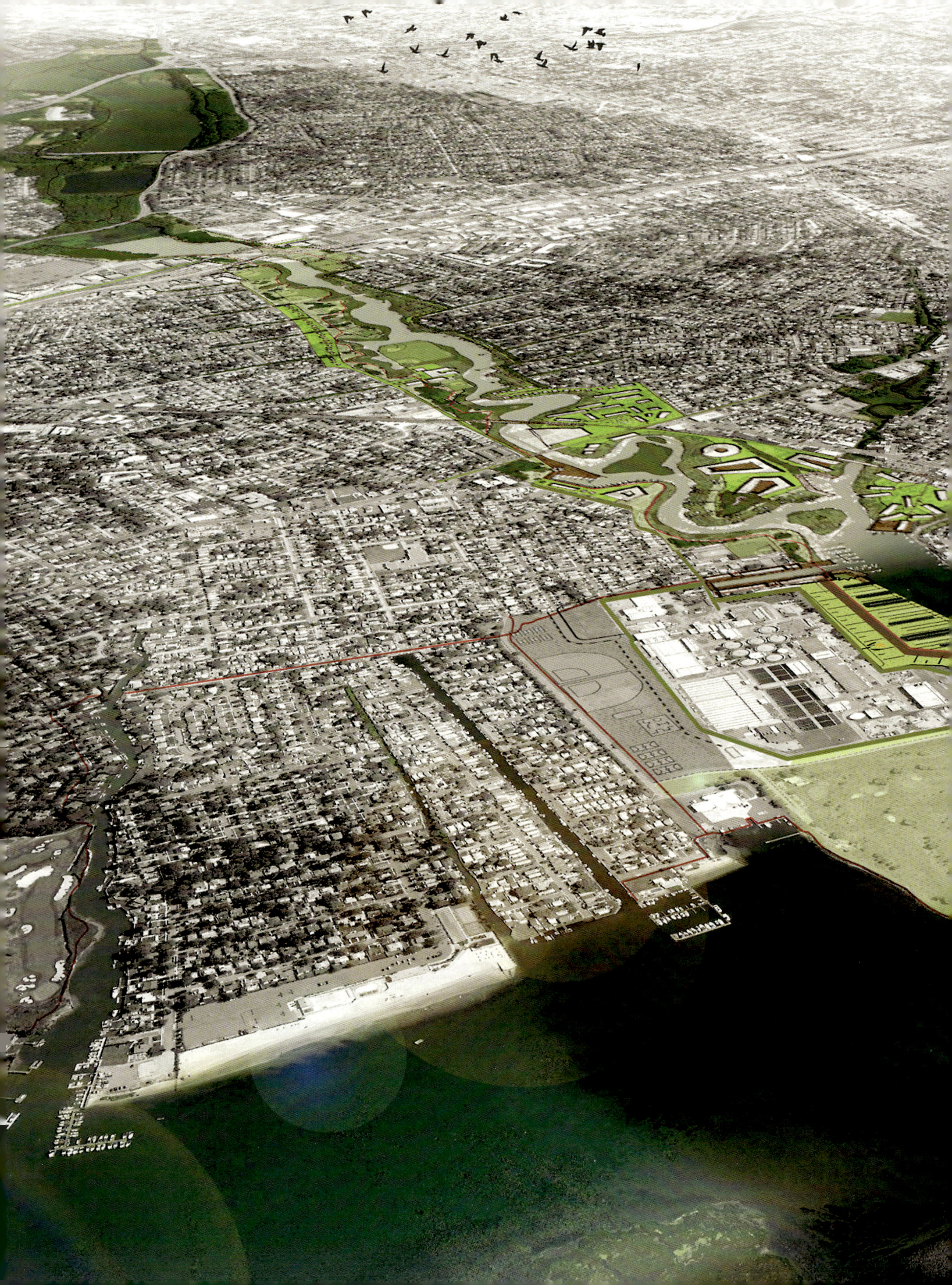

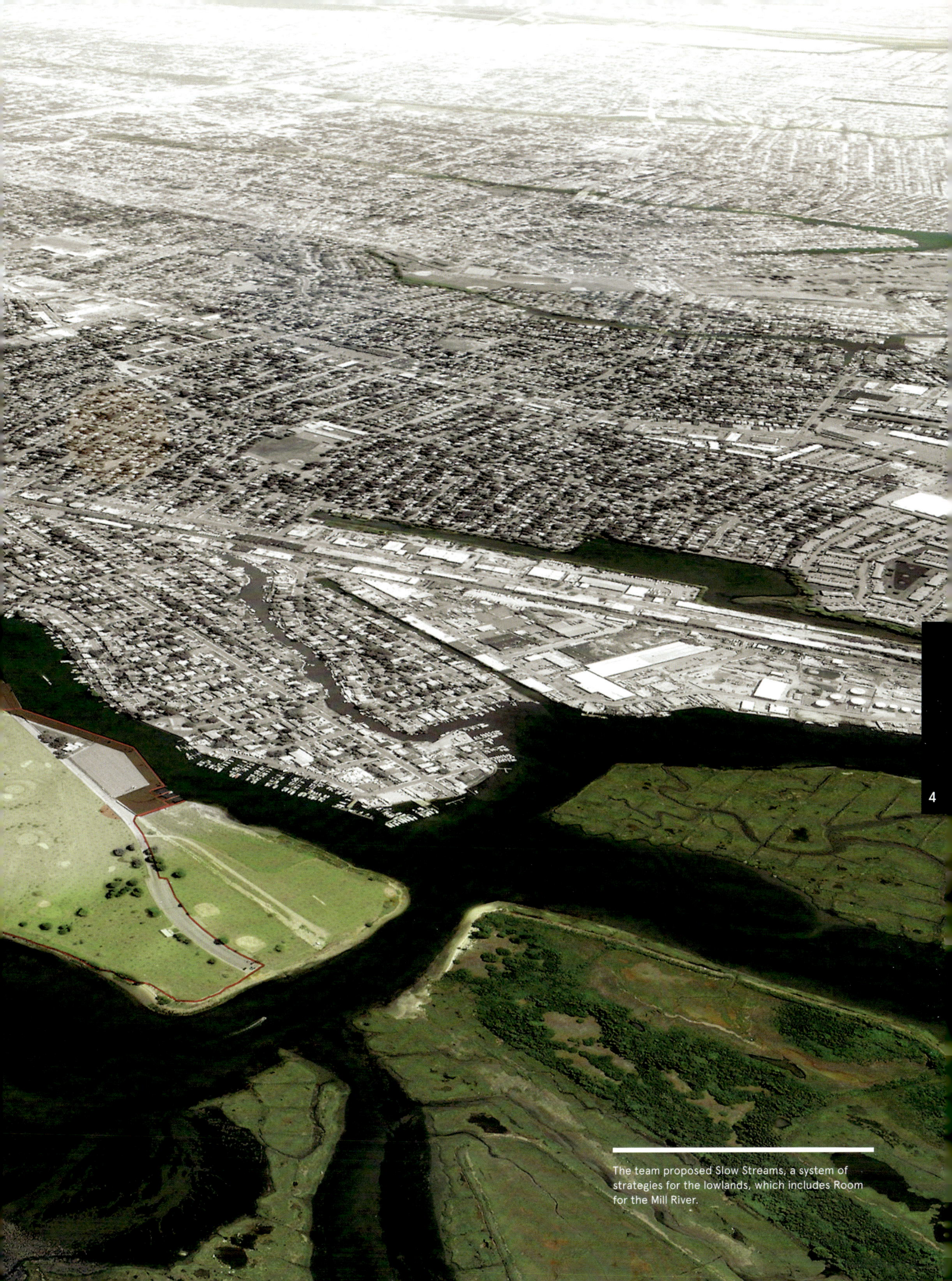

4

The team proposed Slow Streams, a system of strategies for the lowlands, which includes Room for the Mill River.

Design Process

Over the course of its research and design process, the Interboro Team engaged over 100 organizations, including community groups, non-profits, academic institutions, and private companies. It held regular meetings with residents and representatives from these organizations, gaining valuable insights into local conditions. The team also worked closely with governments – municipal, county, and state – to move the design toward implementation.

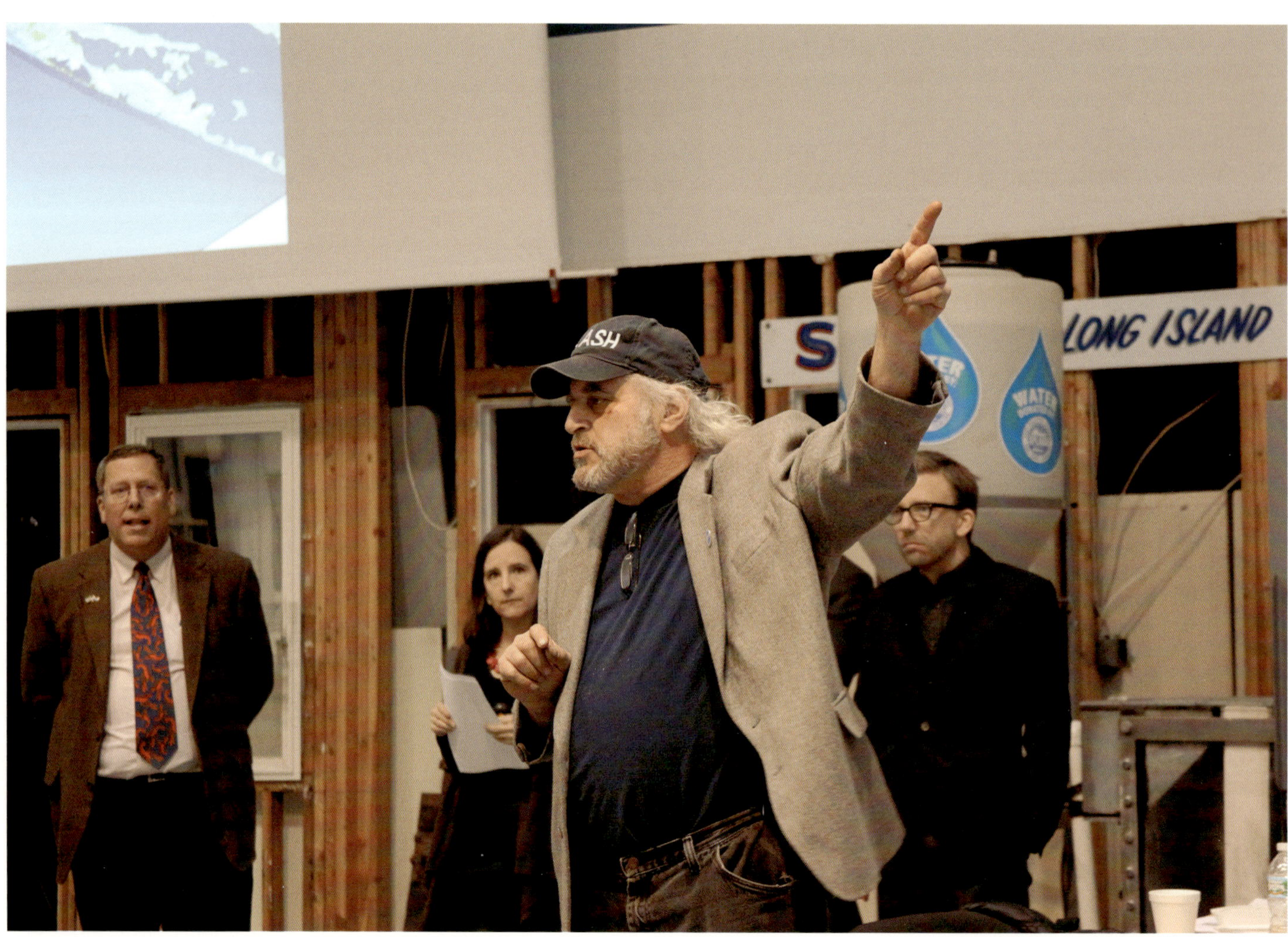

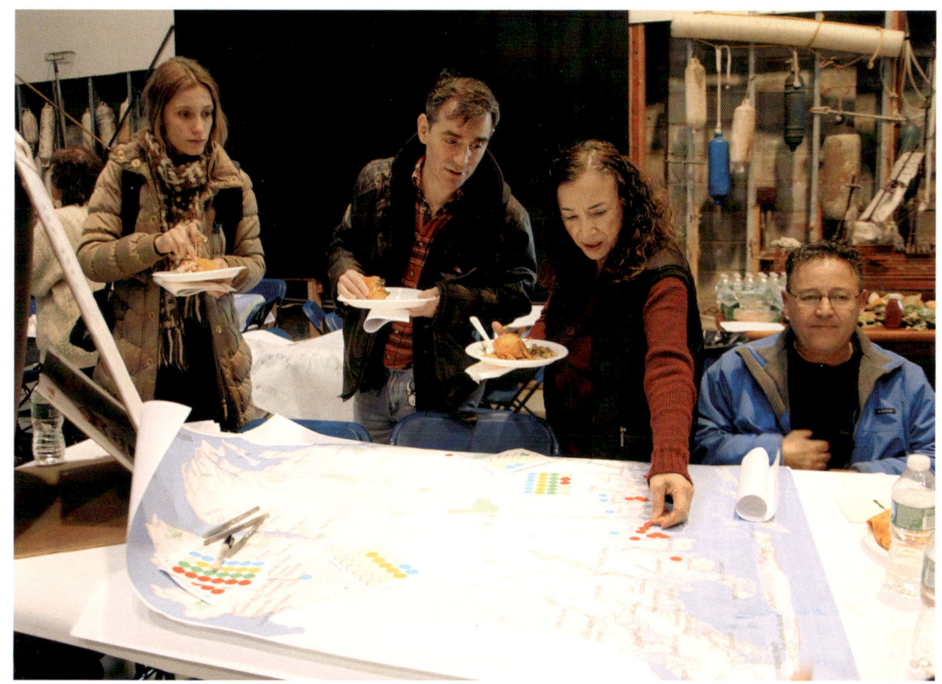
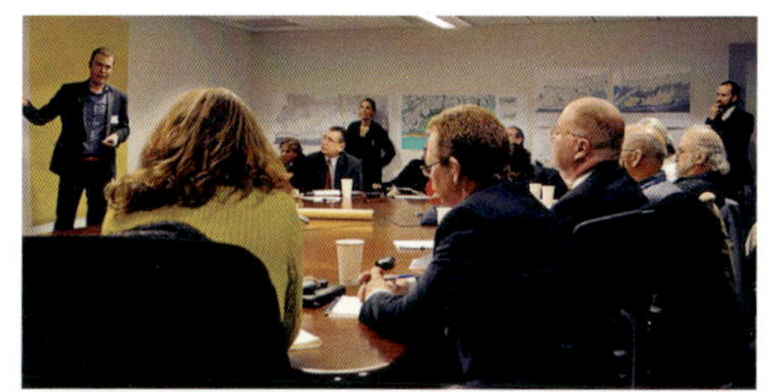
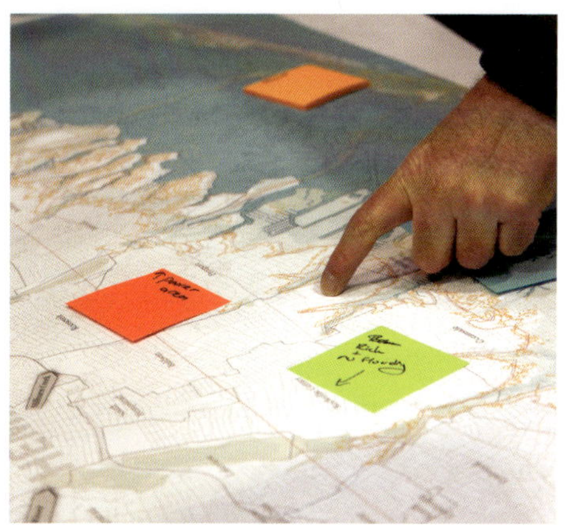
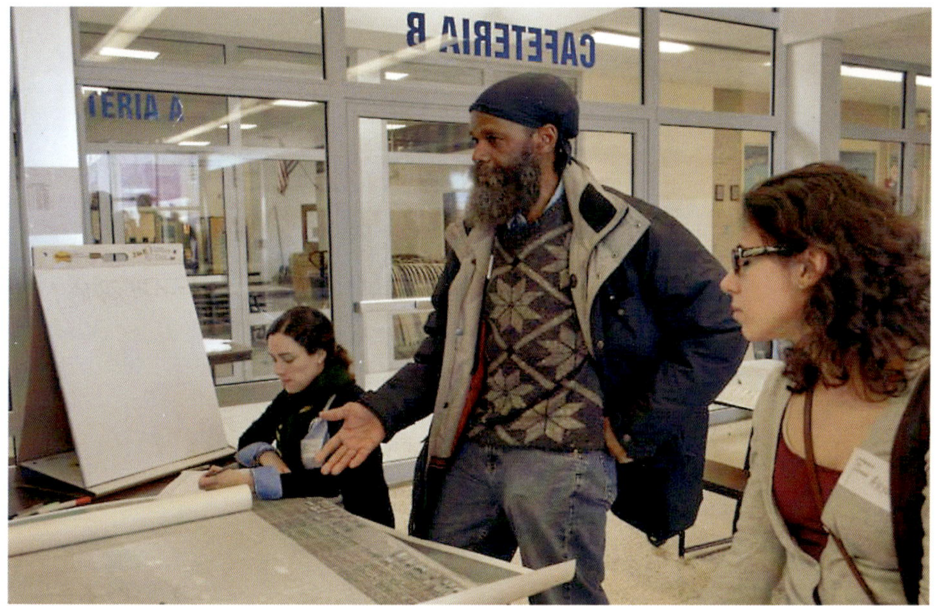
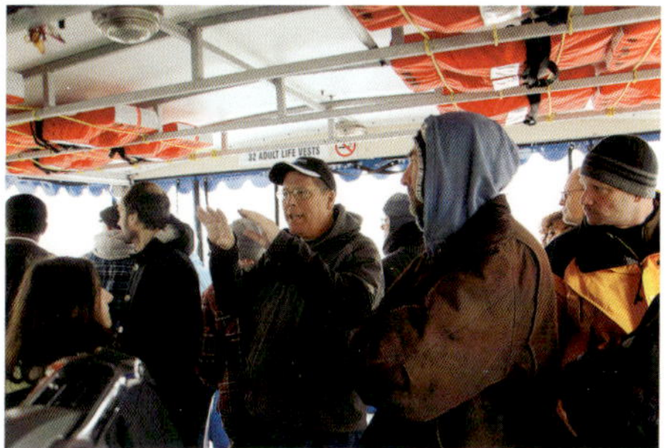
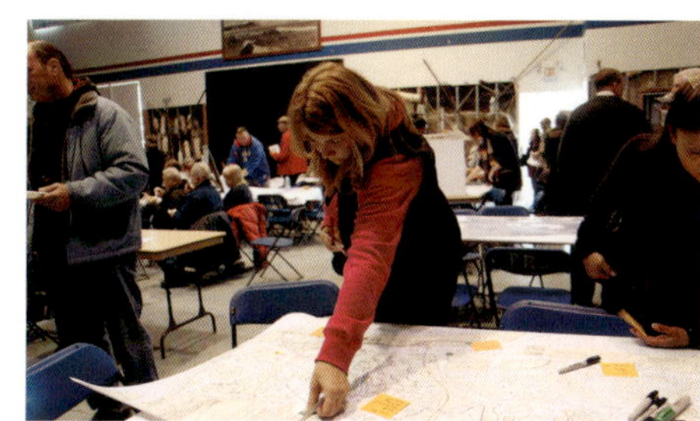
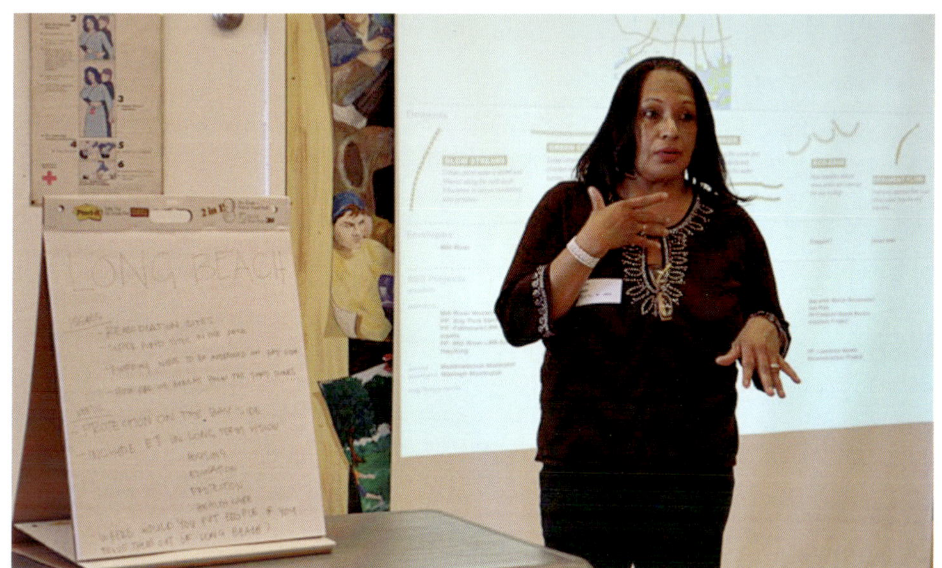

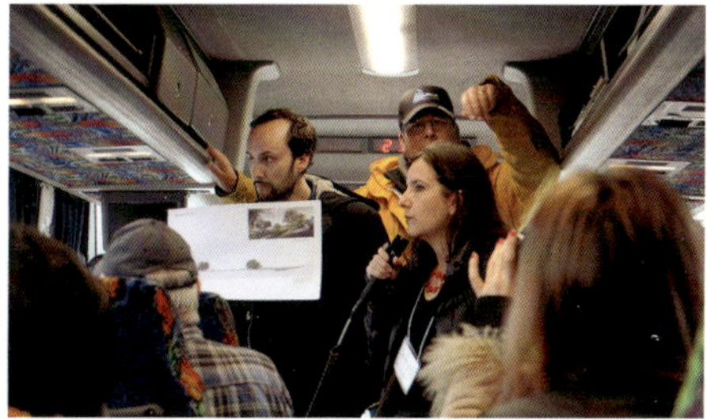
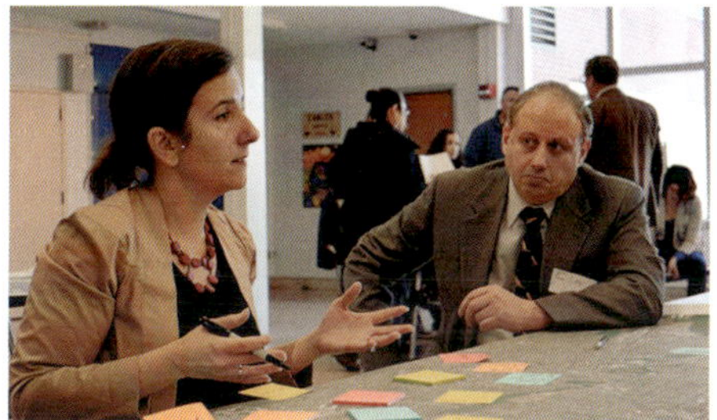

4

NEW MEADOWLANDS

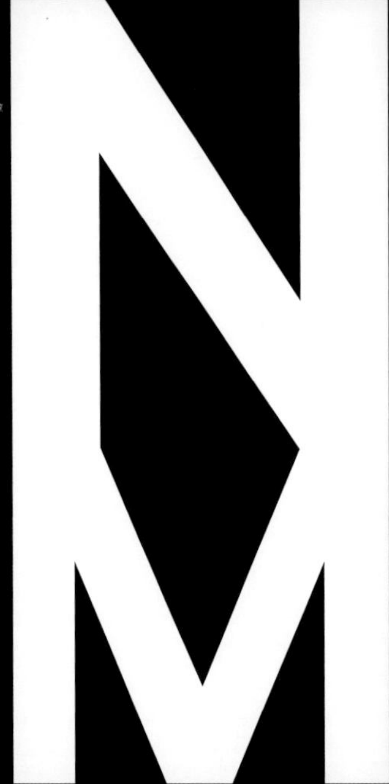

Team Leads
MIT Center for Advanced Urbanism (CAU)
Zones Urbaines Sensibles (ZUS)
DE URBANISTEN

Eco-Engineering
Deltares

Infrastructure Engineering
Volker Infradesign

Graphic and Communication Design
75B

MIT CAU + ZUS + URBANISTEN

The MIT CAU + ZUS + URBANISTEN team developed an analytical method to spatialize federal investment priorities, working from the premise that a dollar is best spent when it addresses the biggest variety of risks for the largest plurality of stakeholders, including vulnerable populations and economies.

The team's proposal for the "New Meadowlands" project articulates an integrated vision to protect, connect, and develop this area, which is a critical asset to both New Jersey and the metropolitan area of New York. A regional analysis that layered a maximum spectrum of risks and vulnerabilities – combining flood risk with social vulnerability, vital network vulnerability, and pollution risk – identified the Meadowlands as a key investment priority.

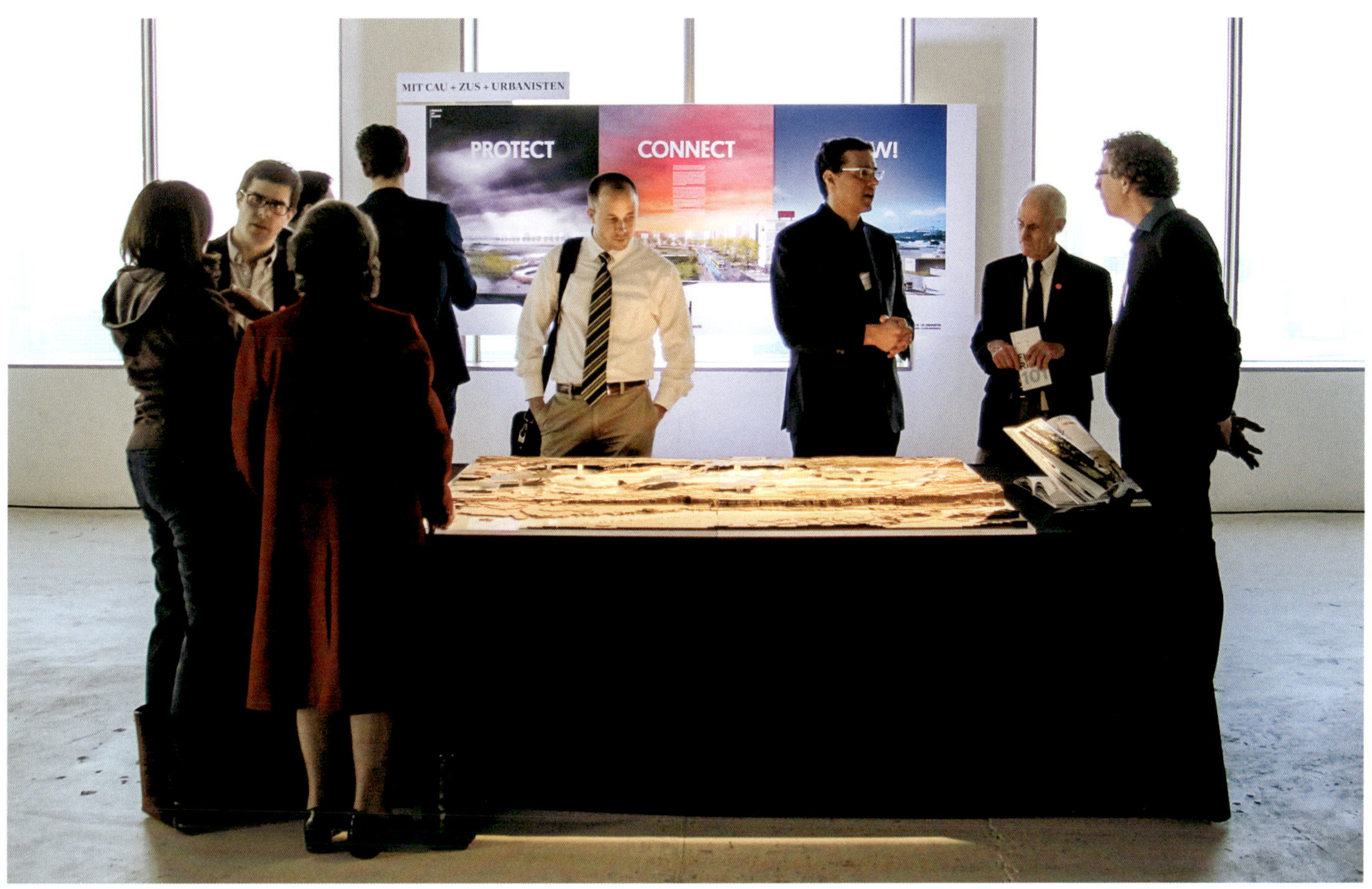

4

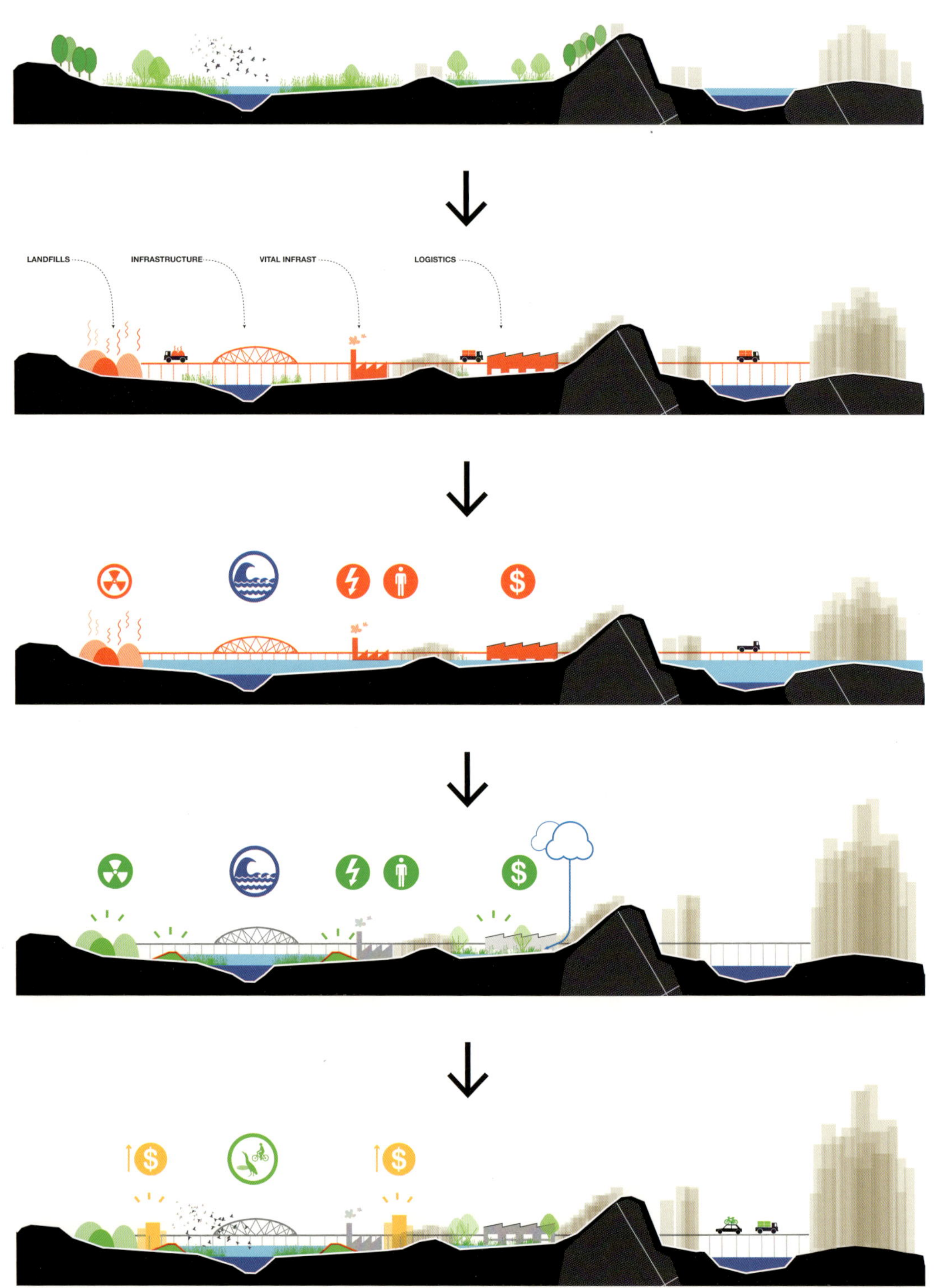

Sectional diagram of the history and the future of the Meadowlands basin. The last two sections illustrate the project scenario.

An Approach to Identifying Risks and Priorities

Natural events only become disasters when human practices are not able to accommodate extreme environmental conditions and resilience is low; otherwise, they would simply be bouts of bad weather.
To a certain degree, this outcome is a conflict in scales. Regional dynamics cause extreme environmental conditions (sea level rise, global warming, watershed dynamics, geomorphology, etc.), that are systemic and work across scales. Projects and interventions that can be realistically implemented, such as objects of architecture or infrastructure, however, have dimensional constraints based on capital availability, land structure complexity, and levels of government (municipal, county, and state).

Taking this into account, the team's approach addressed the scale difference between analysis and intervention, proposing a somewhat new, intermediate scale level: regional design – a series of discrete projects and fragments that add up to a large intervention over time in one of the most critical intersections of systems in the metropolitan area.

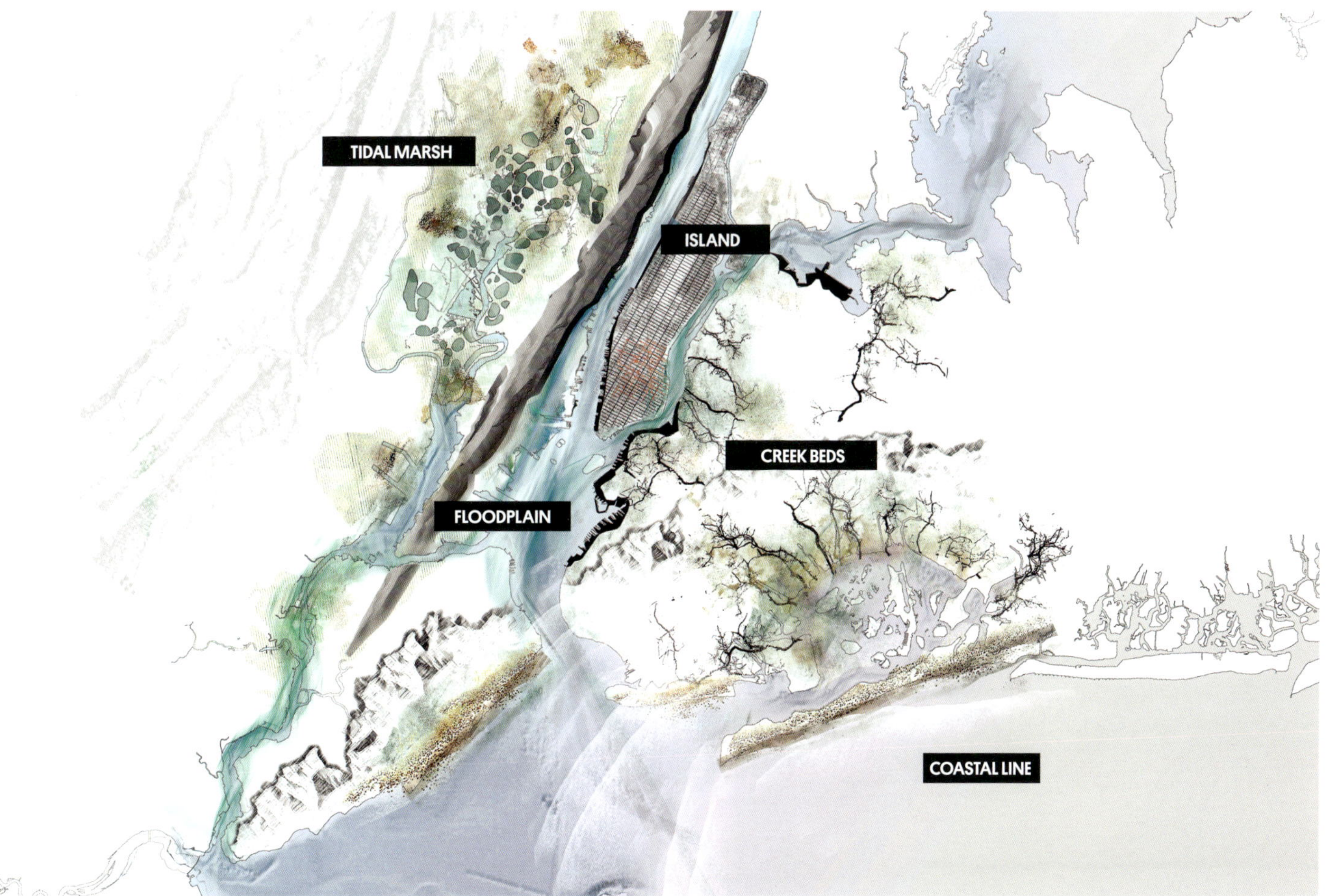

Five types of flood landscapes present distinct patterns of urbanism and resilience.

4

Design Opportunities

The MIT CAU+ZUS+Urbanisten team proposed a grouping of resilience districts along the edges of flood zones at sites across the New York-New Jersey metropolitan area. Resilience adaptations would enhance the capacity of inhabitants to cope with extreme weather, but they would also make changes in the built environment to mitigate damage, injury, and death. The team's research throughout the tri-state area led it to focus on the metropolitan economy centered around Manhattan, representing the most extreme confluence of population density, concentration of value creation, and vital infrastructure networks.

Even with these important assets, the area faces high exposure to hazards, including, but not limited to, extreme weather events. The impact of Hurricane Sandy underscored this at-risk condition. Power blackouts, severely contaminated storm waters, and the shutdown of public transportion were just a few examples of system-wide failures. By layering maps of those risks, the team determined where interventions could address the largest portfolio of threats. A precise location and associated risk definition allowed the team to create context-specific design concepts. In most cases, these design principles would not only

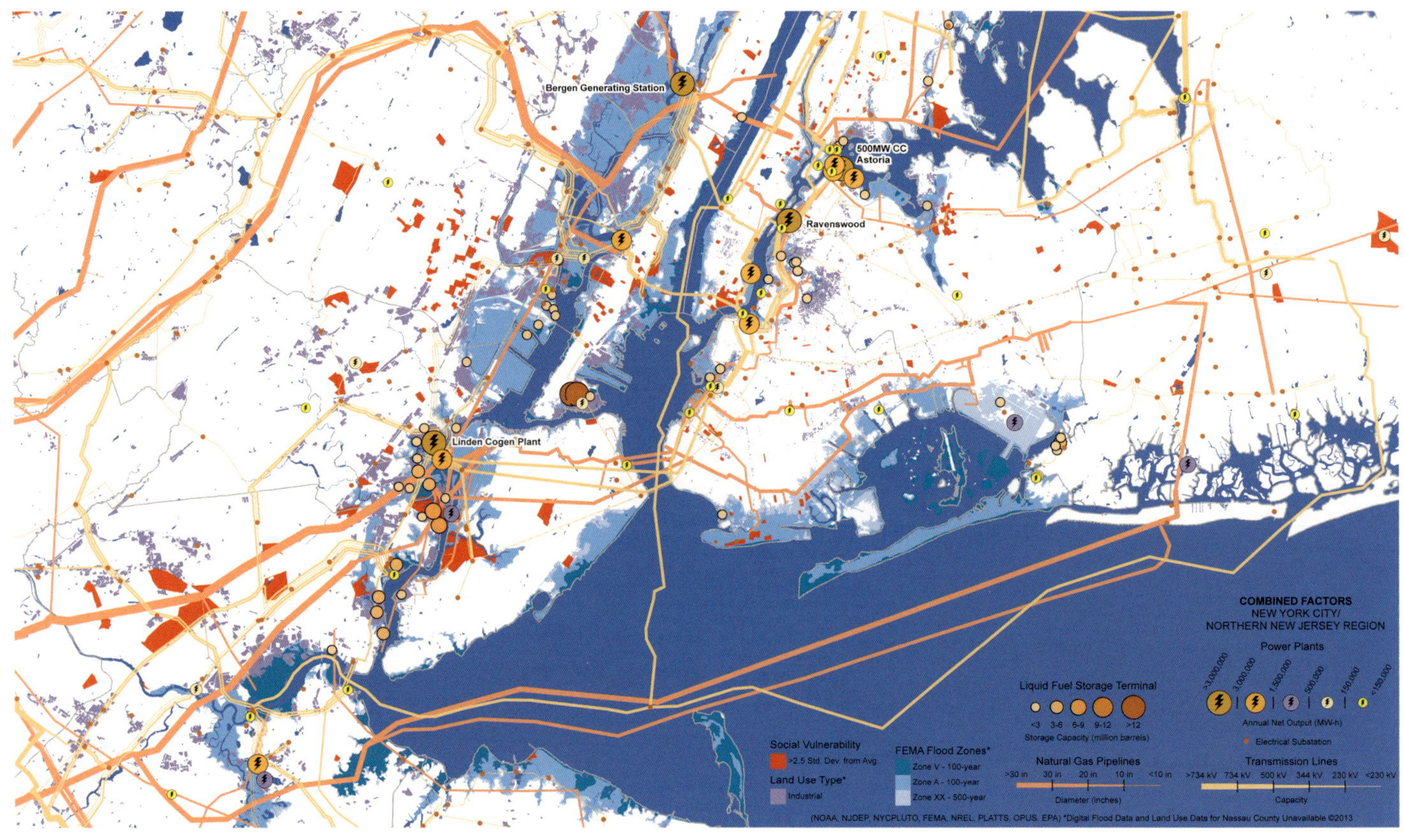

Combining geo-referenced data on both risk and vulnerability spectra, the team identified potential sites for design interventions along river deltas, where rising seawater penetrates inward and urban storm water flows outward. Most importantly, the low-lying flood zones of these deltas contain, almost without exception, a combination of critical infrastructures, polluted land, compromised ecosystem services, and vulnerable neighborhoods. The densest juxtapositions can be found in the metropolitan area of New York City/Northern New Jersey, where roughly 2.5 million people live in the flood zone. Roughly 66% of the most vulnerable populations (2.5 standard deviations from the mean) live a half-mile from the FEMA Flood Zone. About 29% of the most vulnerable populations (2.5 standard deviations from the mean) live in the FEMA flood zones. 39 of the 52 liquid fuel storage terminals in this area are located within the flood plain and these contain 80% of the total area fuel. 75% of the net annual generation comes from 27 power stations that are in flood zones.

mitigate risks, but they would also create new opportunities for community life and development.

These resilient districts would include emergency infrastructure, evacuation capacity, ecological protection, and public landscape infrastructure. They would integrate light manufacturing and warehousing within residential areas, to stimulate economic development.

The team's analysis pointed to four potential resilient districts, highlighted as immediate investment priorities: the Meadowlands basin with a close proximity of residential, wetlands, and industrial land uses; Jersey City and Hoboken, where various vital infrastructure systems cross the Hudson River, connecting New Jersey and New York; the Lower East Side of Manhattan, where persistent drainage issues exacerbate flooding and storm water; and Newtown Creek, between Brooklyn and Queens, where the pollution from long-standing industrial use in the floodplain created environmental challenges.

MULTIPLE VULNERABILITIES / THE HAZARD SANDWICH

	MARSH	RIVER	ISLAND	CREEK	COAST
GEOGRAPHY					
DENSITY					
INUNDATION					
WAVES					
SOCIAL VULNERABILITY					
ECONOMIC LOSS	$	$ $	$	$ $	$
POLLUTION					
HEAT EFFECT					
VITAL NETWORKS					
TRANSPORT NETWORKS					

REGIONAL ANALYSIS

GEOMORPHOLOGICAL TYPOLOGIES + WETLANDS EVOLUTION: **85%** OF THE REGIONAL HISTORIC WETLANDS HAS BEEN DEVELOPED OR LOST

FLOOD + SEA LEVEL RISE: **2.5** MILLION INHABITANTS IN THE NEW YORK & NEW JERSEY METROPOLITAN AREA LIVE IN THE FLOOD ZONE

SOCIAL VULNERABILITY + POPULATION DENSITY: **66%** OF THE MOST VULNERABLE COMMUNITIES LIVE WITHIN A 1/2 MILE OF THE FLOOD ZONE

HEAT STRESS + SEDIMENT CONTAMINATION: **80%** OF THE REGIONAL FUEL STORAGE IS IN THE FLOOD ZONE

75% OF THE NET ANNUAL POWER GENERATION IS IN THE 100 YEAR FLOOD ZONE

Mapping risks and vulnerabilities across the region for each of the coastal flood landscapes yielded the Meadowlands as a priority investment area.

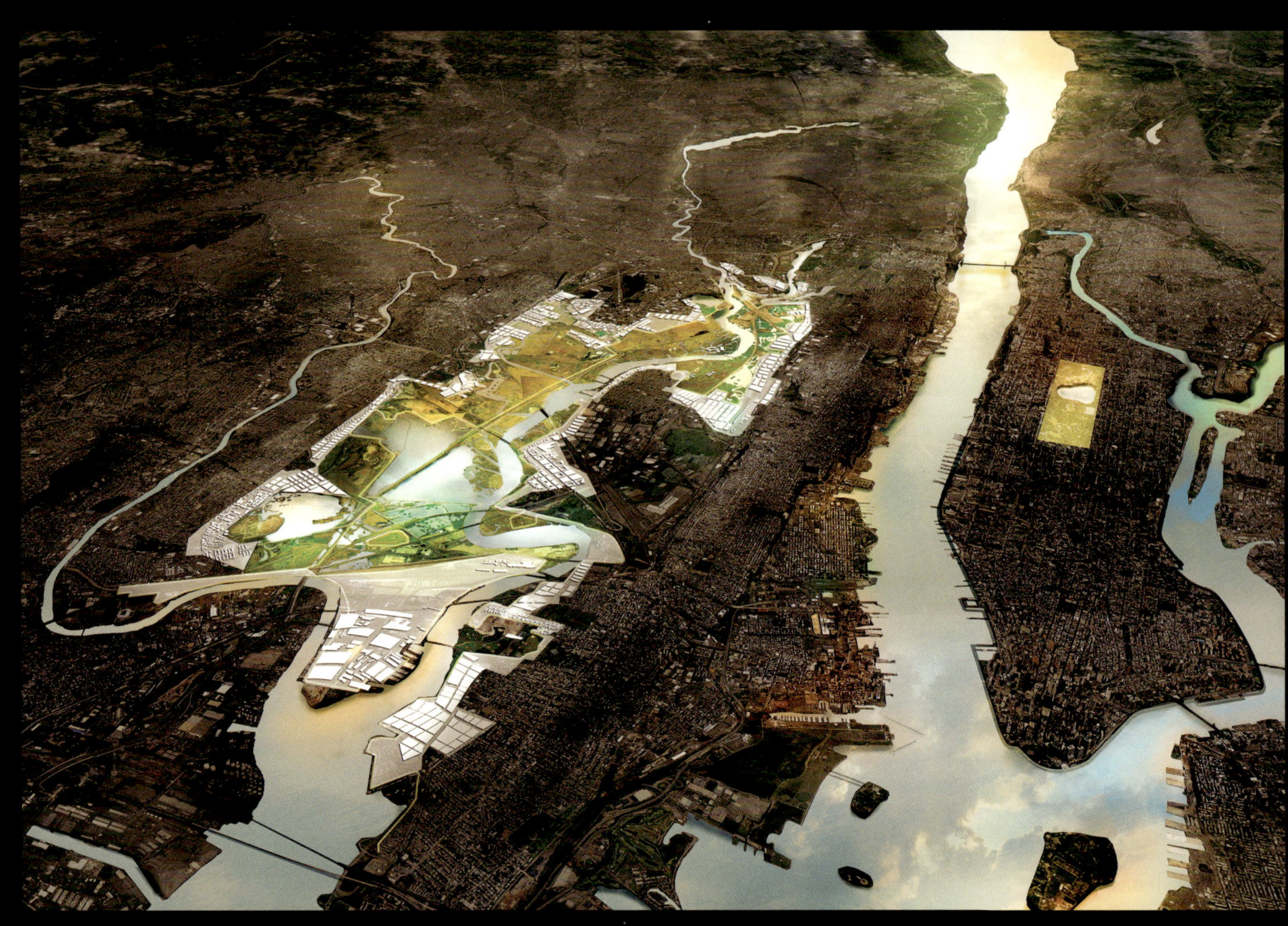

Overview of the New Meadowlands project as a regional attractor for New Jersey and the New York metropolitan area.

Final Proposal: New Meadowlands

For its final design proposal, the team turned to the Meadowlands, a low-lying area in New Jersey, home to critical infrastructure, part of the broader New York City metropolitan area, and prone to flooding. They articulated three guiding principles: protect, connect, and grow. Though there are many elements to the design, two features – Meadowpark and Meadowband – provide consistency across the vast site.

The Meadowpark connects existing and new marshes and freshwater basins with an intricate system of higher and lower berms, providing flood protection from ocean surges and rainwater. With custom dimensions, these berm-formed chambers would capture water. Some would contain polluted waters, while others would separate fresh or brackish water. This system would provide flood protection beyond the municipalities within whose jurisdiction the berms would be constructed. The team conceived the system in such a way that it would result in a contiguous landscape providing public accessibility along the berms and occasional recreational and cultural opportunities. The name Meadowpark underscores the landscape infrastructure's public, recreational character.

The berm along the outer perimeter, which the team has termed the Meadowband, defines the boundary between open landscape and developed urban areas. The team designed the linear topography to act as a civic amenity, with a berm covered by a street lined with commercial, retail, and residential buildings overlooking the park. The street would allow for local traffic, including an affordable mass transit option, preferably Bus Rapid Transit. Entry points to the park, as well as a chain of public spaces – boardwalks, sports fields, sculptures, playgrounds – define the Meadowband as a civic amenity. Development opportunities line the band, all facing the Meadowpark. A series of 'park addresses' line up along this stretch, guiding the ongoing real estate pressure for residential development in a cohesive way. While ground-level development would remain rooted in logistics, upper stories would orient toward the new street and park. The team included each of the project elements – Meadowpark, berms, Meadowband, and redevelopment zones – in each of the pilot areas.

Based on its research of land use throughout the area, the team positioned the Meadowband to fill a gap, becoming a missing link for the Meadowlands basin: a public space that would mediate between different systems (ecology and development) and different scales (hyperlocal to interstate). As the team found, current transportation infrastructure tends to be either supra-regional (Interstate 95) or very local (roads within a small municipality). The proposal would include something in between. For the 14 towns of the Meadowlands, the proposal would provide a common thoroughfare between them using multiple forms of transportation. In doing so, Meadowband would provide a critical connective tissue on the scale of the Meadowlands itself. The team envisions that the audience for this linear, meandering amenity would consist of the inhabitants of existing towns and the residents in new developments that would line the Meadowband. It would also cater to tourists and

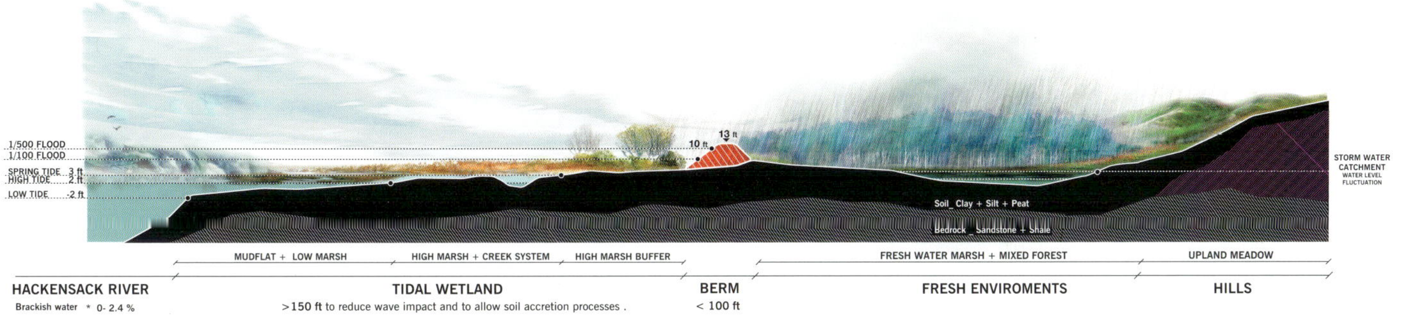

4

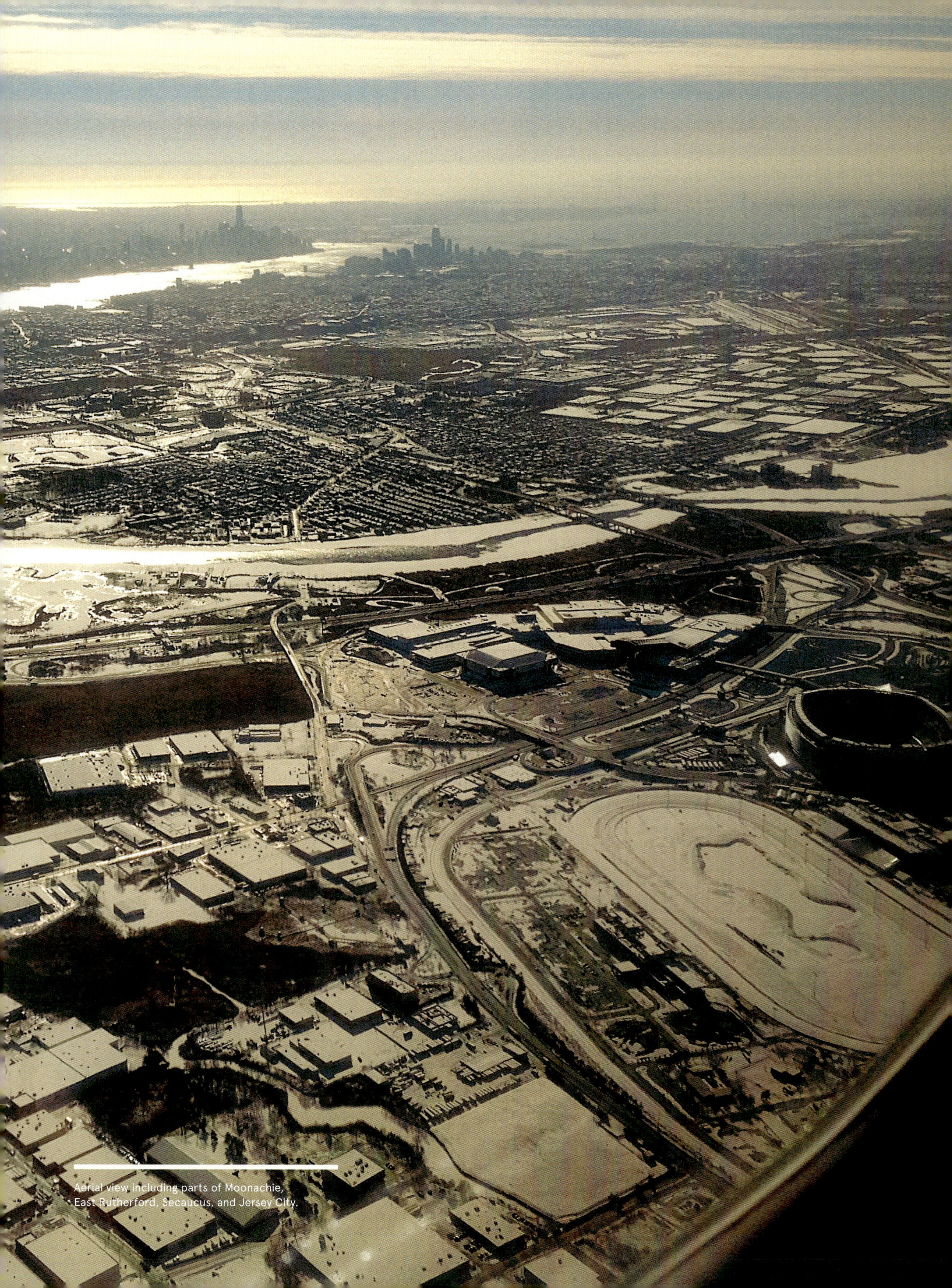

Aerial view including parts of Moonachie, East Rutherford, Secaucus, and Jersey City.

visitors from the region seeking access to what would be its biggest park, providing a chance to explore the area in a recreational way.

Though the project is multi-faceted, the team ensured that each element was completely integrated with the others. By considering both of the main systems – Meadowpark and Meadowband – in full integration, the design delivers the most benefits to wildlife ecology, as well as economic development that otherwise risks going overlooked. The proposed design would also complement various past and ongoing marshland restoration efforts from the Meadowlands Commission. Together, these would become legible as one large, regional wildlife refuge, made accessible to visitors at appropriate places. By tying these different strands together, the project would catalyze value in different developments in the area.

The project would need to be rolled out in phases, allowing designers and stakeholders to evaluate changes incrementally. Within the Meadowlands basin, the team identified three pilot areas for the initial stage of the project. The southern tip consists of South Kearny and the western waterfront of Jersey City. The eastern edge includes Secaucus and a portion of Jersey City. Finally, the northern edge contains sections of Little Ferry, Moonachie, Carlstadt, Teterboro, and South Hackensack. In each pilot, the project consists of multiple elements: first, the Meadowband berms and public space design and construction; second, rezoning; and, third, integration with other ongoing initiatives.

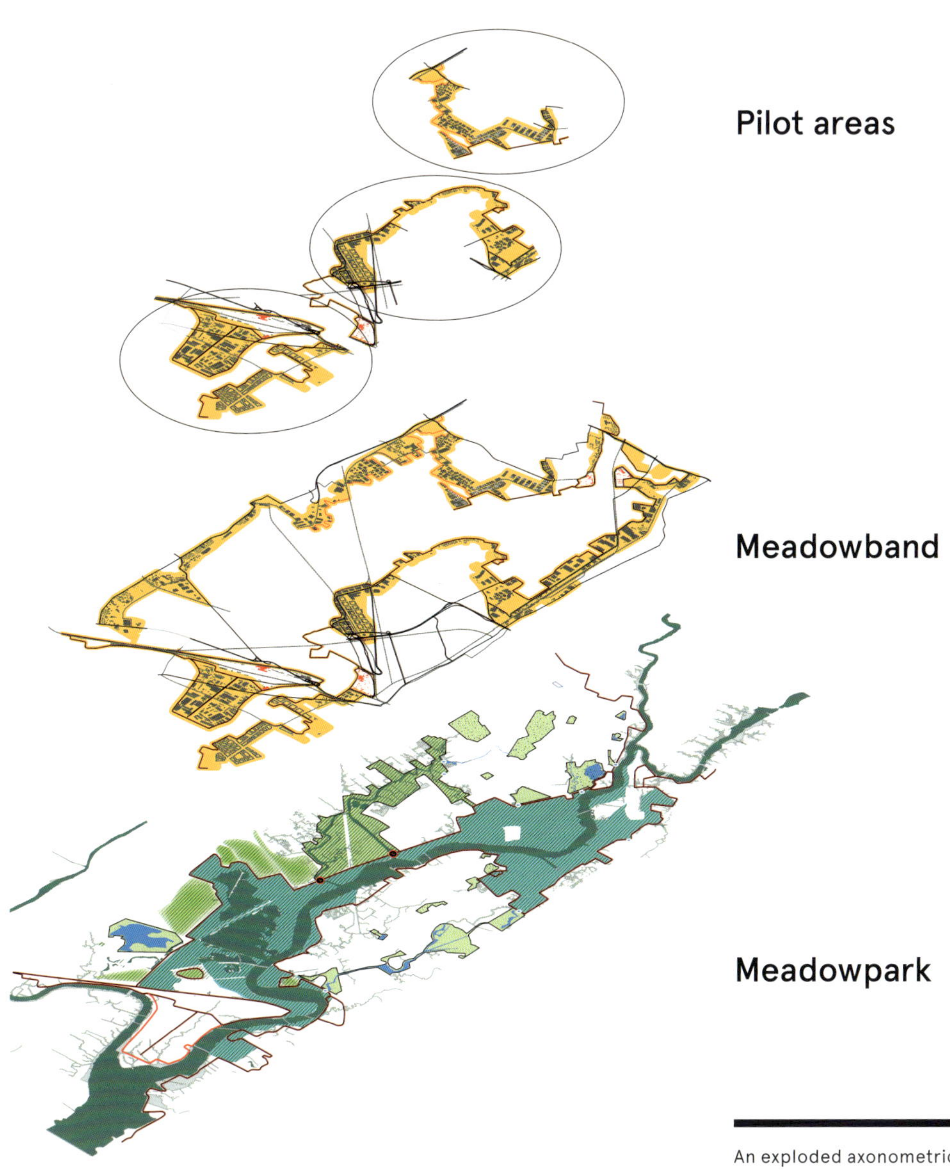

An exploded axonometric shows the Meadowband and Meadowpark elements as well as the three priority pilot areas on the very top.

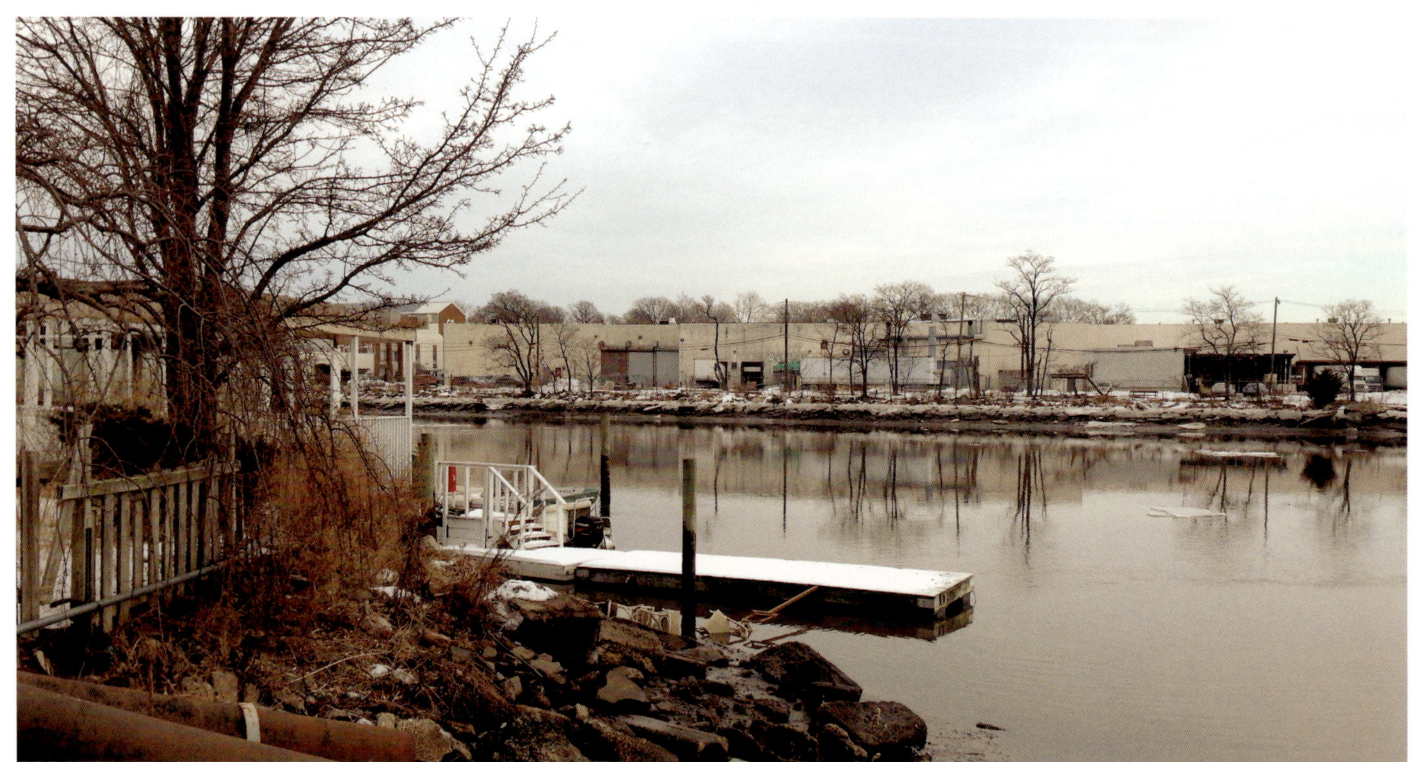

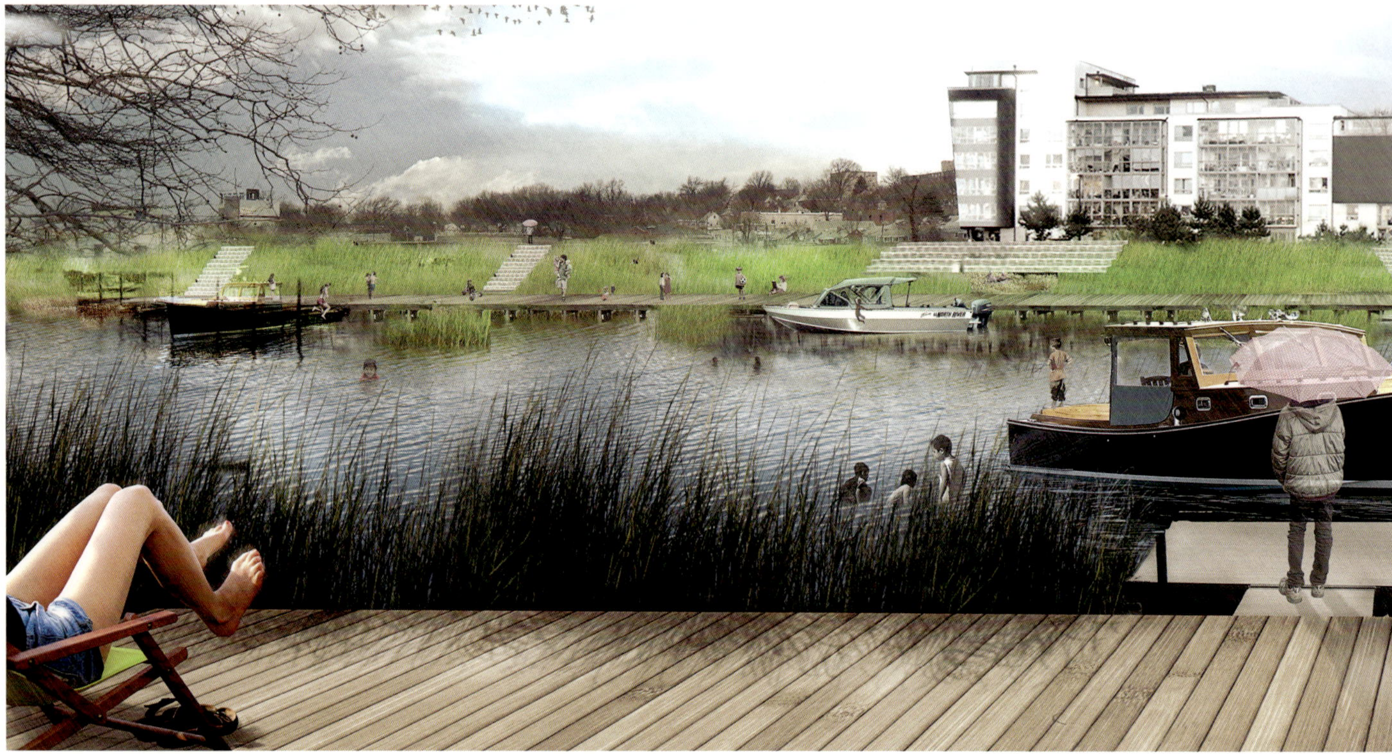

Development patterns for offices, warehouses, and more recently, multi-family residential complexes in the Meadowlands area have been largely of the suburban type: large lots, ground-level parking surrounding buildings, buffer zones around the lots,and direct access to limited-access highways. This project would serve as an opportunity to transform the land-use dynamic into a more dense, durable and multifunctional urban pattern. This would necessitate decreasing parcel sizes, eliminating buffer zones, placing parking in basements, and using the local streets to make better connections with adjacent areas.

The outer Meadowband berm would help protect low-lying areas from ocean surges. Composed of different sections in different locations, it would range from completely soft to hybrid to hard, in response to availability of sediment material (sand, clay, or soil) and available space. It would emulate the innovative and tested third-generation Dutch dike system, which abandons the hard-wall approach in favor of building with nature, providing multifunctional use and flexibility toward changing performance criteria. Multifunctional dikes can also anchor the status and maintenance of the berm. Despite their flexibility, they have proven to be extremely durable.

Positioning the berm in the landscape would ensure maximum stability by coupling with robust existing elements. Marshlands in front of the berm, for example, would reduce wave velocity and generate extra dike stability. The berm could also run adjacent to existing landfills. Besides providing stability, such a location would also cap pollution leakage from the landfills into the wetland. To cut the overall cost, the team proposed configurations with the shortest possible perimeter.

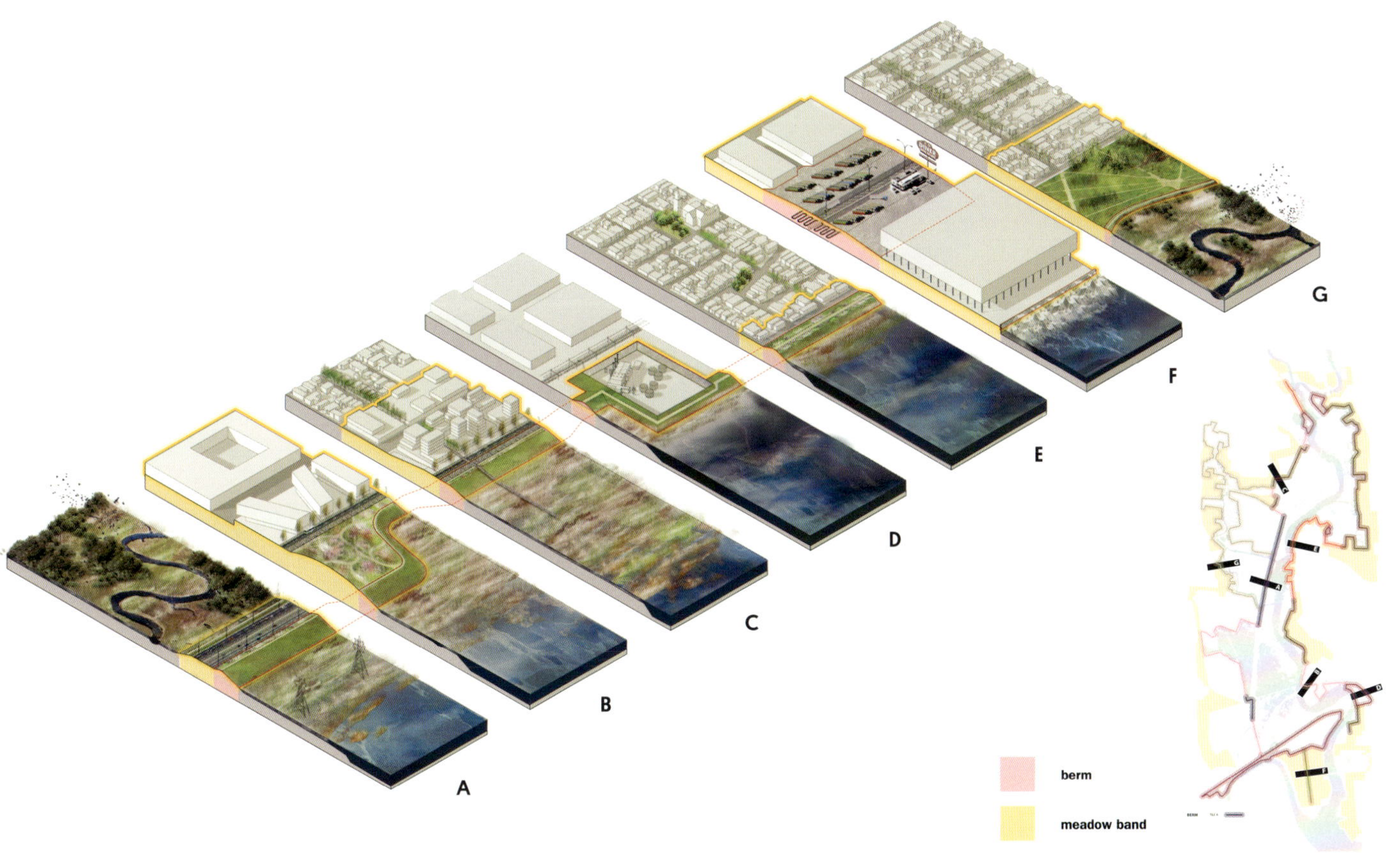

4

Various sections of the Meadowband could have different context-specific identities along different stretches of the outer berm. Recurring elements in every section would include a boardwalk/sidewalk, a bike path, and a local street for emergencies and for access to newly emerging residential developments along its protected edge. The team would widen the local street enough to have a dedicated line for Bus Rapid Transit. Along these linear systems, various accents would widen the boardwalk, allowing for playgrounds, park entrances, sculptures, bike stations, etc. These accents would activate the boardwalk and help draw an audience. The boardwalk itself would have enough room to accommodate terraces and patios for adjacent restaurants.

Streets – the oldest and most affordable public spaces of almost any city – tend to be the public backbone of cities. A great street offers the most iconic views, valuable addresses, and, of course, access to different neighborhoods. The Meadowlands has long lacked such a street. Taking that into account, the team proposed a street that would ring the outer edge of the Meadowpark, linking the park on one side and the new developments on the other. This street would provide access to both sides. It would connect disjointed fragments, taking advantage of the adjacencies and proximities between different fragments of the Meadowlands.

As built, marshes and the ecological reserve abut the backsides of properties, reducing the accessibility of the open space system by effectively removing it from public view. The team proposed to reverse this relationship between road, property, and marsh, orienting buildings to the park with their street-facing sides. With this simple flip, the park would gain visibility, and property addresses would be linked with the public amenity.

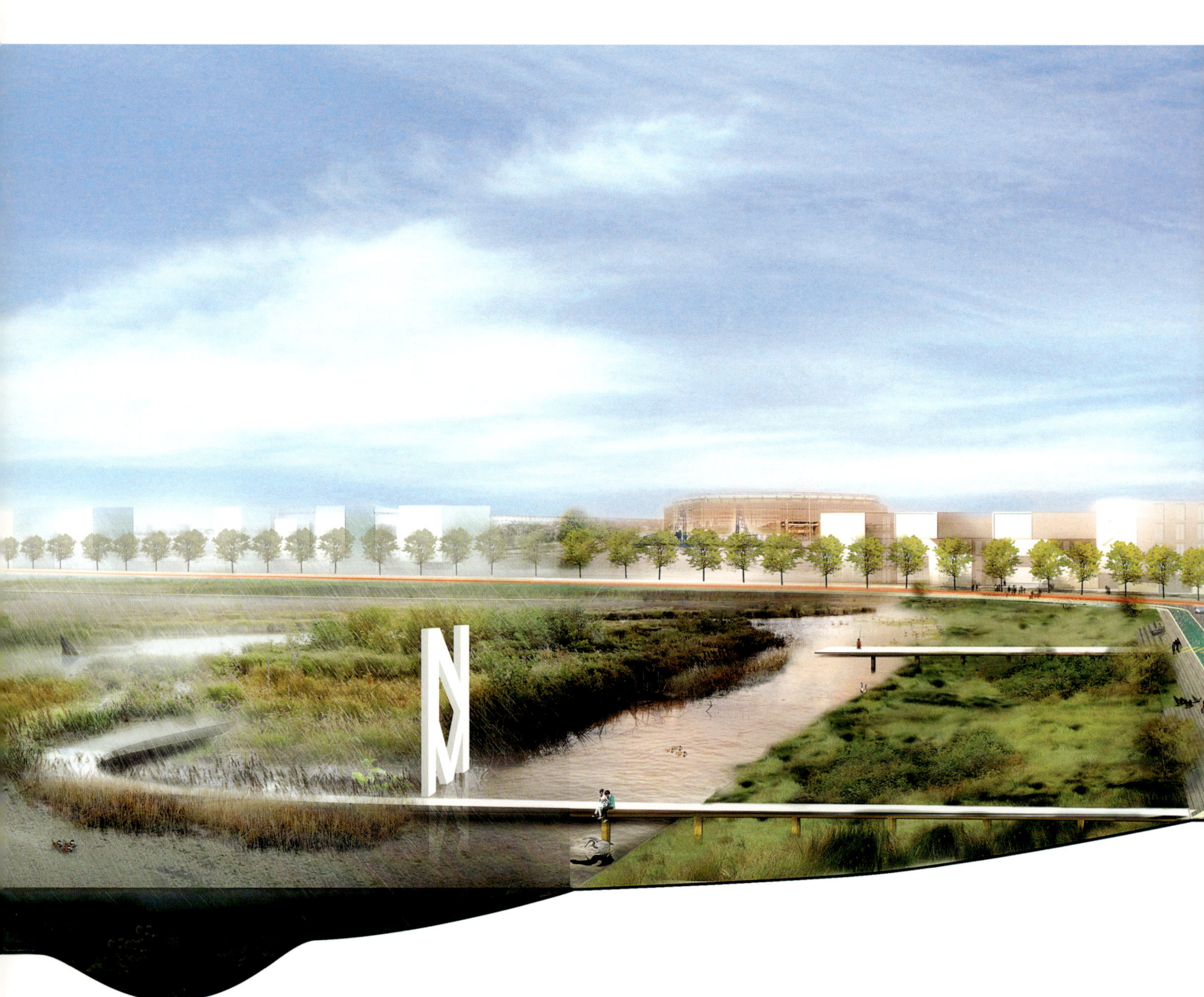

The Meadowband would provide a form of connective public space. Designed on the scale of the Meadowlands, it would become an icon that would generate park access, and it would provide a venue to understand and read the basin as a whole. It would allow for adjacent towns and neighborhoods to be connected without the need to move to a higher-order transportation system (from foot to bike to mass-transit to car). Once connected in this way, the various parts of the Meadowlands would start to add value to each other, rather than existing autonomously. The park, for example, would make the neighborhoods more valuable, park access would make the park more valued, and some local circulation would be taken off the major limited-access highways. A new public boardwalk would start to draw both inhabitants and visitors. When Boardwalks do not have sufficient foot traffic, they fail, and the few visitors walking, running, or cycling on them feel insecure. To counter this, the team's design includes a local street along the boardwalk meant to diminish that risk, and to increase passage, flow, and visibility on the Meadowband.

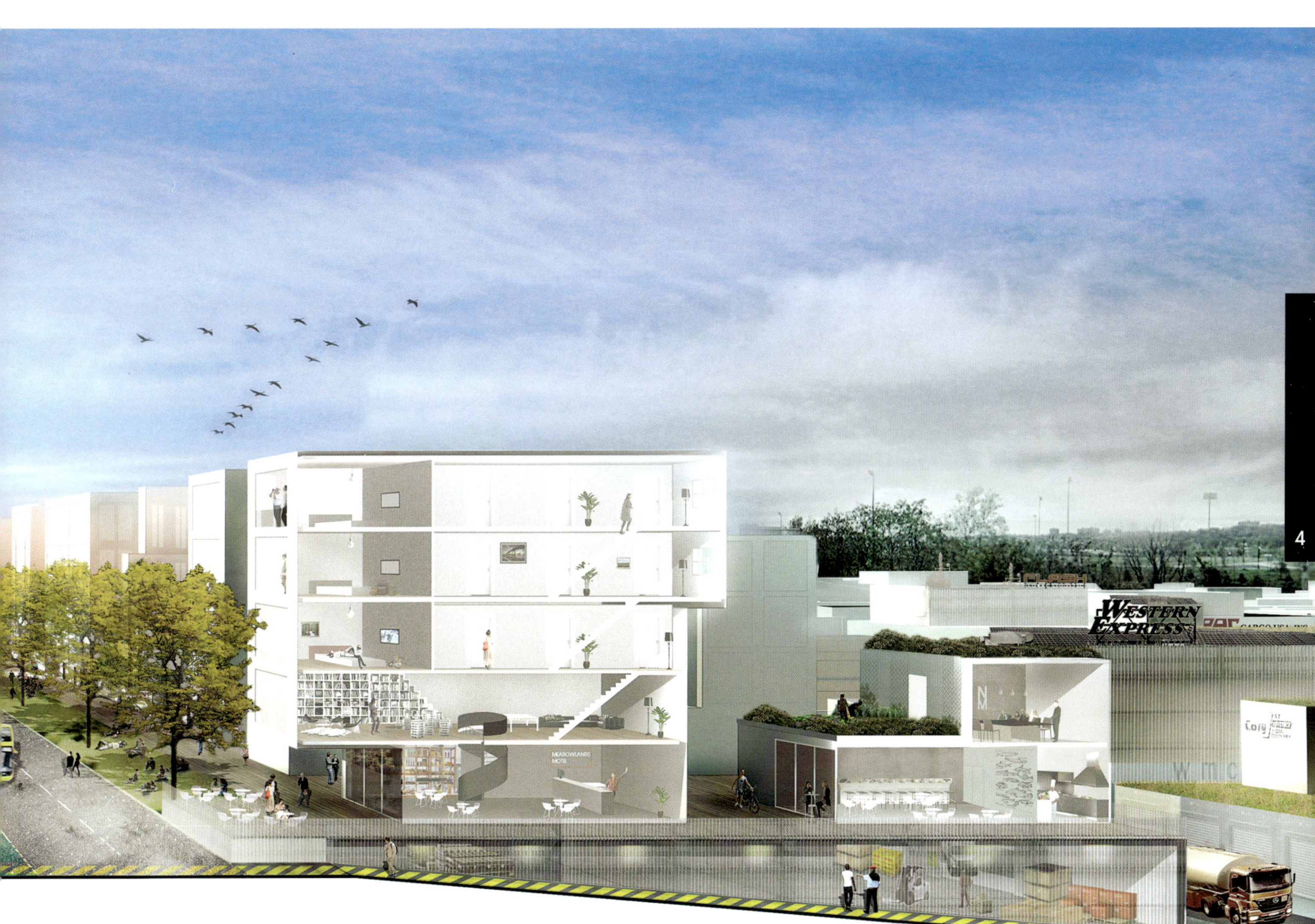

4

The Meadowband connects disparate development fragments and allows multiplier effects between park, neighborhood, and intensified use of existing warehousing zones to become tangible. It is not only a civic amenity and a public space. It also acts as the opportunity creator for a series of (re-)developments. Residential projects along the Meadowband, with an address at and a view of the park, will be an attractive opportunity.

Design Process

The team identified a diverse set of opportunities, at the crossroad of which it proposed a project to make the Meadowlands more resilient. It developed a coalition of area stakeholders, including mayors of municipalities, ecological activists, business owners, and developers, who together articulated a desire to think beyond the status quo and transform the Meadowlands into a stronger, more ecologically sound, more economically attractive area. The team's design had to extend benefits beyond protection against flooding alone.

The area faces mounting development pressure to increase its logistics capacity, expand its role as part of the region's supply chain, and create more opportunities for residential living. The team found that these pressures could be accommodated in the region if appropriate mass transit options were made available. Furthermore, the parkland, industrial, and residential components would each add value to the other.

The team emphasized the need to focus on design integration, weaving different intervention strategies together in a masterplan that addressed the area's complex interests and uses. This would help ensure a holistic approach to building resilience that would answer the needs of different stakeholders.

To help justify substantial federal investment toward protecting land from future flooding, the team argued that it was imperative to use that land more effectively. For that reason, it proposed shifting from suburban to urban-style zoning and land use. Single-story warehouse zones, where freestanding buildings are surrounded by open parking lots, would be up-zoned to encourage multi-story development; additionally, areas around the Meadowband would be rezoned to include multi-story residential uses. The development vision along the Meadowband was therefore created to grow structures with smaller footprints and taller elevations.

These stakeholders also voiced the need to bring public perception of the area up to reality. The Meadowlands had long existed in the public imagination as an isolated industrial zone or even a dumping ground, but the Meadowlands Commission's protracted efforts at ecological restoration and other district-wide improvements have helped the landscape turn a new leaf. The notion of the Meadowlands becoming a landscaped park and a wildlife refuge is no longer a remote dream: with the New Meadowlands project, it is now a pressing reality.

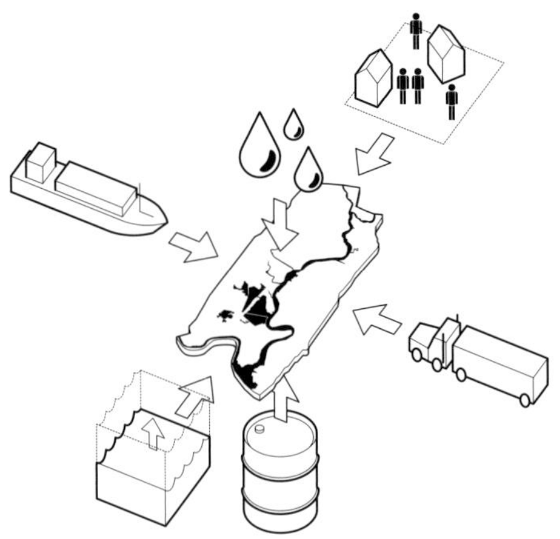

Today's challenges include high-risk flooding, competing residential and supply chain development pressure, pollution, ecological remediation pressures, lack of intermediate connectivity. No science-driven scenarios foresee a future reduction in flooding. Most see a sea level rise and an increase in precipitation, both of which increase risks for the region. In addition, the arrival of large post-Panamax ships in the New York harbor will likely increase the demand for supply chain functions (warehousing, railroads, etc.). At the same time, projected population growth for the greater New York metropolitan area includes 1.5 million new residents over the next two decades. For both of these development pressures, planning experts largely agree that their occurrence in closer proximity to main urban centers may reduce travel times and concurrent carbon dioxide emissions, therfore yielding a more sustainable growth pattern. In other words, current evolutions will only aggravate the tensions between ecological, residential, and supply chain needs for space, and existing developments will face higher flood risks in the near future. On a more local level, the connections within the Meadowlands do not take advantage of adjacencies that may offer temporary relief during emergencies.

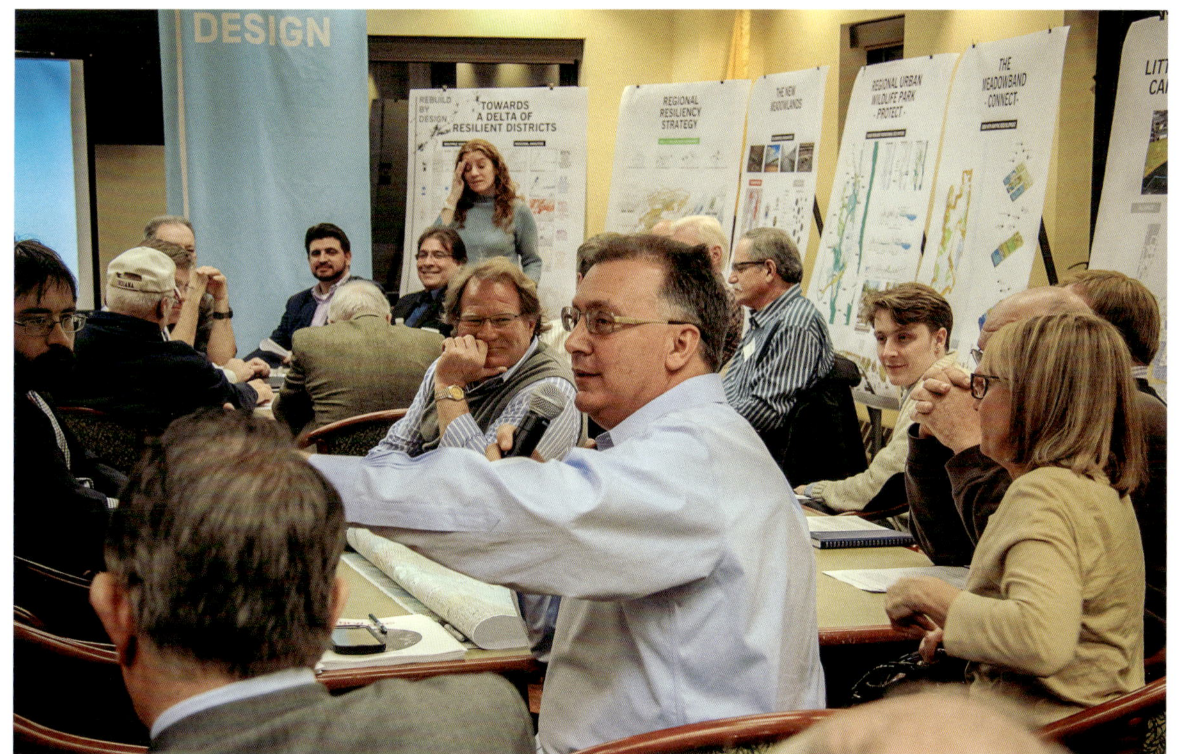

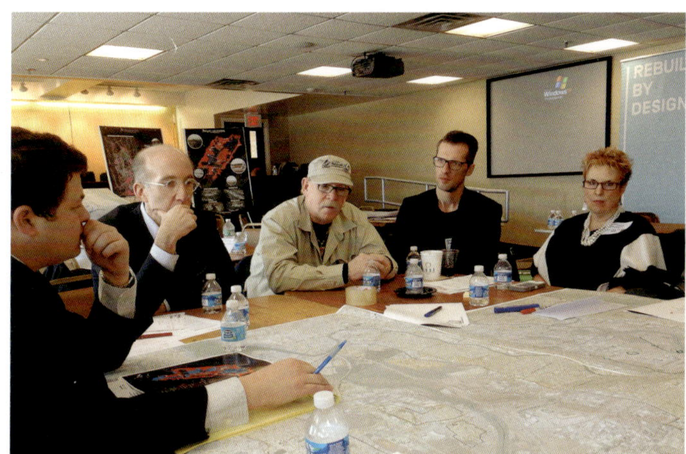

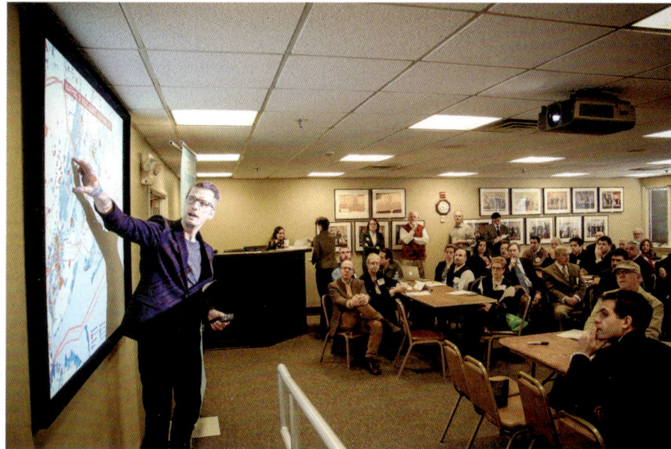

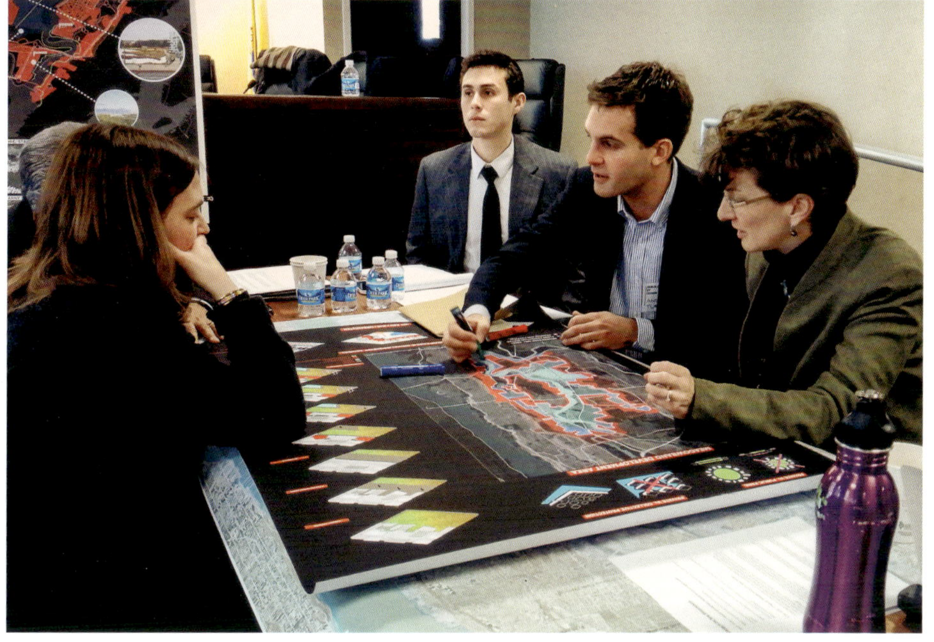

The team engaged in substantive outreach efforts with the State of New Jersey, the Meadowlands Commission, and various municipalities in the area. It worked closely with environmental groups such as Hackensack Riverkeeper, as well as with the Meadowlands Chamber of Commerce. It also included major vital network operators and owners such as the Port Authority of New York & New Jersey and PSEG.

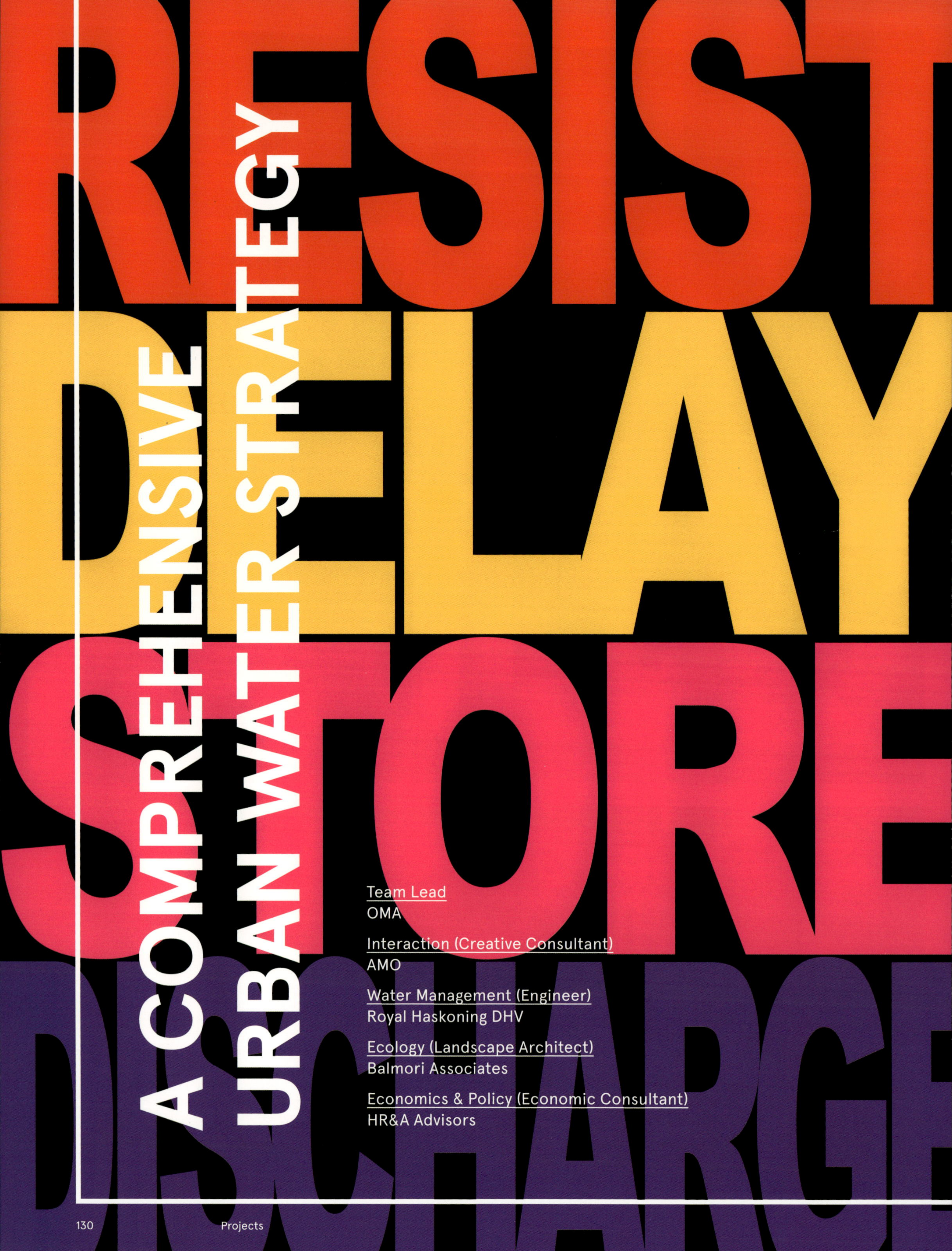

A COMPREHENSIVE URBAN WATER STRATEGY

Team Lead
OMA

Interaction (Creative Consultant)
AMO

Water Management (Engineer)
Royal Haskoning DHV

Ecology (Landscape Architect)
Balmori Associates

Economics & Policy (Economic Consultant)
HR&A Advisors

OMA Team

Within the Sandy-affected region, New Jersey's communities of Jersey City, Hoboken, and Weehawken are susceptible to both flash flood and storm surge. The team recognized that in these integrated urban environments, discreet one-house-at-a-time solutions do not make sense. What is required is a comprehensive approach that acknowledges the density and complexity of the context, galvanizes a diverse community of beneficiaries, and defends the entire city including its assets and citizens.

The OMA team's proposal includes a four-pronged comprehensive urban water strategy which would deploy programmed hard infrastructure and soft landscape for coastal defense (resist); policy recommendations, guidelines, and urban infrastructure to slow rainwater runoff (delay); a circuit of interconnected green infrastructure to store and direct excess rainwater (store); and water pumps and alternative routes to support drainage (discharge).

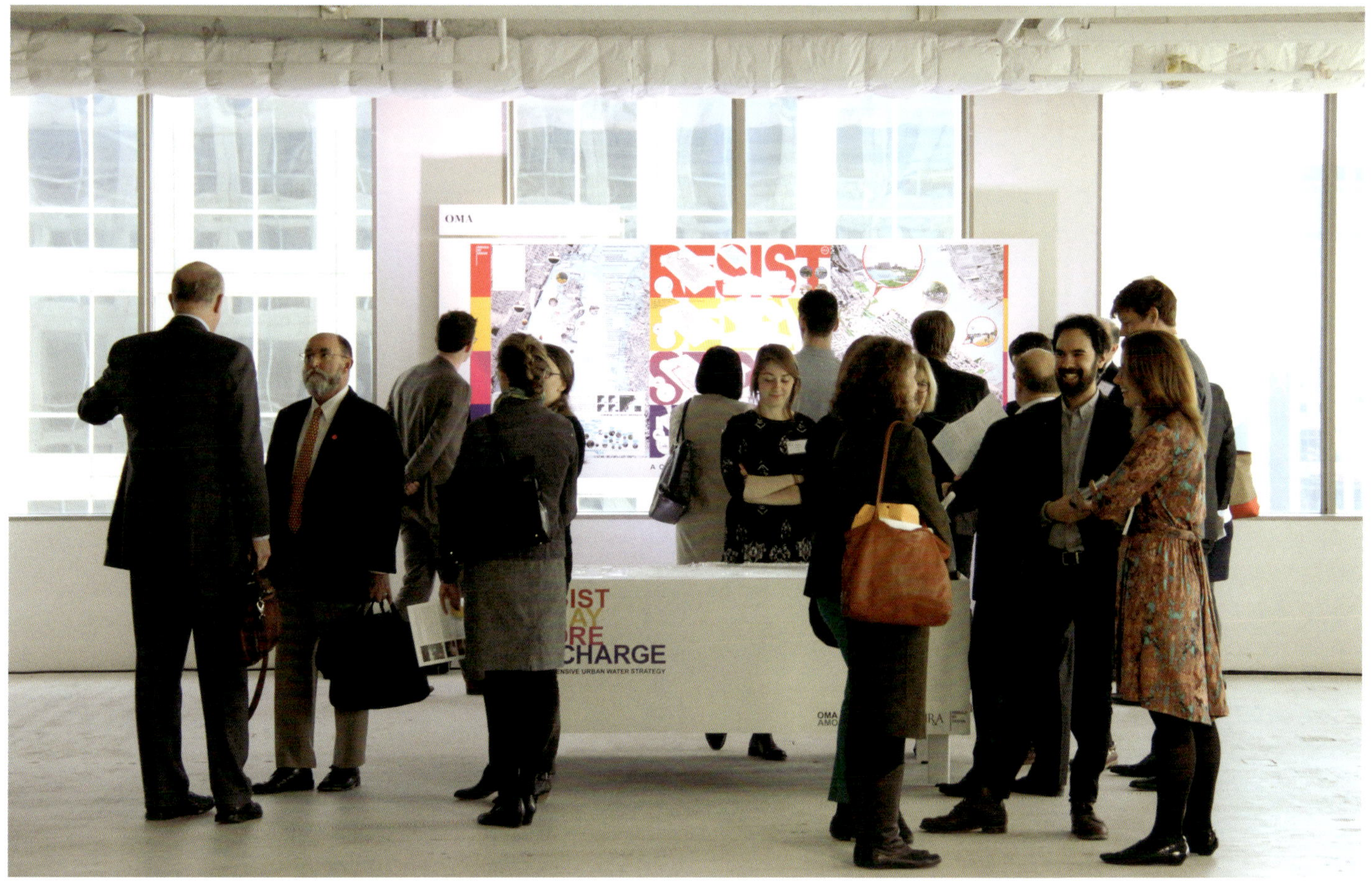

4

Approach to Quantifying Risk

The Sandy-affected region is a long coastline with many assets at risk. To reach a fully comprehensive solution, the team needed to prioritize, build smart, and recognize where best to focus resources. The team felt that investments in risk reduction should not only be integrated into built environments, but also empower communities and the economy, allowing the region to grow resiliently.

OMA's approach was framed by a desire to understand and quantify flood risk. In doing so, the team was better positioned to identify those opportunities that present the greatest impact, the best value, and the highest potential – the priority areas of focus.

Flood risk in the Sandy-affected region is increasing due to the effects of sea level rise and development. The team ruled out doing nothing as an option that would be too costly. To make the region resilient, a comprehensive approach would be needed but is considered beyond the city's means and not feasible. Therefore investments must be prioritized to achieve effective resilience. The OMA team plans to approach this extremely large and complex challenge via the concept of flood risk, which takes into account both the region's vulnerability and the assets at risk.

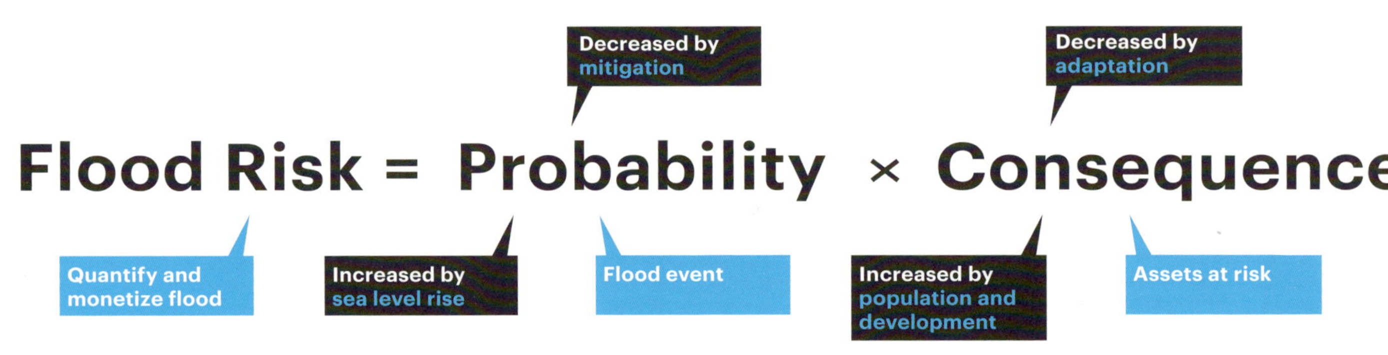

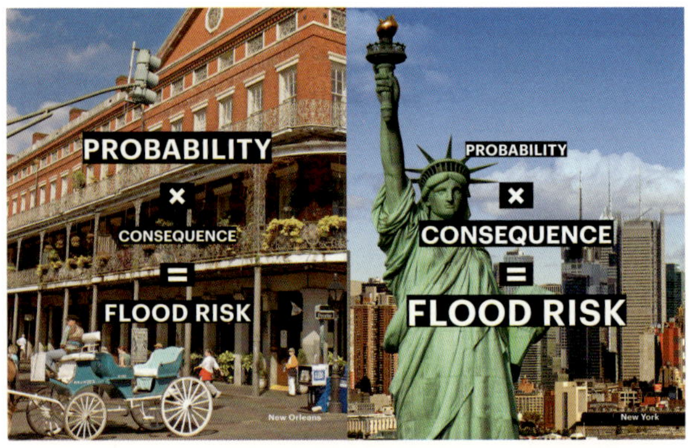

What factors should be considered? Hurricanes are more frequent in New Orleans than in the tri-state area but present a lower flood risk because that region has fewer people and assets.

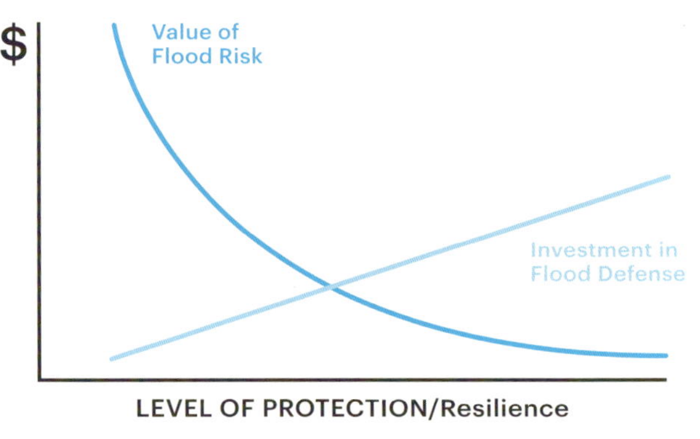

Planning Principle: Defend existing concentration of value, where cost effective.

Measuring flood risk, value, and impact allowed the team to identify the areas of highest potential for intervention, becoming their areas of focus.

RISK

VALUE

IMPACT

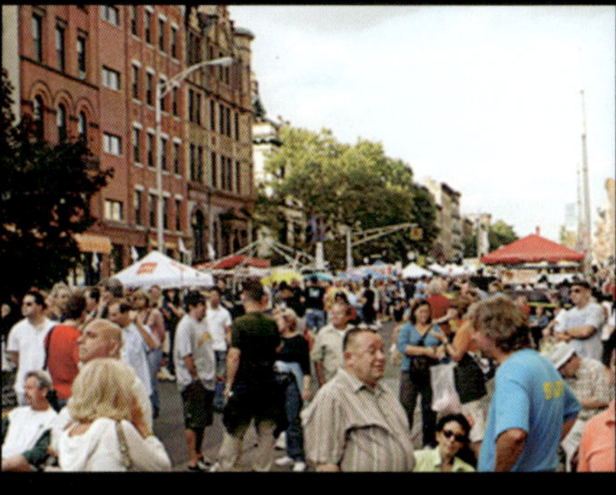

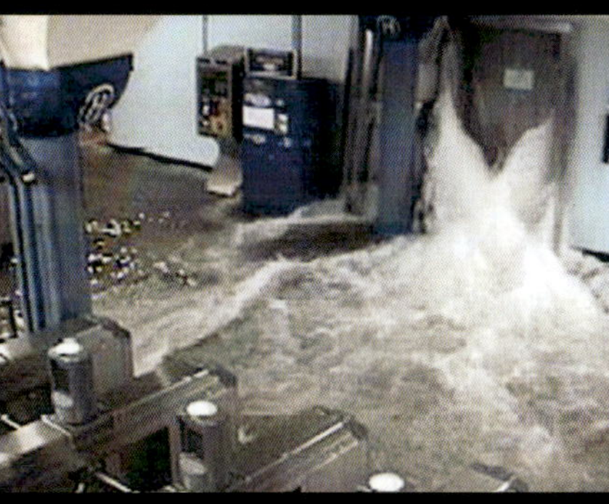

Hoboken is the nation's fourth densest city

30% population rise 2000 to 2010

50K daily transit users x three-month shutdown

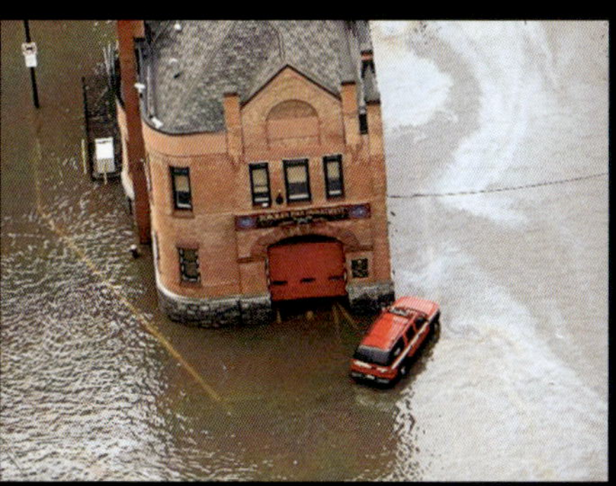

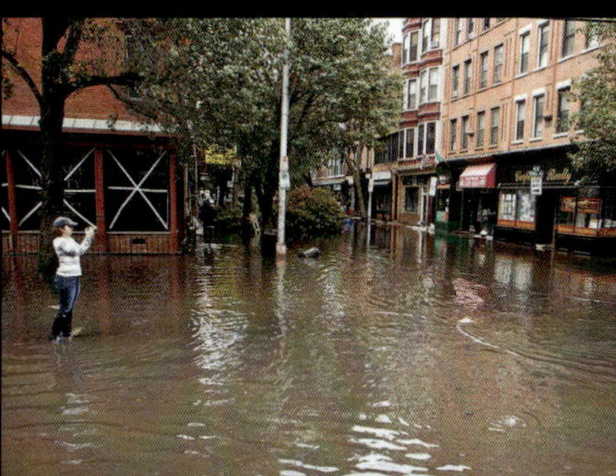

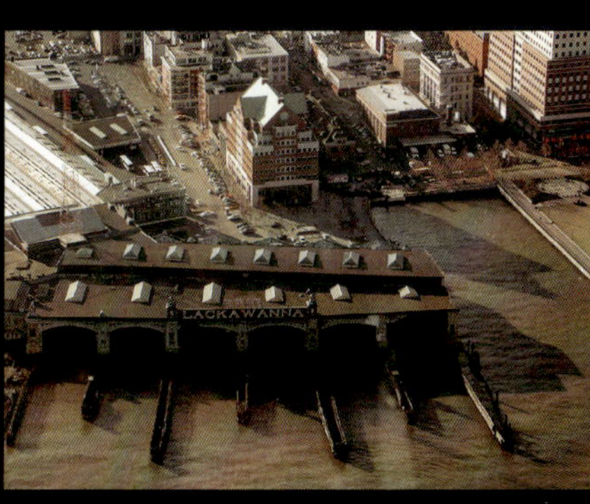

94% of urban surface area is impermeable

Estimated value of real estate and economic assets: +/- $2.5B

100% of regional utility infrastructure lies in the flood zone

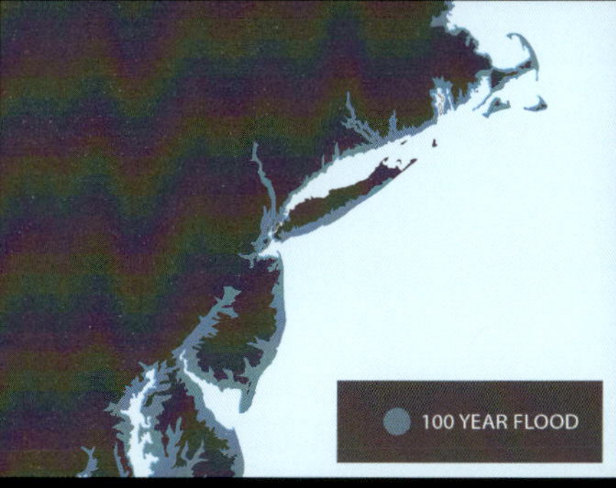

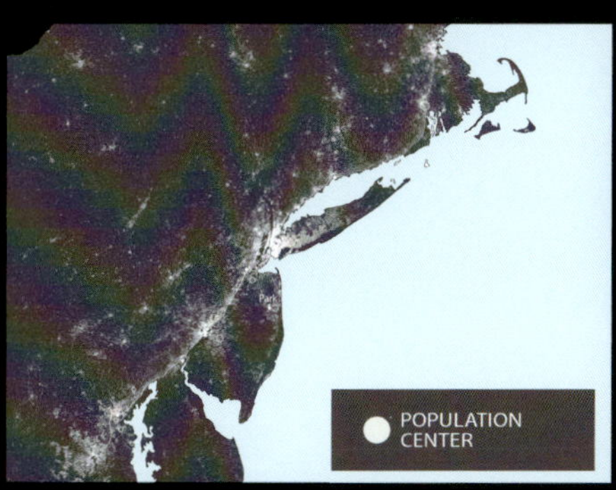

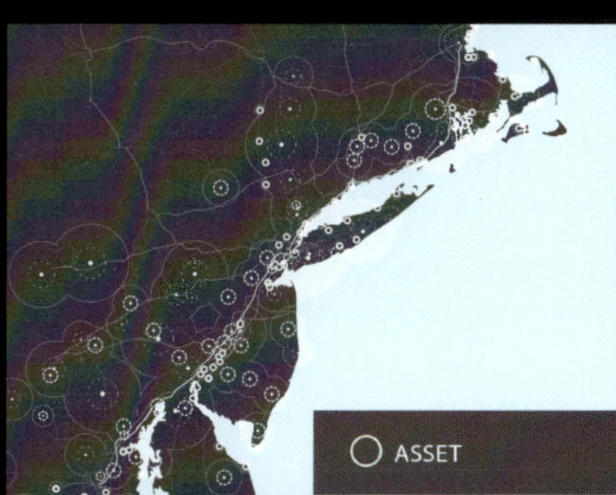

100-year flood line. Source: Federal Emergency Management Agency

Population density. Source: 2010 Census

High-impact centers of industry, tourism and infrastructure. Source: US Energy Information Administration

FOCUS

OMA focused on the high-impact nodes of the network system which defines today's modern built society. These nodes are highly vulnerable, yet very productive, physical locations in a network that has stacked functions and a larger regional impact. Making these critical nodes resilient improves the resilience of a larger region.

Together, risk, value, and impact justify the scale of investment required for a comprehensive solution.

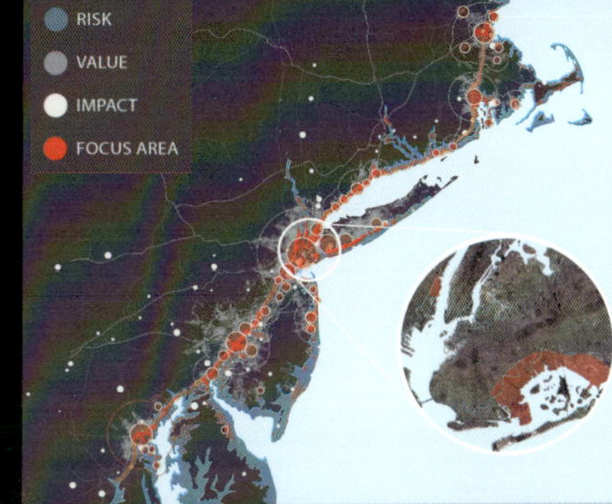

Design Opportunities

OMA's matrix of opportunities charts focus areas at different geographic scales against the spectrum of solutions represented by the team's expertise. The resulting opportunities are a selection of case studies that showcase how the team's approach might be used to transform the region.

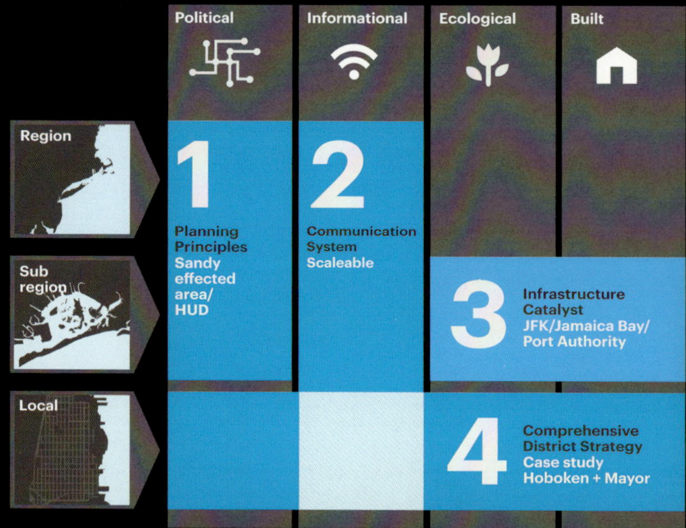

Planning Principles

To support the future growth of the region in an environment constrained by flood risk, deciding where to grow will be critical. This will mean focusing new growth in those areas that can be optimally defended and, conversely, limiting exposure in those areas that cannot - citadel cities versus amphibious villages - remaining safe, but also enjoying the shore.

Communication Systems

Challenges are posed to communications before, during, and after a flood event. In anticipating floods and building resilience, it is essential for all stakeholders to share a common understanding of the risks and their implications. Although efforts continue to be made at outreach and capacity building, more can be done to make information accessible — a Flood Risk 101.

A profusion of information must be negotiated in navigating a flood event. Consolidating and filtering this information into a Bloomberg or ESPN for flood events can better serve users - whether government decision makers, first responders, community groups, or private citizens - but in the event of a disruption or failure, what alternative systems of communication are at the community's disposal? How can resilience be built into communication systems?

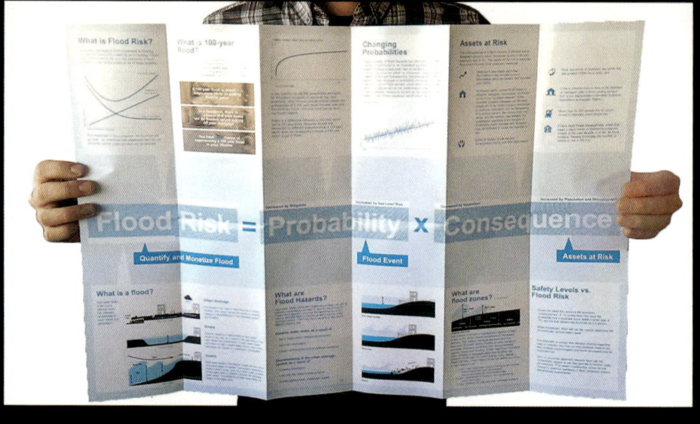

Food Risk 101

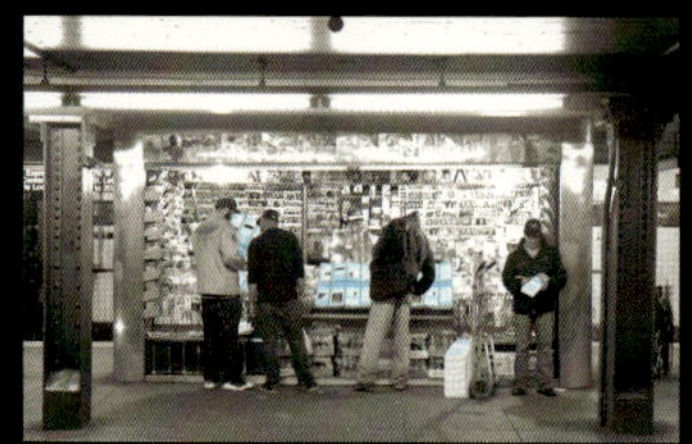

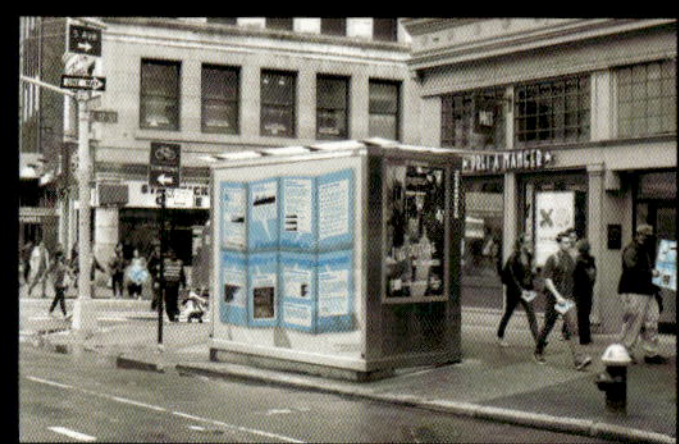

Distribution Tactics
Newstand,Advertisements, Apps

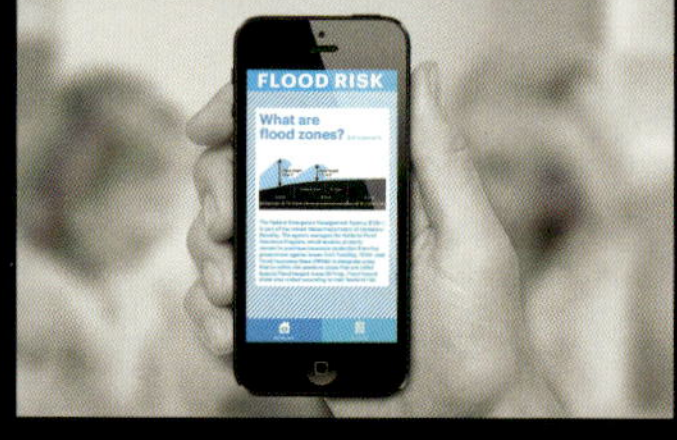

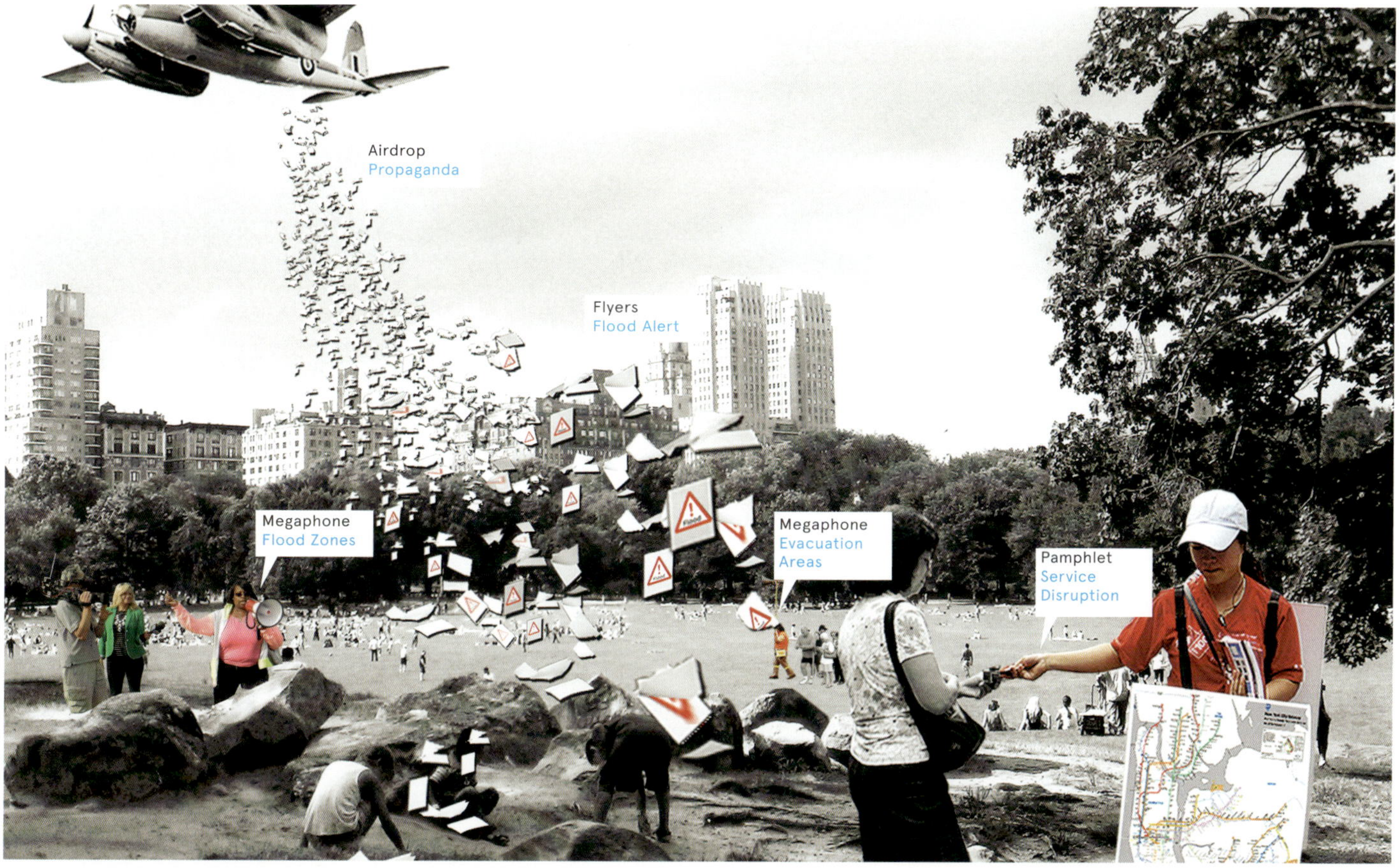

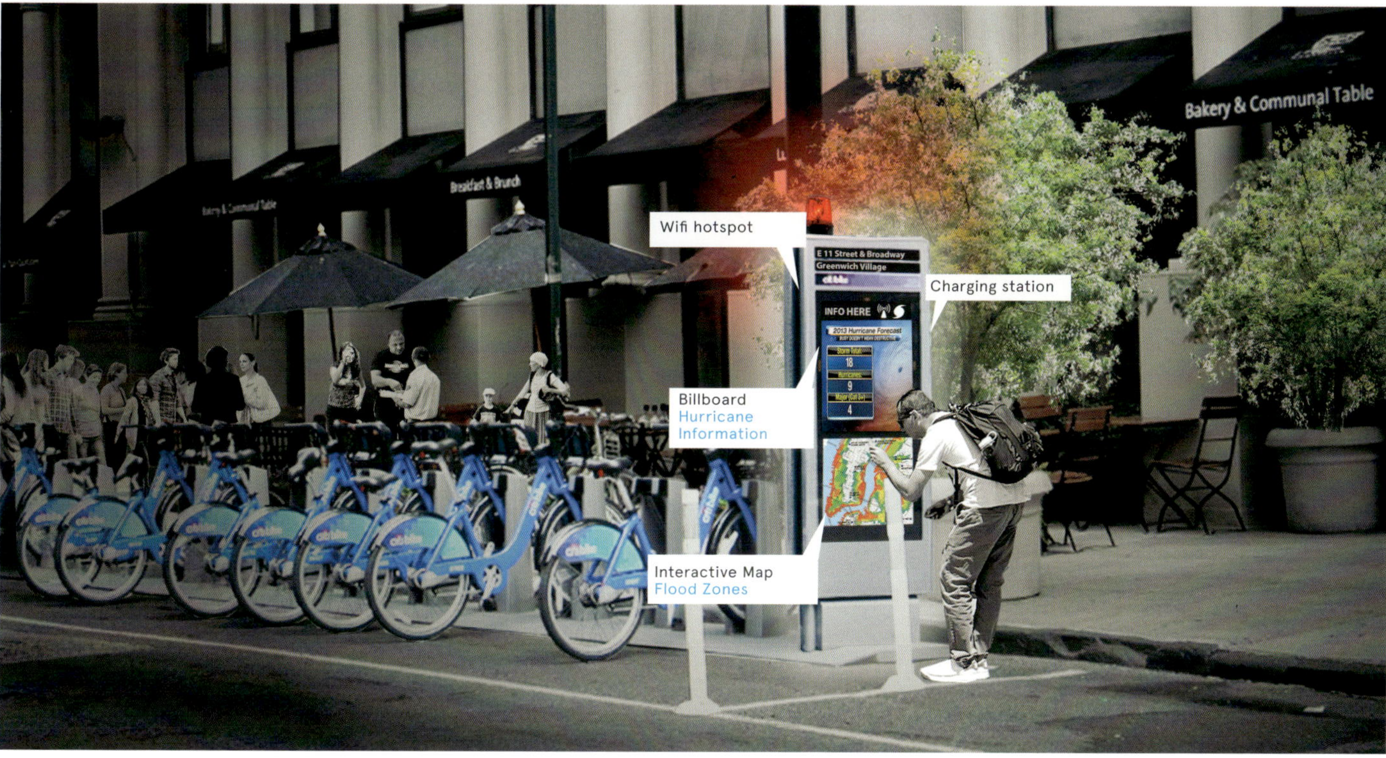

4

Alternative Information Delivery:
During the event of a disruption or failure, how can resilience be built into communication systems? Alternative methods of distributing information could utilize existing signage to communicate instant updates (above) or adapt existing amenities to respond to emergency need (below).

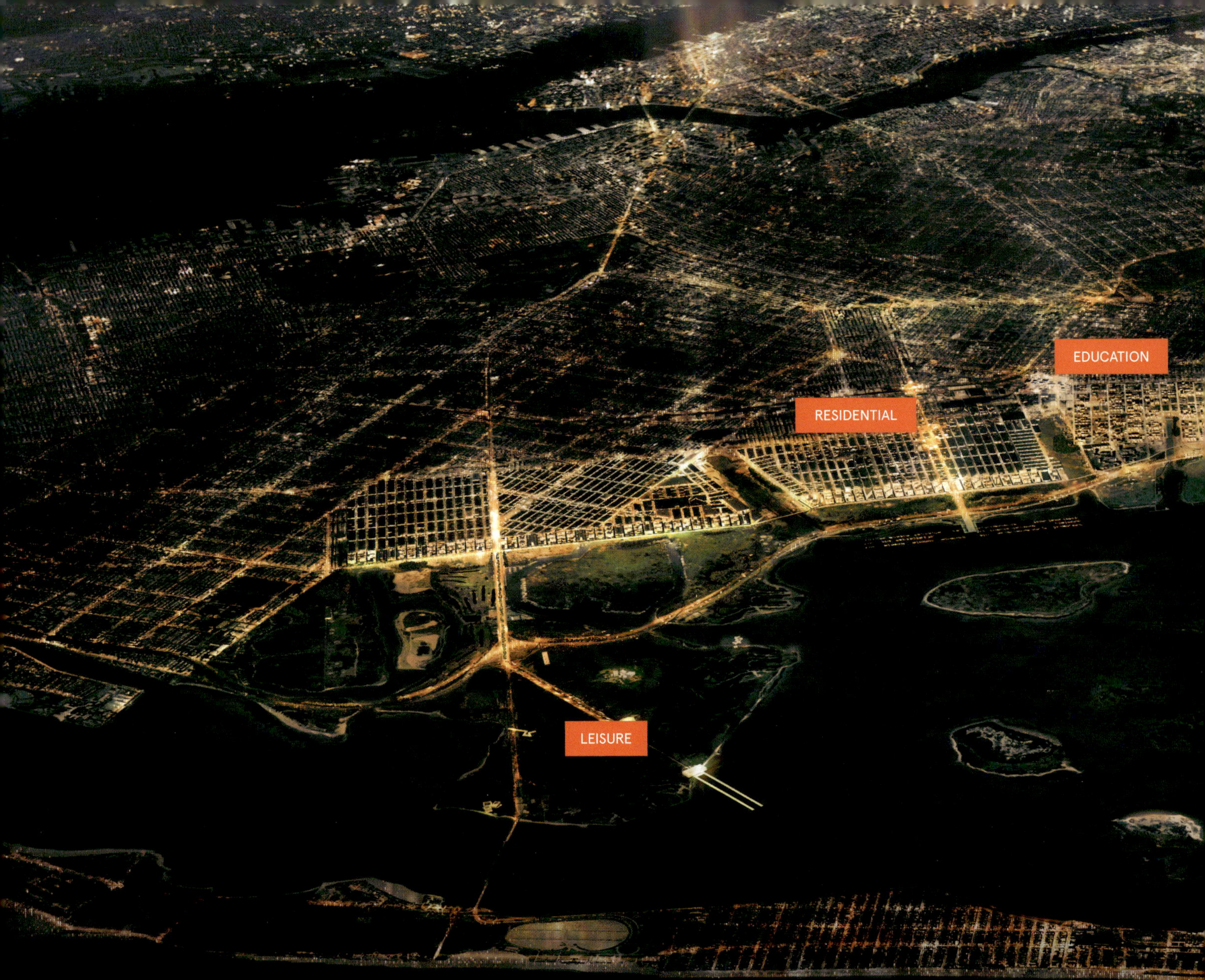

Infrastructure Catalyst

JFK International Airport is a vital node in the region's infrastructure. As part of Jamaica Bay, it is also highly vulnerable to flood risk. Although the airport is capable of "taking care if its own problems," this asset could be leveraged to promote the common flood defense of the Jamaica Bay area. That means integrating the airport into a larger tiered defense system and using it as a catalyst for growth — growth that will help fuel and fund the transformation of the area and position Jamaica Bay as a future economic driver for New York City.

Clockwise from above:
Airport City
Aerial View Showing Flood Defense Strategy
Enabling Transit

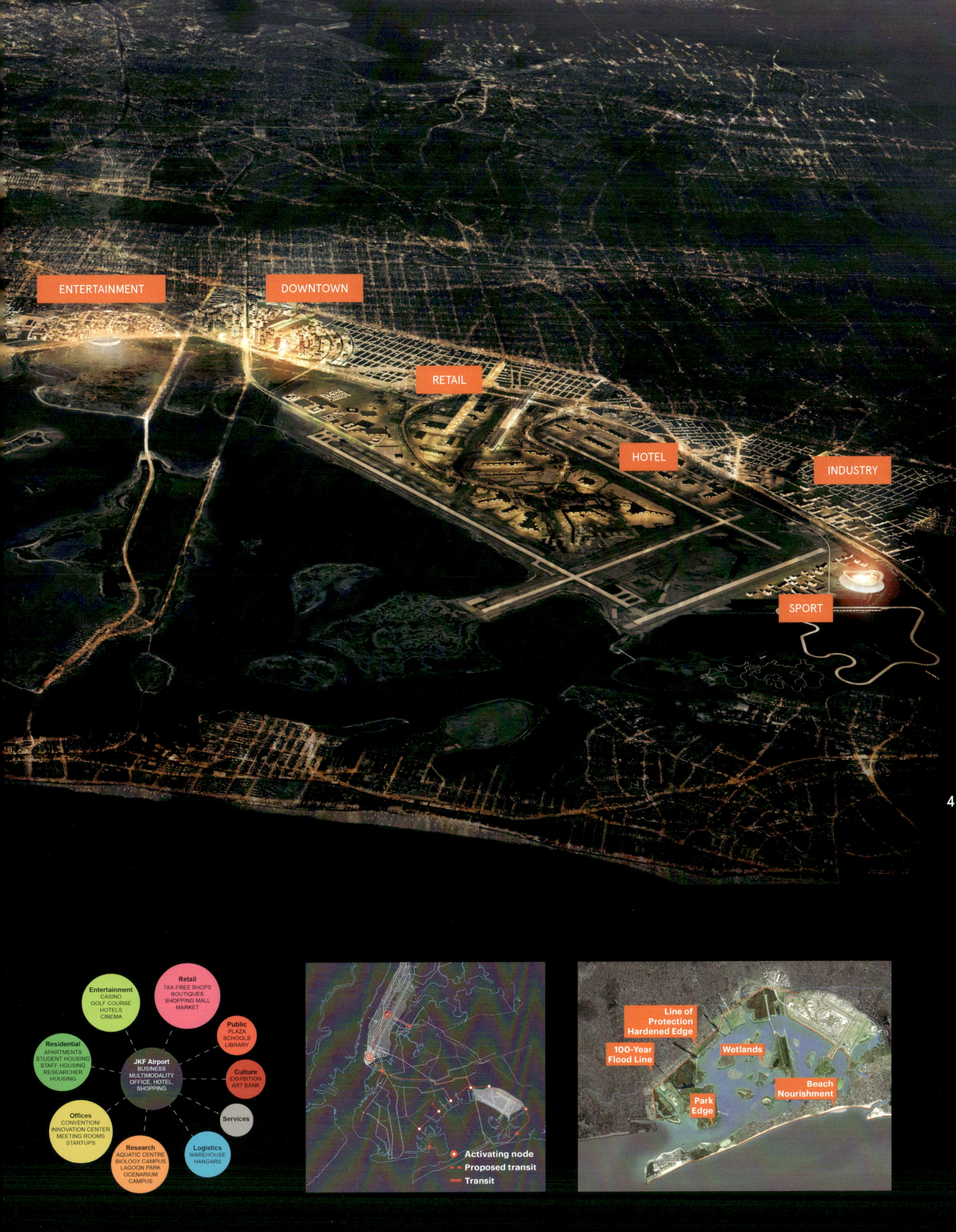
ENTERTAINMENT
DOWNTOWN
RETAIL
HOTEL
INDUSTRY
SPORT
4
Entertainment
CASINO
GOLF COURSE
HOTELS
CINEMA
Retail
TAX-FREE SHOPS
BOUTIQUES
SHOPPING MALL
MARKET
Public
PLAZA
SCHOOLS
LIBRARY
Residential
APARTMENTS
STUDENT HOUSING
STAFF HOUSING
RESEARCHER
HOUSING
JKF Airport
BUSINESS
MULTIMODALITY
OFFICE, HOTEL,
SHOPPING
Culture
EXHIBITION
ART BANK
Services
Offices
CONVENTION/
INNOVATION CENTER
MEETING ROOMS
STARTUPS
Research
AQUATIC CENTRE
BIOLOGY CAMPUS
LAGOON PARK
OCENARIUM
CAMPUS
Logistics
WAREHOUSE
HANGARS
Activating node
Proposed transit
Transit
Line of
Protection
Hardened Edge
100-Year
Flood Line
Wetlands
Park
Edge
Beach
Nourishment

Final Proposal: Resist, Delay, Store, Discharge

Objectives

- Manage Water (for disaster and for growth)
- Mitigate Flood Insurance (reasonable premiums through redrawing flood map and/or applying "Zone X" federal flood insurance exemptions)
- Deliver Co-Benefits (civic, cultural, recreational, and commercial amenities)

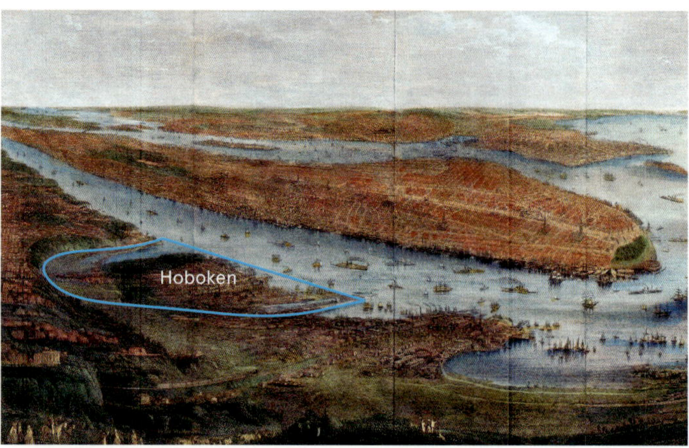

View of Hoboken, NJ and Manhattan, NY, Shanon and Rogers, 1868

Hoboken exemplifies the conditions desired for a comprehensive flood-defense strategy. It is susceptible to both flash flood and storm surge, but its single watershed, single jurisdiction, and combination of high-impact factors (high density, value, influence, and potential) lend themselves to creating a multi-faceted solution that both defends the entirety of the city and enables commercial, civic, and recreational amenities to take shape.

Two-thirds of Hoboken lies within the FEMA 100-year flood zone. It is the fourth densest city in the country and represents a sizeable concentration of value. Its exposed infrastructure, such as the NJT/PANYNJ transit complex at Hoboken station and the NHSA sewage works, play significant roles in the region. Sandy clearly demonstrated the consequence of such vulnerabilities to flood risk, and it is the combination of these factors and others that warrants such significant investment in flood defense. Leadership with the capacity to move quickly and an engaged citizenry provide the conditions for a swift political process.

The objectives of this manifold strategy are to manage water for both disaster and long-term growth; to mitigate the financial pressures of flood insurance – enabling reasonable premiums, or exemption from the Federal flood insurance program, through the redrawing of the FEMA flood maps; and to deliver co-benefits including civic, cultural, recreational, and commercial amenities that enhance the quality of the built environment.

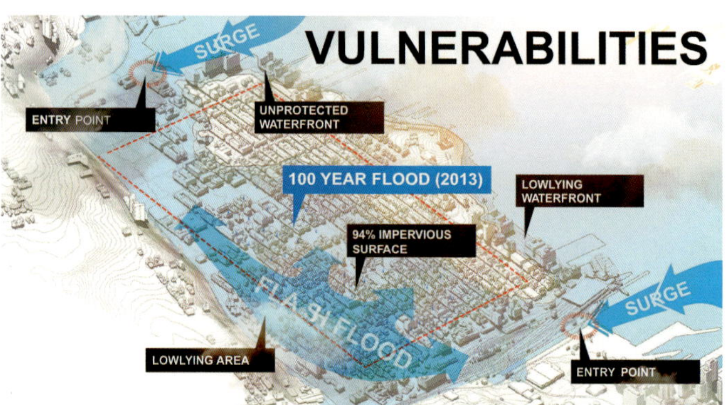

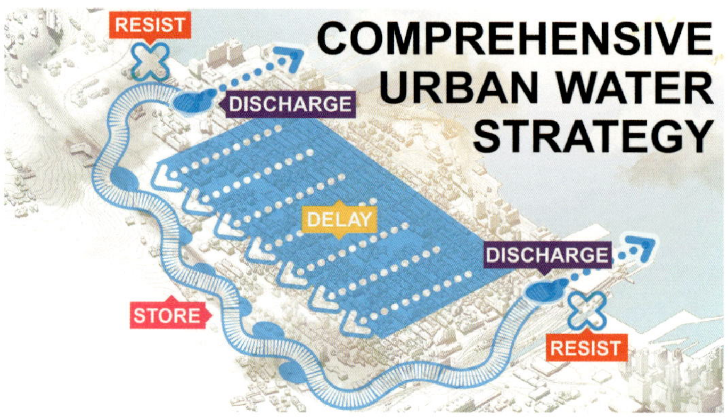

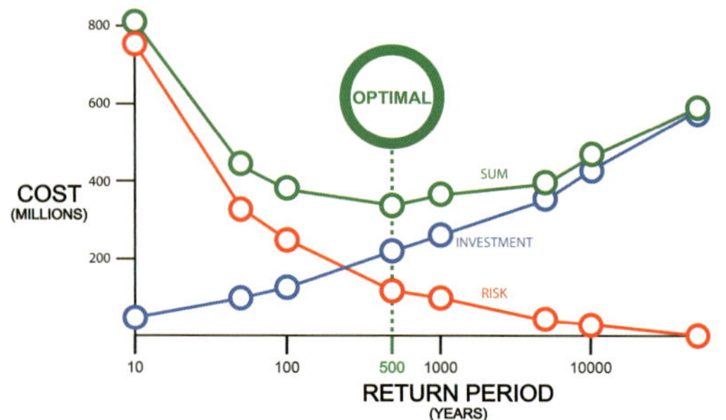

PROPOSED SAFETY LEVEL

500 YEAR
Safety level for STORM SURGE

10 YEAR
Safety level for FLASH FLOOD

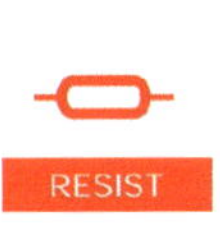

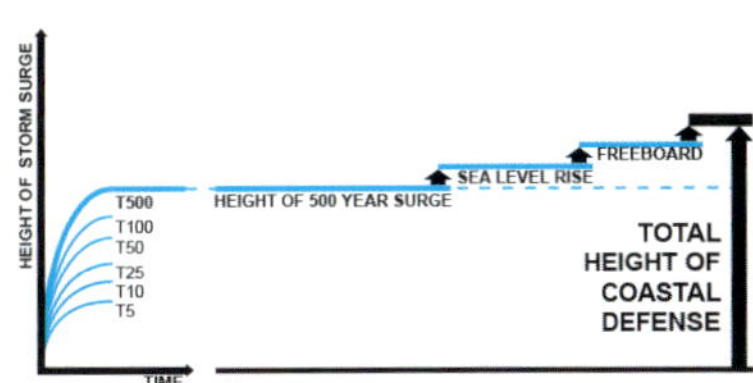

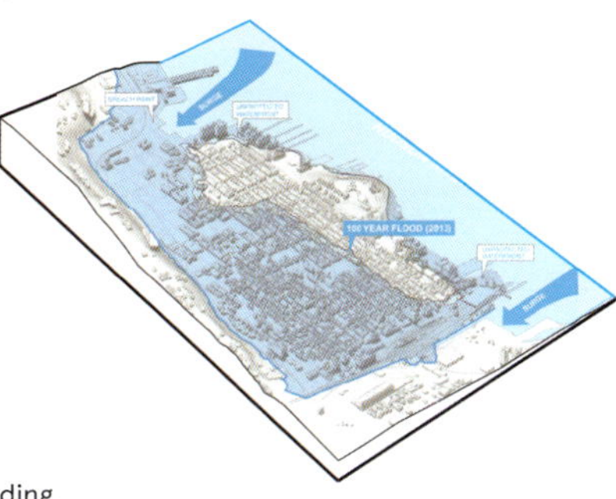

Hoboken's flood risk stems from both surge from the Hudson and flash flooding from rainfall within the city. While flash flooding is much more common, surge events can have devastating impacts on the city.

DELAY

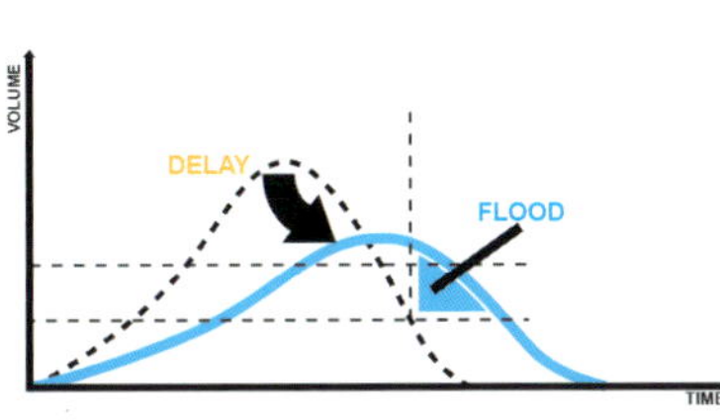

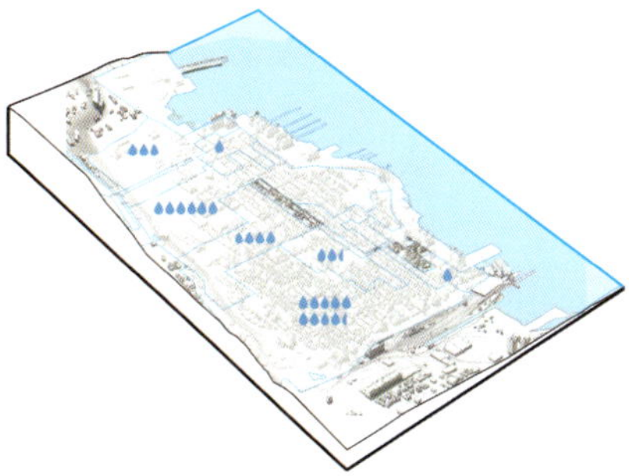

Each rain drop in the diagram to the left represents 100,000 cubic feet of excess water that causes flooding in the city. To prevent flooding, this excess water (over 2.5 million cubic feet) must be managed.

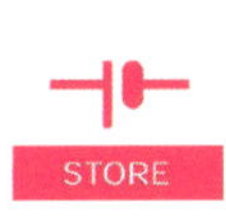

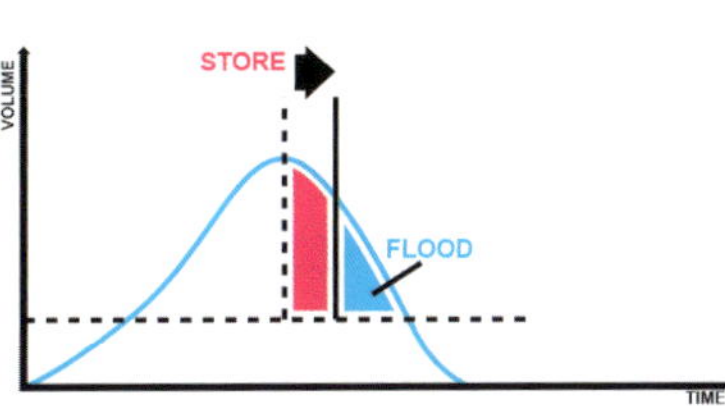

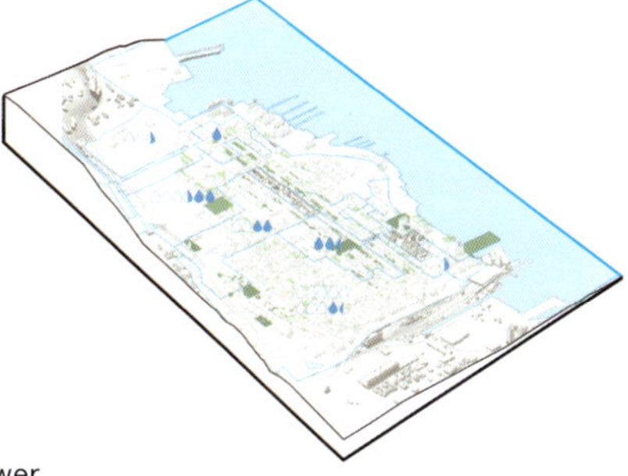

After water is absorbed into the city, the remaining water flows into the sewer system where it is stored or pumped out into the Hudson. The dark blue water drops represent water that has not yet been absorbed into the city and requires storage.

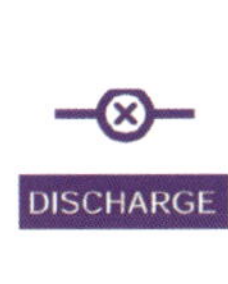

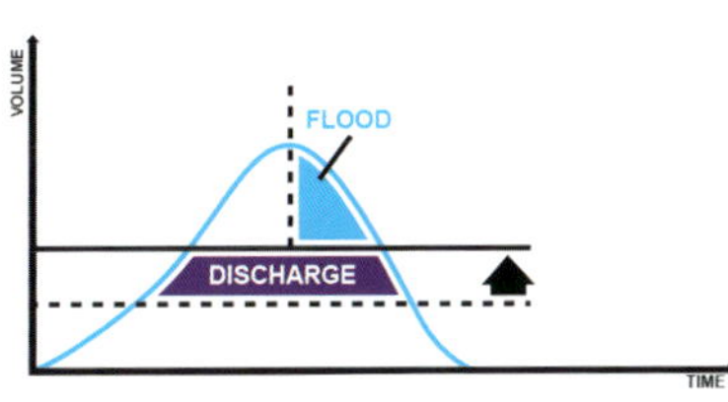

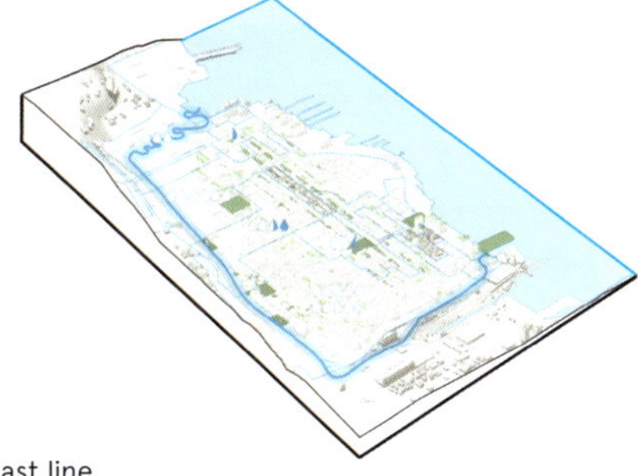

Water that has been stored needs to be evacuated from the city. As the last line of defense, pumping allows for the disposal of trapped rainwater within the city.

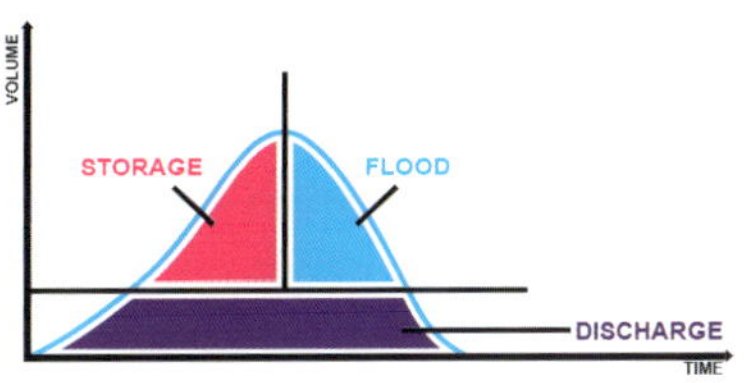

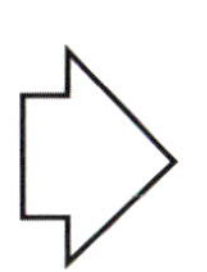

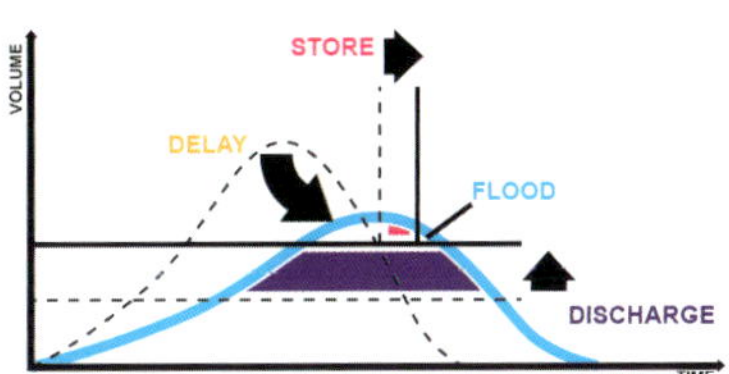

A comprehensive approach allows for a robust protection system.

RESIST

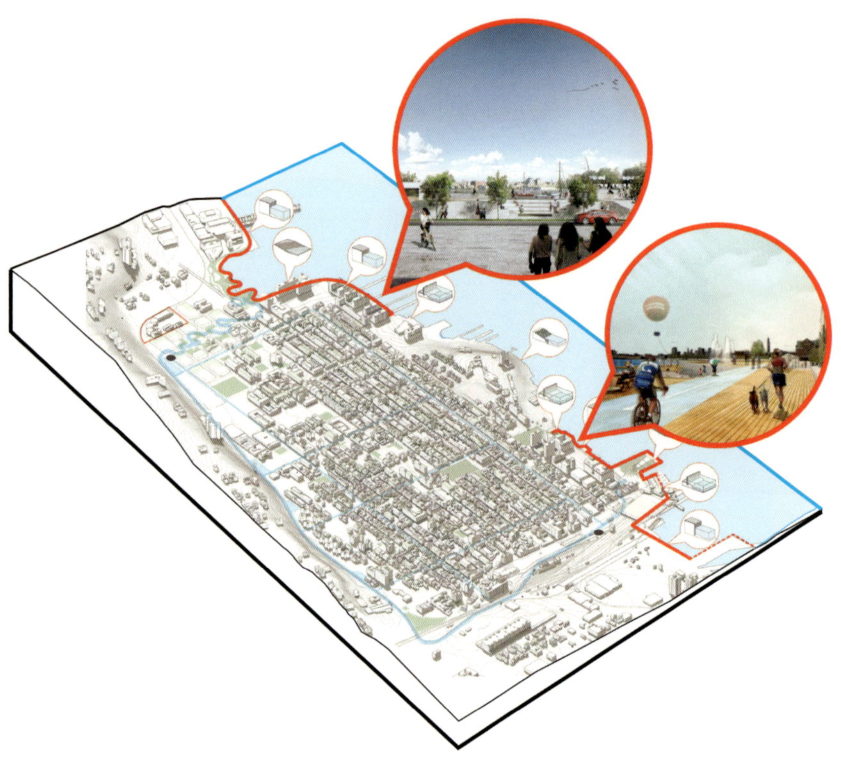

Programmed hard infrastructure and soft landscape improve coastal defense.

Defense against storm surge is primarily a question of elevation. The height of flood-defense measures is determined by an extreme water level analysis, which is based on storm surge water levels to defend against – in this case, a one-in-five-hundred-year storm surge water level – and expected sea-level rise.

DELAY

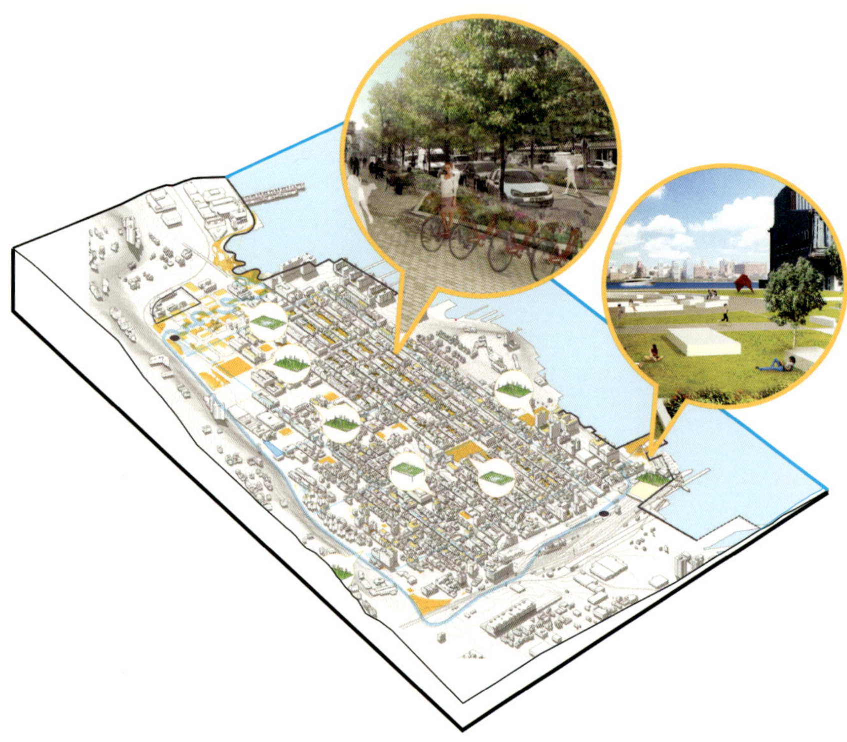

Policy recommendations, guidelines, and urban infrastructure slow rainwater runoff.

Flash flooding from rainfall occurs when rainwater overwhelms the capacity of the drainage system – water goes in faster than it can come out. The intended level of defense against this systemic seasonal flooding is a one-in-ten-year flood level.

Delay strategies act like a sponge by slowing rainwater down. This slower rate of flow gives more time for the drainage to do its job.

STORE

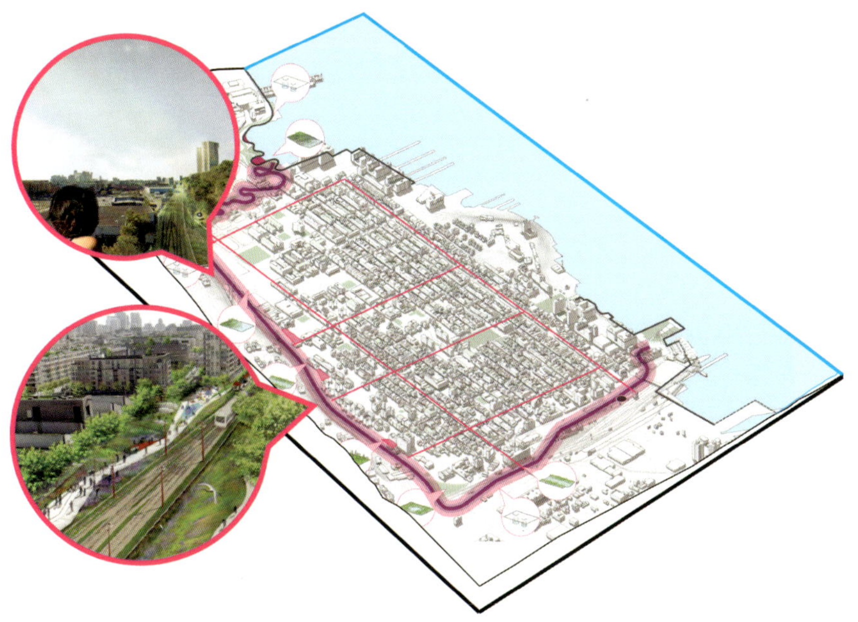

A circuit of interconnected green infrastructure stores and directs excess rainwater.

Storage strategies temporarily take excess water out of the drainage system. This water can later be returned once the system has recovered capacity.

DISCHARGE

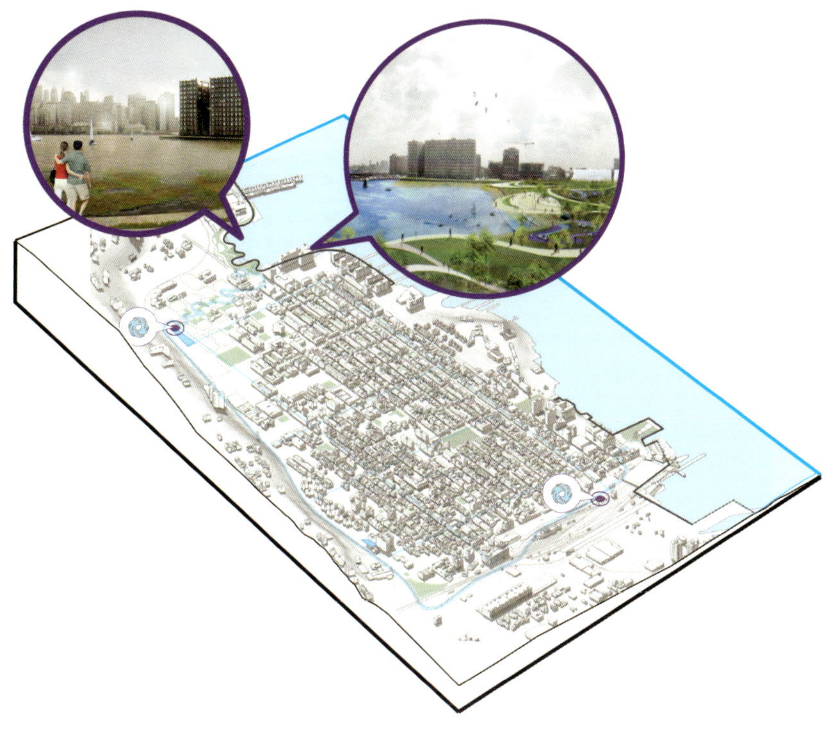

Water pumps and alternative routes support drainage.

While Delay and Store address water going in, Discharge strategies address water going out, removing water from the system. Additional pumps and alternative drainage routes increase the rate in which this can occur.

Together, these complementary strategies provide a robust, cost-effective system of defense that no single strategy can deliver.

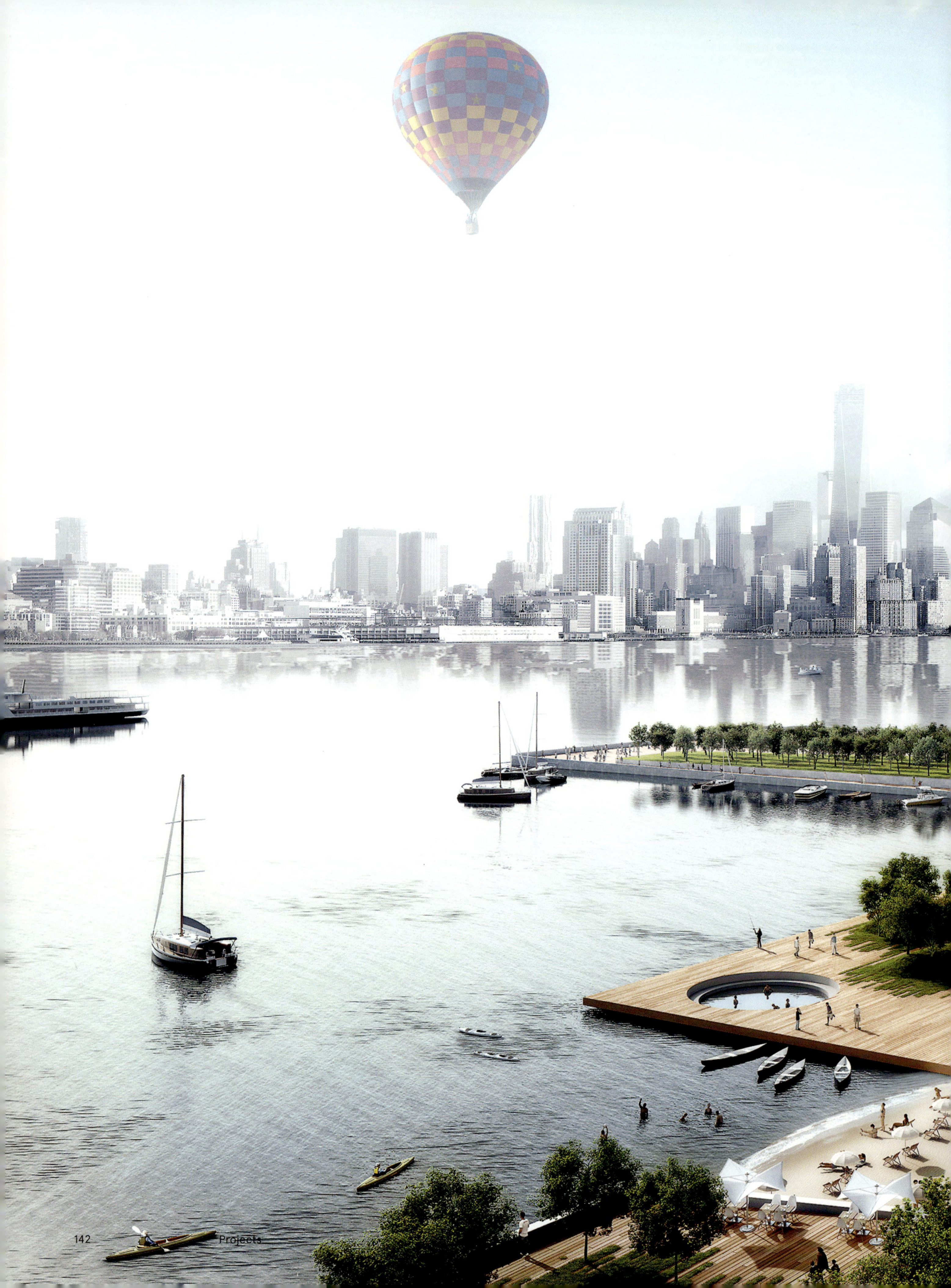

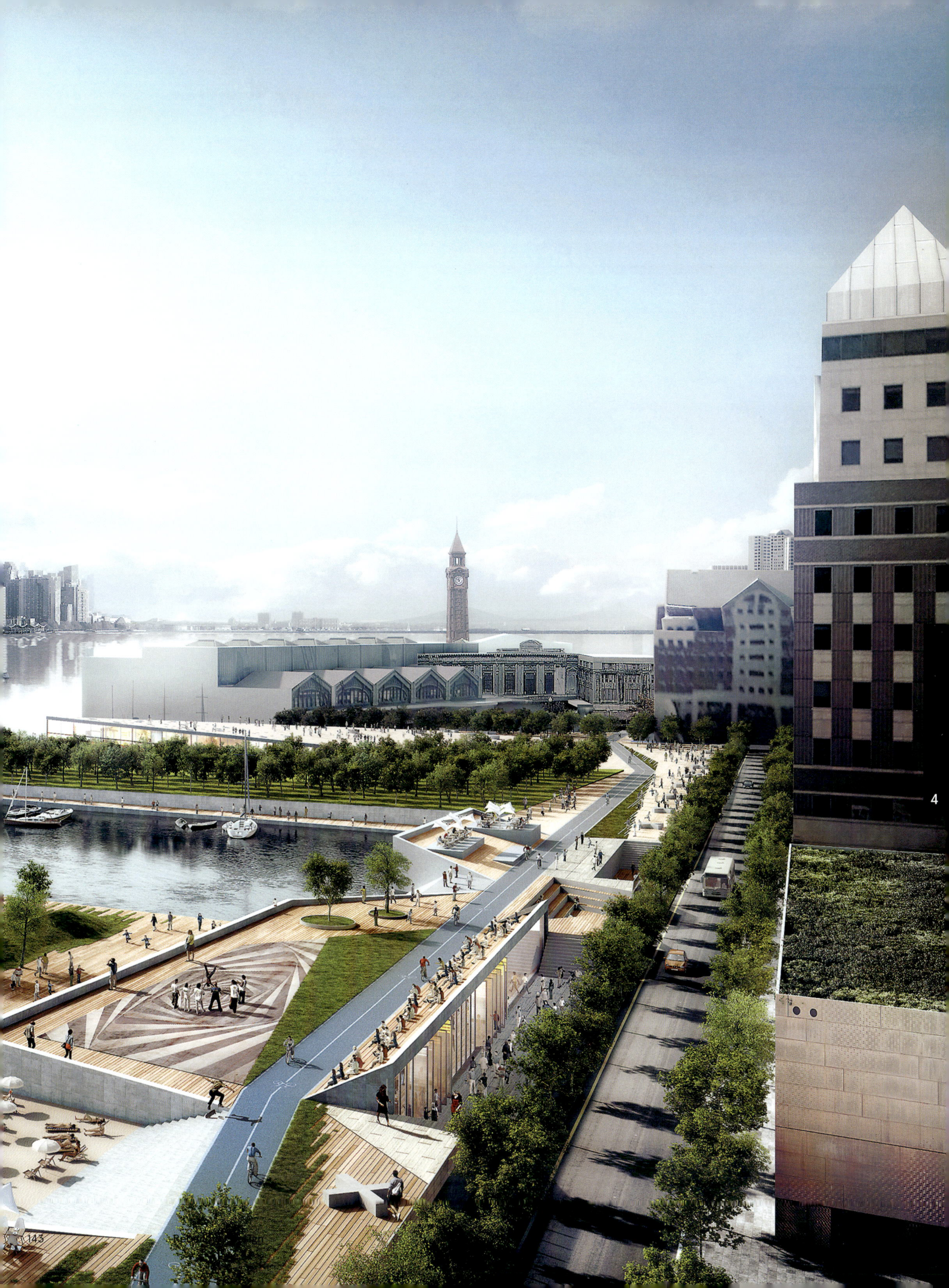

4

Design Process

The OMA team's strategy is based on a series of innovations: a comprehensive approach to flood risk, a coalition of stakeholders and a collaborative funding framework, an umbrella of communication and education, and integrated multi-faceted design solutions. Inherent to each innovation is the opportunity for replication across the region, both to ensure positive impact from the built solution and to propogate its underlying ideas.

A comprehensive strategy towards a resilient Hoboken requires an understanding of flood risk and an aligning of values and priorities. The team has actively engaged a range of stakeholders through presentations, workshops, and meetings. The goal was to educate the community and the team itself on the costs and benefits of protecting Hoboken and living with water. The team spent long days and nights presenting, listening, and even teaching what resilience is through the lens of politics, mediating differences between groups through the shared objective of resilience.

The notes and feedback from public showcases and web-based surveys shaped the team's proposals and were the first phase of a rigorous stakeholder process that had broad and impressive support, from the federal government level to the individual level. A selection of letters of support for Resist, Delay, Store, and Discharge (shown on the right) illustrates the success and efficacy of the stakeholder process and provides a basis for the successful implementation of the proposed solutions for resilience.

The team's strategy will be implemented over a number of years and leverage a broad program of funds across government, philanthropy, business, and community sources. The keystone investment will be HUD CDBG-DR funding.

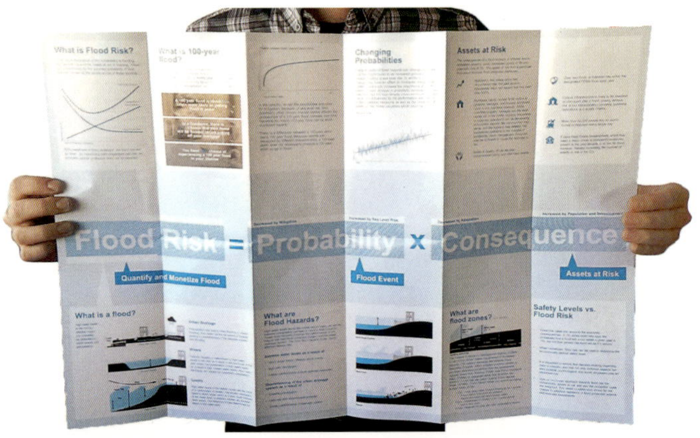

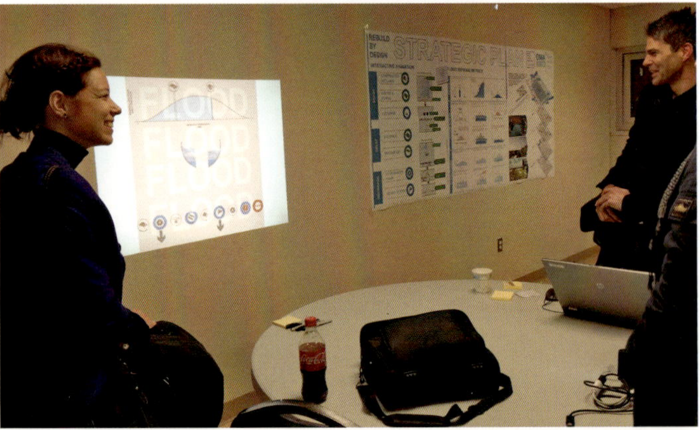

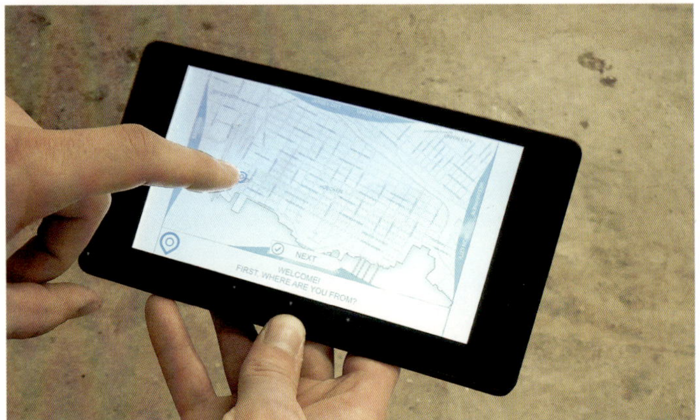

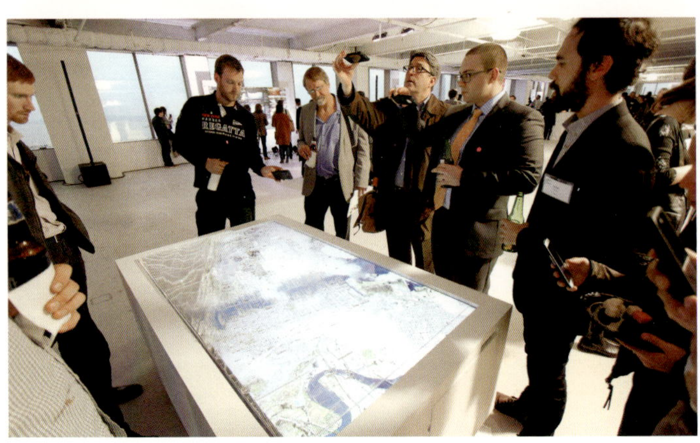

Outreach Tools

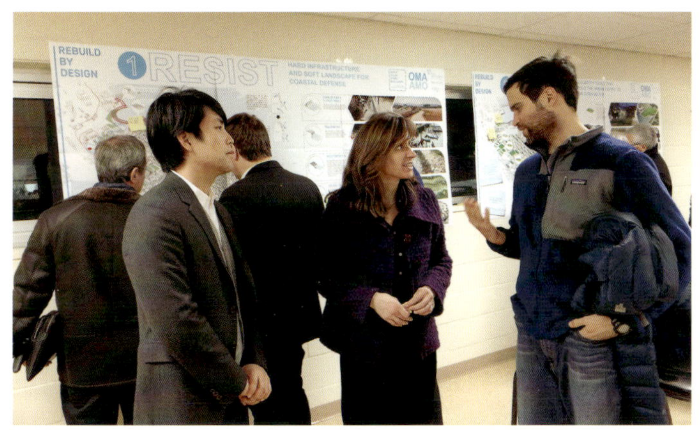

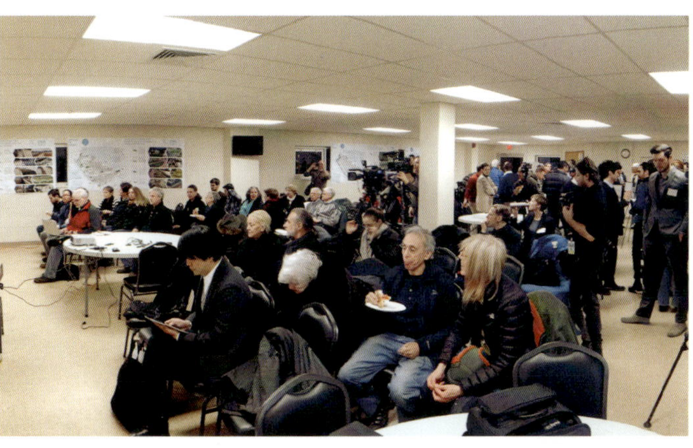

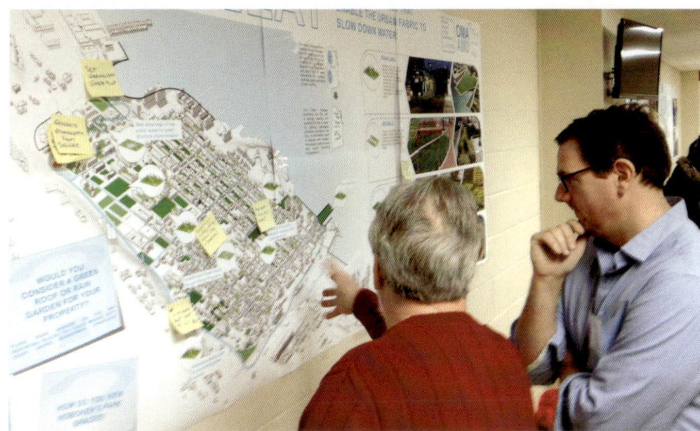

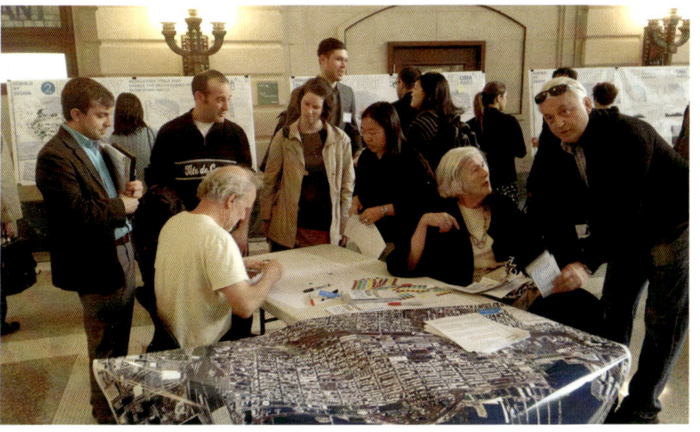

Engagement & Feedback

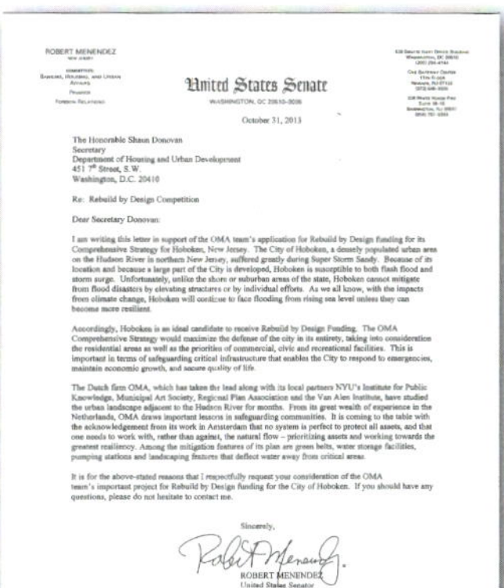

ROBERT MENENDEZ

United States Senate
WASHINGTON, DC 20510-3005

October 31, 2013

The Honorable Shaun Donovan
Secretary
Department of Housing and Urban Development
451 7th Street, S.W.
Washington, D.C. 20410

Re: Rebuild by Design Competition

Dear Secretary Donovan:

I am writing this letter in support of the OMA team's application for Rebuild by Design funding for its Comprehensive Strategy for Hoboken, New Jersey. The City of Hoboken, a densely populated urban area on the Hudson River in northern New Jersey, suffered greatly during Super Storm Sandy. Because of its location and because a large part of the City is developed, Hoboken is susceptible to both flash flood and storm surge. Unfortunately, unlike the shore or suburban areas of the state, Hoboken cannot mitigate from flood disasters by elevating structures or by individual efforts. As we all know, with the impacts from climate change, Hoboken will continue to face flooding from rising sea level unless they can become more resilient.

Accordingly, Hoboken is an ideal candidate to receive Rebuild by Design Funding. The OMA Comprehensive Strategy would maximize the defense of the city in its entirety, taking into consideration the residential areas as well as the priorities of commercial, civic and recreational facilities. This is important in terms of safeguarding critical infrastructure that enables the City to respond to emergencies, maintain economic growth, and secure quality of life.

The Dutch firm OMA, which has taken the lead along with its local partners NYU's Institute for Public Knowledge, Municipal Art Society, Regional Plan Association and the Van Alen Institute, have studied the urban landscape adjacent to the Hudson River for months. From its great wealth of experience in the Netherlands, OMA draws important lessons in safeguarding communities. It is coming to the table with the acknowledgement from its work in Amsterdam that no system is perfect to protect all assets, and that one needs to work with, rather than against, the natural flow – prioritizing assets and working towards the greatest resiliency. Among the mitigation features of its plan are green belts, water storage facilities, pumping stations and landscaping features that deflect water away from critical areas.

It is for the above-stated reasons that I respectfully request your consideration of the OMA team's important project for Rebuild by Design funding for the City of Hoboken. If you should have any questions, please do not hesitate to contact me.

Sincerely,

ROBERT MENENDEZ
United States Senator

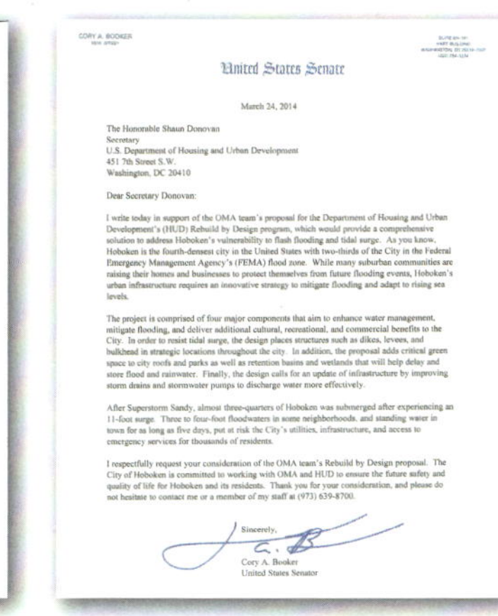

CORY A. BOOKER

United States Senate

March 24, 2014

The Honorable Shaun Donovan
Secretary
U.S. Department of Housing and Urban Development
451 7th Street S.W.
Washington, DC 20410

Dear Secretary Donovan:

I write today in support of the OMA team's proposal for the Department of Housing and Urban Development's (HUD) Rebuild by Design program, which would provide a comprehensive solution to address Hoboken's vulnerability to flash flooding and tidal surge. As you know, Hoboken is the fourth-densest city in the United States with two-thirds of the City in the Federal Emergency Management Agency's (FEMA) flood zone. While many suburban communities are raising their homes and businesses to protect themselves from future flooding events, Hoboken's urban infrastructure requires an innovative strategy to mitigate flooding and adapt to rising sea levels.

The project is comprised of four major components that aim to enhance water management, mitigate flooding, and deliver additional cultural, recreational, and commercial benefits to the City. In order to resist tidal surge, the design places structures such as dikes, levees, and bulkhead in strategic locations throughout the city. In addition, the proposal adds critical green space to city roofs and parks as well as retention basins and wetlands that will help delay and store flood and rainwater. Finally, the design calls for an update of infrastructure by improving storm drains and stormwater pumps to discharge water more effectively.

After Superstorm Sandy, almost three-quarters of Hoboken was submerged after experiencing an 11-foot surge. Three to four-foot floodwaters in some neighborhoods, and standing water in town for as long as five days, put at risk the City's utilities, infrastructure, and access to emergency services for thousands of residents.

I respectfully request your consideration of the OMA team's Rebuild by Design proposal. The City of Hoboken is committed to working with OMA and HUD to ensure the future safety and quality of life for Hoboken and its residents. Thank you for your consideration, and please do not hesitate to contact me or a member of my staff at (973) 639-8700.

Sincerely,

Cory A. Booker
United States Senator

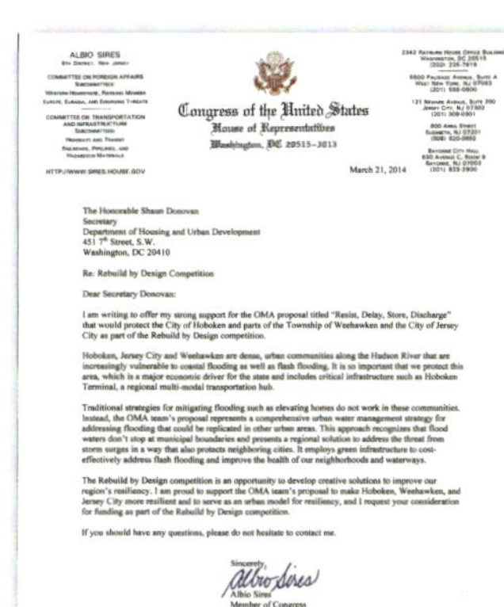

ALBIO SIRES

Congress of the United States
House of Representatives
Washington, DC 20515–3013

HTTP://WWW.SIRES.HOUSE.GOV

March 21, 2014

The Honorable Shaun Donovan
Secretary
Department of Housing and Urban Development
451 7th Street, S.W.
Washington, DC 20410

Re: Rebuild by Design Competition

Dear Secretary Donovan:

I am writing to offer my strong support for the OMA proposal titled "Resist, Delay, Store, Discharge" that would protect the City of Hoboken and parts of the Township of Weehawken and the City of Jersey City as part of the Rebuild by Design competition.

Hoboken, Jersey City and Weehawken are dense, urban communities along the Hudson River that are increasingly vulnerable to coastal flooding as well as flash flooding. It is so important that we protect this area, which is a major economic driver for the state and includes critical infrastructure such as Hoboken Terminal, a regional multi-modal transportation hub.

Traditional strategies for mitigating flooding such as elevating homes do not work in these communities. Instead, the OMA team's proposal represents a comprehensive urban water management strategy for addressing flooding that could be replicated in other urban areas. This approach recognizes that flood waters don't stop at municipal boundaries and presents a regional solution to address the threat from storm surges in a way that also protects neighboring cities. It employs green infrastructure to cost-effectively address flash flooding and improve the health of our neighborhoods and waterways.

The Rebuild by Design competition is an opportunity to develop creative solutions to improve our region's resiliency. I am proud to support the OMA team's proposal to make Hoboken, Weehawken, and Jersey City more resilient and to serve as an urban model for resiliency, and I request your consideration for funding as part of the Rebuild by Design competition.

If you should have any questions, please do not hesitate to contact me.

Sincerely,

Albio Sires
Member of Congress

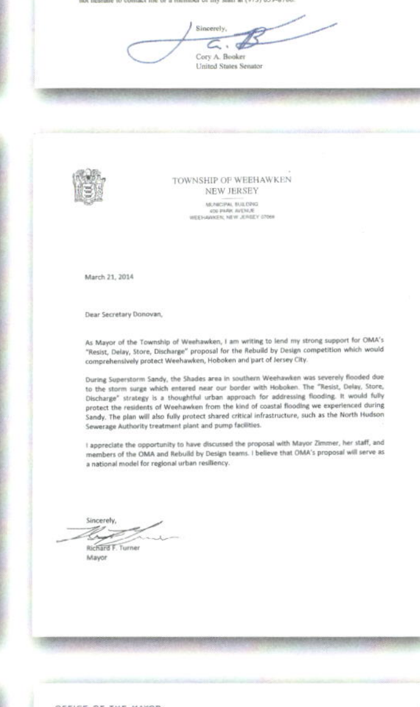

TOWNSHIP OF WEEHAWKEN
NEW JERSEY
MUNICIPAL BUILDING
400 PARK AVENUE
WEEHAWKEN, NEW JERSEY 07086

March 21, 2014

Dear Secretary Donovan,

As Mayor of the Township of Weehawken, I am writing to lend my strong support for OMA's "Resist, Delay, Store, Discharge" proposal for the Rebuild by Design competition which would comprehensively protect Weehawken, Hoboken and part of Jersey City.

During Superstorm Sandy, the Shades area in southern Weehawken was severely flooded due to the storm surge which entered near our border with Hoboken. The "Resist, Delay, Store, Discharge" strategy is a thoughtful urban approach for addressing flooding. It would fully protect the residents of Weehawken from the kind of coastal flooding we experienced during Sandy. The plan will also fully protect shared critical infrastructure, such as the North Hudson Sewerage Authority treatment plant and pump facilities.

I appreciate the opportunity to have discussed the proposal with Mayor Zimmer, her staff, and members of the OMA and Rebuild by Design teams. I believe that OMA's proposal will serve as a national model for regional urban resiliency.

Sincerely,

Richard F. Turner
Mayor

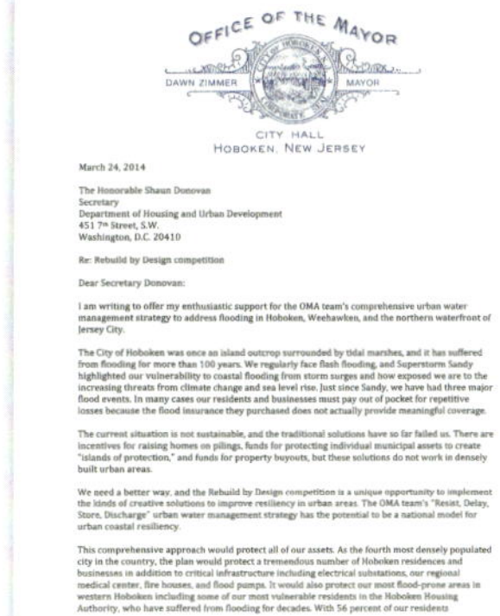

OFFICE OF THE MAYOR
DAWN ZIMMER MAYOR
CITY HALL
HOBOKEN, NEW JERSEY

March 24, 2014

The Honorable Shaun Donovan
Secretary
Department of Housing and Urban Development
451 7th Street, S.W.
Washington, D.C. 20410

Re: Rebuild by Design competition

Dear Secretary Donovan:

I am writing to offer my enthusiastic support for the OMA team's comprehensive urban water management strategy to address flooding in Hoboken, Weehawken, and the northern waterfront of Jersey City.

The City of Hoboken was once an island outcrop surrounded by tidal marshes, and it has suffered from flooding for more than 100 years. We regularly face flash flooding, and Superstorm Sandy highlighted our vulnerability to coastal flooding from storm surges and how exposed we are to the increasing threats from climate change and sea level rise. Just since Sandy, we have had three major flood events. In many cases our residents and businesses must pay out of pocket for repetitive losses because the flood insurance they purchased does not actually provide meaningful coverage.

The current situation is not sustainable, and the traditional solutions have so far failed us. There are incentives for raising homes on pilings, funds for protecting individual municipal assets to create "islands of protection," and funds for property buyouts, but these solutions do not work in densely built urban areas.

We need a better way, and the Rebuild by Design competition is a unique opportunity to implement the kinds of creative solutions to improve resiliency in urban areas. The OMA team's "Resist, Delay, Store, Discharge" urban water management strategy has the potential to be a national model for urban coastal resiliency.

This comprehensive approach would protect all of our assets. As the fourth most densely populated city in the country, the plan would protect a tremendous number of Hoboken residences and businesses in addition to critical infrastructure including electrical substations, our regional medical center, fire houses, and flood pumps. It would also protect our most flood-prone areas in western Hoboken including some of our most vulnerable residents in the Hoboken Housing Authority, who have suffered from flooding for decades. With 56 percent of our residents

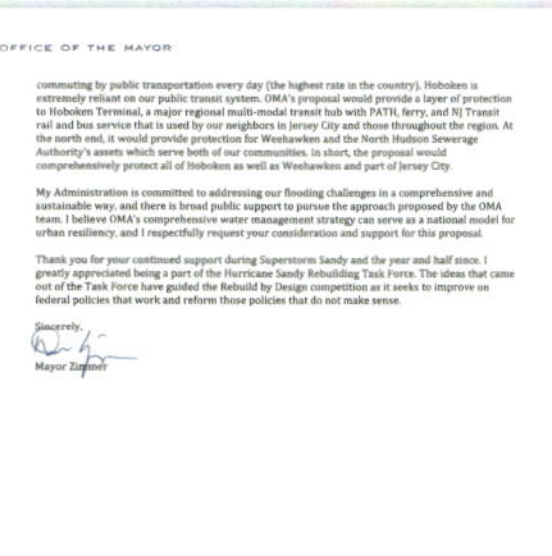

OFFICE OF THE MAYOR

commuting by public transportation every day (the highest rate in the country), Hoboken is extremely reliant on our public transit system. OMA's proposal would provide a layer of protection to Hoboken Terminal, a major regional multi-modal transit hub with PATH, ferry, and NJ Transit rail and bus service that is used by our neighbors in Jersey City and those throughout the region. At the north end, it would provide protection for Weehawken and the North Hudson Sewerage Authority's assets which serve both of our communities. In short, the proposal would comprehensively protect all of Hoboken as well as Weehawken and part of Jersey City.

My Administration is committed to addressing our flooding challenges in a comprehensive and sustainable way, and there is broad public support to pursue the approach proposed by the OMA team. I believe OMA's comprehensive water management strategy can serve as a national model for urban resiliency, and I respectfully request your consideration and support for this proposal.

Thank you for your continued support during Superstorm Sandy and the year and half since. I greatly appreciated being a part of the Hurricane Sandy Rebuilding Task Force. The ideas that came out of the Task Force have guided the Rebuild by Design competition as it seeks to improve on federal policies that work and reform those policies that do not make sense.

Sincerely,

Mayor Zimmer

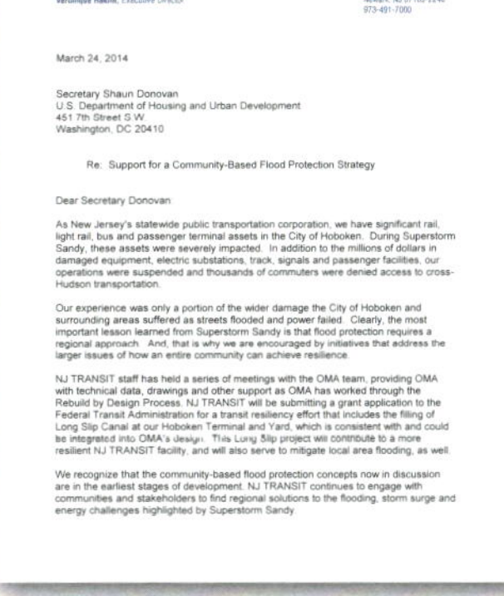

Chris Christie, Governor
Kim Guadagno, Lieutenant Governor
James S. Simpson, Board Chairman
Veronique Hakim, Executive Director

NJTRANSIT
One Penn Plaza East
Newark, NJ 07105-2246
973-491-7000

March 24, 2014

Secretary Shaun Donovan
U.S. Department of Housing and Urban Development
451 7th Street S.W.
Washington, DC 20410

Re: Support for a Community-Based Flood Protection Strategy

Dear Secretary Donovan

As New Jersey's statewide public transportation corporation, we have significant rail, light rail, bus and passenger terminal assets in the City of Hoboken. During Superstorm Sandy, these assets were severely impacted. In addition to the millions of dollars in damaged equipment, electric substations, track, signals and passenger facilities, our operations were suspended and thousands of commuters were denied access to cross-Hudson transportation.

Our experience was only a portion of the wider damage the City of Hoboken and surrounding areas suffered as streets flooded and power failed. Clearly, the most important lesson learned from Superstorm Sandy is that flood protection requires a regional approach. And, that is why we are encouraged by initiatives that address the larger issues of how an entire community can achieve resilience.

NJ TRANSIT staff has held a series of meetings with the OMA team, providing OMA with technical data, drawings and other support as OMA has worked through the Rebuild by Design Process. NJ TRANSIT will be submitting a grant application to the Federal Transit Administration for a transit resiliency effort that includes the filling of Long Slip Canal at our Hoboken Terminal and Yard, which is consistent with and could be integrated into OMA's design. This Long Slip project will contribute to a more resilient NJ TRANSIT facility, and will also serve to mitigate local area flooding, as well.

We recognize that the community-based flood protection concepts now in discussion are in the earliest stages of development. NJ TRANSIT continues to engage with communities and stakeholders to find regional solutions to the flooding, storm surge and energy challenges highlighted by Superstorm Sandy.

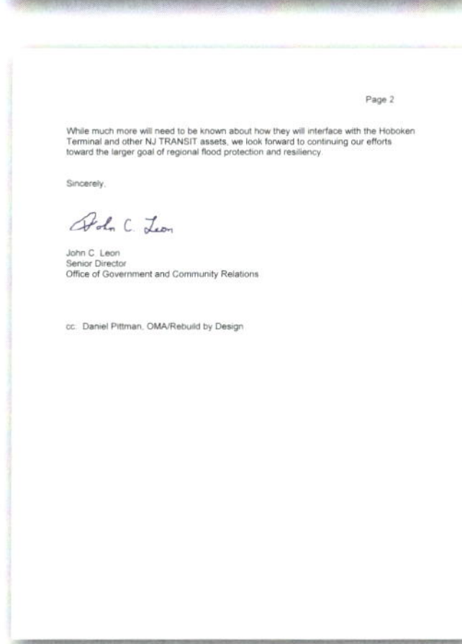

Page 2

While much more will need to be known about how they will interface with the Hoboken Terminal and other NJ TRANSIT assets, we look forward to continuing our efforts toward the larger goal of regional flood protection and resiliency.

Sincerely,

John C. Leon
Senior Director
Office of Government and Community Relations

cc: Daniel Pittman, OMA/Rebuild by Design

Selected Letters of Support

HUNTS POINT LIFELINES

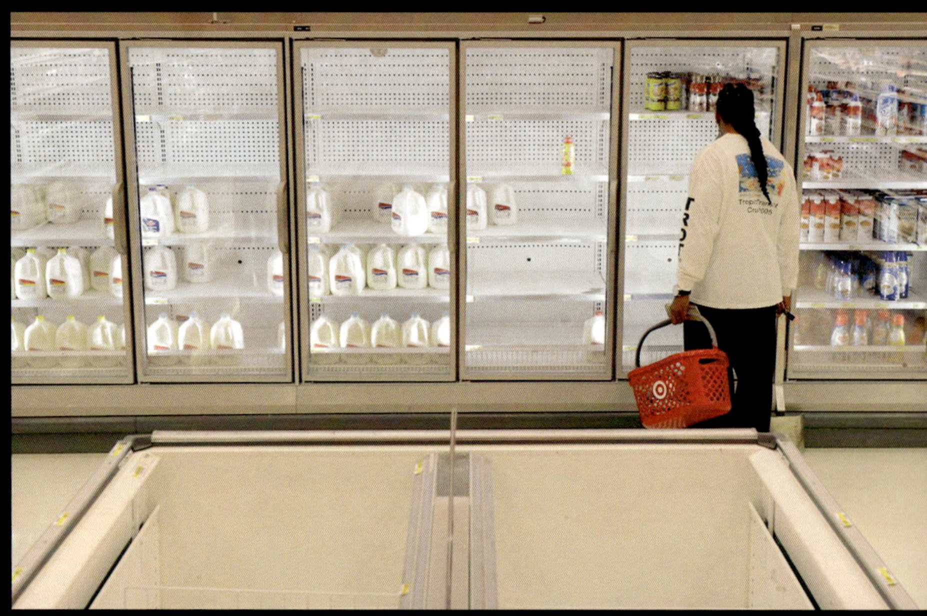

Team Lead
PennDesign/OLIN

Community Engagement
Barretto Bay Strategies

Environmental Engineering
eDesign Dynamics

Infrastructure Planning
Level Infrastructure

Economic Strategy
HR&A Advisors

Marine Engineering
McLaren Engineering Group

Civil and Transportation Engineering
Philip Habib & Associates

Structural Engineering
Buro Happold

PennDesign/OLIN

The PennDesign/OLIN team investigated the square mile of the Hunts Point peninsula. Hunts Point represents the intersection of the local and the regional in rebuilding by design. What is at risk there is the hub of the food supply for 22 million people, a $5 billion annual economy, over 10,000 direct jobs, and the livelihoods of residents in the poorest Congressional District in the United States. The team was excited by the potential for a cultural shift in Hunts Point that could create a new way of working and living with water.

Hunts Point Lifelines builds on assets and opportunities of regional importance and a coalition of leaders in community environmental action, business, and labor to create a working model of social, economic, and physical resilience. The project presents a formula for a working waterfront, working community, and working ecology that grows out of long-term community plans.

Left: Sandy exposed the vulnerability of the region's food supply. If the storm had hit six hours later, when the Bronx was at high tide, the food supply for the region would have been decimated.

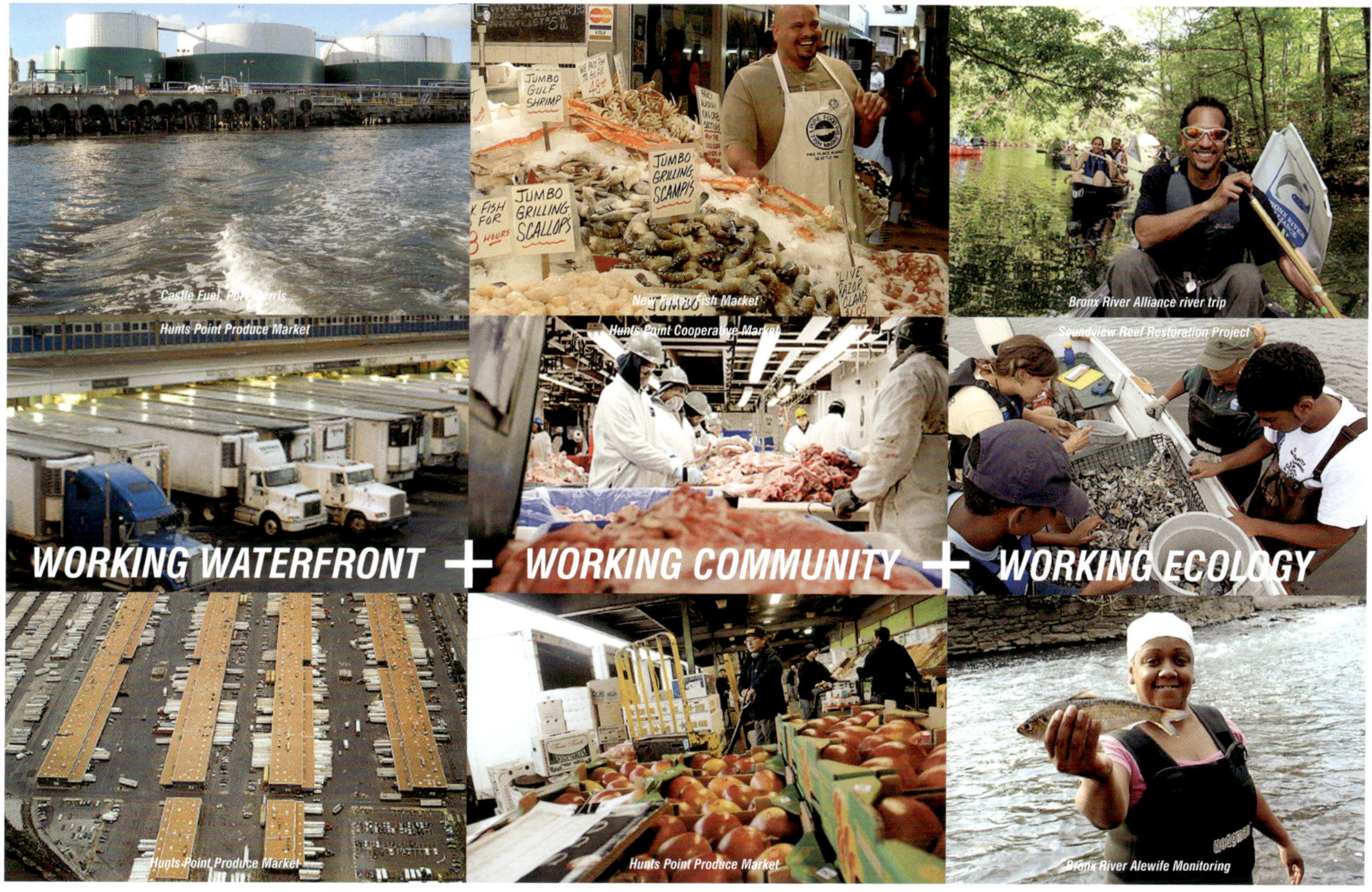

4

An Approach for Everyday Resilience

The PennDesign/OLIN team's regional analysis concentrated on economic and social vulnerability, recognizing that these barriers to resilience are often more immediate and significant than the physical risks. In a region where capital is highly mobile, rising flood insurance rates and the costs of repetitive storm damage could create two different coastal development trajectories: one in which concentrations of high-end housing where residents have the means to self-insure, and another, in which concentrations of housing and industry that decline in quality, density, and economic activity after capital takes flight. As analysis of communities at risk progressed, the team grew increasingly certain that a community-based response to adaptation would be most effective.

The team's focus on socioeconomic vulnerability and community capacity led to the selection of Hunts Point, the hub of the region's food supply chain, as the site for its proposal. Hunts Point is a physically, socially, and economically vulnerable place, and at the same time, a place with the community assets and business capacity to build deep-rooted resilience. An investment in resilience at Hunts Point would be felt throughout the region, providing food security, protecting living-wage jobs, and modeling authentic community-based action on the adaptation of working waterfronts.

Regional Importance

The Hunts Point Food Distribution Center is the heart of a network that feeds 22 million people, generates $5 billion in annual revenues, and employs more than 10,000 people, most of whom are in unionized positions. Hurricane Sandy exposed the vulnerability of Hunts Point to flooding, as well as to power and fuel outages, and highlighted the need to protect this critical asset. The City's PlaNYC analysis identified Hunts Point as a high priority, and its value in terms of the region's food supply creates an extraordinarily high benefit-cost ratio of 1.6 to 2.1 for investment in protection.

Vulnerability

Much of the Food Distribution Center and many related businesses are in the floodplain now; by 2050, much more of the peninsula will be flood prone due to sea level rise. Very few businesses have flood insurance or contingency plans in place. The Hunts Point Waste Water Treatment Plant is at a very low elevation and is the City's highest priority plant for protection. Hunts Point is located in the poorest Congressional District in the US (NY-15) and scores very high on multiple dimensions of HUD's storm vulnerability factors. The neighborhood is challenged by poverty, low pedestrian safety and air quality due to truck traffic, and decades of environmental degradation.

Capacity

The food hub efficiently moves enormous quantities of food to every scale of buyer in the region, from push carts to hospitals to large grocery chains. Representing the interests of many businesses and thousands of employees, the management and labor unions of the three cooperative markets – produce, meat, and fish – view resilience planning and implementation as imperative. Hunts Point's community-based organizations, including THE POINT Community Development Corporation, Sustainable South Bronx, Rocking the Boat, and Bronx River Alliance, are nationally recognized as leaders in environmental education, action, and green jobs strategies. Local organizations have cooperated with the City on major projects for improvement of waterways and the community.

Opportunity

Through patient, long-term consultation, Community Board 2 and local organizations have generated thoughtful strategic plans that align with an integrated flood protection system at the edge of the peninsula. In addition to the Food Distribution Center itself, the City owns the four continuous miles of the shoreline needed to build perimeter protection.

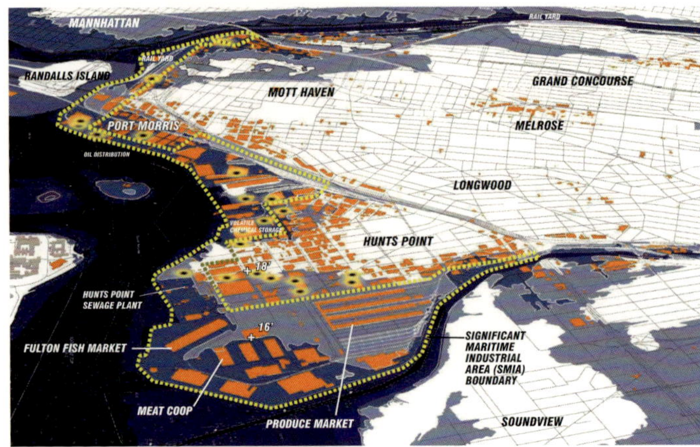

Design Opportunities

Before focusing on Hunts Point, the team identified design opportunities in three other communities at risk of major asset dissolution and decline. By design, the focus sites represented different mixes of vulnerabilities and potentials, allowing an exploration of a range of methods and leverage points. The design opportunities represented major communities, economies, and landscape geomorphologies in the region where economic and social capital is at risk and an increase in long-term value is possible: promising sites for demonstration of new approaches to economic and social resilience that might produce a culture shift and mobilize long-term investment in adaptation.

Staten Island, NY

Geomorphology on this five-mile long coastal plain lends itself to an integrated solution: multiple new folds in the coastal plain, from reefs to new platforms for development.

Toms River, NJ

In a town of 92,000 on the verge of change, the team considered alternate scenarios for future growth, identity, and relationship to the water.

Jersey City and Hoboken, NJ

In dense cities with different income profiles, the team explored the potential for a resilience project shared by two cities.

Opposite Page: Flood vulnerability of Hunts Point: Dark blue indicates 100-year flood risk; light blue 500-year risk. By 2030 all areas will fall into the 100-year flood risk due to sea level rise.

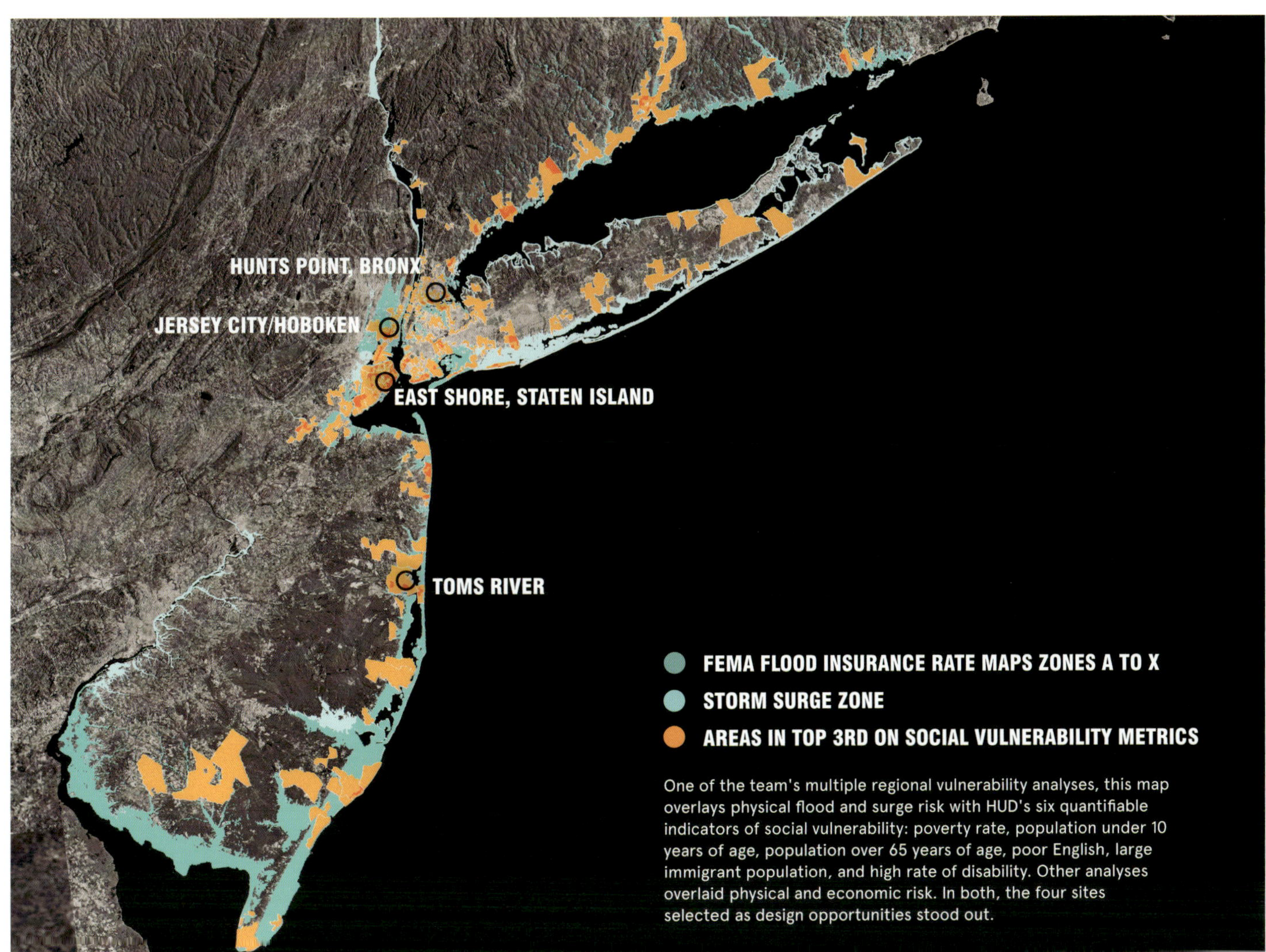

One of the team's multiple regional vulnerability analyses, this map overlays physical flood and surge risk with HUD's six quantifiable indicators of social vulnerability: poverty rate, population under 10 years of age, population over 65 years of age, poor English, large immigrant population, and high rate of disability. Other analyses overlaid physical and economic risk. In both, the four sites selected as design opportunities stood out.

4

Design Process

Co-Producing Change

Intense, sustained engagement led by the team along with its community partners produced a broad coalition of support for Hunts Point Lifelines as a shared vision for a modernizing, thriving economic hub tied to a healthy community and ecology. The plan recognizes living-wage jobs as a critical piece of resilience infrastructure for lower income communities. It also recognizes the barriers to regional adaptation and calls for a culture shift that brings businesses, community organizations, and government together to co-produce resilience. The three major wholesale markets – Hunts Point Terminal Market (fresh produce), Hunts Point Cooperative Market (meat), and the New Fulton Fish Market – endorsed the project as an essential measure to ensure the viability of the Food Distribution Center (FDC). Leaders of the major organized labor locals in the FDC – Teamsters Local 202 and United Food and Commercial Workers Locals 342 and 359 – endorsed the proposal and praised its contribution to the long-term competitiveness of the wholesale markets.

Bronx Community Board 2 and many non-profit organizations in the area – including THE POINT CDC, Mothers on the Move, Rocking the Boat, the Hunts Point Economic Development Corporation, the Hunts Point Chamber of Commerce, and Sustainable South Bronx endorsed the plan as a step forward in their plans to improve the quality of life in the peninsula and creating jobs, environmental justice, and climate security. The Lifelines proposal has received broad support from elected officals representing the Bronx at all levels. Congressman Jose E. Serrano (NY-15), who represents Hunts Point, offered opening remarks at the final public meeting. Many leaders in city, borough, state, and federal agencies helped shape the proposal, contributing key ideas, implementation strategies, and partnerships. At the final jury interview with HUD Secretary Donovan, 65 representatives of community organizations, businesses, and labor unions provided a resounding answer to the question of why Hunts Point matters. They talked about investments they were prepared to make if government joined with them to make the peninsula secure.

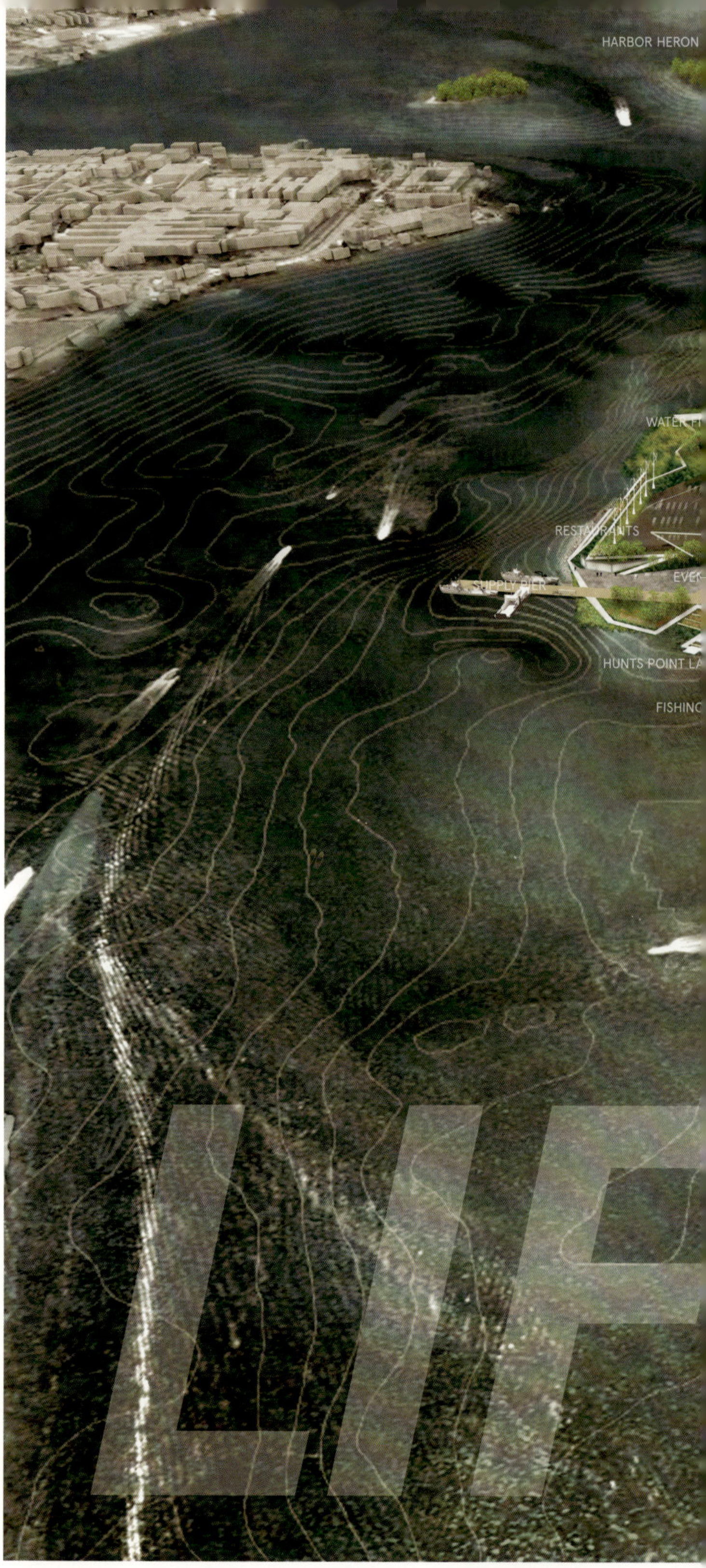

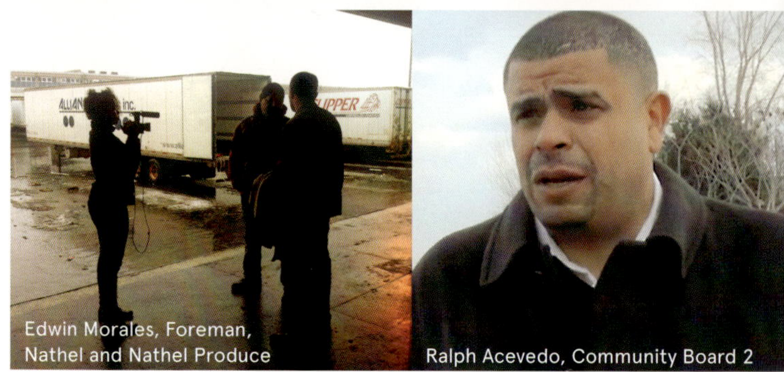

Edwin Morales, Foreman, Nathel and Nathel Produce

Ralph Acevedo, Community Board 2

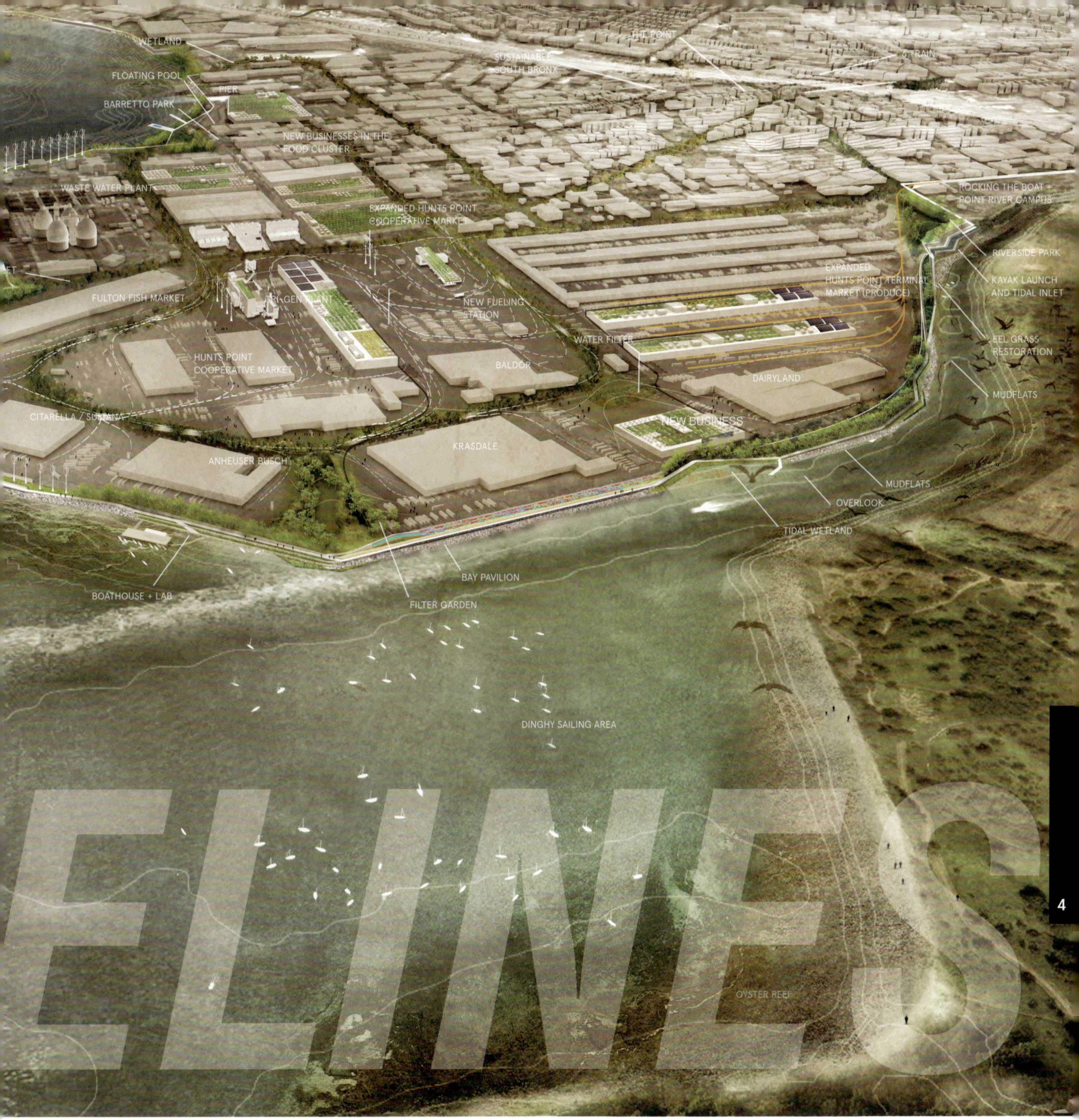

4

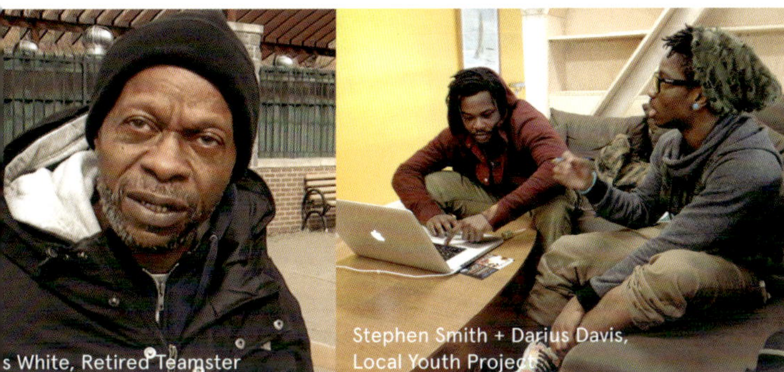

Above: The long-term vision for a growing, modernizing regional Food Distribution Center and Waste Water Treatment Plant, wrapped by a compact flood protection greenway that opens public access to the Bronx and Harlem Rivers and enriches the ecologies of the Bronx.

Left: To help people see the interests of others, the team initiated a video project that captured the resilience ideas of businesses, workers, community members and youth – in their own environments.

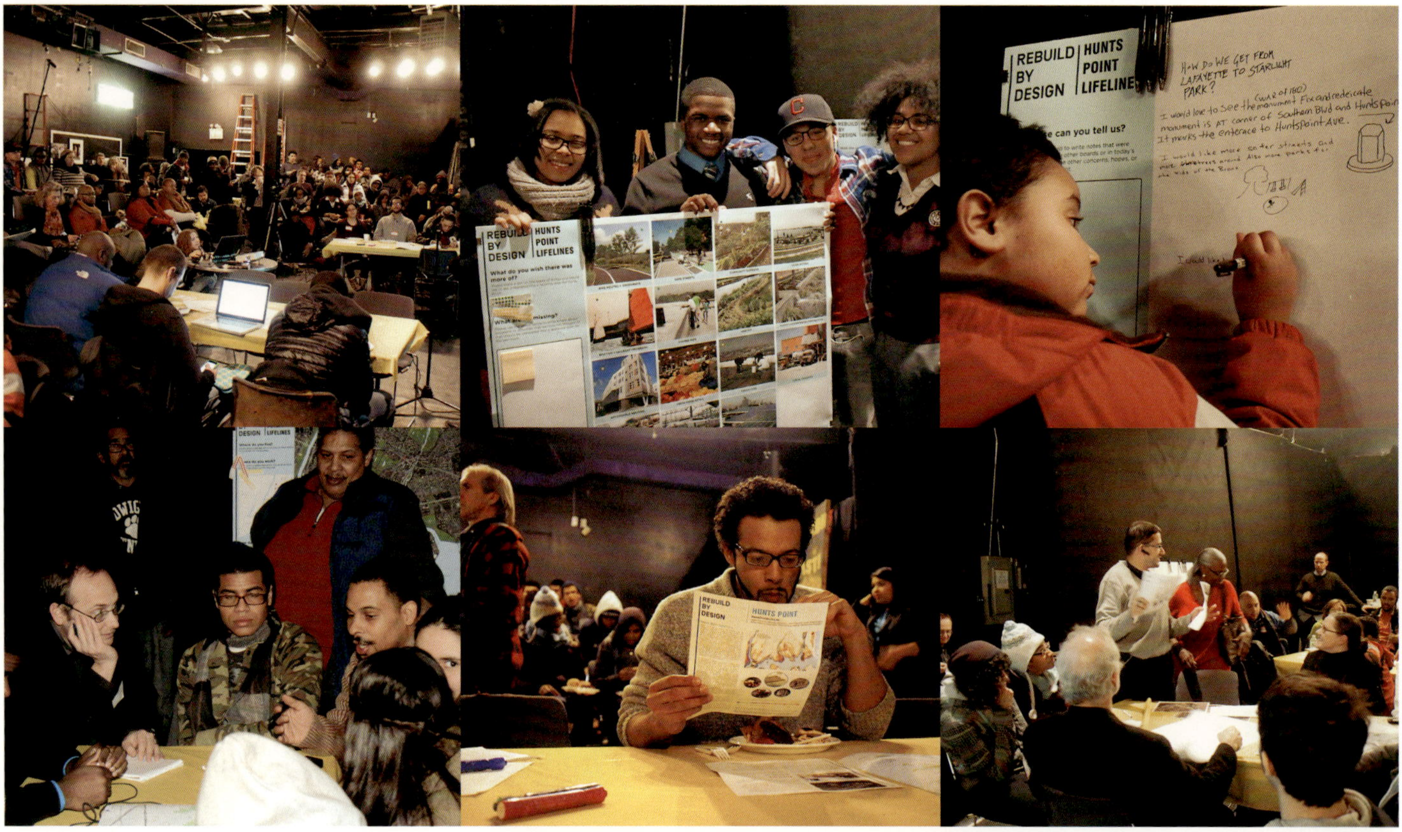

A "Slam Bake" brought the small business community, wholesalers, labor, residents, community groups, and youth together over a topic of mutual interest: food. The event, an Iron Chef-inspired cooking competition hosted by Baron Ambrosia, the host of "Bronx Flavor" on the Cooking Channel, attracted over 300 people to discuss Hunts Point Lifelines.

The event created a new sense of common cause that prompted 65 leaders of community organizations, businesses, unions, and elected officials to support the team's presentation to the HUD Secretary and jury. They came to say they were willing to work with government to co-produce climate adaptation — proof of the culture shift needed for sustained investment.

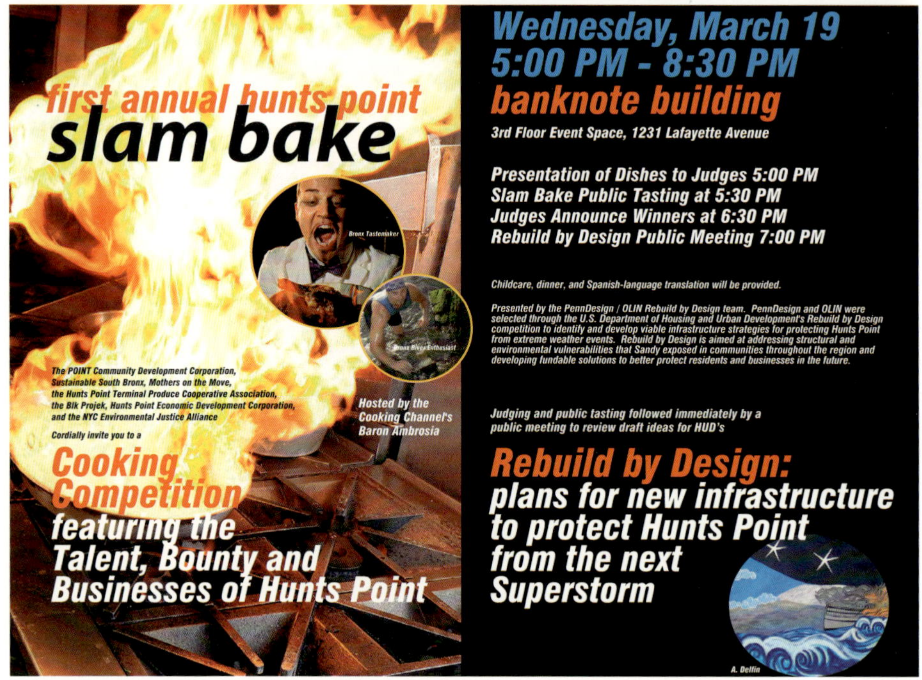

Strong community-based plans laid the ground work for new engagement on resilience. THE POINT CDC, lead community-based partner, helped shape and host meetings in the neighborhood. Working with Barretto Bay strategies, Penn/Olin reached out to the business community. While community groups had been collaborating to improve the Bronx River and advance many other projects, business, labor, and the community have had few opportunities to work together.

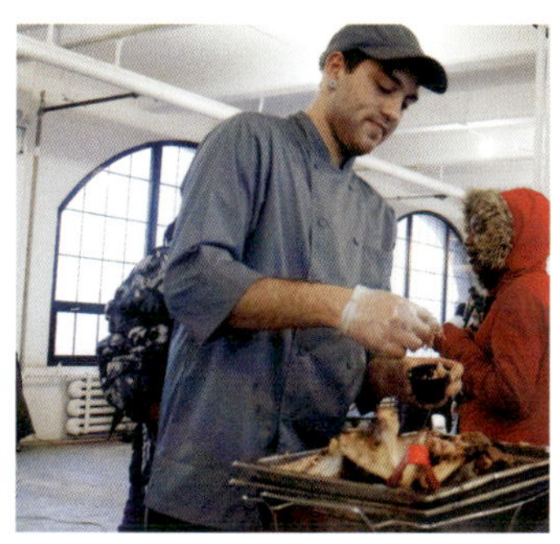
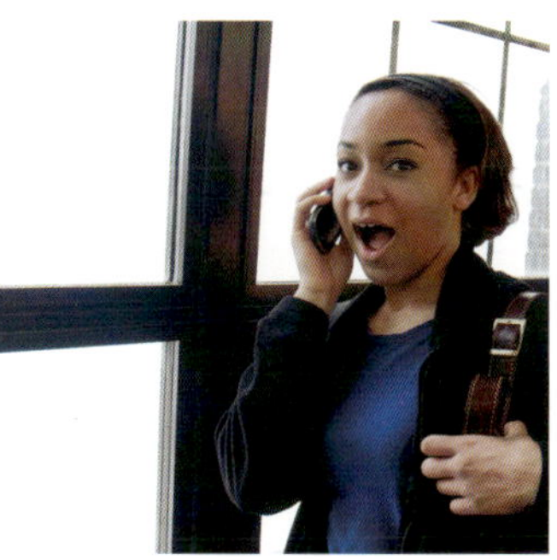
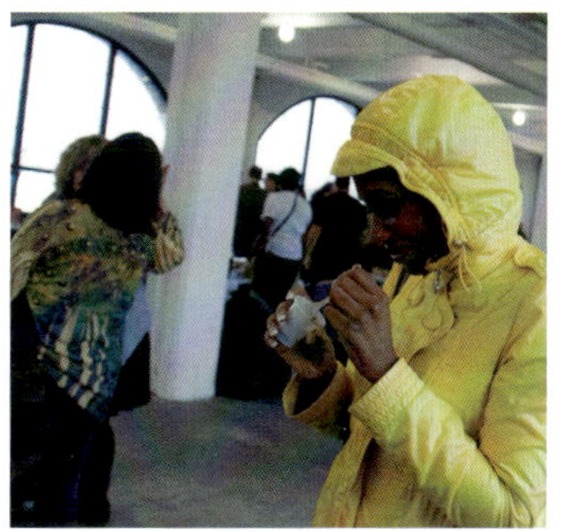
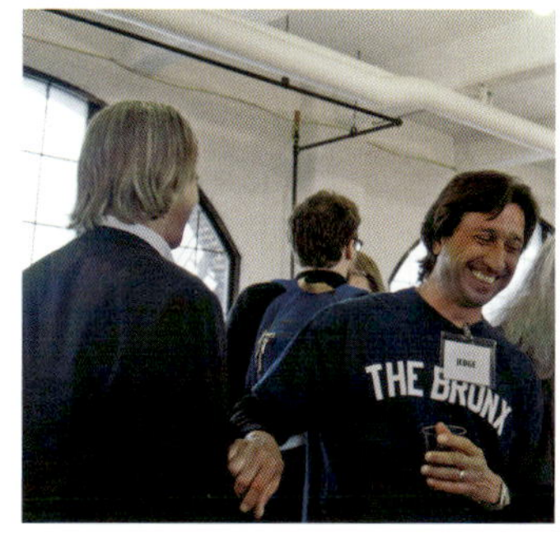

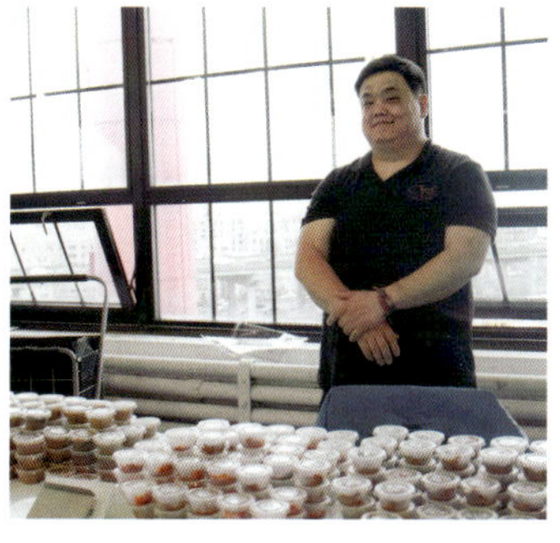
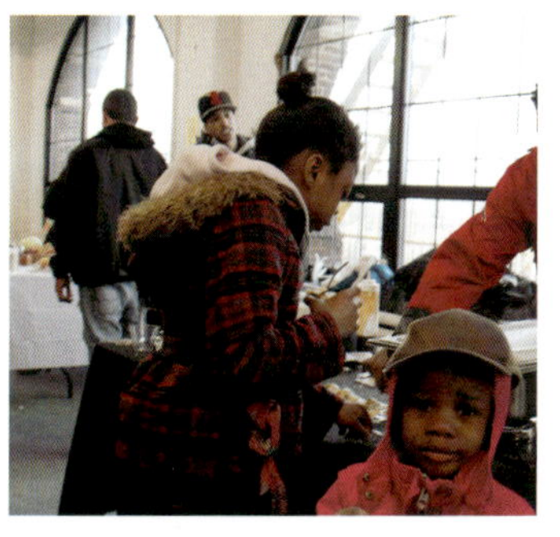
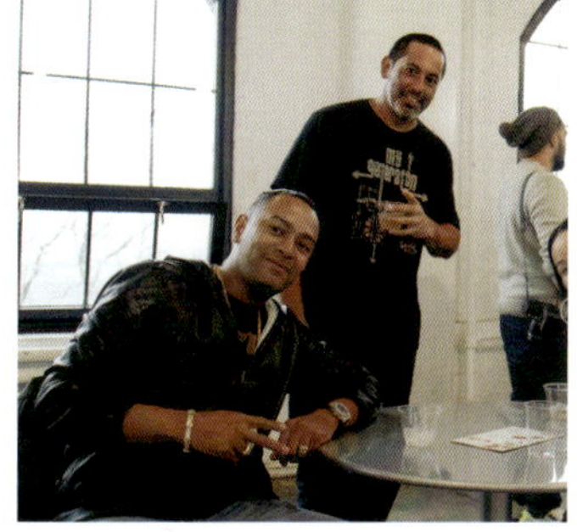
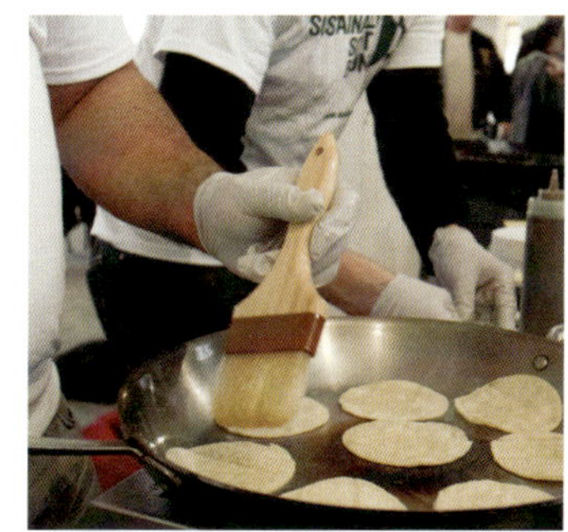
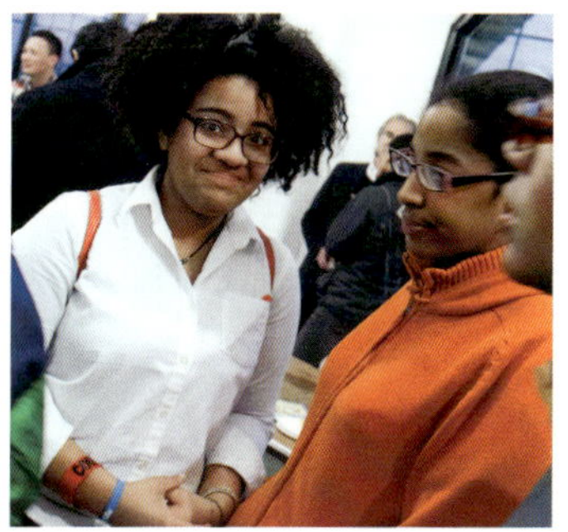
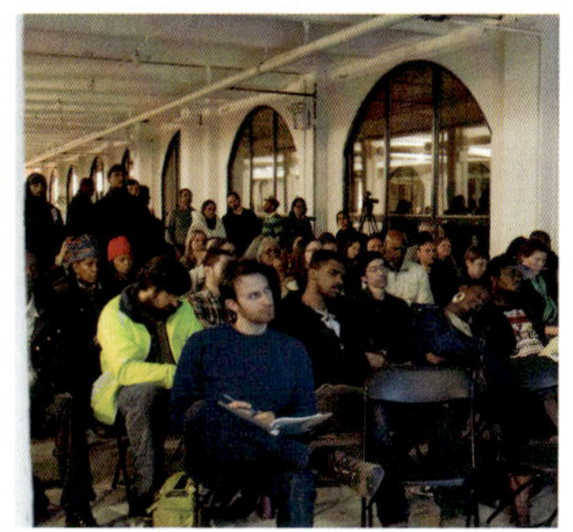
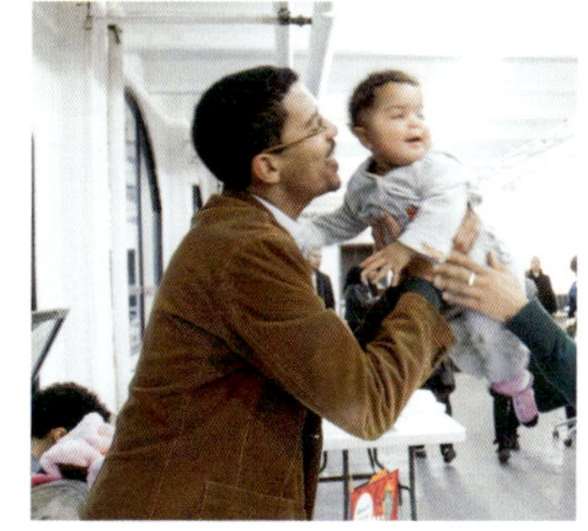
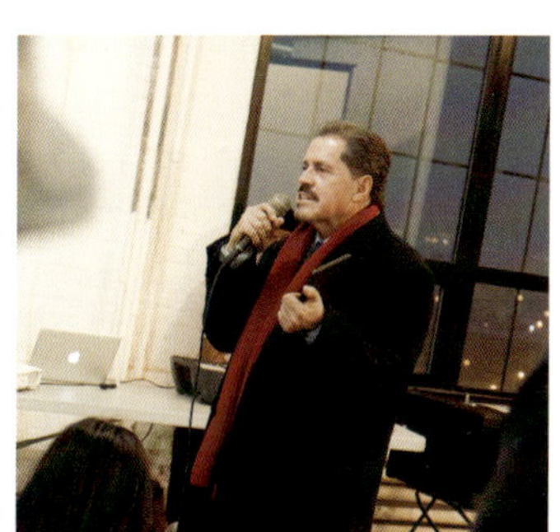
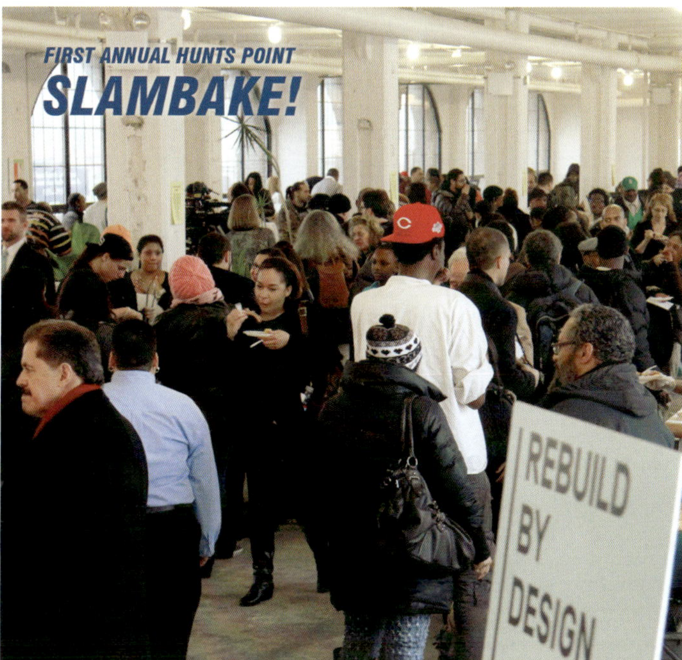

FIRST ANNUAL HUNTS POINT
SLAMBAKE!
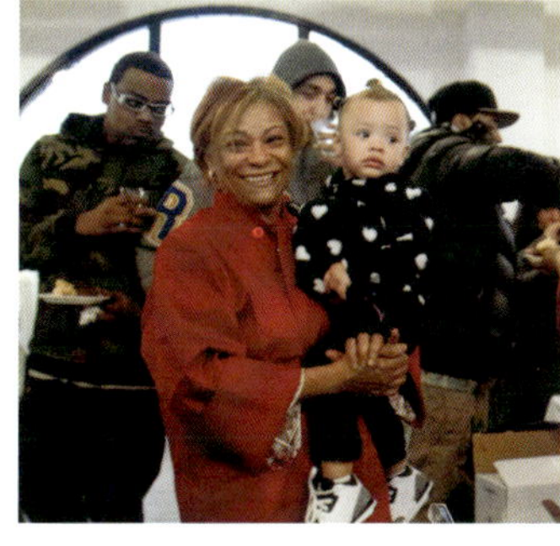
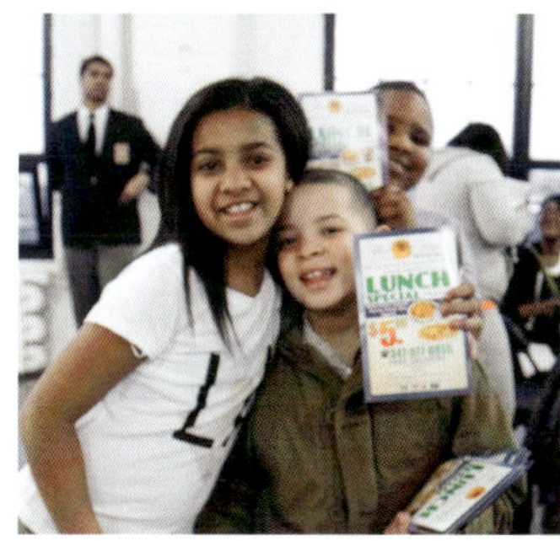

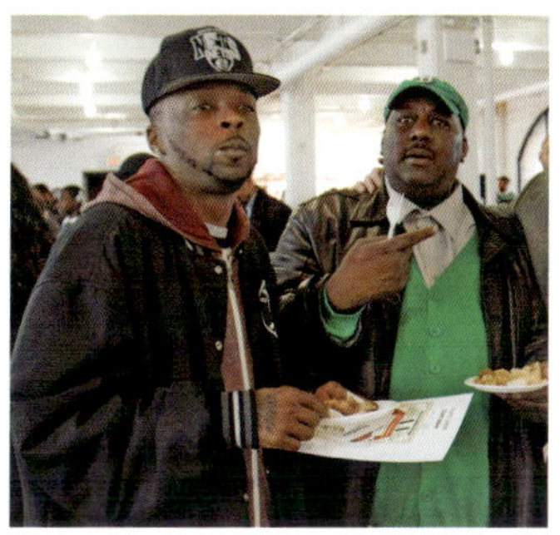
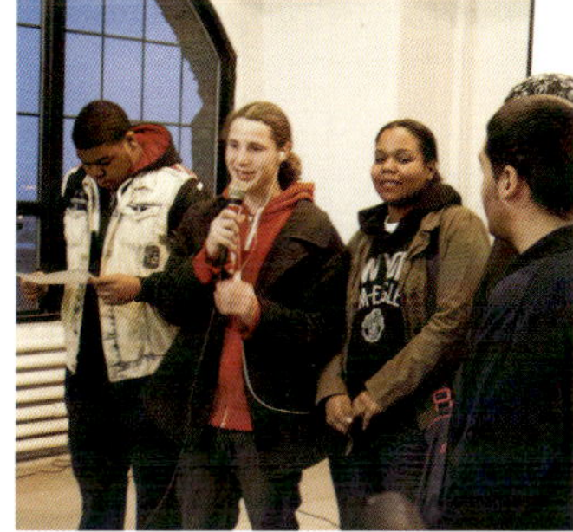

4

Final Proposal: Hunts Point Lifelines

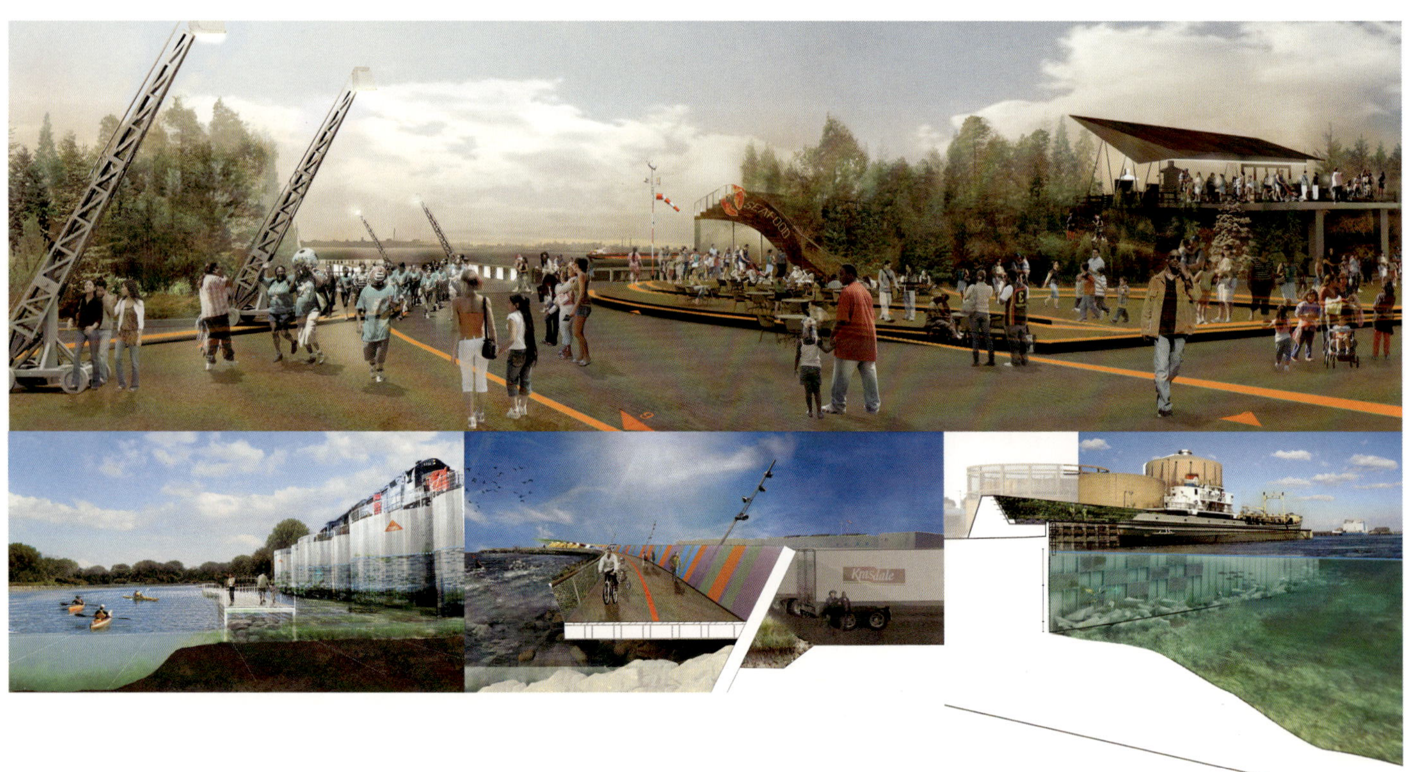

Above: Buoyant flood gates accommodate large openings in the levee for a new pier and restaurants proposed by the Fulton Fish Market. The operations area doubles as a generous public space for the annual Hunts Point Fish Parade and other events.

1 Levee Lab

Hunts Point Lifelines focuses on flood protection that keeps the food supply on-line and stimulates reinvestment in Hunts Point. Flood protection is integrated with the South Bronx Greenway, a cornerstone of the Hunts Point Vision Plan developed by the community and the New York City Economic Development Corporation. New awareness of the need for protection makes it possible to expand the scale, ambition, and functions of the original greenway proposal.

Lifelines builds on the diversity of edge and energy conditions in the Bronx and East Rivers to propose a proactive research model called Levee Lab: a series of designed ecologies, applied materials research, and pilots that test new techniques for climate adaptation on industrial waterfronts. Collectively, these projects can contribute to a new regulatory framework and demonstrate an intelligent approach to scaling up climate adaptation.

The design opens dynamic windows on the operations and spectacle of the working waterfront – the eclectic mix of things that people like about the working waterfront. Levee Lab takes many forms as it negotiates the conditions of the site, supporting ecologies suited to the slow, shallow water of the Bronx River and the deep, high-energy water of the East River.

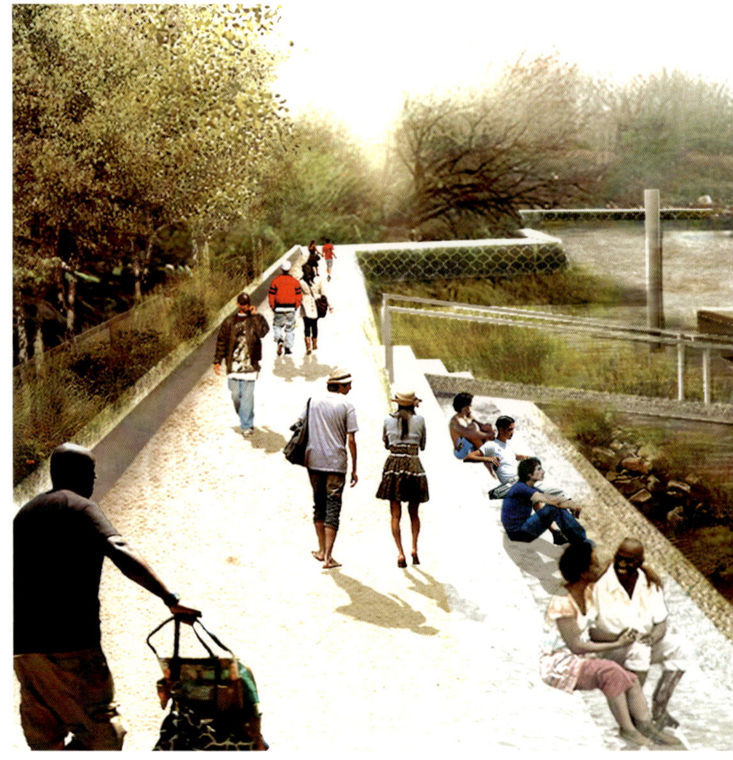

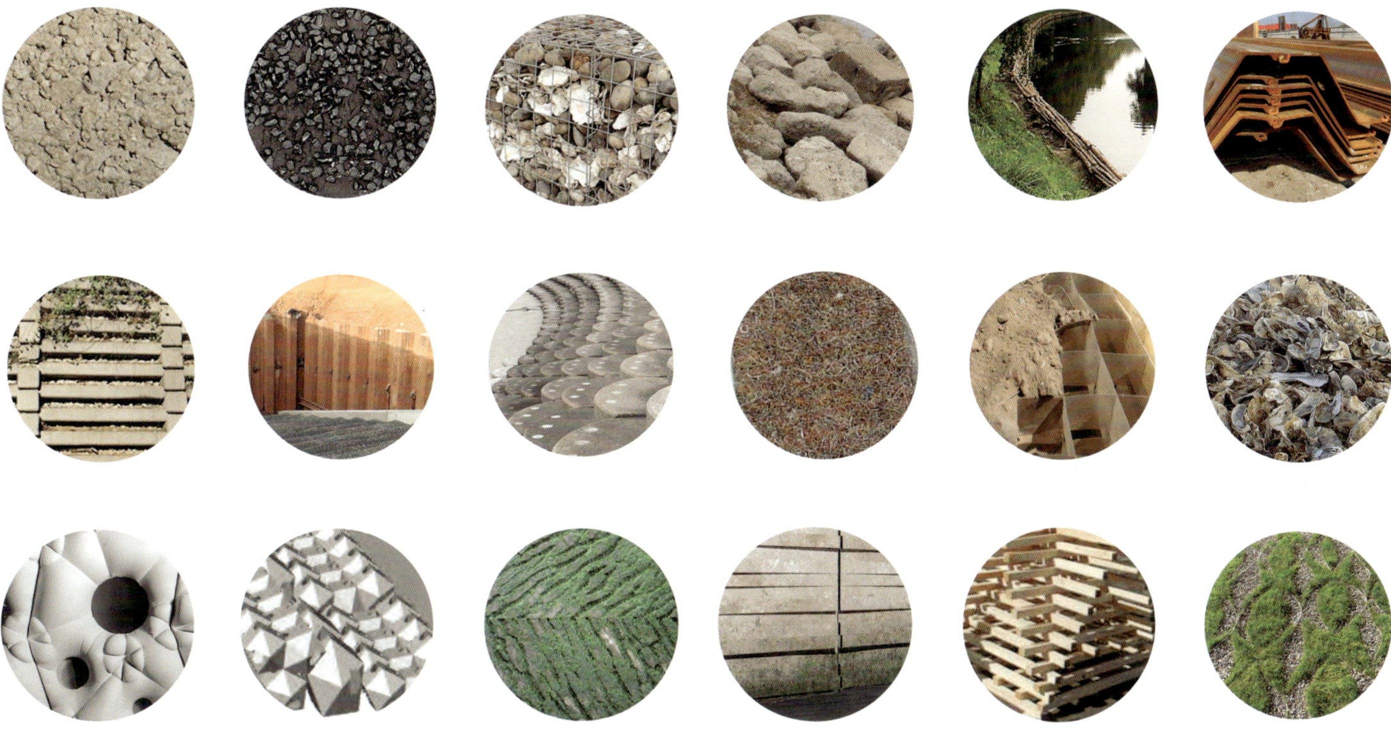

Because the length of the flood protection edge is long and the uses are practical, a considerable stretch of the integrated levee and greenway will use an efficient, "workhorse" palette of materials but deploy these materials to maximum experiential and ecological effect. In selected areas, the team also proposes experimenting with new materials and techniques, rigorously evaluating the effects to determine if the materials merit wider application. The locations for experimentation will be dictated by constraints that make standard approaches challenging. NYS DEC suggested investigating alternatives to fill such as cantilevered decks and decking on light structures where operations make it impossible to build the greenway on land. Problem-solving for selected locations involves accommodation of loaded freight trains on top of a coffer dam, sludge boat service to the waste water treatment plant, and other pragmatics of the working waterfront and intermodal access.

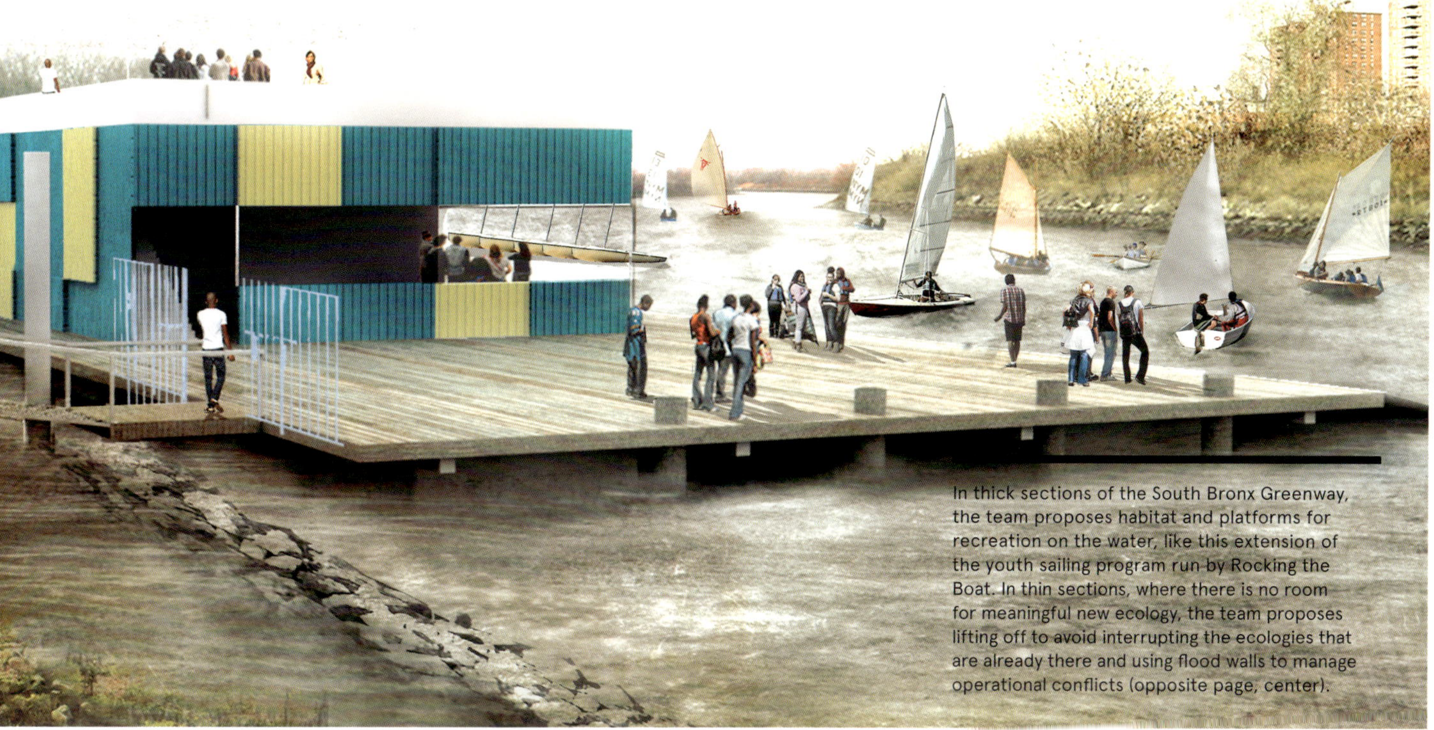

In thick sections of the South Bronx Greenway, the team proposes habitat and platforms for recreation on the water, like this extension of the youth sailing program run by Rocking the Boat. In thin sections, where there is no room for meaningful new ecology, the team proposes lifting off to avoid interrupting the ecologies that are already there and using flood walls to manage operational conflicts (opposite page, center).

2 Livelihoods

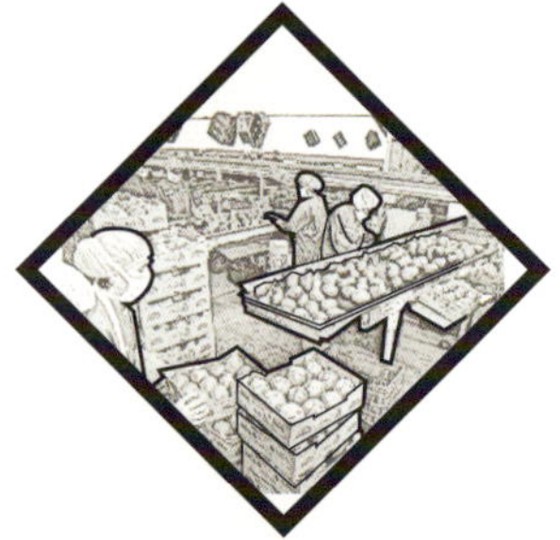

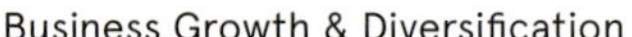

Business Growth & Diversification

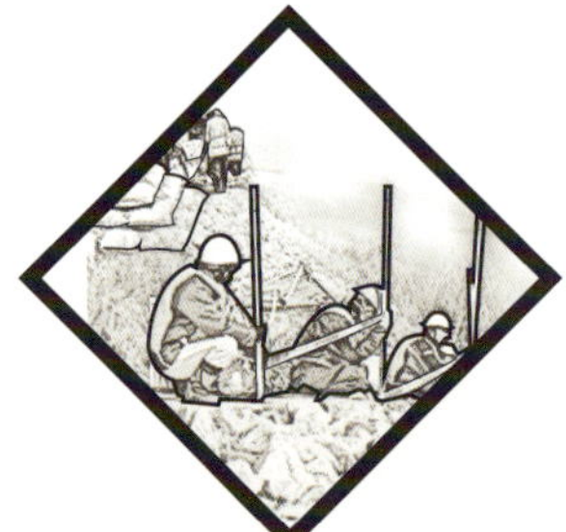

Operations

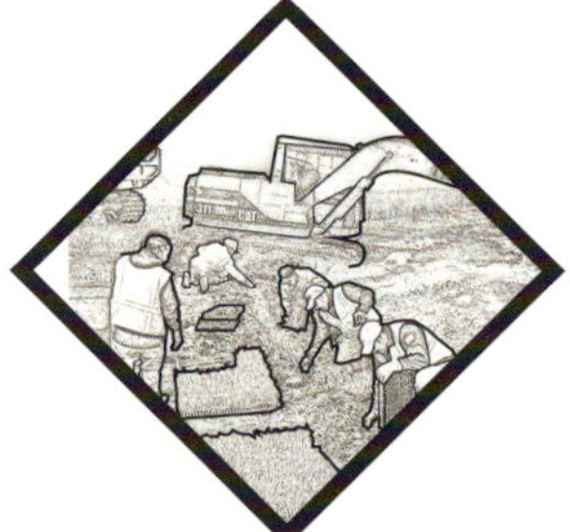

Construction

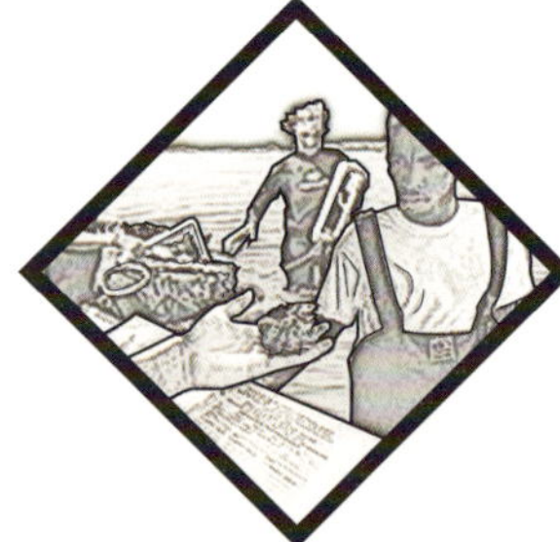

Research and Monitoring

In addition to supporting private sector growth, Lifelines incorporates new approaches to construction, maintenance, and research into the Levee Lab. Attention to job creation recognizes that employment is an essential part of resilience infrastructure in communities where poverty creates major vulnerability to storms and other disasters.

An important aim of Lifelines is to demonstrate that local communities can participate in climate adaptation, understand its dynamics and risks, and benefit from public and private sector investments in resilience. Local procurement and labor force strategies not only build community economic assets needed for resilience, but also generate a range of benefits including learning, awareness of waterfront dynamics, perception of risk, informed citizenship, and a deeper sense of locality and personal investment. These are all meaningful contributions to the cultural shift required for the larger transformation that Rebuild by Design seeks to catalyze.

If the value of resilience investment is felt every day in new jobs, community economic assets, and awareness of the waterfront, the community will be more likely to sustain the on-going commitment that climate adaptation demands.

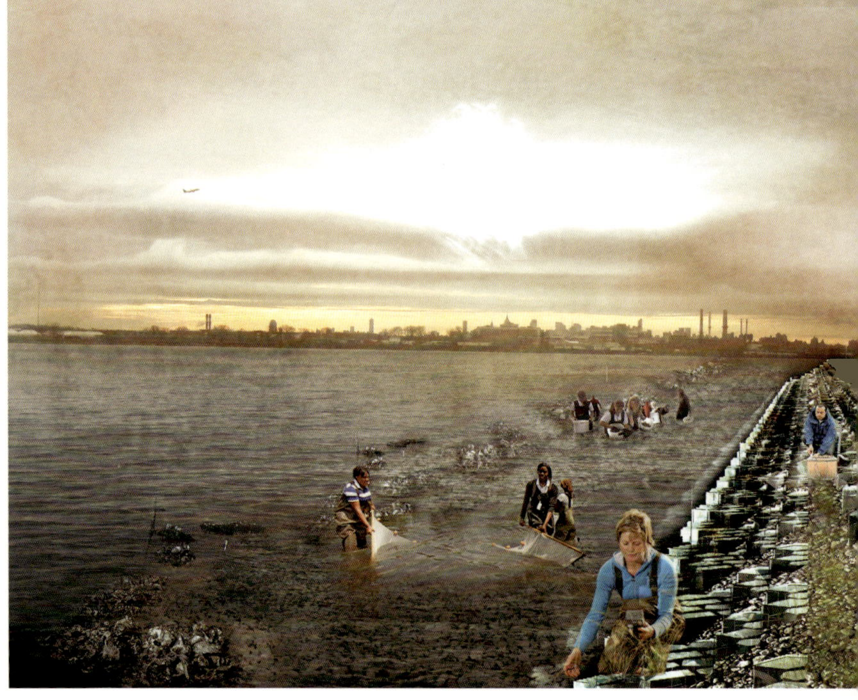

View of the South Bronx Greenway and flood protection infrastructure. The waterfront becomes a space not just for recreation, but also for work, engagement, and awareness. Youth involvement is high, building on the demonstrated expertise Hunts Point organizations have in habitat creation and monitoring programs.

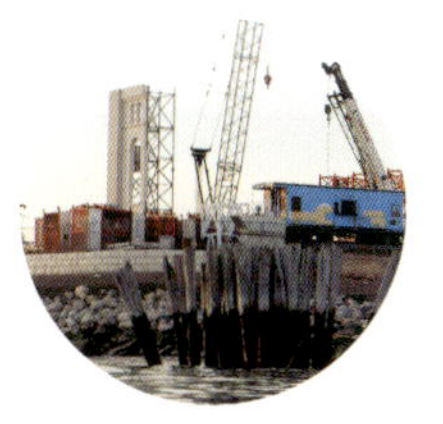
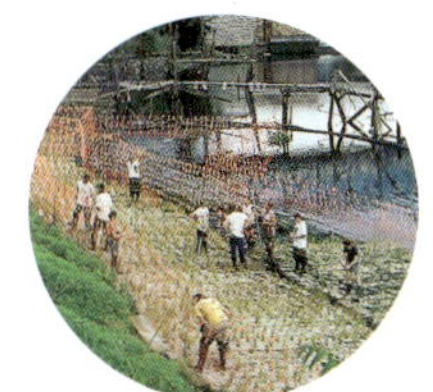
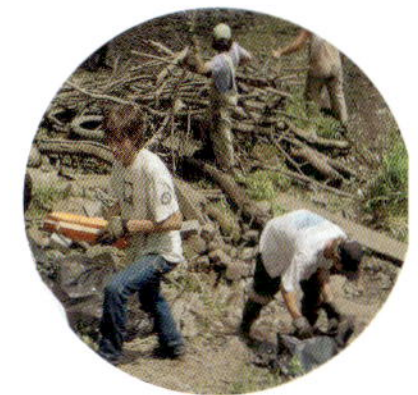
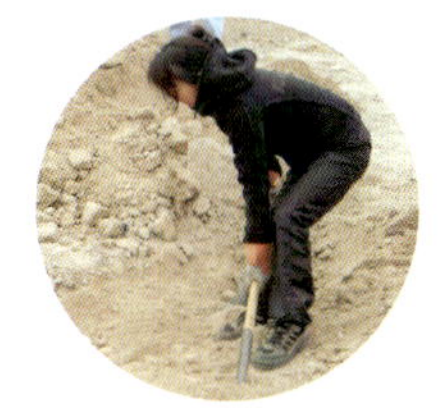
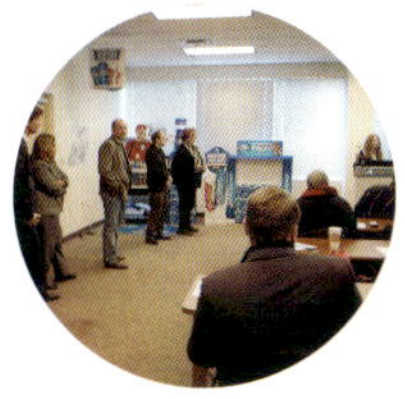
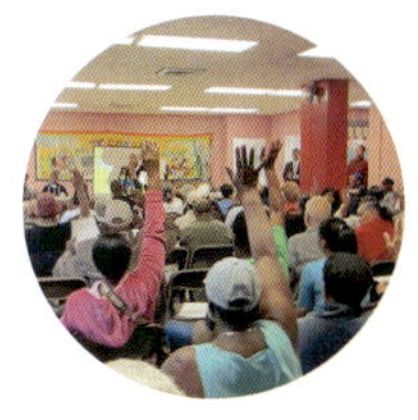
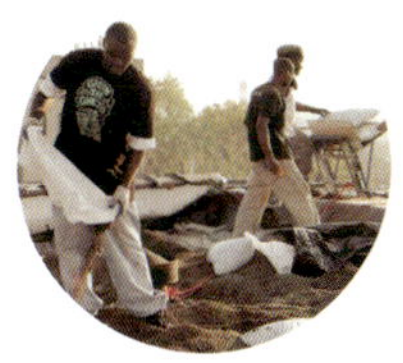
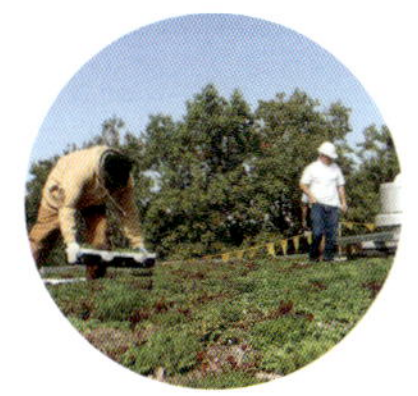
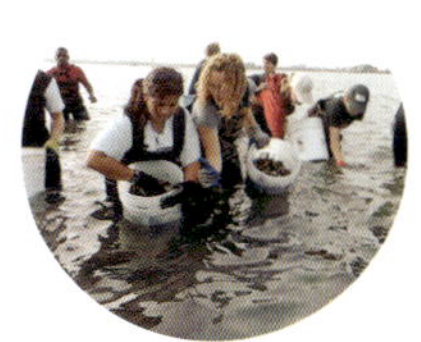
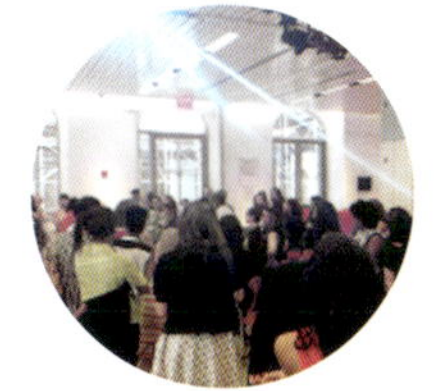
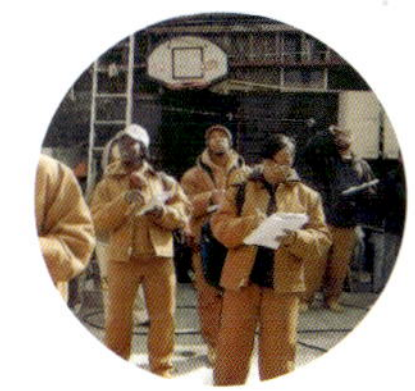
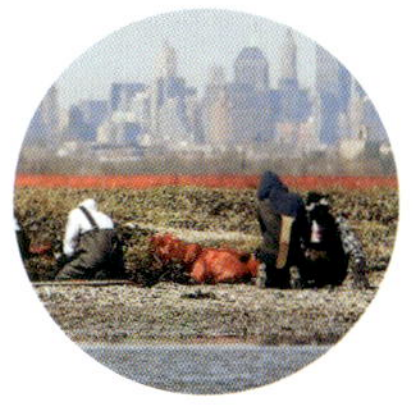

To help project partners and potential funders think constructively about the best way to integrate jobs and economic resilience benefits into the physical design of the levee, the team developed a palette of options for consideration by government and the community.

Penn/OLIN outlined a number of possible arrangements rather than preferred options. Job opportunities include specific construction roles, maintenance, ecological productivity monitoring, as well as private sector growth.

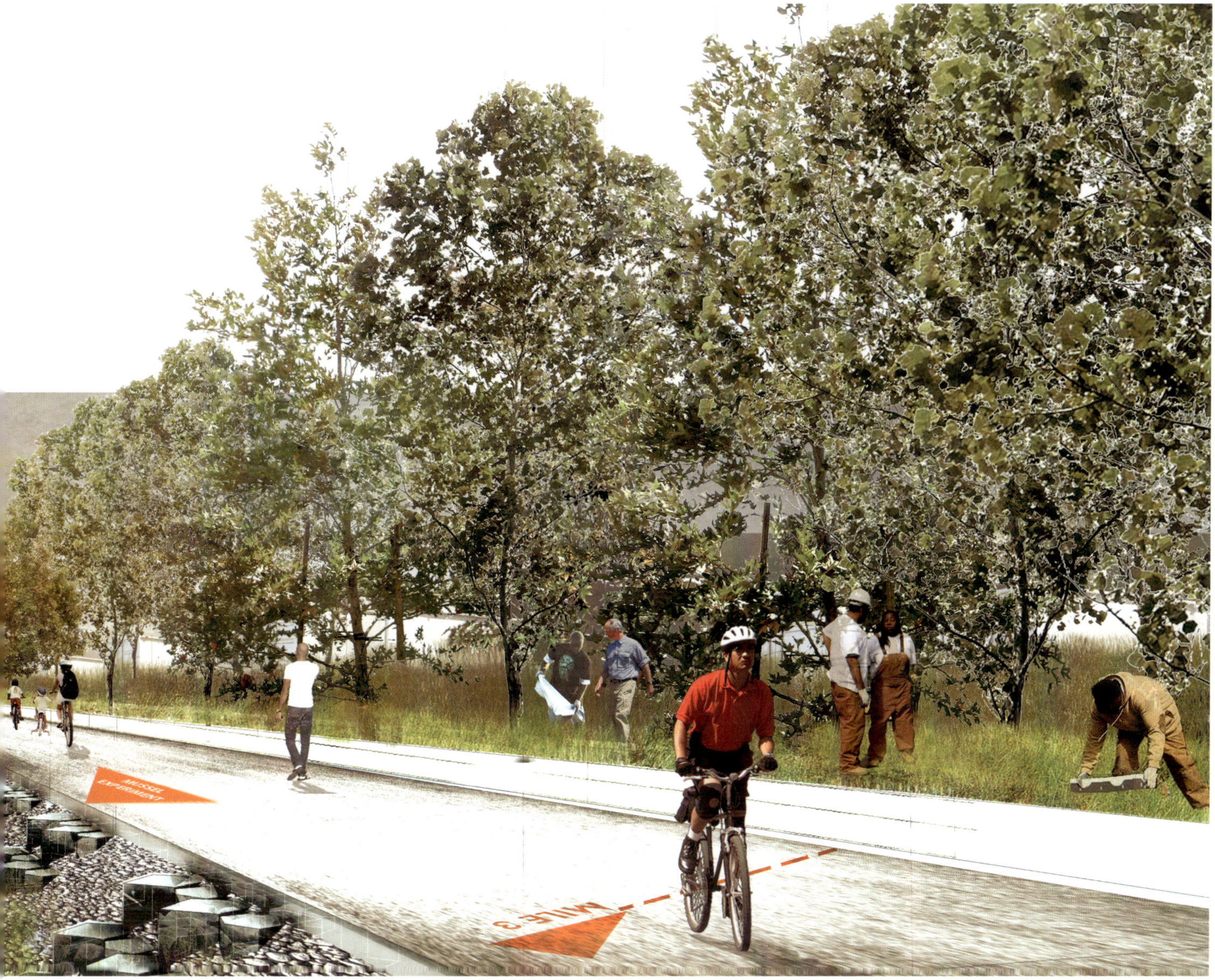

3 Cleanways

The Cleanways are a series of infrastructure elements that improve connectivity, sociability, air quality, safe passage for pedestrians through truck routes, food access, and filtration of stormwater. They connect the new amenity and open space of the waterfront to inland neighborhoods. The Cleanways also help to recenter the community around public transit and the new Metro North station to be built in Hunts Point.

The most ambitious element of the Cleanways lifeline is a proposal to move beyond back-up generation and create a clean Tri-Gen Power Generating Station that turns waste heat into chilled water, designed for the huge thermal load of a district dependent on refrigeration. The creation of a Tri-Gen plant would make it possible for the Hunts Point peninsula to act as a microgrid island when the City grid goes down. While the public investment required to leverage private operator investment is significant, there are major energy cost reductions for power to food businesses in Hunts Point, as well as reductions in air pollution and the carbon tab of the Food Distribution Center.

CLEANWAY CONNECTIONS

- Greenways/Pedestrian and Bike Corridors
- Truck Routes + Air Quality Corridors
- Cultural Corridor
- Jobs Corridor

CLEANWAY POWER

- Resilient Energy

CLEANWAY ZONES

- Stormwater Infiltration
- Residential Area
- Light Industrial Area
- Proposed Metro North Station
- Existing Subway Station

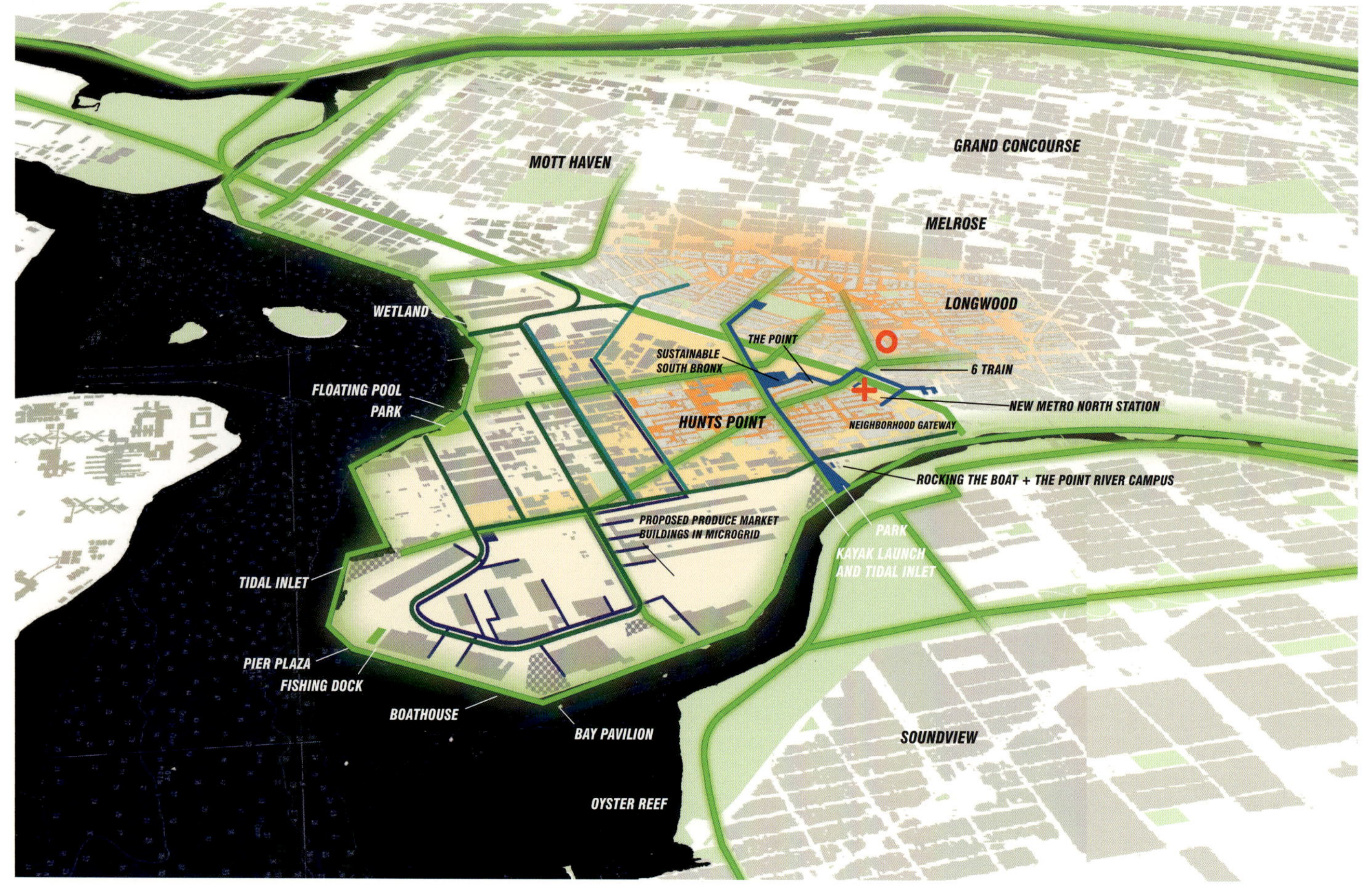

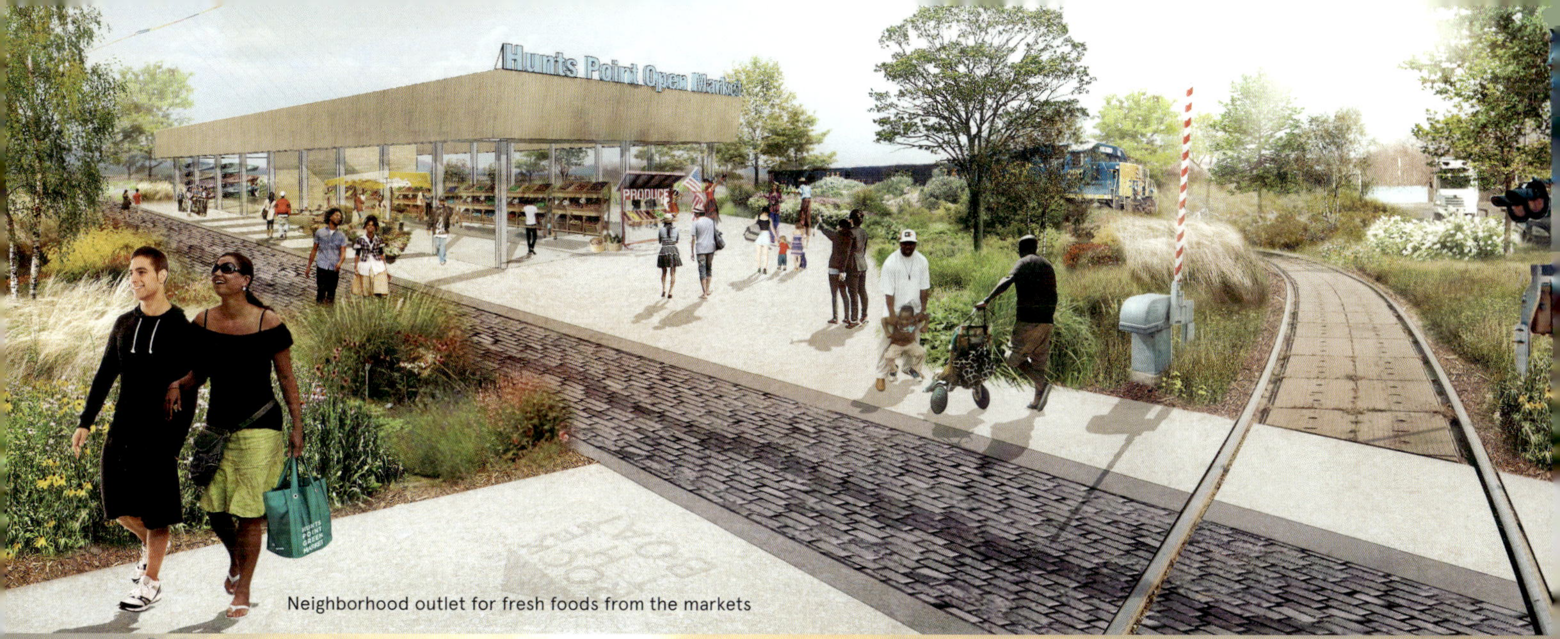

Neighborhood outlet for fresh foods from the markets

Tidal inlet and freshwater wetland for storm treatment

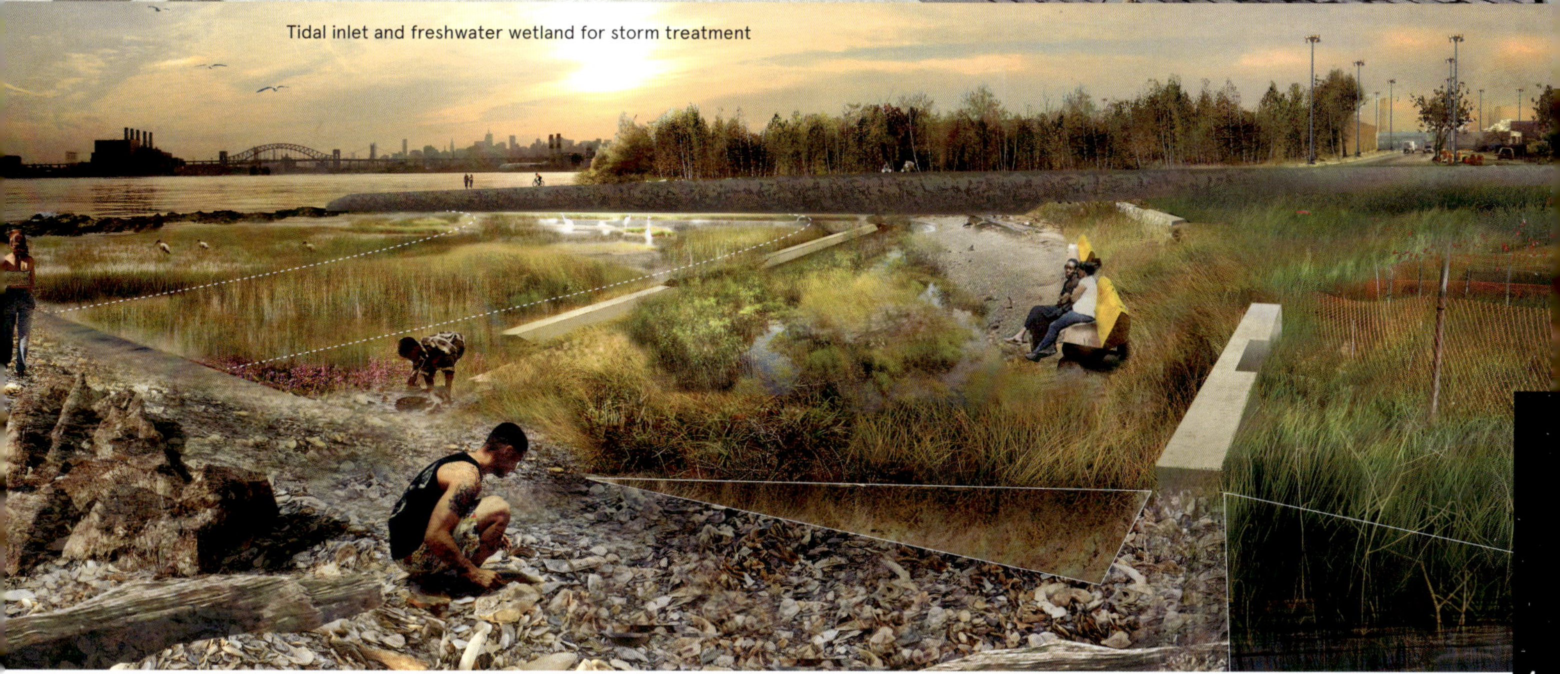

4

To investigate the feasibility of flood protection, Penn/OLIN studied flood vulnerability, sea level rise, stormwater quantity, and wave and surge heights.The levee design considers the modernization of buildings and infrastructure over time.

To avoid a bathtub condition in storms with both high rainfall and surge, the design creates a system of high-volume stormwater treatment wetlands that improve water quality and habitat in typical storms, augmented with passive and active pumping systems.

Flood protection and fresh water treatment basins are engineered to hold and treat stormwater in 95% of all rain events.

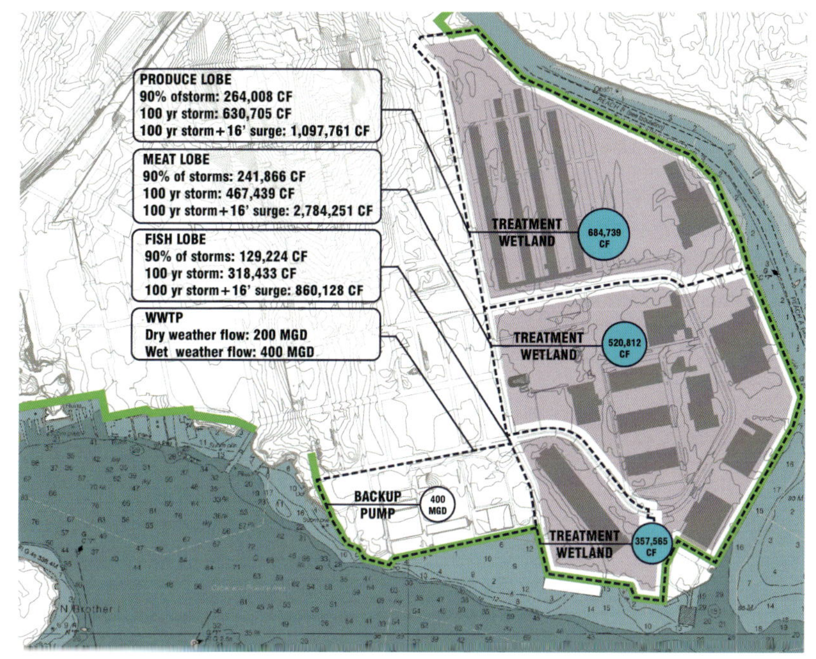

4 Maritime Emergency Supply

The 1997 blizzard, September 11 attacks, 2003 blackout, and the 2011 and 2012 hurricanes demonstrated the vulnerability of New York's road and subway-based transportation network. Maritime access can often be restored before other modes, and more than 15 million people in the New York metropolitan area live within a few miles of navigable waterways, including New York Harbor, the East River, Long Island Sound, and the Hudson, Passaic, and Raritan rivers.

The PennDesign/OLIN team identified an opportunity to create a base of operations in Hunts Point for the maritime distribution of goods, personnel, and equipment to areas under emergency, particularly when roads, tunnels, and bridges are down. Hunts Point Lifelines builds on the Marine Highways, Cities Readiness Initiative, and Disaster Relief and Mitigation programs of the federal government to explore the viability of establishing an emergency maritime supply chain for the east coast, with Hunts Point as a distribution node and potential supply stockpile site. Once built, the necessary pier infrastructure would make it possible to increase use of marine highways for regular maritime commerce, increasing resilience, reducing carbon, and stimulating growth in Hunts Point.

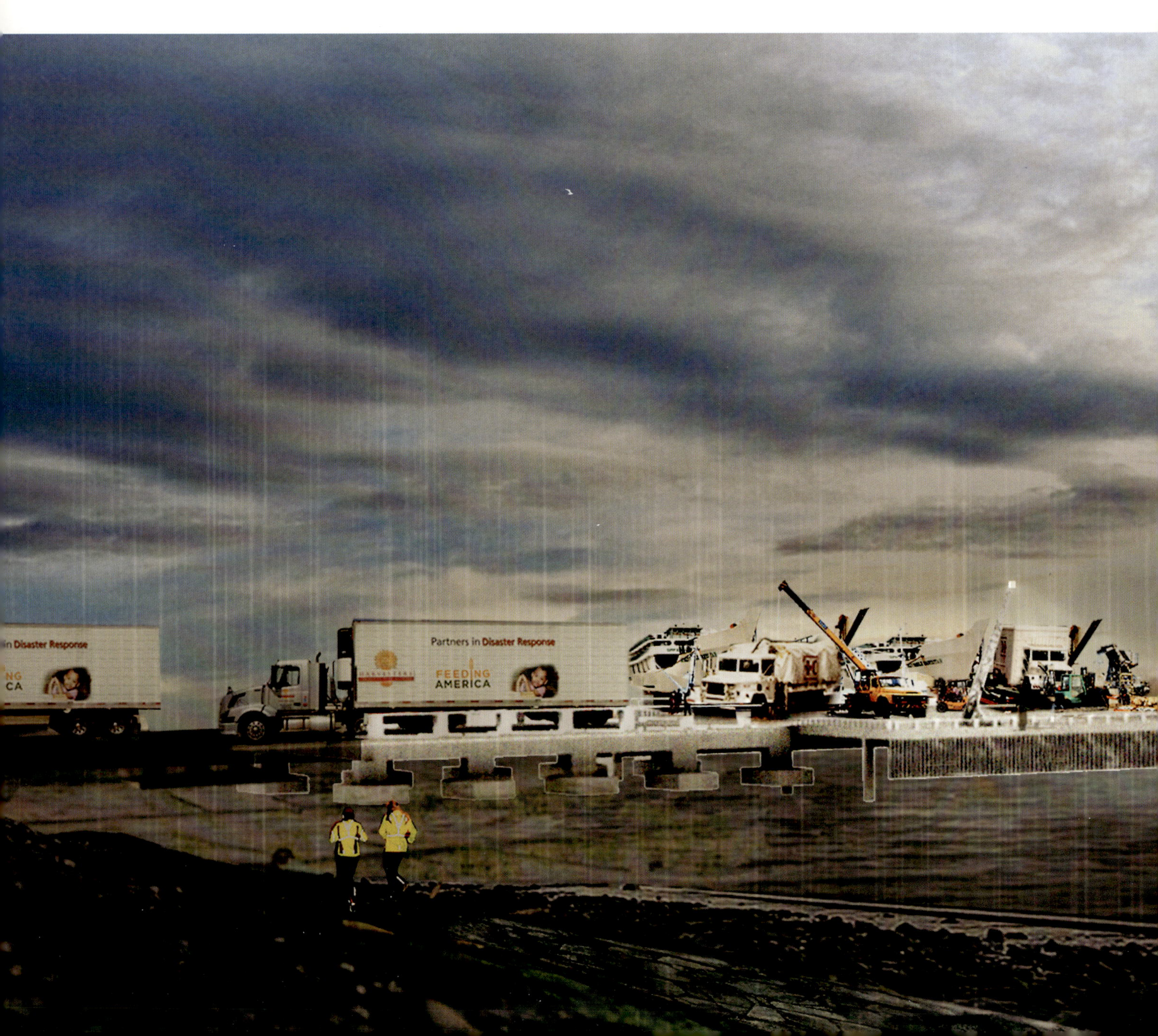

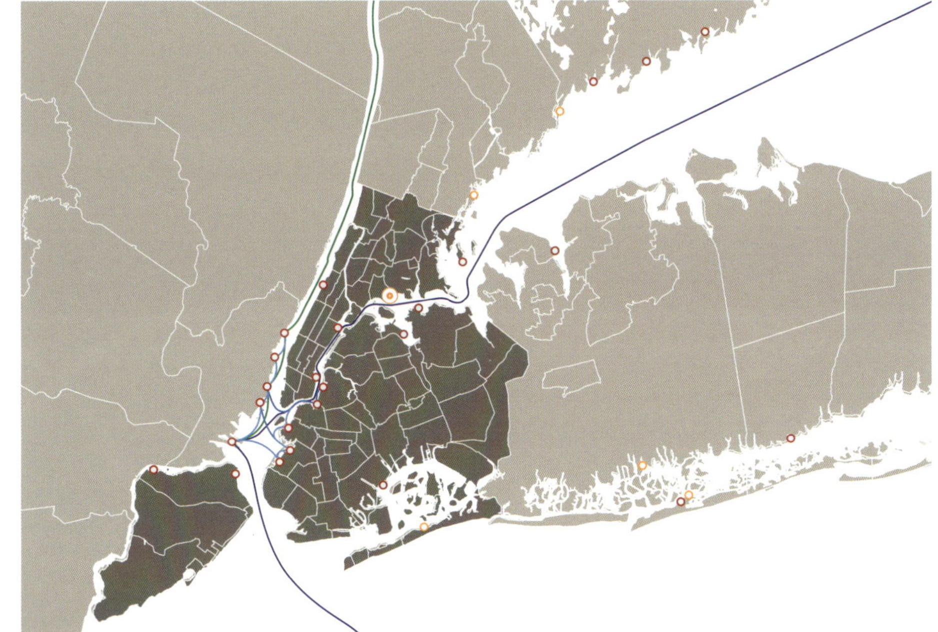

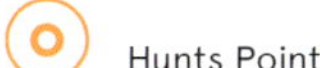 Hunts Point

Destination with existing pier

Destination with new or improved pier

Trans-Hudson Freight Connector Project

New England Marine Highway Project

Hudson River Food Corridor Initiative

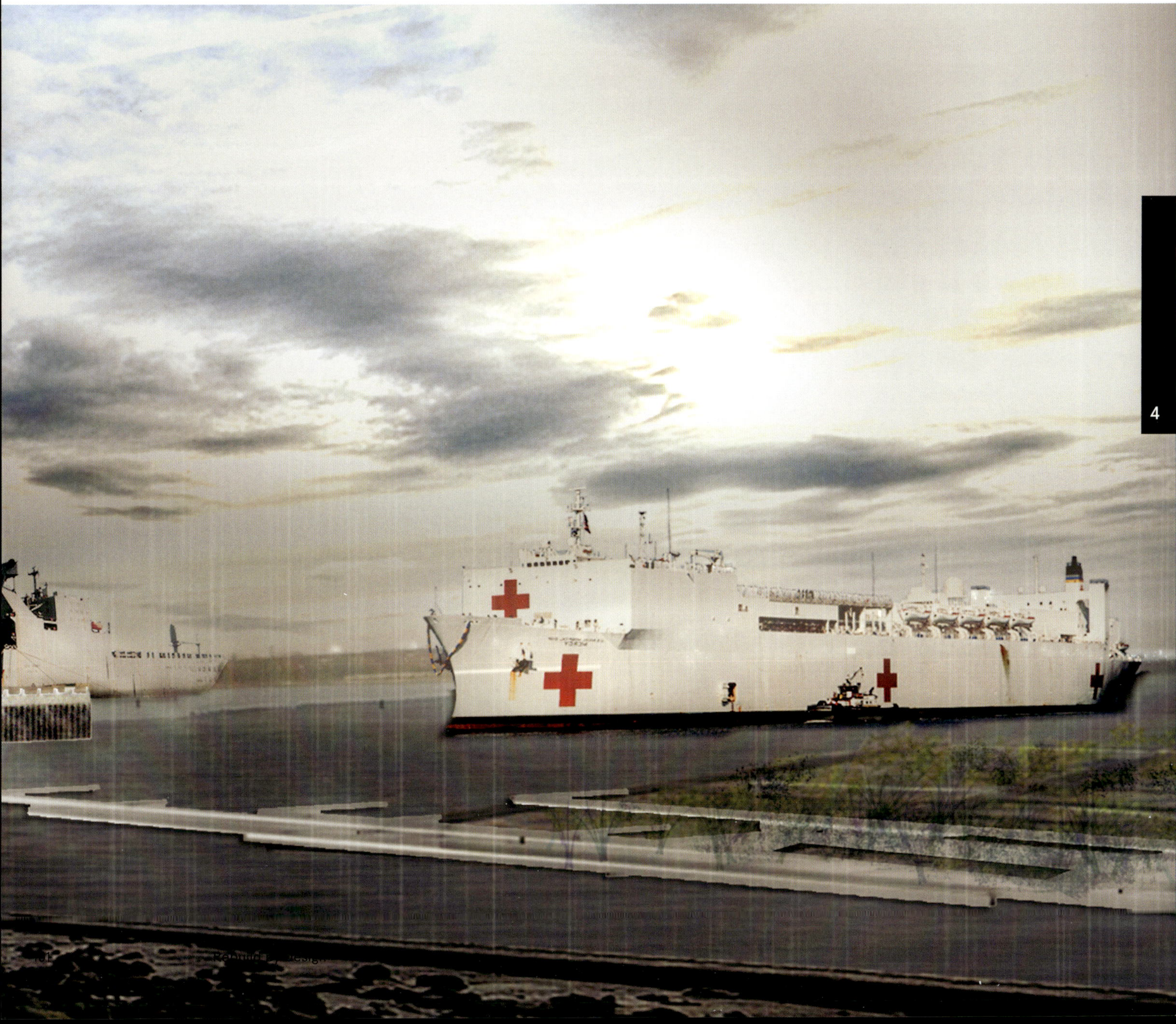

RESILIENCE + THE BEACH

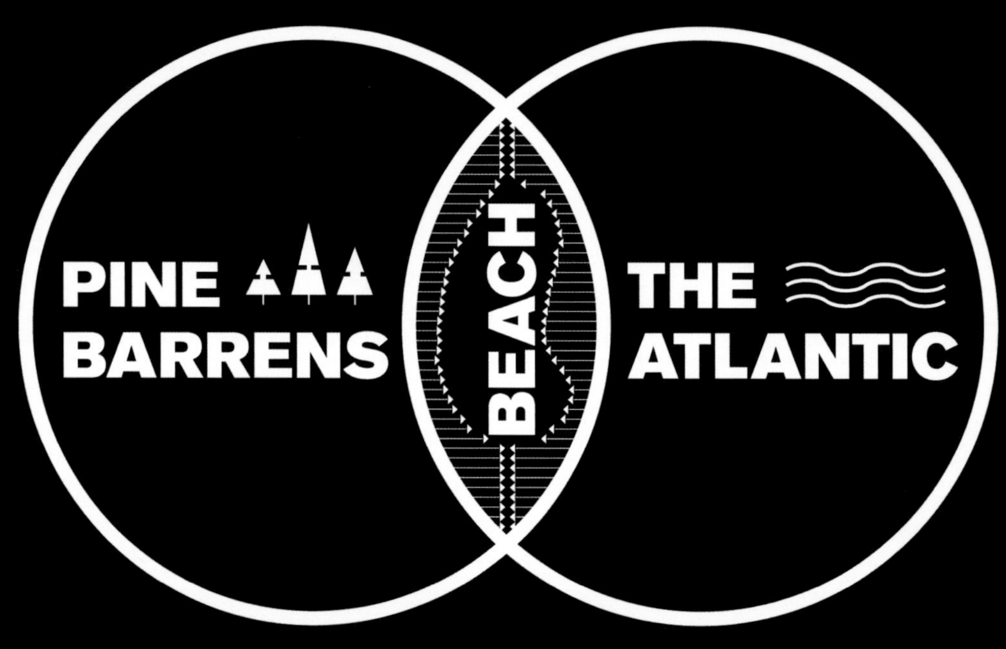

Team Lead
Sasaki Associates, Inc.

Ecology, Biology, and Sociology
Rutgers University

Coastal Engineering
ARUP

Sasaki/Rutgers/Arup

New Jersey's beaches constitute a complex system of fluctuating populations, transit and development patterns, and ecological conditions unique to the Atlantic coast. Three coastal landform typologies - barrier islands, headlands, and inland bays - each face particular vulnerabilities that require specific solutions and regional collaboration. The Sasaki/Rutgers/Arup Team's design drew from both an environmental analysis of each typology and from the cultural memory of this storied place. The project aims to protect future communities and ensure the beach's role as an economic driver for the state. Adaptations to ecological structures, infrastructure, tourism, and settlement must be made to meet these twin goals. Integrated solutions for each typology create a new type of resilience — one that protects the beach and enhances social capital.

Barrier Islands [Barnegat Bay]
Significant development has occurred on the Jersey Shore barrier islands in recent decades, but Hurricane Sandy brought to light their vulnerability. Sasaki's proposal encourages inland development meant to support a diversified, resilient tourism economy.

Headlands [Asbury Park]
The site of the Shore's boardwalk, this landscape is attractive to tourists, but not supportive to habitat. Sasaki's design explores a more organic boardwalk form that captures sand and forms dunes, creating protection while serving as habitat for beach wildlife. The design would improve inland lakes and green streets to absorb surge and improve urban character.

Inland Bay [Natco Lake]
The inland bay integrates industry, dense maritime communities, New York City connections, and the ecology of the estuary. Sasaki's design rethinks the local marina to make it multifunctional, augmenting it with marshlands to increase coastal protection, providing new sources of value for ecosystems and communities, and mitigating contamination.

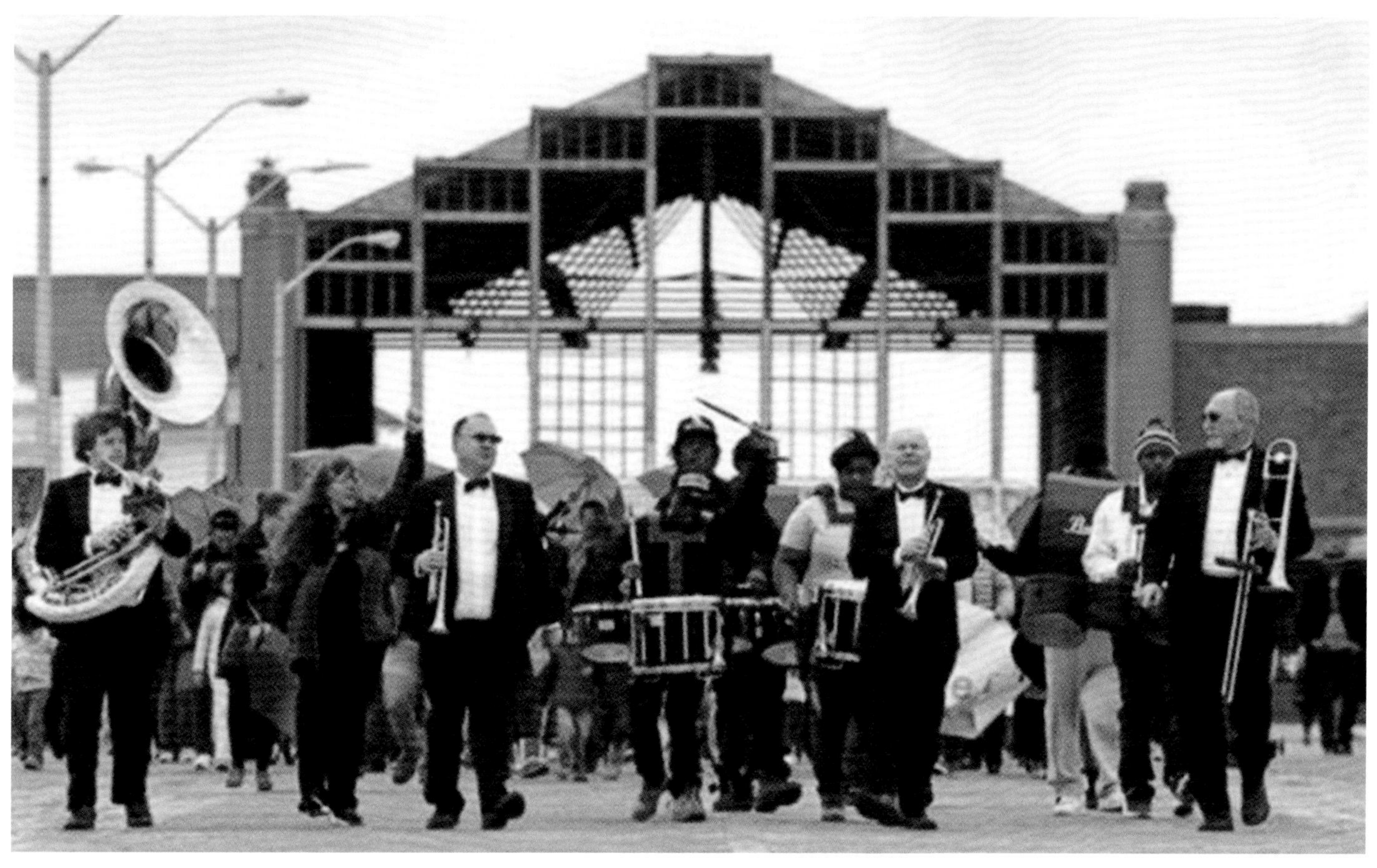

Approach to Varying Typologies

The team's research and design strategies focused on the value of "the beach." Even though the beach is particularly significant to cultural memory, state and local economies, and coastal ecosystems, it is also incredibly vulnerable to the impact of sea level rise. Over the past century, Jersey Shore tourism has grown to play a significant role in the state's economy and the region's identity. At the same time, practices to support tourism and other development negatively impacted the underlying ecology and resilience of the beach and its communities. Sasaki defined the Shore far beyond the narrow strip of sand typically associated with the

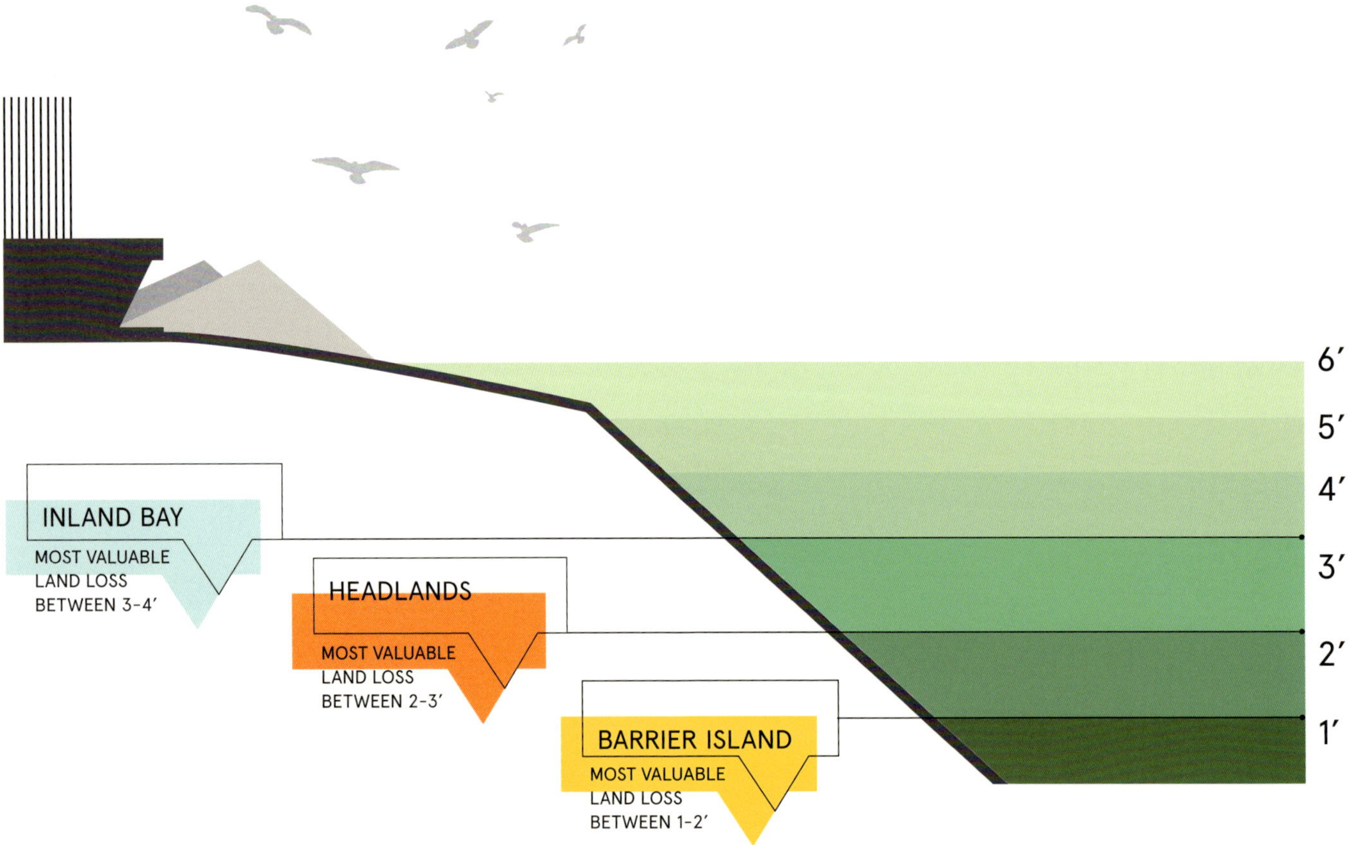

Impact of Variations in Sea Level Rise

The analysis of sea level rise was intended to retain its dynamic nature when characterizing potential losses and threats to three coastal typologies. Using NOAA sea level rise data and parcel-level data from Monmouth and Ocean Counties, parcels were reclassified according to their relationship to inundation envelopes for one to six feet of sea level rise as well as their location in the three coastal types. By linking sea level rise projections, coastal typologies, and county assessor's data, the Sasaki team was able to understand the magnitude of losses (land, value, and tax income) for each coastal typology within a range of sea level rise scenarios. The findings on overall magnitude of projected physical land and land value losses showed steady increases between each one-foot increment and an eventual leveling off in the rate of growth of losses at the five-foot mark.

However, a critical finding was the pronounced variation across coastal typologies in rate of change in value per acre lost in each foot of sea level. This illuminated the differences in how proximity to the water is valued and mediated in each of the coastal typologies in New Jersey. For example, in the Jersey Shore barrier island study area, the highest value land is lost between one- and two-feet of sea level rise, while in the Inland Bay, the most valuable land is lost between three- and four-feet of sea level rise. Ultimately, across all three typologies in Ocean and Monmouth counties, $526.6 million in annual tax dollars (measured in 2013 dollars) will be lost by 3-feet of sea level rise. This analysis helped frame the threats, confirming the team's understanding that the Barrier Island typology is the most immediately vulnerable, and helped structure a greater intervention in the Barrier Islands vs. the other typologies.

beach. Instead, the team asserted that for the beach to be resilient in the future, it would need to be conceived of as deeper – ecologically, socially, and economically.

In New Jersey, sandy soils reach inland to the Pine Barrens, an expansive and ecologically diverse pine forest. A series of 22 coastal lakes and myriad rivers and creeks bring estuarine and wetlands environments miles into shore. While storm surge and coastal flooding pose increasing threats to the coastline, stormwater from inland watersheds also contributes to significant flood risk. The team took this broad view, contending that resilience would not be achieved with engineering solutions for the immediate coast, but that a resilient beach would need to be linked to projects that deepen the physical extent, ecological reach, and cultural understanding of the beach. Informed by a close reading of the coastal typologies that exist along the Jersey Shore, the Sasaki team developed a regional strategy and local solutions for long-term resilience along the Jersey Shore. This multi-scaled approach could be replicated at sites across the eastern seaboard.

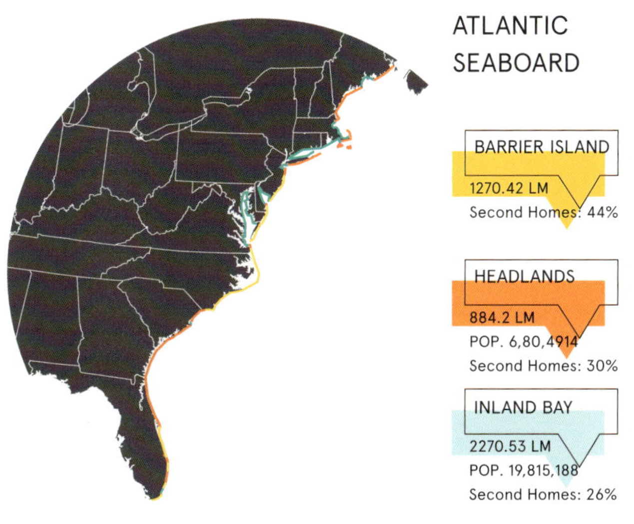

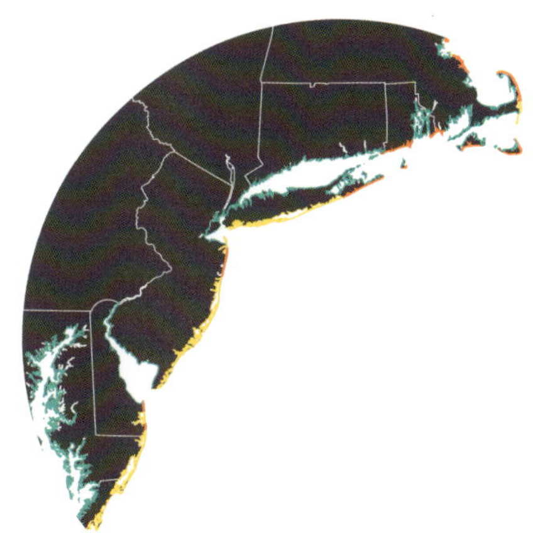

SANDY
AFFECTED AREAS

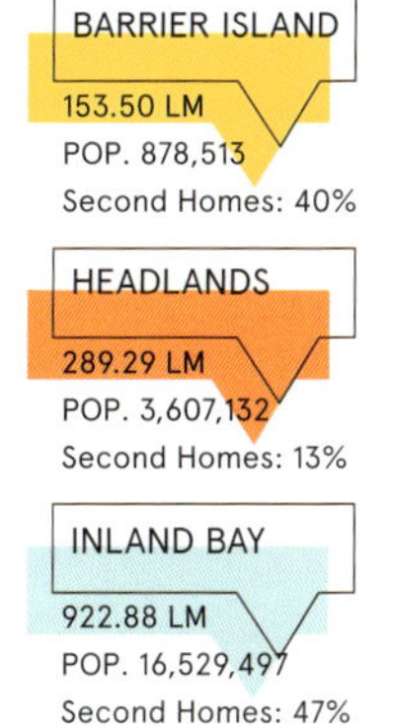

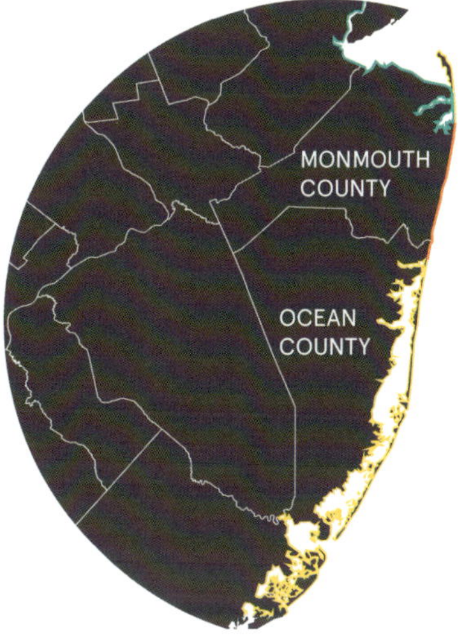

NEW
JERSEY SHORE

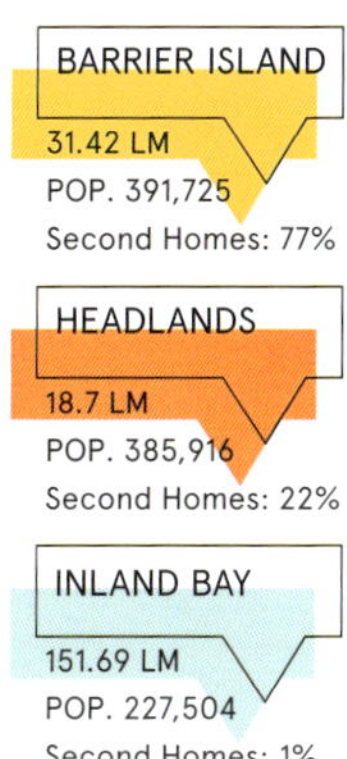

Regionally and nationally relevant typologies

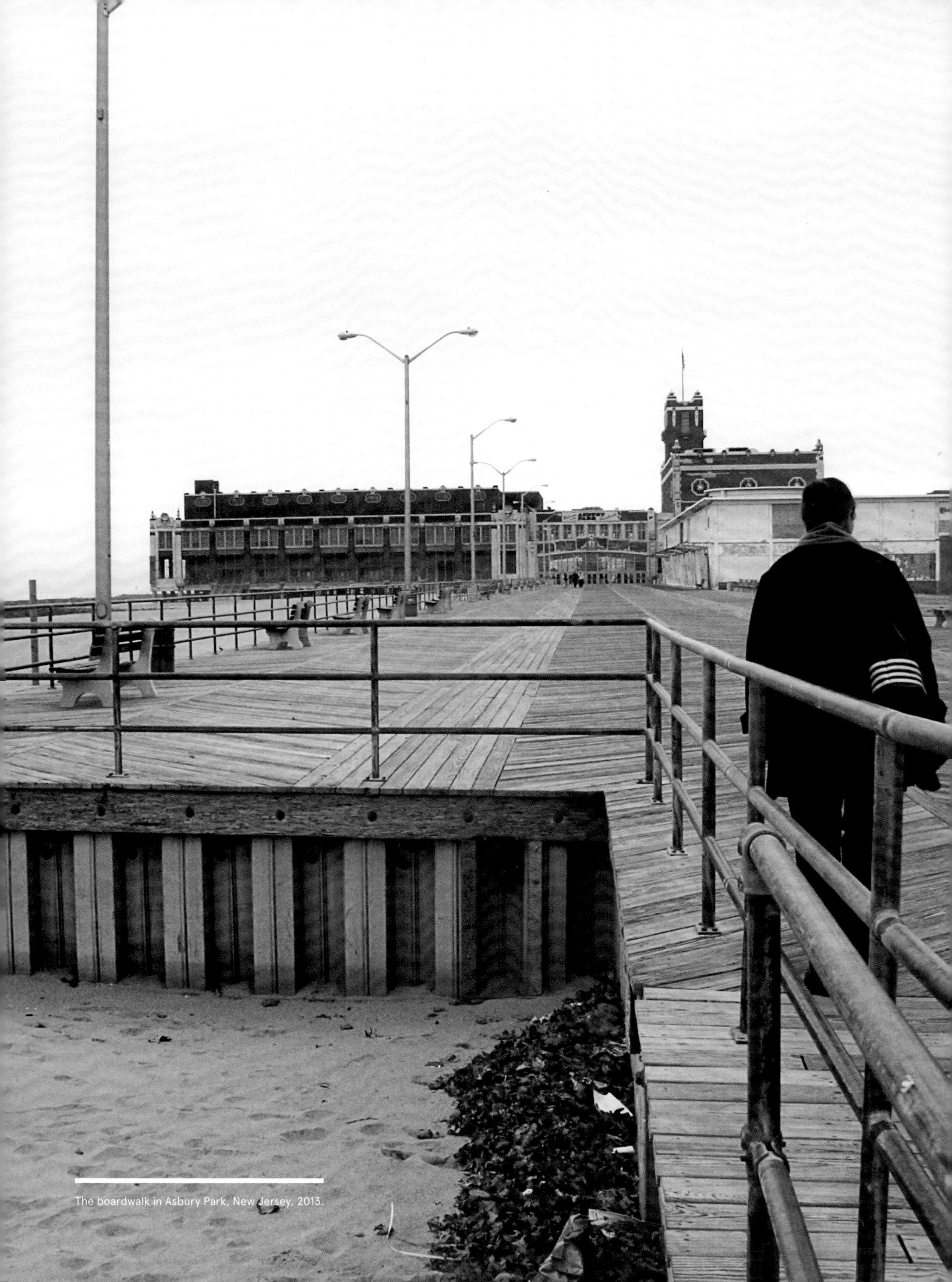

The boardwalk in Asbury Park, New Jersey, 2013.

Design Opportunities

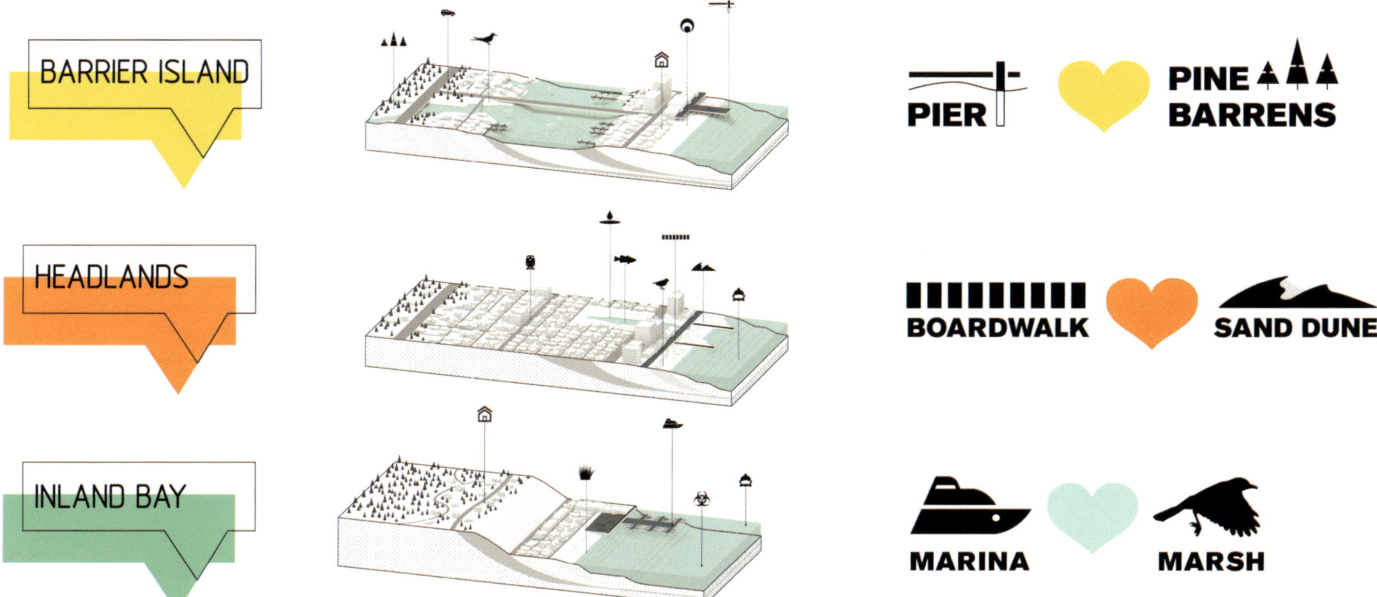

While many economies are driven by dense cities, the economies of American beaches are an exception, fueled instead by the diverse, underlying coastal ecology. The team's research focused on understanding the characteristics and vulnerabilities of the coast based on an analysis of its physical landscape. Every stretch of the US Atlantic coast can be categorized into three distinct environmental typologies: the barrier island, the headlands, and the inland bay. The Sasaki team used these three classifications to develop strategies for a more resilient region.

The team also looked at land-use patterns throughout the region and found a close relationship between the coast's phyiscal characterization and the development that takes place around it. The team found that coastal types directly relate to an area's vulnerability to sea level rise. For example, the Jersey Shore's headlands communities are typified by a public waterfront, with a linear boardwalk and several blocks deep of waterfront commercial property. In contrast, barrier island communities tend to have private waterfronts with individual houses built up to the water's edge. Inland bay communities, which emerged around waterfront industries, have more varied and industrial- or marina-based waterfronts.

Along the Shore, an average headlands community is typically "higher and drier" (at an average elevation of 13 feet) than those on barrier islands (average 3 feet). Hence, barrier island communities in New Jersey, with densely developed, high-value land along ocean or bay edges are highly susceptible to very early levels of sea level rise (1-2 feet), which pose a significant threat to private property. Rising tides compound risks for inland bay communities that are already vulnerable to regular flooding from drainage and storms. When measured against other Atlantic Coast barrier island communities, New Jersey's have a high concentration of second homes, a trait that leads to additional challenges around flood insurance and community cohesion.

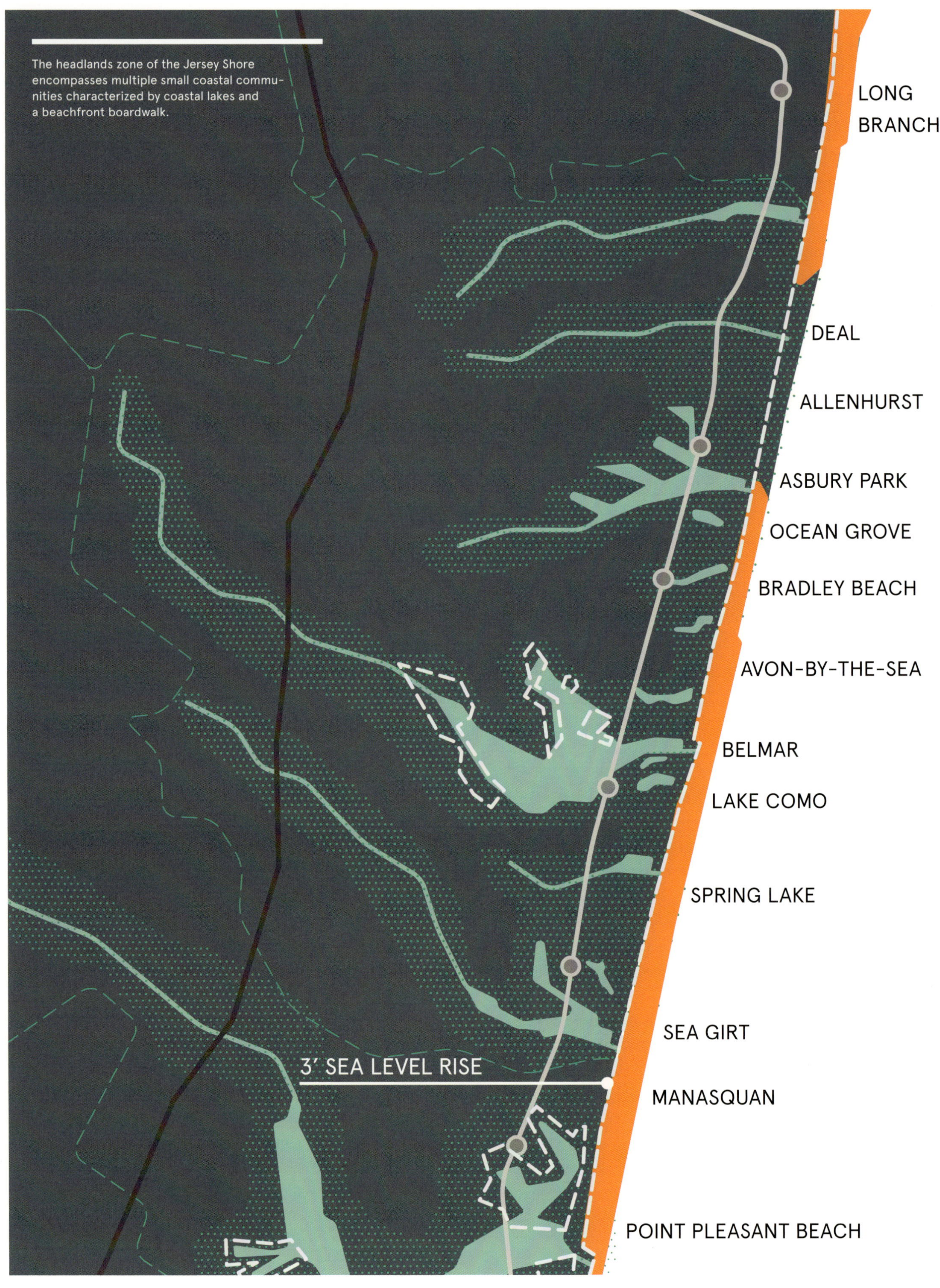
The headlands zone of the Jersey Shore encompasses multiple small coastal communities characterized by coastal lakes and a beachfront boardwalk.
LONG BRANCH
DEAL
ALLENHURST
ASBURY PARK
OCEAN GROVE
BRADLEY BEACH
AVON-BY-THE-SEA
BELMAR
LAKE COMO
SPRING LAKE
SEA GIRT
3′ SEA LEVEL RISE
MANASQUAN
POINT PLEASANT BEACH

Sasaki grounded its research in a study of beach culture: the human experience of the Shore that continues through generations. The proposal drew inspiration from the iconic elements that animate those experiences: the pier, the boardwalk, and the marina. Each of the three coastal types doubles as a distinct cultural emblem for each environmental typology: the barrier islands with piers, the headlands with the boardwalk, and the inland bay with marinas. The proposal integrates these three cultural icons with ecological designs meant to help coastal communities adapt in the face of sea level rise and storm threats.

Like watershed planning approaches, which cross jurisdictional boundaries to promote better and more cohesive water management, Sasaki's project would use regional strategies for each of the coastal typologies. The team tailored each element of its project to development patterns and vulnerabilities specific to each landform, but integrated everything into a full regional approach.

The team identified three pilot sites, one for each of the three coastal typologies. The barrier island strategy would be tested in a district comprised of Berkeley Township, Toms River Township, and Seaside Heights. Asbury Park would represent the headlands condition, and several communities surrounding Natco Lake – Keansburg, Union Beach, and Hazlet – would provide a pilot site for the inland bay condition. While the team addressed local needs for each specific site, it was also able to explore general conditions that the sites embodied, allowing them to be replicable across other communities on the Jersey Shore as well as the entire Atlantic seaboard.

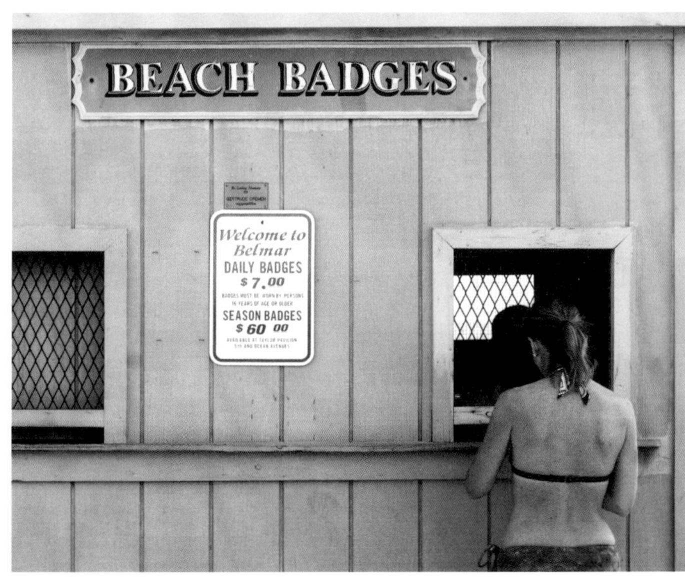

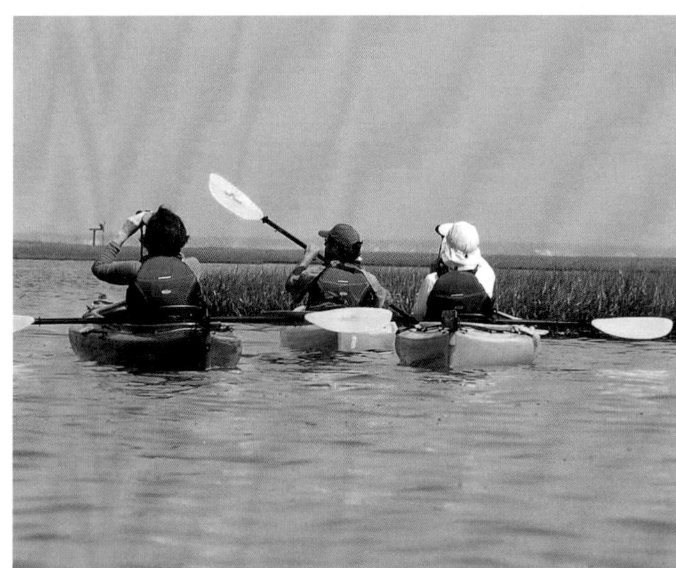

While the Shore's economy is linked to beach pleasures – hotels, amusements, and local restaurants – the future could involve visits to other local ecotourism opportunities, such as kayaking or visiting the Pine Barrens forest.

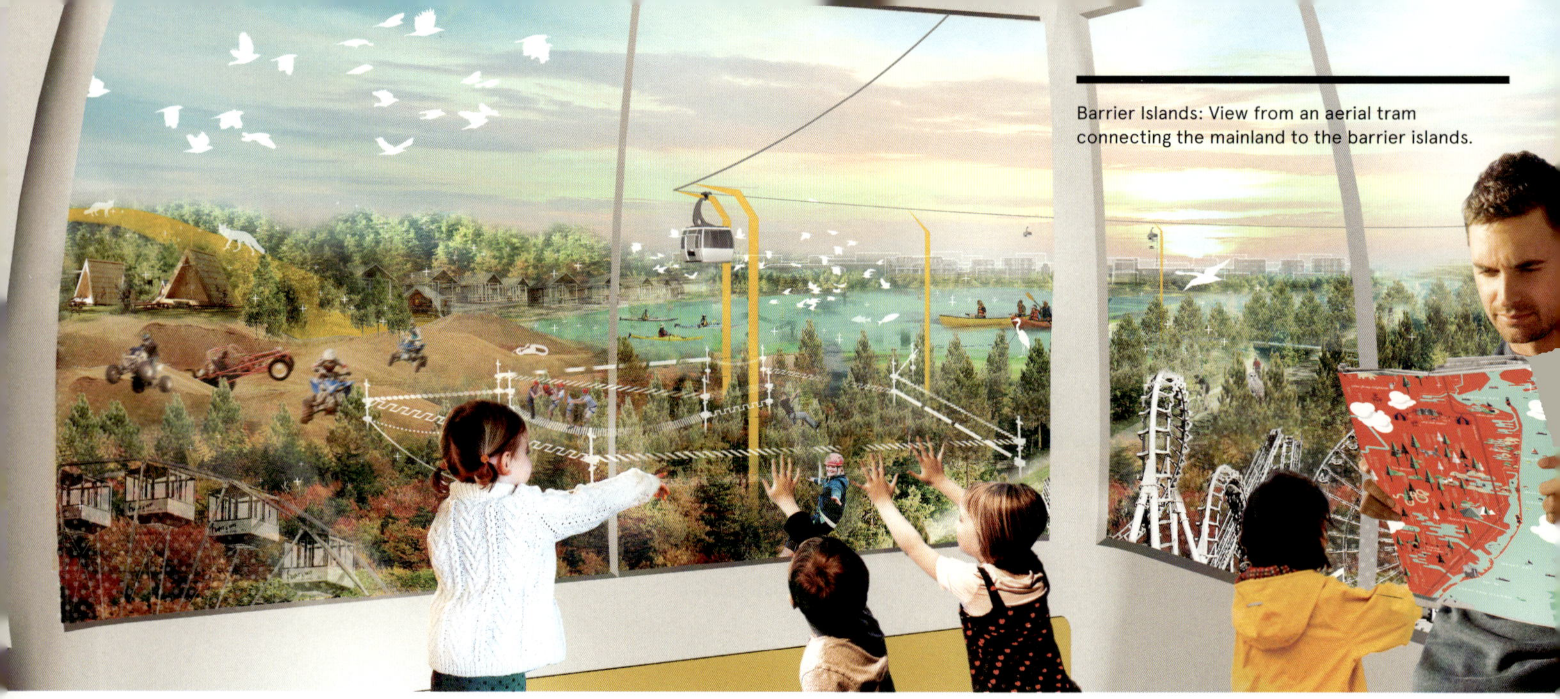

Barrier Islands: View from an aerial tram connecting the mainland to the barrier islands.

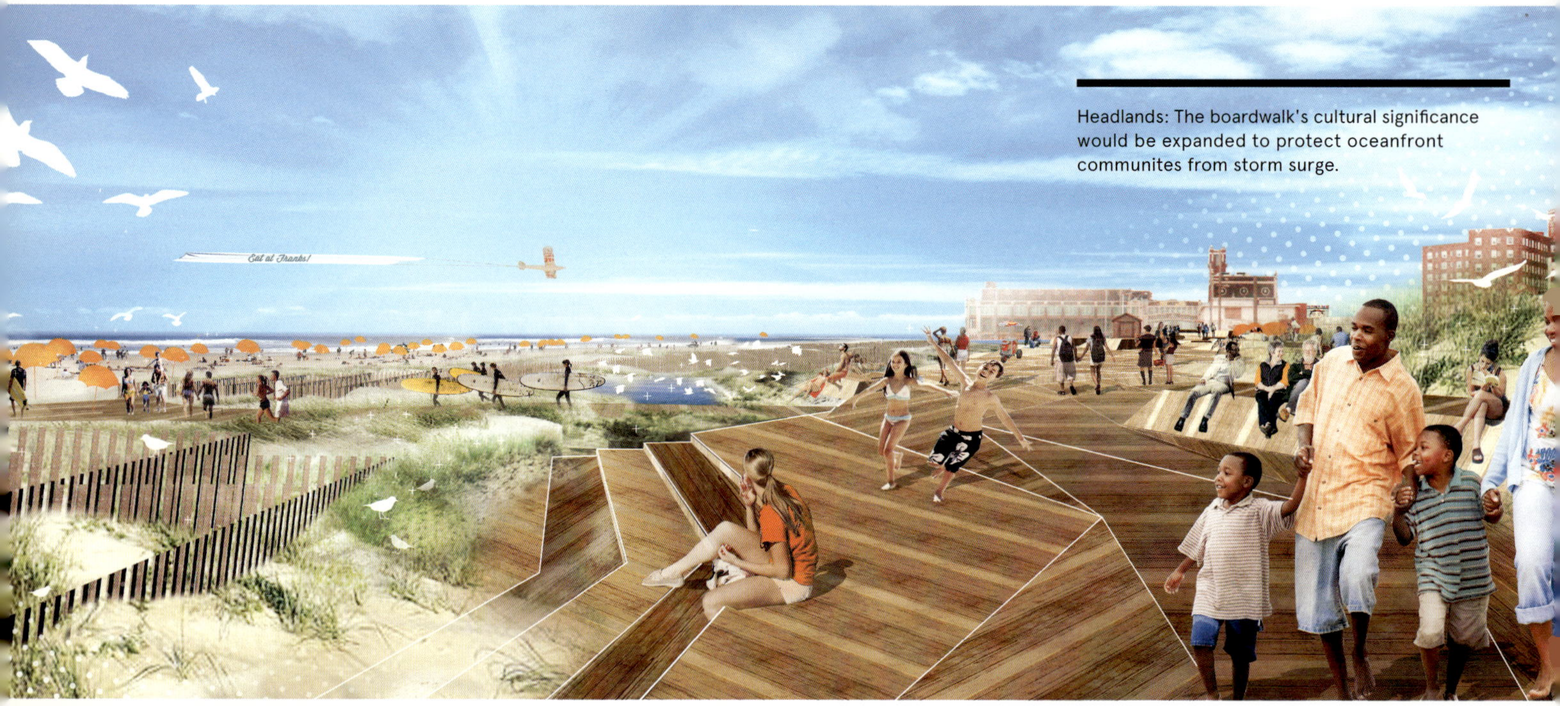

Headlands: The boardwalk's cultural significance would be expanded to protect oceanfront communites from storm surge.

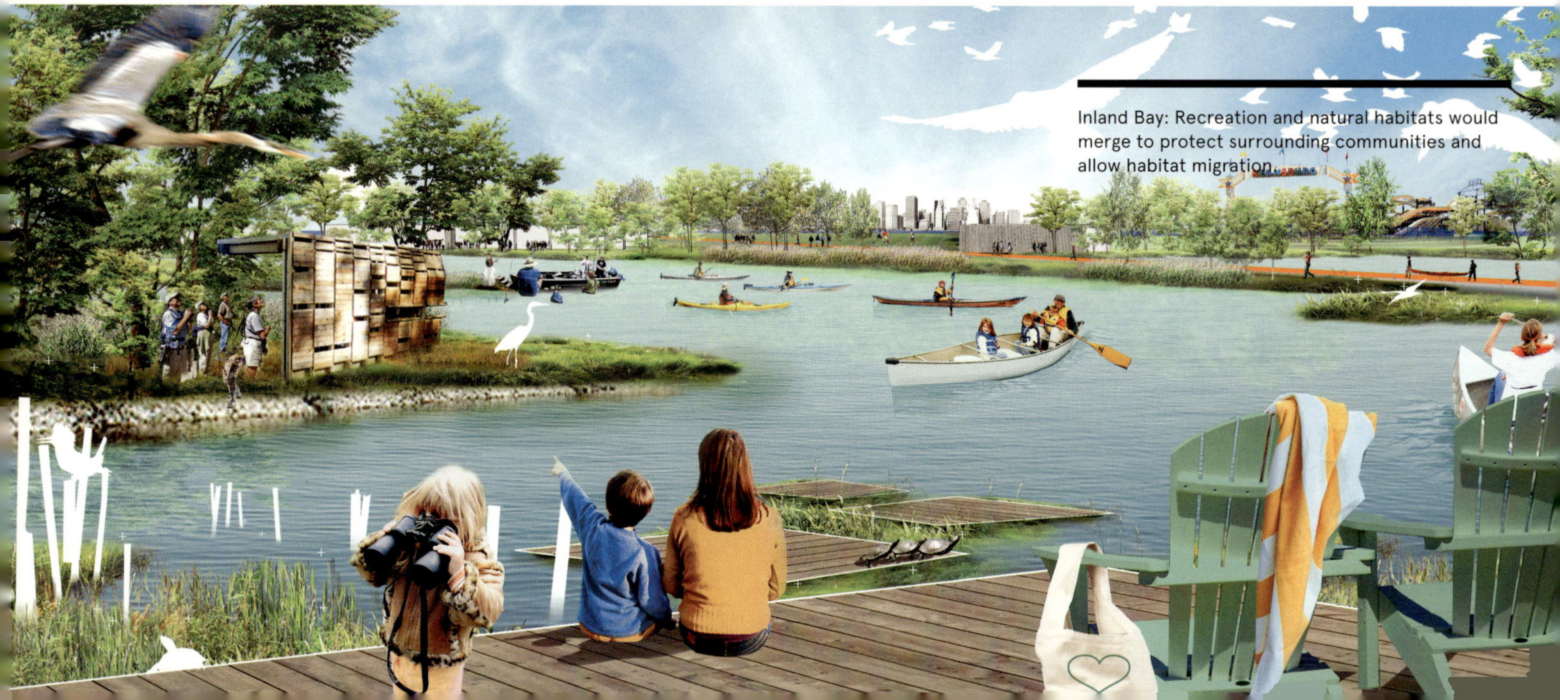

Inland Bay: Recreation and natural habitats would merge to protect surrounding communities and allow habitat migration.

Final Proposal: Resilience + The Beach

Resilience for the Jersey Shore and other American beach communities necessitates a combination of both regional cooperation and local solutions. Sasaki's strategy for New Jersey's Ocean and Monmouth Counties used the lens of coastal typologies to gain insights into local vulnerabilities and to develop potential solutions. At the regional scale, these solutions included improving ecology, protecting tourism economies, and strengthening social cohesion through a cross-jurisdictional resilience network. The Shore is fractured into dozens of small, discrete municipalities that range in size from a few thousand people to around 90,000 residents. This individualized governance structure of small communities with limited local capacity hampers resilience planning along the Shore. Sasaki urged a role for coalitions of nonprofits, citizens, and governments that could scale up or down, serve as resource-sharing platforms, and be mechanisms to support disaster response in emergency situations as well.

One of the proposal's core principles was to position the beach's ecological function as foundational to regional resilience. "Jersey Strong" would need to be more than just a descriptor of people. It would also have to apply to environmental strength. By defining the coastline as deeper than the physical water edge, the design would allow the experience of the beach to cover diverse ecologies and reach miles inland. For the Jersey shore, this transect would reach from the Atlantic Ocean to the Pine Barrens, a heavily forested national reserve nearly the size of Grand Canyon National Park. The team proposed a "Habitat Engine" to support migration and enhance the sustainability of living coastal features in this deeper coast. To maintain critical resources, all habitat elements would be moved to appropriate conditions as sea levels rise. Since it is impossible to accurately predict the speed or scope of sea level changes, the Habitat Engine would set the stage for the inevitable movement of coastal resources by preparing to work with hydrological changes. Like a mechanical engine, the Habitat Engine would draw along living communities as the vegetation structure matures and conditions for animal life become available.

In addition to proposing an overall regional strategy for social and ecological resilience, the team also considered specific strategies for the barrier island, headlands, and inland bay conditions.

Barrier Island: "Pier-to-Pinelands"

The barrier islands are the most dynamic stretch of the Jersey Shore, constantly shifted by tidal and storm energy.

While ecological dynamism has long been a source of value for barrier island tourism economies, it also presents a prevailing risk. Under three feet of sea level rise, barrier islands are projected to lose half their land area. Under six feet, they would completely disappear. Compounded by sensitivity to tidal change and storm surge, New Jersey's barrier islands could be uninhabitable a century from now. Rather than fight this reality, Sasaki's project, with pilot sites in Seaside Heights, Toms River, and Berkeley Township, would diversify the traditional beach economy and its location, allowing the economic, social, and ecological health of the barrier island communities to persist flexibly over time.

The team identified a new role for the public amusement pier. Now limited to a discrete element along the beach, it could be extended on shore to deepen the experience of barrier island ecosystems and encourage development in higher zones. This new inland pier could be an ecotourism link reconnecting different ecological patches and allowing habitats to migrate to higher ground. It could also draw tourism economies to lower-risk sites.

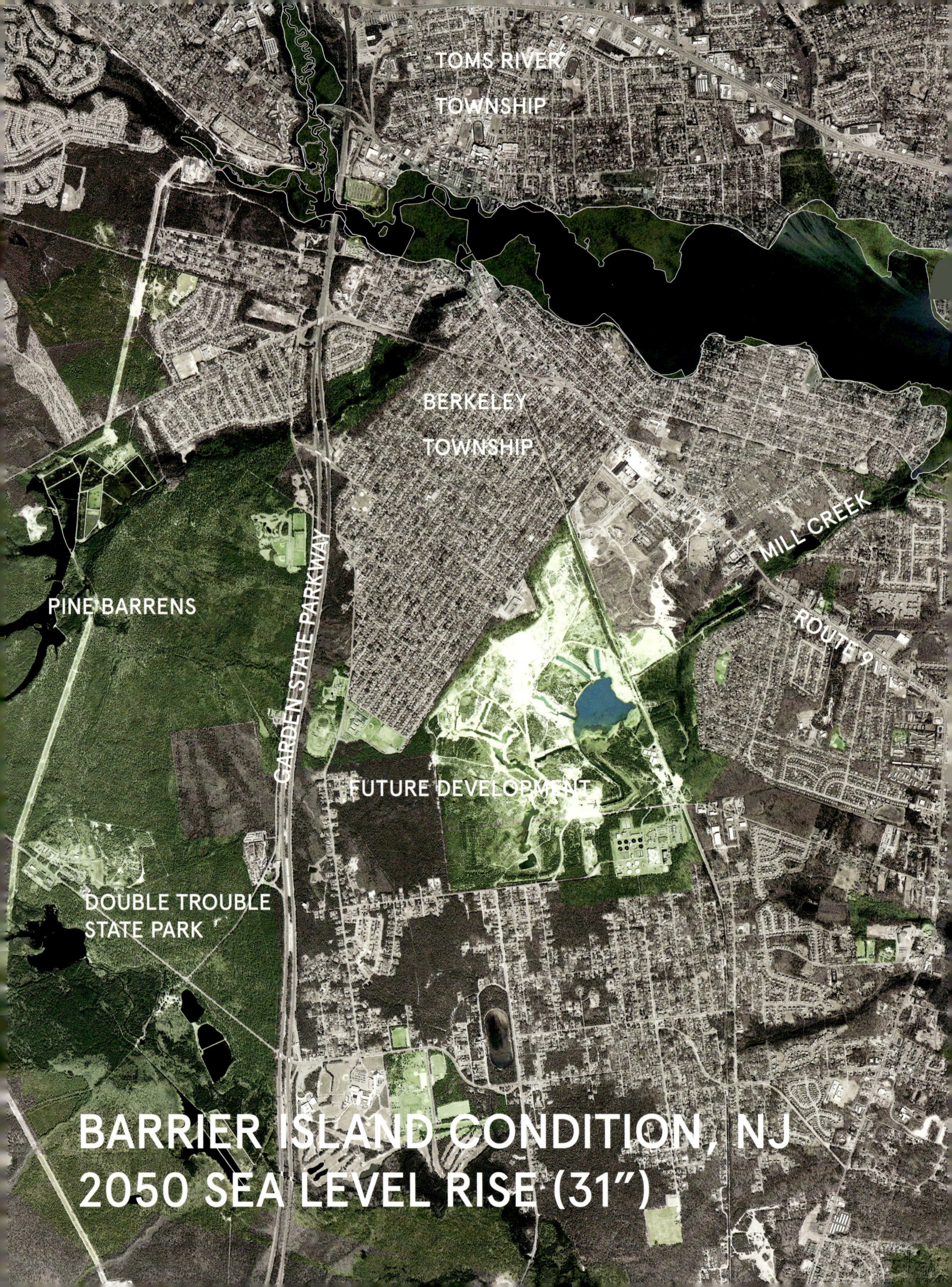

TOMS RIVER TOWNSHIP

BERKELEY TOWNSHIP

MILL CREEK

ROUTE 9

PINE BARRENS

GARDEN STATE PARKWAY

FUTURE DEVELOPMENT

DOUBLE TROUBLE STATE PARK

BARRIER ISLAND CONDITION, NJ
2050 SEA LEVEL RISE (31”)

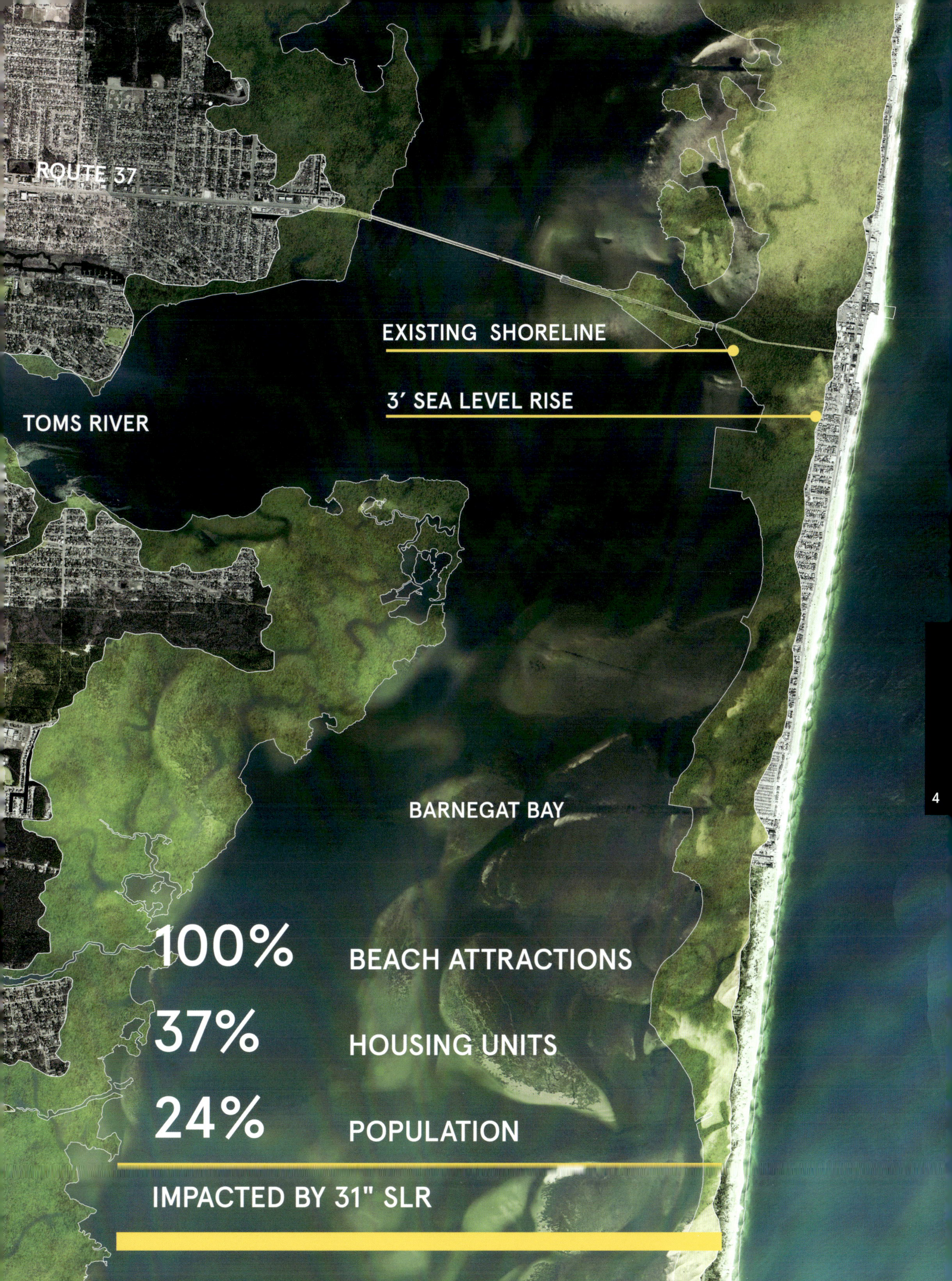
ROUTE 37
EXISTING SHORELINE
3′ SEA LEVEL RISE
TOMS RIVER
BARNEGAT BAY
100% BEACH ATTRACTIONS
37% HOUSING UNITS
24% POPULATION
IMPACTED BY 31" SLR

Headlands: "Boardwalk-Dune"

The headlands are the most exposed stretch of the New Jersey shore, with open ocean views subject to the direct action of wind and wave.

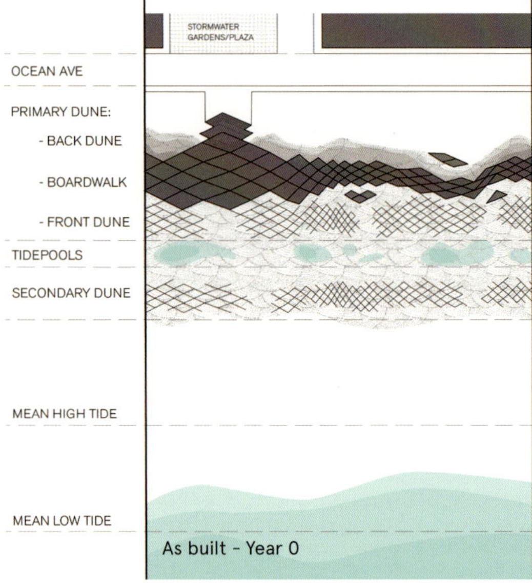

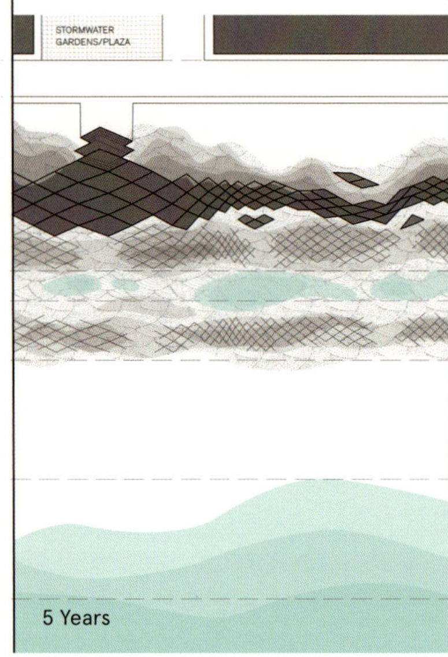

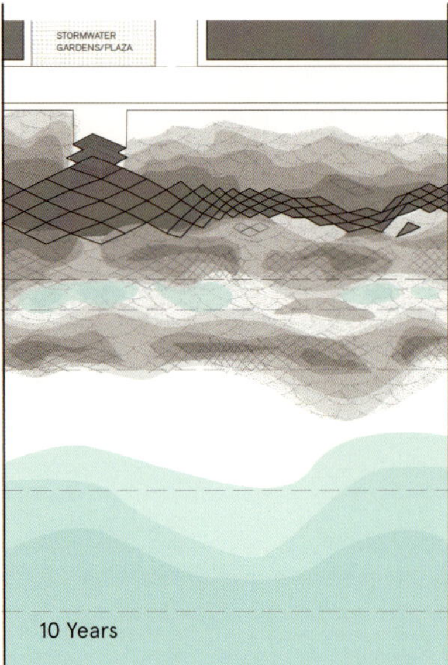

Evolution: Dune-Building Boardwalk Time is a central element of all ecologically driven design solutions, so Sasaki considered the long-term time horizon.

For Asbury Park, a boardwalk would slowly help to form protective dunes over time, creating a socially and ecologically rich protective waterfront.

For the Barnegat Bay region around Toms River (images at right) a new inland development site and a focus on ecotourism opportunities beyond the beach would support diversification of the tourism economy so that it could withstand future storms. Over time, permanent structures would migrate to higher ground, with destination visits to the evolving barrier islands.

New Jersey's headlands were the first major tourism sites along the North Jersey coast. Resorts, hotels, and vacation communities sprung up there in the late 19th and early 20th century. The boardwalk was built in this era. The team developed its headlands project for Asbury Park, where an iconic boardwalk provides popular public space, and where prevailing winds and tidal flows naturally capture sand, making it a safer location for investment and occupation. Still vulnerable to sea level rise and storm surge, the coastal community has the infrastructure and high elevation to develop into a protected, resilient coastal community. Sasaki included the boardwalk as part of a three-pronged strategy – protection, absorption, and connectivity – piloted in Asbury Park. The boardwalk would be integrated into a dune system for protection from coastal flooding, hyper-absorbent coastal lakes and streets would mitigate watershed flooding, and better east-west connections would link all parts of the community to the oceanfront.

Inland Bay: "Marina-Marsh"

The Inland Bay is a complex region with a legacy of industrial uses, densely-populated maritime communities, increasing levels of integration into the Greater New York City economy, and a rich estuarine environment.

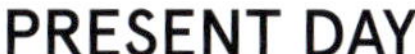

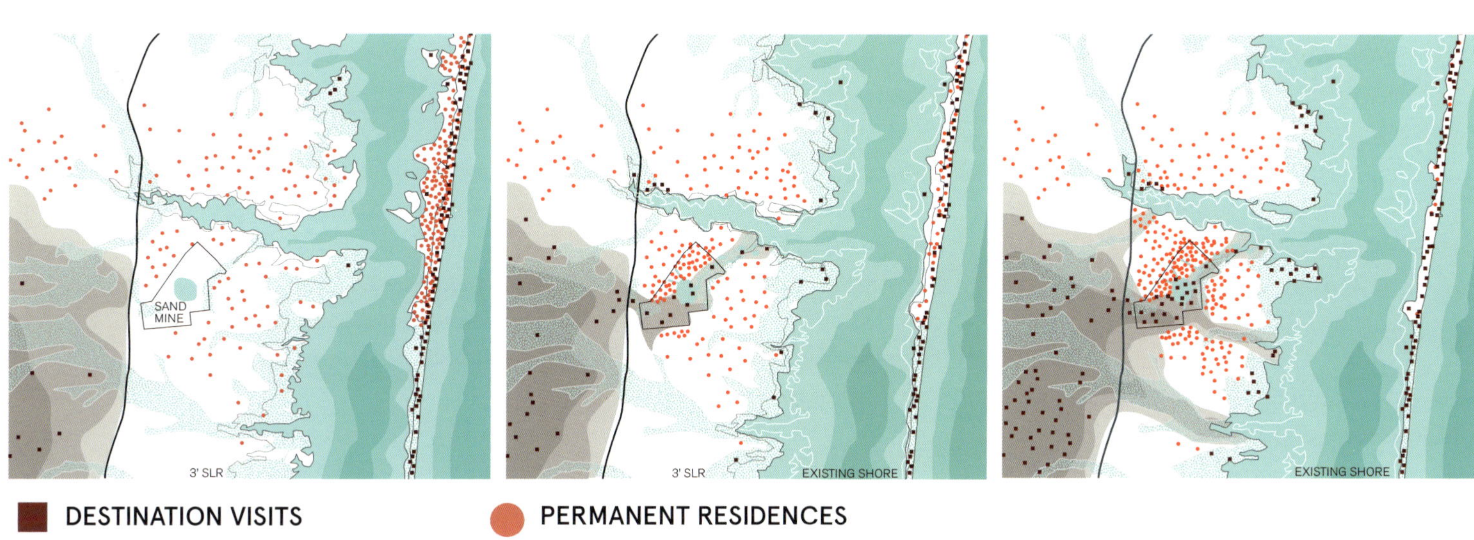

Evolution: Diversification The drawings above describe the evolving Barrier island situation.

New Jersey's inland bay communities grew around the Raritan Bay's protected, brackish, and contaminated waters. The bay's complex conditions create different risks for storms and sea level rise, necessitating a multi-layered approach. Flooding in upland areas presents risks to a network of creeks, wetlands, and small lakes that line the shore. Sasaki proposed to build on the recreational and commercial role of these water bodies to enhance coastal protection.

The Natco Lake District, located at the nexus of Union Beach, Hazlet, and Keansburg, encompasses dense residential neighborhoods, post-industrial lands, and a diverse ecosystem centered on the lake. The team identified an opportunity to give this ecological and community asset the capacity to protect the area from storms and floods. Both Union Beach and Keansburg are waterfront towns that border Natco Lake and that were heavily impacted by Hurricane Sandy through storm surge and bowl conditions. To create long-term resilience in all dimensions, Natco Lake, an artificial lake created by industry, and the surrounding marshland would be nurtured and transformed into an ecological system that would help manage storm surge and water inflow, as well as provide a destination for recreational boating and wildlife viewing.

Design Process

With the physical and emotional trauma of Sandy in the foreground, and with the sustained dialogue of Rebuild by Design, disparate groups on the Shore have had the opportunity to develop a common resilience language and set of shared values. Yet, one of the main challenges persists: to link individual community voices into a concerted effort. In order to facilitate a conversation across the broad geography of the Shore, Sasaki held a series of community meetings and events in its three pilot sites, and it utilized the CrowdGauge tool, which, through an online game-like interface, helped communities achieve better public participation and develop shared values.

CrowdGauge is an open-source framework for creating educational online maps and surveys. It first asks users to rank a set of priorities, and then gives them a limited number of coins, asking them to put their symbolic money toward the actions they would support most. A meter at the bottom of the priorities page lets survey users know how their priorities increase or decrease sea level rise risk behaviors. After it had been implemented, the survey showed that the Jersey Shore's first priority value was a very fundamental one: to have clean air, water, and land.

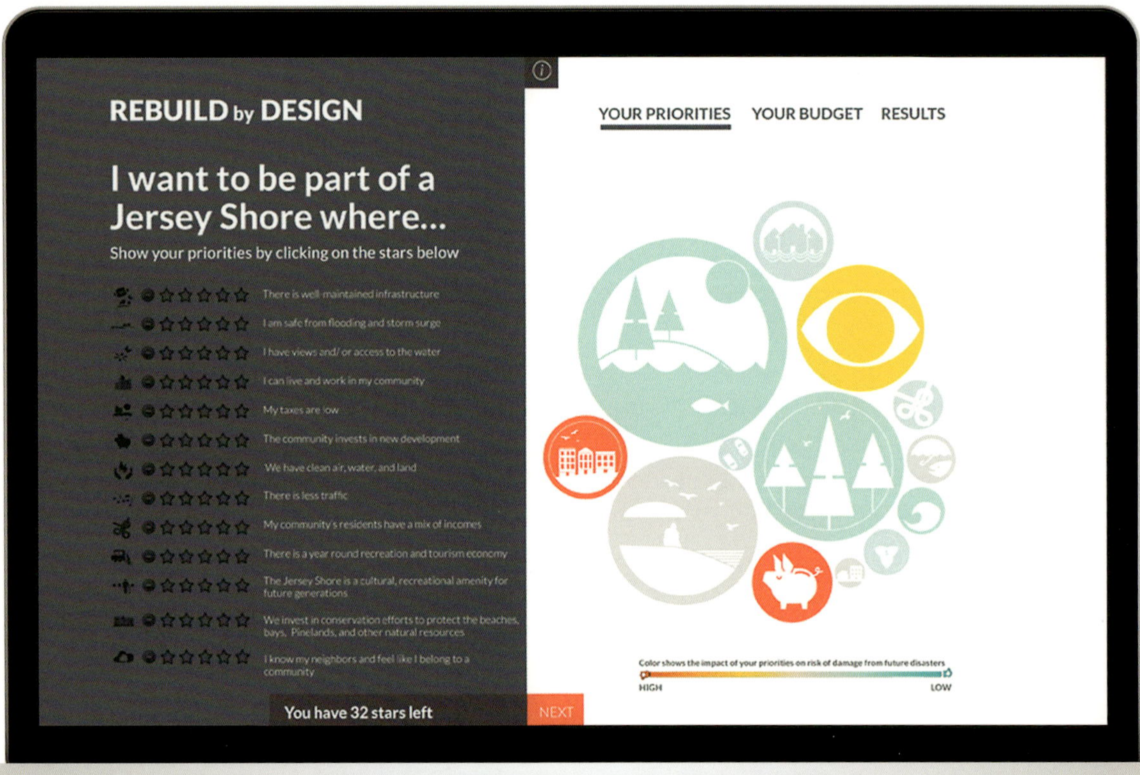

Working with local partners in and around each community, the coalition-building process facilitated many conversations among diverse groups and across different boundaries. Each community demonstrated its strength and commitment to creating a resilient future. For example, Asbury Park residents threw their support behind the project in a compelling and inspiring way. Grassroots outreach produced unprecedented attendance, open dialogue, sharing of issues and concerns, a strong local identity, and a community that asked "How can we help? How can we do more?" The community demonstrated its commitment and spirit at a parade and event focused on creating a new Asbury Park more resilient to change and risk.

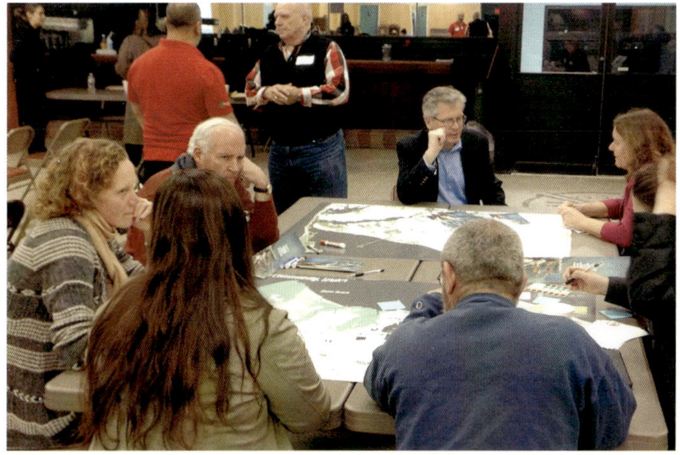

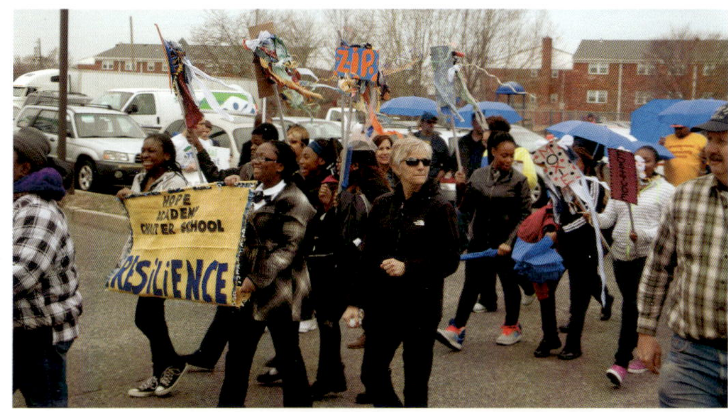

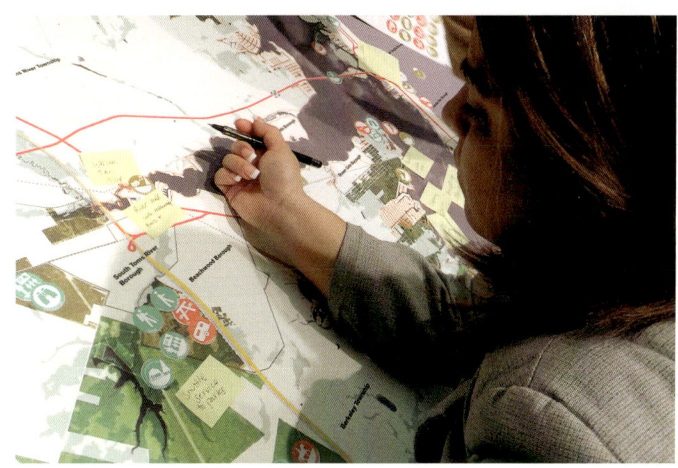

Community meetings like the ones held in Keansburg and Toms River and the Scale it Up parade for Asbury Park are examples of the engagement process along the Jersey Shore to promote and understand current resilience measures being undertaken and future needs as sea levels rise.

LIVING BREAKWATERS

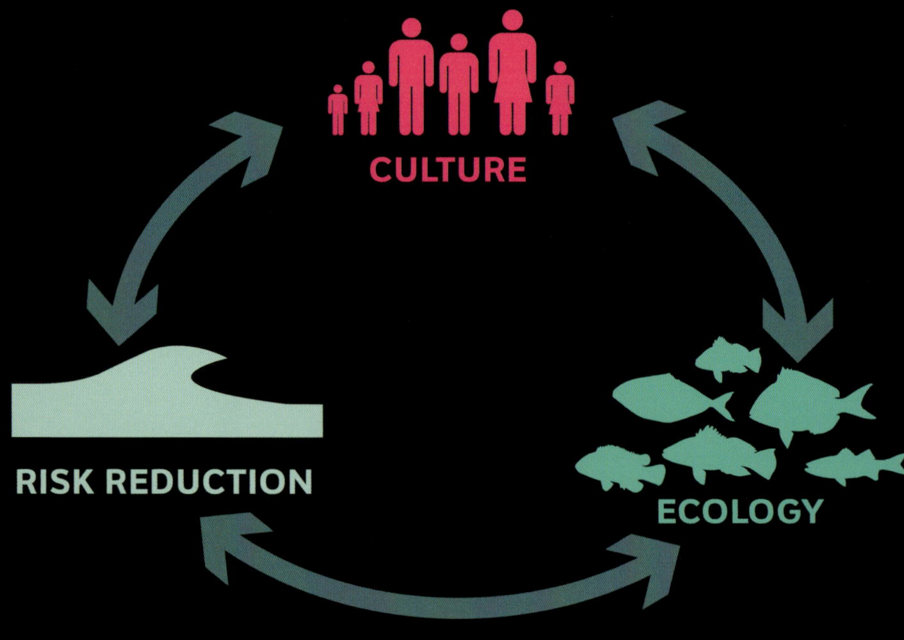

Team Lead
SCAPE/LANDSCAPE ARCHITECTURE

Engineering/Planning
Parsons Brinckerhoff

Hydrodynamic Modeling
Stevens Institute of Technology

Coastal Engineering
Ocean and Coastal Consultants

Marine Biology
SeArc Consulting

Education/Oyster Restoration
The New York Harbor School

Architecture
LOT-EK

Graphic Design
MTWTF

Advisor/Author of "Four Fish"
Paul Greenberg

SCAPE/LANDSCAPE ARCHITECTURE

The SCAPE Team's Living Breakwaters project reduces risk, revives ecologies, and connects educators to the shoreline, inspiring a new generation of harbor stewards and a more resilient region over time. These structures provide valuable wave attenuation, reducing erosion along the otherwise exposed shoreline, as well as critical rocky habitat for juvenile fish, oysters, and other marine organisms. This combination of rigorously modeled coastal resilience infrastructure with habitat enhancement techniques and new community engagement models allow for a layered strategy that links in-water protective forms to on-shore interventions. The team is committed to advancing ideas that help protect from periodic weather extremes while improving the quality of the everyday lives of Staten Islanders for long-term resilience.

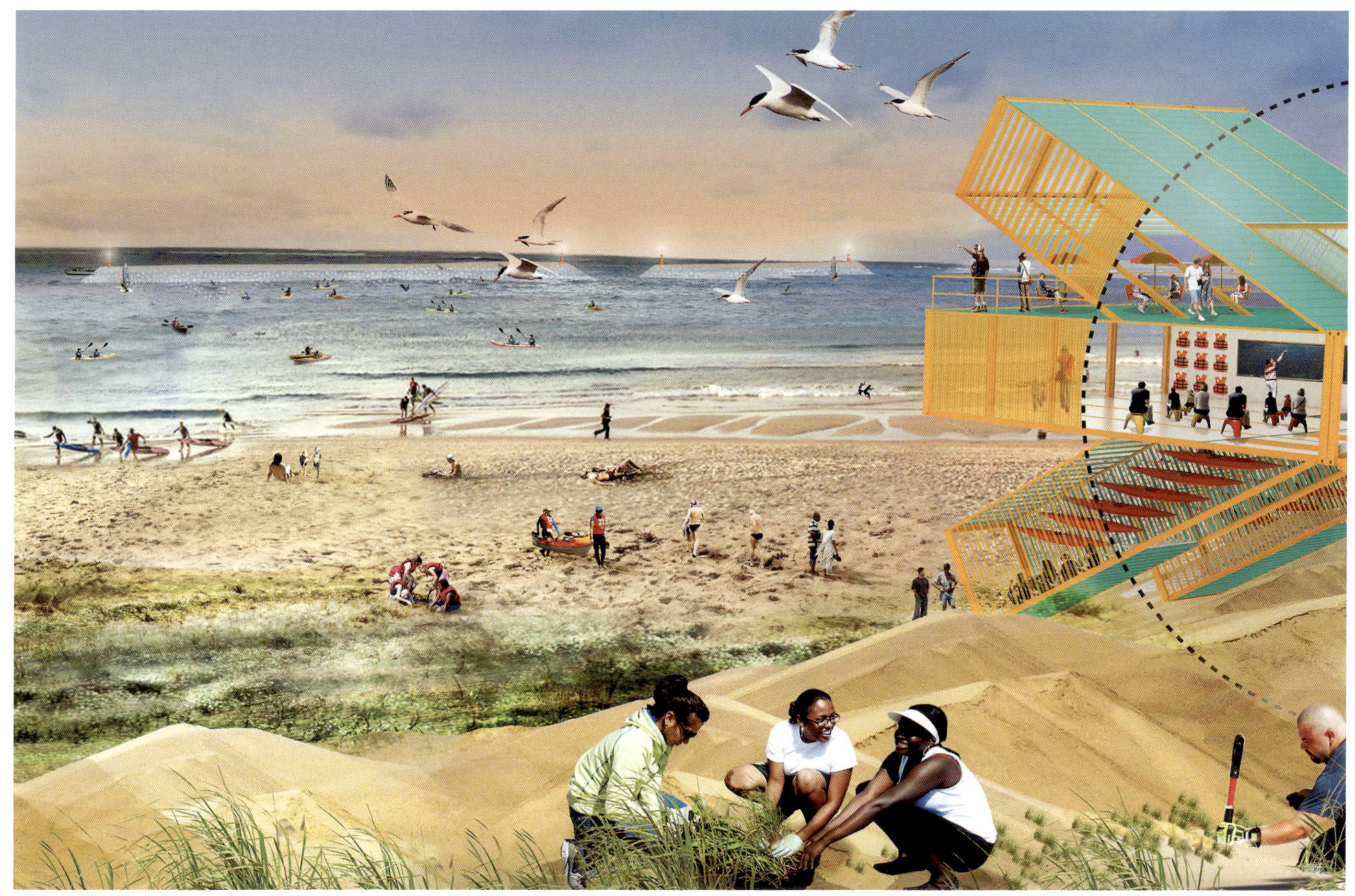

4

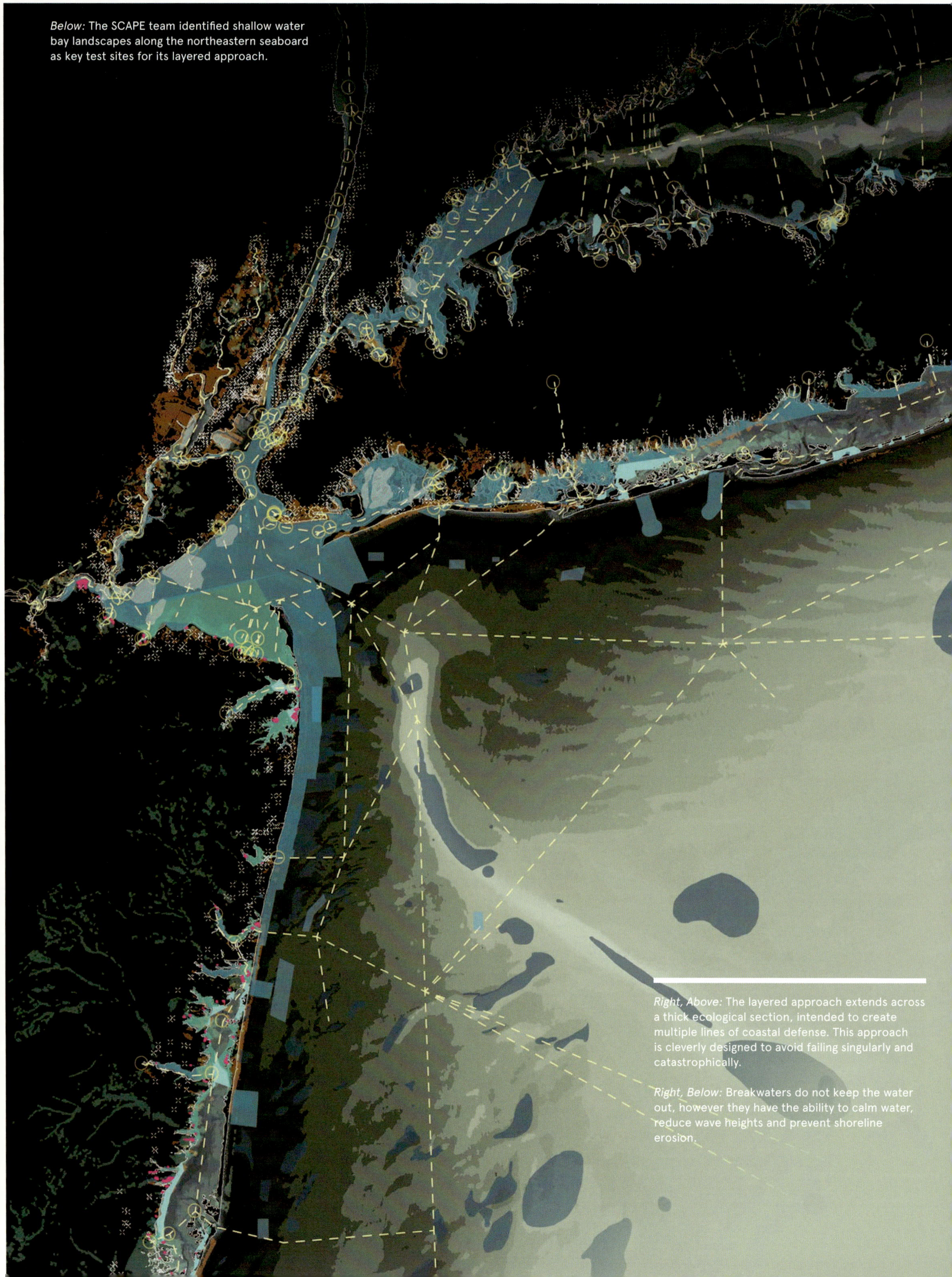

Below: The SCAPE team identified shallow water bay landscapes along the northeastern seaboard as key test sites for its layered approach.

Right, Above: The layered approach extends across a thick ecological section, intended to create multiple lines of coastal defense. This approach is cleverly designed to avoid failing singularly and catastrophically.

Right, Below: Breakwaters do not keep the water out, however they have the ability to calm water, reduce wave heights and prevent shoreline erosion.

A Layered Approach

The SCAPE team focused its research on shallow bay ecosystems, including Raritan Bay, Jamaica Bay, and Barnegat Bay, by exploring the potential for ecological infrastructure based on hard and soft, land and water, human-made and "natural" habitats. Bays have a diverse array of protective elements, including marshes, dunes, mud flats, shrub lands, reefs and barrier islands – what the team has called "The Shallows." These spaces all have a multiplicity of functions: providing habitat for wildlife, enhancing ecosystem health, and supporting local economic and cultural activity.

Shallow waters in the Northeast were directly affected by Hurricane Sandy and face continued risks from urbanization, contamination, sediment starvation, and sea level rise. These phenomena put critical estuaries and bays at risk of disappearing within decades. With their shallow bathymetry and delicate balance of vulnerable marine life, a loss of these endangered waters would threaten not only the places where communities live, work, and play but also cultural connection to the water.

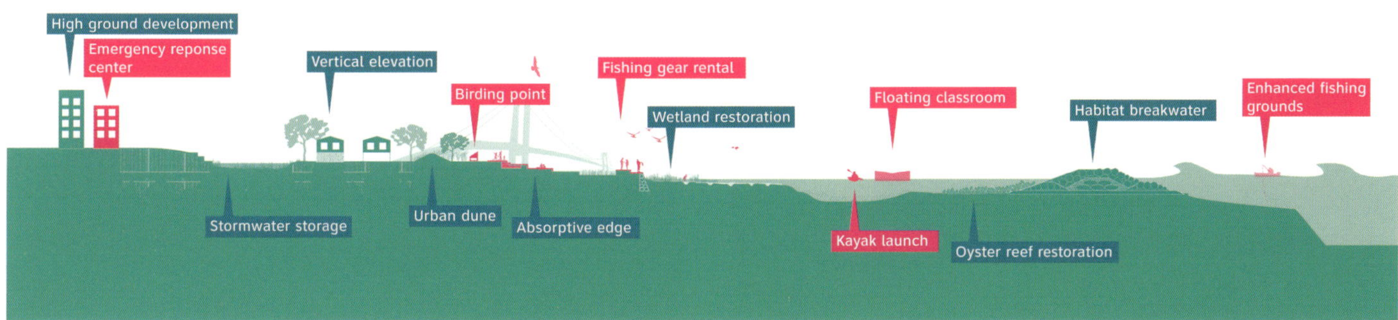

EXPOSED BREAKWATER

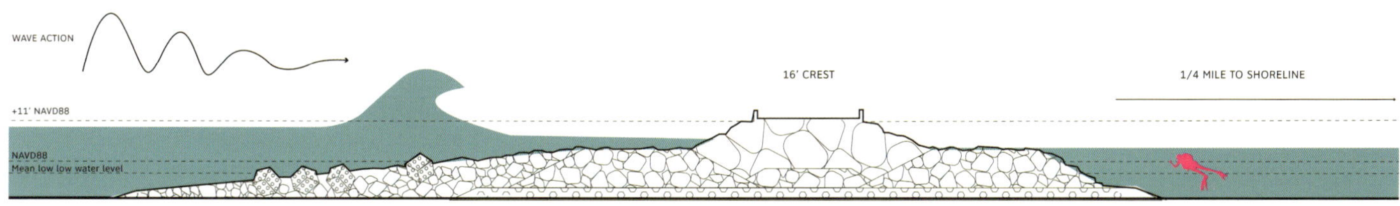

SUBTIDAL BREAKWATER

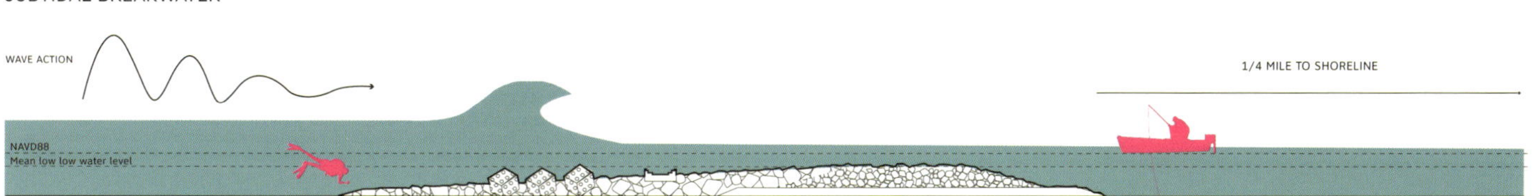

4

Design Opportunities

The SCAPE team identified five strategies and applicable design opportunities within the Sandy-affected region as a response to its research findings.

Living Breakwaters

This opportunity addresses the vulnerabilities facing the coastline of Raritan Bay, on Staten Island's South Shore. Rather than building a single protective barrier, the SCAPE team designed a series of living reefs that would collectively offer both protection from wave action and enhanced habitat, paired with protective on-shore interventions and increased opportunities for the public to connect with the waterfront.

Barnegat Bay Remade

The team also considered opportunities in New Jersey's Barnegat Bay, engaging networks of localized dredging. Framed in part by Long Beach Island, the bay is a beloved recreational area, popular among beach and fishing enthusiasts. The replenishment of coastal wetlands through small-scale dredge recycling could serve to absorb surge waters and reduce wave impacts within coastal communities.

Gardening the Bay

Situated in a dense urban environment, Jamaica Bay is particularly vulnerable. It shares its ecology with

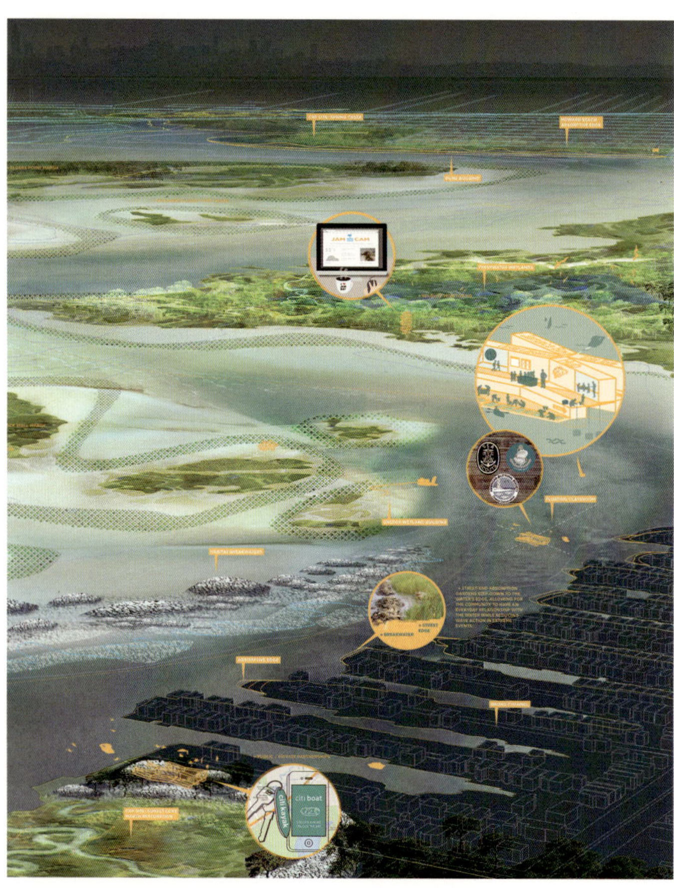

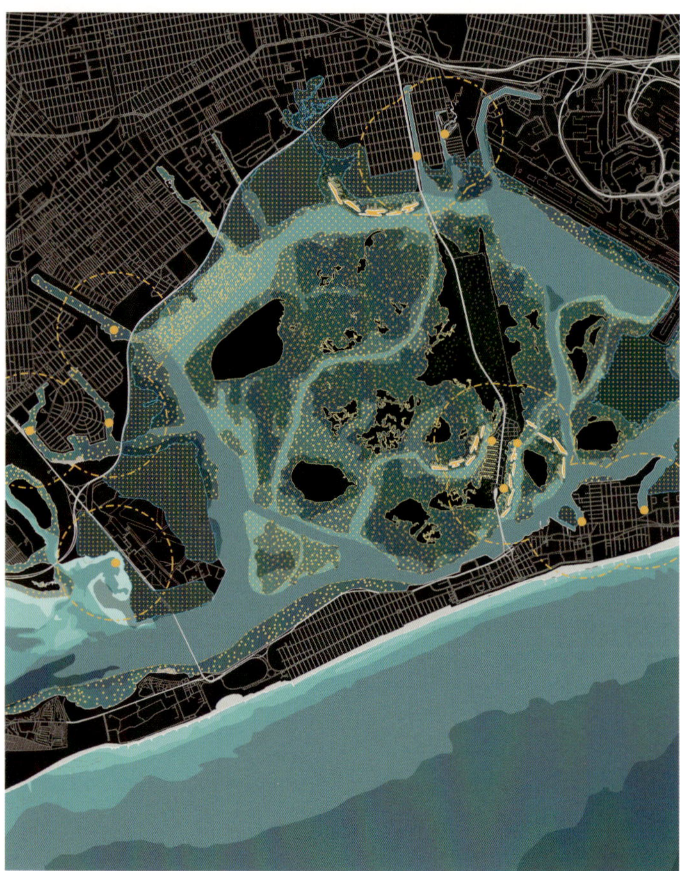

The opportunities at Jamaica Bay show how society can shift its approach to resilience, and offer the potential to test a range of different strategies depicted here within the bay's disappearing marshes and shoals.

a large urban population, which has led to a changed set of sediment regimes and water dynamics within the bay. The team proposed exploring a layered approach through bay nourishment alternatives, including wetland restoration, absorptive edge retrofits, and maritime friction forests.

Hudson Habitat

The impacts of Hurricane Sandy were felt far up the Hudson River Estuary, devastating communities such as Piermont, New York. The team recommended looking at the modification and restoration of historic marsh and shellfish ecosystems along these shorelines.

More Wet Meadow, Less Lands

Furthering its research into shallow water ecosystems, the team considered the Hackensack River, a heavily industrialized waterway running through the New Jersey Meadowlands. Having been extensively dredged for shipping routes, the river provides less flood protection than it would have with its historically shallow waters. The SCAPE Team identified an opportunity to undertake a gradual shallowing there, which, coupled with wetland restoration, would provide more robust flood protection.

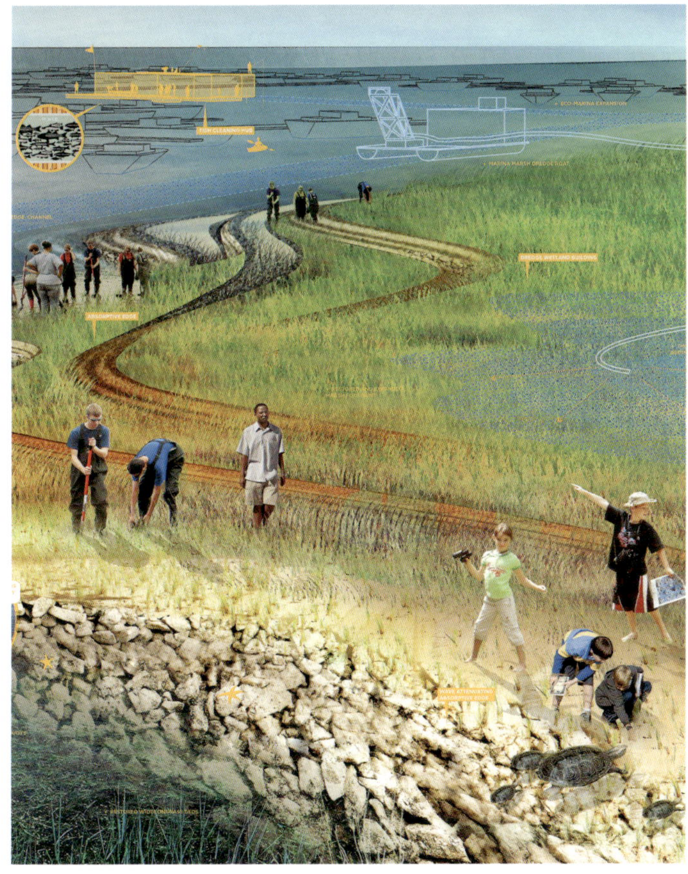

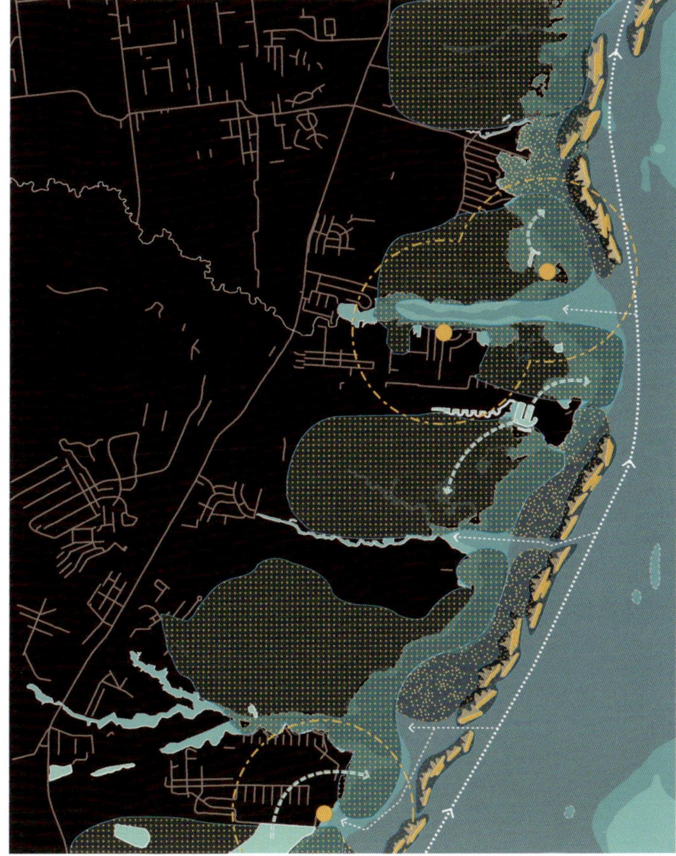

Within Barnegat Bay, man-made sediment cycles could be linked with natural cycles, helping ensure a productive and resilient bay landscape for future generations.

Final Proposal: Living Breakwaters

Staten Island's South Shore, the SCAPE team's site, is highly vulnerable to high-velocity coastal flooding and erosion. Though it was once buffered by a shallow bathymetric shelf known as the "West Bank," dredging and the diminishment of natural and farmed oyster reefs have left it more exposed to wave action over time. One of the hardest hit areas during Hurricane Sandy, the task of rebuilding there is particularly urgent and complex. The team focused its approach on the vulnerable area between the Tottenville neighborhood, originally known as "the town the oyster built," to the south and Great Kills Park to the north.

Living Breakwaters seeks to create a multi-layered section between land and water, providing a thickened edge that would absorb the energy from wave action and not fail singularly and catastrophically. Stevens Institute of Technology, part of the SCAPE team, carried out extensive hydrological modeling to test the proposal against different storm scenarios. It found that exposed breakwaters, by causing partial wave breaking, could lead to up to a four-foot wave height decrease during storms like Hurricane Sandy as well as reducing base flood elevations.

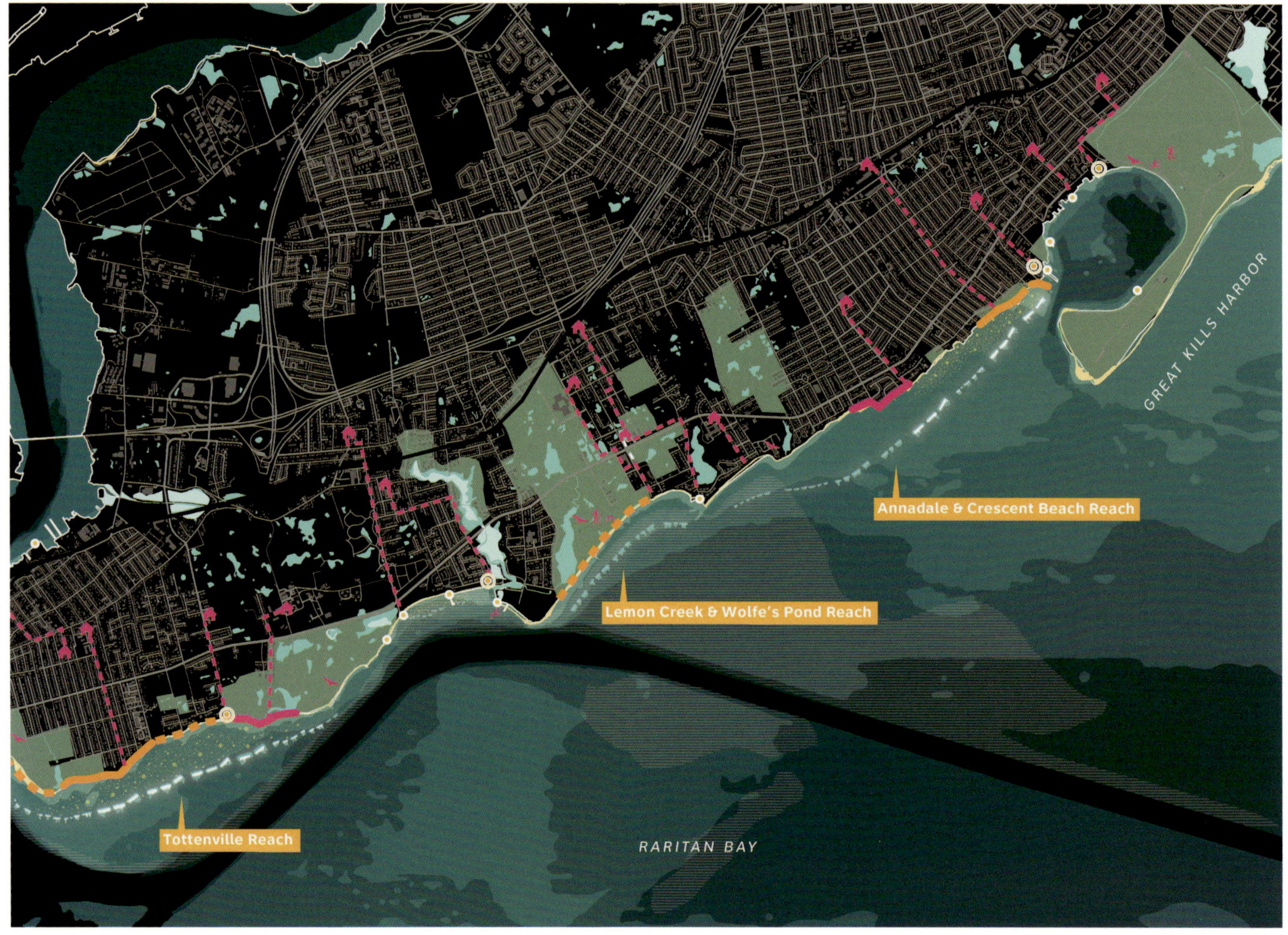

Dispersed across 13,000 linear feet of shoreline, Living Breakwaters would form a thick patchwork of coastal defenses both above and below the water. A pilot project along the Tottenville shoreline has been proposed to implement and monitor all elements of the project: physical, ecological, and social. This approach would allow for adjustments to changing conditions on the ground, tailoring each element to the site's particularities as well as taking into close account input from the community. The lessons learned from this pilot can then be applied to similar sites throughout the region.

Conventional techniques that attempt to protect people by erecting a barrier between communities and the water ultimately sever their visual and physical relationship with the water. The SCAPE Team aims to reduce actual risk while increasing the perception of risk by building a landscape scale intervention that integrates aquatic habitat and community access.

Breakwaters do not keep the water out; however, they have the ability to calm water, reduce wave heights, and prevent shoreline erosion. High velocity water – such as when a levee is overtopped – can be fatal.

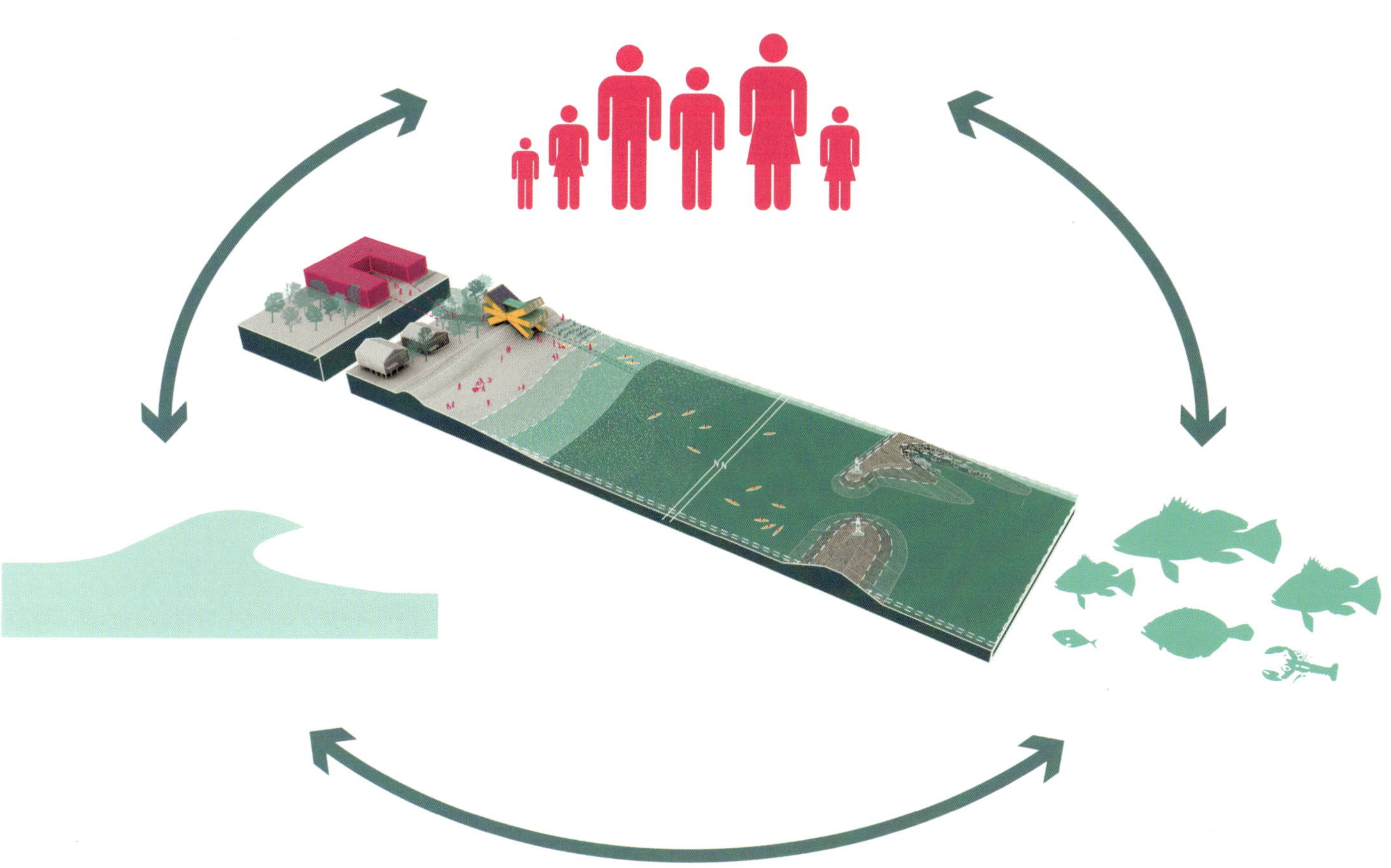

Left: The southeast coast of Staten Island is particularly vulnerable to wave action and erosion. The team's proposal is broken into three phases, or reaches, starting with the southern Tottenville reach, which would be implemented first.

SCAPE's proposals are replicable in waterfront communities along the northeast seaboard. They center around fostering vibrant water-based culture, investing in students, promoting shoreline ecologies, and developing local economies.

A cross-section of the proposed breakwaters demonstrates how the project has the potential to reduce wave heights while enhancing ecological diversity and ecosystem health.

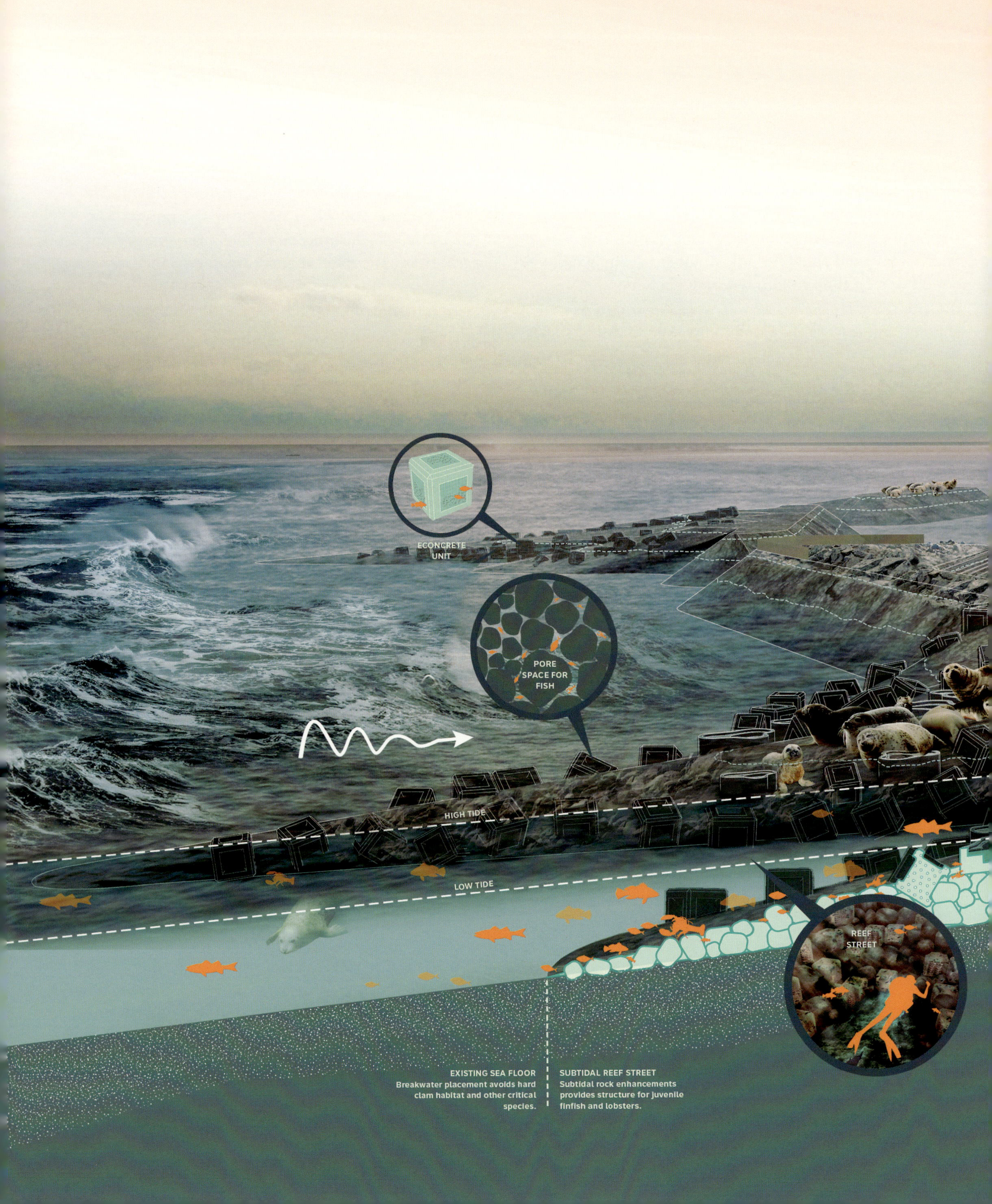

Breakwaters absorb wave energy and create slow moving water, saving lives, reducing damage to structures, and lowering floodwater elevations. Calm water in turn encourages sedimentation, which replenishes protective beaches. Designed with attention to materiality, scale, and location, these breakwaters will enhance maritime ecosystems and link risk reduction with a renewed stewardship of a biodiverse and activated Raritan Bay shoreline. Conceived as living systems, they build up biogenically in parallel with future sea level rise.

Raritan Bay is prime habitat for juvenile fish that shelter in the bay before venturing out into the Atlantic Ocean as adults. Many of these fish species require rocky habitat and tiny pore spaces for shelter during this crucial phase of life. The breakwaters are designed to maximize complexity and habitat for a diversity of species, including finfish, lobsters, and shellfish. Pockets of maximum complexity, known as "reef streets," mimic the historic reef habitats of Raritan Bay while serving as fishing and recreational attractions. Other species, such as muddy-bottom loving eelgrass and hard clams, thrive in the lightly sedimented zone in the lee of the breakwater.

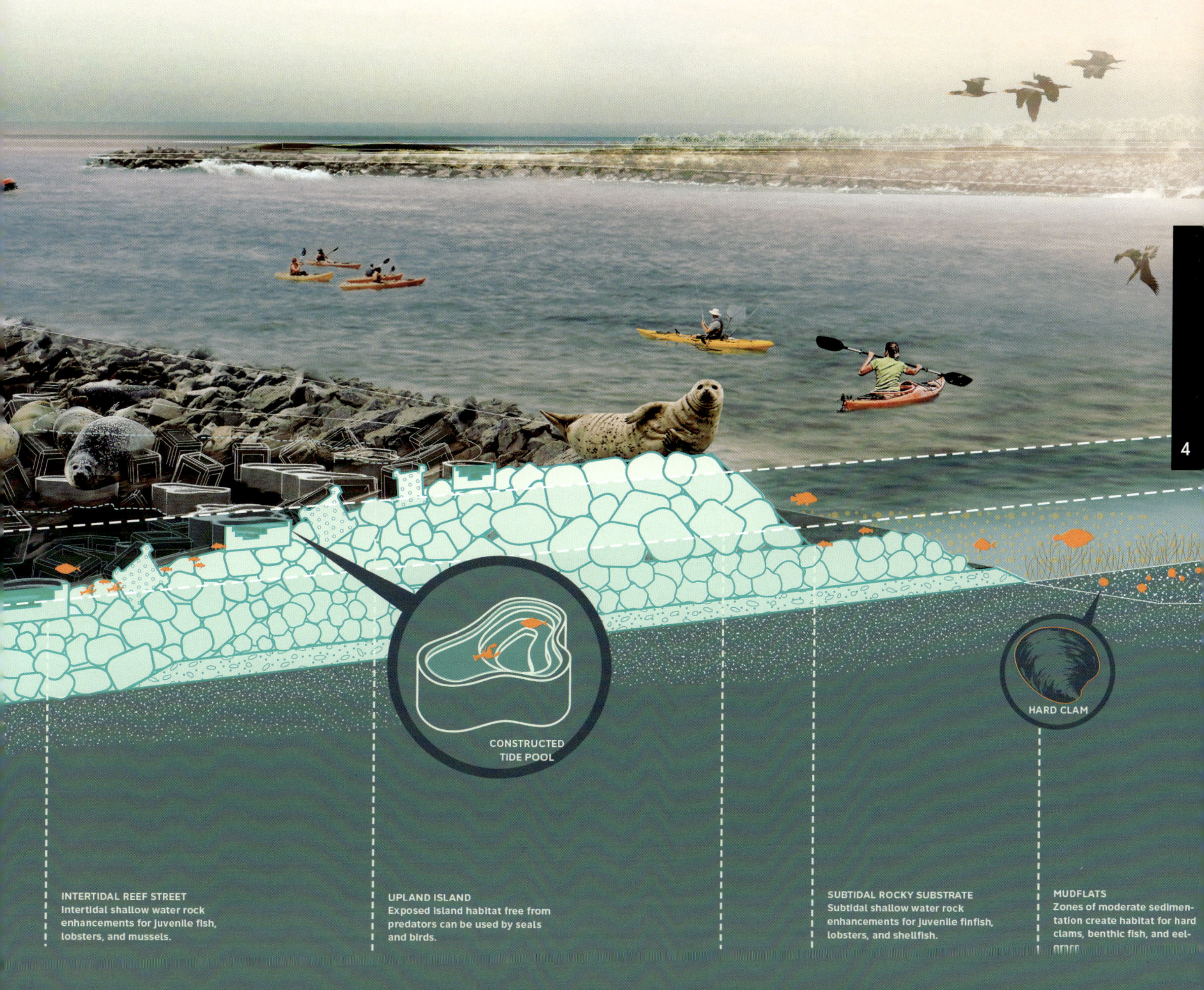

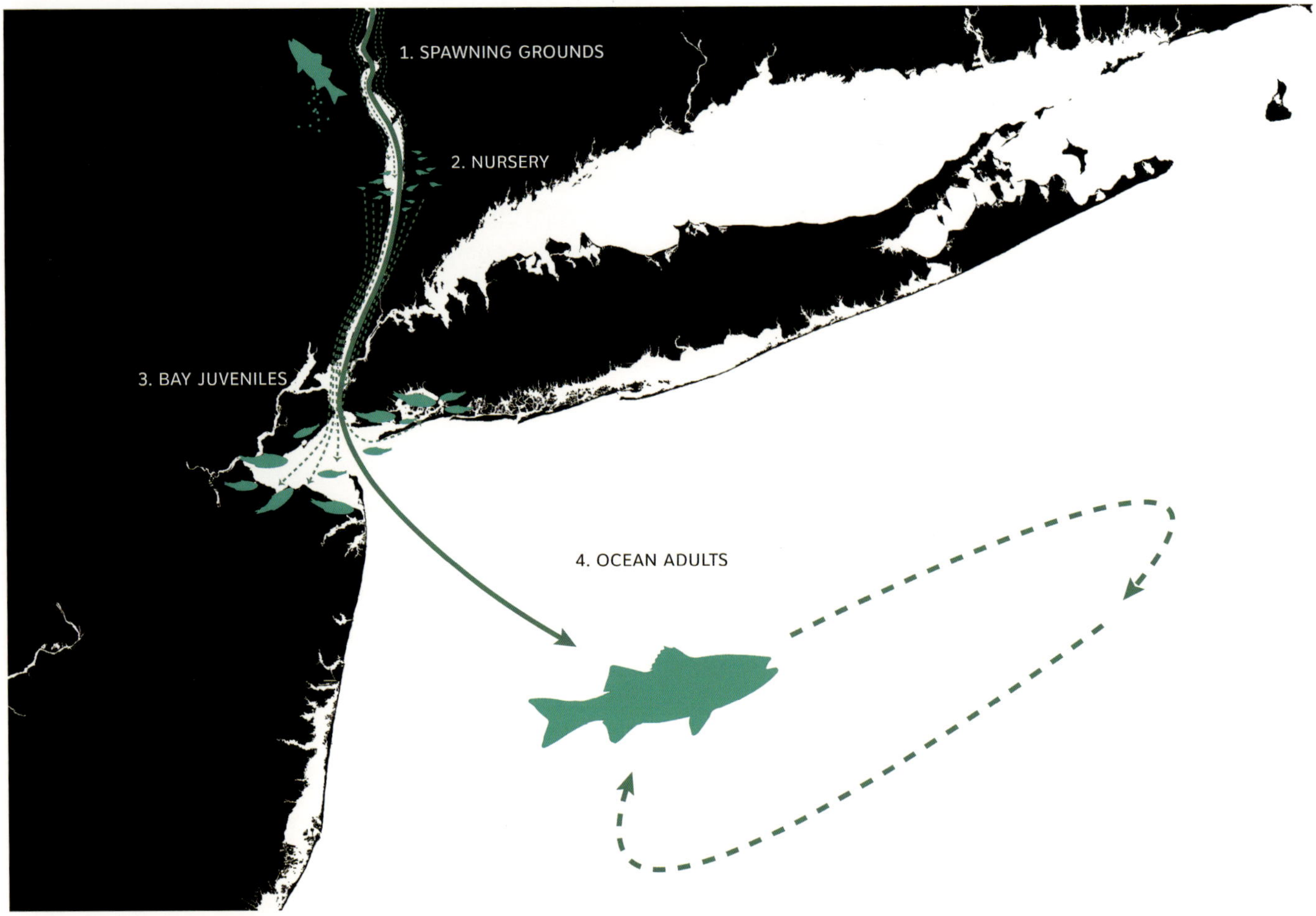

1. SPAWNING GROUNDS
2. NURSERY
3. BAY JUVENILES
4. OCEAN ADULTS

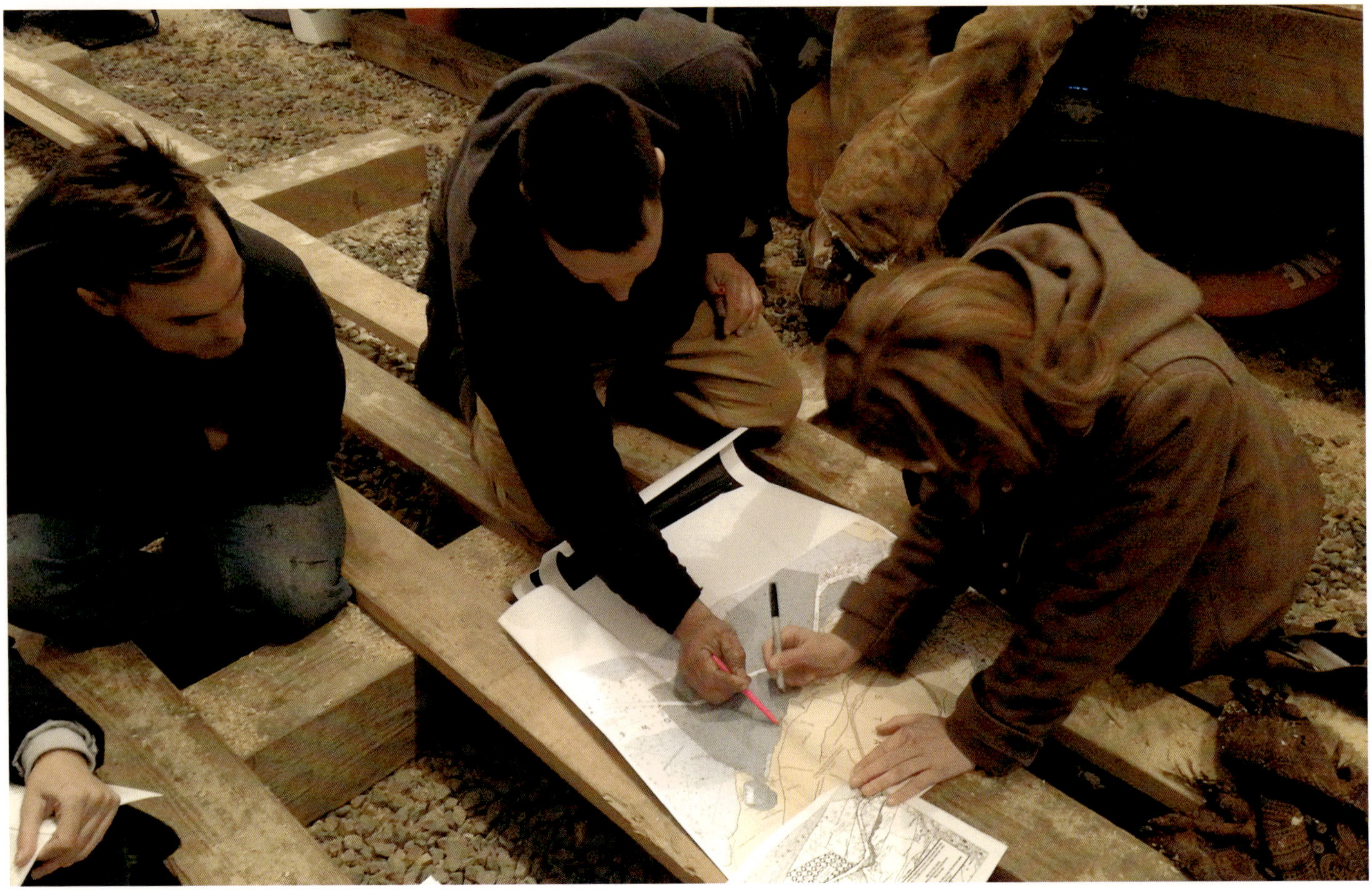

Harbor seals and birds use the exposed uplands for basking and perching. ECOncrete, an innovative low pH concrete mix for maritime construction, is formed into special units that line the reef streets. Their composition of micro- and macro-surface textures is proven to increase biological recruitment and shelter filter-feeding organisms. Ultimately, biogenic buildup will protect the structures from damage and prolong their operational life span.

Rather than cut communities off from the water with a levee or wall, the SCAPE Team emphasizes the need to embrace the water and its economic and recreational opportunities through creating closer cultural connections with the water itself. The proposal includes a series of community "water hubs" that provide social and educational spaces along the coastline.

Community members and visitors will be able to bird watch, rent kayaks, garden oysters, or gather for events and educational initiatives. The New York Harbor School, a SCAPE team member, is currently developing programs and curricula that treat the New York harbor as a classroom through the Billion Oyster Project, giving locals the opportunity to learn more about the marine ecosystem and reinforcing a substantive appreciation for coastal resilience.

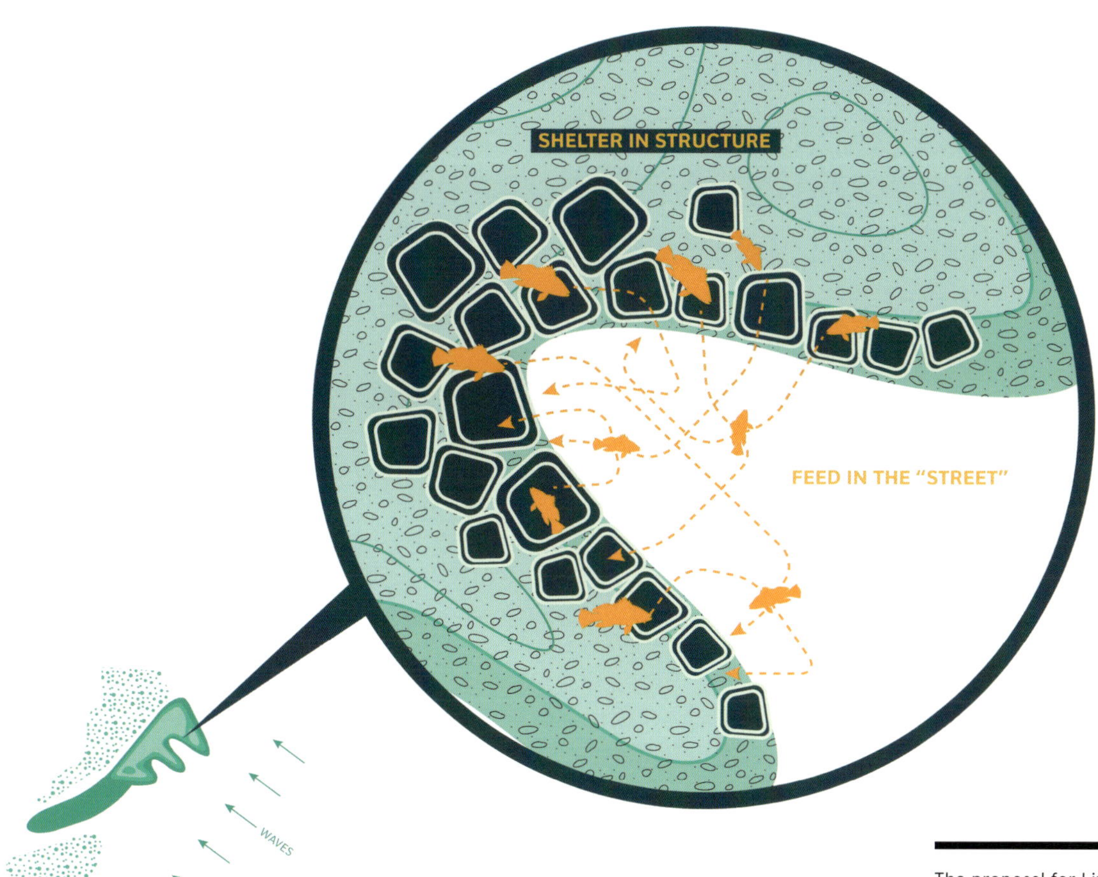

The proposal for Living Breakwaters incorporates underwater small-scale pockets, or reef streets, which provide foraging and shelter for juvenile fish.

Opposite Above: Protecting aquatic habitat and the maritime economy is critical to the team's proposal. Inside Raritan Bay, juvenile fish are a target species group for habitat creation.

Opposite, Below: The team met with a local group of Staten Island clammers to learn more about the link between ecosystems and economies.

4

The project allows for layered, on-shore interventions to be protected and gain efficacy, increasing their value for the neighboring communities and creating a coordinated approach to coastal resiliency. Creating a zone of calmer water in the lee of the breakwaters, the shoreline can become activated through kayaking, safer beaches and parks, and simply enjoying the coastline.

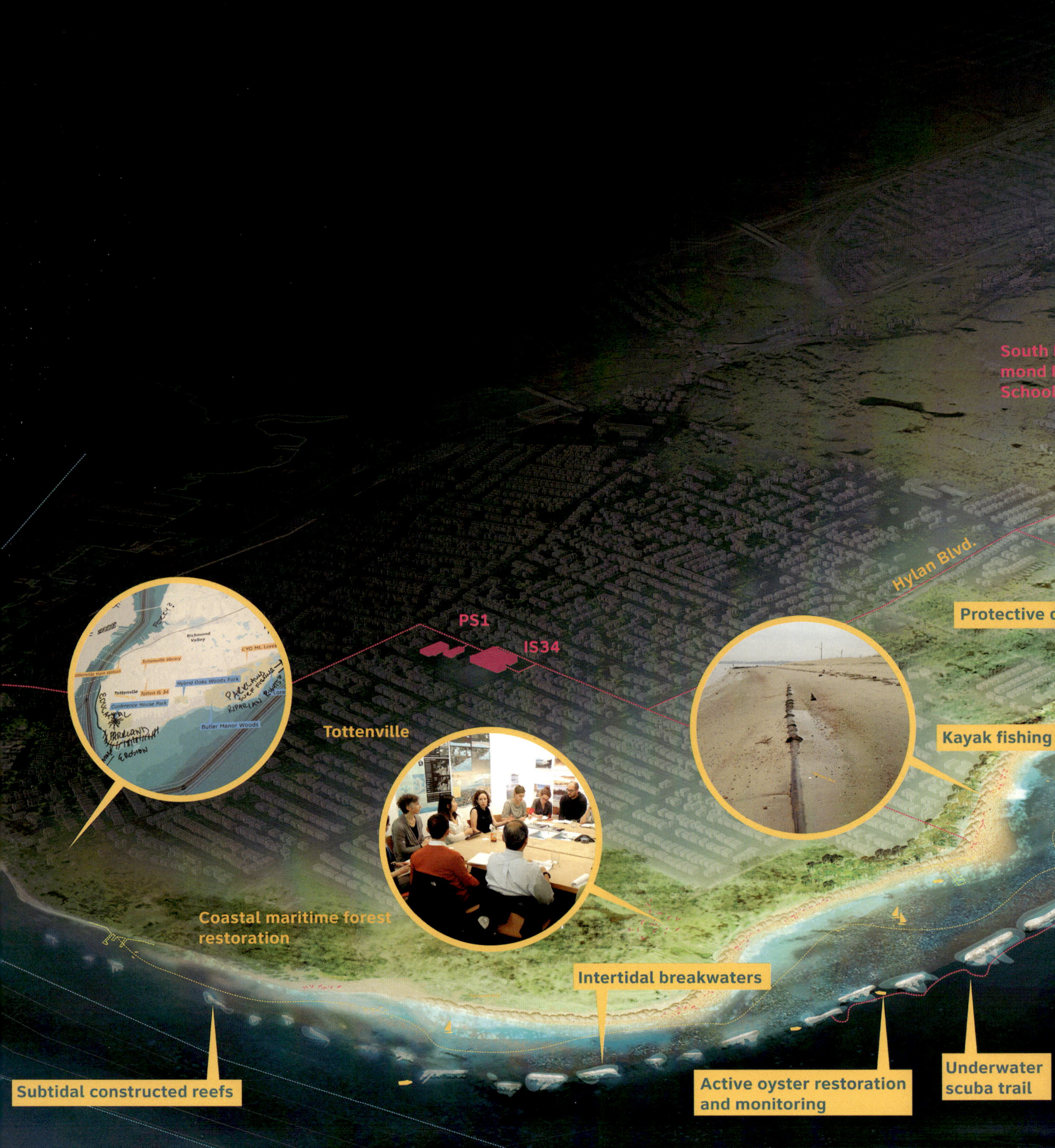

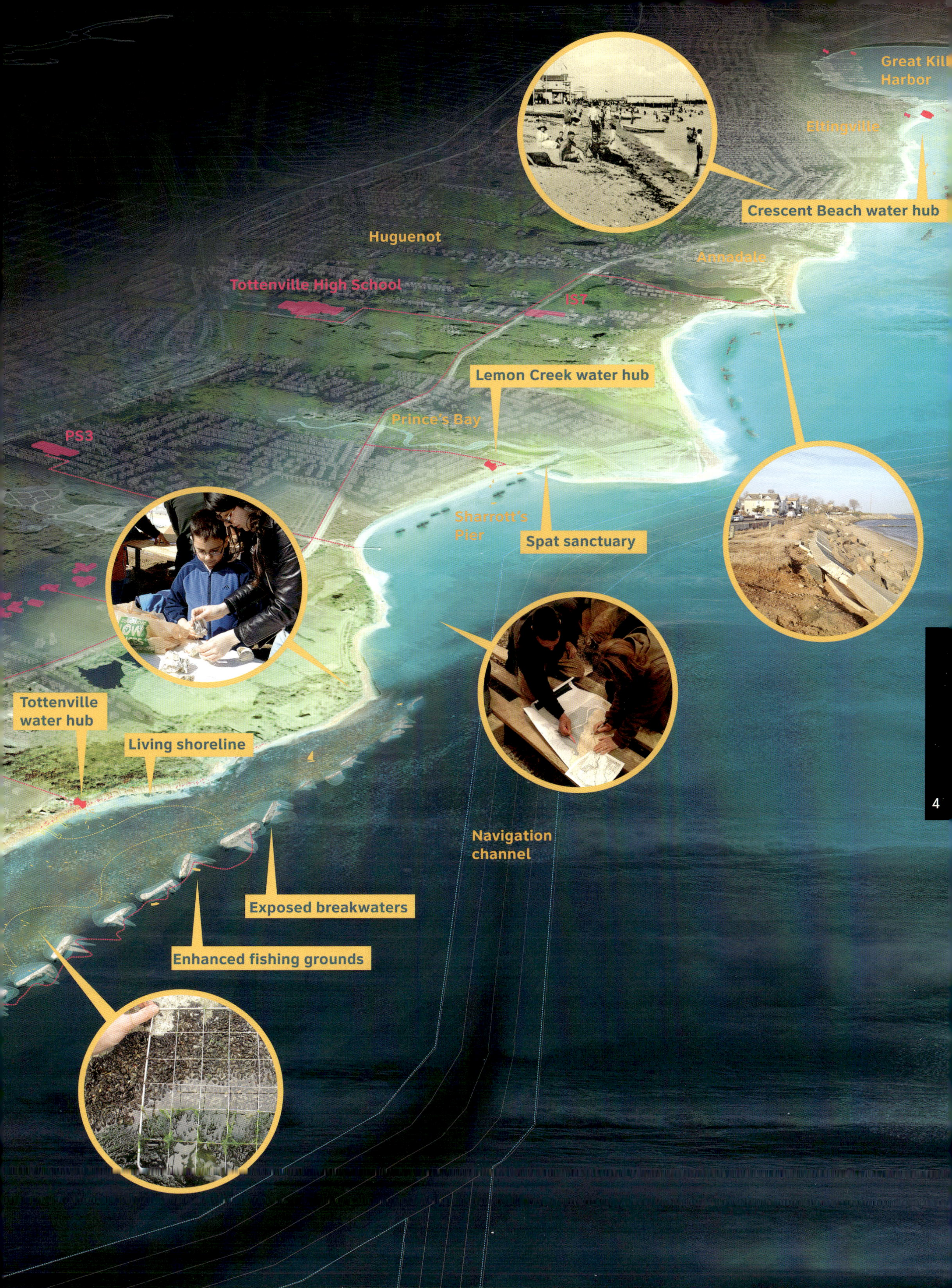
Great Kill
Harbor
Eltingville
Crescent Beach water hub
Huguenot
Tottenville High School
IS7
Annadale
Lemon Creek water hub
Prince's Bay
PS3
Sharrott's
Pier
Spat sanctuary
Tottenville
water hub
Living shoreline
Navigation
channel
Exposed breakwaters
Enhanced fishing grounds

Design Process

Throughout the design process, the SCAPE team actively engaged community members, learning about the area's aspirations and priorities. The team worked with organizations such as Kayak Staten Island, Friends of Conference House Park, and other community and agency stakeholders to gather input on the proposed design. In addition to gathering feedback at roundtable meetings, the team worked with the New York Harbor School to hold several trainings in order to engage public school teachers with the concept of using oyster gardening as an educational focal point. Beyond classroom applications, the experiential learning continued on the ground when the team worked with the community to build a large-scale model of an oyster reef cross section that was then displayed at the Staten Island Museum and later at Conference House Park.

As the design progresses, team members will continue to meet with resident stakeholders in community design charrettes. Once built, the community water hubs will create spaces for this kind of community dialogue, giving a platform for residents to continue shaping community and design decisions.

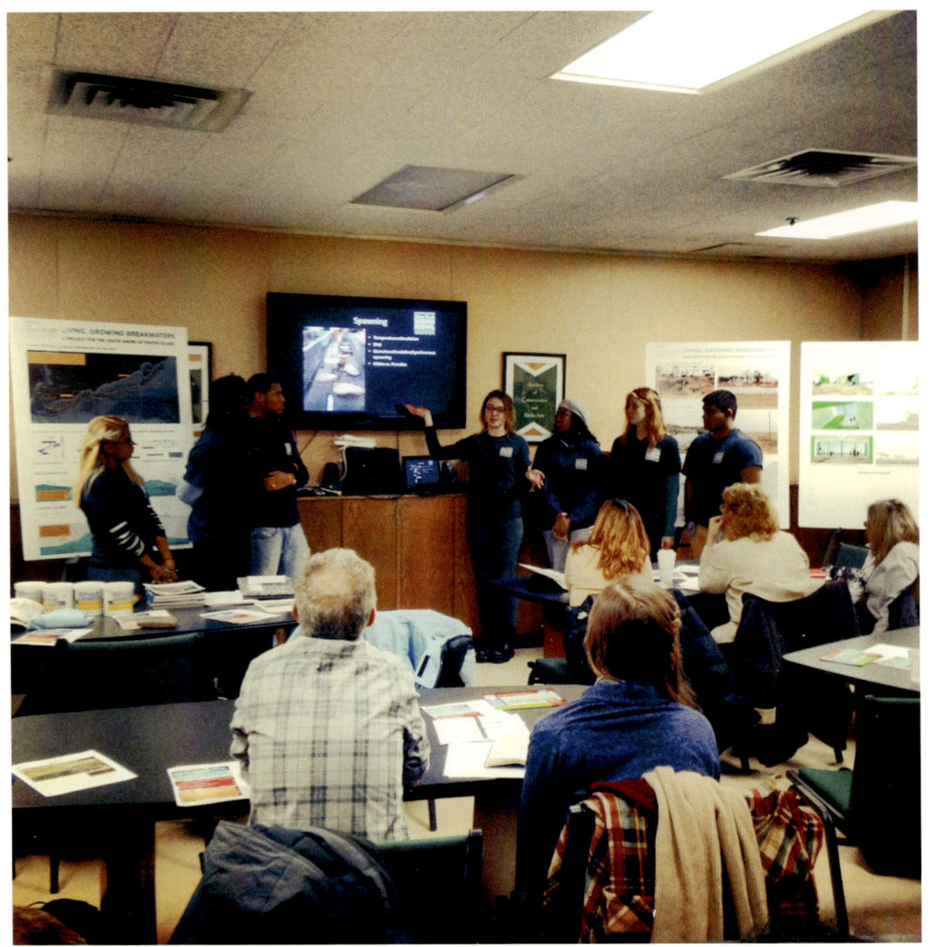

Left: SCAPE held several teacher trainings to gain insight from Staten Island teachers on how they could incorporate the Harbor School's curriculum for the Billion Oyster Project into their own classrooms.

Opposite, Above: A community project to build a model oyster reef brought together people from neighborhoods from all over Staten Island, an important component of SCAPE's strategy for incorporating social resilience into its work.

Opposite, Below: "I <3 My Shoreline," a Rebuild by Design Scale It Up community event showcased the reef model as an example of how the breakwaters improve ecological diversity, bring people together, and provide risk reduction for Staten Island's fragile shoreline.

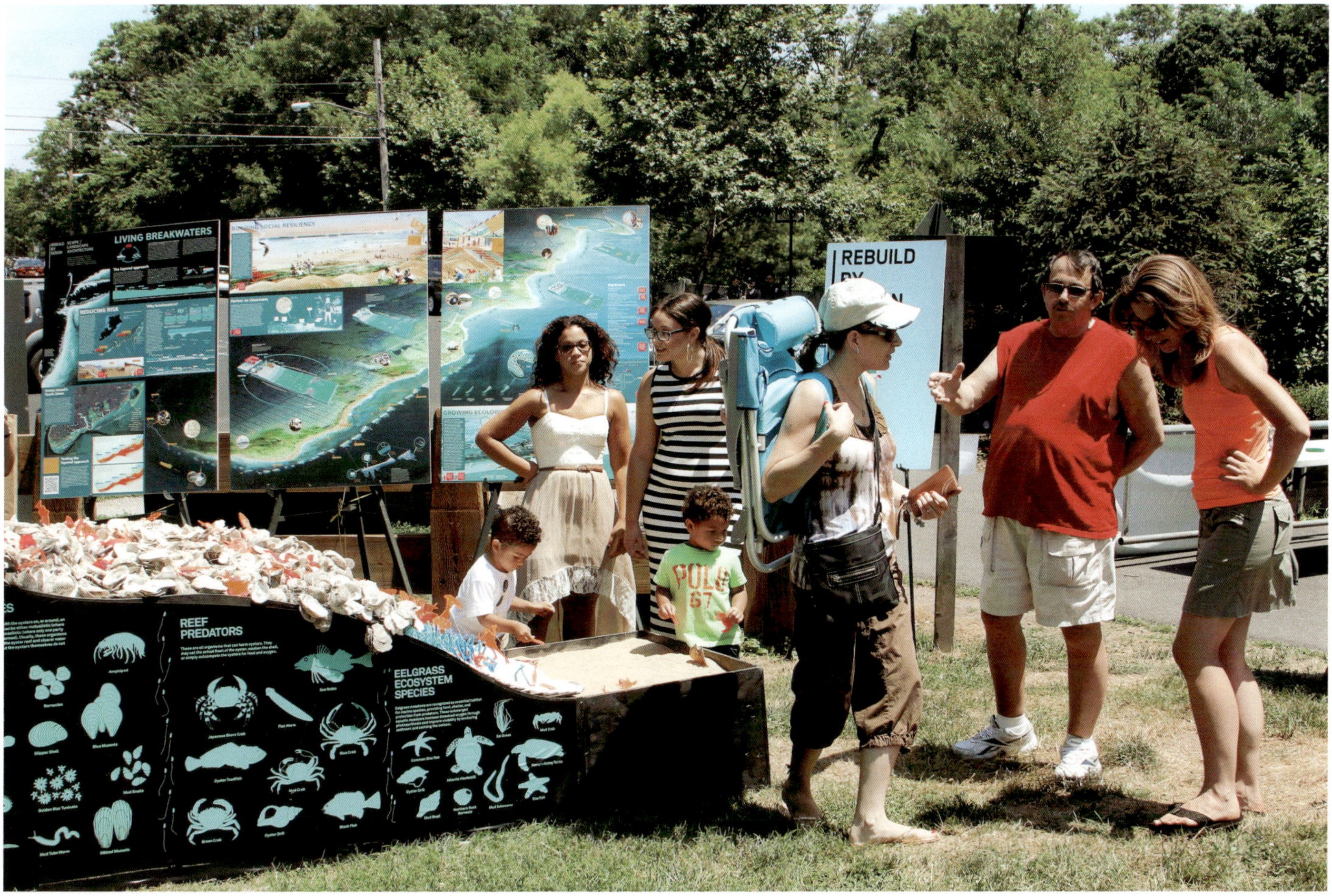

4

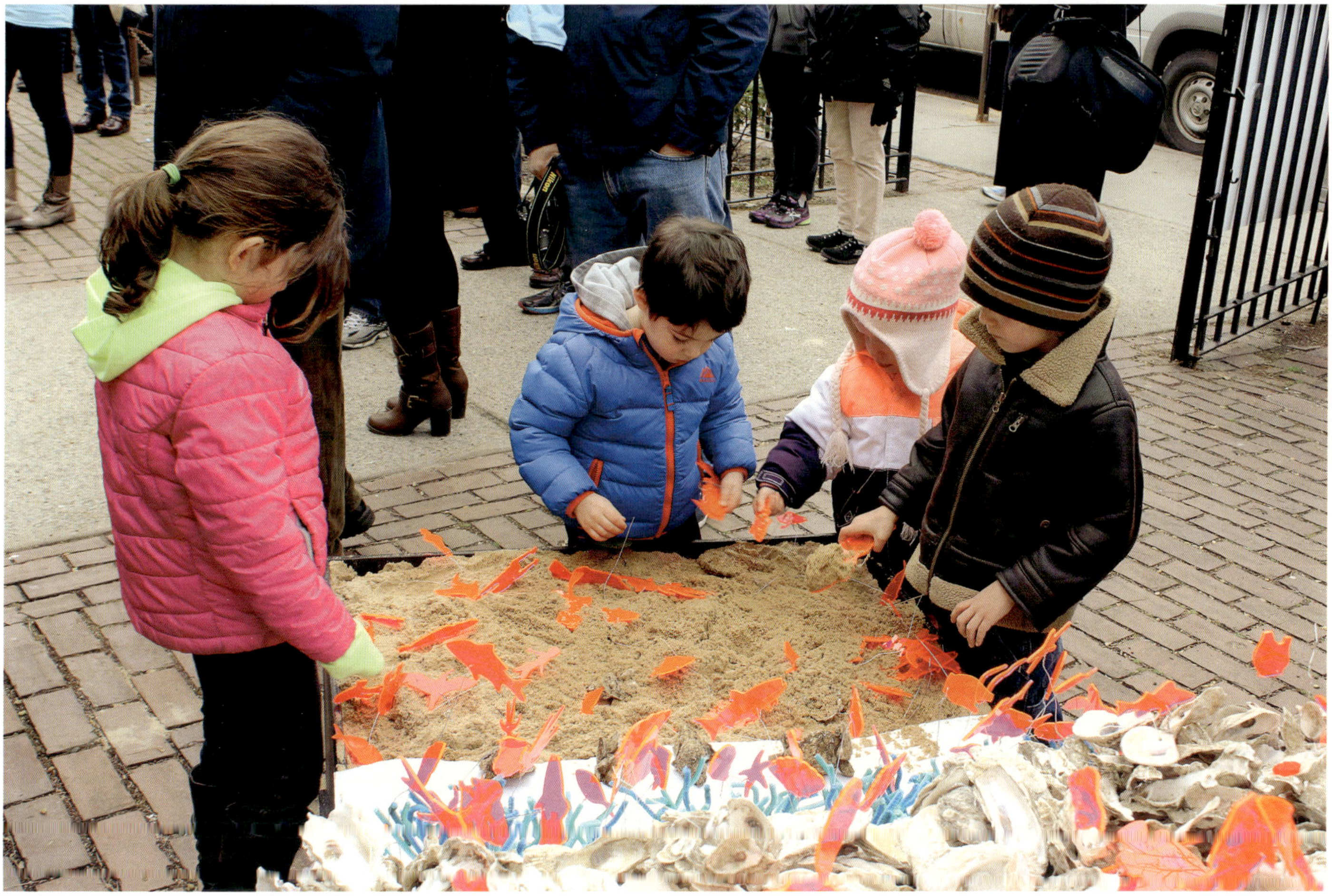

RESILIENT BRIDGEPORT

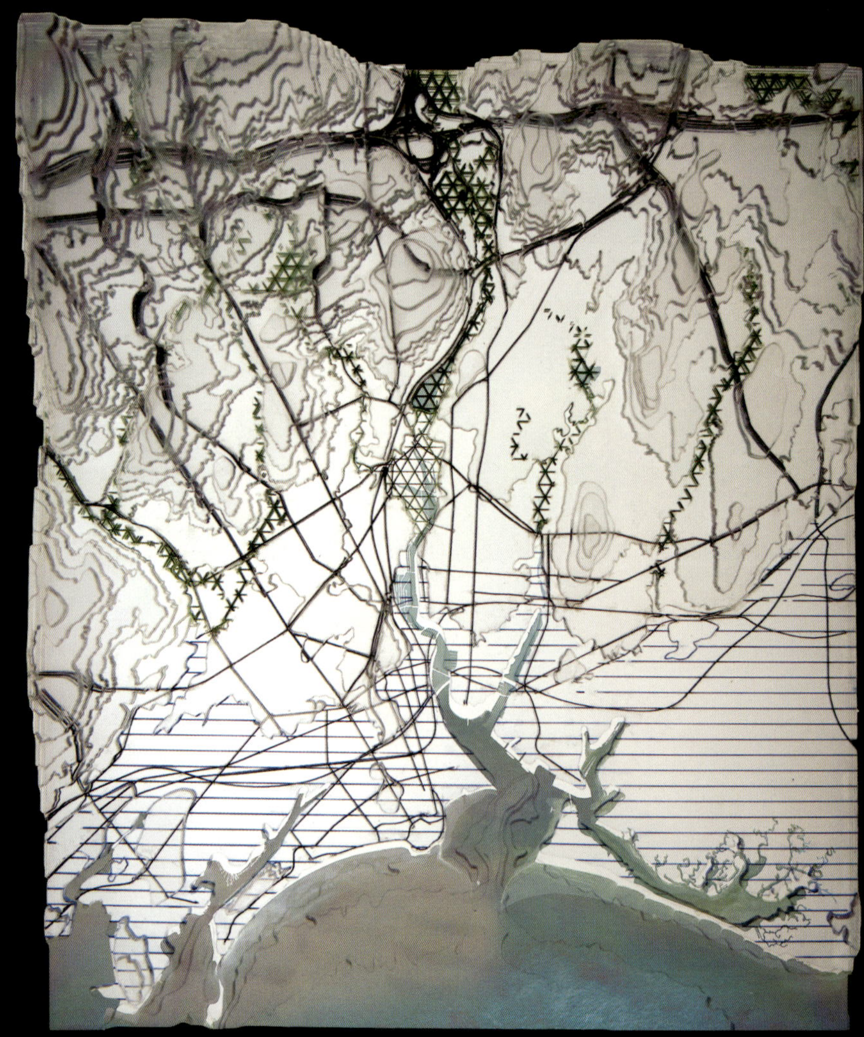

<u>Team Leads</u>
Waggonner & Ball Architects
unabridged Architecture

<u>Landscape, Planning and Community Engagement</u>
Gulf Coast Community Design Studio

<u>Ecology, Urban and Landscape Design</u>
Yale University

<u>Coastal Engineering and Stormwater Management</u>
ARCADIS

<u>Affiliates</u>
Carl Pucci
Kathy Dorgan
Robbert DeKoning
Derek Hoeferlin
Don Watson

WB unabridged with Yale ARCADIS

Living and working along Connecticut's coastline and waterways can be done in ways that restore the environment, strengthen connectivity, enhance the urban and regional economy, reduce long-term risk, restore the primacy of the city's coast and waterways, and stimulate downtown to make it central to the city's identity. The Resilient Bridgeport proposal provides for incremental change through catalytic projects, and for the integration of urban development with natural systems, so that Bridgeport can become a model for other cities along the Long Island Sound and throughout New England.

The team conceived combinations of natural and fortified solutions to facilitate more resilient forms of inhabitation in the places most at risk from sea level rise and severe weather. The resultant proposal integrates riparian, urban, and coastal strategies across four economic development and environmental restoration zones: Downtown, South End, Black Rock Harbor, and throughout the Lower Pequonnock Watershed.

Waggonner & Ball, unabridged Architecture, and the Gulf Coast Community Design Studio brought 24 years of experience living in and designing for disaster-affected communities along the Gulf Coast of the United States. Yale's Urban Ecology and Design Laboratory and ARCADIS provided expertise in ecology, urban and landscape design, coastal engineering, and stormwater management, as well as specific knowledge of the Long Island Sound and the northeast Atlantic region.

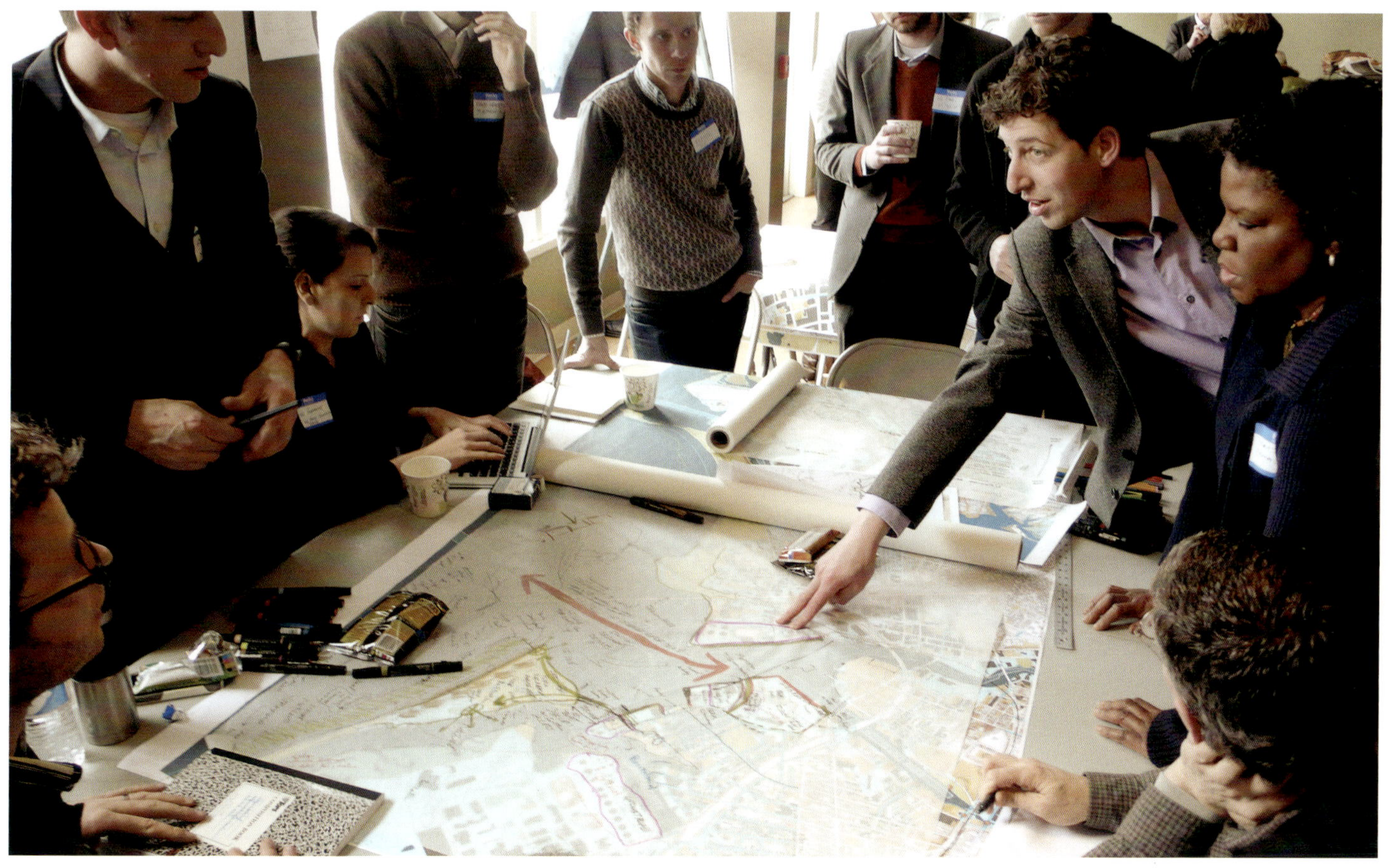

4

Approach to Estuarine Watersheds

A basic unit of resilience is the watershed. The way in which water flows through and around a community has a direct effect on safety and flood risk in cases of both regular rainfall events and exceptional storms. Using a watershed-based planning approach, the WB unabridged w/ Yale ARCADIS team identified twenty-nine possibilities across the region and grouped them according to estuary type. The team then selected five representative sites for further study as design opportunities in Phase II: Bridgeport, Rockville Centre, Far Rockaway, Long Branch, and Toms River.

In addition to estuary type, criteria for choosing sites included comparisons of elevation, population density, connectivity, populations at risk, and proximity to water.

For its final proposal, the team focused on Bridgeport, Connecticut. At the regional and city scales, the team mapped risks, assets, and land use to determine the value of varying forms of interventions along the Connecticut coast and the densely settled I-95/Metro North Railroad Corridor. The team considered interventions including variegated edges of hard

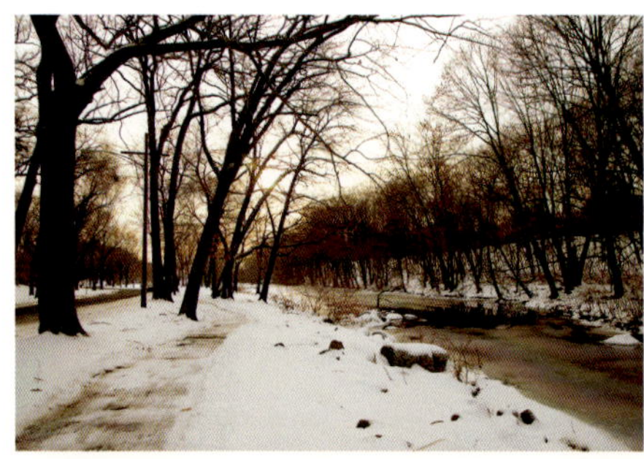

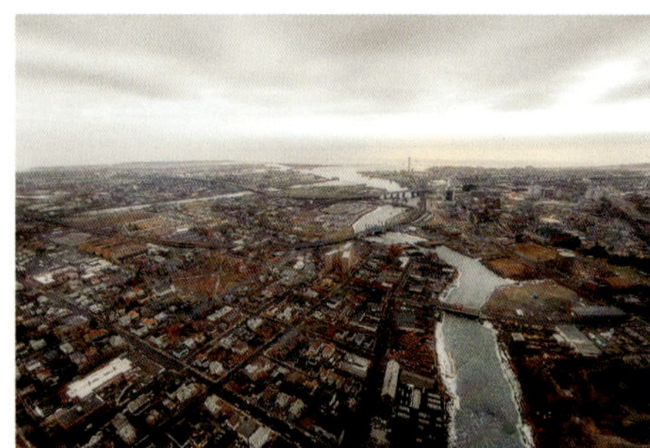

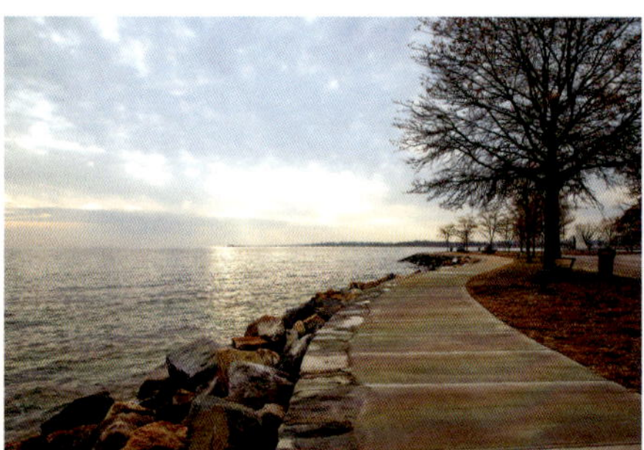

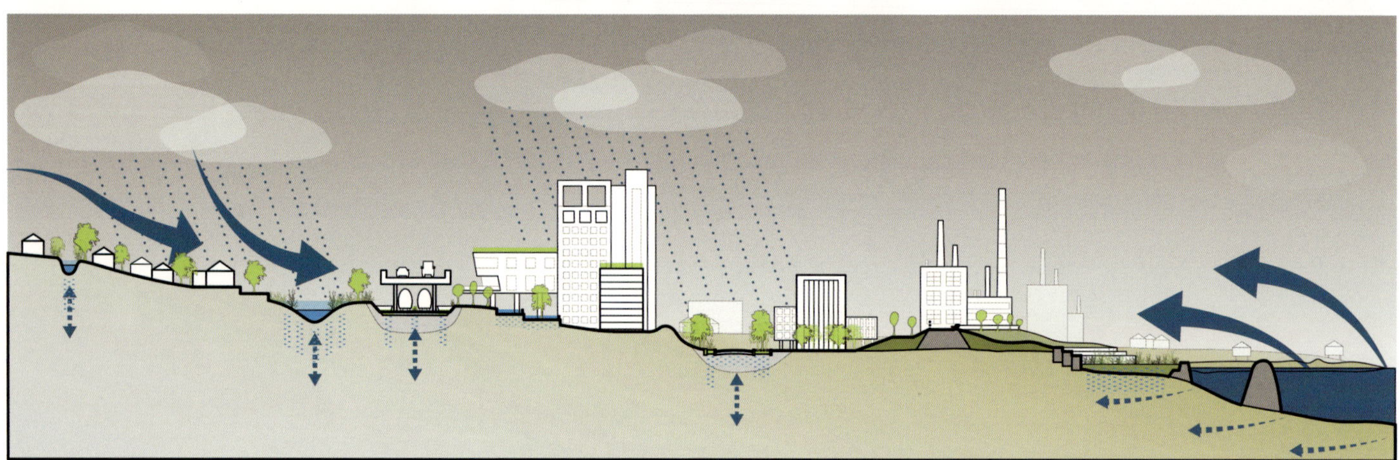

Riparian Strategies
River/Watershed Restoration
Stream Daylighting
Stream Capacity Enhancement
Park-to-Riparian Corridor Connections

Urban Strategies
Green Stormwater Infrastructure
Combined Sewer Separation
Floodproofing/Building Elevation
Cross-City Connections/Networks

Coastal Strategies
Shoreline Stabilization and Enhancement
Berms and Storm Surge Barriers
Critical Facilities Protection
Relocation of Floodplain Development

and soft protection zones with multiple lines of defense, providing higher levels of risk reduction.

Each project in the Resilient Bridgeport proposal is founded upon: 1) integrating multiple lines of defense and resilience to provide redundancy and higher levels of safety; 2) facilitating the flow of materials and people along waterways and waterfronts in order to strengthen the regional economy and ecology; and 3) connecting residents to water resources and restoring the centrality of water to Bridgeport's identity.

The proposal consists of two types of projects: immediately practicable projects that can be constructed in the near term, and more advanced concepts that require further planning and study in order to pave the way for their implementation in the coming years. The siting and design of each project arose out of an extensive community engagement process that shaped and informed the team's work.

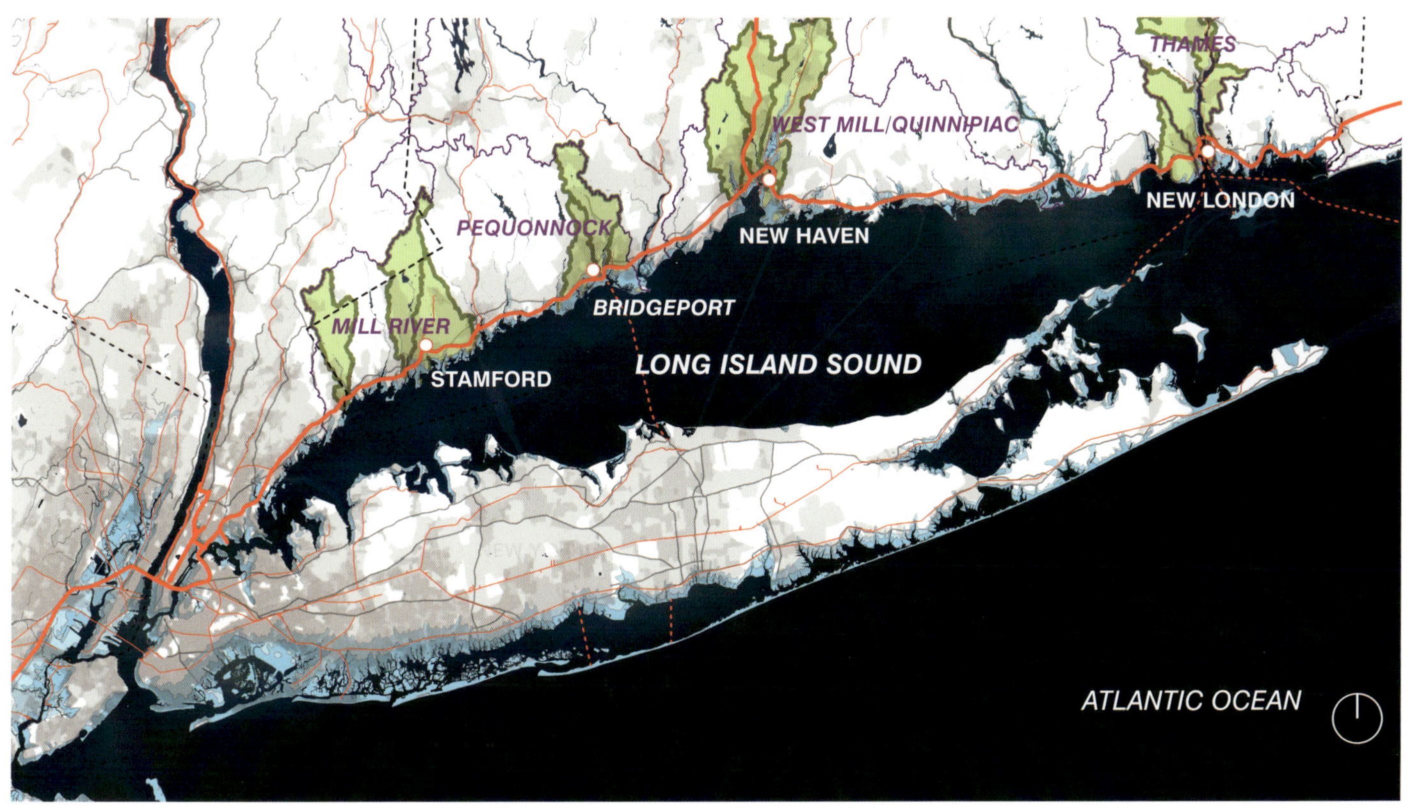

The Connecticut Coast
The coastal ecology and economy exist because of the exchanges that are only possible at this juncture. Transportation infrastructure, utilities, and information networks link Bridgeport to regional markets and centers. Coastal hydrology, too, moves sediment and other materials, constantly reshaping the line between land and water.

Population Density
Regional Rail Corridor
Primary Watershed
Secondary Watershed
2080 Severe Surge/SLR Risk

4

Design Opportunities

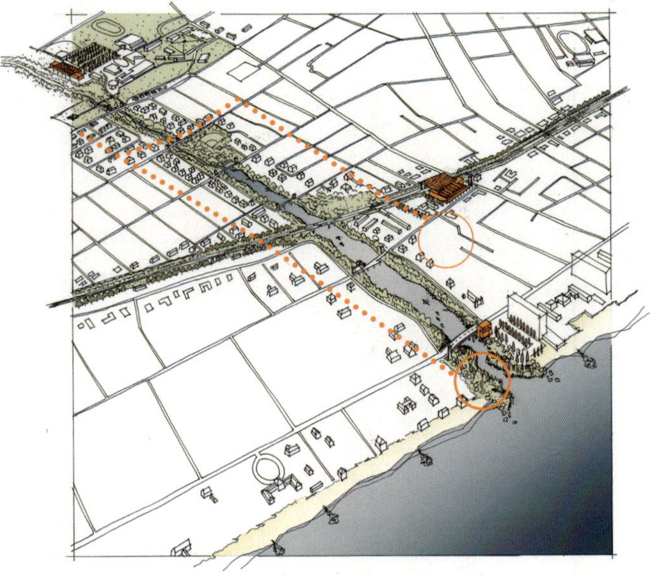

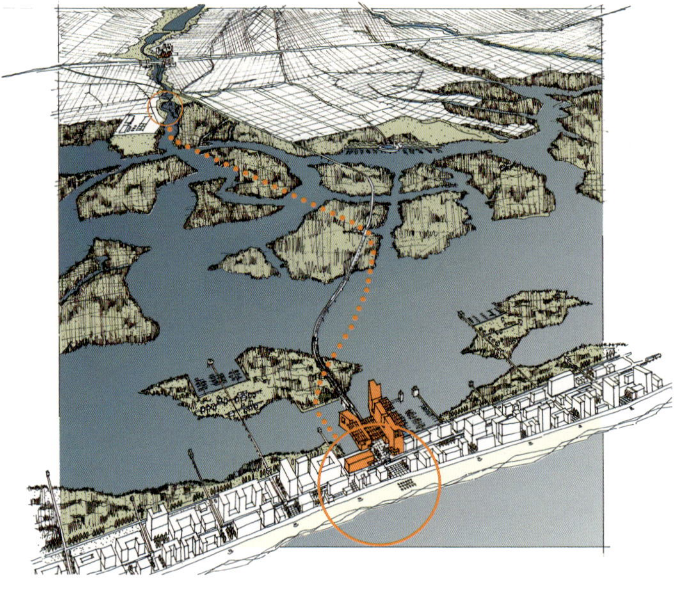

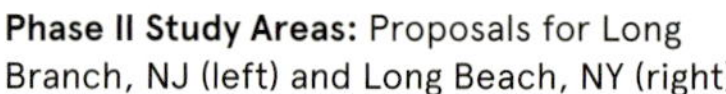

Phase II Study Areas: Proposals for Long Branch, NJ (left) and Long Beach, NY (right)

Before focusing in on Bridgeport, the design team studied five coastal communities, each situated on a different kind of estuary. They identified opportunities for landscape and urban design interventions as well as resilience centers that would catalyze safer and more sustainable forms of inhabitation and economic development.

Far Rockaway, NY

A cut through the peninsula to restore water circulation to the east side of Jamaica Bay is under study by the Army Corps of Engineers. Retrofits to multi-family housing that move residences and critical infrastrucuture out of the floodplain could allow residents to shelter in place, as would features that facilitate self-sufficiency. The construction of a resilient community center could support everyday activities as well as emergency functions.

Long Branch, NJ

Along the coast are a number of impounded tidal inlets that have changed from desirable development sites to unpleasant landscapes, often with poor water quality and flooding. Restoring tidal flow would reconnect inland locations with the beach and improve the health of estuaries and recreational amenities. The Resilience Center at Monmouth University links to the research initiatives already underway for rapid response along urban coasts.

Rockville Centre, NY

Sea level rise and more powerful storm surges will require intensification of land use and development along the high ground of both Long Island and the Long Beach Barrier Island. By 2080, the team expects that much of the barrier island will be underwater, with access via water taxi or an elevated rail line. The team envisions the lower bayside of the island becoming marshland, with colonies of stilt houses. An elevated east-west streetcar along Broadway would connect the remaining communities. Ground floor inhabitation exists predominantly as floodproof retail and commercial spaces. Inland, Rockville Centre would demonstrate safe elevation, net-zero utility use, restored estuary edges, and water-based recreation, with denser patterns of housing along the Long Island Rail Road line.

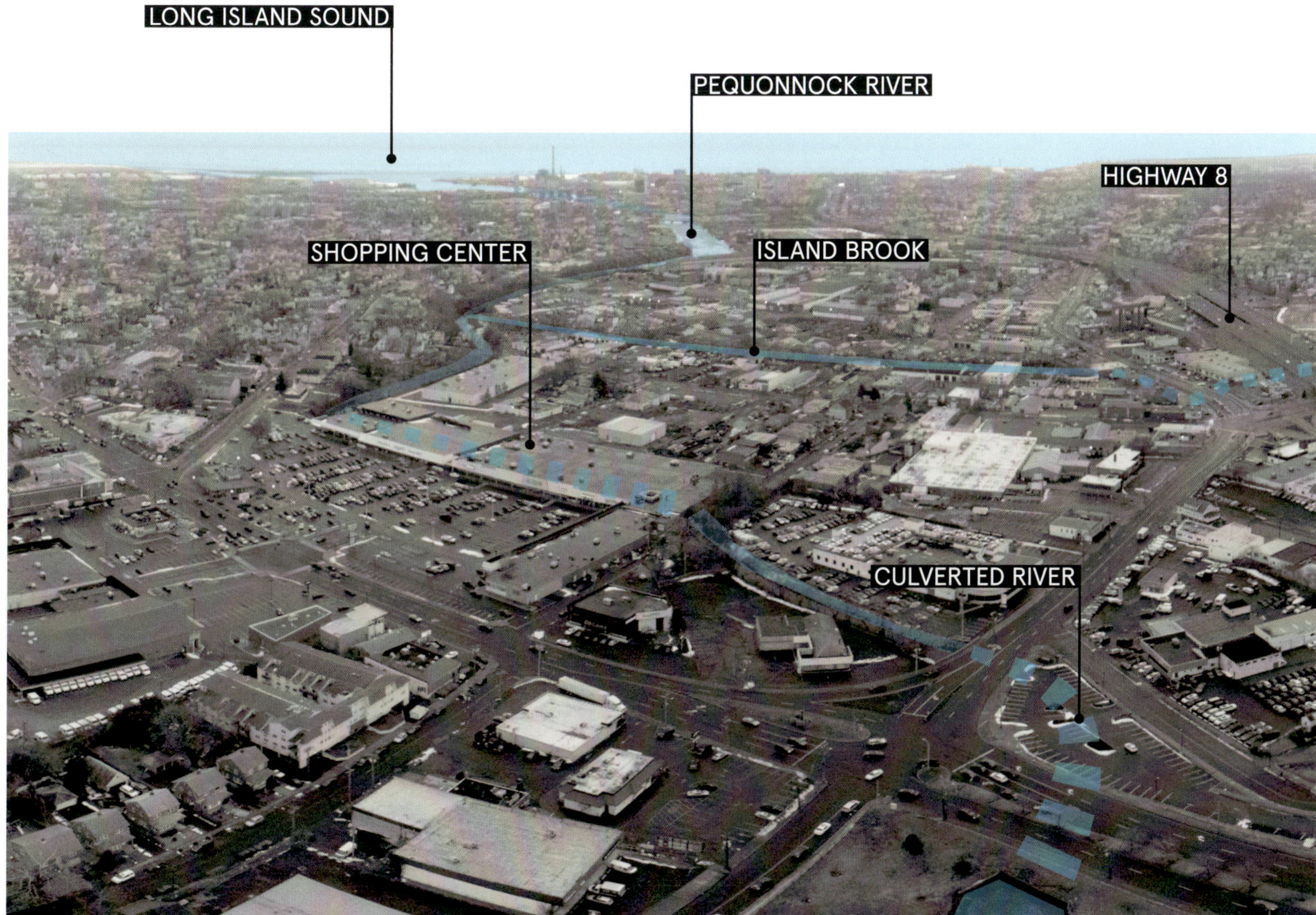

Daylighting Opportunities: Uncovering the Pequonnock River at key junctures will reveal connections from upland areas down to the coast.

4

Toms River, NJ

The coastal barrier islands of the Jersey Shore have been summer destinations for over a century. By 2080, the team envisions that water taxis would replace roads and bridges because automobile access may no longer be possible. Boardwalks could link communities along the high ground and provide a spine of hardened infrastructure. Ferry stops would be interspersed with public amusements on barges: a natatorium, arcades, restaurants, and rides. The mainland community of Toms River then provides safe harbor for these mobile features during the winter months, with the advantage of roughly +30′ elevation and strong public facilities.

Bridgeport, CT

The Resilient Bridgeport proposal is a prototype for integrating coastal, riparian, and urban strategies into a resilience framework. It focuses on how to protect Bridgeport against climate change and flooding caused by storm surge and rainfall, while stimulating environmental restoration, economic development, and neighborhood revitalization. The design proposals are place-specific design solutions ranging from green streets in upland areas to wetland park buffers in coastal areas. Included, too, are places throughout the city that provide shelter and services in storm events, and instruct people on how to transition to a way of living and thriving with water.

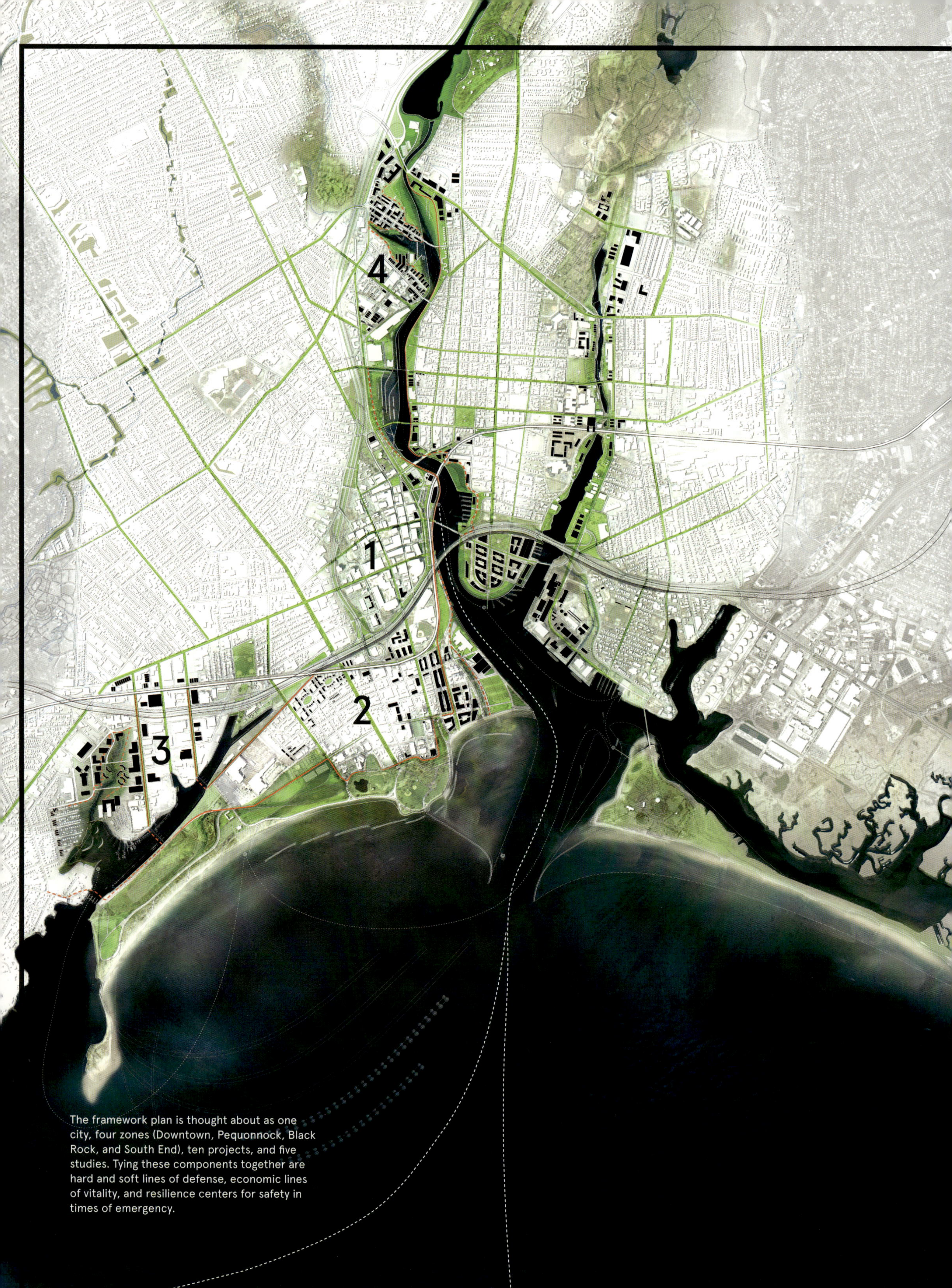

The framework plan is thought about as one city, four zones (Downtown, Pequonnock, Black Rock, and South End), ten projects, and five studies. Tying these components together are hard and soft lines of defense, economic lines of vitality, and resilience centers for safety in times of emergency.

Final Proposal: Resilient Bridgeport

Bridgeport is a sound place for investment and innovation. It has a long history of manufacturing, and played an important role in the defense of the nation during World War II as the "Arsenal of Democracy." The city has a rich tradition, too, of welcoming immigrants and diverse talents, with more than 70 languages spoken in the city today. It is also a heavily-trafficked crossing point within the Northeast Corridor, and sits at the juncture of the Pequonnock and Yellow Mill Rivers and the Long Island Sound.

The Resilient Bridgeport proposal came out of careful study of the city's geography and history. What became evident is that roads that were primary connectors in the 18th century continue to hold together the fabric of the modern city. Park Avenue and Main Street are still the major north/south routes on the west side of the city, while Kings Highway and Fairfield Avenue link Bridgeport to neighboring cities.

Over time, the city's residents filled in shallows and wetlands, and narrowed or covered waterways. Commercial corridors were situated along the high ground of Bridgeport's peninsulas, following Native American and Colonial trading routes that predate the city. More recent development, however, has placed critical infrastructure, institutions, and residential areas in harm's way, either immediately adjacent to the Pequonnock and Yellow Mill Rivers or in low-lying coastal areas most at risk from storm surge flooding and sea level rise.

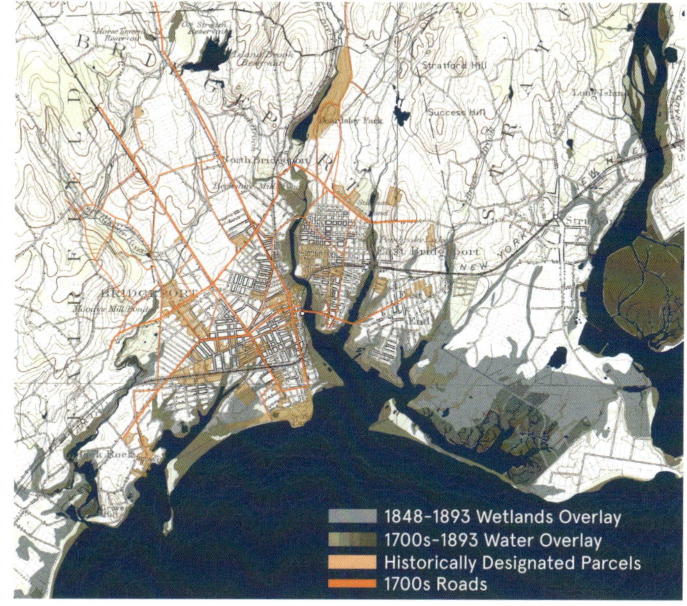

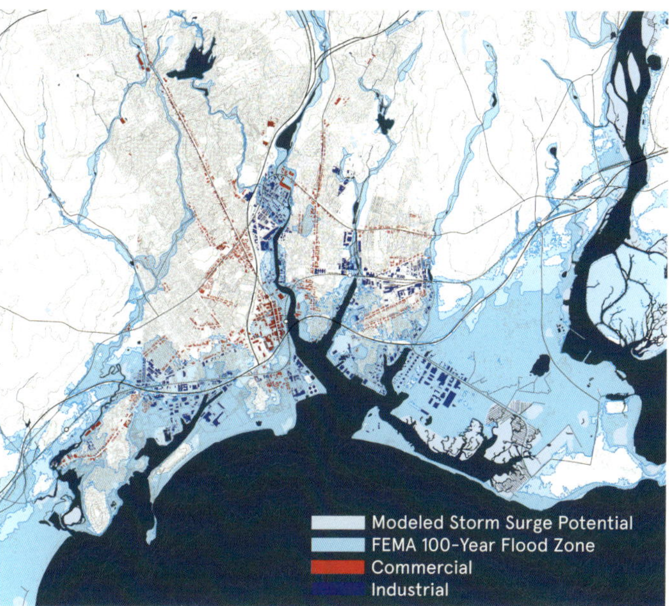

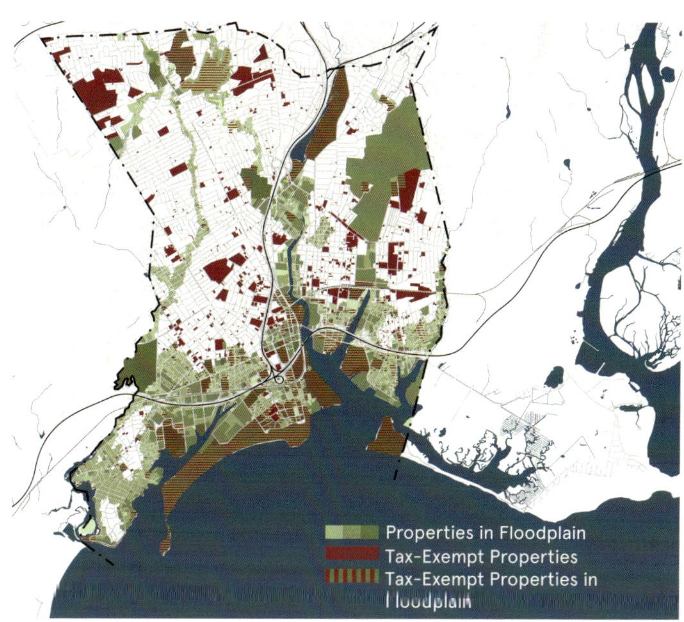

Historic Analysis
Above, Right: 18th century roadways remain important connectors today.

Commercial Corridors & Flood Risk
Middle, Right: Commercial areas are arrayed in long lines along the high ground of Bridgeport's peninsulas.

Tax Exempt Properties
Below, Right: Bridgeport is land-constrained and property tax dependent.

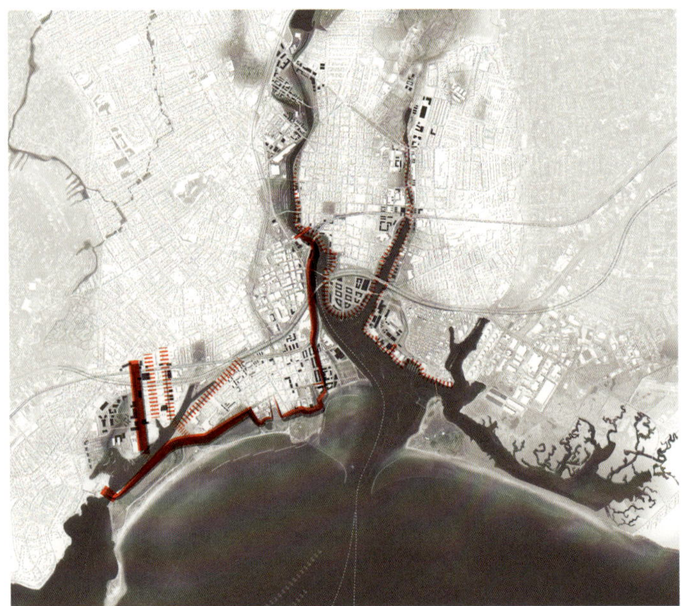

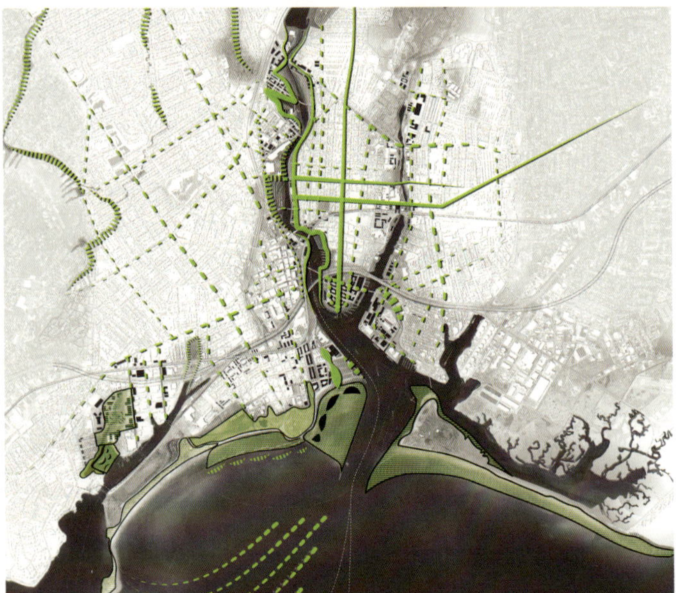

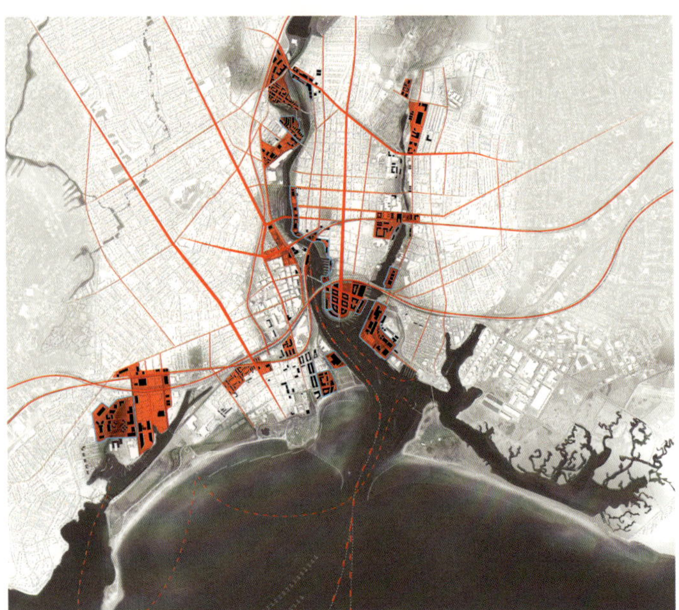

Close to $4 billion in assessed property value lie in the floodplain — power and sewage treatment plants, the University of Bridgeport, and a variety of vital facilities. Resilient Bridgeport provides clear opportunities to demonstrate resilience measures that allow for the continued inhabitation of the coastline while protecting critical historic and infrastructural assets, enhancing the regional ecology and economy, and building the strength of the city's neighborhoods and urban core.

The Resilient Bridgeport proposal integrates three systems:

Hard Lines consist of natural and fortified solutions that link communities and form stronger edges in places most at risk during storms, in order to improve safety, retain insurability, and thus gain opportunity. These living lines of defense extend and enable habitation at the waterfront, are aligned with the topography and geology of the coastal zone, and are designed for adaptation to changing situations.

Soft Lines include the Pequonnock River, Inland Waterways, and Offshore Habitats. The Pequonnock River Watershed is an ideal area for integrative and comprehensive water-based planning for redevelopment. The targeted restructuring and rezoning of land uses within the watershed, as well as the opening up and reclaiming of buried portions of the Pequonnock River and other impaired inland waterways, can reduce risks, increase development value, and improve the local ecology.

Economic Lines encompass neighborhood revitalization and economic development. Like other similarly sized, post-industrial cities, Bridgeport faces many obstacles to revitalization because of low employment rates,

Hard Lines
Above, Left: Solid red lines indicate an integrated berm, floodwall, and raised corridor systems. Dashed lines indicate possible alignments in Black Rock Harbor.

Soft Lines
Middle, Left: Solid green lines indicate Phase 1 green infrastructure interventions, both on land and offshore.

Economic Lines
Below, Left: Key commercial corridors and thoroughfares are rendered as solid orange lines. Areas outlined in blue indicate water-sensitive development.

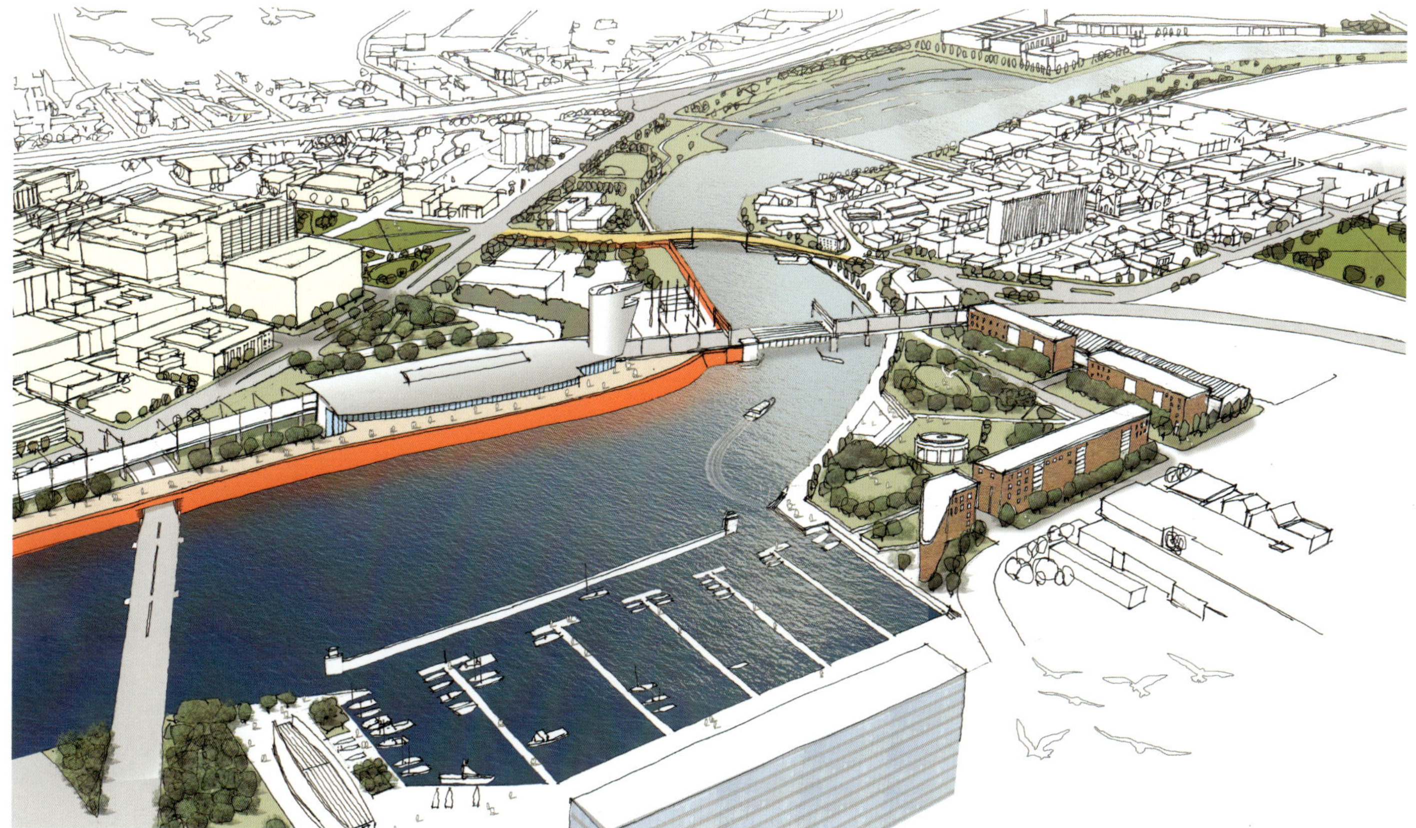

a stagnant housing market, and many blighted properties. Of the city's 12.9 square miles of parcel area, nearly one fourth are tax exempt, which constrains the city's tax revenues and creates the need for greater economic productivity throughout the city and especially along its waterfronts. The proposal looks to Bridgeport's past as well as long-term economic trends, and outlines a staged revitalization for Bridgeport and its diverse communities by fostering connectivity, innovation, production, and exchange.

Resilient Bridgeport provides a framework for the city's residents to take value from the water by restoring their connection to it. The team proposes peeling open boxed-in rivers, connecting water-rich Olmsted parks at either end of the watershed, and embracing the flow as a true water city. Ten projects and five studies center around four zones: Downtown, South End, Black Rock Harbor, and the Pequonnock River.

Downtown: Bridge and Port

Cars, trucks, and trains pass through Downtown, the locus of Bridgeport's health and resilience. The ferry connects at the Port across the Sound to Long Island. Yet too few people stop and walk, shop, or eat here. In an era of globalization and regionalism, and given the centrality of Manhattan and the proximity of Bridgeport, development is nearly inevitable. Protection and connection are provided by a Waterside Promenade that coordinates and aligns with train platforms in current or shifted locations. Long term Northeast Corridor highway and rail system relocations need further study, though benefits to Downtown are evident. An Urban Design Center, operating in conjunction with universities, will focus on smart adaptation strategies. Rebuilding the Congress Street Bridge will give Bridgeport back its lost connections from the East Side and Washington Square to Downtown. This vital investment will regenerate commerce, and is crucial to a holistic understanding of resilience.

Downtown at the Pequonnock River
Above: A strengthened city core includes a new riverfront train station. Orange lines indicate perimeter lines of defense.

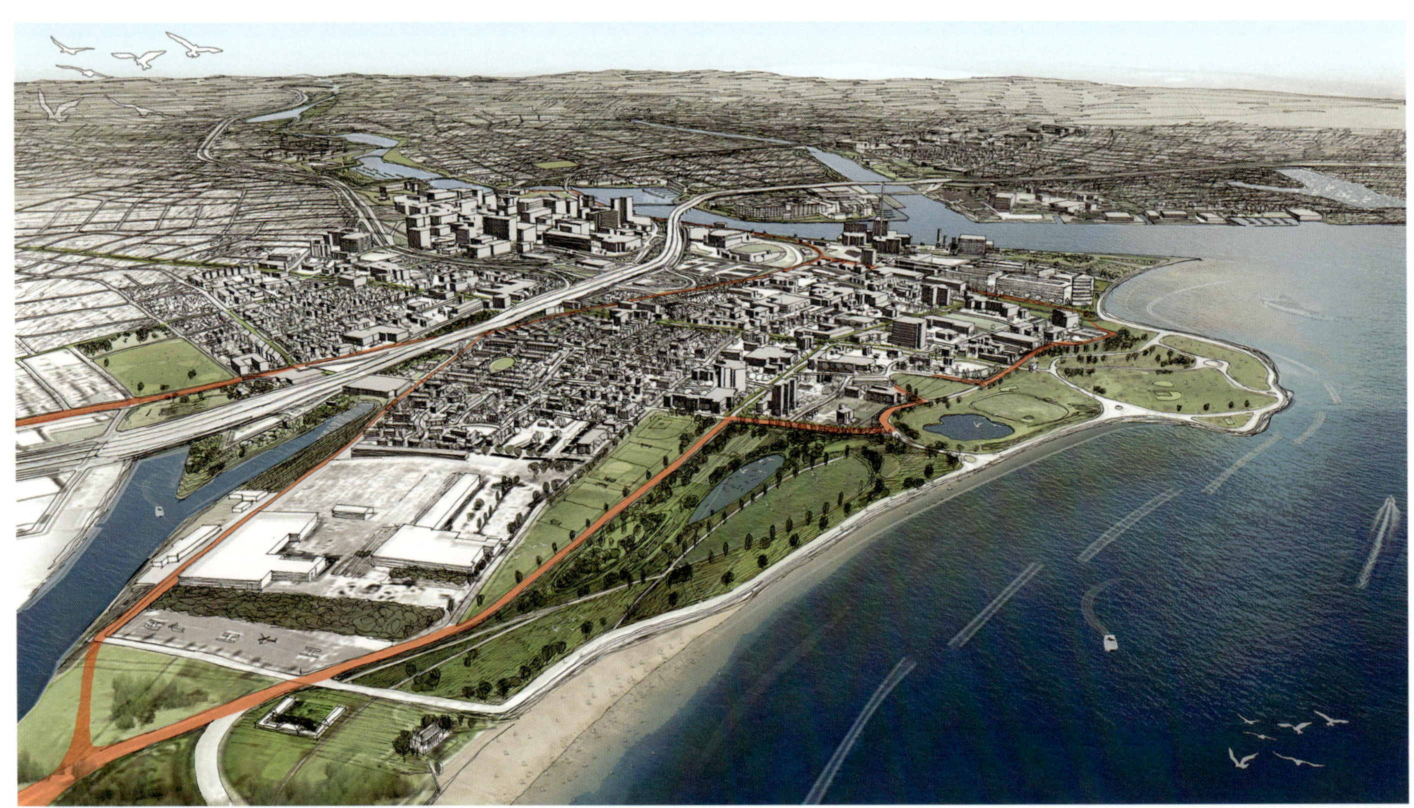

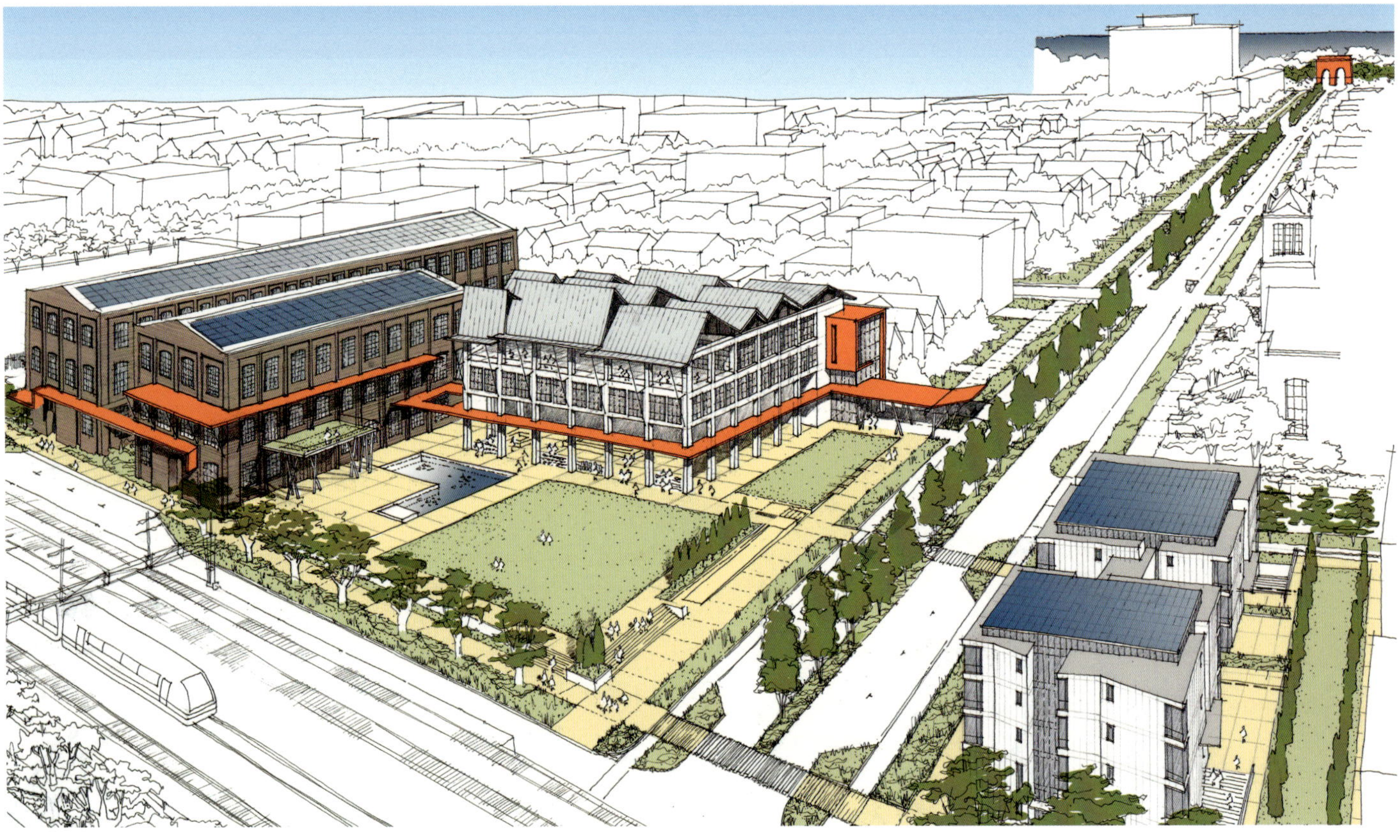

Seaside Park

Above: The neighborhood, University of Bridgeport, and historic Seaside Park are protected with integrated lines of resilience and improved connections to downtown. Orange lines indicate perimeter lines of defense.

South End Resilience Center

Below: A resilience center is a catalyst for the transformation of the neighborhood and serves 12,600 residents and workers with a wide range of community-driven programming.

South End: Protecting the Community

Beginning at the back of Olmsted's Seaside Park and protecting the neighborhood with its historic buildings and developments, including the University of Bridgeport, a multipurpose berm continues both west through the park and north towards Downtown. This new landscape asset, combined with an onshore stormwater treatment park and offshore breakwaters, adds value and creates opportunities in spatial as well as risk-reduction terms at the center of the community.

Black Rock Harbor: Powering the City

Setting new standards, technical innovations to protect the bourgeoning Eco-Industrial Park are proposed and planned, including a later-phase Bridge with Integral Storm Surge Barrier. The Elevated Infrastructure Corridor network is a key public investment, with large stormwater and utility distribution benefits, and is the first step in a series of needed public and private adaptations. These include phased improvements for the housing development up the corridor from the Offshore Treatment Park as well as for other parts of Black Rock, the battery that powers Downtown.

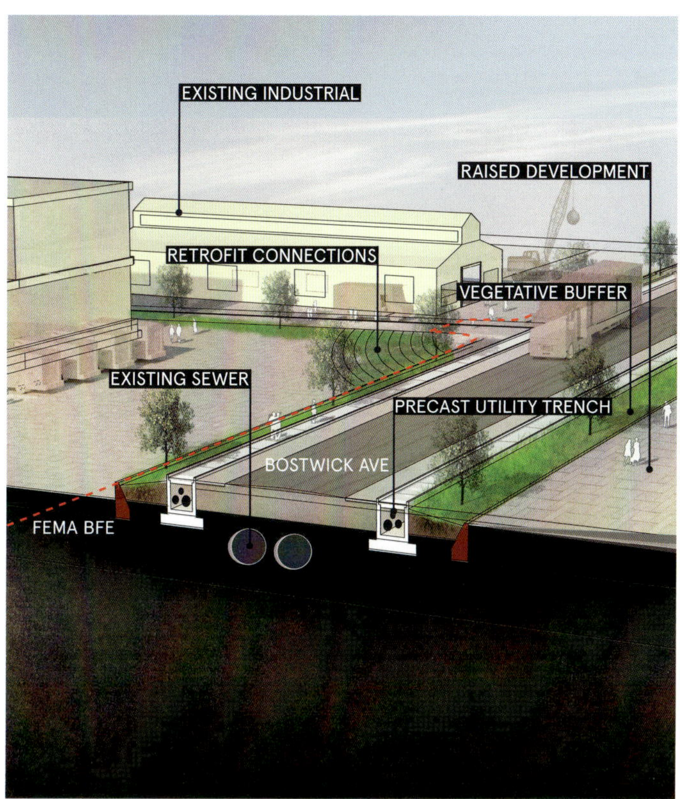

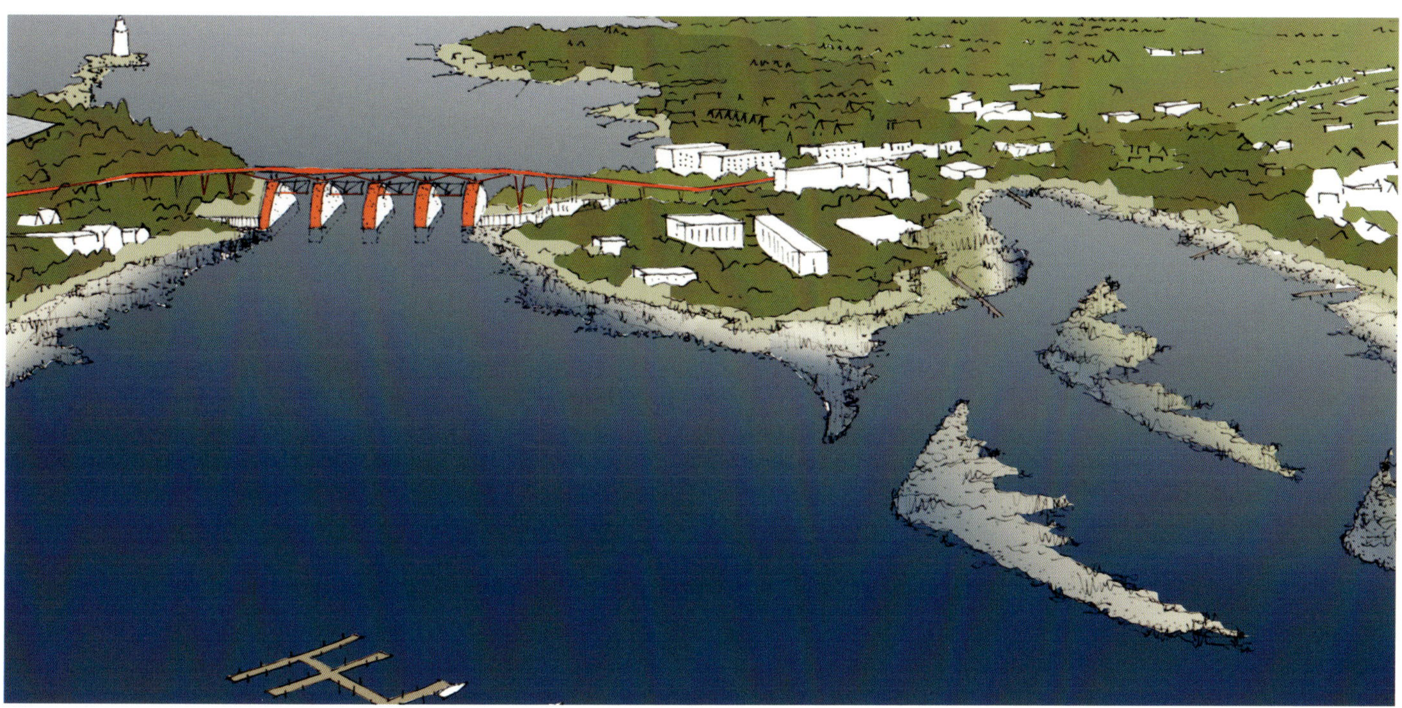

Elevated Infrastructure Corridor
Above: Bostwick Avenue serves as a pilot for a network of elevated streets and utility corridors in the Eco-Industrial Park and surrounding areas. In later phases, the raised utility corridors align and integrate with broader surge protection.

Black Rock Closure Structure
Below: Offshore reef and wetland structures improve water quality year-round, while the addition of a surge barrier at the mouth of the harbor provides critical assets and protection from storm surge to coastal neighborhoods.

4

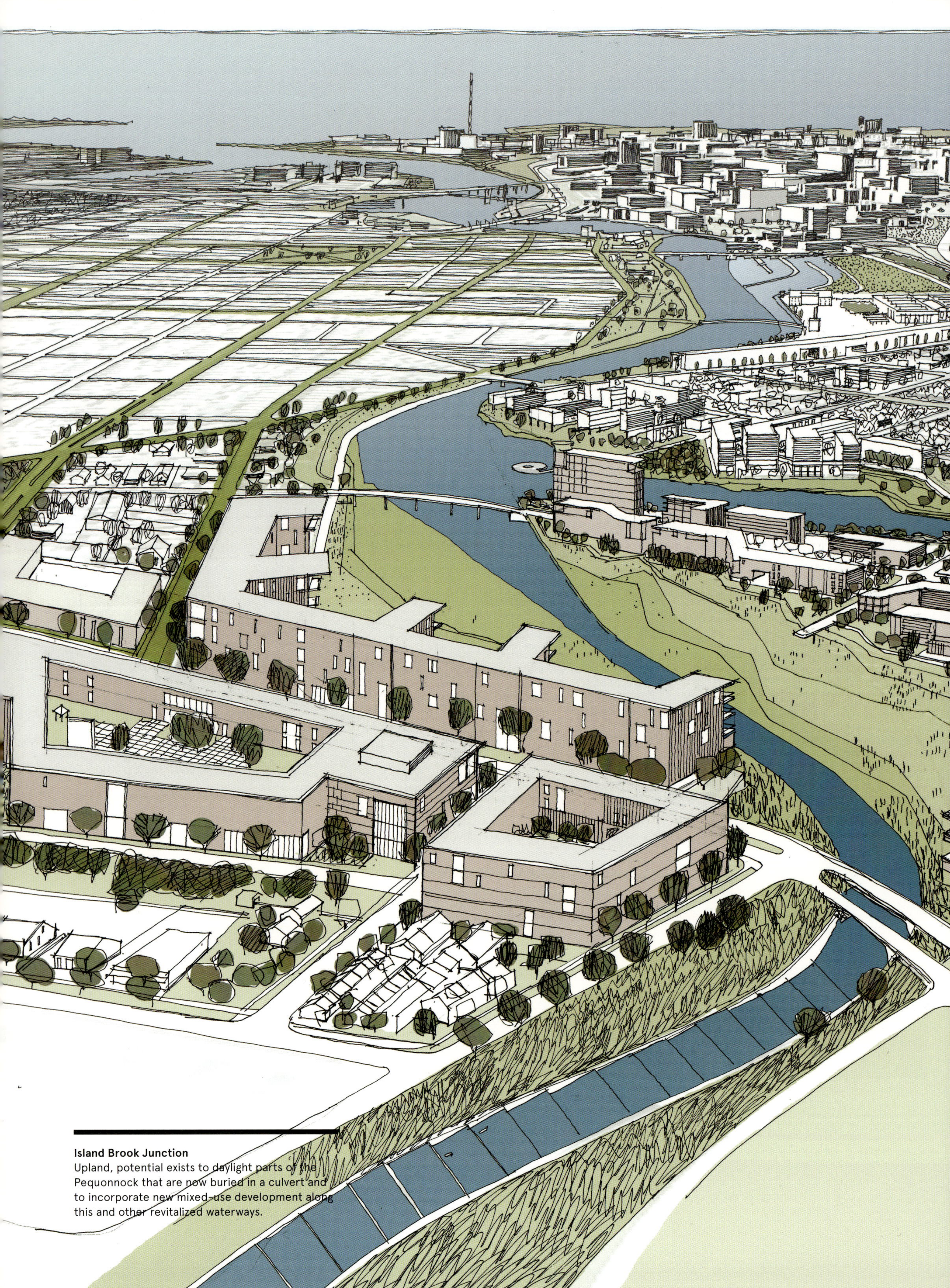

Island Brook Junction
Upland, potential exists to daylight parts of the Pequonnock that are now buried in a culvert and to incorporate new mixed-use development along this and other revitalized waterways.

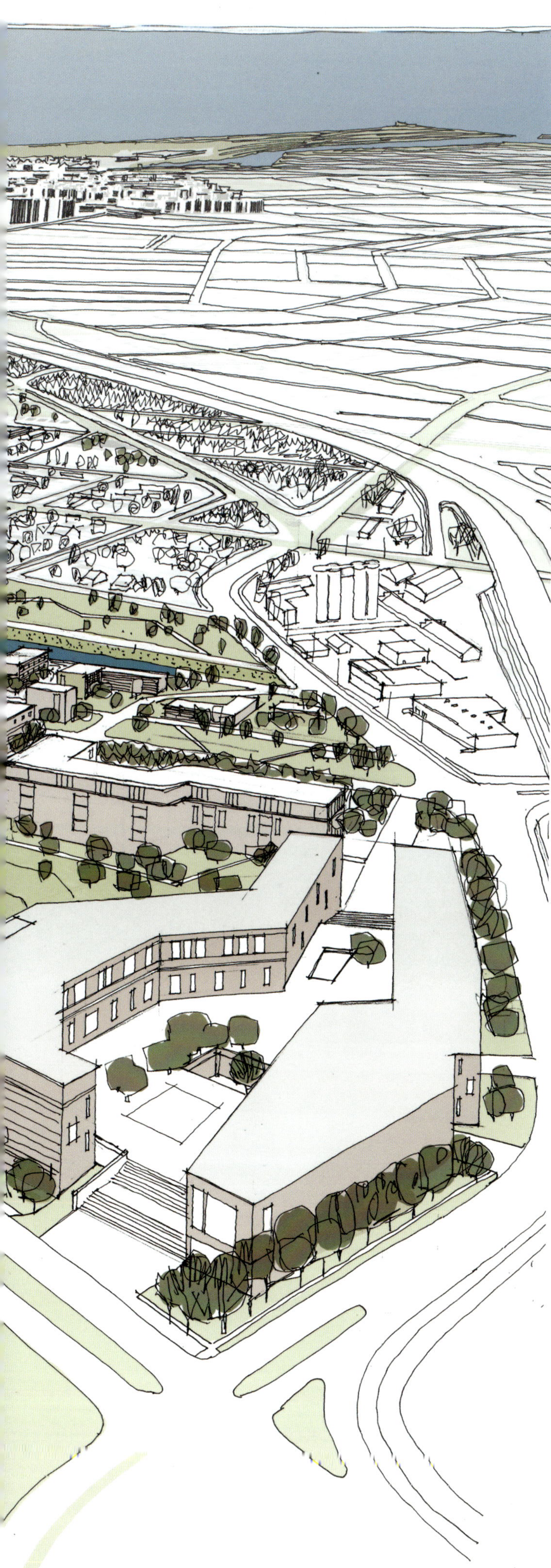

Pequonnock River: Claim the Edge

Rarely is a river so ripe for reclamation as the Pequonnock. Connecting water and park systems from Olmsted's freshwater Beardsley Park to brackish Seaside Park allows for a string of improvements that nurture resilience. Conditions and locations needed for aquaculture are prioritized as room is given back to the floodplain. The network of East Side Green Streets mitigates runoff and pollution, demonstrating watershed benefits on a neighborhood scale. Repetitive loss of properties near the intersection of the river with US 1, where a marginal shopping center is built on top of the confluence with Island Brook, are targeted for reorganization to allow for daylighting the water system, commercial revitalization, upscaling and reorientation of development to the water, and creation of a new upland entry for Bridgeport.

Bridgeport Next

Once a place where the rivers structured the local economy, organizing flows of materials and the shapes of people's lives, activities have abated, and Bridgeport has lost its connection to its waterways and waterfronts, turning its back on its prime assets and reason to be: the water system.

Despite the presence of the Sound and a plethora of rivers and creeks – including the Pequonnock, Yellow Mill, and Rooster Rivers and Cedar, Burr, Island Brook, and Johnson Creeks – water is too often out of sight and out of mind. After recent storms and floods, it may be counterintuitive to pivot towards the water. There is, however, nothing more important to the physical, economic, and ecological health and resilience of the place and the people.

Each proposal demonstrates three key principles of the resilience framework. First, integrated lines of resilience are critical to inhabiting the coast, with site- and district-level measures complementing engineered solutions and natural buffers. Second, the city's coastal and riparian edges are productive places of exchange and the restoration of these zones can be the basis for a revived regional ecology and economy. Third, Bridgeport's identity is founded upon the relationship of its people and industries to its watercourses, estuaries, and beaches. Reclaiming this identity and redefining what it means to live at the water's edge are critical to the city's safety and long-term prospects.

Design Process

For the design team, integrating the design process and community engagement efforts has allowed for the participation of diverse local and regional stakeholders in the development of a resilience framework for Bridgeport. Workshops with community partners, ongoing conversations with government officials, design charettes with critical stakeholders, and a series of public open houses and educational activities with both youth and adults have been instrumental in shaping the focus and content of the design team's work.

Each event has been an opportunity to share water management strategies and principles for resilient design with the community, to empower citizens to engage in the conversation about their city's future, and to build together towards a shared vision and implementation strategy.

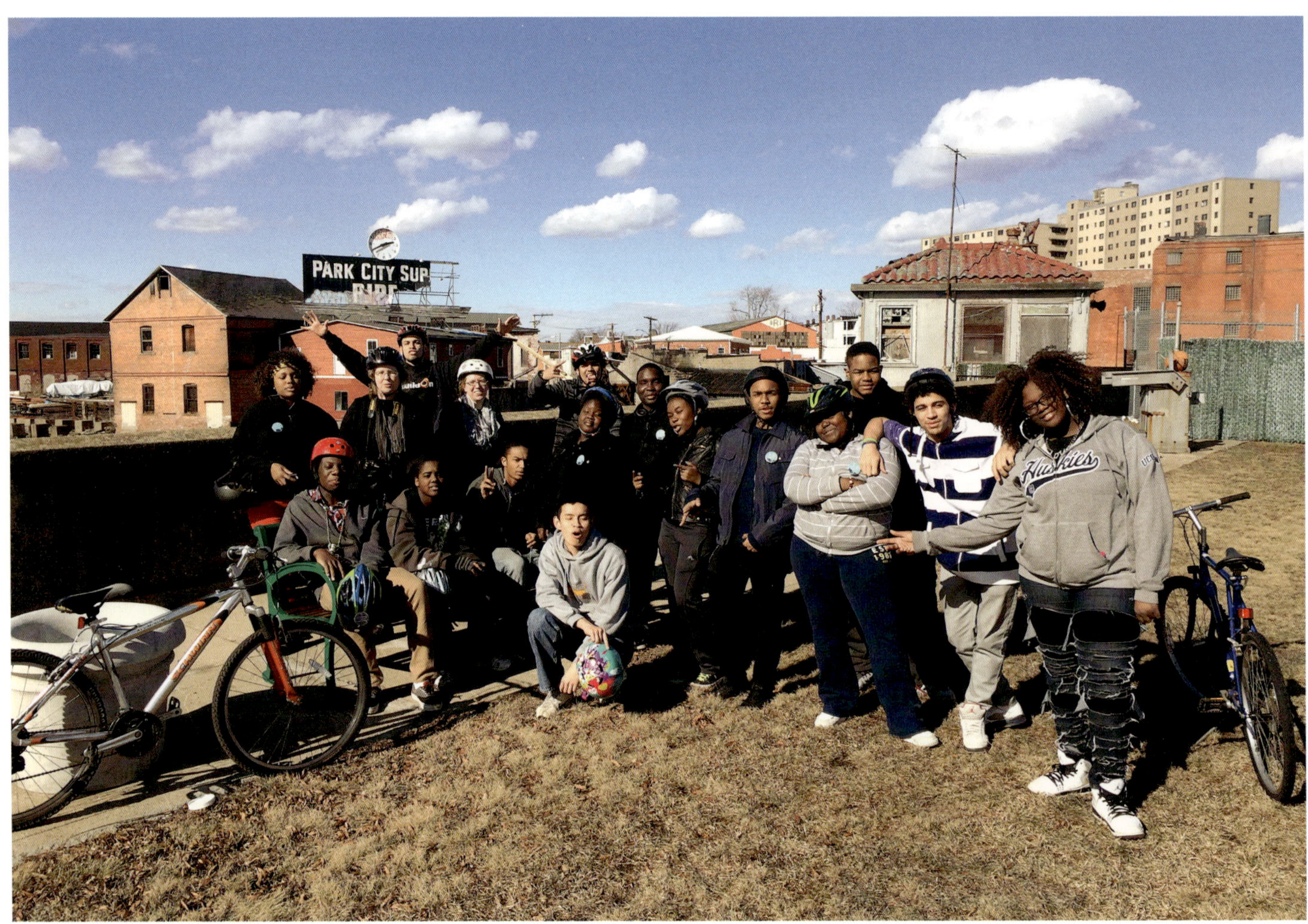

A group of Bridgeport teenagers joined design team members and cycling activists for a bike ride along the Pequonnock River during the CityMaking Scale It Up! event.

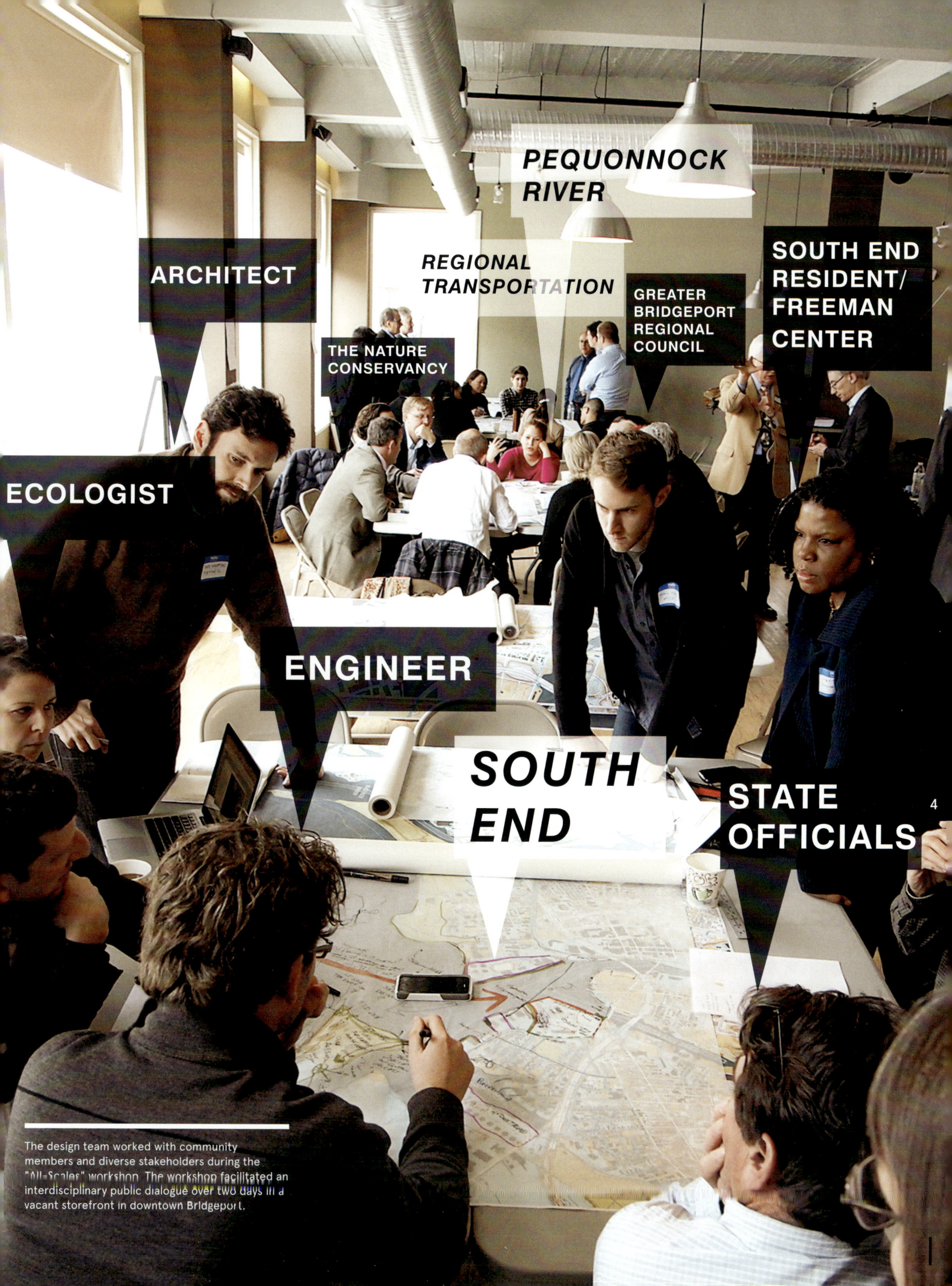

The design team worked with community members and diverse stakeholders during the "All-Scales" workshop. The workshop facilitated an interdisciplinary public dialogue over two days in a vacant storefront in downtown Bridgeport.

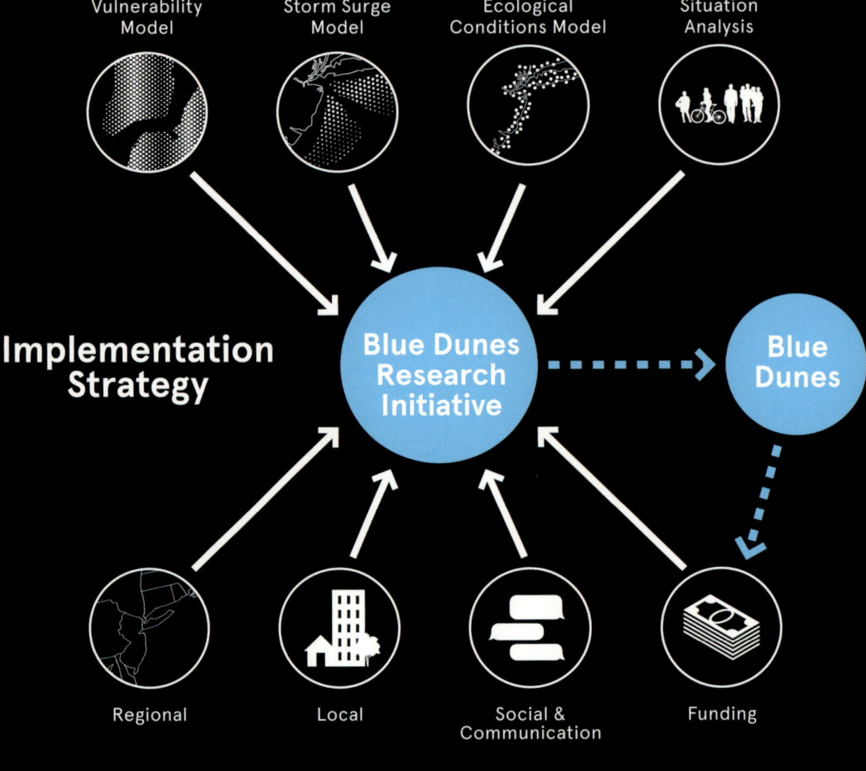

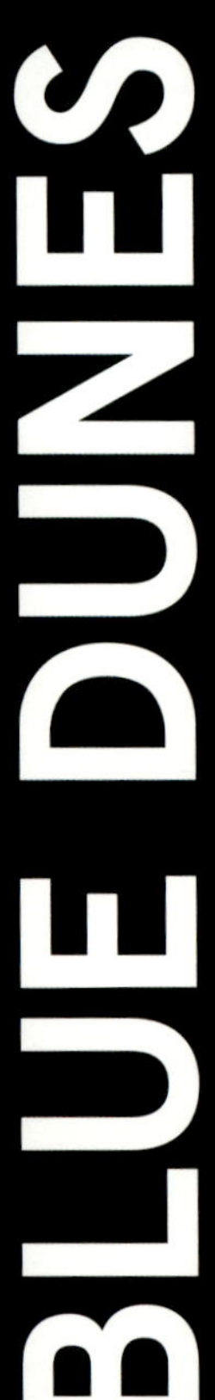

Team Leads
WXY Architecture + Urban Design
West 8 Urban Design & Landscape Architecture

Climate Science Leads
Dr. Alan Blumberg, Dr. Sergey Vinogradov, Dr. Thomas Herrington, Stevens Institute of Technology

Risk Modeling
Andrew Kao, AIR Worldwide

Engineering & Technical Feasibility
Daniel Hitchings, ARCADIS

Financial Modeling
Kei Hayashi, BJH Advisors

Landscape Ecology
Kate John-Alder, Rutgers University

Planning & Design
Maxine Griffith, Griffith Planning & Design

Graphic Design
Yeju Choi, NowHere Office

Real Estate Development
Jesse Keenan, Columbia University Center for Urban Real Estate

Community & Planning
William Morrish, Parsons the New School for Design

WXY/West 8

The WXY/West 8 team focused its research toward developing a new regional model for resilience: a network of man-made barrier islands.

Through an empirical process, the team tested scientific projections and performed extensive hydrological modeling to establish the efficacy of protecting large areas within the region. Stevens Institute and AIR Worldwide integrated projections into the model to account for the storms of greater intensity and frequency that the region will face as climate change takes effect.

The team also facilitated dialogue and debate within the research community, inviting scientists from the University of Connecticut, Columbia University, the University of Delaware, and Rutgers University to join in the conversation about the challenges of long-term and system-wide approaches to reversing environmental degradation and reducing risk.

As a result of this research, the team proposed Blue Dunes, a system of constructed dunes built offshore in the Atlantic Ocean from Cape Cod to Cape May. The team contended that the region's tremendous risk required robust regional protections. But rather than building a sea wall or dike system, the team advocated a less intrusive approach that would mimic ecological systems. Along with this proposal, it called for the creation of a research program – the Blue Dunes Research Initiative – that would study climate risk throughout the region.

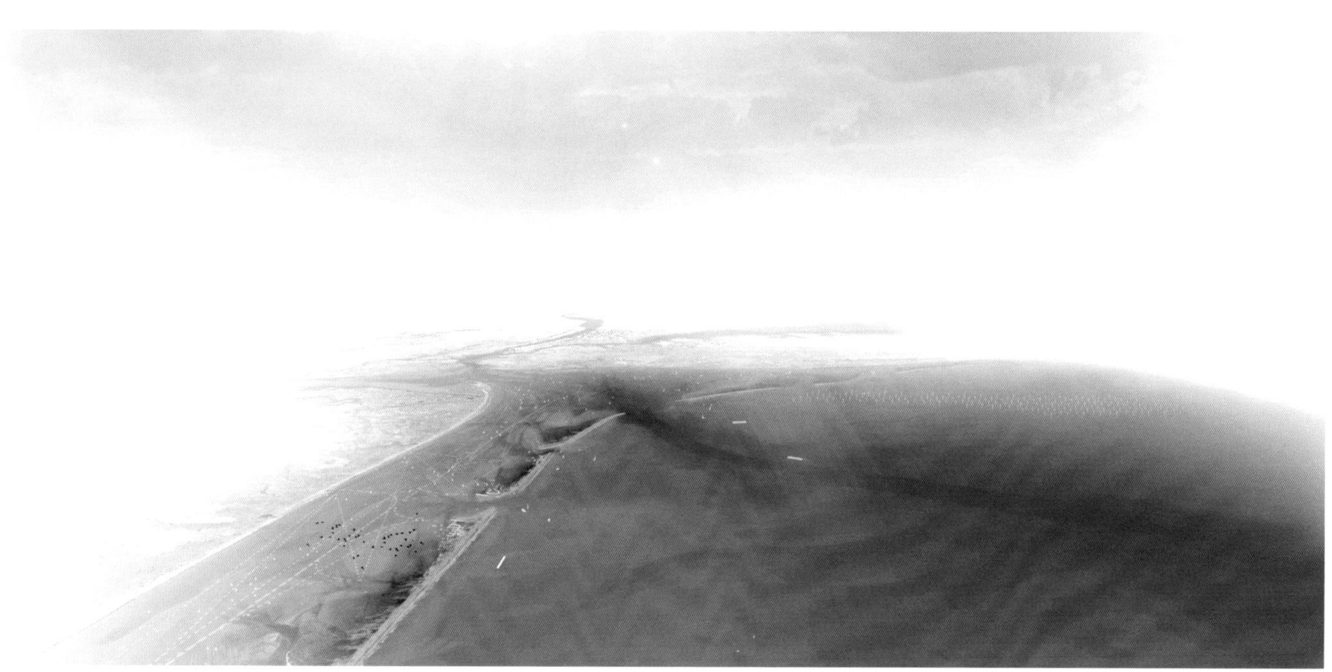

Blue Dunes proposes a series of offshore barrier island chains that would mitigate the damaging effects of storm surges.

A Regional Approach to Resilience

Throughout its research process, WXY/West 8 focused on the many different dimensions of risk.

The team's approach considered that every local design intervention depends on regional systems that are themselves at risk. Considering these regional systems as possible solutions – climate risks, insurance mechanisms, communication strategies – the team emphasized the advantages of this innovative approach, such as its ability to bypass onshore complexities and to avoid the problems of incremental interventions that may protect some areas while endangering others.

The more precisely it could quantify risk based on science and calculation, the team reasoned, the more effectively it could design systems that would mitigate those risks. Not only did the team take a broad view in terms of geography, but also in its interpretation of risk: in addition to flood risks, it considered economic and infrastructural risks, and the insurance formulations meant to distribute their costs

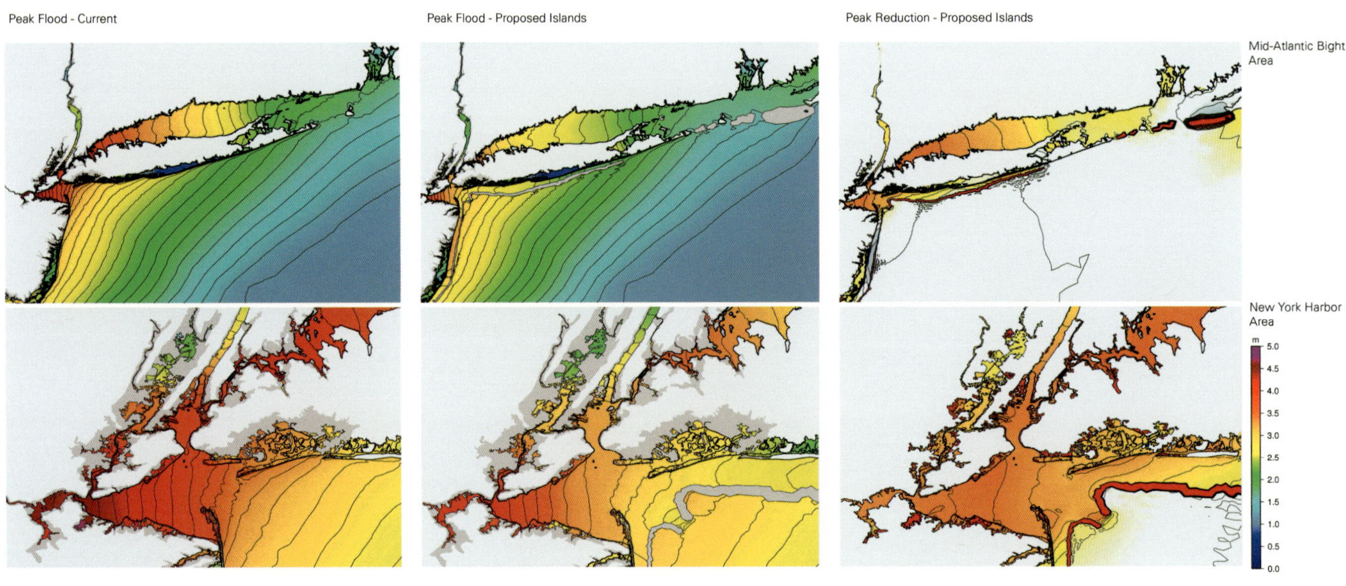

Computational Modeling

Using storm data from 1960 Hurricane Donna, the 1992 Nor'Easter, and 2012 Hurricane Sandy, Stevens Institute of Technology modeled surge levels on various barrier island configurations.

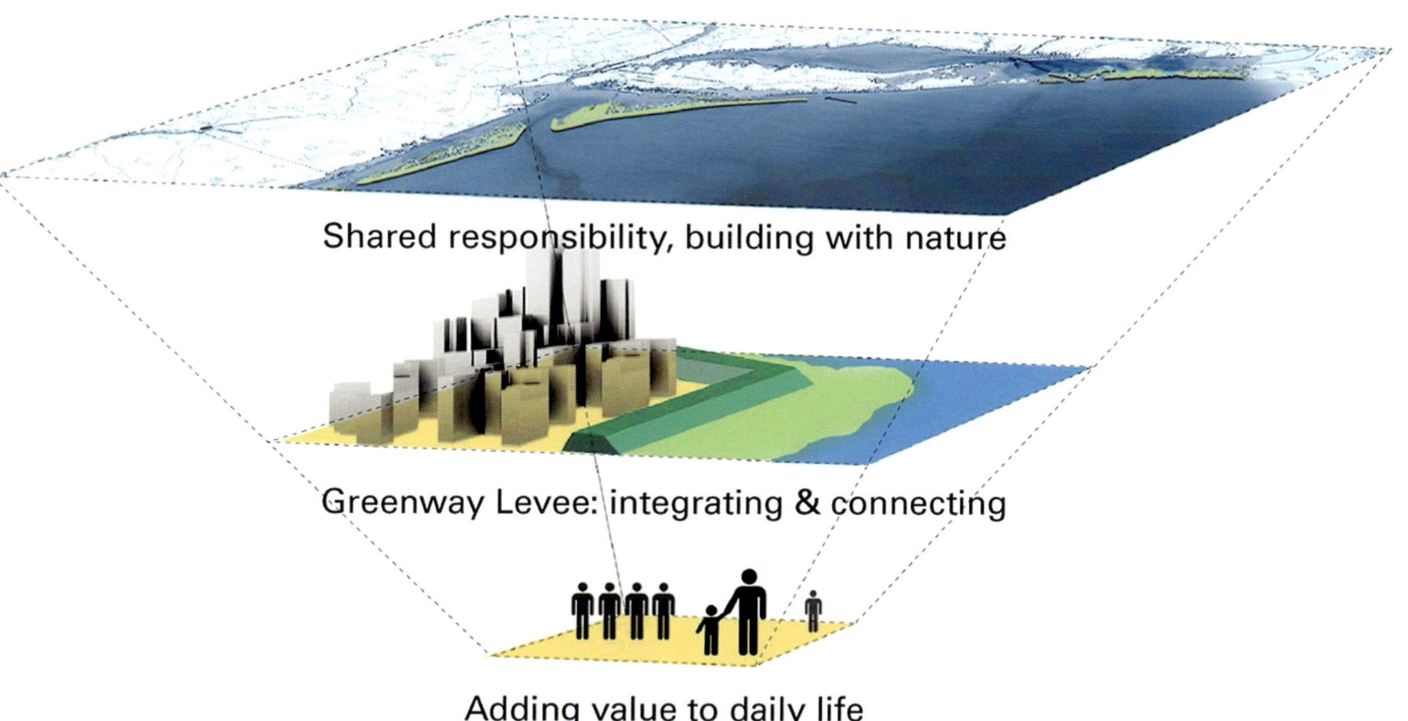

A Multi-Layered Defense System

4

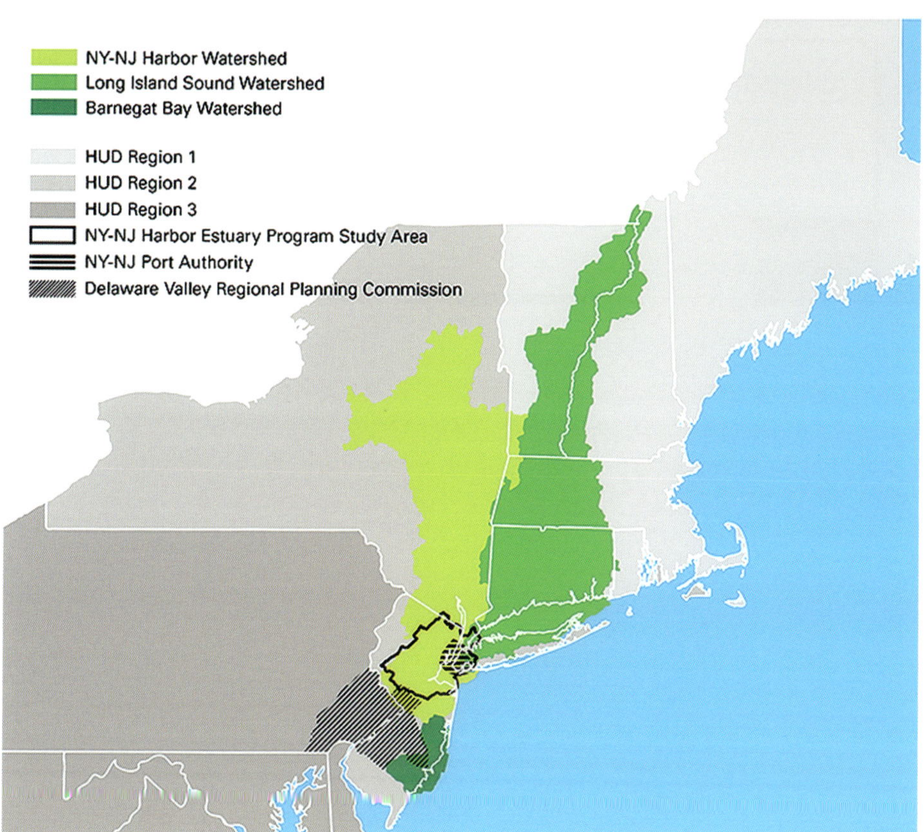

Above: Quality of life becomes a shared responsibility on the regional scale as the team thought about building up resilience.

Left: Identifying political boundaries demonstrates the necessity of regional cooperation to manage the risk of future storms as their effects cross multiple state and authority lines.

In New York and New Jersey, a system of constructed barrier islands could reduce the necessity for unsightly high walls and barriers at the shoreline, and the impact of these flood defenses on valuable waterfront spaces.

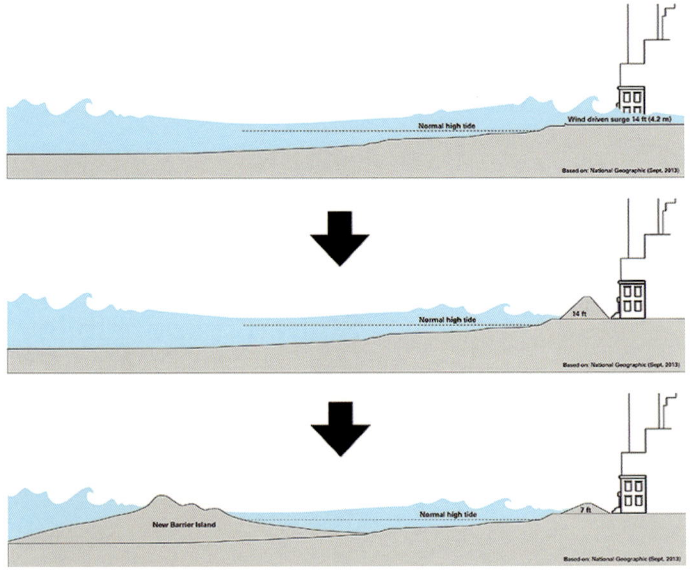

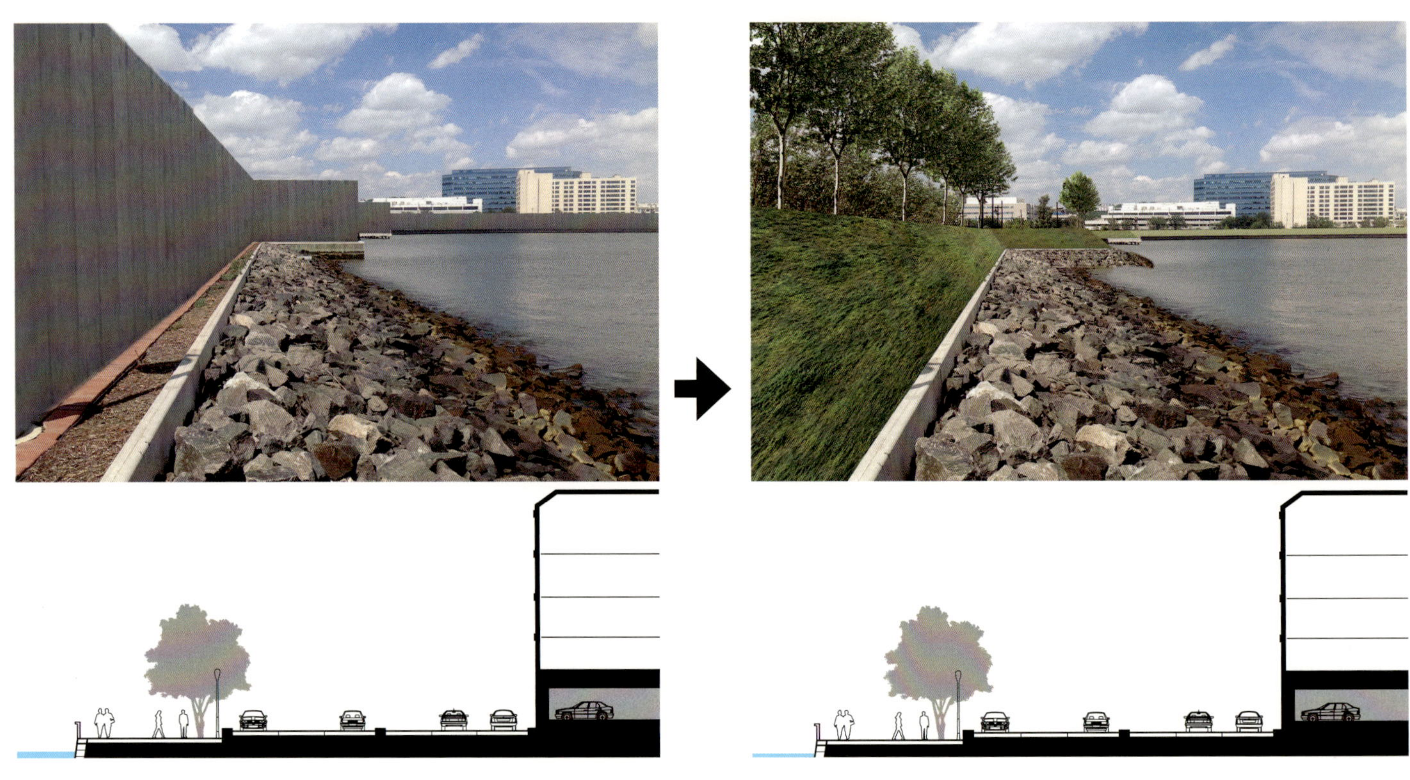

Ecological impacts were also taken into consideration, as the construction of barrier islands of such a large scale would affect natural habitats for marine lifeforms. The seabed and hundreds of species were thoroughly researched and considered in the conceptualization of the barrier island chain.

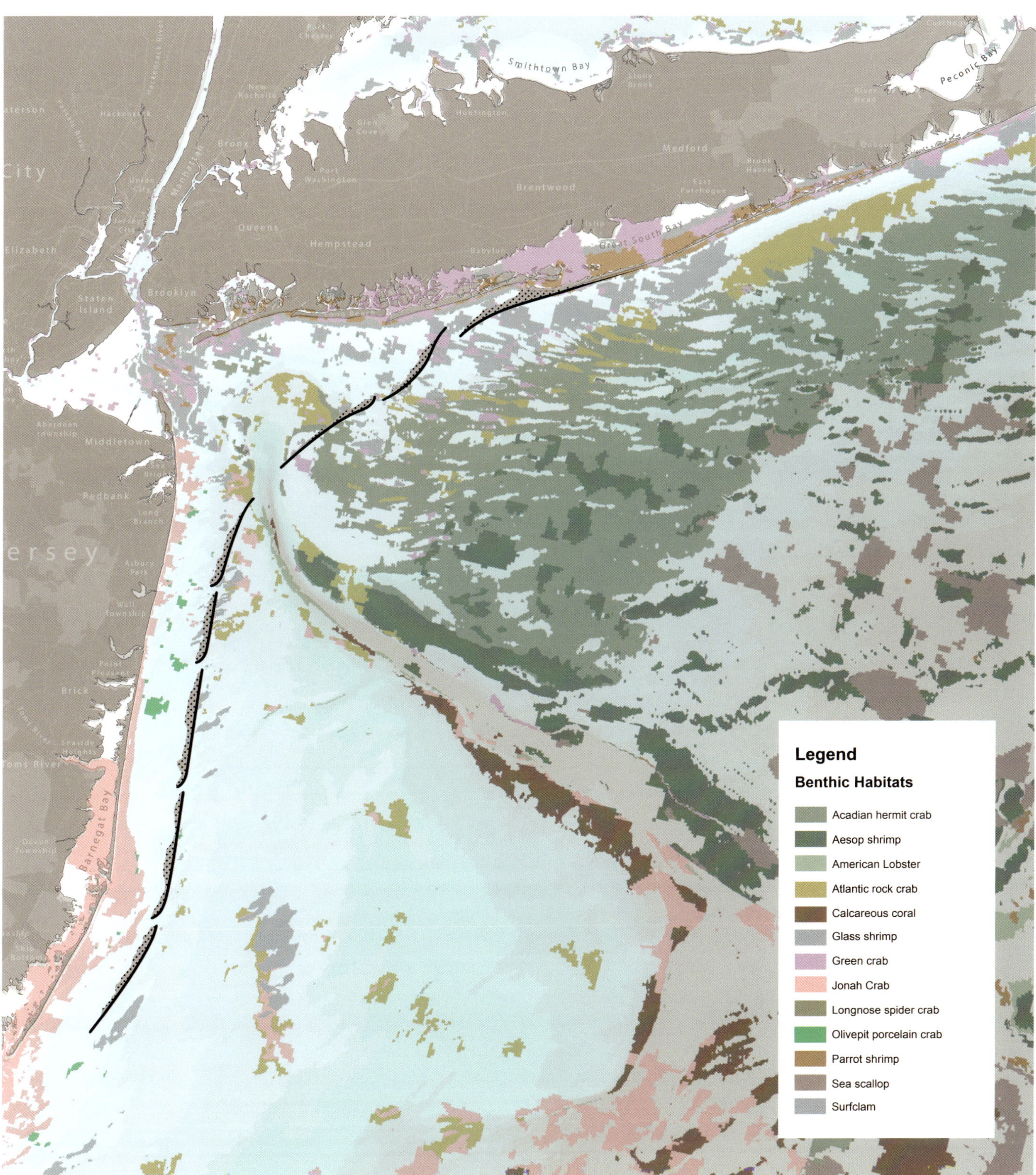

4

Design Opportunities

In response to its research, WXY/West 8 proposed five design opportunities. In the first, Eco-Government Strategies for the Atlantic Ocean, which held the seed of what would become its finalist project, the team suggested a multi-layered coastal defense strategy for the New Jersey Shore. Islands, constructed off shore with dredge material, would attenuate wave energy without interfering with the culture of the coast. Working on this scale would demand extensive cooperation between federal, state, and municipal governments, so the proposal also included provisions to facilitate that inter-governmental collaboration.

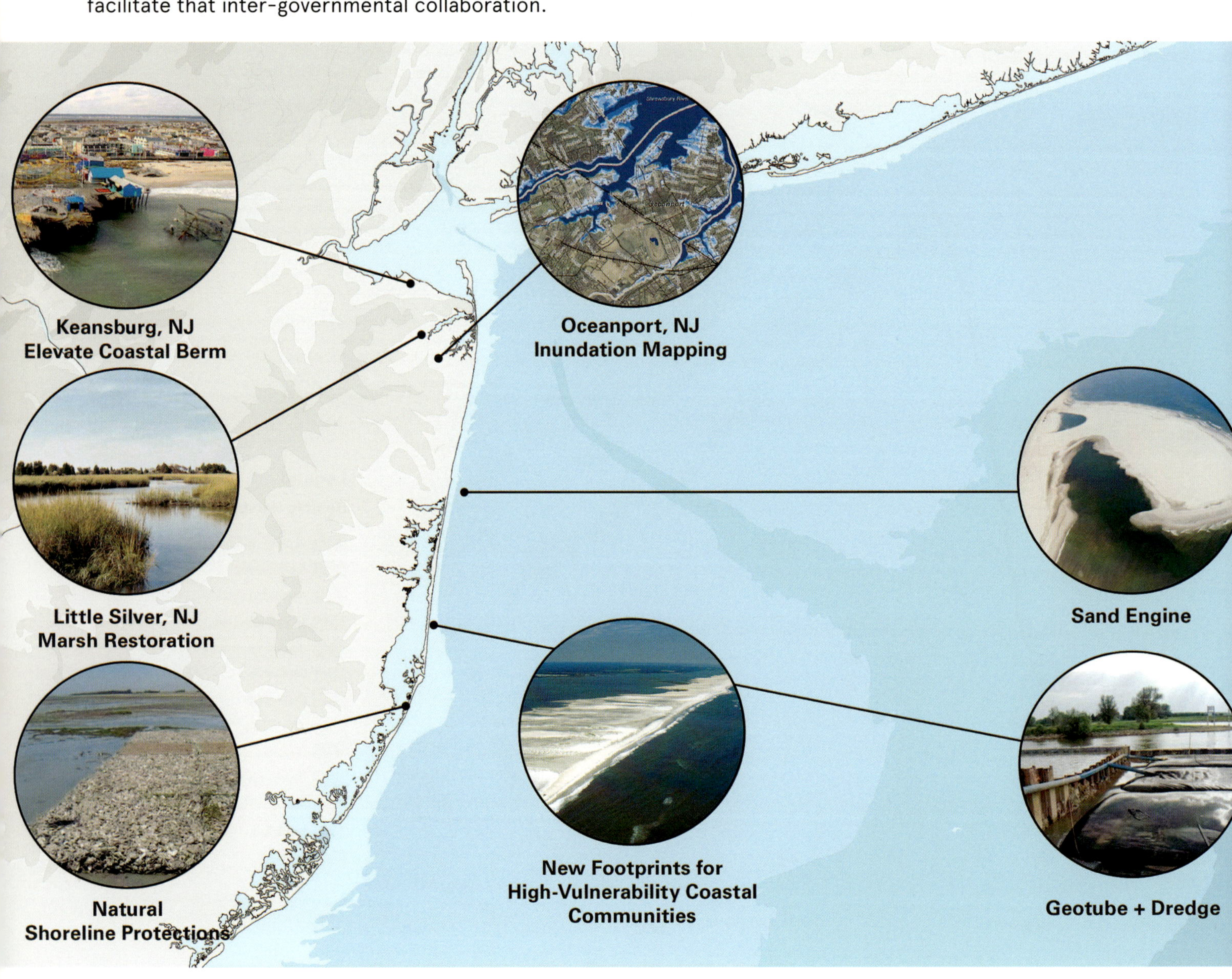

For sites across the very flood-prone banks of New York's Jamaica Bay, the team considered landscape architecture strategies that would make communities safer by working with neighborhood-specific approaches. With widely divergent land use patterns throughout the bay – including industrial, public parks, single-family houses, and high-density housing – different stretches have remarkably different cultural connections to the water. With this in mind, the team developed a catalogue of different coastal protections that communities could use in ways most appropriate to particular sites.

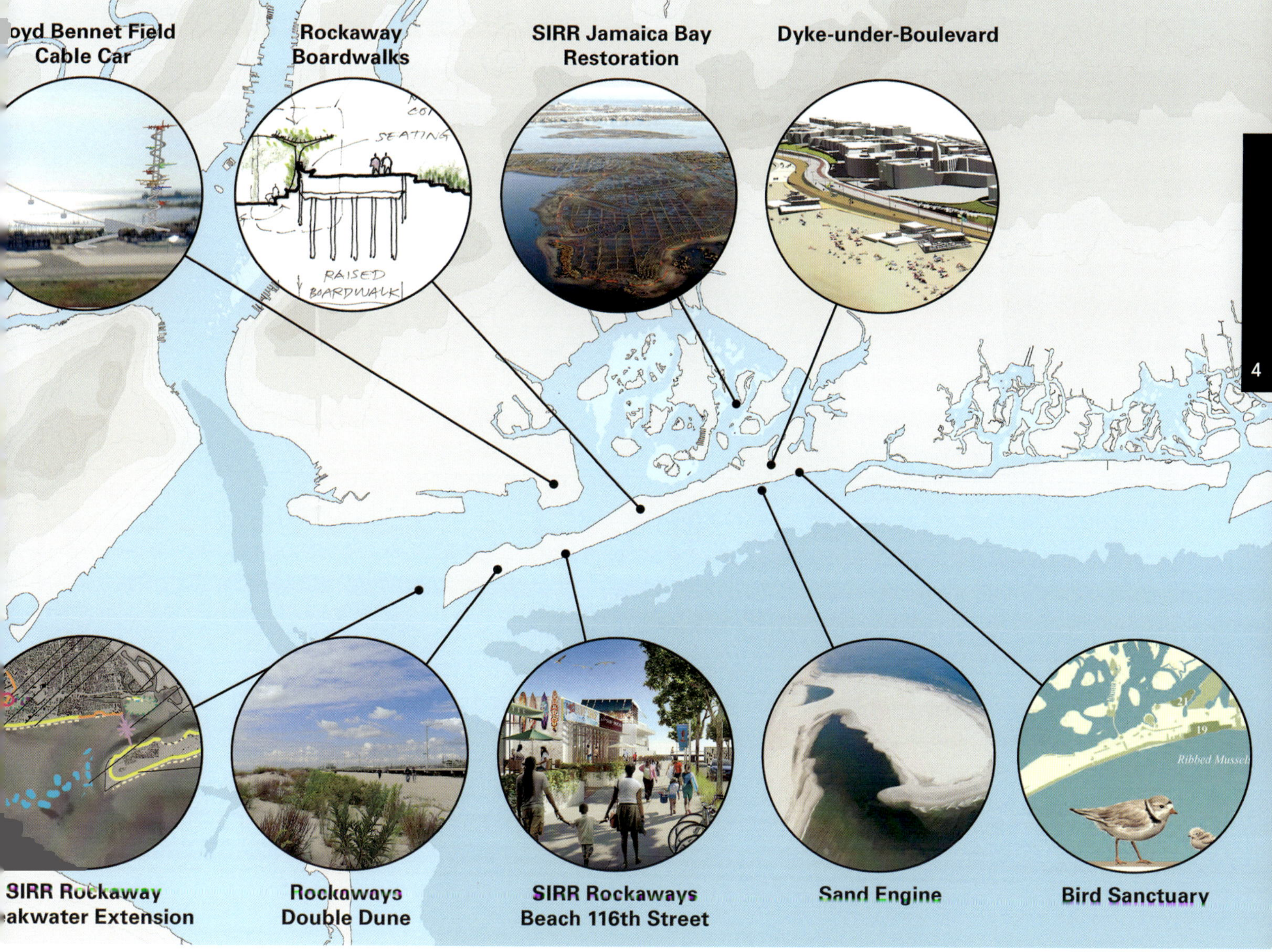

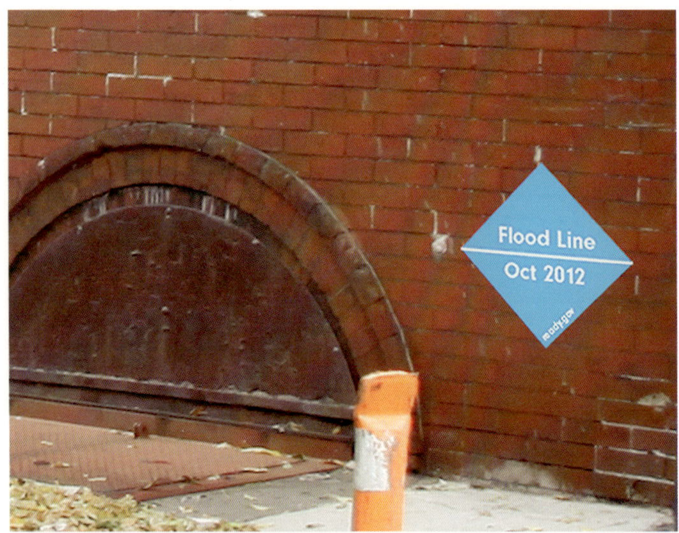

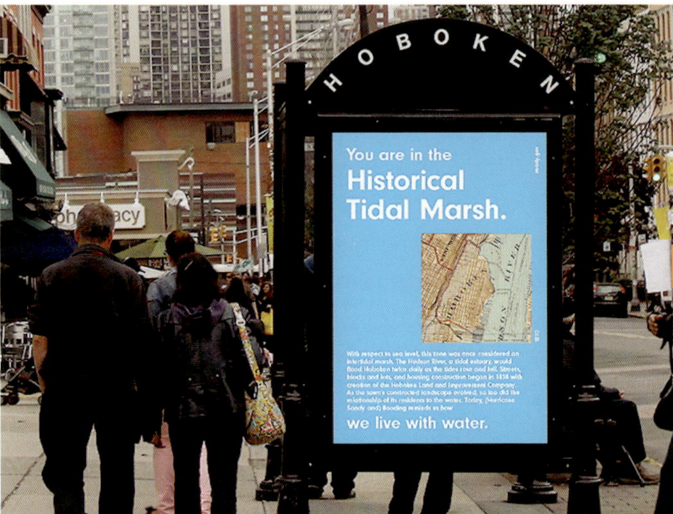

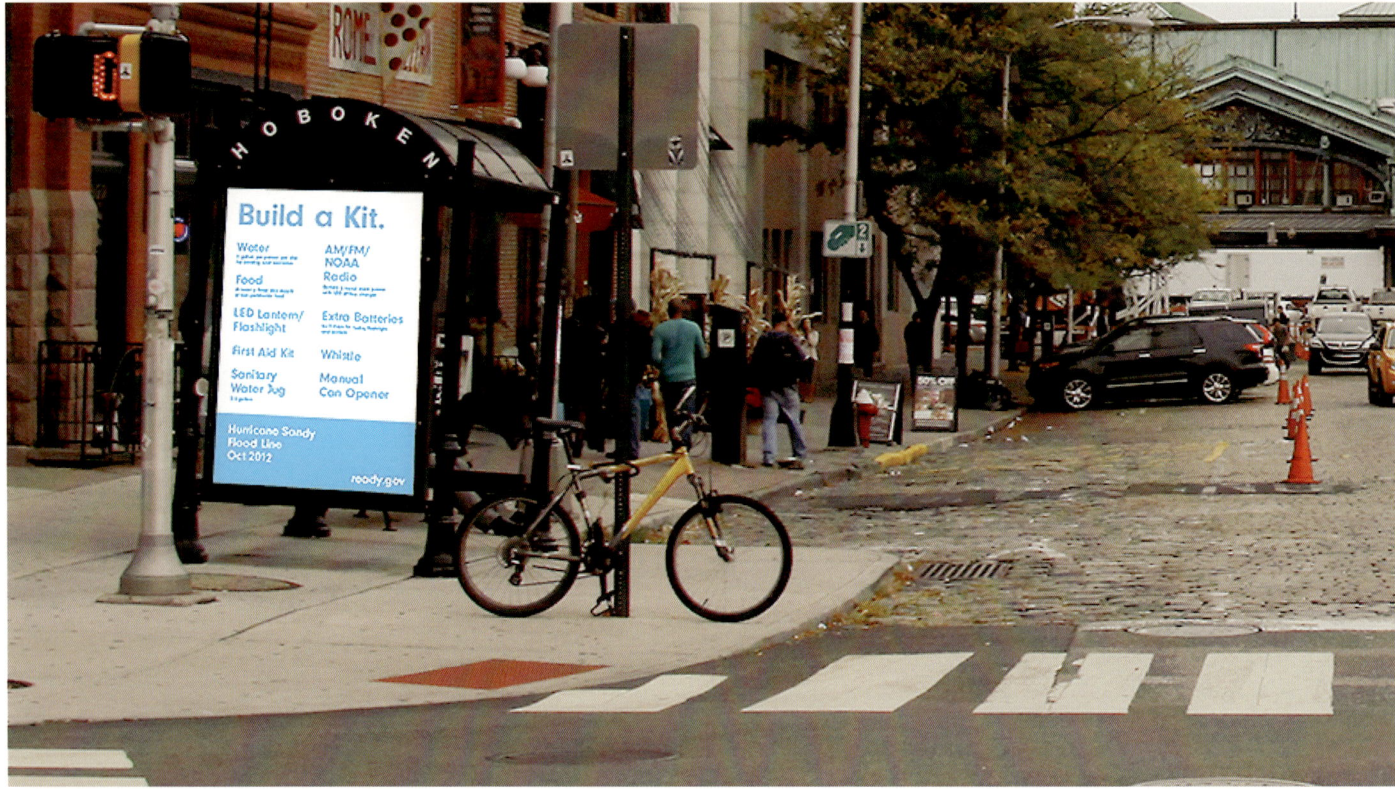

Designing methods for community outreach and engagement were an important dimension in the team's approach. Signage and graphics (depicted above) were designed to encourage people to consider and become aware of their changing environment.

For its proposal along the Long Island Sound, WXY/West 8 identified the need to clarify the cryptic risk assessments sent to homeowners in the flood zone. The housing stock on the Long Island Sound is predominantly single-family, and many homeowners must face a daunting choice to stay put, move inland, or make what can be costly protective retrofits. With this in mind, the team saw an opportunity to clarify risk, making an easy-to-understand cost-benefit tool for homeowners.

Coastal ecologies can be similarly perplexing, so, for the Hudson River region, the team proposed a communication strategy that would provide a resource for community members to better understand the environmental complexities of hydrology and the Hudson estuary. This would help communities make more informed choices about risks associated with the environment.

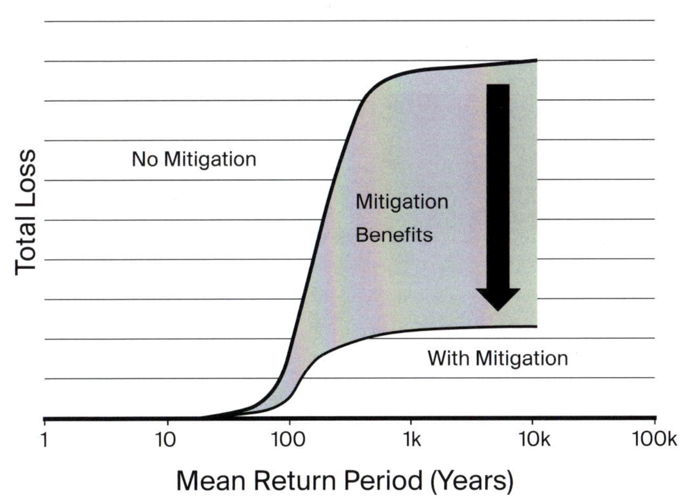

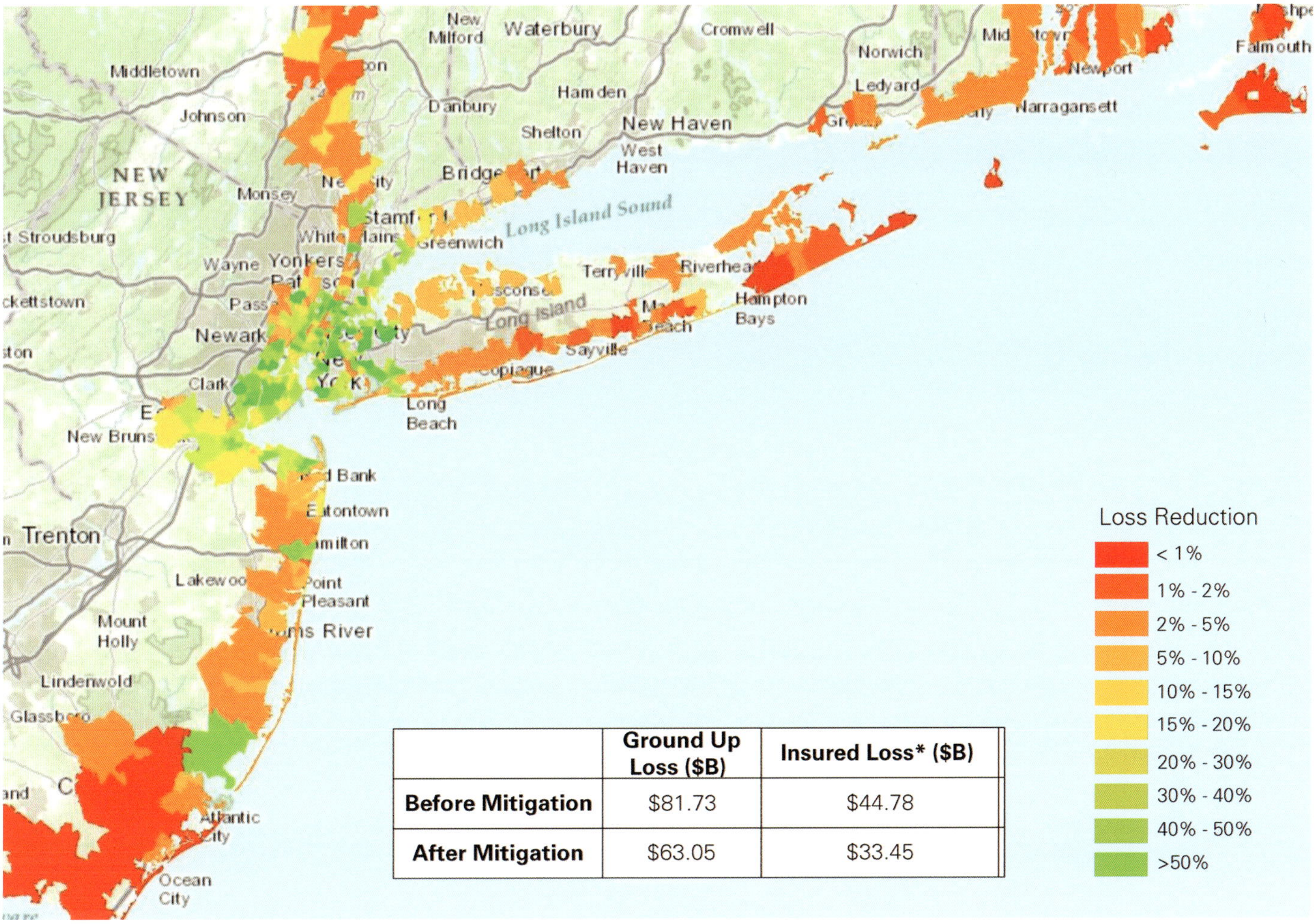

	Ground Up Loss ($B)	Insured Loss* ($B)
Before Mitigation	$81.73	$44.78
After Mitigation	$63.05	$33.45

Loss Reduction
< 1%
1% - 2%
2% - 5%
5% - 10%
10% - 15%
15% - 20%
20% - 30%
30% - 40%
40% - 50%
>50%

An image from AIR's proprietary modeling software illustrates how the reduction in losses that the barrier islands would bring about.

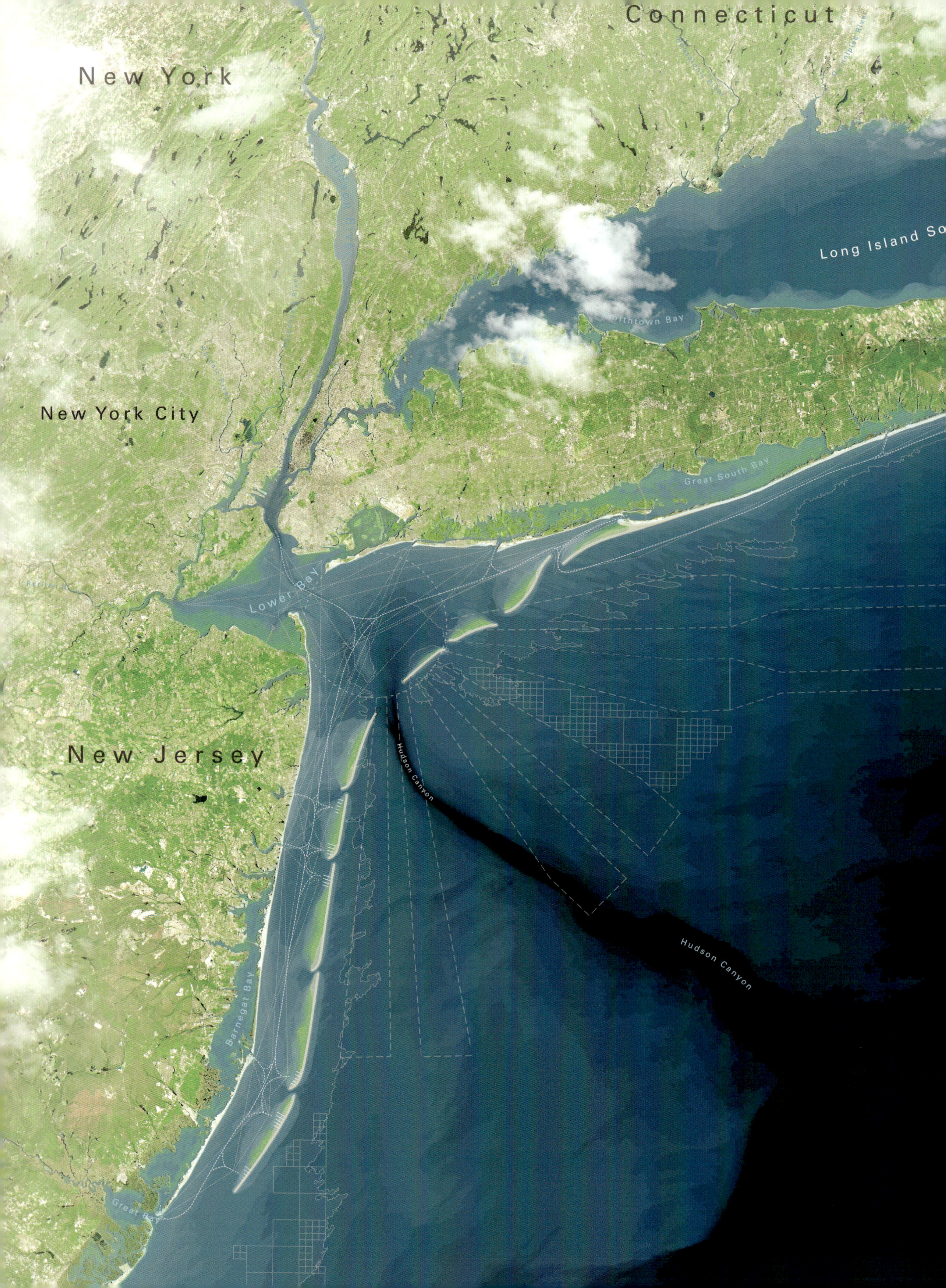
Connecticut
New York
Long Island So
New York City
Great South Bay
Lower Bay
New Jersey
Hudson Canyon
Hudson Canyon
Barnegat Bay

Final Proposal: Blue Dunes

For Blue Dunes, its final proposal, WXY/West 8 synthesized elements from each of its design opportunities into a single project with many layers. The project would build a string of dunes in the Atlantic, stretching from the southern reaches of New Jersey up to Massachusetts. Located roughly nine miles off shore, the seascape features would provide robust coastal protection without imposing the hard infrastructure – dikes and sea walls – that could otherwise sever the cultural, ecological, and economic relationship between coastal communities and the ocean. Built using material found in that environment, the dunes would also provide marine habitats, and, in some cases, recreational opportunities.

Building on the cost-benefit analyses it did for its research along the Long Island Sound, WXY/West 8 made an economic argument for the Blue Dunes, treating risk as an informed calculation rather than as an abstract concept. After quantifying the economic value embedded in the Sandy-affected region, the team calculated the value of risk mitigation provided by the project, finding it would reduce insured losses by more than $10 billion and ground-up losses by nearly $20 billion. These numbers would be closely felt by individuals and communities, not just by high-value waterfront real estate. For example, coastal tourism for fishing and recreation would not suffer the consequences of construction on the shoreline. In many cases, the project would be additive, providing enhanced – not diminished – economic opportunities for area stakeholders.

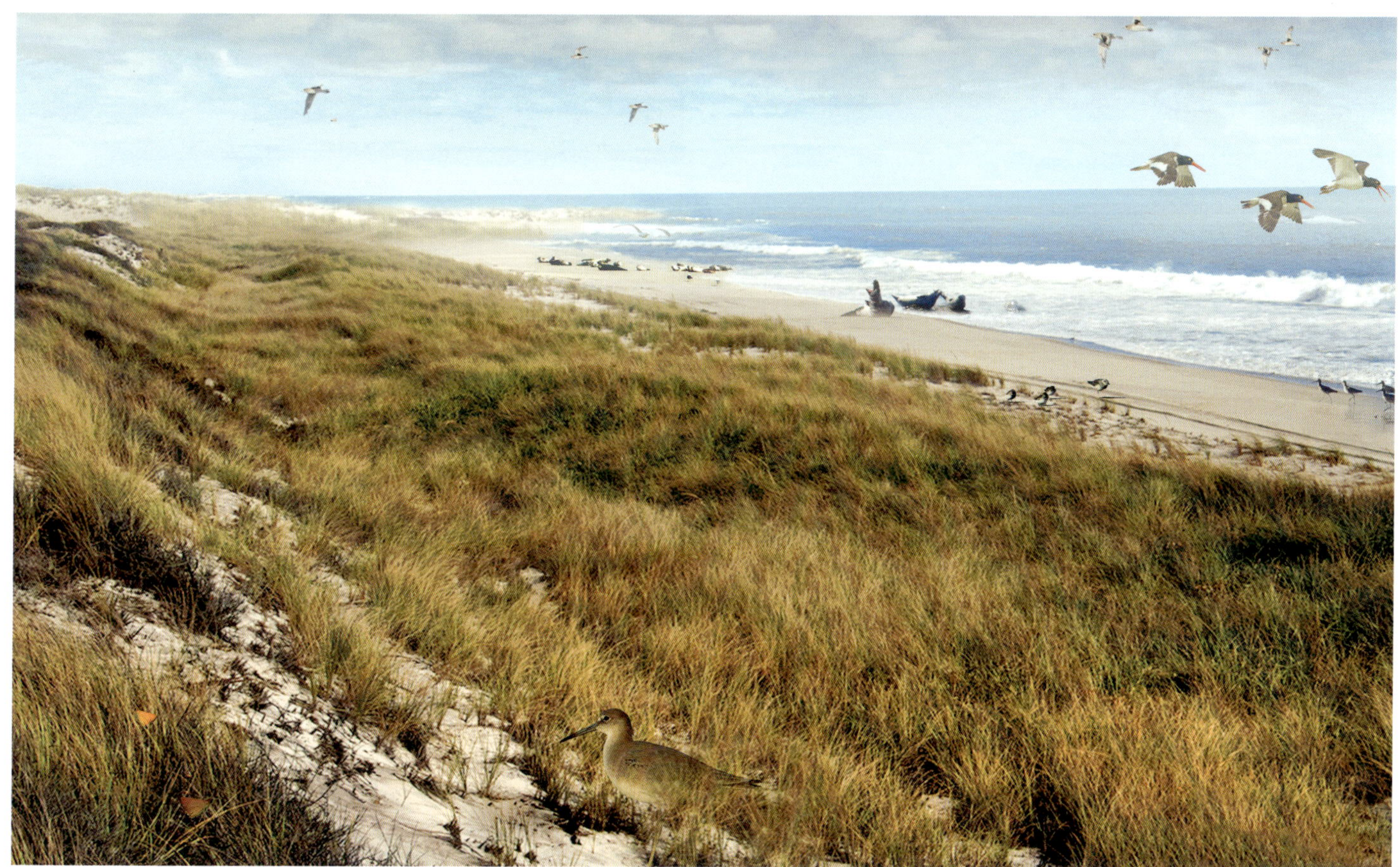

4

Plans and renderings show the Blue Dunes close up and illustrate its relationship to the continental shelf and Atlantic shipping routes.

The project, which sets out to protect approximately 4,000 miles of coastline, was not designed to be implemented in a single stroke. The team conceived of the intervention as something that could be broken down into constituent increments, carried out in phases, and tailored to site ecologies. Unlike reinforced concrete barriers, the dunes could evolve over time, becoming a dynamic part of the surrounding environment.

Because communication and education were pillars of the team's process, the project also proposes to launch the Blue Dunes Research Initiative, a science-based non-profit institute that would carry out research into coastal environments, and that would then communicate those findings to a broader public.

This initiative highlights one of the team's central research findings: risk mitigation must be multi-layered, involving both physical adaptations and also changes to perception and awareness. The goal was to build a regional predictive model for the benefit of understanding how various local projects work together, since water and environment are connected systems.

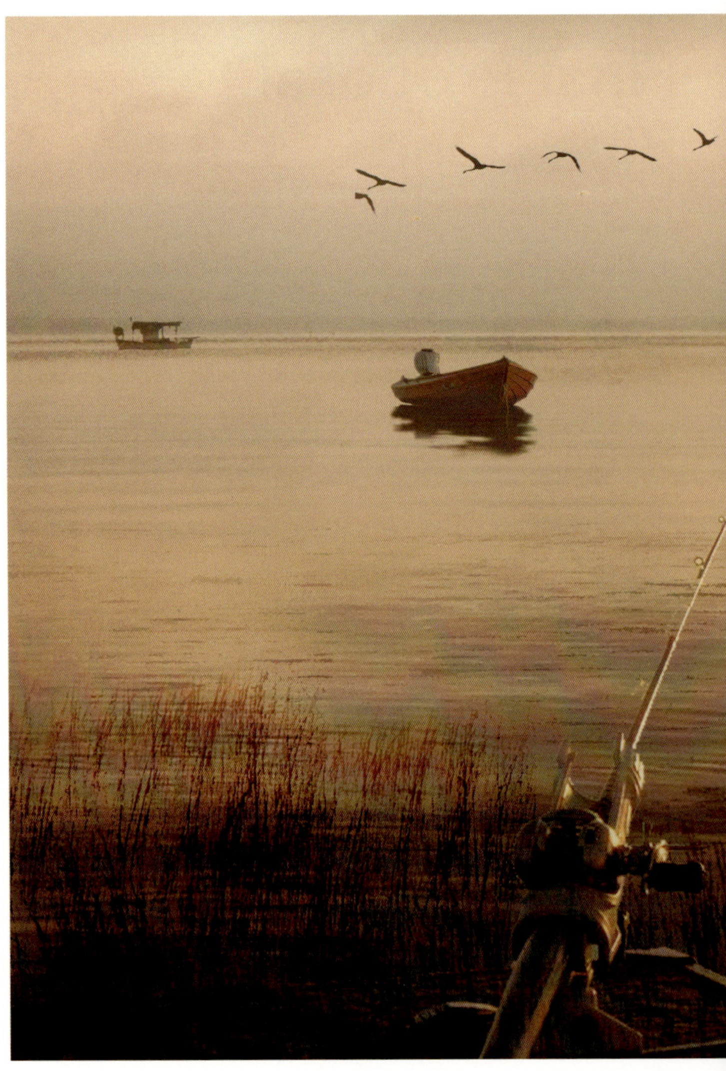

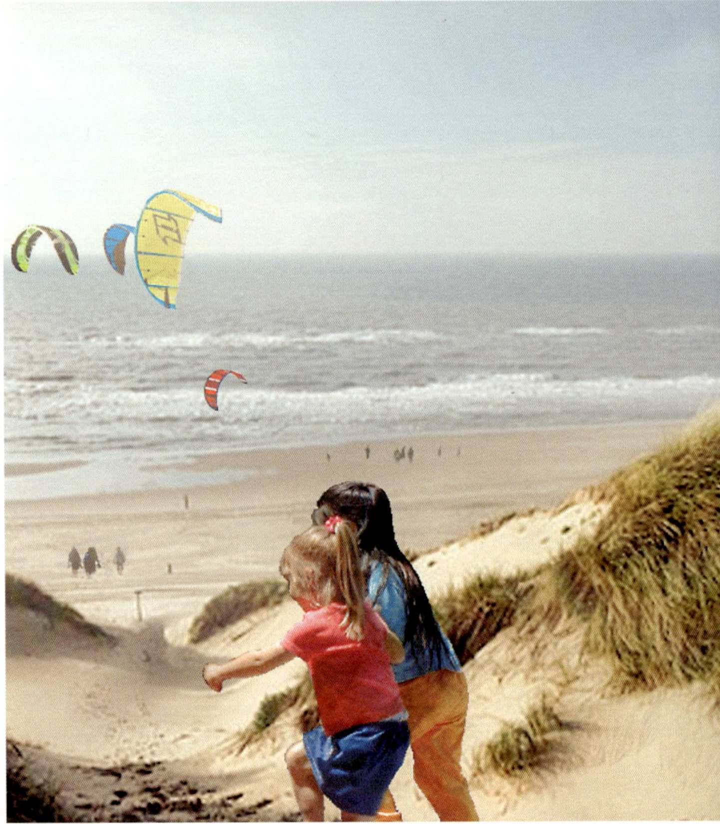

Offshore islands, once stabilized, may provide recreational and educational opportunities for those in the region. Over time, the islands will build up naturally and their ecologies will mature to provide habitats for various species.

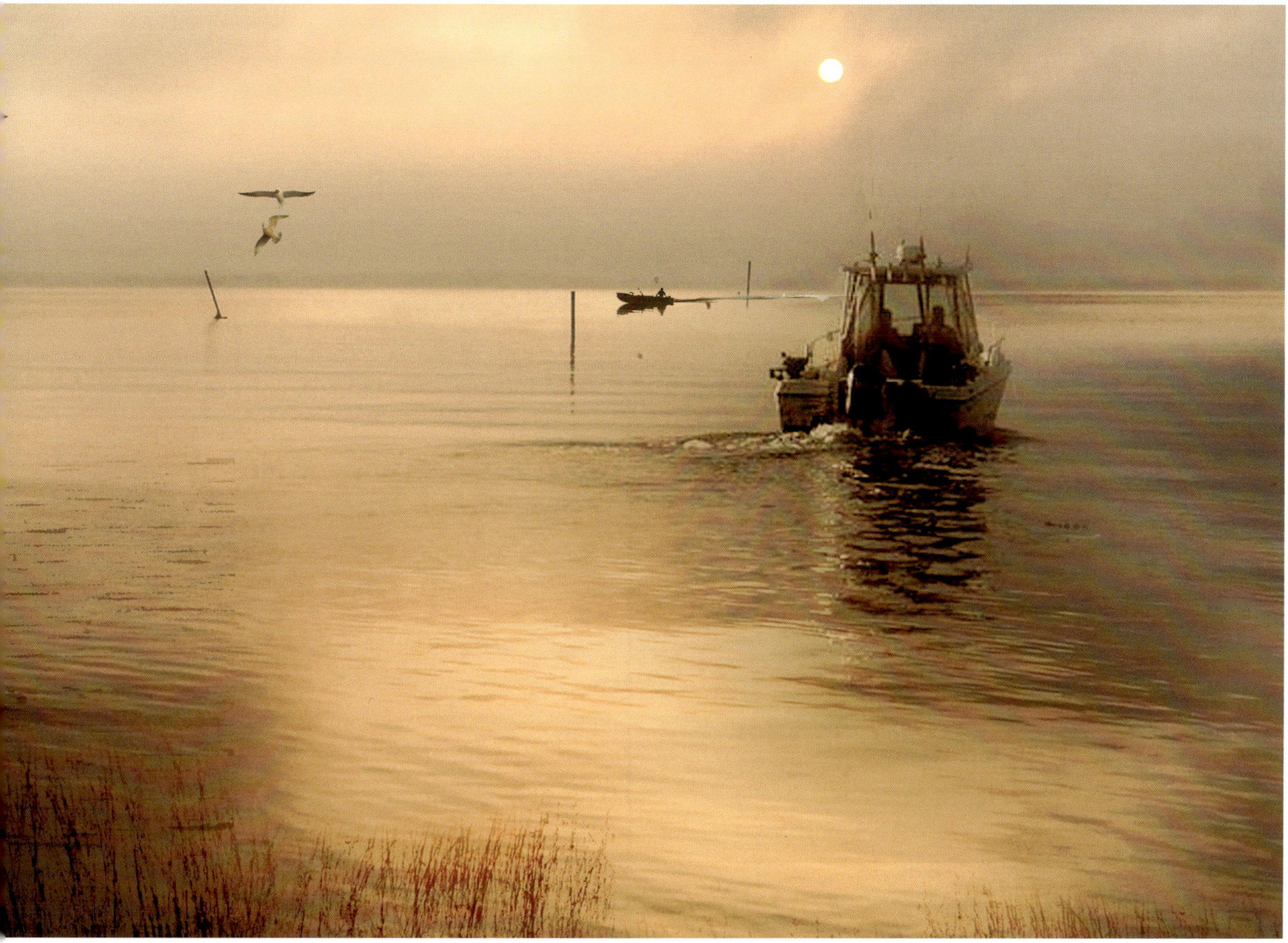

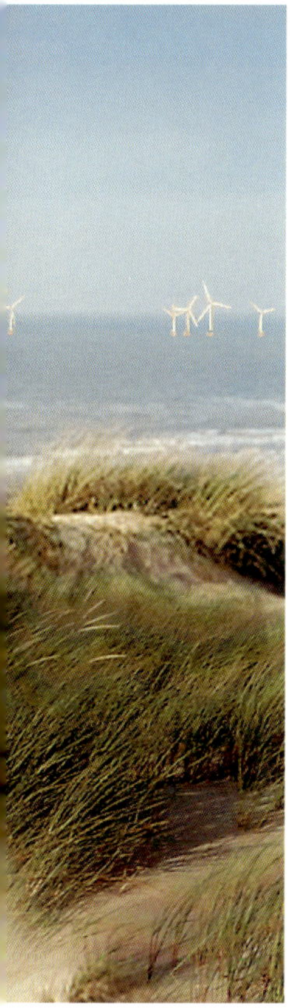

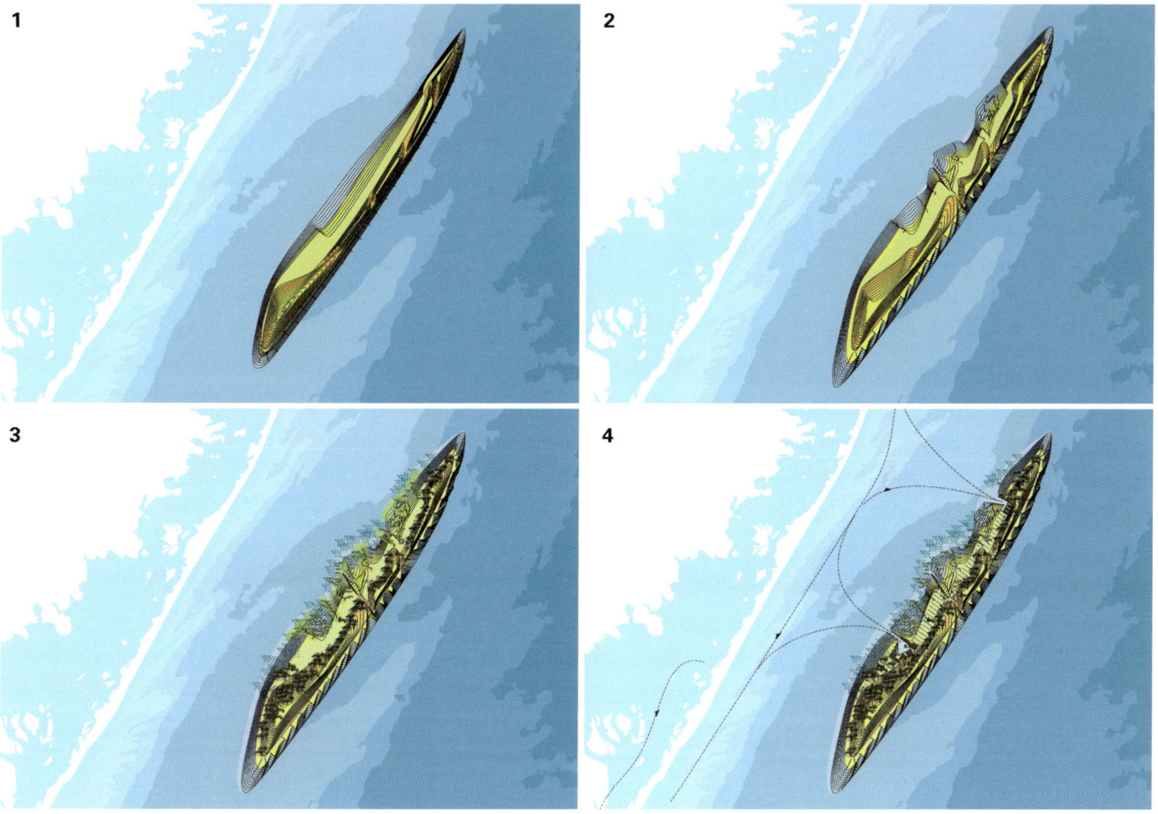

1

2

3

4

4

Design Process

Stemming from its science-based approach, WXY/ West 8 convened a series of research colloquia that brought together experts from the diverse fields of hydrology, economics, insurance, and policy to exchange ideas and help guide the Blue Dunes project. These public forums allowed the team to learn from outside experts, while broadening the discussion of risk for an open audience. In a session on the science of coastal landscapes, panelists including team member Alan Blumberg, from the Stevens Institute of Technology, analyzed the hydrological impact of coastal land formations. A second session analyzed the economy of risk, particularly the economic effects of implementing part of or all of the Blue Dunes. As part of this discussion, Andy Kao of AIR and economist Kei Hayashi led an array of invited experts in a debate on the economic dimensions of risk and catastrophe.

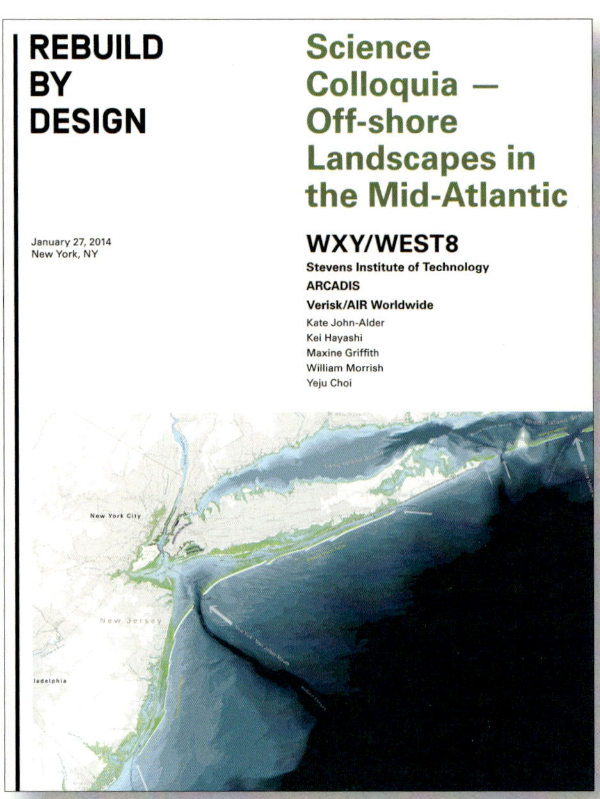

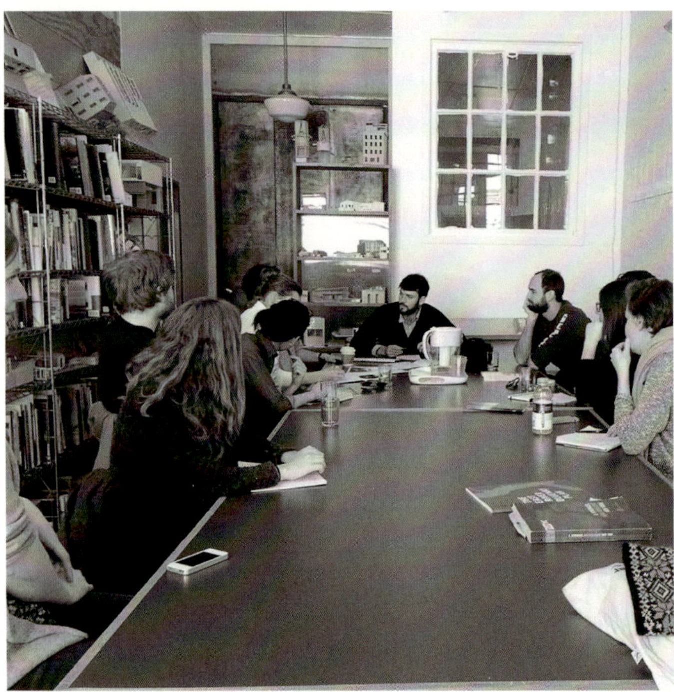

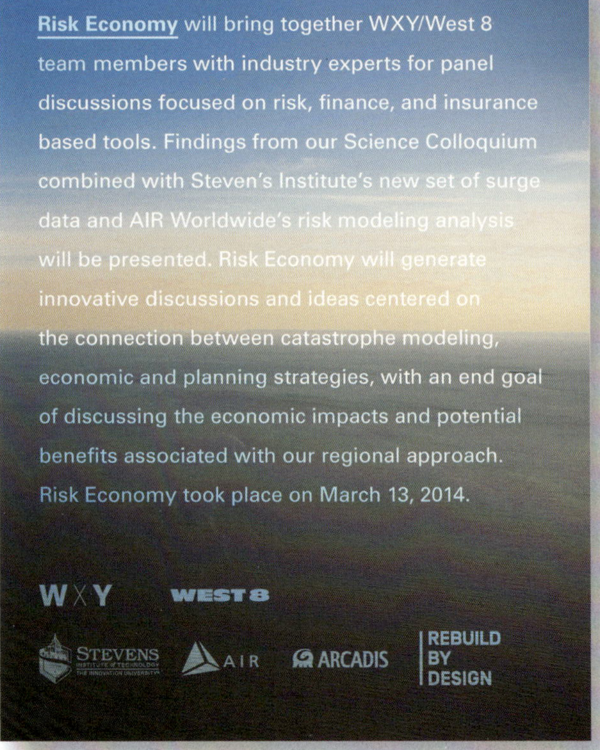

The team hosted wo major colloquia involving experts, academics, and professional consultants as well as community members and local stakeholders. One focused on science and ecology; the other, on the economic impact of such a project.

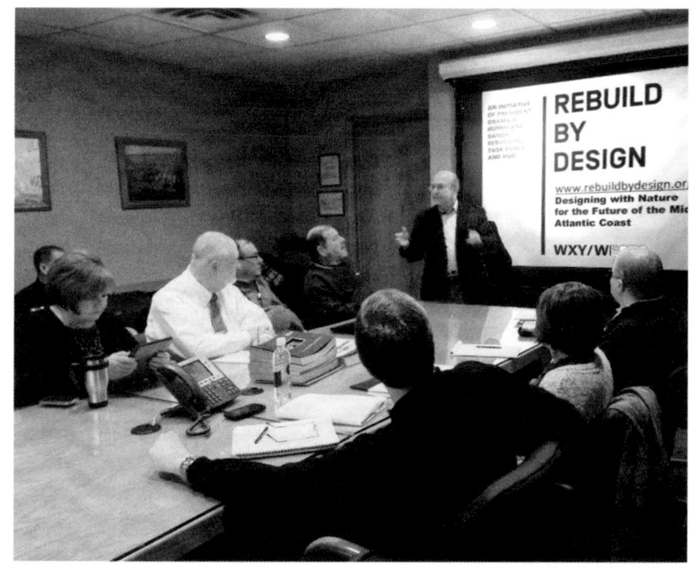
REBUILD
BY
DESIGN
Designing with Nature
Atlantic Coast

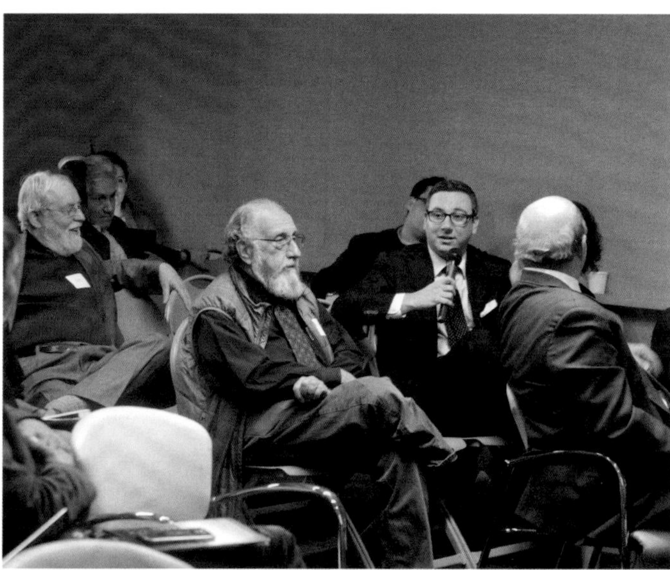

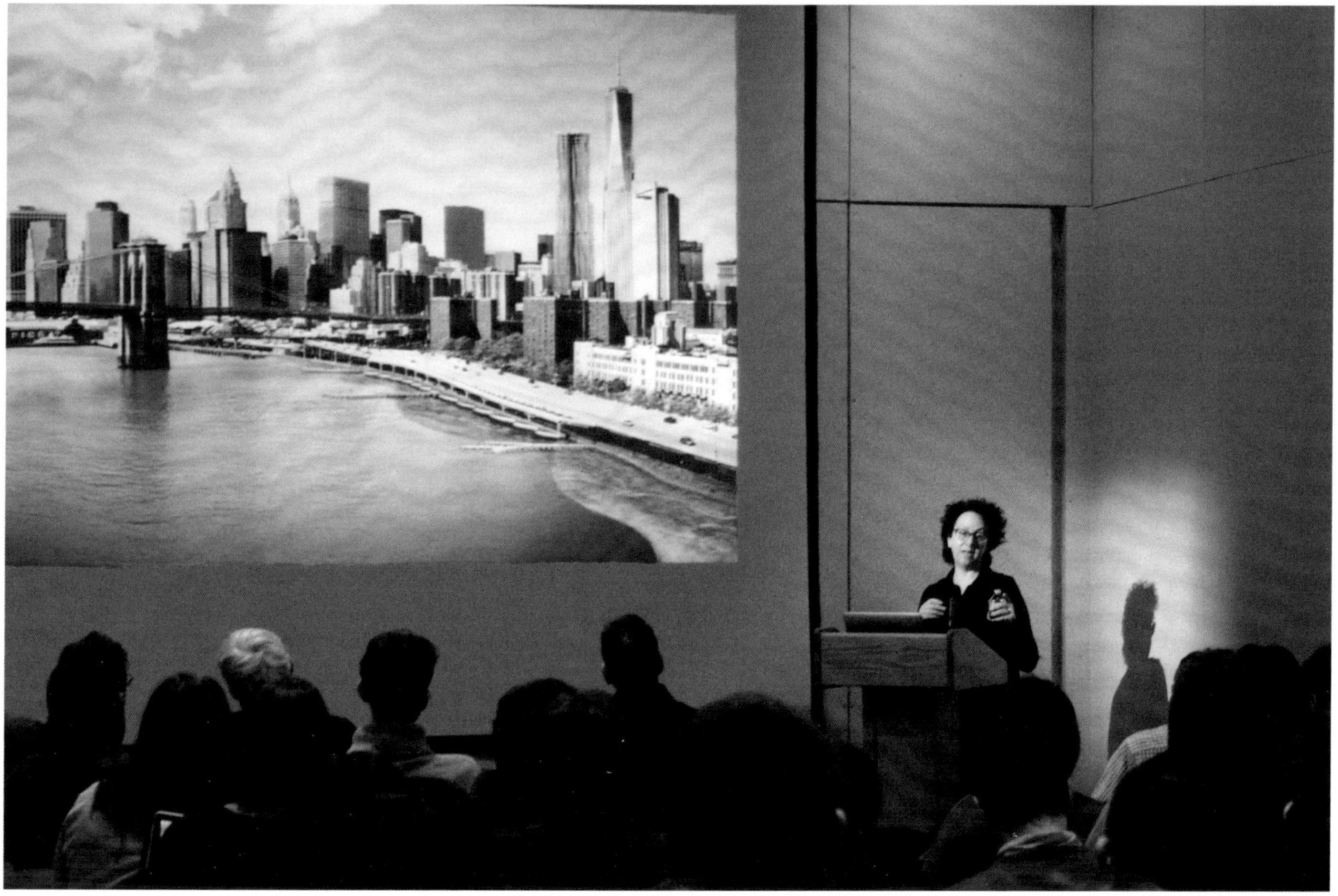

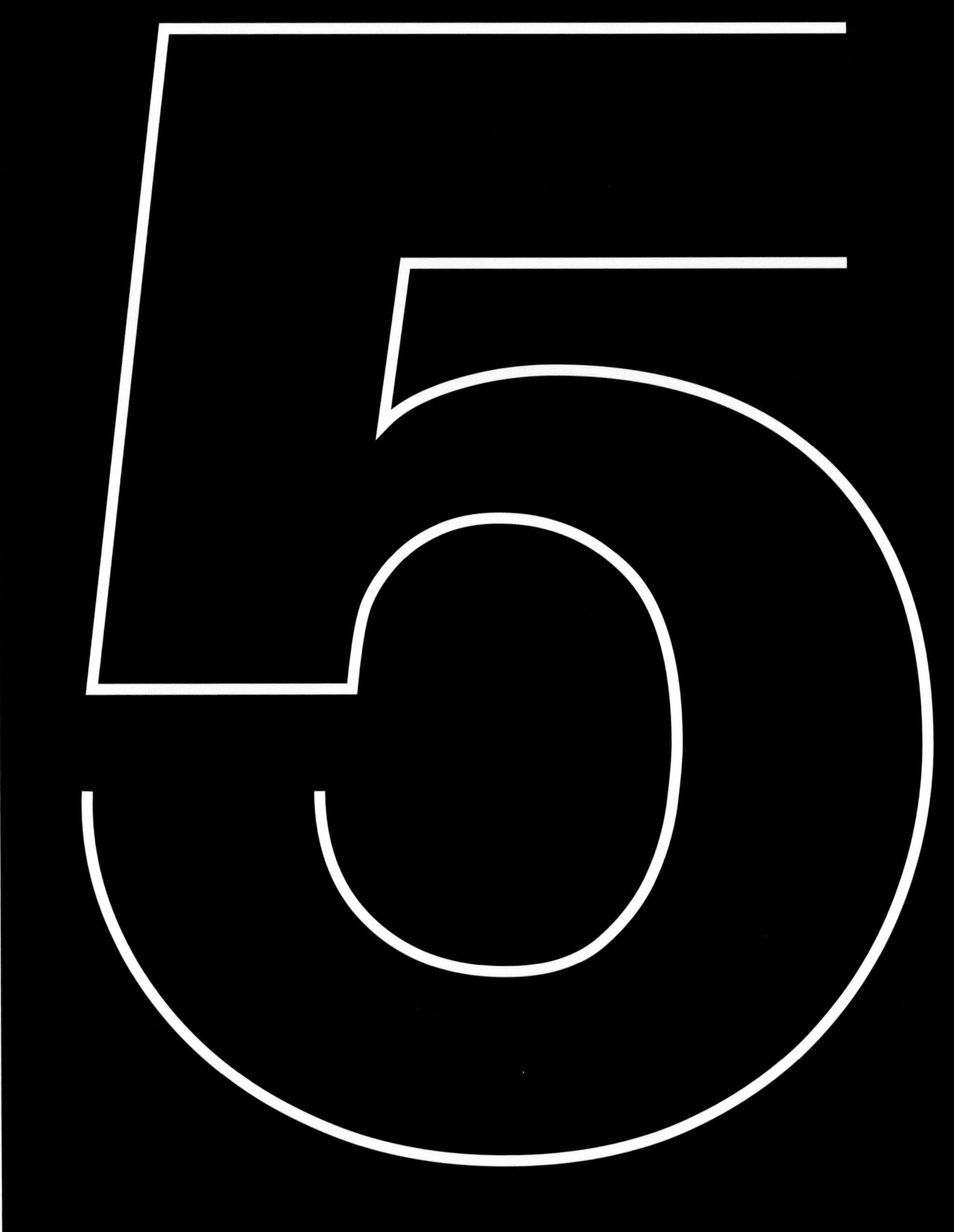

UNVEILING THE PROPOSALS

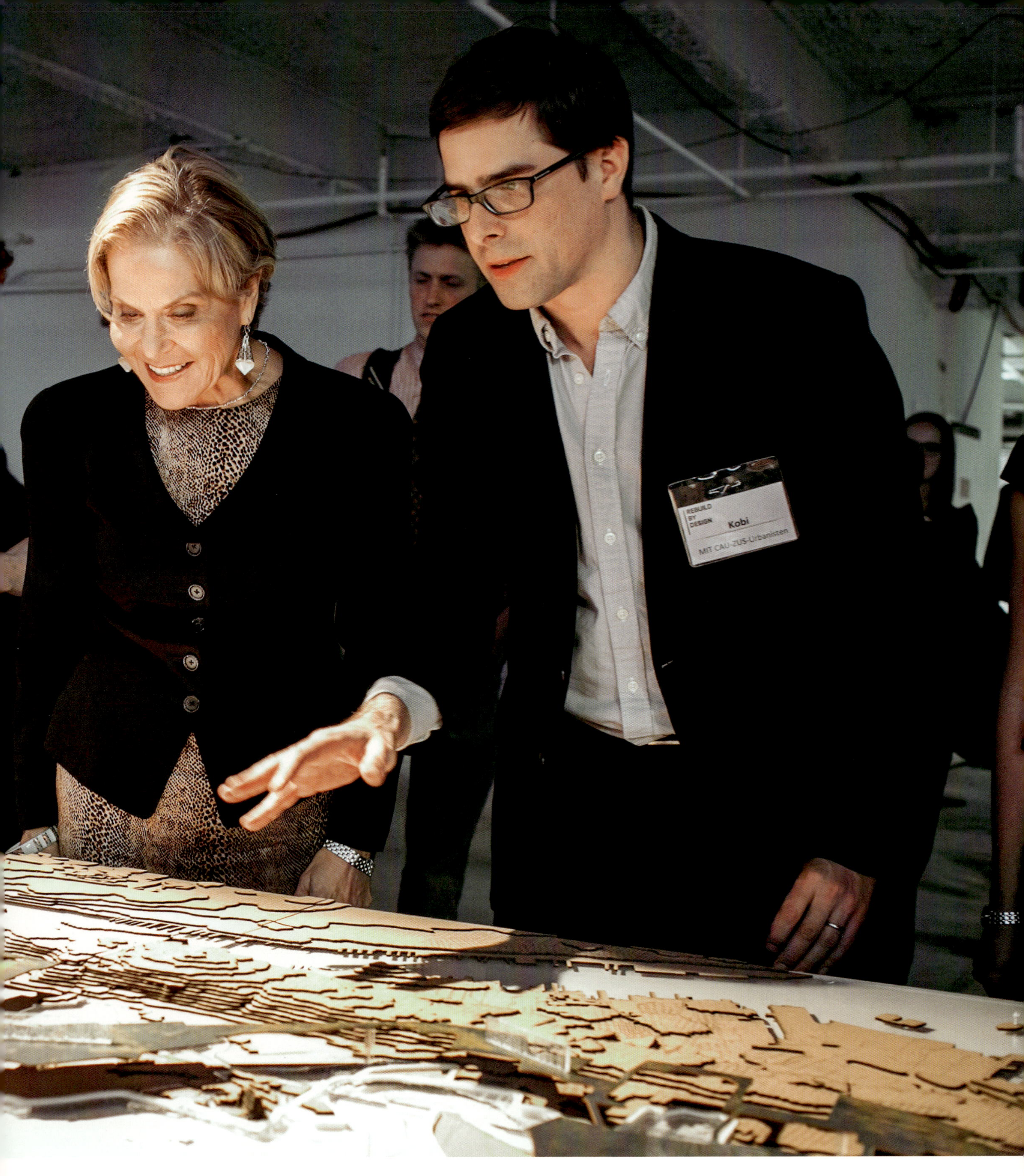

Judith Rodin, president of The Rockefeller Foundation, with Kobi Ruthenberg of the MIT CAU + ZUS + URBANISTEN Team explore a model of the New Meadowlands proposal.

Final Design Exhibitions

In April 2014, less than a year after the ambitious competition's genesis, the design teams unveiled their ten visionary design proposals at public exhibitions in New York and New Jersey.

More than 1,000 members of the public came to the Liberty Science Center in New Jersey and the World Financial Center in New York City to see the final designs. The design teams were joined by many of the government and community stakeholders with whom they had worked during the research and design stages. Excitement pervaded the atmosphere as those who had been part of the process celebrated their hard work, and together with new audiences, marveled at its innovative results.

At a panel discussion accompanying the morning's event, Henk Ovink hosted a public discussion among influential officials, philanthropists, and academics. Participants in the discussions highlighted the ways in which Rebuild by Design had set a new standard for planning and funding community-based infrastructure development. At an evening event in New York, Ovink, HUD Secretary Shaun Donovan, and The Rockefeller Foundation President Judith Rodin spoke about the proposals themselves and the transformative precedent that the Rebuild by Design process set for creating resilience in the region and around the globe.

"Rebuild by Design has become a future-oriented project of historic proportions: seeding, designing, and building a resilience network that now may serve as a cross-disciplinary, collaborative model for coastal regions around the world."

—

David van der Leer, Executive Director, Van Alen Institute

5

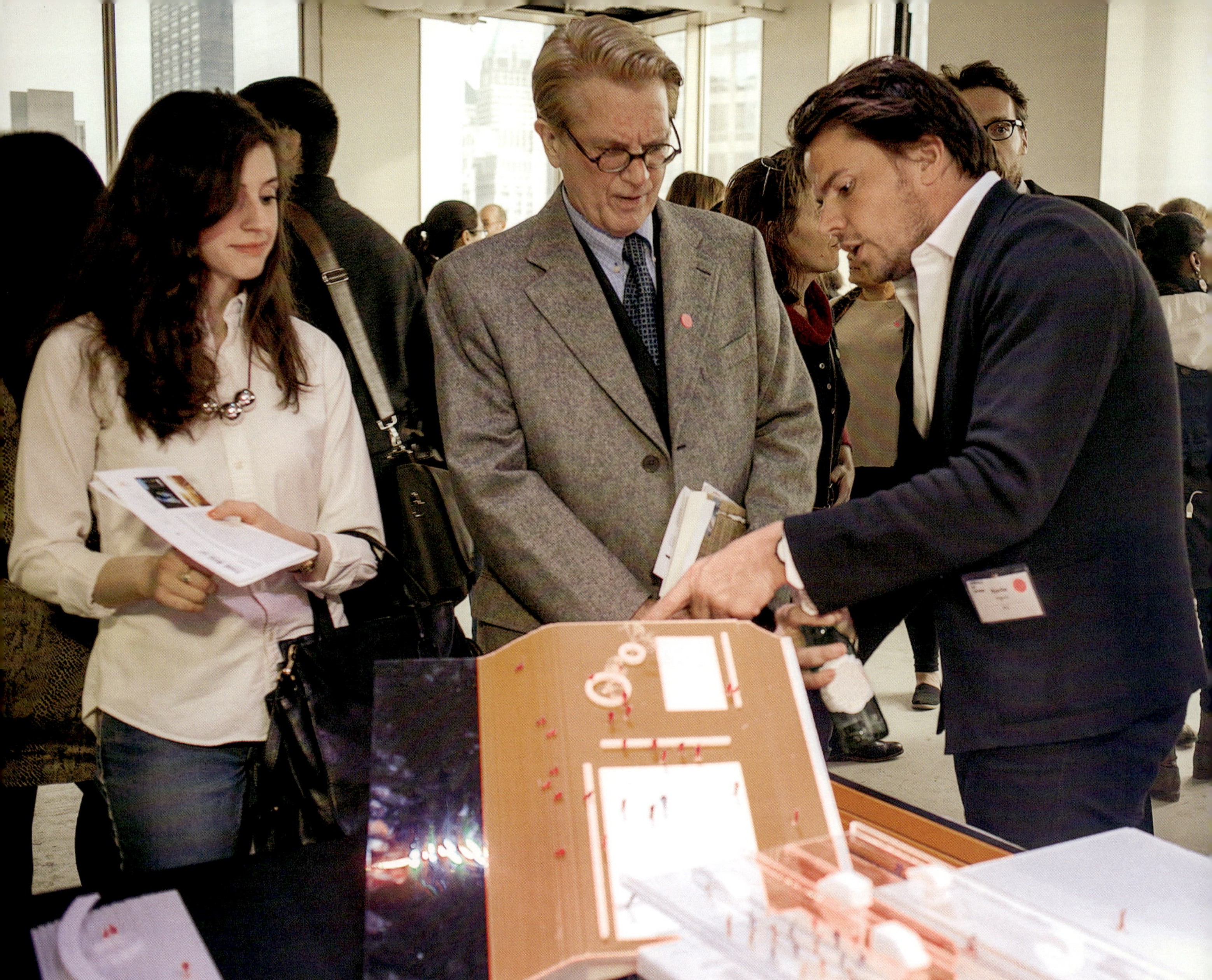

"Rebuild by Design has been a perfect marriage of regional planning and innovation around the topic of resilience. By establishing relationships across boundaries and disciplines, these projects are poised to make a lasting impact in our region."

—

Tom Wright, President,
Regional Plan Association

Bjarke Ingels, principal at BIG, demonstrates the intricacies of the BIG U by showing members of the public the insides of a three-dimensional model.

Evaluating the Proposals

Following the exhibitions, the teams entered the final part of the competition: presentations to a jury that would evaluate the proposals. The eleven-member jury, chaired by HUD Secretary Donovan, brought a broad spectrum of expertise to the deliberations. Jury members were instructed to evaluate each proposal under four categories: research and analysis, demonstration of participatory process and stakeholder coalition, the design solution and proposal, and implementation strategy. Their mission was to identify the proposals that stood to achieve the highest standards of design, innovation, and resilience.

Each team presented the details of its proposal and responded to the jury's questions, discussing the project, engagement process, implementation plan, and cost-benefit analysis. Teams were encouraged to bring members of their community coalitions and other project stakeholders into the process to help present the designs. Many brought scientists, research advisors, and representatives from the local governments and community organizations with whom they had worked. These key collaborators traveled from far and wide to demonstrate their support for the projects they had co-created.

At the start of the deliberations, the jurors were briefed on their roles and on the parameters of the America COMPETES Act, as well as given a memo with comments on each proposal from federal agencies and local government bodies that could potentially be responsible for implementing the winning designs. As jury members carefully reviewed the ten proposals, each juror contributed observations, insights, and recommendations that informed the final determination of winning proposals by the jury chair.

Jury

Jury members provided expertise, insight, and leadership from a variety of fields.

Shaun Donovan, Chair
Secretary, US Department of Housing and Urban Development and Chair, Hurricane Sandy Rebuilding Task Force

Henk Ovink, Co-Chair
Principal, Rebuild by Design, and Senior Advisor to the Secretary of Housing and Urban Development, Hurricane Sandy Rebuilding Task Force

Lauren Alexander Augustine
Director, Office of Special Projects on Risk, Resilience, and Extreme Events, National Academy of Sciences

Julie Bargmann
Founding Principal, D.I.R.T. Studio and Associate Professor, University of Virginia School of Architecture

Ole Bouman
Creative Director, Shenzhen Biennale for Architecture and Urbanism

Ricky Burdett
Professor of Urban Studies at the London School of Economics and Political Science (LSE), Head, Department of Sociology, and Director, LSE Cities and the Urban Age Program

Susan Cutter
Carolina Distinguished Professor and Director, Hazards and Vulnerability Research Institute, University of South Carolina

Jeanne Gang
Founding Principal, Studio Gang Architects

Eric Klinenberg
Director, Institute for Public Knowledge, and Professor of Sociology, New York University

Guy Nordenson
Partner, Guy Nordenson and Associates, Commissioner, NYC Public Design Commission, and Professor, Princeton University

Mitchell J. Silver *
Chief Planning and Development Officer and Director, Department of City Planning, Raleigh, NC

Mark Tercek
President and Chief Executive Officer, The Nature Conservancy

*Mitchell Silver recused himself during final deliberations due to his appointment as NYC Parks Commissioner

5

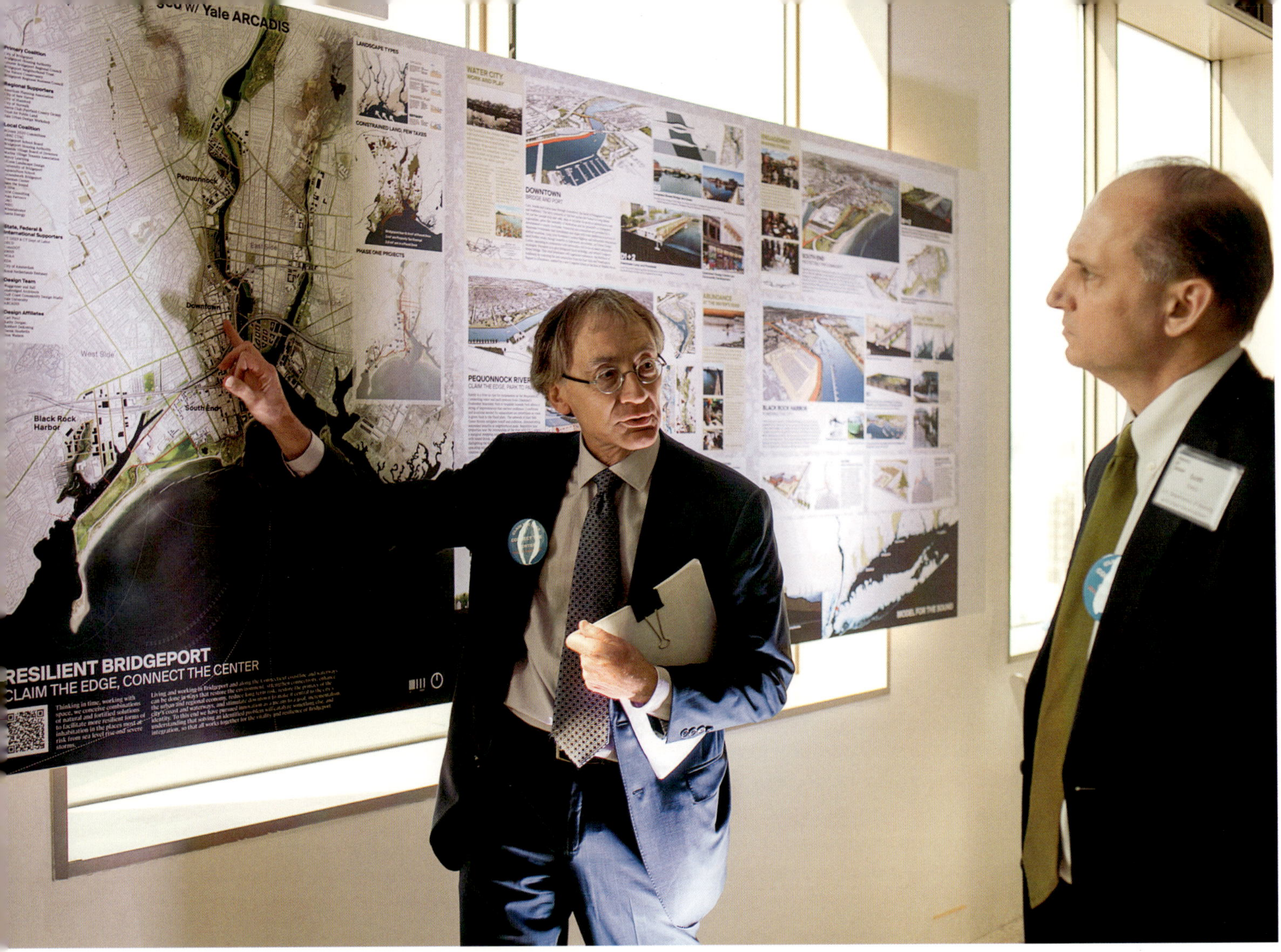

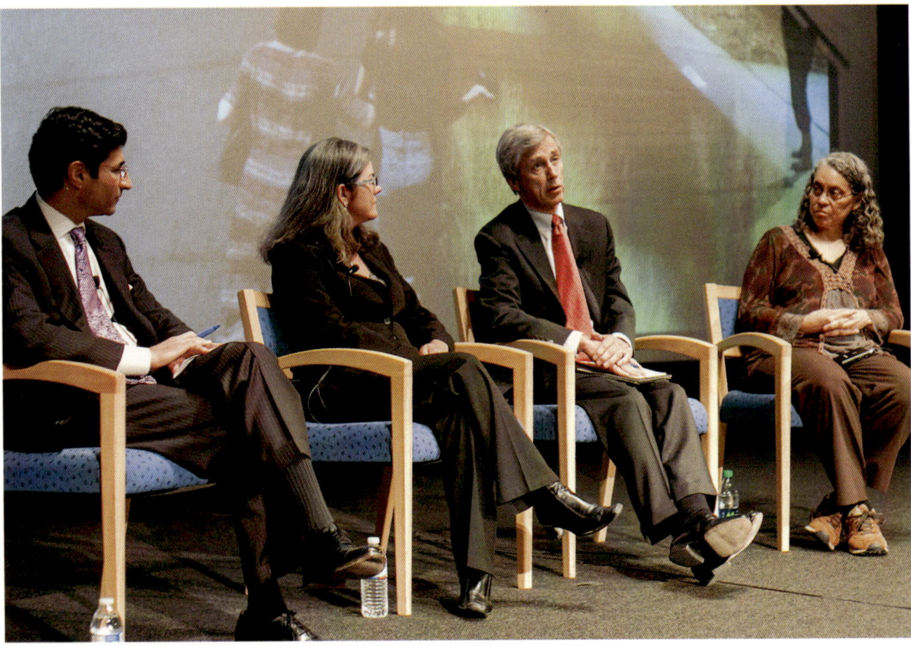

Above: David Waggonner explains the WB unabridged with Yale ARCADIS team's plan for Resilient Bridgeport to Scott Davis of HUD.

Below: A panel at the Liberty Science Center explores how the competition set a new standard for government, community, and funder collaboration. From left to right: Marc Ferzan, New Jersey Governor's office; Holly Leicht, HUD; Chris Daggett, Dodge Foundation; and Mindy Fullilove, Columbia University.

Right: HUD Secretary Shaun Donovan congratulates the teams and community members on the final design proposals.

Middle: Amy Chester, Rebuild by Design's Project Manager, at the final design exhibition in New York City.

Bottom: The SCAPE team worked with communities on Staten Island to build a model breakwater reef section, which they then displayed at the final exhibition.

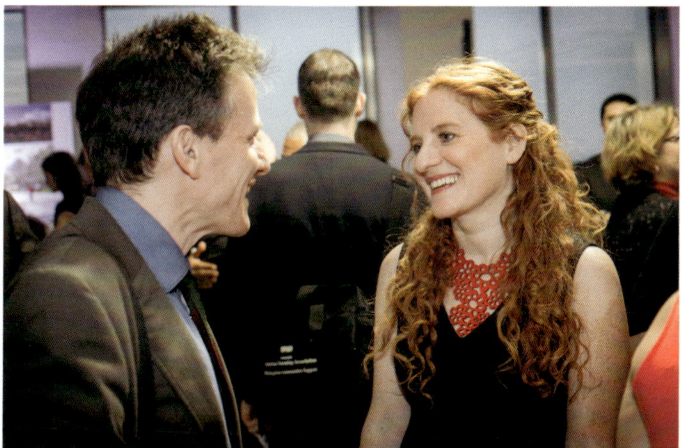

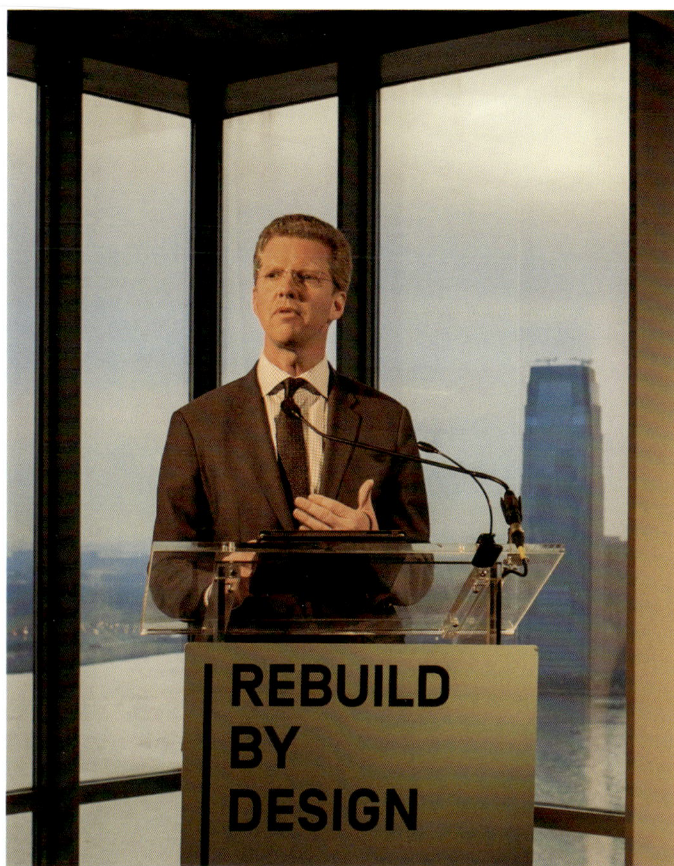

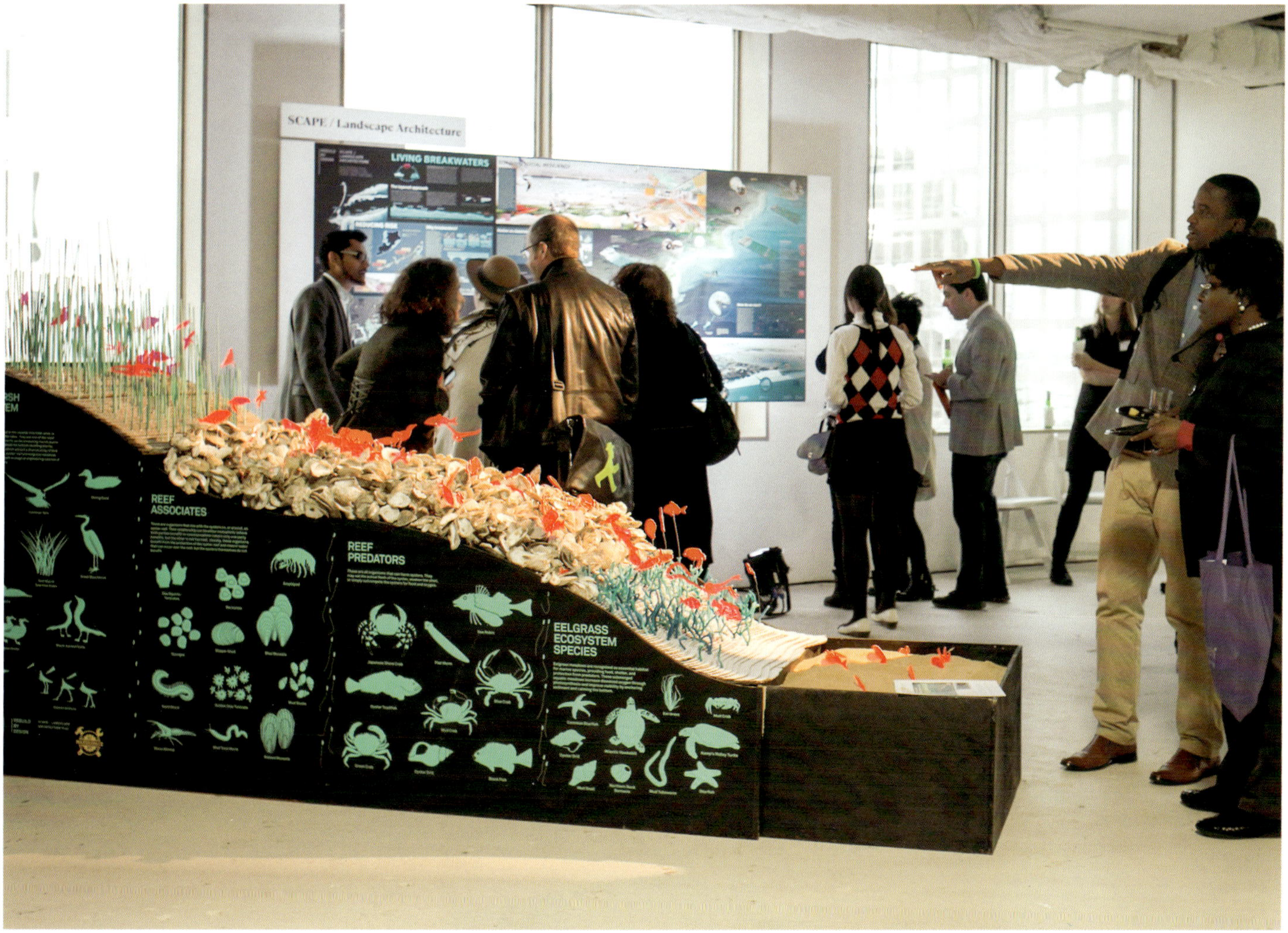

5

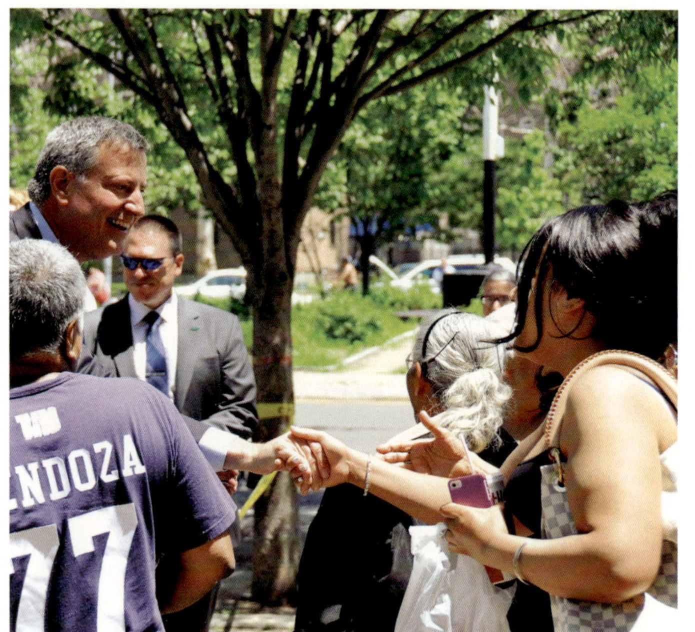

"There's no question: Superstorm Sandy made clear just how vulnerable we are when it comes to climate change. The risks are real – and growing – and it's vital that we continue to innovate toward a stronger and more resilient New York. Rebuild By Design has been a great partner as we identify and meet these challenges."

—

New York City Mayor Bill de Blasio

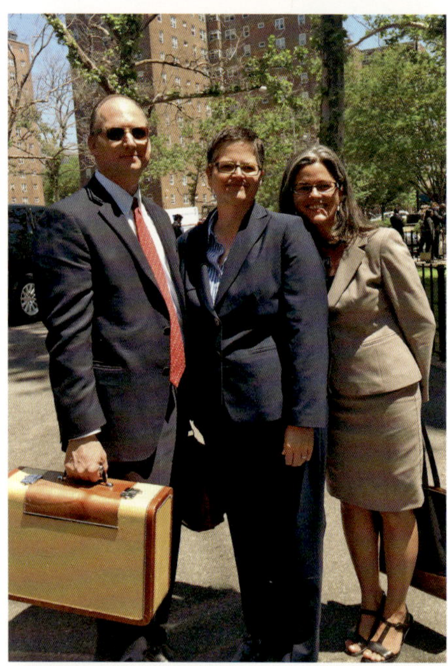

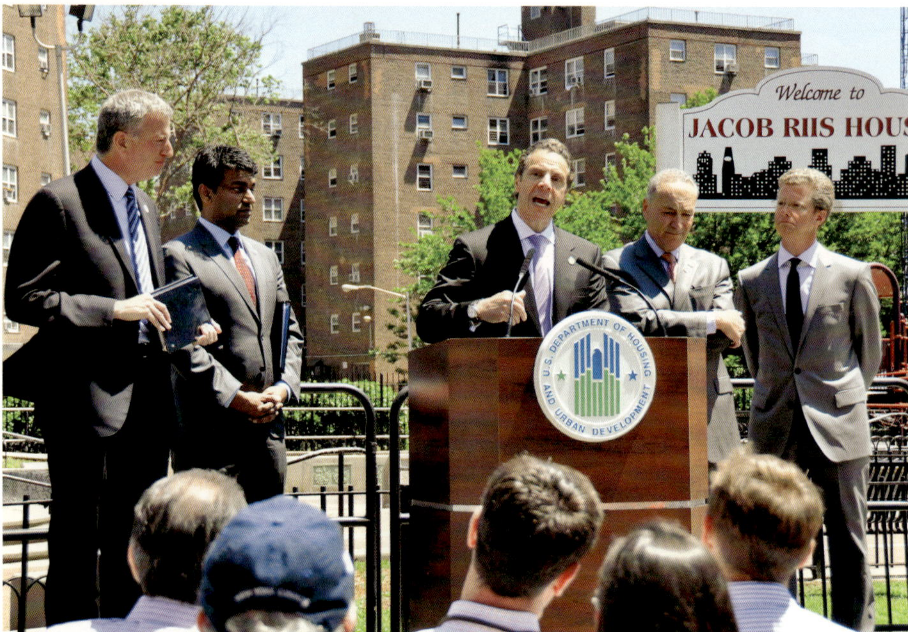

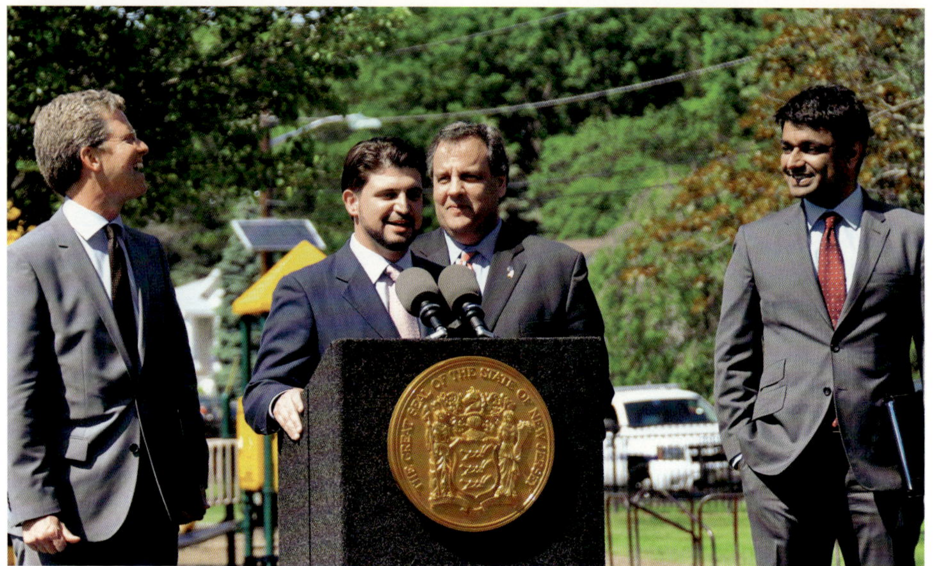

Above: New York City Mayor Bill DeBlasio congratulates members of the Lower East Side community following the announcement of the winning proposals.

Middle Left: Scott Davis, left, Marion McFadden, center, and Holly Leicht of HUD were instrumental in facilitating the Rebuild by Design competition.

Middle Right: New York City Mayor Bill DeBlasio, The Rockefeller Foundation Vice President Zia Khan, New York Governor Andrew Cuomo, US Senator Chuck Schumer, and HUD Secretary Shaun Donovan gather on June 2, 2014 to announce the winning proposals for New York City and State.

Bottom: HUD Secretary Shaun Donovan joins New Jersey Governor Chris Christie and Little Ferry Mayor Mauro Raguseo in Little Ferry, New Jersey, to announce New Jersey's winning projects.

Announcing the Winners

On June 2, 2014, Secretary Donovan announced the competition's winning designs at press events in New York and New Jersey, joined by New York Governor Andrew Cuomo, New Jersey Governor Chris Christie, New York City Mayor Bill de Blasio, and other officials.

The selection represented an award of great distinction for the design teams. The six winning projects were the BIG U, from the BIG Team; Living with the Bay, from the Interboro Team; New Meadowlands, from MIT CAU + ZUS + URBANISTEN; Resist, Delay, Store, Discharge, from OMA; Hunts Point Lifelines, from PennDesign/OLIN; and Living Breakwaters from SCAPE/Landscape Architecture.

HUD announced allocations totaling $930 million to begin implementing the six winning proposals plus one finalist: Resilient Bridgeport, from WB unabridged with Yale ARCADIS. The funding was granted to New York City, the State of New York, the State of New Jersey, and the State of Connecticut, who are in charge of implementing the projects themselves. HUD issued guidelines for this process in a Federal Register Notice, including requirements that these state and city governments would have to meet before the funds could be handed down. Among these, each grantee would have to incorporate its Rebuild by Design projects into a broader Disaster Recovery Action Plan, specifying its strategies for developing the proposals and plans for continuing to involve community stakeholders. HUD would review and approve each action plan before releasing the funds, first for pre-construction and later, after final engineering specifications and cost estimates were completed, for construction itself. Grantees have until September 30, 2022 to use the funding.**

"The winning proposals are truly transformative and serve as blueprints for how we can safeguard the region and make it more environmentally and economically resilient. By investing in these proposals, we are going to ensure that when the next storm comes, the region will be safer and better prepared."

—

HUD Secretary Shaun Donovan

Winning Proposal Allocations* to City and States

$335,000,000
The BIG U in Manhattan, NY (The BIG Team)

$230,000,000
Resist, Delay, Store, Discharge in Hoboken, Weehawken, Jersey City, NJ (OMA)

$150,000,000
New Meadowlands in Little Ferry, Moonachie, Carlstadt, Teterboro, NJ (MIT CAU+ZUS+URBANISTEN)

$125,000,000
Living with the Bay in Nassau County, Long Island (The Interboro Team)

$60,000,000
Living Breakwaters in Tottenville, Staten Island, NY (SCAPE/Landscape Architecture)

$20,000,000
Lifelines in Hunts Point, Bronx, NY (PennDesign/OLIN)

$10,000,000***
Resilient Bridgeport in Bridgeport, CT (WB unabridged with Yale ARCADIS)

* HUD's authority to administer the competition was provided under the America COMPETES Act; the authority to allocate disaster recovery funds was provided under The Disaster Relief Appropriations Act of 2013.

** The 2022 deadline is inclusive of waiver authority provided in the appropriation law allowing expenditure beyond the default 2019 deadline.

*** Resilient Bridgeport received implementation funding, but was not a winner in the competition.

5

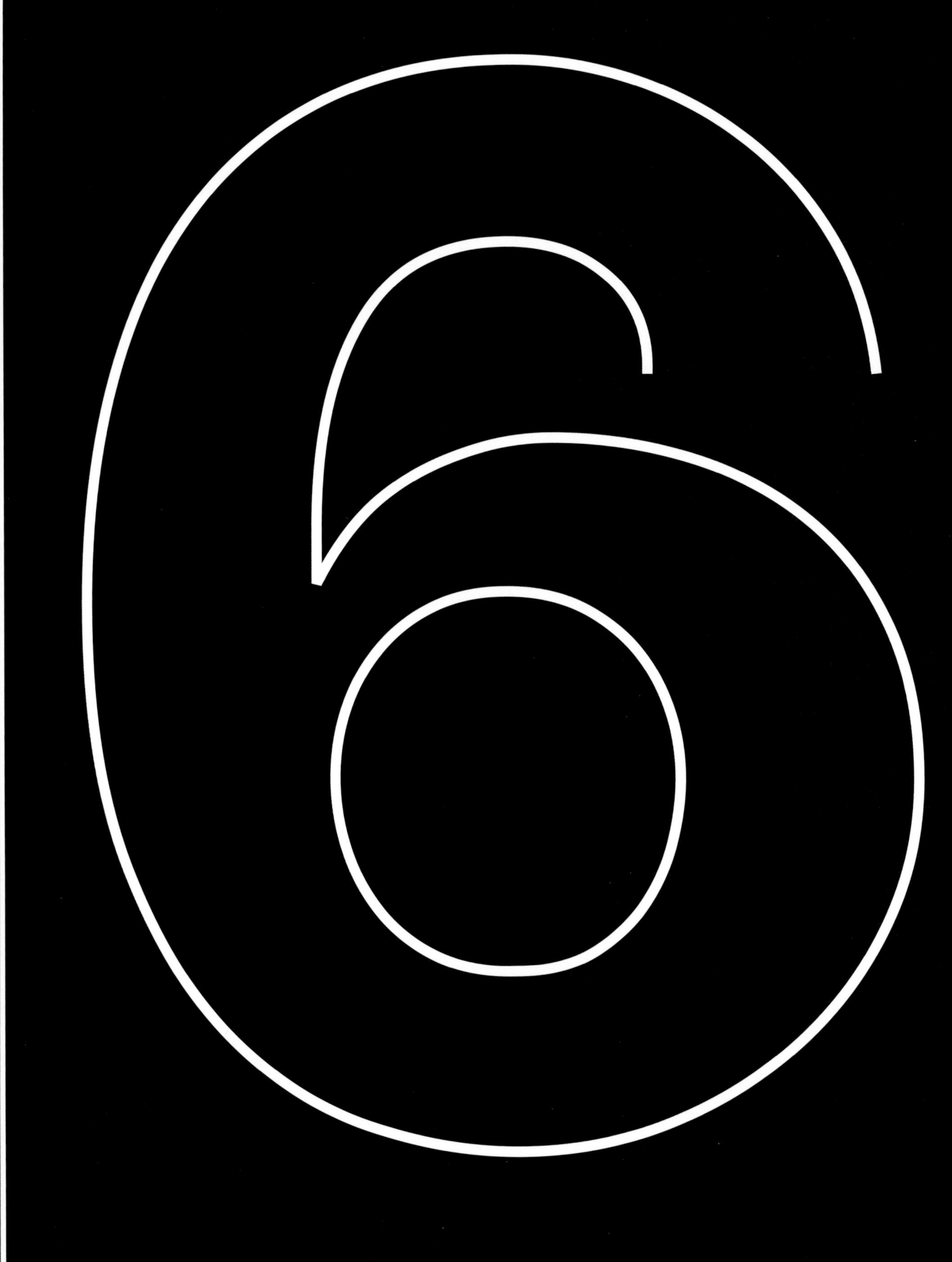

A LASTING IMPACT

A New Standard for Designing Resilience

As the competition entered its final stages, HUD, The Rockefeller Foundation, and the JPB Foundation partnered with the Urban Institute to design and implement a formative evaluation of the Rebuild by Design process. The evaluation assessed four primary areas: (1) Rebuild by Design's overall concept, including its explicit and evolving goals and objectives; (2) the competition model and its components; (3) strategies used for community engagement; and (4) state and local policymakers' receptivity to the proposals.

"The evaluation," wrote Dr. Carlos Martín, one of its primary authors, "found that Rebuild by Design brings hope and inspiration that communities and decision makers can collectively 'build back better' by responding in innovative and creative ways and working as a region to become more resilient."

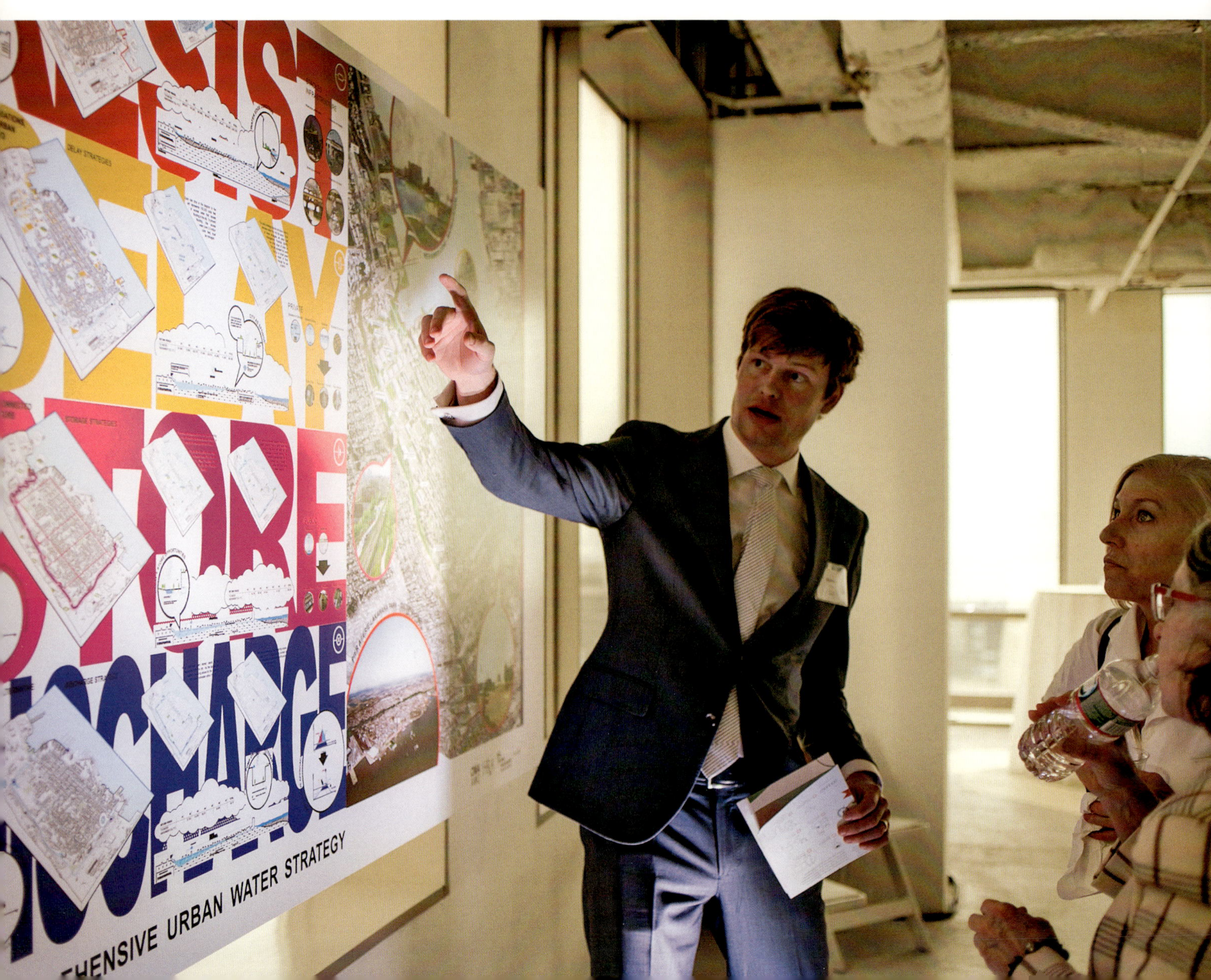

Synopsis of the Urban Institute's Evaluation on Rebuild by Design

Vision
Rebuild by Design's implementation held true to its innovative vision for integrating design competition into disaster recovery and to its ambition for regional and resilient infrastructure. Leadership among the core partners and the magnitude of nearly $1 billion in federal funding for awards motivated all of the key stakeholders in spite of an expedited time frame and daunting requirements.

Innovation
The Rebuild by Design competition was an especially innovative strategy for meeting resilience goals. The model contained many innovations, such as the use of architecture and planning to address resilience, the harnessing of talent through the competition and prize framework, and the involvement of public-philanthropic financing to complement traditional public procurement. These innovations produced a novel and effective organizational structure, increased community awareness, provoked a reconsideration of regional connections and shared needs among policymakers, and laid the groundwork for producing more innovation in the long term.

Resilience strategies
The competition placed design thinking in the foreground for developing problem statements and solutions, and developed an administrative structure that remained flexible, approachable, and outside of the federal bureaucracy. This structure has promoted a high degree of responsiveness from the administrative staff, including the Rebuild by Design project manager, HUD's advisor, and the Rebuild by Design liaisons to the design teams and communities.

Design as the strategy
The process provides preliminary evidence that design methods can be used to coordinate multidisciplinary inquiry for the purpose of developing problem statements that then require design solutions. Traditionally, design thinking is spurred by clear project scopes and parameters. Rebuild by Design has pushed the design envelope beyond this legacy by focusing design on a central environmental and social issue. Rebuild by Design's vision is, in this way, a direct contribution to a longer history of promoting design in land, infrastructure, and building development among federal and local governments.

Competitions for generating the best design
Rebuild by Design broke the mold of traditional design competitions with its approach to teamwork and encouragement of creativity. By charging its design teams with the responsibility for creating the problem statements, rather than prescribing the project scope, parameters, and budget, the competition engendered the creation of truly visionary design approaches. By having design teams share concepts, information, research, and feedback, the competition helped the teams function as a network of participants rather than competing contestants, strengthening all of their proposals.

Integrating local stakeholders in the competition's work
Including the public in the early stages of design development and continually incorporating their feedback was vital to creating proposals that represented the needs of large groups of stakeholders and gathered support from a number of different sectors of society.

The highly positive findings of the evaluation indicate that, even though Rebuild by Design itself is limited in scope to the Sandy recovery area and its projects are still under development, it has the potential to be transformational in the way disaster recovery efforts are designed, funded, and implemented at a broader scale. In sum, the evaluation team noted that Rebuild by Design has moved the mark on resilience planning and action in the country.

At a public exhibition of the final proposals, Marten Hillen of the OMA Team describes how Resist, Delay, Store, Discharge will help the city of Hoboken manage its stormwater.

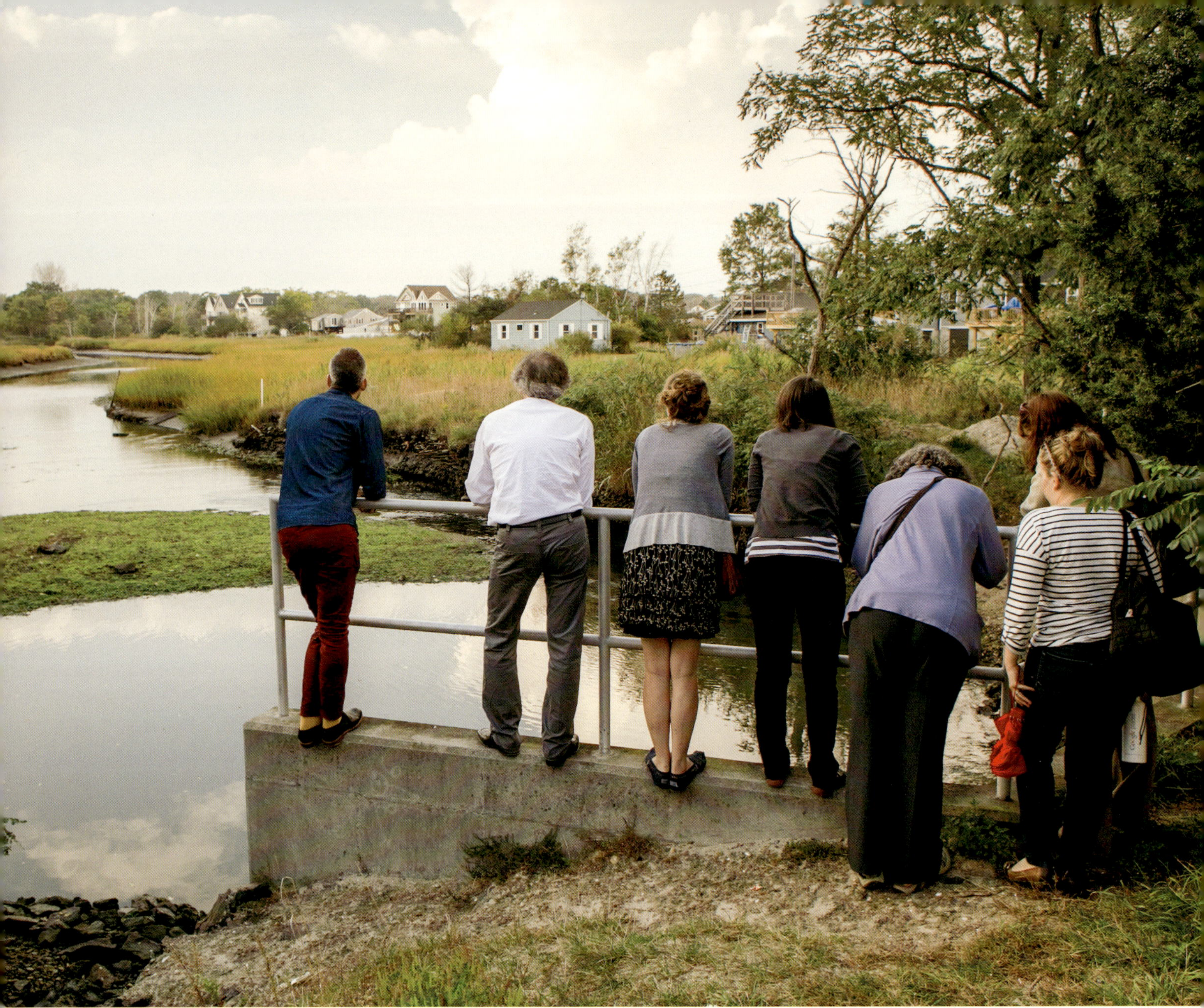

"By starting from a regional perspective and focusing on the future, Rebuild by Design not only worked to build resilience where Sandy's impact was most immediate, but also developed a broader understanding of the future vulnerabilities and the interdependencies of our region."

—

Nancy Kete, Managing Director, The Rockefeller Foundation

The design teams explored Bridgeport's natural landscape to examine ecological vulnerabilities and devise green infrastructure solutions.

The Horizon Ahead

Around the world, climate change is confronting cities and societies with unprecedented challenges. After Hurricane Sandy, Rebuild by Design pioneered a uniquely effective, collaborative, and innovative method for designing, funding, and implementing resilient solutions to these challenges.

Using Rebuild by Design as their standard, community organizations are now holding government planners accountable to a higher level of engagement. Design and planning schools are teaching its process so that their next generation will be better prepared to build forward instead of repeating the mistakes of the past. Government agencies are looking for ways to use the Rebuild by Design process to address their own regions' pressing needs.

In the United States, President Obama launched the National Disaster Resilience Competition in June 2014, "inspired by the success of Rebuild by Design." The national competition brings Rebuild by Design's high standards of stakeholder inclusion and cross-sector collaboration to disaster preparedness throughout the country.

In the international sphere, the Global Resilience Partnerships launched a multi-phase resilience design challenge in 2014 modeled after Rebuild by Design. The Grand Challenge focuses on three regions – the Horn of Africa, the Sahel, and South and Southeast Asia – and gathers interdisciplinary teams to collectively research and diagnose problems, and "develop locally driven, high-impact solutions that can build resilience at scale."

The Rebuild by Design competition produced not only tangible design solutions, but also an innovative process that will continue to serve as inspiration for communities and governments. As the first projects mature and bear fruit in the Sandy-affected region, the Rebuild by Design process has evolved into a powerful tool for enhancing regional resilience across the country and world, helping other cities rethink resilience before disaster strikes.

Special Thanks

In addition to all the team members, partners, advisors, and numerous supporters mentioned throughout the book, Rebuild by Design would like to thank our consortium of agencies, organizations, and stakeholders, without whom, this process would not have been possible.

Hurricane Sandy Task Force and Federal Agencies
Army Corps of Engineers
Corporation for National and Community Service
Council of Economic Advisers
Council on Environmental Quality
Department of Commerce
Department of Education
Department of Veterans Affairs
Department of Agriculture
Department of Energy
Department of Health and Human Services
Department of Homeland Security
Department of Housing and Urban Development
Department of the Interior
Department of Labor
Department of Transportation
Department of the Treasury
Economic Development Administration
Environmental Protection Agency
Federal Emergency Management Agency
Fish and Wildlife Service
National Oceanic and Atmospheric Administration
National Endowment for the Arts
Occupational Safety and Health Administration
Office of Management and Budget
Office of Science and Technology Policy

Small Business Administration
White House Office of Cabinet Affairs

Partner Organizations
Municipal Art Society
New York University's Institute for Public Knowledge
Regional Plan Association
Van Alen Institute

Philanthropy
The Rockefeller Foundation
Community Foundation of New Jersey
Dodge Foundation
Deutsche Bank Americas Foundation
Hearst Foundation
JPB Foundation
New Jersey Recovery Fund
Surdna Foundation

Advisory Groups
Research Advisory Group
Jury Members
Special Advisors

Kingdom of the Netherlands
Ministry of Infrastructure and Environment
Ministry of Foreign Affairs
Dutch Embassy in Washington, DC
Dutch Consulate in New York

Grantees
Governor's Office of Storm Recovery, New York
Governor's Office of Recovery and Rebuilding, New Jersey
Office of Recovery and Resiliency, New York City Mayor's Office
Department of Housing, State of Connecticut

State and Local Government Stakeholders
Asbury Park Planning Department
Bergen County
Berkeley Township
Borough of Moonachie
Bridgeport Housing Authority
Bridgeport Mayor's Office
Bronx River Alliance
City of Asbury Park
City of Bridgeport
City of Bridgeport Department of Health and Social Services
City of Bridgeport Office of Emergency Management and Health Services
City of Highlands
City of Hoboken
City of Jersey City
City of Jersey City Planning
City of Keansburg
City of Kearny
City of Long Beach
City of Lyndhurst
City of Middletown
City of Milford
City of Monmouth Beach
City of North Arlington
City of Ridgefield Park
City of Rutherford
City of Sea Bright
City of Seaside Heights
City of Secaucus
City of South Hackensack
City of Stamford Capital Use Board
City of Teterboro
Connecticut Department of Energy and Environmental Protection
Connecticut Department of Emergency Management and Homeland Security
Connecticut Department of Economic and Community Development
Connecticut Historic Preservation and Museum Division
Connecticut State Senate
Deputy Chief Engineer & Director of Land Use
District 2 New York City Council
Empire Justice
Empire State Development Corporation
Fairfield County
Fire Department of New York
Hoboken City Council
Hoboken Housing Authority
Hoboken Office of Emergency Management
Hoboken Planning Board
Hudson River Park Trust
Little Ferry City Government
Long Island Index
Long Island Rail Road
Long Island Regional Economic Development Council
Long Island Regional Planning Commission
Metropolitan Transportation Authority
Monmouth County
Nassau County Department of Public Works
Nassau County Executive Office
Nassau County Legislature
National Center for Suburban Studies
New Jersey Department of Environmental Protection
New Jersey Department of State: Department of Environmental Protection, Department of Planning Advocacy, Division of Travel & Tourism
New Jersey Department of Transportation
New Jersey Economic Development Authority
New Jersey Legislature
New Jersey Meadowlands Commission
New Jersey Planning Division
New Jersey Secretary of State
New Jersey State Senate
New Jersey Transit
New York Department of Transportation
New York City Council
New York City Comptroller's Office
New York City Community Boards
New York City Department of City Planning
New York City Department of Citywide Administrative Services
New York City Department of Design and Construction
New York City Department of Environmental Protection
New York City Department of Parks & Recreation
New York City Department of Small Business Services

New York City Department of Transportation
New York City Department of Sanitation
New York City Economic Development Corporation
New York City Housing Authority
New York City Housing Preservation and Development
New York City Landmarks Preservation Commission
New York City Manhattan Community Districts
New York City Mayor's Office of Environmental Remediation
New York City Office of Emergency Management
New York City Office of Management and Budget
New York City Police Department
New York Empire State Development Corporation
New York Rising
New York State Assembly Districts
New York State Department of State
New York State Department of Environmental Conservation
New York State Department of Environmental Protection
New York Department of Health
New York State Department of Planning
New York State Homes and Community Renewal
New York State Office of Parks, Recreation, and Historic Preservation
New York State Office for the Aging
New York State Senate
Ocean County
Port Authority of New York and New Jersey
Staten Island Borough President's Office
Staten Island Foundation, District Attorney's Office
Staten Island Council
Staten Island Assembly
Suffolk County Department of Economic Development and Planning
Suffolk County Department of Public Works
Suffolk County Fire, Rescue, and Emergency Services
Suffolk County Police Department
Suffolk County Office of Ecology
Town of Hempstead Department of Conservation and Waterways
Town of Hempstead Department of Engineering
Trust for Governors Island
Union Beach
Valley Civic Association
Village of East Rockaway
Village of Freeport
Village of Lynbrook
Village of Rockville Centre
Weehawken City Council

Non-Government Stakeholders

116th St Merchant Association
Action for Community Development
Adelante of Suffolk County
Adelphi University
Afikim Foundation
Agriculture Program
Ain't No Stopping Radio
Alchemy Park
Allen Chapel AME
Alliance for a Just Rebuilding
Alliance For The Arts
Alliance of Resident Theatres
Alspector Architecture
Alzheimer's Association
American Littoral Society
American Planning Association
American Red Cross
Amsterdam Business
Amtrak
Anheuser-Busch Distributors, Hunts Point Distribution Center
Appleseeds, NY
Archdiocese of New York
Architectural League of New York
Architecture for Humanity
Artemis Landscaping
Arts Horizons
Arverne by the Sea
Asbury Can
Asbury Park Press
Asbury Park Environmental and Shade Tree Commission
Ashe Cultural Arts Center
Asian Americans for Equality
Association for Energy Affordability Consulting
Association for Neighborhood & Housing Development
Association of Marine Industries
AVR Realty Company
Baldwin Civic Association
Barnegat Bay Partnership
Battery Park Conservancy
Battery Urban Farm
Beach 116th St Partnership
Beach Packaging Design
Beacons of Hope New Orleans
Belle Harbor Property Owners Association
Bellport High School Students for Environmental Quality
Bike Hoboken
Bloomberg LP
Bridgeport Board of Education
Bridgeport Child Advocacy Coalition
Bridgeport Daycare
Bridgeport Emergency Operations Center
Bridgeport Neighborhood Trust
Bridgeport Regional Business Council
Bright Temple African Methodist Episcopal Church
Brighton Beach Long Term Recovery
Broad Channel Athletic Club
Broad Channel Community
Bronx Council on the Arts
Bronx Long Term Recovery Group
Bronx on the Go
Brookfield Properties
Brookhaven Baymen's Association
Brookhaven League of Women Voters
Brooklyn Center for Independence of the Disabled
Brooklyn Community Foundation
Brooklyn Heights Association Inc.
Brooklyn Recovery Fund
Brotherhood of Teamsters Local 202
Brottworks Design Studio
Bungalow Bar & Restaurant
Business Intelligence Associates, Inc
Cameron Engineering
Canarsie Disaster Relief Committee
Canarsie Long Term Recovery Group
Captain Don's Nautical Adventures, Bay Park Fishing Station, NY
Carnegie Endowment for International Peace
Carroll Gardens Association
Carrollton-Hollygorve Community Development Corporation
Catholic Charities, NY
Cazzeek Brothers
Center for Estuarine, Environmental and Coastal Oceans Monitoring
Center for New York City Neighborhoods
Chartier Group
Chase Bank
Child Care Council of Long Island
Child First/Bridgeport Hospital
Chinatown Partnership
Chinese Consolidated Benevolent Association
Chinese-American Planning Council
Citizen's Campaign for the Environment
City University of New York, Hunter and Jamaica Bay Institute
Clean Ocean Action
Clemente Solo Vélez Cultural Center
Coalition for Asian American Children & Families
Coastal Habitat for Humanity
Coastal Protection and Restoration Authority of Louisiana
Coastal Research and Education Society of Long Island
Columbia University
Community Affairs & Resource Center
Community Development Corporation of Long Island
Community Emergency Response Team
Coney Island Long Term Recovery Group
Connecticut Coalition for Environmental Justice/HCA
Connecticut Green Building Council
Council on the Arts and Humanities for Staten Island
County of Hudson Division of Planning
Creative New Jersey
Crow Hill Community Association

Culinary Kids Culinary Arts Initiatives Inc.
D+G Industries Inc
Deal Lake Commission
Dean Sakamoto Architects LLC
Defender Homes
Department of Planning Advocacy
Dermot
Destination Chelsea
Division of Travel & Tourism
Donor's Collaborative
DoTank BPT
Downtown Alliance
Downtown Special Services District
Dry Dock
East End Neighborhood Resilience Zone
East Village Community Coalition
Ecological Engineering of Long Island
Edison Properties
Empire Justice Center
Empire State Future
Enterprise Community Partners
Environmental Quality, Hunter
EPA Region 6 Urban Waters Partnership
ERASE Racism
Fair Share Housing Center
Fairfield Business Council
Fairfield County Community Foundation
Faith Based Initiative Group
Family Service League
Federal Employees Benefit Association
Federation Employment & Guidance Service
Federation of Protestant Welfare Agencies
Feel the Music!
Fire Island Association
First National Bank
Fisherman's Conservation Association
Flickinger Glassworks
Food Bank for New York City
Foresee Community
Forsgate Industrial Partners
Fort Defiance Café and Bar
Freeport Church of Wazerene
Friends of Conference House Park
Friends of Rockaway Beach
Friends of the High Line
Gans Studio
Garden Club of Long Island
Gay Men's Health Crisis
Georgica Green Ventures
Gerritsen Beach Cares, Inc. Sandy Recovery Program
Gerritsen Beach Long Term Recovery Group
Goldman Sachs
Good Jobs New York
Good Old Lower East Side
Gowanus Dredgers
Grace City Church
Grand Street Settlement
Great Lakes Dock and Dredging
Great South Bay Audubon Society
Greater Bridgeport Community Enterprises
Greater Bridgeport Regional Council
Greater Media Newspapers
Greater New Orleans, Inc
Greater New York Lecet / Laborers 66
Green Faith
Green Map
Greenberg Nature Center
Greenwich Village Society
Guyon Rescue
Habitat for Humanity
Hackensack Riverkeeper
Hammer Magazine
Hartley House
Hartz Mountain Industries
Hatch Mott MacDonald
HDR/HydroQual
Health and Welfare Council of Long Island
Heffernan Realty
Henry Street Settlement
Hill Neighborhood House
Hispanic Federation
Hoboken Boys and Girls Club
Hoboken Catholic Academy
Hoboken Chamber of Commerce
Hoboken Commuter Community
Hoboken Cove Community Boathouse
Hoboken Day Care
Hoboken Developers
Hoboken Dual Language Charter School
Hoboken Green Infrastructure Strategic Plan
Hoboken Jubilee Center
Hoboken Museum CFM
Hoboken Rail Yards Task Force
Hoboken Resident Community Hopes
Hofstra University Suburban Studies Program
Home/Made
Hoop Dancers of Connecticut
Hope Academy
Hopes Cap, Inc.
Housatonic Community College
Howard Hughes Corporation
Hudson Riverkeeper
Hunts Point Cooperative Market
Hunts Point Economic Development Corporation
Ice + Iran
Ikea
Il Forno Bakery
Institute for a Resilient Economy
Institute Of Indian Culture
Institute on Water Resources Law and Policy
Integrated Ocean Observing System
Interfaith Neighbors, Inc.
International Flavors and Fragrances
Irish Arts Center
Islip Town Leaseholders Association
iStar
Italian-American Museum
Iwa Construction
Jacobs Engineering Group
Jamaica Bay Ecowatchers
Jamestown Properties
Jaral Properties
Jennie Curé
Jersey City Division of City Planning
Jersey Shore Partnership
JHM Financial Group LLC
Jonathan Rose Companies
Kayak Staten Island
Kearny Point Industrial Park
Keio University
Kevin's Restaurant
Kimmel Housing Foundation
KIPP New Orleans
Kips Bay Neighborhood Alliance
Knights of Columbus
Krzysztof Sadlej
KSK Architects, Planners, Historians Inc.
Kuchma Corps
Land Use Ecological Services
Langosta Lounge
League of Municipalities
Leg Dave Denenberg
LGBT Community Center
Linda Tool
LiRo Group
Living Systems Design and Planning
Local Initiatives Support Corporation
Local New York Laborers 66
Local Office Landscape Architecture
Long Island Association
Long Island Contractors' Association
Long Island Housing Partnership
Long Island Road Runner's Club
Long Island Sierra Club
Long Island Sound Futures
Long Island Voluntary Organization Active in Disaster Long-Term Recovery Group
Long Island Volunteer Center
Louis Berger Group
Louisiana Office of Community Development
Low Income Investment Fund
Lower East Side Girls Club
Lower East Side Ready Long-Term Recovery Group
Lower East Side Tenement Museum
Lower Manhattan Cultural Council
Lutheran Counseling Center
Lutheran Social Services
Madison Marquette
Make the Road New York
Maracoos
Mary and Eliza Freeman Center
Mary Queen of Vietnam CDC
Mastic Beach Property Owners Association
Materials Conservation Co.
Meadowlands Chamber of Commerce
Meadowlands Commission
Melillo + Bauer Associates
Mercy Learning Center
Merrick Fire Department
Metis Association
Metropolitan Waterfront Alliance
Mid-Atlantic Association Coastal Ocean Observing System
Mile Mesh
Mississippi River Delata Restoration Project
Mo Gridder's BBQ
Monmouth University
Mothers on the Move

Museum of Jewish Heritage
Nathel & Nathel
National Coalition for Arts Preparedness
National Institute for Coastal Harbor & Infrastructure
National Marine Fisheries Service
National Museum of The American Indian
National Wildlife Federation
Natural Resources Protective Association
Nautilus International
Nazareth Housing
Neighborhood Housing Services of New York City
Neighborhood Partnership Network
New England Interstate Water Pollution Control Commission
New Fulton Fish Market at Hunts Point
New Haven Home Recovery
New Jersey Audubon
New Jersey Bike/ Walk Coalition
New Jersey Enterprise Development Center
New Jersey Environmental Federation
New Jersey Future
New Orleans Coalition on Open Governance
New Orleans Office of Coastal and Environmental Affairs
New Orleans Redevelopment Authority
New School for Social Research
New York Academy of Medicine
New York Building Congress
New York Chapter of the United States Green Building Council
New York City Environmental Justice Alliance
New York Committee for Occupational Safety and Health
New York Resilience System Organization
New York Rising Community Reconstruction Program
New York Sea Grant
New York Seafood Council
New York Smart Grid Consortium
New York Sportfish Fererat/ SPLASH
New York Sportfishing Federation
New York Times, The Lens
New York/New Jersey Audubon
New York/New Jersey Baykeeper
NewCorp
Newport Associates
NJ.com, TrueJersey
North Hudson Sewerage Authority
North Jersey Transportation Planning Authority
Northstar Fund and Adam Leibowitz Consulting
Nuyorican Poets Café
Oak Restaurant & Grill
Oakland Beach Buyout
Occupy Sandy
Ocean Bay Community Development Corporation
Old Seaport Association
Old Town Civic
Operation SPLASH
Orange Industries
Our Lady of Mt. Carmel 21st Century Learning Center
Our World Neighborhood Charter School
Parsons New School
Pattersquash Creek Civic Association
Peconic Baykeeper
Peconic Land Trust
Phillips, Preiss, Grygiel, LLC,
Pleasant Plains, Prince's Bay, and Richmond Valley Civic Association
Poko Partners, LLC
Point Lookout Civic Association
Point Partners
Portside
Powell Communications
Pratt Center for Community Development
Pratt Institute
Presbytery of Long Island
Prince's Bay and Richmond Community Association
Proactive Transportation and Planning
Project Home Again
Project Hope
Project Hospitality
Project Rebirth
Pryceless Consulting/ DoTank
Public Housing Resident Network
Public Service Enterprise Group
Quality of Life Coalition
Rare Find Nursery
RDK Landscape
Real Estate Board of New York
Rebuilding Together New York
Rebuilding Together of Long Island
Recovery Management Office
Red Cross
Renaissance Downtowns
Restore Red Hook
Richmond Senior Services
Ridgefield Park
River Terminal Developments
Rockaway Artists Alliance
Rockaway Civic
Rockaway Waterfront Alliance
Rockaway Youth Task Force
Rocking the Boat
Rutgers University
Ruth Green Team
Sandyhook Pilots
Santa Energy
Sara Roosevelt Park Coalition
Save Energy Project
Scenic Hudson
Seatuck Environmental Association
Secaucus Town Council
Second City Bikes
Sheepshead Bay Long Term Recovery Group
SheerSerendipity
Sheet Metal Workers Local 28
Sierra Club
Smitty's Filet House
Snug Harbor
Society of Vincent de Paul
Soho Alliance
Solar One
Solar Thin Films Group INC Eco Homes + Cleaning Tech Solutions
South Bay Cruising Club
South End Neighborhood Revitalization Zone
South Shore Audubon Society
South Shore Bayhouse Owners Association
South Shore Estuary Reserve
South Shore Waterfowlers Association
Southeast Louisiana Flood Protection Authority East
Southwest Brooklyn Industrial Development Corporation
St Ame Zion Church
St Bernard Parish Economic Development Commission
St Bernard Parish Public Schools
St Marks Center for Community Renewal
St Stephens
Staten Island Baymen's Association
Staten Island Civic Coallition
Staten Island Green Charter School
Staten Island Historic Society
Staten Island Legal Services
Staten Island Long Term Recovery Organization
Staten Island MakerSpace
Staten Island YABC Program
Steve's Authentic Key Lime Pies
Stony Brook University Department of Geosciences
Strategic Decisions Group
Structures of Coastal Resilience
Suffolk County Alliance of Sportsmen
Surfrider Foundation Jersey Shore Chapter
Sustainable Long Island
Sustainable Society Network
Sustainable South Bronx
T&M Associates
Table Talk
Tanner Senior Center
Task Force on Emergency Planning and Response for Special Needs Populations
Tear New York
The Blk Projek
The Bridgeport Area Youth Ministry
The Center for Architecture
The City College of New York
The Coastal YMCA
The College of Staten Island
The Council of Churches of Greater Bridgeport
The Design Trust
The Gift is Love
The Human Impacts Institute
The Hunts Point Terminal Produce Cooperative Association
The Idea Village
The Nature Conservancy
The Nature of Cities
The Point Community Development Corporation

The Trust for Public Land
The Urban Conservancy: Stay Local
The Urban Institute
The Workplace
Together North Jersey
Tom Fox Associates
Toms River/Berkley Township
Tottenville Civic Association
Touro Law School
Town of Secaucus
Tribeca Partnership
Trout Unlimited
TruFund Financial Services
Two Bridges Neighborhood Council
Ukranian-American Youth Association
Union Beach Strong
Unitarian Universalists Disaster Responder
United Food and Commercial Workers
United Methodist Church
United Nations International Strategy for Disaster Reduction
United Way of Long Island
University of Bridgeport
University of Connecticut
University of Delaware
Urban Coast Institute at Monmouth University
Urban Conservancy
URS Corporation
Vidaris
Vision Long Island
Visiting Nurse Service of New York
Vista Food Exchange
Walsh Properties
Warehouse owners
WaterWonks LLC
West Side Community Ceakh
Western Bays Coalition
Wheelabrator Technologies
Wildcat Academy Charter School
Yale Urban Design Workshop
youarethecity; The Design Trust
Youth Ministries for Peace and Justice
Zone A New York

Image Credits

All images in chapters 1, 2, 3, 5, 6 credited to Cameron Blaylock, unless otherwise noted.

1: The Storm & The Response
10 NJ Governor's Office/Tim Larsen; 11 NASA, NJ Governor's Office/Tim Larsen; 12-13 Iwan Baan/Getty Image News/Getty Images; 14 SCAPE/Landscape Architecture; 15 White House; 16-17 NJ Governor's Office/Tim Larsen; 18 Michael Premo/sandystorelines.com, White House/Pete Souza; 20-21 State Island Advance/Bill Lyons; 22-23 White House/Chuck Kennedy; 27 The Rockefeller Foundation (right); 28-31 Rebuild by Design

2: Researching the Region
36-37 John Gendall (Jamaica Bay and Jersey Shore); 38-39 Rebuild by Design; 42-43 MIT CAU+ZUS+URBANISTEN Team; 45 BIG Team

3: Designing Resilience
52 WB Unabridged with Yale ARCADIS Team; 54 Rebuild by Design; 55 WB Unabridged with Yale ARCADIS Team, Rebuild by Design; 58-61 Rebuild by Design

All images in chapter 4 credited to their respective teams, unless otherwise noted.

4: Projects
133 City of Hoboken, Port Authority of New York and New Jersey, hobokenhighhorse.com, latimes.com, Bob Jagendorf; 146 Michael Reynolds/epa/Corbis; 147 Ellen Neises, Hunts Point Produce Market, Hunts Point Cooperative Market, Bronx River Alliance, Rocking the Boat, bottom row image 2: c 2010 Viorel Florescu / northjersey.com; 151 bottom row image 1- Ivan Rodriguez, Sheena Olimpo, Yuna Kubota, David Vuong, Hadrian Predock, image 2- Cricket Day, image 3- WORKSHOP Ken Smith Landscape Architect, image 6- PEG Office of Landscape Architecture; 153 Sustainable South Bronx, Bronx River Alliance, Rocking the Boat, Youth Voices, Melissa Mark Viverito, The Stop, NYC EDC, FEMA, Eric Rothstein